The Best of
Girl

THIS IS A PRION BOOK

First published in the UK in 2006

This paperback edition published
in the UK in 2011 by Prion
an imprint of the Carlton Publishing Group
20 Mortimer Street
London
W1T 3JW

10 9 8 7 6 5 4 3 2 1

A catalogue record of this book can be obtained from the British
Library.

ISBN: 978 1 85375 832 4

Edited and compiled by Lorna Russell

Art Director: Lucy Coley
Design: Barbara Zuñiga
Production: Caroline Alberti
Production for paperback edition: Janette Burgin

Printed in China

The Best of Girl

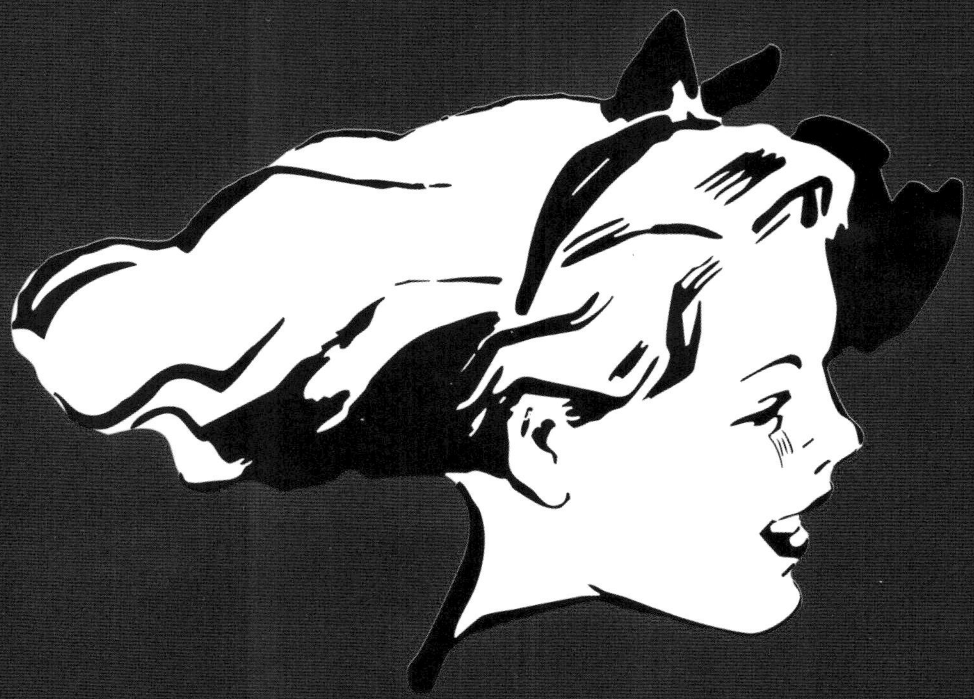

PRION

CONTENTS

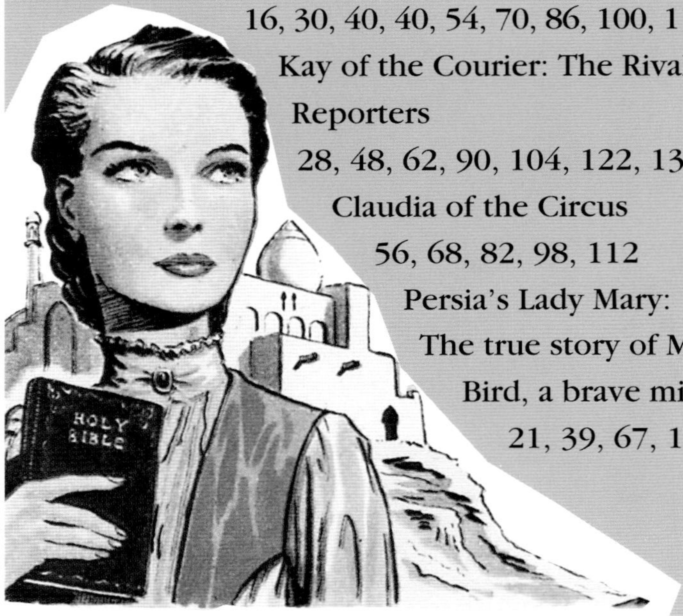
HOLY BIBLE

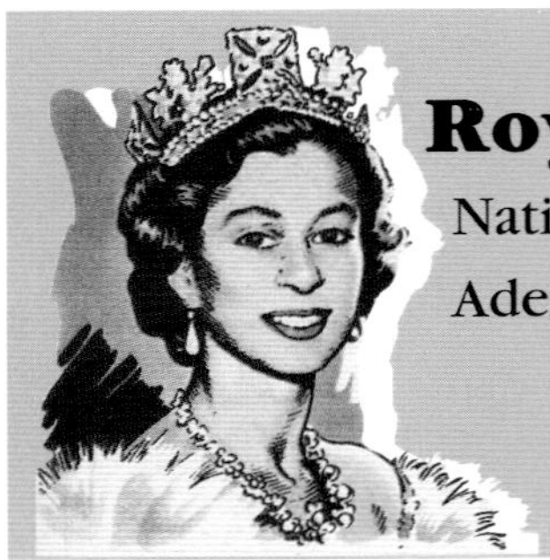

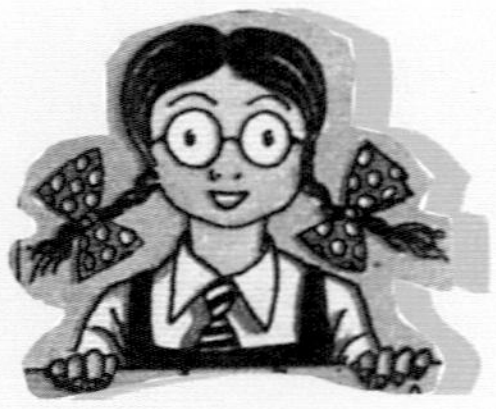

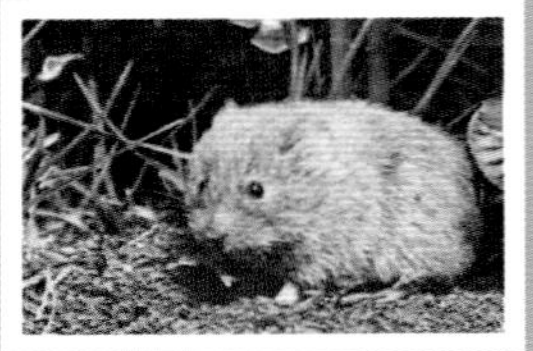

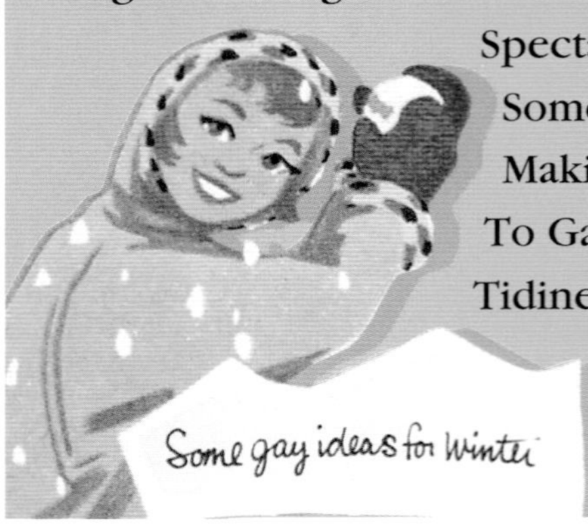
Some gay ideas for Winter

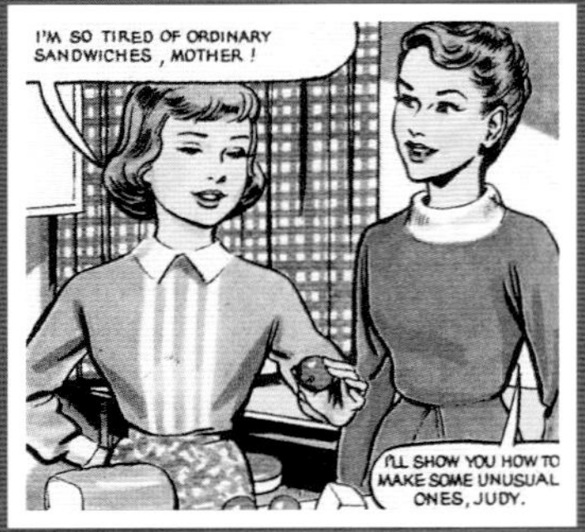
I'M SO TIRED OF ORDINARY SANDWICHES, MOTHER!
I'LL SHOW YOU HOW TO MAKE SOME UNUSUAL ONES, JUDY.

INTRODUCTION

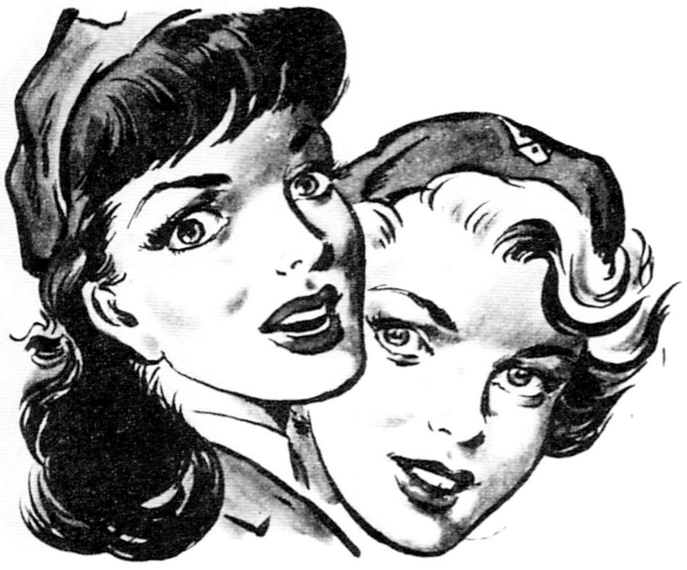

Back in the austere days of the early 1950s, there was very little excitement in a trip to the local newsagents for a young girl. A new generation of post-war baby boomers was growing up and there seemed to be nothing new to cater for them unless you read *School Friend* or *Girls' Crystal*, both of which had their origins in the 1920s when mummy was growing up.

That situation changed in the last week of October 1951. That week, any young reader pushing back the door, was almost certain to be greeted by a new tabloid-sized paper with the banner headline 'The New Super-Colour Weekly for Every Girl.' Unlike anything previously published for girls, *Girl* was to become a welcome weekly friend, an inspiration and confidant for over half a million girls for the next thirteen years.

Girl was the brainchild of the Reverend Marcus Morris, founder of the famous boys' paper the *Eagle*. When *Eagle* was launched in 1950, it soon became obvious that a large portion of the audience were girls, and the astute Reverend Morris was not slow in recognising the fact, noting in his first editorial in *Girl* that 'for a long time we have been wanting to produce another paper especially for girls—and we have had hundreds of letters asking us to do so.'

Putting together this new paper was the responsibility of a team that were still relatively inexperienced. *Eagle* was only eighteen months old and, at first, *Girl* was perhaps a little too close to its older brother to make its female readers feel they had something special of their own. Morris's plea for letters ('as that's the only way I can know for certain what sort of things you like') soon led to changes. The first ever cover (dated November 2nd) featured the opening episode of 'Kitty Hawke'. Kitty and her all-girl crew flew a Tadcaster for her father, head of Hawke Air Charter, and, despite the snide comments of Captain Smedley that 'gels are only gels,' Kitty was the best pilot they had and soon proved it. But soon 'Kitty' gave way to 'Wendy and Jinx', the inseparable chums of Manor School, and other newcomers over the next few months included 'Robbie of Red Hall', an orphaned Scots girl who found herself in charge of a large, neglected estate, and 'Belle of the Ballet', the star ballerina at Madame Arensa's dancing school.

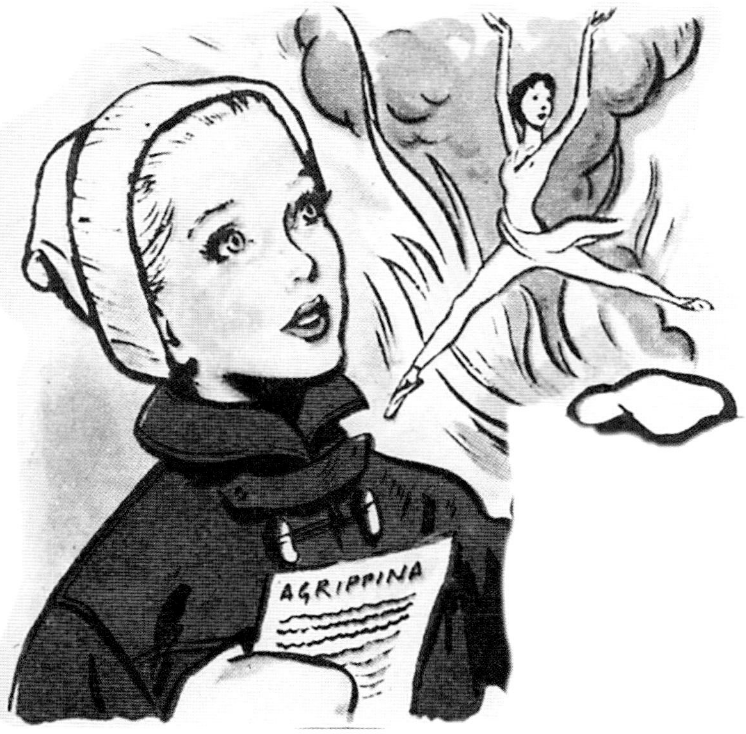
AGRIPPINA

There were some fixed stars in the firmament. The *Girl* logo is said to have been modelled on Julia Lockwood who, even at the age of nine, was already following in her mother's footsteps as an actress, Margaret Lockwood being a friend of Marcus Morris's actress wife, Jessica Dunning. A friend of Julia's, Jacky Curtis, became Girl's roving reporter, visiting all manner of shops and factories, interviewing celebrities from Joan Collins to Eamonn Andrews, or happily plunging into a diving tank in a 200lb amphibious suit complete with goldfish bowl helmet.

And there was always 'Lettice Leefe, the greenest girl in the school'. Lettice, with her polka-dot bows and big round glasses, was the only character to appear in every issue of *Girl*, and even survived a move to the later *Princess and Girl* for three years, making a grand total of sixteen years. The artist was John Ryan, better known as the creator of 'Captain Pugwash', in whose hands Lettice survived over 800 encounters with the rotund Miss Froth, headmistress of St. Addledegga's, and the ghastly

Miss Tantrum, forever sending Lettice off to write lines in her study.

The back cover was given over to biographies of famous women, from historical figures like Miriam, the sister of Moses ('Daughter of the Nile'), and Joan of Arc to scientist Marie Curie and missionary Mary Bird ('Persia's Lady Mary'). Author Chad Varah (founder of the Samaritans) claimed that these beautifully painted strips (primarily by Gerald Haylock) were *Girl*'s most popular feature.

Although the inclusion of religious figures may be seen as a logical extension of having a vicar at the helm of the magazine, Marcus Morris was not the only hand on the tiller; throughout the 1950s – generally considered *Girl*'s finest era – the day-to-day running of the paper was the responsibility of Morris's assistant editors, Joan ('Jodi') Hyland, Laurie Purden, Jean Crouch and Patricia Jackson, who made sure that the stories in *Girl* relied less on the physical danger that was the cliff-hanger ending of the boy's adventure strip and more on emotional crisis. *Girl* also carried a problem page ('What's Your Worry?') compiled by educational psychologist James Hemmings whose honest replies to everything from 'Are all teachers honest?' to what to do if you have a crush on an older girl or boy, were key to earning *Girl* the trust of many young readers.

Competitions to win holidays abroad and scholarships to the famous Sadler's Wells ballet school helped draw in readers and the wide variety of spin-off books and licensed merchandise proved that *Girl* was a powerful brand name. The editorial staff tried to make *Girl* as interactive as possible, through letters pages, running pictures of readers and sending staff out to photograph a variety of readers' activities. Girl was more of a club than a comic; indeed, there was a 'Girl Adventurers' Club' which attracted more than 16,000 members in six weeks.

The popularity of *Girl* meant that the paper could attract some big names as contributors. Jean Plaidy, horse riding champion Pat Smythe, Kathleen Peyton, Judith M. Berrisford, Peter Ling (often sharing the credit with his wife, Sheilah Ward) and Anne Digby were amongst the authors to contribute serials. Elizabeth Cruft (granddaughter of Charles Cruft, founder of the famous dog show) and Barbara Woodhouse were both stars of factual strips about animals, whilst Bebe Daniels and Valerie Hobson were amongst the presenters of 'Girl Hobbies Corner'.

As *Girl* entered the swinging sixties, practical features on how to make a bed or iron a blouse gave way to beauty and fashion tips. However, events behind the scenes began to be reflected in the contents of the paper. Hulton Press, the original publisher, was taken over first by Odhams Press and then by I.P.C. I.P.C.'s comics division, Fleetway Publications, had launched *Princess* as a strong rival to *Girl* in 1960. When Fleetway took control of *Girl* a year later, they dropped many of the features that had made *Girl* so individual. Three years later, in October 1964, *Girl* was merged with *Princess* to create new *Princess and Girl*, but only 'Belle and Mamie' – as 'Belle of the Ballet' was renamed in 1962 – and 'Lettice Leefe' survived.

Choosing a selection from the over 10,000 pages that were published in *Girl* is no easy task – and, happily, it was not my task! Finding space to mention even a fraction of the beautifully drawn comic strips and finely written serials and features has been hard enough but, hopefully, this brief canter through the history of one of the mostly fondly remembered of all girls' comics has whetted your appetite for the main course to come.

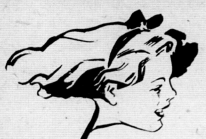

A Letter from the Editor

GIRL OFFICE, 18 FURNIVAL ST., LONDON E.C.4

29th October, 1952

HAPPY Birthday to all of you – and all of us! Here's a birthday we all can share, the birthday of our GIRL, who is a year old this week! Our birthday present to all you readers is this Special Birthday issue and all it contains. We only wish that all of you could have been with Jacky and the happy group of readers at the surprise Birthday Party in Cambridge. Your birthday present to us is the continued friendship of you all throughout the year – and we hope during the years to come. We are planning a lot of exciting things to happen in the pages of GIRL during the year which lies ahead, and we hope you are going to find it more and more interesting as the months pass.

Birthday news for *Girl Adventurers* is that a special First Year Diamond for you to hang on your Adventurer badges is being prepared at the moment and we shall be making a thrilling announcement about it soon.

For those of you who are enjoying our serial, *Island of Secrets*, here is an interesting item of news about Arthur Catherall, its author. Next Tuesday, November 4th, he will be broadcasting a talk on the subject of looking for material for books and stories. The talk is called 'Excitement is my business' and will be heard at 9.55 a.m. – so if you are at home at that time, we know you'll enjoy listening in; if not, perhaps your mother will listen for you.

Yours sincerely,

SPECIAL 'GIRL' CONCERT

Famous people will be there!

Grand Festival of Girl Choirs

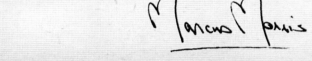

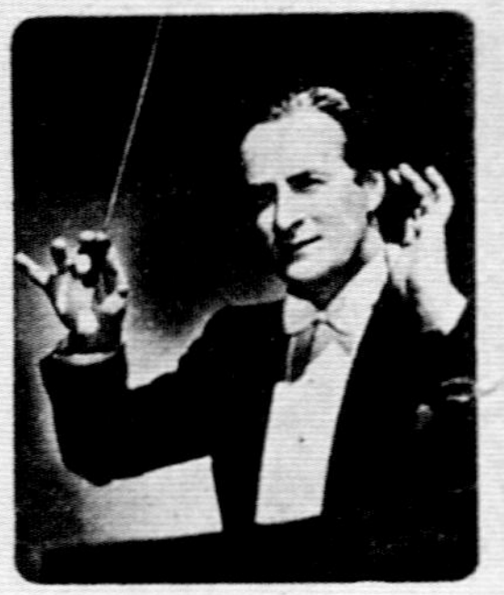

George Melachrino

THERE is a little more than a week left before the Grand Festival of Girl Choirs organized by GIRL to aid the funds of the National Playing Fields Association.

Have you secured your ticket yet? Tickets can now be obtained by writing to or calling at the Royal Festival Hall, London S.E.1, where the concert is to be held on Saturday, 8th Nov., or from your local ticket agency.

This wonderful feast of music is to be given by the combined Girl Choirs of Eastbourne, Hastings, Ilford and Leicester, supported by Fela Sowande on the organ and Tommy Reilly who will play his harmonica. The George Melachrino Concert Orchestra, conducted by George Melachrino, will accompany the choir and also render several items including *Memories of the Ballet*.

Glyn Jones, the famous B.B.C. Choral Conductor, will lead community singing and the compere will be Frank Phillips, also of the B.B.C.

If you have not already made arrangements to go to the concert why not form a party with all your friends? It is a wonderful opportunity to hear these famous choirs and artistes as well as see the famous Festival Hall.

Remember, too, that all the profits are to be donated to the National Playing Fields Association of which the Duke of Edinburgh is President.

- **Doors open 7 p.m., the concert begins 7.30 p.m.**
- **Tickets 4/-, 7/6, 10/- obtainable by writing to or calling at the Royal Festival Hall, London, S.E.1., or from your local ticket agency.**
- **ALL PROFITS will be donated to the National Playing Fields Association.**

READERS' PETS

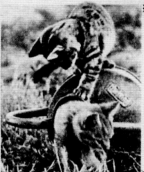

The names of my two kittens playing in the watering-can are Muff and Jennifer. Muff is all ginger and Jennifer is black and grey. They are now about six months old. One day we lost Jennifer and on saying to Muff, "Where is Jennifer?" he went to the watering-can and there she was, fast asleep. – *Marjory Churchyard, Lawford, Nr Manningtree, Essex.*

Girl Window No. 15 ★ The GIRL Hoodscarf ★

THE Hoodscarf is the companion to the GIRL Scarf which we recommended on October 8th, and will come in useful now that the winter months are upon us. It is made of beautifully soft wool and fits snugly over the head, with scarf ends attached to tie under the chin. The GIRL head emblem is embroidered in matching colours on one of the scarf ends. There are four colours from which to choose – gold, camel, red and royal blue – and the price is 8/11d.

This is an Ariel production which should be in stock at your local shop.

BIKE-A-WEEK COMPETITION

ARE YOU GOOD AT CROSSWORDS?

This one may win you a bike!

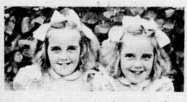

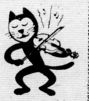

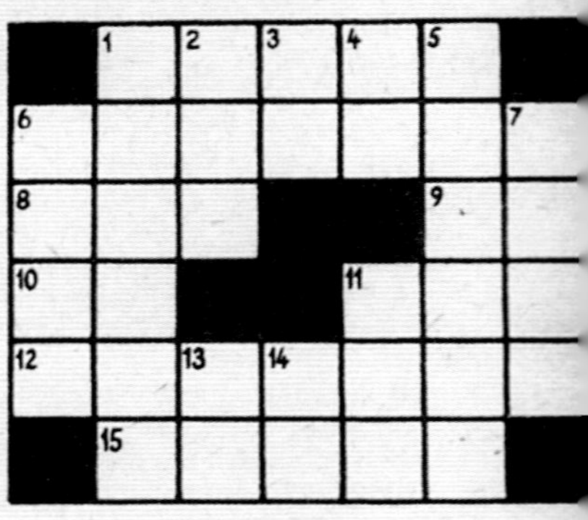

IT'S GIRL's First Birthday this week and once more you have the chance to win a wonderful new B.S.A. bicycle. All you have to do is solve this easy crossword puzzle and send your entry to us.

Read the rules carefully before posting off your solution.

RULES:

1. Solve the crossword puzzle and copy out the answers (with clue numbers alongside) on to a postcard.
2. Remember that neatness of handwriting and age will be taken into consideration in the judging as well as the correct solution.
3. Send no money; this is FREE.
4. Write your name, address and age last birthday on the same card and post it to GIRL Bike-a-Week Competition No. 35, GIRL, Long Lane, Liverpool 9, to reach there by November 10th, 1952.
5. The decision of the Editor will be final and no correspondence will be entered into about any entries.
6. This competition is open to all readers.

CLUES:

Across: 1. Haughty; 6. You may learn this at school; 8. Past tense of eat; 9. Automobile Association; 10. I am the object; 11. Cone-bearing tree. 12. *"Oh, to be in – now that April's there!"* 15. Frog-like creatures.

Down: 1. Powerful; 2. The eggs o fishes; 3. Slang expression for 'a right'; 4. Cue without a head; 5 Runs away; 6. Arrived; 7. Thre feet make one; 11. Hobby or craze 13. Depart; 14. Law with no end.

READERS' LETTERS **5/-** will be paid for every reader's letter printed on this page.

Could you tell us apart?

THIS PHOTOGRAPH is of my twin sister Valerie and me taken in our aunt's garden. We wore blue dresses and had blue ribbons in our hair. We are celebrating our tenth birthday next week. Everybody has great difficulty in telling us apart as we look so alike. – *Shirley Skennerton, London, S.E.*

* * *

Idea from GIRL

I THINK your paper is the best I have ever read; it's so exciting. I look forward to it very much. Mummy and I took such an interest in the serial, *Daughter of the Nile* that when the time for our local carnival came round we decided to do a tableau on the theme. We called it *The Finding of Moses*. We took all patterns for the costumes and the colours of the dresses from GIRL. You can guess how delighted we were when we were awarded the first prize! – *Joan Haskins, East Portishead, Nr Bristol.*

* * *

The Cat and the Fiddle

DURING TEA one day I was surprised to hear a sudden musical strumming sound. It kept on repeating so I set out to track it down. I was so surprised when I discovered our cat plucking the strings of my brother's toy violin. – *Coral Henshaw, Mold, Flintshire.*

GIRL OF THE WEEK

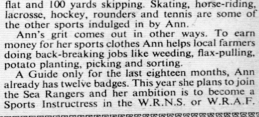

Ann's a successful athlete

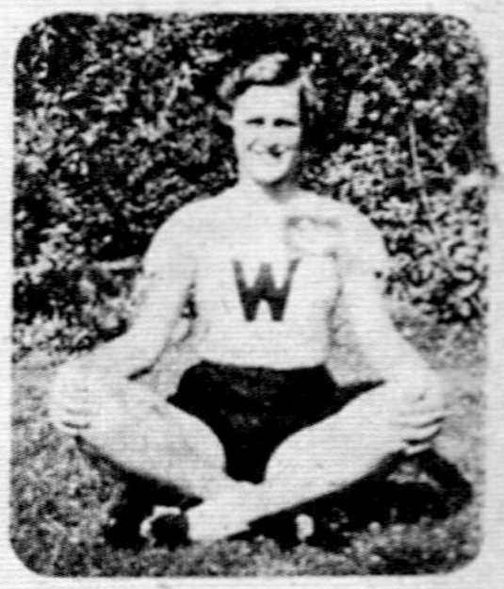

ANN CLARK (15) who lives at the Police Station, Wilton, Nr Salisbury, Wilts., has several strong claims to become 'Girl of the Week' for she has achieved a high position as an all-round athlete and a proficient Guide. But we chose her for something different – the grit and initiative which got her there.

Ann was born with a great handicap – a hip defect which affected her feet and legs. Many children would have given in but not so Ann. Encouraged by her mother, she proceeded to take up ballet and tap dancing, and by the age of ten passed three exams.

Now take a look at her athletics record. She was a member of the Wiltshire Junior Girls' team which won the 440 yards relay at the All-England Country School Championships at Bradford, Yorks, in the summer. Last year she was champion athlete of Salisbury, winning the high jump, 100 yards flat, 50 yards flat and 100 yards skipping. Skating, horse-riding, lacrosse, hockey, rounders and tennis are some of the other sports indulged in by Ann.

Ann's grit comes out in other ways. To earn money for her sports clothes Ann helps local farmers doing back-breaking jobs like weeding, flax-pulling, potato planting, picking and sorting.

A Guide only for the last eighteen months, Ann already has twelve badges. This year she plans to join the Sea Rangers and her ambition is to become a Sports Instructress in the W.R.N.S. or W.R.A.F.

ARTING TODAY: the story of a girl with one ambition

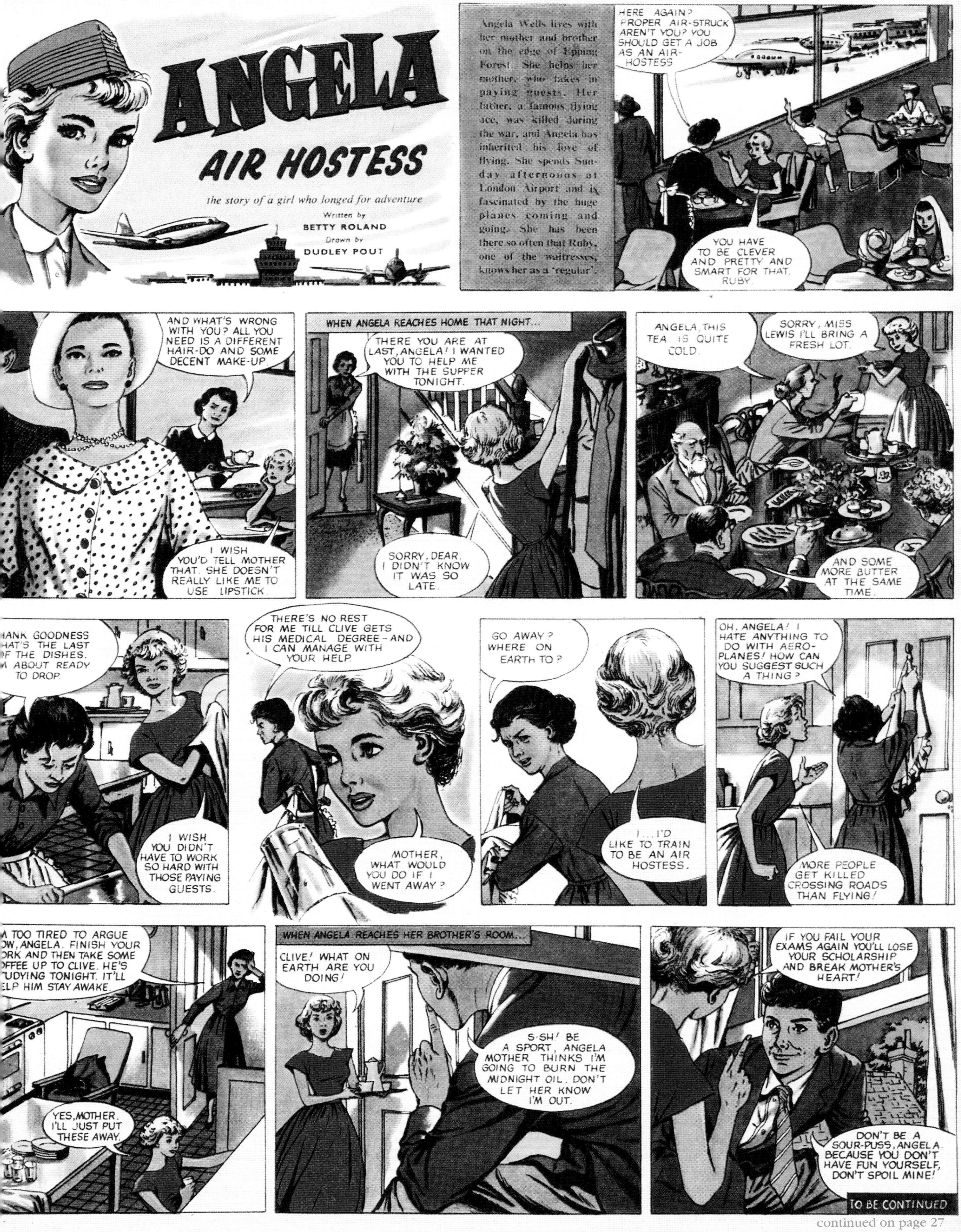
ANGELA
AIR HOSTESS
the story of a girl who longed for adventure
Written by BETTY ROLAND
Drawn by DUDLEY POUT
Angela Wells lives with her mother and brother on the edge of Epping Forest. She helps her mother, who takes in paying guests. Her father, a famous flying ace, was killed during the war, and Angela has inherited his love of flying. She spends Sunday afternoons at London Airport and is fascinated by the huge planes coming and going. She has been there so often that Ruby, one of the waitresses, knows her as a 'regular'.
HERE AGAIN? PROPER AIR-STRUCK AREN'T YOU? YOU SHOULD GET A JOB AS AN AIR-HOSTESS
YOU HAVE TO BE CLEVER AND PRETTY AND SMART FOR THAT, RUBY.
AND WHAT'S WRONG WITH YOU? ALL YOU NEED IS A DIFFERENT HAIR-DO AND SOME DECENT MAKE-UP.
I WISH YOU'D TELL MOTHER THAT. SHE DOESN'T REALLY LIKE ME TO USE LIPSTICK.
WHEN ANGELA REACHES HOME THAT NIGHT...
THERE YOU ARE AT LAST, ANGELA! I WANTED YOU TO HELP ME WITH THE SUPPER TONIGHT.
SORRY, DEAR. I DIDN'T KNOW IT WAS SO LATE.
ANGELA, THIS TEA IS QUITE COLD.
SORRY, MISS LEWIS I'LL BRING A FRESH LOT.
AND SOME MORE BUTTER AT THE SAME TIME.
HANK GOODNESS HAT'S THE LAST F THE DISHES. M ABOUT READY TO DROP.
I WISH YOU DIDN'T HAVE TO WORK SO HARD WITH THOSE PAYING GUESTS.
THERE'S NO REST FOR ME TILL CLIVE GETS HIS MEDICAL DEGREE–AND I CAN MANAGE WITH YOUR HELP.
MOTHER, WHAT WOULD YOU DO IF I WENT AWAY?
GO AWAY? WHERE ON EARTH TO?
I...I'D LIKE TO TRAIN TO BE AN AIR HOSTESS.
OH, ANGELA! I HATE ANYTHING TO DO WITH AERO-PLANES! HOW CAN YOU SUGGEST SUCH A THING?
MORE PEOPLE GET KILLED CROSSING ROADS THAN FLYING!
M TOO TIRED TO ARGUE OW, ANGELA. FINISH YOUR ORK AND THEN TAKE SOME OFFEE UP TO CLIVE. HE'S TUDYING TONIGHT. IT'LL ELP HIM STAY AWAKE.
YES, MOTHER. I'LL JUST PUT THESE AWAY.
WHEN ANGELA REACHES HER BROTHER'S ROOM...
CLIVE! WHAT ON EARTH ARE YOU DOING!
S-SH! BE A SPORT, ANGELA. MOTHER THINKS I'M GOING TO BURN THE MIDNIGHT OIL. DON'T LET HER KNOW I'M OUT.
IF YOU FAIL YOUR EXAMS AGAIN YOU'LL LOSE YOUR SCHOLARSHIP AND BREAK MOTHER'S HEART!
DON'T BE A SOUR-PUSS, ANGELA. BECAUSE YOU DON'T HAVE FUN YOURSELF, DON'T SPOIL MINE!
TO BE CONTINUED

continued on page 27

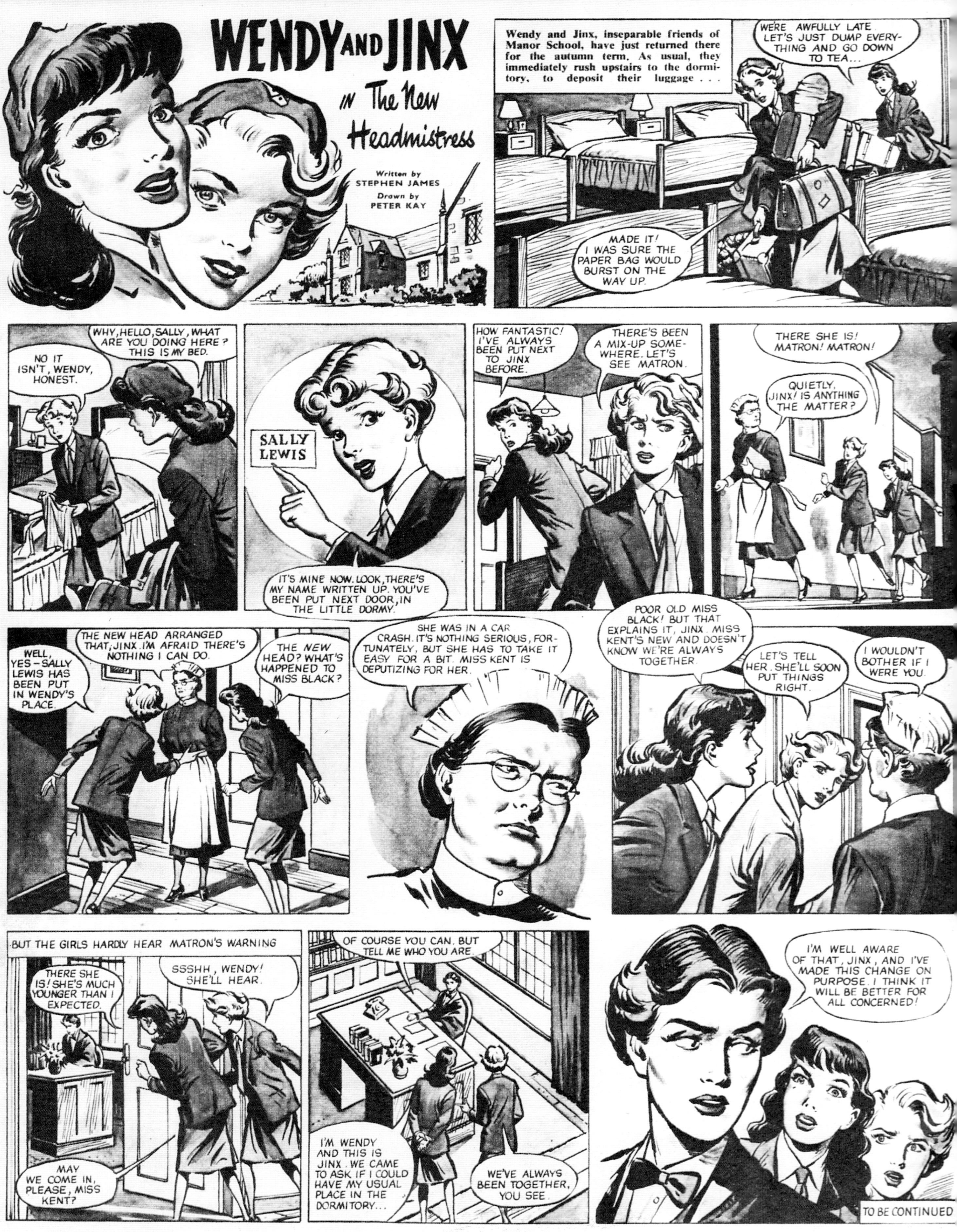
WENDY AND JINX
IN The New Headmistress
Written by STEPHEN JAMES
Drawn by PETER KAY
Wendy and Jinx, inseparable friends of Manor School, have just returned there for the autumn term. As usual, they immediately rush upstairs to the dormitory, to deposit their luggage . . .
WE'RE AWFULLY LATE. LET'S JUST DUMP EVERYTHING AND GO DOWN TO TEA...
MADE IT! I WAS SURE THE PAPER BAG WOULD BURST ON THE WAY UP.
WHY, HELLO, SALLY, WHAT ARE YOU DOING HERE? THIS IS MY BED.
NO IT ISN'T, WENDY, HONEST.
SALLY LEWIS
IT'S MINE NOW. LOOK, THERE'S MY NAME WRITTEN UP. YOU'VE BEEN PUT NEXT DOOR, IN THE LITTLE DORMY.
HOW FANTASTIC! I'VE ALWAYS BEEN PUT NEXT TO JINX BEFORE.
THERE'S BEEN A MIX-UP SOMEWHERE. LET'S SEE MATRON.
THERE SHE IS! MATRON! MATRON!
QUIETLY, JINX! IS ANYTHING THE MATTER?
WELL, YES–SALLY LEWIS HAS BEEN PUT IN WENDY'S PLACE.
THE NEW HEAD ARRANGED THAT, JINX. I'M AFRAID THERE'S NOTHING I CAN DO.
THE NEW HEAD? WHAT'S HAPPENED TO MISS BLACK?
SHE WAS IN A CAR CRASH. IT'S NOTHING SERIOUS, FORTUNATELY, BUT SHE HAS TO TAKE IT EASY FOR A BIT. MISS KENT IS DEPUTIZING FOR HER.
POOR OLD MISS BLACK! BUT THAT EXPLAINS IT, JINX. MISS KENT'S NEW AND DOESN'T KNOW WE'RE ALWAYS TOGETHER.
LET'S TELL HER. SHE'LL SOON PUT THINGS RIGHT.
I WOULDN'T BOTHER IF I WERE YOU.
BUT THE GIRLS HARDLY HEAR MATRON'S WARNING
THERE SHE IS! SHE'S MUCH YOUNGER THAN I EXPECTED.
SSSHH, WENDY! SHE'LL HEAR.
MAY WE COME IN, PLEASE, MISS KENT?
OF COURSE YOU CAN. BUT TELL ME WHO YOU ARE.
I'M WENDY AND THIS IS JINX. WE CAME TO ASK IF I COULD HAVE MY USUAL PLACE IN THE DORMITORY...
WE'VE ALWAYS BEEN TOGETHER, YOU SEE.
I'M WELL AWARE OF THAT, JINX, AND I'VE MADE THIS CHANGE ON PURPOSE. I THINK IT WILL BE BETTER FOR ALL CONCERNED!
TO BE CONTINUED

continued on page 24

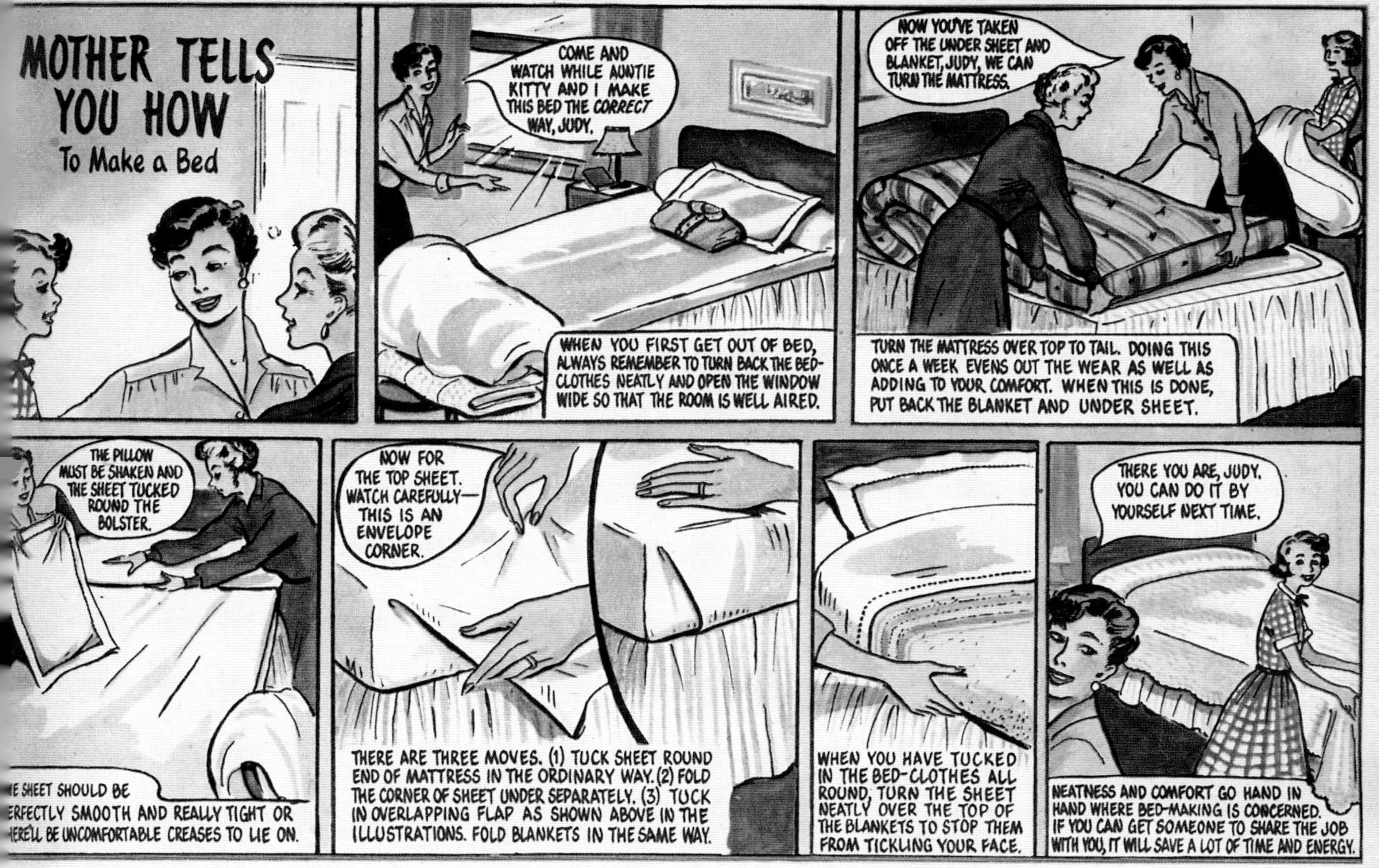
MOTHER TELLS YOU HOW
To Make a Bed
COME AND WATCH WHILE AUNTIE KITTY AND I MAKE THIS BED THE CORRECT WAY, JUDY.
WHEN YOU FIRST GET OUT OF BED, ALWAYS REMEMBER TO TURN BACK THE BED-CLOTHES NEATLY AND OPEN THE WINDOW WIDE SO THAT THE ROOM IS WELL AIRED.
NOW YOU'VE TAKEN OFF THE UNDER SHEET AND BLANKET, JUDY, WE CAN TURN THE MATTRESS.
TURN THE MATTRESS OVER TOP TO TAIL. DOING THIS ONCE A WEEK EVENS OUT THE WEAR AS WELL AS ADDING TO YOUR COMFORT. WHEN THIS IS DONE, PUT BACK THE BLANKET AND UNDER SHEET.
THE PILLOW MUST BE SHAKEN AND THE SHEET TUCKED ROUND THE BOLSTER.
HE SHEET SHOULD BE ERFECTLY SMOOTH AND REALLY TIGHT OR HERE'LL BE UNCOMFORTABLE CREASES TO LIE ON.
NOW FOR THE TOP SHEET. WATCH CAREFULLY— THIS IS AN ENVELOPE CORNER.
THERE ARE THREE MOVES. (1) TUCK SHEET ROUND END OF MATTRESS IN THE ORDINARY WAY. (2) FOLD THE CORNER OF SHEET UNDER SEPARATELY. (3) TUCK IN OVERLAPPING FLAP AS SHOWN ABOVE IN THE ILLUSTRATIONS. FOLD BLANKETS IN THE SAME WAY.
WHEN YOU HAVE TUCKED IN THE BED-CLOTHES ALL ROUND, TURN THE SHEET NEATLY OVER THE TOP OF THE BLANKETS TO STOP THEM FROM TICKLING YOUR FACE.
THERE YOU ARE, JUDY. YOU CAN DO IT BY YOURSELF NEXT TIME.
NEATNESS AND COMFORT GO HAND IN HAND WHERE BED-MAKING IS CONCERNED. IF YOU CAN GET SOMEONE TO SHARE THE JOB WITH YOU, IT WILL SAVE A LOT OF TIME AND ENERGY.

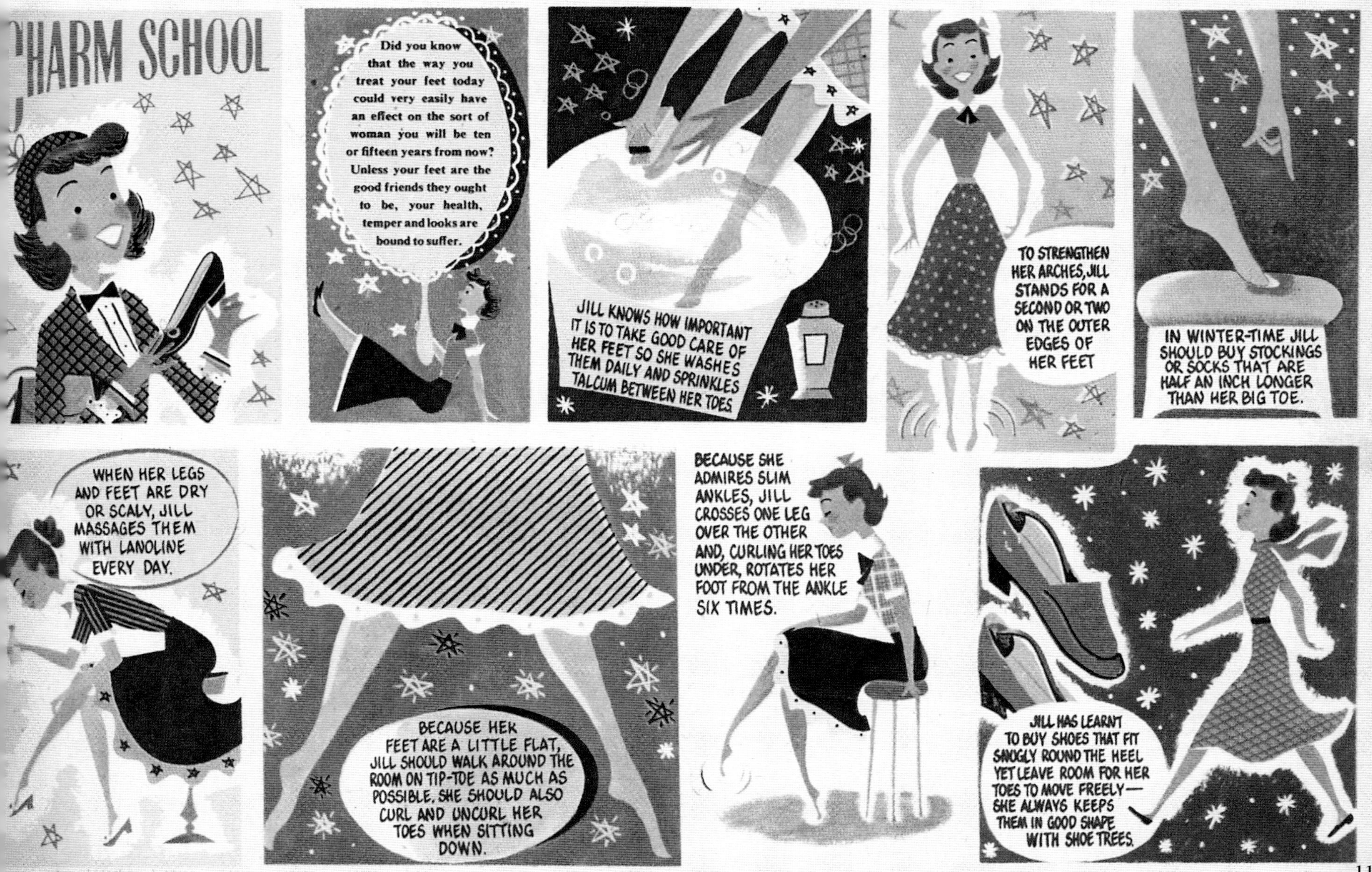
CHARM SCHOOL
Did you know that the way you treat your feet today could very easily have an effect on the sort of woman you will be ten or fifteen years from now? Unless your feet are the good friends they ought to be, your health, temper and looks are bound to suffer.
JILL KNOWS HOW IMPORTANT IT IS TO TAKE GOOD CARE OF HER FEET SO SHE WASHES THEM DAILY AND SPRINKLES TALCUM BETWEEN HER TOES.
TO STRENGTHEN HER ARCHES, JILL STANDS FOR A SECOND OR TWO ON THE OUTER EDGES OF HER FEET
IN WINTER-TIME JILL SHOULD BUY STOCKINGS OR SOCKS THAT ARE HALF AN INCH LONGER THAN HER BIG TOE.
WHEN HER LEGS AND FEET ARE DRY OR SCALY, JILL MASSAGES THEM WITH LANOLINE EVERY DAY.
BECAUSE HER FEET ARE A LITTLE FLAT, JILL SHOULD WALK AROUND THE ROOM ON TIP-TOE AS MUCH AS POSSIBLE. SHE SHOULD ALSO CURL AND UNCURL HER TOES WHEN SITTING DOWN.
BECAUSE SHE ADMIRES SLIM ANKLES, JILL CROSSES ONE LEG OVER THE OTHER AND, CURLING HER TOES UNDER, ROTATES HER FOOT FROM THE ANKLE SIX TIMES.
JILL HAS LEARNT TO BUY SHOES THAT FIT SNUGLY ROUND THE HEEL YET LEAVE ROOM FOR HER TOES TO MOVE FREELY— SHE ALWAYS KEEPS THEM IN GOOD SHAPE WITH SHOE TREES.

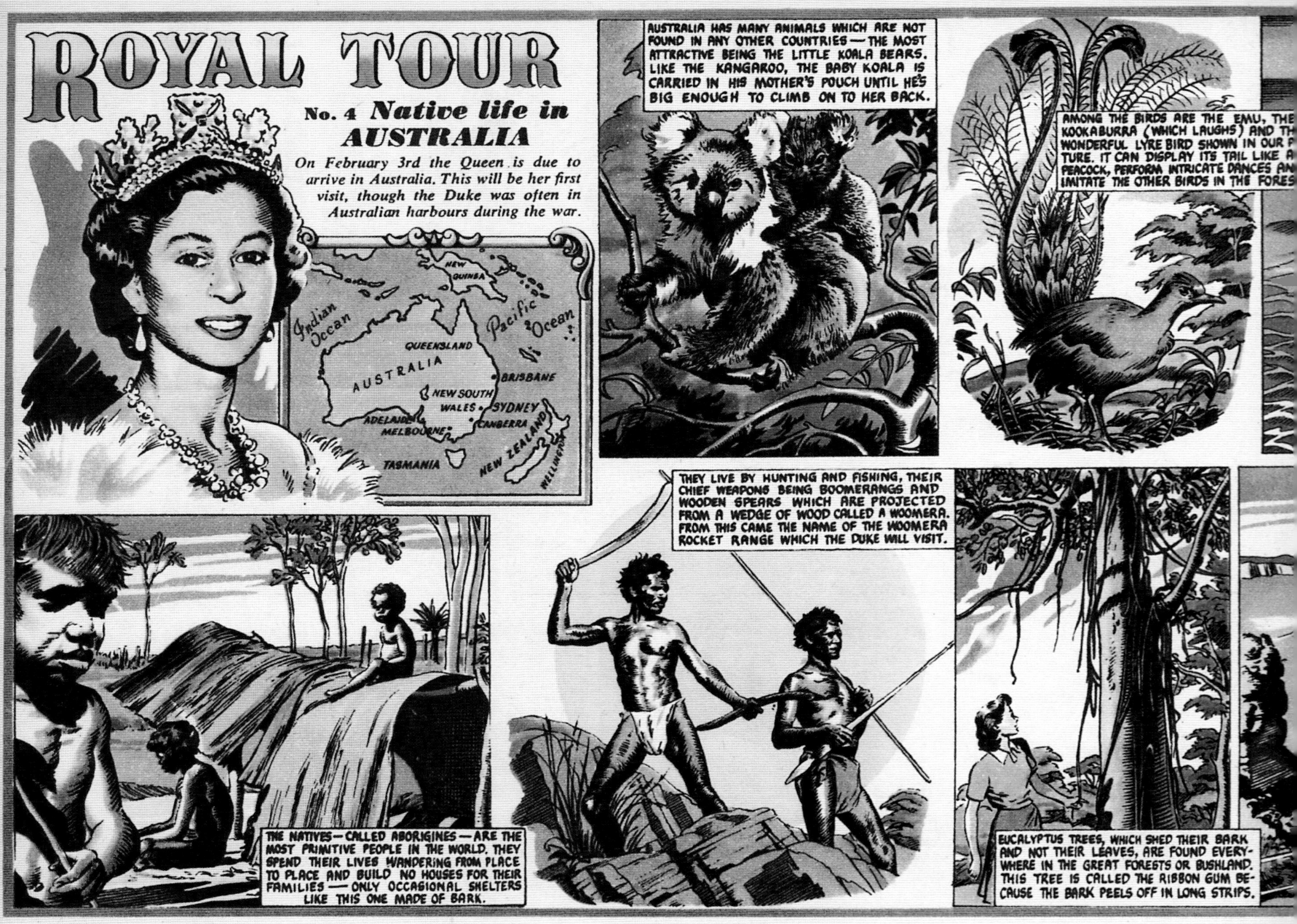
ROYAL TOUR
No. 4 Native life in AUSTRALIA
On February 3rd the Queen is due to arrive in Australia. This will be her first visit, though the Duke was often in Australian harbours during the war.
Indian Ocean
Pacific Ocean
NEW GUINEA
QUEENSLAND
AUSTRALIA
BRISBANE
NEW SOUTH WALES
SYDNEY
ADELAIDE
MELBOURNE
CANBERRA
TASMANIA
NEW ZEALAND
WELLINGTON
AUSTRALIA HAS MANY ANIMALS WHICH ARE NOT FOUND IN ANY OTHER COUNTRIES — THE MOST ATTRACTIVE BEING THE LITTLE KOALA BEARS. LIKE THE KANGAROO, THE BABY KOALA IS CARRIED IN HIS MOTHER'S POUCH UNTIL HE'S BIG ENOUGH TO CLIMB ON TO HER BACK.
AMONG THE BIRDS ARE THE EMU, THE KOOKABURRA (WHICH LAUGHS) AND TH WONDERFUL LYRE BIRD SHOWN IN OUR P TURE. IT CAN DISPLAY ITS TAIL LIKE A PEACOCK, PERFORM INTRICATE DANCES AN IMITATE THE OTHER BIRDS IN THE FORES
THE NATIVES—CALLED ABORIGINES—ARE THE MOST PRIMITIVE PEOPLE IN THE WORLD. THEY SPEND THEIR LIVES WANDERING FROM PLACE TO PLACE AND BUILD NO HOUSES FOR THEIR FAMILIES — ONLY OCCASIONAL SHELTERS LIKE THIS ONE MADE OF BARK.
THEY LIVE BY HUNTING AND FISHING, THEIR CHIEF WEAPONS BEING BOOMERANGS AND WOODEN SPEARS WHICH ARE PROJECTED FROM A WEDGE OF WOOD CALLED A WOOMERA. FROM THIS CAME THE NAME OF THE WOOMERA ROCKET RANGE WHICH THE DUKE WILL VISIT.
EUCALYPTUS TREES, WHICH SHED THEIR BARK AND NOT THEIR LEAVES, ARE FOUND EVERYWHERE IN THE GREAT FORESTS OR BUSHLAND. THIS TREE IS CALLED THE RIBBON GUM BECAUSE THE BARK PEELS OFF IN LONG STRIPS.

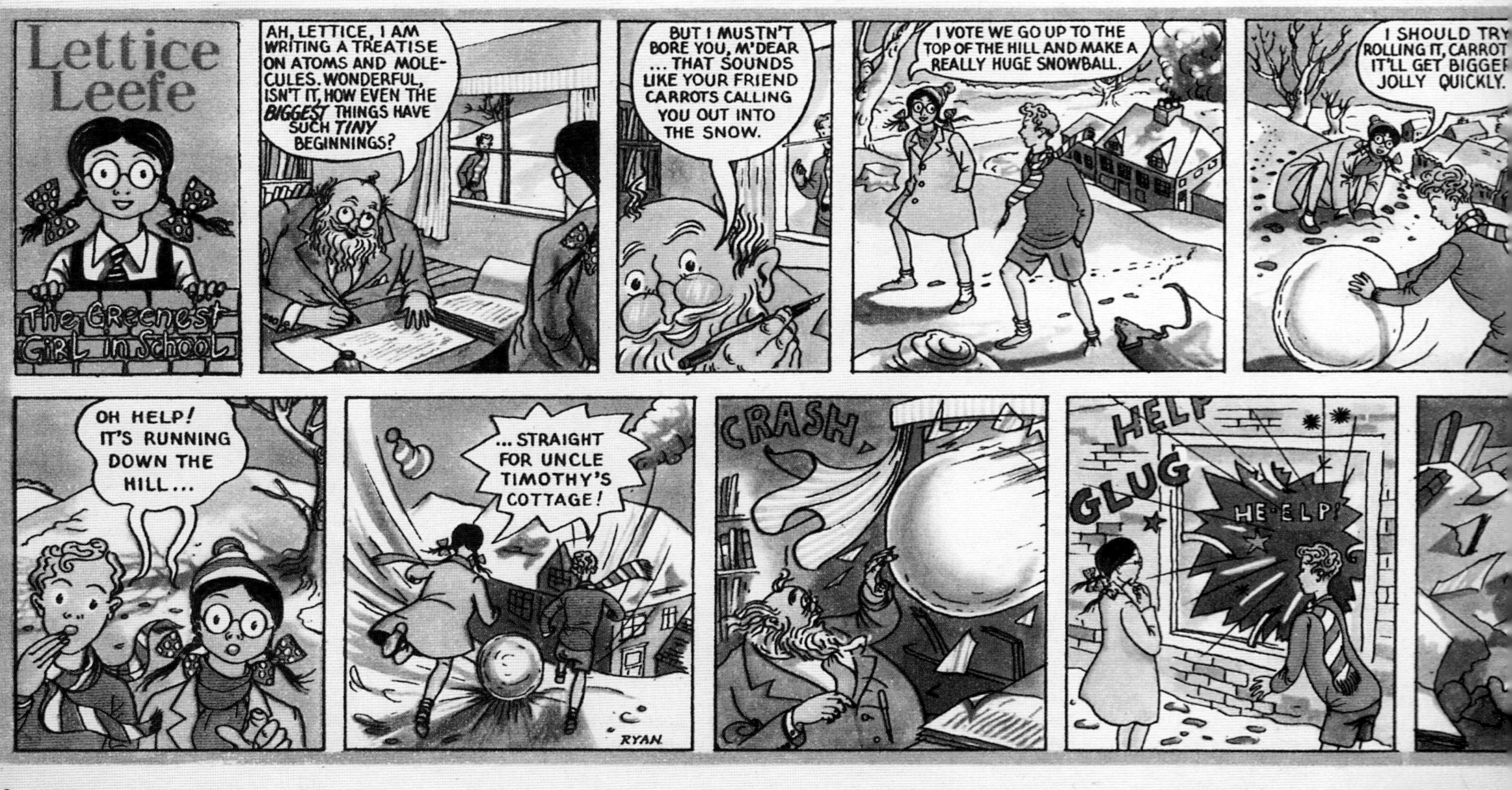
Lettice Leefe
The Greenest Girl in School
AH, LETTICE, I AM WRITING A TREATISE ON ATOMS AND MOLECULES. WONDERFUL, ISN'T IT, HOW EVEN THE BIGGEST THINGS HAVE SUCH TINY BEGINNINGS?
BUT I MUSTN'T BORE YOU, M'DEAR ... THAT SOUNDS LIKE YOUR FRIEND CARROTS CALLING YOU OUT INTO THE SNOW.
I VOTE WE GO UP TO THE TOP OF THE HILL AND MAKE A REALLY HUGE SNOWBALL.
I SHOULD TRY ROLLING IT, CARROT IT'LL GET BIGGER JOLLY QUICKLY.
OH HELP! IT'S RUNNING DOWN THE HILL...
...STRAIGHT FOR UNCLE TIMOTHY'S COTTAGE!
RYAN
CRASH
HELP
GLUG
HE-ELP!

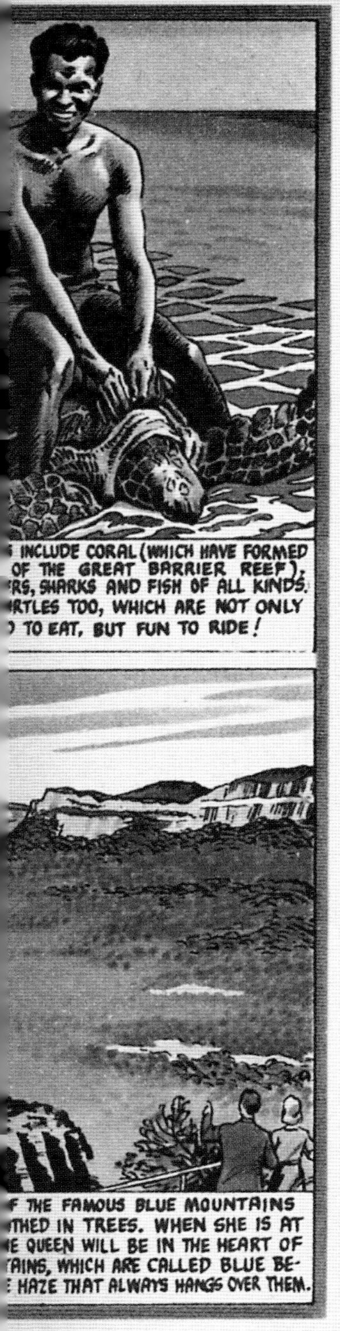
INCLUDE CORAL (WHICH HAVE FORMED
OF THE GREAT BARRIER REEF),
RS, SHARKS AND FISH OF ALL KINDS,
RTLES TOO, WHICH ARE NOT ONLY
TO EAT, BUT FUN TO RIDE!
F THE FAMOUS BLUE MOUNTAINS
THED IN TREES. WHEN SHE IS AT
E QUEEN WILL BE IN THE HEART OF
TAINS, WHICH ARE CALLED BLUE BE-
E HAZE THAT ALWAYS HANGS OVER THEM.

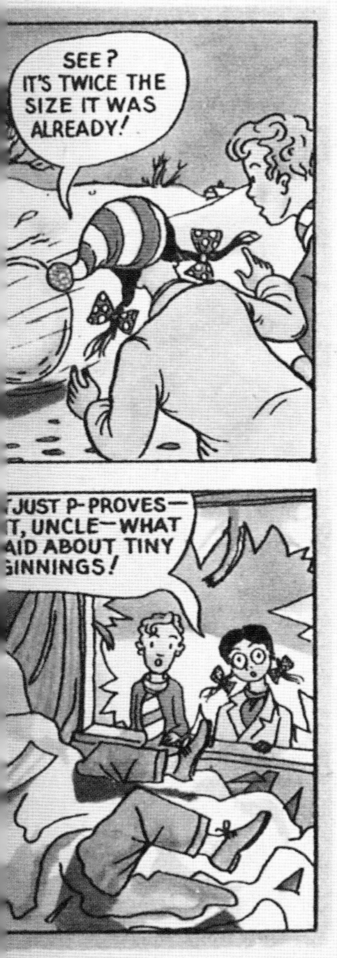
SEE? IT'S TWICE THE SIZE IT WAS ALREADY!
JUST P-PROVES— T, UNCLE—WHAT AID ABOUT TINY GINNINGS!

Girl Picture Gallery

No. 310

This talented performer leads a band, composes, writes and draws, but is best known to you as one of our foremost jazz trumpeters.

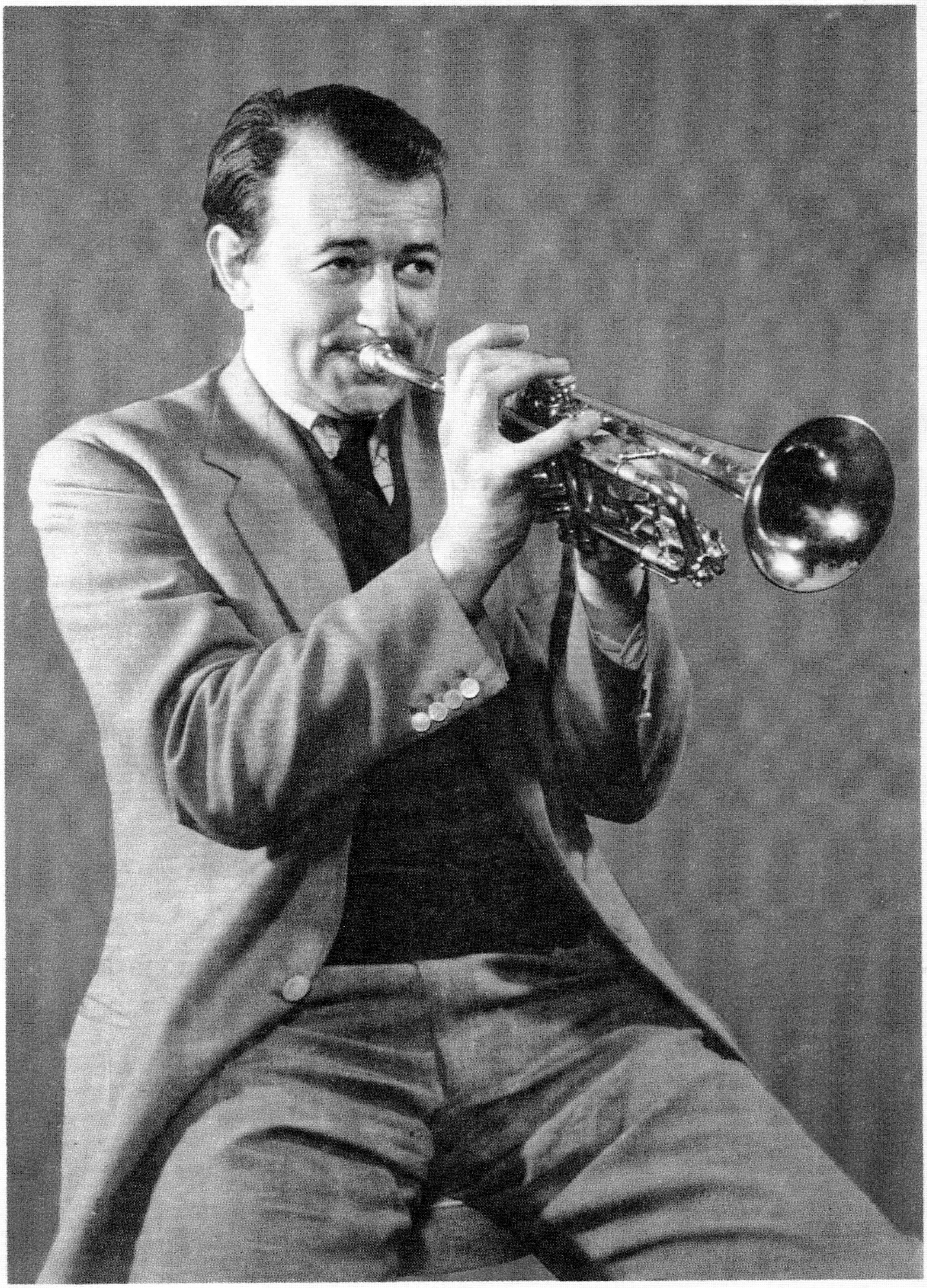

HUMPHREY LYTTELTON

Specially photographed for GIRL by Bert Hardy

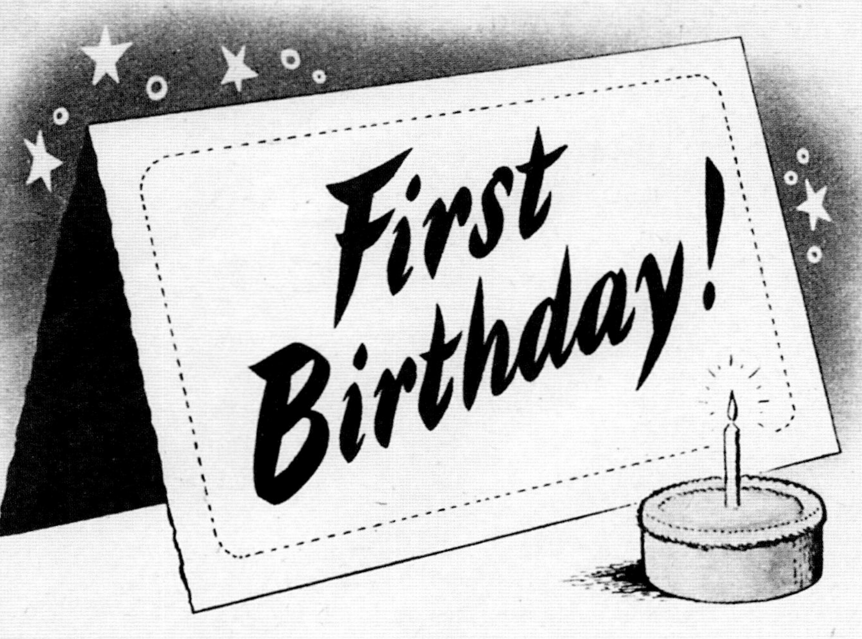
First Birthday!

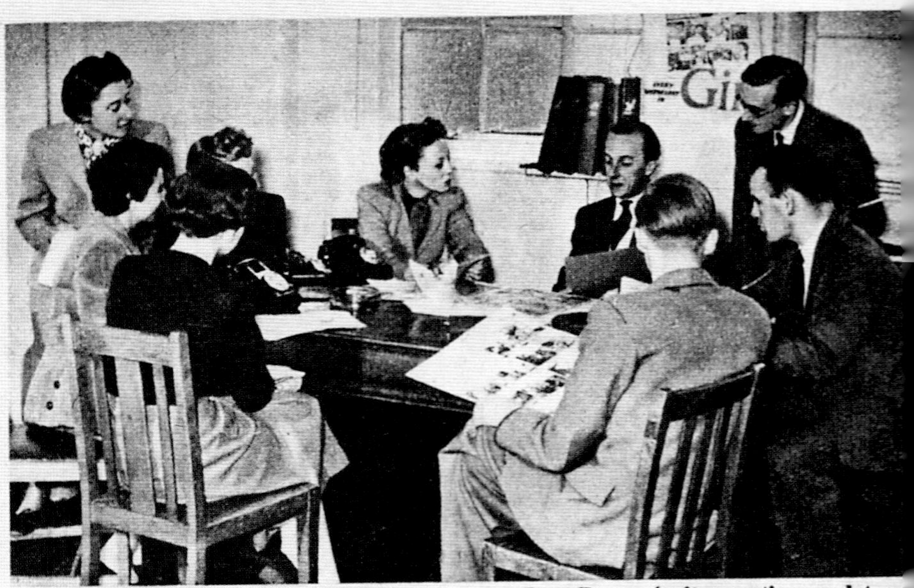
GIRL

How GIRL is planned. Round the table are Jean Brown (writes captions and type Maureen Levene (chief sub-editor), Win Gordine (secretary), Beth Featherston (Edito secretary), Jodi Hyland (Assistant Editor), Marcus Morris (Editor), Derek Lord (editor assistant), Arthur Roberts (Art Editor) and Roy (a lettering artist).

IT'S been a wonderful year in the offices of GIRL – ever since that time, over a year ago now, when we all sat up nearly all night putting the finishing touches to the very first issue!

We made 'Adventure' our key-word on GIRL, and the contributors and staff have had as many adventures preparing the stories, pictures and strips, as there are weeks in the year. Each week has brought some new adventure to us – and we hope to you as well. We have tried to make it so.

We have made a lot of new friends and we have had a great many new and exciting experiences. We thought you'd like to share our friends and our experiences with us, so we are going to introduce to you on this page some of the people who have helped us to make GIRL possible, and remind you of some of the fun we have had during GIRL's first year.

As well as the staff members you will see in the conference photo above there is also a team of busy people who sort all the letters that you write to us, and who cope with the typing and despatching of the answers. There is a gang dealing with all the competitions, seeing that the winners receive their prizes and that every single competition entry is looked at and fairly judged. There are our two office boys, Owen and John, who scurry about looking for lost parcels and taking late packets to the station for despatch to the printer. There's Margaret, who reminds forgetful artists of press dates. There's Maureen who sees that commas are all put in their right places and that words are spelled correctly, and Sherley who invents the puzzles for Treasure Chest. And, of course, there are the Printers – those important people who often work through the night to see that GIRL is ready on time.

Though we have not space here to mention, everybody there are hundreds of other people who work outside our offices making it possible for GIRL to reach you every week. Outside our office walls there are those people 'behind the scenes' whose work is none the less important though their names do not show on every copy. There are the newsagents and distributors, the van drive and even the ladies who bring round t morning tea. There are people like Barba Wace who goes from her Fleet Street flat find *Girl of the Week* each week; people li J. H. Kisch who drives Jacky all over t countryside on her visits and photographs h There's Mileson Horton who thinks up t Adventures of *Penny Wise* and Arthur Ca erall, Sylvia Little and others who write t exciting serials for you to read.

To all these people we wish a very hap First Birthday.

And to all of you who read our paper – wish you another happy year of reading ahe and hope you'll be with us for many yea

Some of the events of GIRL's first year...

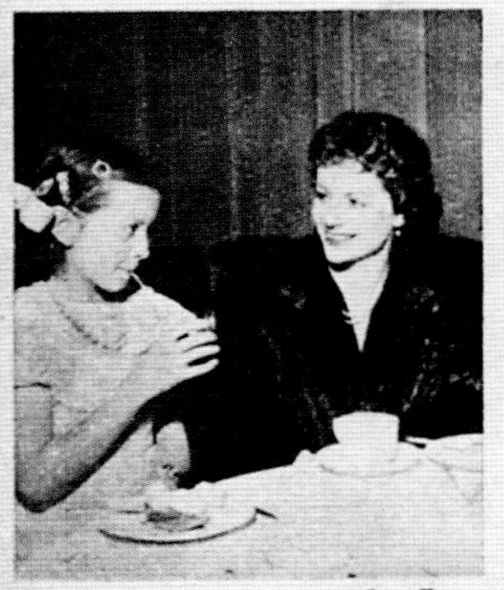

Event of the year for reader Jean Bowman was when she had her wish granted – a tea-party with film star Margaret Lockwood.

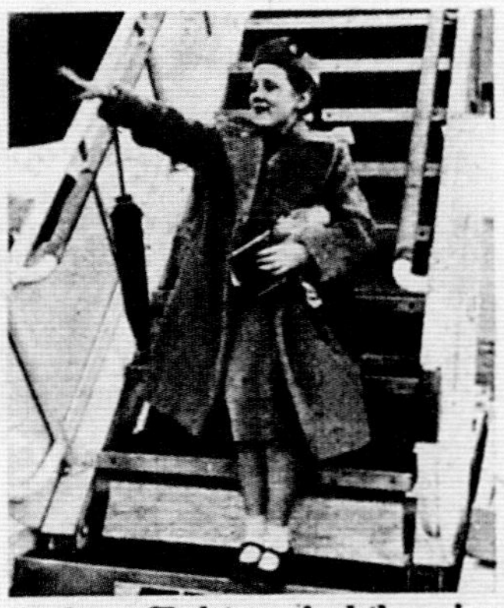

Barbara Christmas had the prize of the year through GIRL's competitions. She won an air trip to New York and a week's stay.

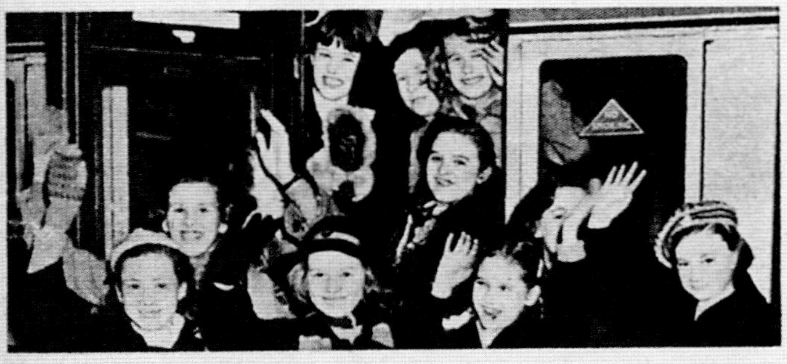

One of the main events last January was the departure for a winter sporting holiday in the French Alps of a large party of GIRL readers.

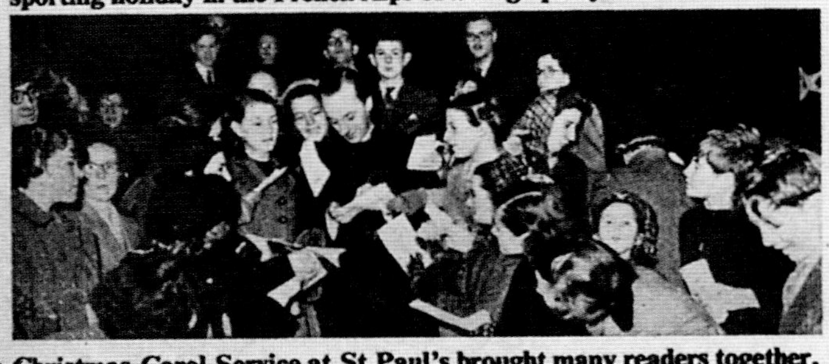

Christmas Carol Service at St Paul's brought many readers together. The Editor, Rev Marcus Morris, signs autographs after the service.

...and some of the people who have made GIRL possible...

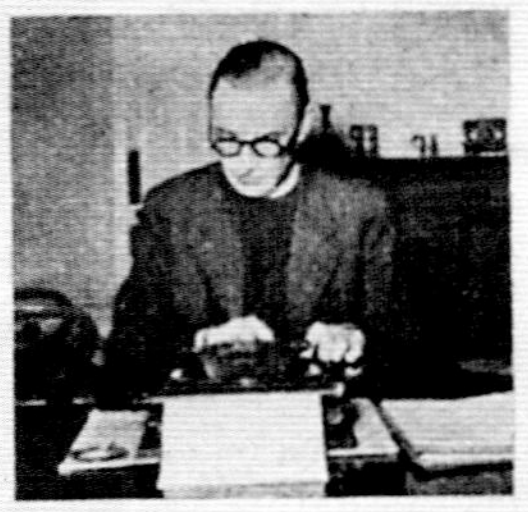

Chad Varah *writes Royal Margaret in his vicarage.*

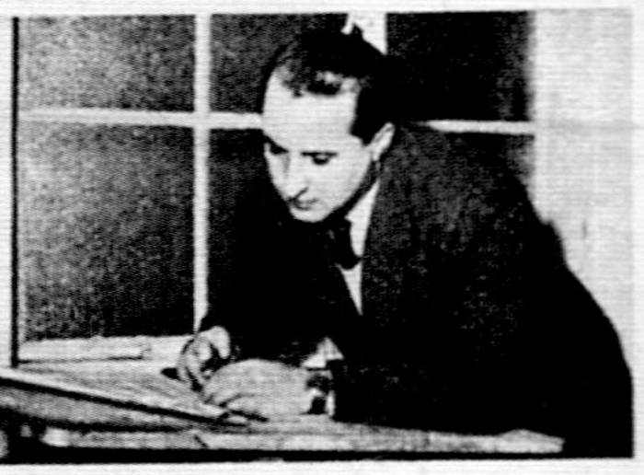

Bernard Greenbaum *draws Penny Wise and the Lesters in his home at Hendon.*

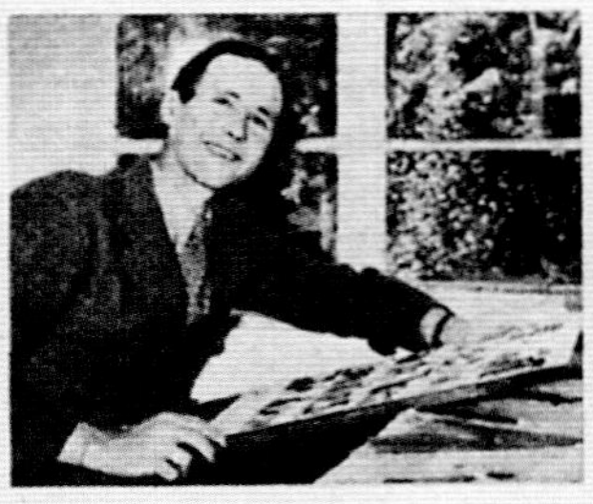

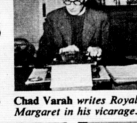

John Ryan *teaches art, thinks up and draws Lettice as well.*

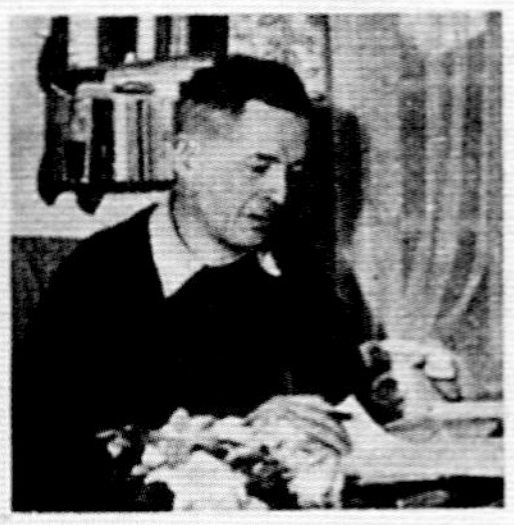

George Beardmore *writes of Robbie and Starling.*

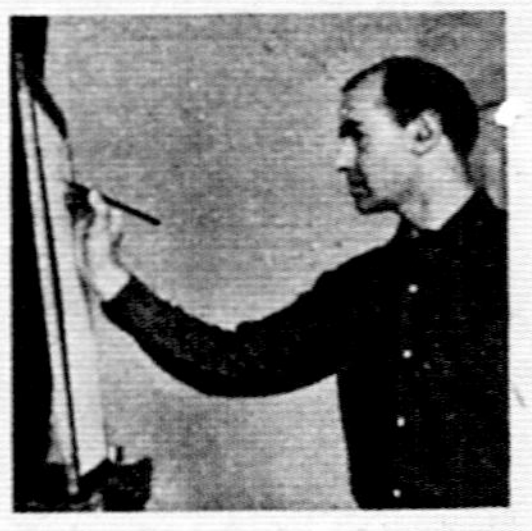

Roy Newby *draws all of Robbie's adventures.*

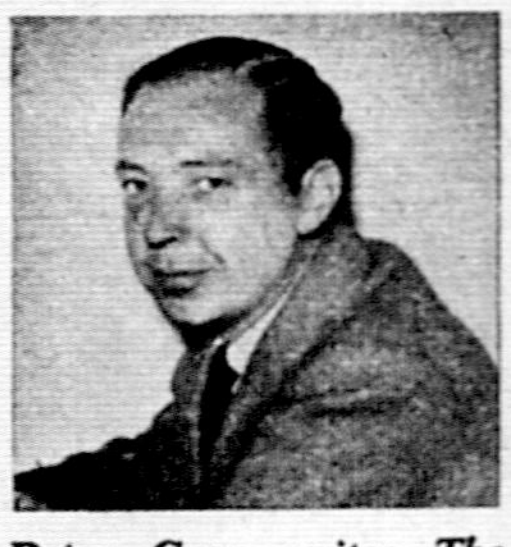

Peter Grey *writes The Lesters and is Fiction Ed.*

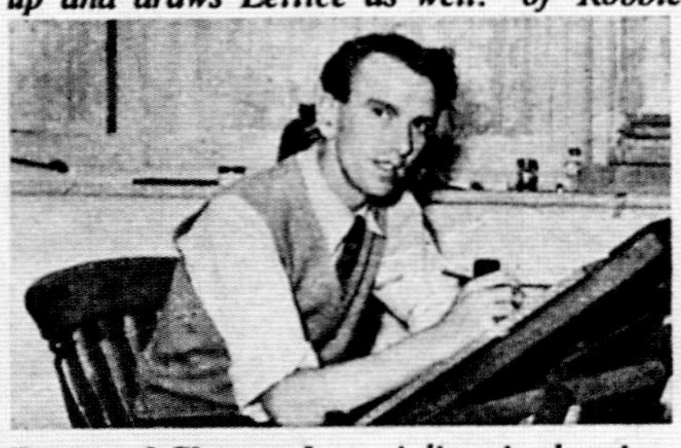

Raymond Sheppard *specialises in drawings of animals – and is the artist of Pets Corner*

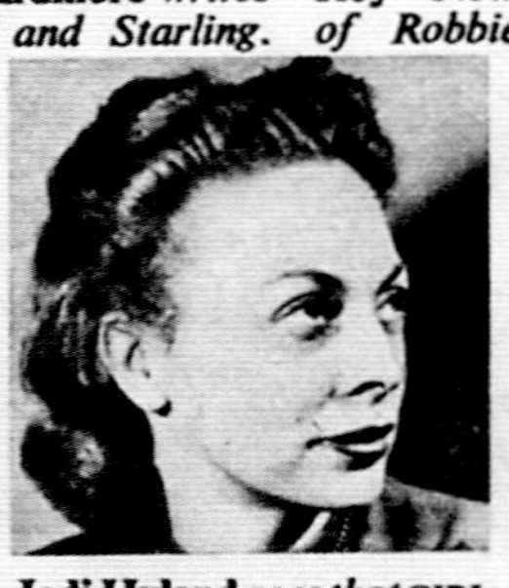

Jodi Hyland *sees that* GIRL *goes to press each week.*

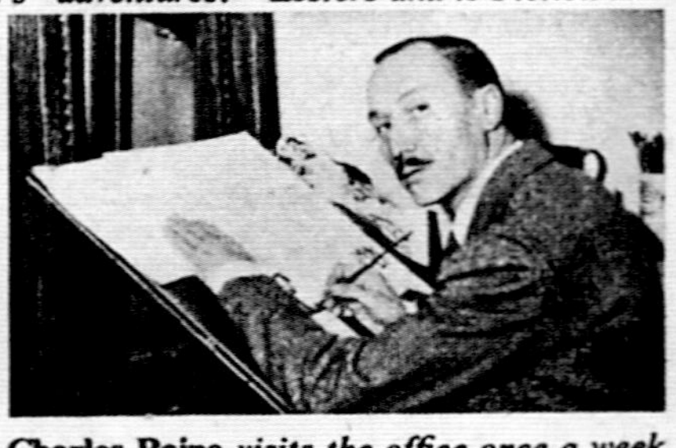

Charles Paine *visits the office once a week bringing in drawings of Jala the Jungle Girl.*

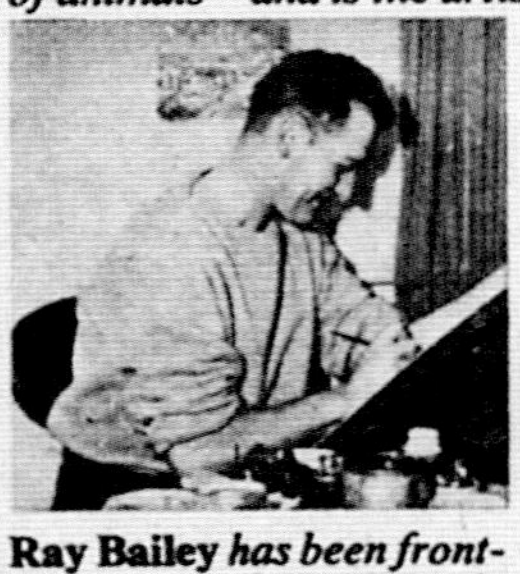

Ray Bailey *has been front-page artist from Issue 1. He lives at Battersea.*

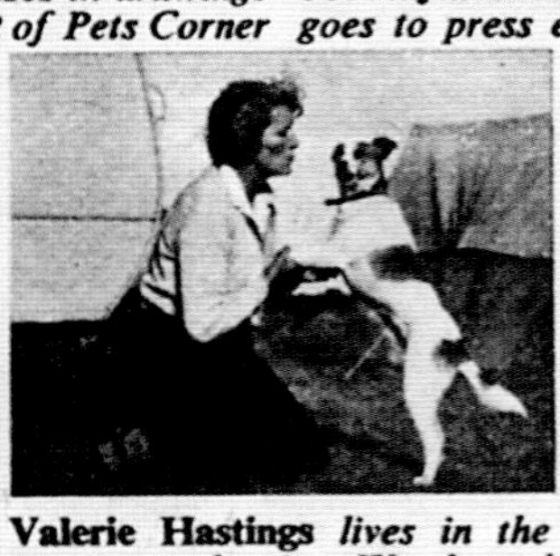

Valerie Hastings *lives in the country and writes Wendy and Jinx. Her husband writes too.*

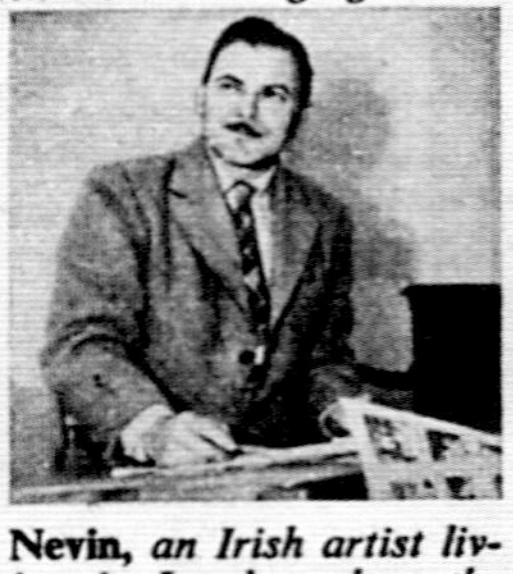

Nevin, *an Irish artist living in London, does the Captain Starling drawings*

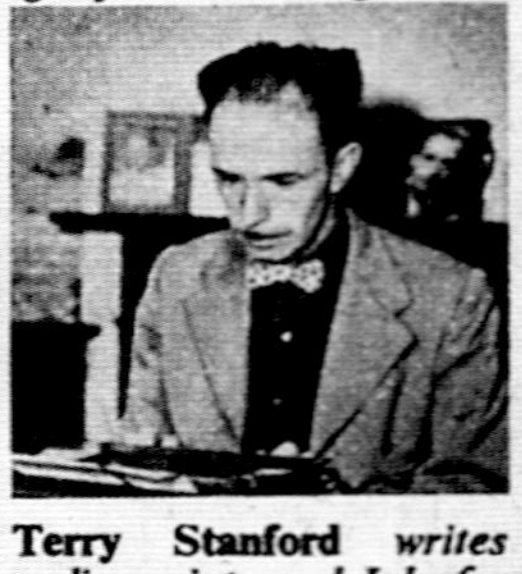

Terry Stanford *writes radio scripts and Jala for us. He's lived in a jungle.*

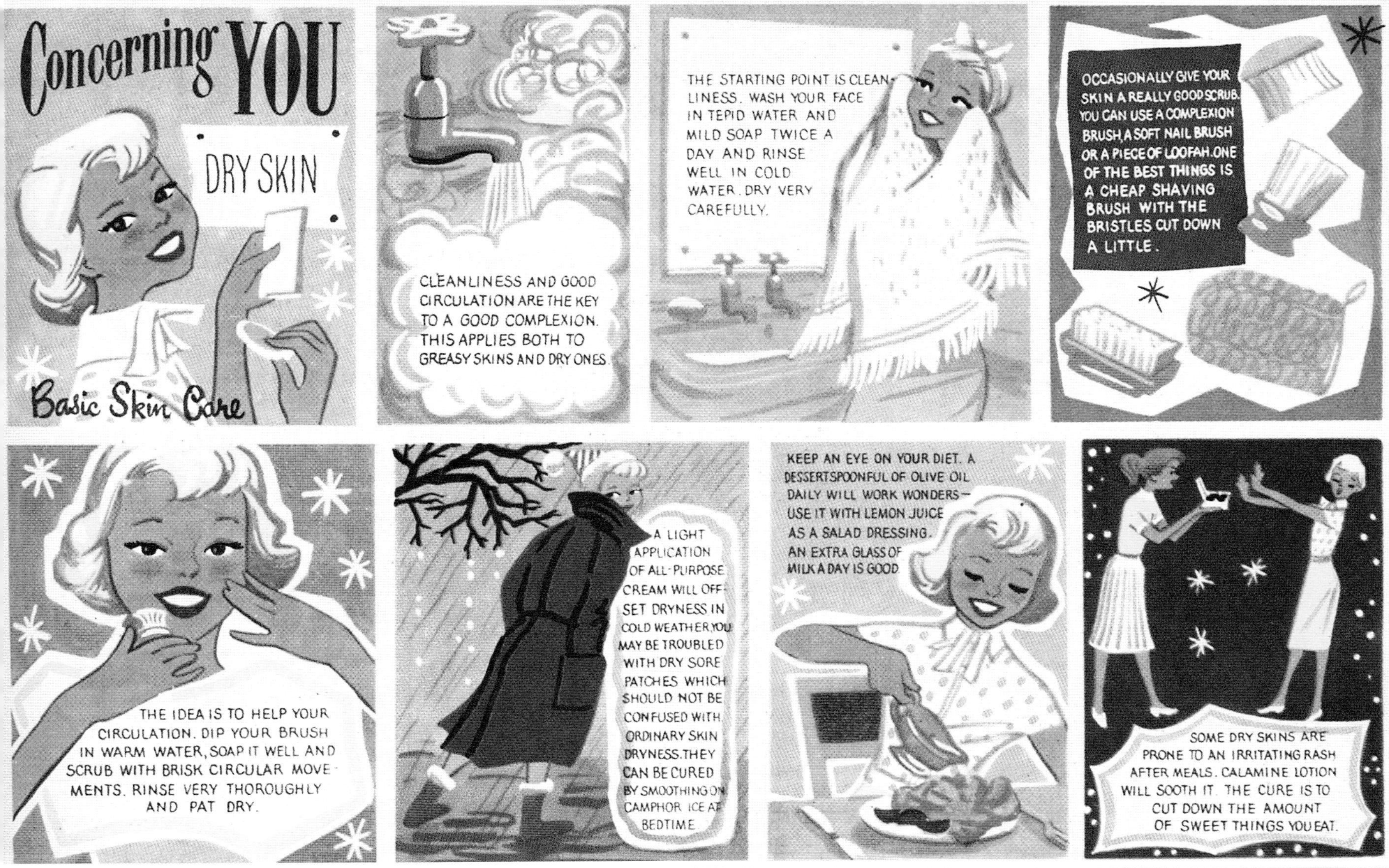
Concerning YOU
DRY SKIN
Basic Skin Care
CLEANLINESS AND GOOD CIRCULATION ARE THE KEY TO A GOOD COMPLEXION. THIS APPLIES BOTH TO GREASY SKINS AND DRY ONES.
THE STARTING POINT IS CLEANLINESS. WASH YOUR FACE IN TEPID WATER AND MILD SOAP TWICE A DAY AND RINSE WELL IN COLD WATER. DRY VERY CAREFULLY.
OCCASIONALLY GIVE YOUR SKIN A REALLY GOOD SCRUB. YOU CAN USE A COMPLEXION BRUSH, A SOFT NAIL BRUSH OR A PIECE OF LOOFAH. ONE OF THE BEST THINGS IS A CHEAP SHAVING BRUSH WITH THE BRISTLES CUT DOWN A LITTLE.
THE IDEA IS TO HELP YOUR CIRCULATION. DIP YOUR BRUSH IN WARM WATER, SOAP IT WELL AND SCRUB WITH BRISK CIRCULAR MOVEMENTS. RINSE VERY THOROUGHLY AND PAT DRY.
A LIGHT APPLICATION OF ALL-PURPOSE CREAM WILL OFFSET DRYNESS IN COLD WEATHER. YOU MAY BE TROUBLED WITH DRY SORE PATCHES WHICH SHOULD NOT BE CONFUSED WITH ORDINARY SKIN DRYNESS. THEY CAN BE CURED BY SMOOTHING ON CAMPHOR ICE AT BEDTIME.
KEEP AN EYE ON YOUR DIET. A DESSERTSPOONFUL OF OLIVE OIL DAILY WILL WORK WONDERS—USE IT WITH LEMON JUICE AS A SALAD DRESSING. AN EXTRA GLASS OF MILK A DAY IS GOOD.
SOME DRY SKINS ARE PRONE TO AN IRRITATING RASH AFTER MEALS. CALAMINE LOTION WILL SOOTH IT. THE CURE IS TO CUT DOWN THE AMOUNT OF SWEET THINGS YOU EAT.

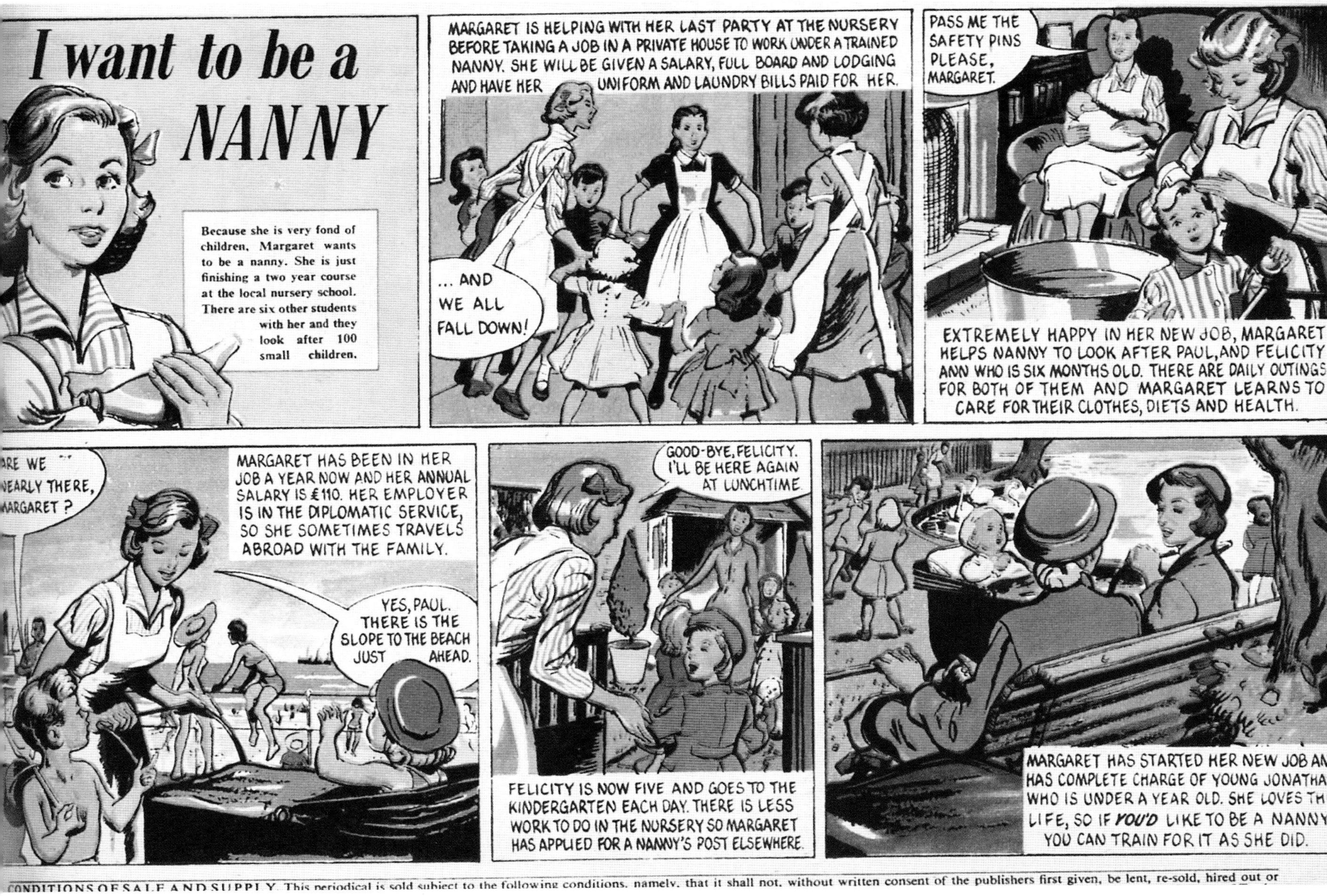
I want to be a NANNY
Because she is very fond of children, Margaret wants to be a nanny. She is just finishing a two year course at the local nursery school. There are six other students with her and they look after 100 small children.
MARGARET IS HELPING WITH HER LAST PARTY AT THE NURSERY BEFORE TAKING A JOB IN A PRIVATE HOUSE TO WORK UNDER A TRAINED NANNY. SHE WILL BE GIVEN A SALARY, FULL BOARD AND LODGING AND HAVE HER UNIFORM AND LAUNDRY BILLS PAID FOR HER.
... AND WE ALL FALL DOWN!
PASS ME THE SAFETY PINS PLEASE, MARGARET.
EXTREMELY HAPPY IN HER NEW JOB, MARGARET HELPS NANNY TO LOOK AFTER PAUL, AND FELICITY ANN WHO IS SIX MONTHS OLD. THERE ARE DAILY OUTINGS FOR BOTH OF THEM AND MARGARET LEARNS TO CARE FOR THEIR CLOTHES, DIETS AND HEALTH.
ARE WE NEARLY THERE, MARGARET?
MARGARET HAS BEEN IN HER JOB A YEAR NOW AND HER ANNUAL SALARY IS £110. HER EMPLOYER IS IN THE DIPLOMATIC SERVICE, SO SHE SOMETIMES TRAVELS ABROAD WITH THE FAMILY.
YES, PAUL. THERE IS THE SLOPE TO THE BEACH JUST AHEAD.
GOOD-BYE, FELICITY. I'LL BE HERE AGAIN AT LUNCHTIME.
FELICITY IS NOW FIVE AND GOES TO THE KINDERGARTEN EACH DAY. THERE IS LESS WORK TO DO IN THE NURSERY SO MARGARET HAS APPLIED FOR A NANNY'S POST ELSEWHERE.
MARGARET HAS STARTED HER NEW JOB AND HAS COMPLETE CHARGE OF YOUNG JONATHAN, WHO IS UNDER A YEAR OLD. SHE LOVES THE LIFE, SO IF YOU'D LIKE TO BE A NANNY YOU CAN TRAIN FOR IT AS SHE DID.

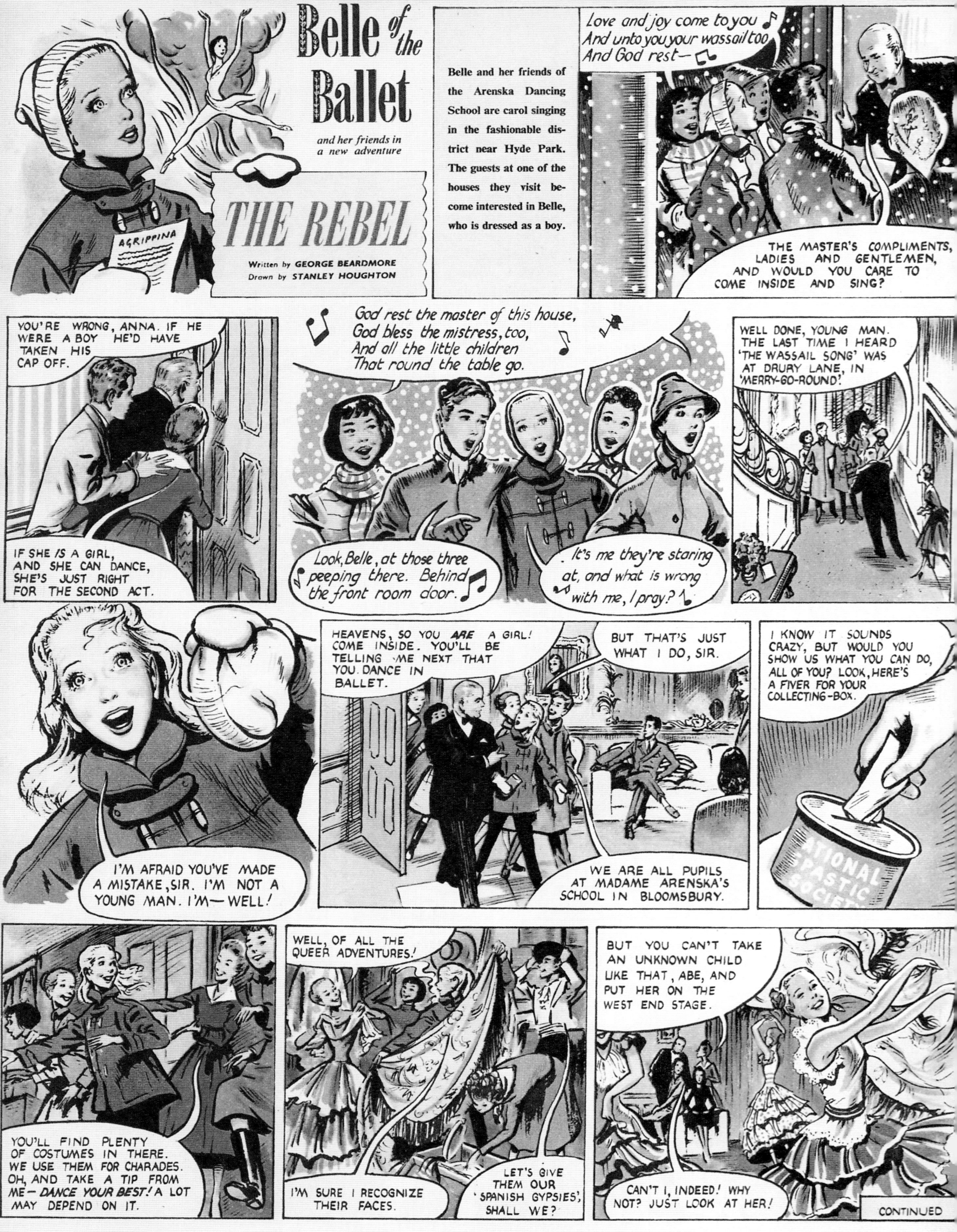

Belle of the Ballet
and her friends in a new adventure
THE REBEL
Written by GEORGE BEARDMORE
Drawn by STANLEY HOUGHTON
AGRIPPINA
Belle and her friends of the Arenska Dancing School are carol singing in the fashionable district near Hyde Park. The guests at one of the houses they visit become interested in Belle, who is dressed as a boy.
Love and joy come to you And unto you your wassail too And God rest—
THE MASTER'S COMPLIMENTS, LADIES AND GENTLEMEN, AND WOULD YOU CARE TO COME INSIDE AND SING?
YOU'RE WRONG, ANNA. IF HE WERE A BOY HE'D HAVE TAKEN HIS CAP OFF.
IF SHE IS A GIRL, AND SHE CAN DANCE, SHE'S JUST RIGHT FOR THE SECOND ACT.
God rest the master of this house, God bless the mistress, too, And all the little children That round the table go.
Look, Belle, at those three peeping there. Behind the front room door.
It's me they're staring at, and what is wrong with me, I pray?
WELL DONE, YOUNG MAN. THE LAST TIME I HEARD 'THE WASSAIL SONG' WAS AT DRURY LANE, IN 'MERRY-GO-ROUND'.
I'M AFRAID YOU'VE MADE A MISTAKE, SIR. I'M NOT A YOUNG MAN. I'M—WELL!
HEAVENS, SO YOU ARE A GIRL! COME INSIDE. YOU'LL BE TELLING ME NEXT THAT YOU DANCE IN BALLET.
BUT THAT'S JUST WHAT I DO, SIR.
WE ARE ALL PUPILS AT MADAME ARENSKA'S SCHOOL IN BLOOMSBURY.
I KNOW IT SOUNDS CRAZY, BUT WOULD YOU SHOW US WHAT YOU CAN DO, ALL OF YOU? LOOK, HERE'S A FIVER FOR YOUR COLLECTING-BOX.
YOU'LL FIND PLENTY OF COSTUMES IN THERE. WE USE THEM FOR CHARADES. OH, AND TAKE A TIP FROM ME—DANCE YOUR BEST! A LOT MAY DEPEND ON IT.
WELL, OF ALL THE QUEER ADVENTURES!
I'M SURE I RECOGNIZE THEIR FACES.
LET'S GIVE THEM OUR 'SPANISH GYPSIES', SHALL WE?
BUT YOU CAN'T TAKE AN UNKNOWN CHILD LIKE THAT, ABE, AND PUT HER ON THE WEST END STAGE.
CAN'T I, INDEED! WHY NOT? JUST LOOK AT HER!
CONTINUED

continued on page 30

Jacky goes Christmas Shopping with Julie Andrews

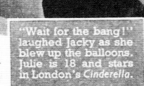

When Jacky called for singing star Julie Andrews she found her putting up Christmas decorations.

"Wait for the bang!" laughed Jacky as she blew up the balloons. Julie is 18 and stars in London's *Cinderella*.

Putting up paper chains the girls had some help from the cat – he kept trying to pull them down again! Julie lives at Walton-on-Thames.

Out shopping they couldn't resist stopping at all the brightly-lit windows.

Julie has 3 brothers and had almost decided to buy them a big toy tractor . . . . .

. . . when she saw the trains! Julie once collected them as a hobby, now prefers ballet, riding and tennis.

There was just time for a fitting of the dress Julie wears in *Cinderella* before they said good-bye and wished each other "Merry Christmas".

I'LL TEACH YOU HOW TO DANCE

by CECILEY FRANK F.I.S.T.D., F.I.D.M.A.
(Championship dancer, teacher and judge)
assisted by VICTOR MORGANS

The photographs illustrating these articles were taken by Carl Sutton.

"May I have the pleasure?"

John invites Pauline to take the floor for a waltz. "Dancing isn't difficult," Miss Frank told Pauline. "Just study the instructions and you'll be able to enjoy your first waltz."

No. I THE WALTZ

IF you can walk, you can dance – it's as easy as that. Learn a few steps to music and you'll be able to enjoy a popular pastime, take healthy exercise and make new friends.

Put a strict tempo waltz on the gramophone and walk round in time to the music. You'll easily distinguish the regular ONE-two-three beat and you must follow the same rhythm, taking one step to each beat of the music.

Always move in an anti-clockwise direction round the room.

This week I show you the main steps in the waltz – known as the Closed Change – then how to fit them in with your partner's. Remember that in all dances you must let your partner *lead*. Don't anticipate his movements, but learn the steps so you can follow intelligently.

The Lady's Hold, for modern dances.

Stand erect, with tummy muscles braced, shoulders softly relaxed and head turned slightly upward and to the left. Use slight pressure when laying your left forearm along your partner's right upper arm. Raise your right hand to same level as your partner's left hand so he can hold it. Do not drag on his left arm. Make your body pliable to his movements.

Here are the Girl's steps for the CLOSED CHANGE...

Starting position (A). Move left foot back (B). Right foot to side and slightly back (C). Close left to right, changing weight to left (D). Repeat, starting with right foot.

...and now try the above steps with your partner

Victor and I dance the step together, so: 1. Boy steps forward with right foot, you step back with left. 2. Boy: side and slightly forward, left foot. You: side and slightly back, right foot. 3. Boy closes right foot to left, while you close left to right, changing weight on to closing foot. 4. Now repeat sequence as follows: Boy: forward left foot (You: back right foot). Boy: side and slightly forward, right foot (You: side and slightly back, left). Boy: close left foot to right. (You: close right to left). Change weight and repeat 1 to 3. Using this step you can dance an elementary waltz but next week I'll teach you a simple variation – the Natural Turn.

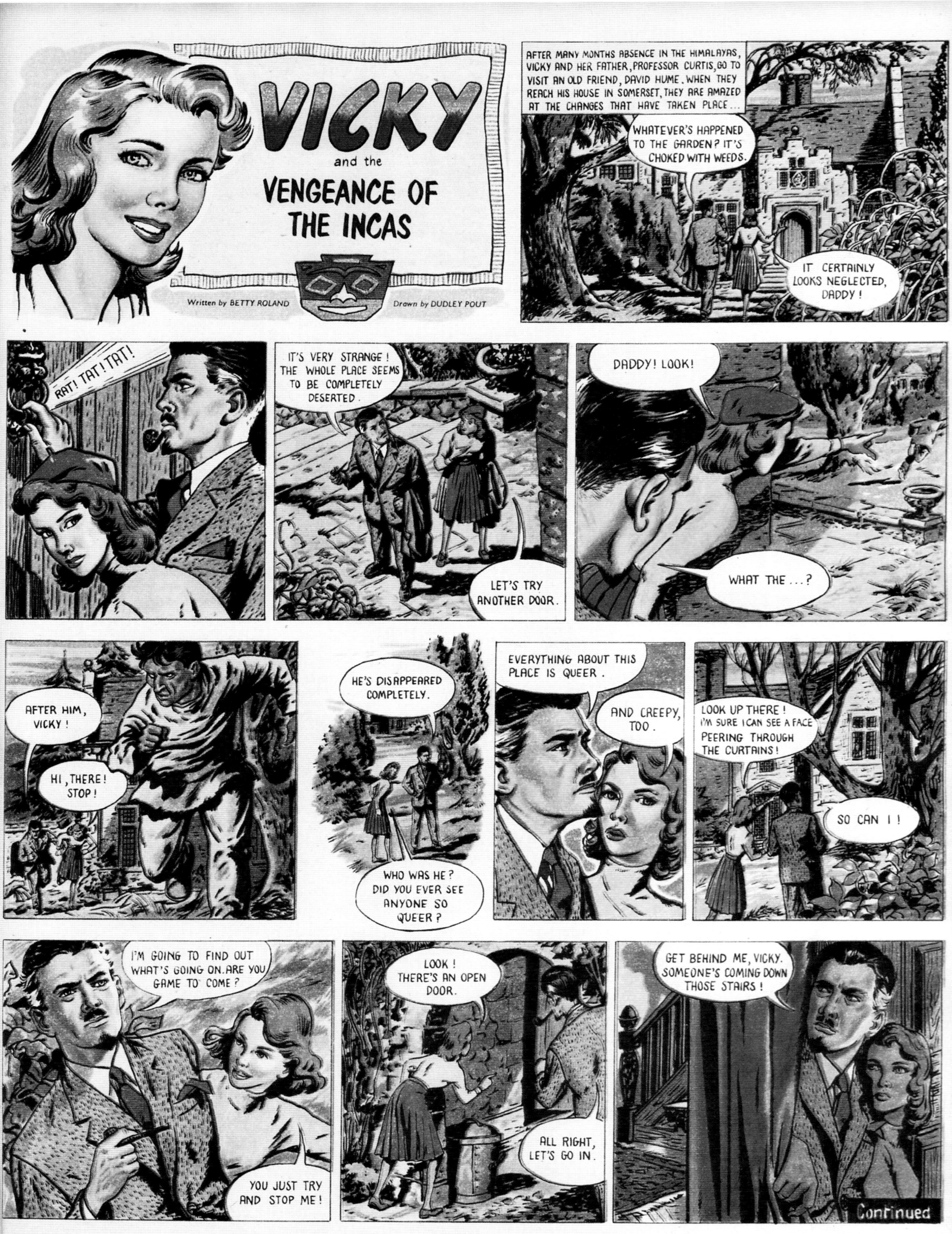
VICKY
and the
VENGEANCE OF THE INCAS
Written by BETTY ROLAND
Drawn by DUDLEY POUT
AFTER MANY MONTHS ABSENCE IN THE HIMALAYAS, VICKY AND HER FATHER, PROFESSOR CURTIS, GO TO VISIT AN OLD FRIEND, DAVID HUME. WHEN THEY REACH HIS HOUSE IN SOMERSET, THEY ARE AMAZED AT THE CHANGES THAT HAVE TAKEN PLACE...
WHATEVER'S HAPPENED TO THE GARDEN? IT'S CHOKED WITH WEEDS.
IT CERTAINLY LOOKS NEGLECTED, DADDY!
RAT! TAT! TAT!
IT'S VERY STRANGE! THE WHOLE PLACE SEEMS TO BE COMPLETELY DESERTED.
LET'S TRY ANOTHER DOOR.
DADDY! LOOK!
WHAT THE ...?
AFTER HIM, VICKY!
HI, THERE! STOP!
HE'S DISAPPEARED COMPLETELY.
WHO WAS HE? DID YOU EVER SEE ANYONE SO QUEER?
EVERYTHING ABOUT THIS PLACE IS QUEER.
AND CREEPY, TOO.
LOOK UP THERE! I'M SURE I CAN SEE A FACE PEERING THROUGH THE CURTAINS!
SO CAN I!
I'M GOING TO FIND OUT WHAT'S GOING ON. ARE YOU GAME TO COME?
YOU JUST TRY AND STOP ME!
LOOK! THERE'S AN OPEN DOOR.
ALL RIGHT, LET'S GO IN.
GET BEHIND ME, VICKY. SOMEONE'S COMING DOWN THOSE STAIRS!
Continued

continued on page 32

Christmas Carol Services

for EAGLE and GIRL readers in some of our great Cathedrals

Write in for your free tickets now!

LAST Christmas we had a magnificent Carol Service for EAGLE and GIRL readers in St Paul's Cathedral. Many thousands of you came and joined in singing the well-known Christmas Carols. The Cathedral was packed.

This year we are again having a Carol Service at St Paul's – and in several other great Cathedrals and Churches as well.

One of them may be near where you live. If so, make sure you come – and bring your parents and friends.

To make sure of getting a seat, write in to us *now*, to Carol Service, GIRL, Long Lane, Liverpool 9, enclosing a large envelope addressed to yourself and bearing a 1½d stamp, asking for tickets for whichever service you want to attend.

Saturday, 20th December	
St Paul's Cathedral, London	**2.15**
Monday, 22nd December	
Manchester Cathedral	**2.30**
Tuesday, 23rd December	
Birmingham Parish Church	**2.30**
Wednesday, 24th December	
St Giles' Cathedral, Edinburgh	**3.00**
Saturday, 27th December	
Bristol Cathedral	**2.30**
Monday, 29th December	
Portsmouth Cathedral	**3.00**

Specially picked EAGLE *and* GIRL *readers will take part in the Service with the Editor.*

NEXT WEEK: Uncle Joe's New Year customs may be odd, but they really welcome it in with a bang!

GIRL's Christmas Book Choice

Do you like to read about animals, adventure or fun? There's something here for everyone, so spend your Christmas present money on a book you'll enjoy, says WILFRED ASHWORTH.

LOOK back to GIRL dated 29th April 1953 and you will find the feature *Jacky visits Janette Scott.* No doubt those pictures gave you a real thrill – specially finding that Jacky had been Janette's stand-in for one of her films. Now Janette has written a book called ***Act One*** (Nelson, 8/6) telling how, at fifteen, she has become an actress on the stage and in films.

This is a happy book and it is so obviously true, because things do not always go right for Janette and because, in spite of all her successes, it's quite evident that she is still a jolly, unaffected girl whom anyone would welcome as a friend. In fact Janette herself says she has been very lucky as she's had 'the most valuable thing there is to be had – and that's friendship'.

All about a pony club

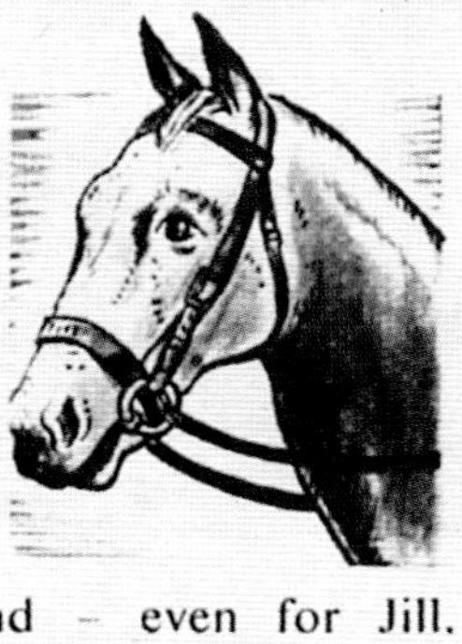

Minda by Kathleen Mackenzie (Evans, 9/6) will delight pony-lovers. It describes how a group of not-very-well-off children start a Pony Club in spite of many difficulties and take part successfully in sporting events. Much trouble is caused by a rich girl, Jill, who jealously plots against Minda, but all comes right in the end – even for Jill.

You may think ***Captain Apple's Ghost*** by Evelyn Lampman (Hodder and Stoughton, 8/6) rather unusual, but it's great fun to read. An old American house, used as a children's museum, is scheduled for demolition, until the ghost of the former owner returns to earth to take a hand in the affair. He has one gift – he can make people say whatever he wishes – and this is quite enough to save the day and make an exciting story.

A book full of magic!

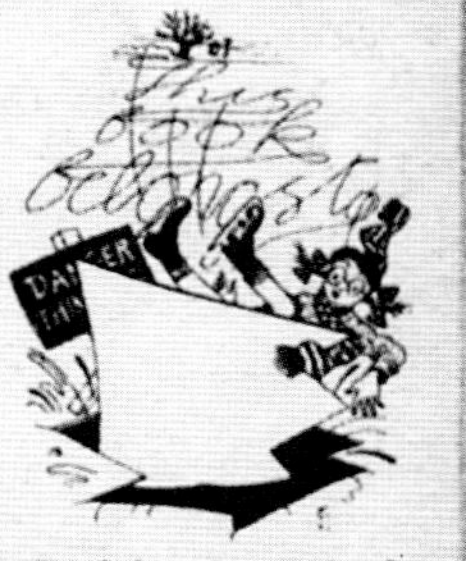

Read about Lettice Leefe in GIRL Annual No. 2.

Twenty-five mystifying tricks and two chapters of good advice make up ***Your Book of Magic*** by Alexander van Rensselaer (Faber and Faber, 5/6) to transform you into a clever conjuror.

And for magic of a different kind – the magic of real enjoyment – don't forget ***GIRL Annual No. 2*** (Hulton Press, 10/6).

If you enjoy more grown-up books and especially if you like 'lives' of people you *must* read ***The Prisoners Friend*** by Patrick Pringle (Harrap, 7/6). It tells of Elizabeth Fry's upbringing in a large Quaker family, of her own marriage and children, and then reaches a climax with her wonderful work for prison reform.

It's hard to imagine how dirty and squalid the old prisons used to be, and almost impossible to picture a staid Quaker mother of a big family setting out to improve them. Elizabeth Fry had real missionary zeal in her difficult task, especially as women were not expected to undertake work of this kind in the early eighteen-hundreds. This is a really worth-while – and fascinating – account of a noble and courageous woman.

All these can be obtained from your local bookshop

WHAT'S YOUR WORRY?

Betraying secrets

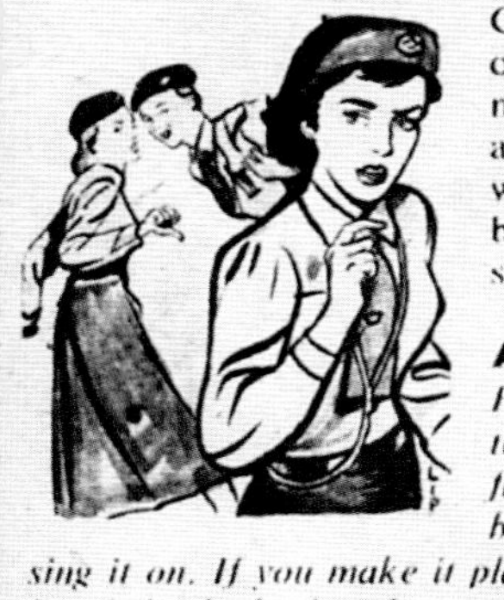

Q. I am a Girl Guide. One day two of my Guide friends told me a secret which I repeated to my best friend, who is not a Guide. She promised not to tell anyone, but when I went to Guides the next week my two friends turned away from me. When I asked what was the matter, they said that my best friend had told them about the secret. What can I do?

A. *Secrets have a habit of spreading. Friends tell friends and then the trouble starts. You and your best friend were both at fault – you for betraying the secret and she for passing it on. If you make it plain to the two Guides that you told her and nobody else, they may be more understanding and forgive you this time. It might be a good idea to get your best friend to join your Guide company with you, then you could form a quartette and have fun sharing all your secrets.*

* * *

A blistered finger

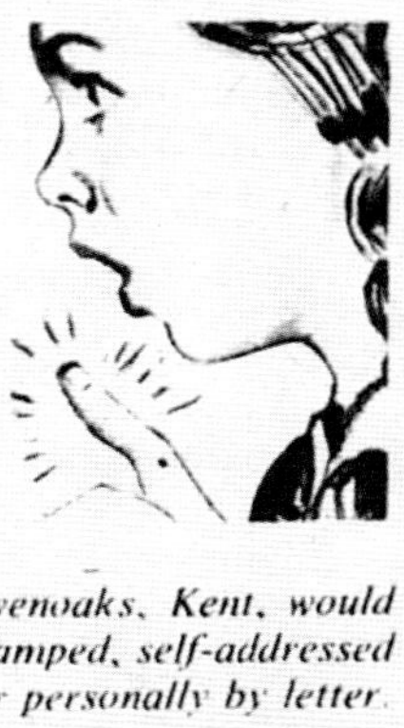

Q. I am very fond of tennis, but after a hard game I get a blister on my first finger. It takes ages for it to heal as the skin keeps coming off. What should I do? I put plaster over it, but it doesn't seem to make any difference.

A. *Stick a piece of crepe adhesive plaster over the finger which blisters before you start to play. Try a different grip on your racket, too. A rubber or string hand-grip in place of the usual leather one sometimes prevents blistering successfully.*

* * *

If the girl who sent us a worry from Sevenoaks, Kent, would care to write in to us again enclosing a stamped, self-addressed envelope we shall be able to reply to her personally by letter.

FILMS *that are fun to see*

Lia Low ***talks about some entertaining pictures.***

Cartoons are not the only kind of films that interest Walt Disney. His latest picture ***ROB ROY*** – which Her Majesty the Queen saw at the Royal Command Performance – is played entirely by live actors. It's a tale about proud Scottish clansmen and their young chief, Rob Roy MacGregor.

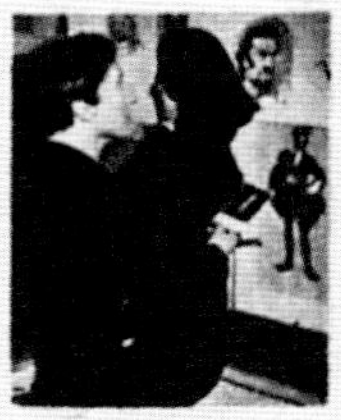

Carmen Dillon

The castles, the fort and the gorgeous costumes were all made to the designs of England's only woman art director, Carmen Dillon. She once studied to become an architect, but then changed over to films. Her designs for *Hamlet* won her an 'Oscar', which is Hollywood's highest film award.

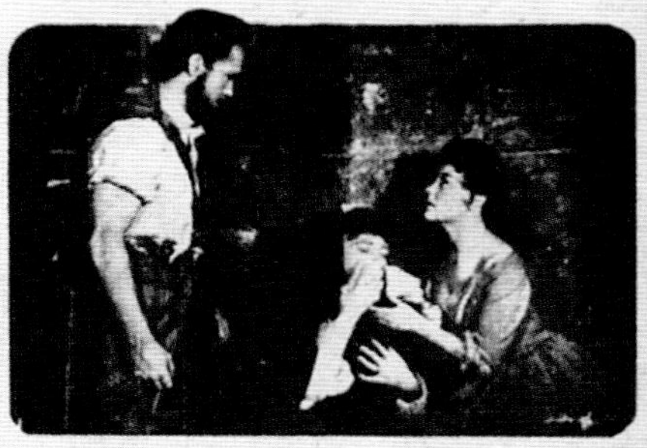

Rob Roy is packed with excitement. The stars of the film are Richard Todd and Glynis Johns.

Nor is Disney's ***BEAR COUNTRY*** a cartoon. Indeed, the mischievous black cubs and their great lumbering parents are very much alive: the camera-man had to photograph them with a special lens from a safe distance!

Bears can't be ordered about, so it took a year's patience to make this story. And a second year was spent sorting out the spools of film, choosing the best shots and sticking them together in the most interesting order. I am sure you will agree that it was worth the trouble.

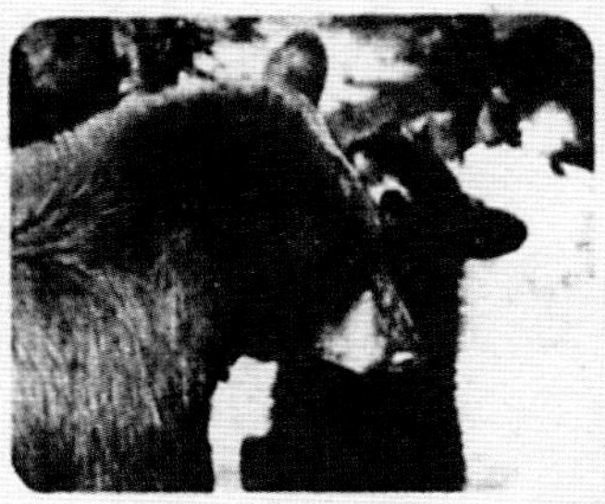

The bears wrestle, play tag and invent new games when they're bored!

Disney characters (like Pluto here) have new rivals – a little boy named Gerald McBoing-Boing and a short-sighted old man called Mr Magoo. Look out for them.

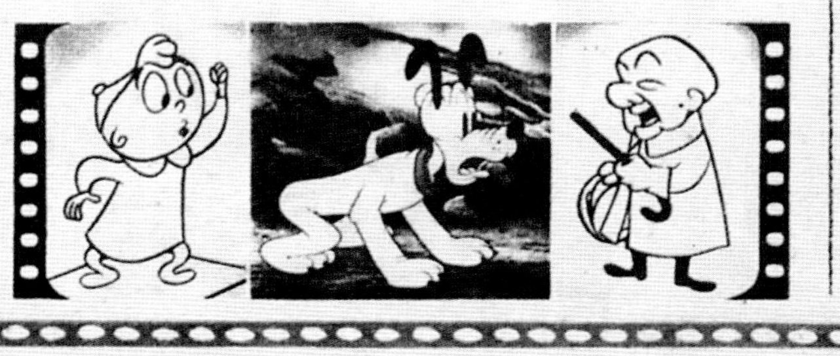

Do you remember the morning of Coronation Day, when the news came through that Edmund Hillary and Sherpa Tensing had reached the summit of Mount Everest? You can now see parts of this great adventure in a film called ***THE CONQUEST OF EVEREST.***

Remember, when you see this film, that the camera-man's fingers were often numb with cold and his feet searching for a hold on the treacherous ice of the highest mountain in the world.

SANDRA'S JUNGLE ADVENTURE

Written by
ROSEMARY GARLAND

Illustrated by
V. J. BERTOGLIO

Sandra always wanted a lion cub, but when she got one . . .

SANDRA sprang to her feet as she saw Tamu come into the compound. He was cradling a small, furry bundle in his strong arms.

"A lion cub!" exclaimed Sandra, as she ran towards the native boy.

Tamu had always promised she should have the first lion cub for a pet. He had told her that occasionally a cub was left motherless when the party came back from big game hunting. But there was no smile of triumph on Tamu's shining black face as she bore her new pet towards her.

Sandra sensed something was wrong. She understood Tamu well for she had lived most of her young life in Africa. Her father had gone out as a mining engineer when she was quite a baby.

"Something wrong?" she asked. Then, as she stood over him, she saw that there was indeed something wrong – the cub was limp.

"Dead?" she whispered.

"No, missie, him not dead . . . but him not live long," said Tamu, shaking his head over the tiny creature.

"What happened?" asked Sandra.

"One fool hunter . . . him miss. She-lion escape but the gun hit this little chappie – through the leg!"

"Oh!" cried Sandra. "One of those young idiots who've never handled a gun before but want to boast that they've been big game shooting! I know the type!"

She examined the little leg, stretched out stiff with the shot. There was a small hole in the thigh.

Sandra led Tamu up the verandah steps and into the room.

"Bring him in," she said. "Can we save him?"

"We try, but I think he die!" said Tamu.

Sandra made the animal comfortable in a corner of the room. Tamu ran out and plucked some leaves. When he returned, he made a poultice which he placed tenderly on the wound.

"We must save him!" said Sandra with fierce determination.

But, the very second after her words were spoken, something more dramatic snatched their attention away. There came shouts and a running of bare feet.

"Tamu! Tamu!" Tamu pulled back the curtains of the window. It was Tamu's mother. The tone of her voice was enough to tell them something terrible had happened. A stream of turbulent words from the woman in her native tongue made it impossible for Sandra to follow.

"What's the matter, Tamu? Tell me! Tell me!" she grabbed at Tamu's arm.

"My little baby brother . . . him lost in jungle . . . him lost in . . . Him pretend to big game shoot like big brother Tamu. Tamu's little sister, she take him in jungle . . . but she come home . . . no baby brother!"

"Oh! Tamu! How awful!" cried Sandra. And as she said this, the twilight closed in about them. Sandra shuddered. She knew that in less than ten minutes inky jungle darkness would make a proper search impossible that night.

"I must come with you!" she said, and snatched up her father's powerful torch. Tamu had already rushed across the compound.

Sandra met Tamu again outside his own hut. Already a small band of natives with flares had collected and the party moved off, spreading fanwise into the jungle.

They searched and searched but it was hopeless, and hours later they returned with no sign of the little boy.

Late that night Sandra watched over the lion cub until she fell into an uneasy sleep, huddled on the floor. At the first light of dawn she awoke. Her first thought was for the baby in the jungle. Suddenly an idea flashed into her head.

Without hesitation, she raced across to Tamu's hut. Tamu was awake. His native ears were sharp and alert to the smallest sound. He went outside.

"It's me – Sandra!" whispered the girl. "Tamu, I've had an idea. Perhaps your sister followed your hunting party? Perhaps she took the same path you took?"

Tamu seemed to think Sandra was right. He needed no further explanation. Together, silently, they crept into the jungle.

After about an hour, long after they realized that they had penetrated farther than the little girl could possibly have gone, Tamu pointed and said: "That's the lair where the lion cub came from!"

Sandra peered through a screen of giant leaves to a craggy sort of ledge like a miniature cliff running to the west of them. In the cliff's side was a cavelike den behind numerous tree roots.

Tamu was making towards it. Sandra was alarmed.

"Don't go too near!" she whispered.

"She-lion out hunting," said Tamu. "See her new marks!"

And he pointed to spoor marks which Sandra would never have detected as being fresh. Since Tamu was so bold, Sandra followed close behind him.

Suddenly they were frozen in their tracks by a muffled wail. It came from the den itself.

"She has another cub!" said Sandra. "I do wish we could have it!" she said.

Tamu was watchful. The tracks of the beast clearly showed that it had left the lair but not returned.

Sandra crept forward on all fours and peered into the shadows. As she did so it came again, a strange wail . . . it was only a few feet away now. She slipped her hand forward to clutch the furry bundle, but what she touched was not fur. She dragged something out into the light. It was a sweet, inky black baby . . . Tamu's brother!

It was Tamu who made the first movement. He darted at the baby and scooped it up from the clay. Then, clasping it to him like a mother, he spoke softly to the child. But the moment of reunion was shattered by the sudden appearance of the lioness. She appeared from nowhere and was in a fighting mood. She had lost one cub and came now to defend the "cub" she had fostered.

Tamu was instantly alive to this situation. He practically flung the baby into Sandra's arms and faced the lioness calmly, steadily – Tamu, the hunter! He did something Sandra did not expect. From the haversack he carried, he drew out a leg of raw meat and flung it far behind the lioness. She smelt its delicious odour and turned an enquiring nose to it. She could not resist it. Sandra and Tamu retreated as the lioness retrieved the meat and hastened with it to her den. She must have thought the baby was still safe inside.

Back in the compound, Tamu raced with his baby brother to his mother while Sandra returned to her pet. She found the cub walking stiffly round the room. Sandra laughed as he growled at her pretending to be a grown-up lion!

As she fed him with bread and milk she saw that he had almost recovered. After the meal he was playful, biting at her hand, and growling as she teased him.

Soon he settled down to sleep, curled up in the crook of her arm. And it was then that she made a momentous decision.

So it was that, when Tamu returned she said, quite simply: "Tamu, will you take me back to the lion's den today?"

"Why, missie?" Tamu was surprised.

"I want to return the cub to its mother!"

"Oh, missie! You want lion cub, all the time you ask Tamu for lion cub. When Tamu come back from big game shooting missie say: 'You got lion cub for me, Tamu?' Tamu not understand."

"Yes, I know, Tamu. But you know how terrible it was for your mother when she thought she had lost her baby? Well, it must be just the same for the lioness. She only took your baby brother because she had lost her own baby. Besides," she added, "she deserves her own cub back as a reward for keeping your baby brother safe!"

The end

Registered at the G.P.O. for transmission by Magazine Post to Canada (including Newfoundland). GIRL printed in Great Britain by Eric Bemrose Ltd., Long Lane, Liverpool 9, for the Proprietors and Publishers, Hulton Press Ltd., 161/166 Fleet Street, London, E.C.4. Sole agents for Australia and New Zealand, Gordon & Gotch (A'sia) Ltd.; South Africa, Central News Agency Ltd. Subscription Rate: Inland, 12 months 28/2, 6 months 14/1; abroad, 12 months 26/-; 6 months 13/-. Postage for single copies: 2d.; Canada 1d. You can have GIRL sent to any address in this country for one year for 28/2, abroad for 26/-, and to Canada at a special rate of 23/10. To readers in U.S.A. or Canada we will mail copies each week for a year at $3.75. Please send your order to Hulton Press Ltd., Subscription Dept., Long Lane, Aintree, Liverpool 9.

PERSIA'S LADY MARY

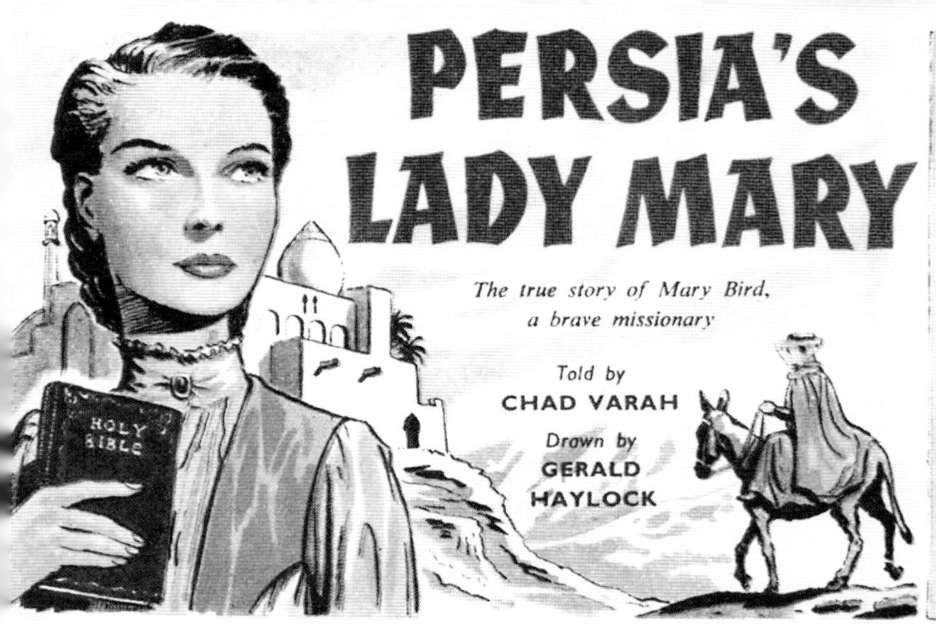
HOLY BIBLE

The true story of Mary Bird, a brave missionary

Told by
CHAD VARAH

Drawn by
GERALD HAYLOCK

Mary Bird, daughter of the rector of Castle Eden, County Durham, was born in 1859. When she was a child she decided that one day she would be a missionary. In May 1891, Mary is sent to Persia and, after many hardships, arrives in Julfa at the house of Doctor Bruce to work among the Moslem women. She tells Mrs Bruce she would give her life to help them out of their misery and suffering. One day, a little girl takes her to see her baby brother. Mary says he is a lovely baby, whereupon the child's mother curses her . . .

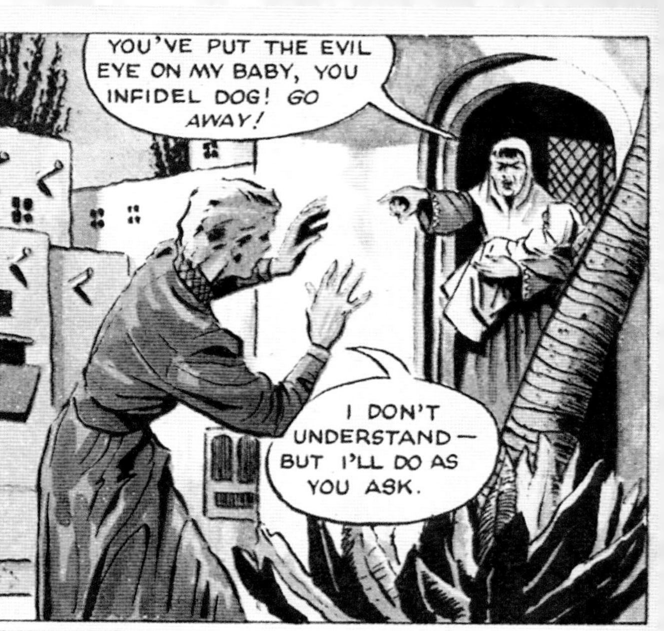
YOU'VE PUT THE EVIL EYE ON MY BABY, YOU INFIDEL DOG! *GO AWAY!*
I DON'T UNDERSTAND — BUT I'LL DO AS YOU ASK.

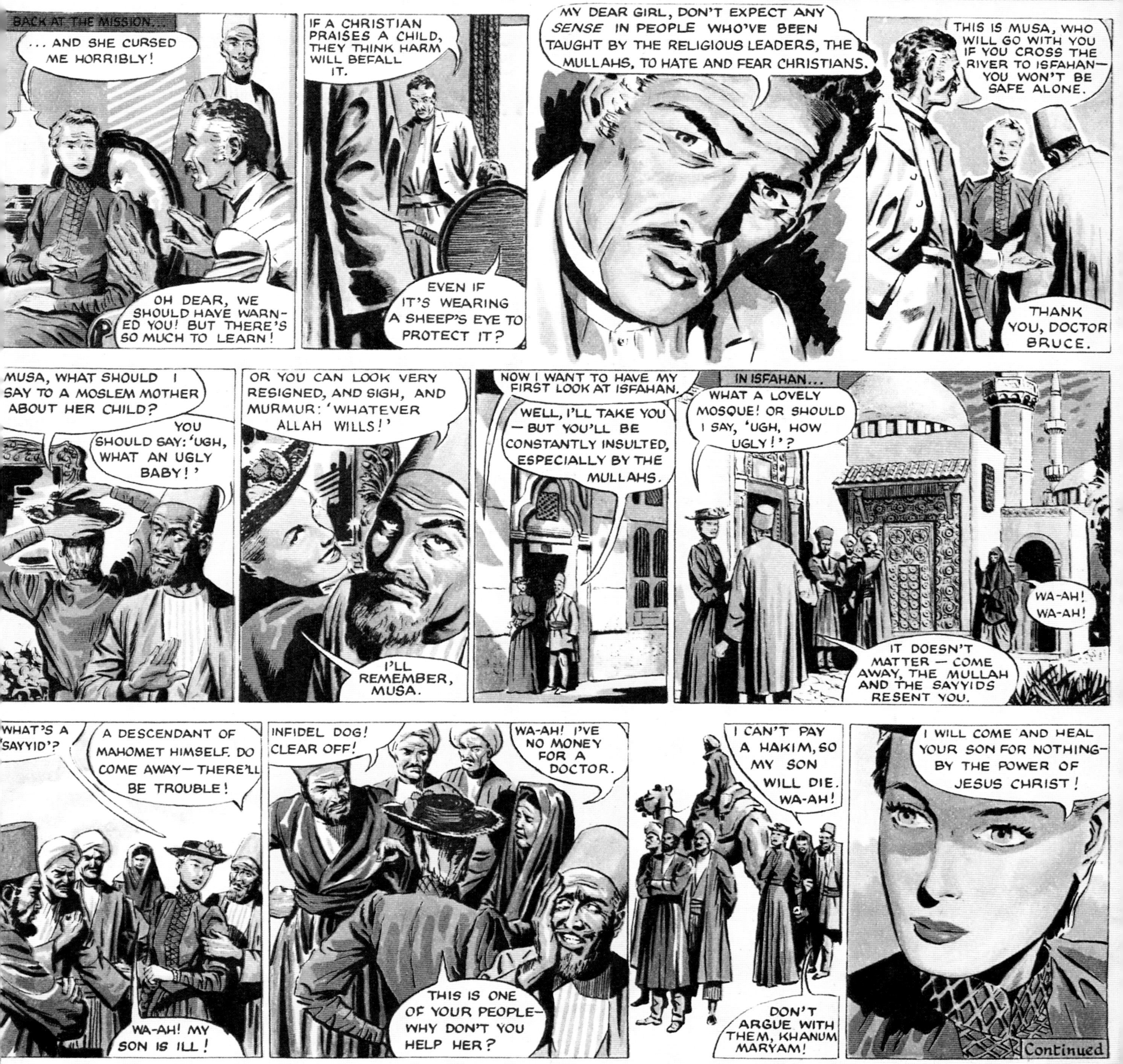
BACK AT THE MISSION...
... AND SHE CURSED ME HORRIBLY!
OH DEAR, WE SHOULD HAVE WARNED YOU! BUT THERE'S SO MUCH TO LEARN!
IF A CHRISTIAN PRAISES A CHILD, THEY THINK HARM WILL BEFALL IT.
EVEN IF IT'S WEARING A SHEEP'S EYE TO PROTECT IT?
MY DEAR GIRL, DON'T EXPECT ANY *SENSE* IN PEOPLE WHO'VE BEEN TAUGHT BY THE RELIGIOUS LEADERS, THE MULLAHS, TO HATE AND FEAR CHRISTIANS.
THIS IS MUSA, WHO WILL GO WITH YOU IF YOU CROSS THE RIVER TO ISFAHAN — YOU WON'T BE SAFE ALONE.
THANK YOU, DOCTOR BRUCE.
MUSA, WHAT SHOULD I SAY TO A MOSLEM MOTHER ABOUT HER CHILD?
YOU SHOULD SAY: 'UGH, WHAT AN UGLY BABY!'
OR YOU CAN LOOK VERY RESIGNED, AND SIGH, AND MURMUR: 'WHATEVER ALLAH WILLS!'
I'LL REMEMBER, MUSA.
NOW I WANT TO HAVE MY FIRST LOOK AT ISFAHAN.
WELL, I'LL TAKE YOU — BUT YOU'LL BE CONSTANTLY INSULTED, ESPECIALLY BY THE MULLAHS.
IN ISFAHAN...
WHAT A LOVELY MOSQUE! OR SHOULD I SAY, 'UGH, HOW UGLY!'?
WA-AH! WA-AH!
IT DOESN'T MATTER — COME AWAY, THE MULLAH AND THE SAYYIDS RESENT YOU.
WHAT'S A 'SAYYID'?
A DESCENDANT OF MAHOMET HIMSELF. DO COME AWAY — THERE'LL BE TROUBLE!
WA-AH! MY SON IS ILL!
INFIDEL DOG! CLEAR OFF!
WA-AH! I'VE NO MONEY FOR A DOCTOR.
THIS IS ONE OF YOUR PEOPLE — WHY DON'T YOU HELP HER?
I CAN'T PAY A HAKIM, SO MY SON WILL DIE. WA-AH!
DON'T ARGUE WITH THEM, KHANUM MARYAM!
I WILL COME AND HEAL YOUR SON FOR NOTHING — BY THE POWER OF JESUS CHRIST!
Continued

continued on page 39

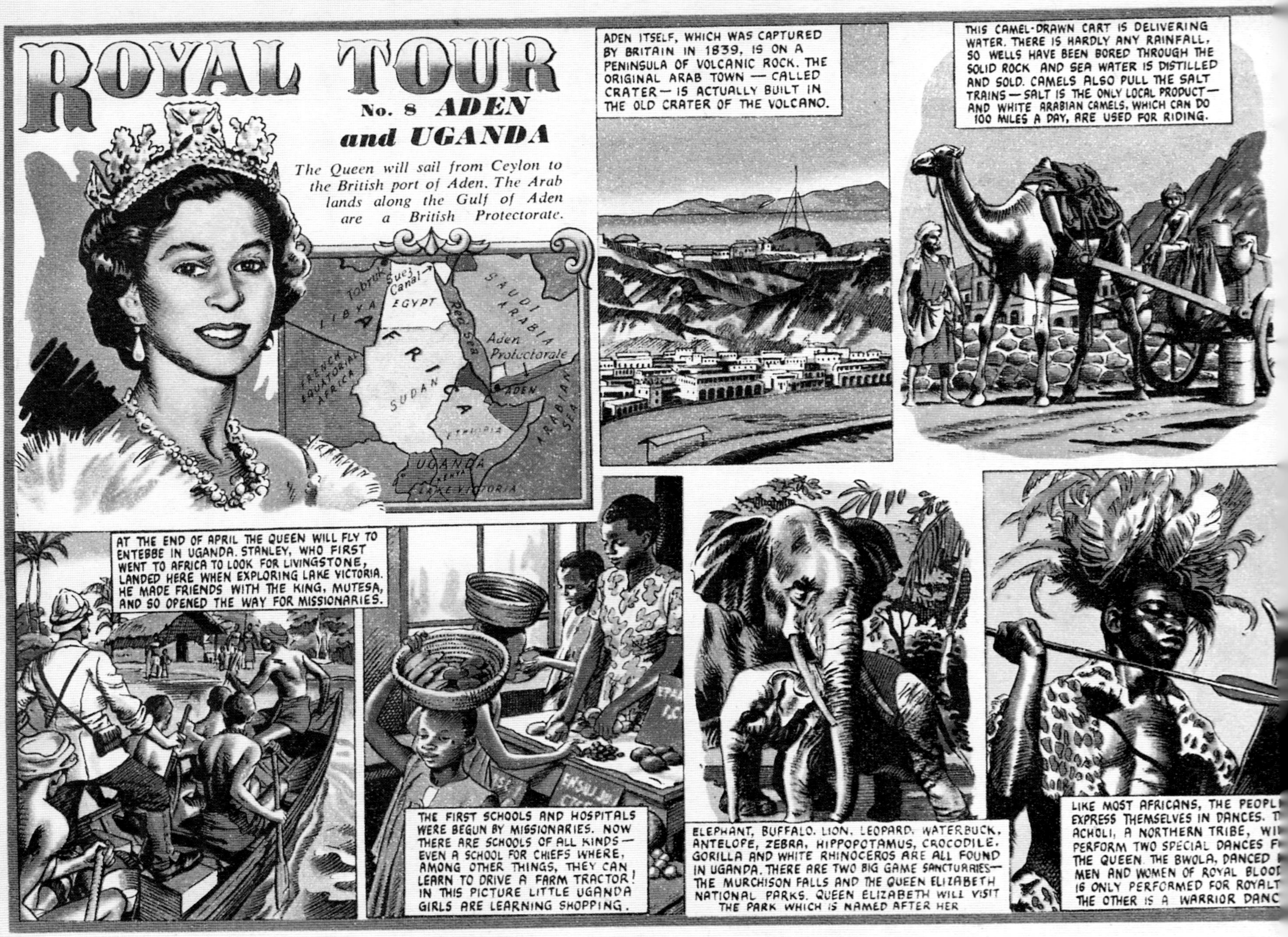
ROYAL TOUR
No. 8 ADEN and UGANDA
The Queen will sail from Ceylon to the British port of Aden. The Arab lands along the Gulf of Aden are a British Protectorate.
Tobruk
Suez Canal
LIBYA
EGYPT
SAUDI ARABIA
Red Sea
AFRICA
Aden Protectorate
FRENCH EQUATORIAL AFRICA
SUDAN
ADEN
ETHIOPIA
ARABIAN SEA
UGANDA
KENYA
LAKE VICTORIA
ADEN ITSELF, WHICH WAS CAPTURED BY BRITAIN IN 1839, IS ON A PENINSULA OF VOLCANIC ROCK. THE ORIGINAL ARAB TOWN — CALLED CRATER — IS ACTUALLY BUILT IN THE OLD CRATER OF THE VOLCANO.
THIS CAMEL-DRAWN CART IS DELIVERING WATER. THERE IS HARDLY ANY RAINFALL, SO WELLS HAVE BEEN BORED THROUGH THE SOLID ROCK AND SEA WATER IS DISTILLED AND SOLD. CAMELS ALSO PULL THE SALT TRAINS — SALT IS THE ONLY LOCAL PRODUCT — AND WHITE ARABIAN CAMELS, WHICH CAN DO 100 MILES A DAY, ARE USED FOR RIDING.
AT THE END OF APRIL THE QUEEN WILL FLY TO ENTEBBE IN UGANDA. STANLEY, WHO FIRST WENT TO AFRICA TO LOOK FOR LIVINGSTONE, LANDED HERE WHEN EXPLORING LAKE VICTORIA. HE MADE FRIENDS WITH THE KING, MUTESA, AND SO OPENED THE WAY FOR MISSIONARIES.
THE FIRST SCHOOLS AND HOSPITALS WERE BEGUN BY MISSIONARIES. NOW THERE ARE SCHOOLS OF ALL KINDS — EVEN A SCHOOL FOR CHIEFS WHERE, AMONG OTHER THINGS, THEY CAN LEARN TO DRIVE A FARM TRACTOR! IN THIS PICTURE LITTLE UGANDA GIRLS ARE LEARNING SHOPPING.
ELEPHANT, BUFFALO, LION, LEOPARD, WATERBUCK, ANTELOPE, ZEBRA, HIPPOPOTAMUS, CROCODILE, GORILLA AND WHITE RHINOCEROS ARE ALL FOUND IN UGANDA. THERE ARE TWO BIG GAME SANCTUARIES — THE MURCHISON FALLS AND THE QUEEN ELIZABETH NATIONAL PARKS. QUEEN ELIZABETH WILL VISIT THE PARK WHICH IS NAMED AFTER HER
LIKE MOST AFRICANS, THE PEOPL EXPRESS THEMSELVES IN DANCES. T ACHOLI, A NORTHERN TRIBE, WI PERFORM TWO SPECIAL DANCES F THE QUEEN. THE BWOLA, DANCED MEN AND WOMEN OF ROYAL BLOOD IS ONLY PERFORMED FOR ROYALT THE OTHER IS A WARRIOR DANC

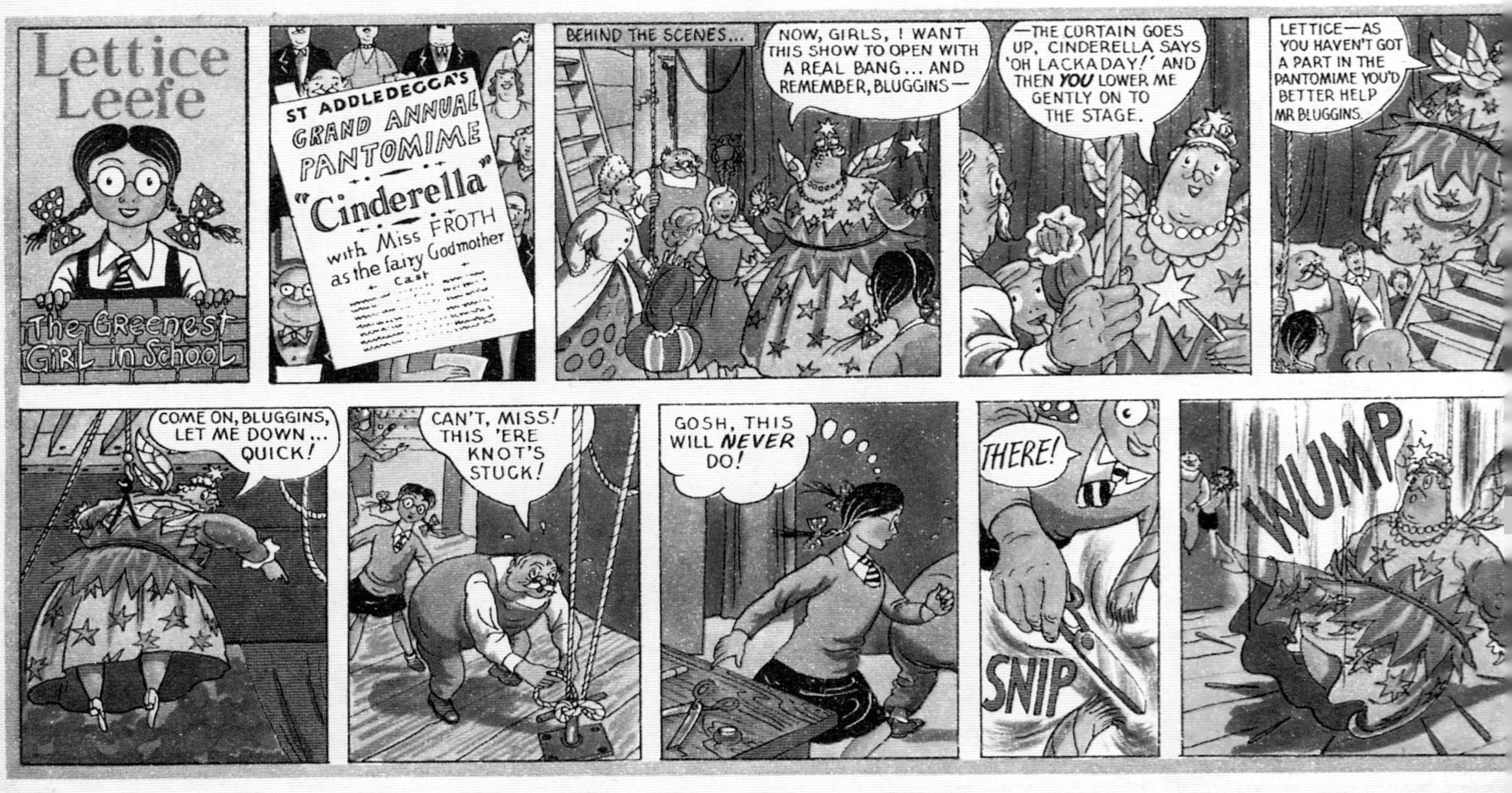
Lettice Leefe
The Greenest Girl in School
ST ADDLEDEGGA'S GRAND ANNUAL PANTOMIME
"Cinderella"
with Miss FROTH as the fairy Godmother
Cast
BEHIND THE SCENES...
NOW, GIRLS, I WANT THIS SHOW TO OPEN WITH A REAL BANG... AND REMEMBER, BLUGGINS—
—THE CURTAIN GOES UP, CINDERELLA SAYS 'OH LACKADAY!' AND THEN YOU LOWER ME GENTLY ON TO THE STAGE.
LETTICE—AS YOU HAVEN'T GOT A PART IN THE PANTOMIME YOU'D BETTER HELP MR BLUGGINS.
COME ON, BLUGGINS, LET ME DOWN... QUICK!
CAN'T, MISS! THIS 'ERE KNOT'S STUCK!
GOSH, THIS WILL NEVER DO!
THERE!
SNIP
WUMP

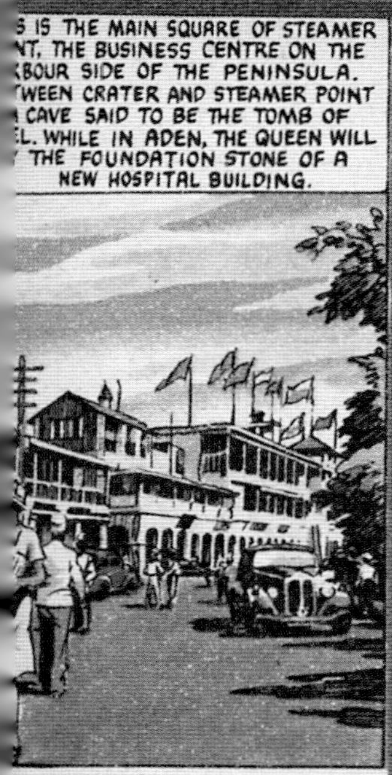
S IS THE MAIN SQUARE OF STEAMER
NT, THE BUSINESS CENTRE ON THE
BOUR SIDE OF THE PENINSULA.
TWEEN CRATER AND STEAMER POINT
CAVE SAID TO BE THE TOMB OF
L. WHILE IN ADEN, THE QUEEN WILL
THE FOUNDATION STONE OF A
NEW HOSPITAL BUILDING.

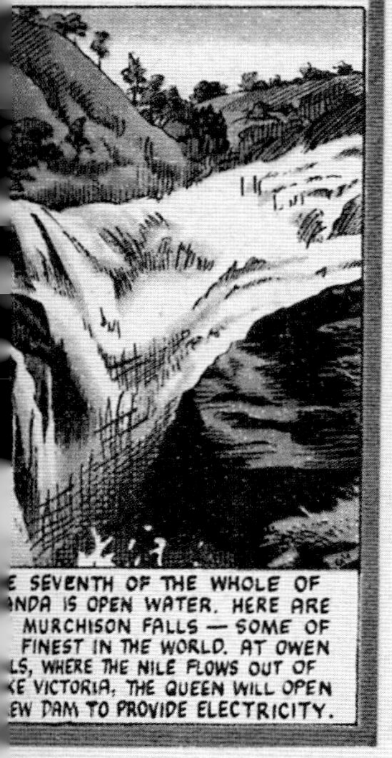
E SEVENTH OF THE WHOLE OF
NDA IS OPEN WATER. HERE ARE
MURCHISON FALLS — SOME OF
FINEST IN THE WORLD. AT OWEN
LS, WHERE THE NILE FLOWS OUT OF
E VICTORIA, THE QUEEN WILL OPEN
EW DAM TO PROVIDE ELECTRICITY.

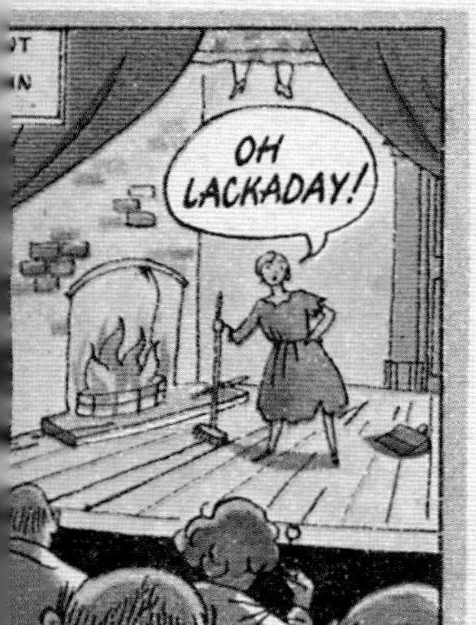
OH LACKADAY!

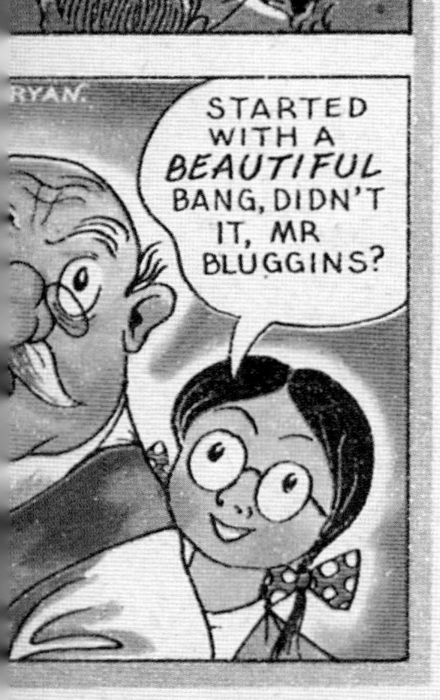
RYAN.
STARTED WITH A BEAUTIFUL BANG, DIDN'T IT, MR BLUGGINS?

Girl Picture Gallery

No. 253

Here is another of the wonderful nature photographs you have been asking for in your letters.

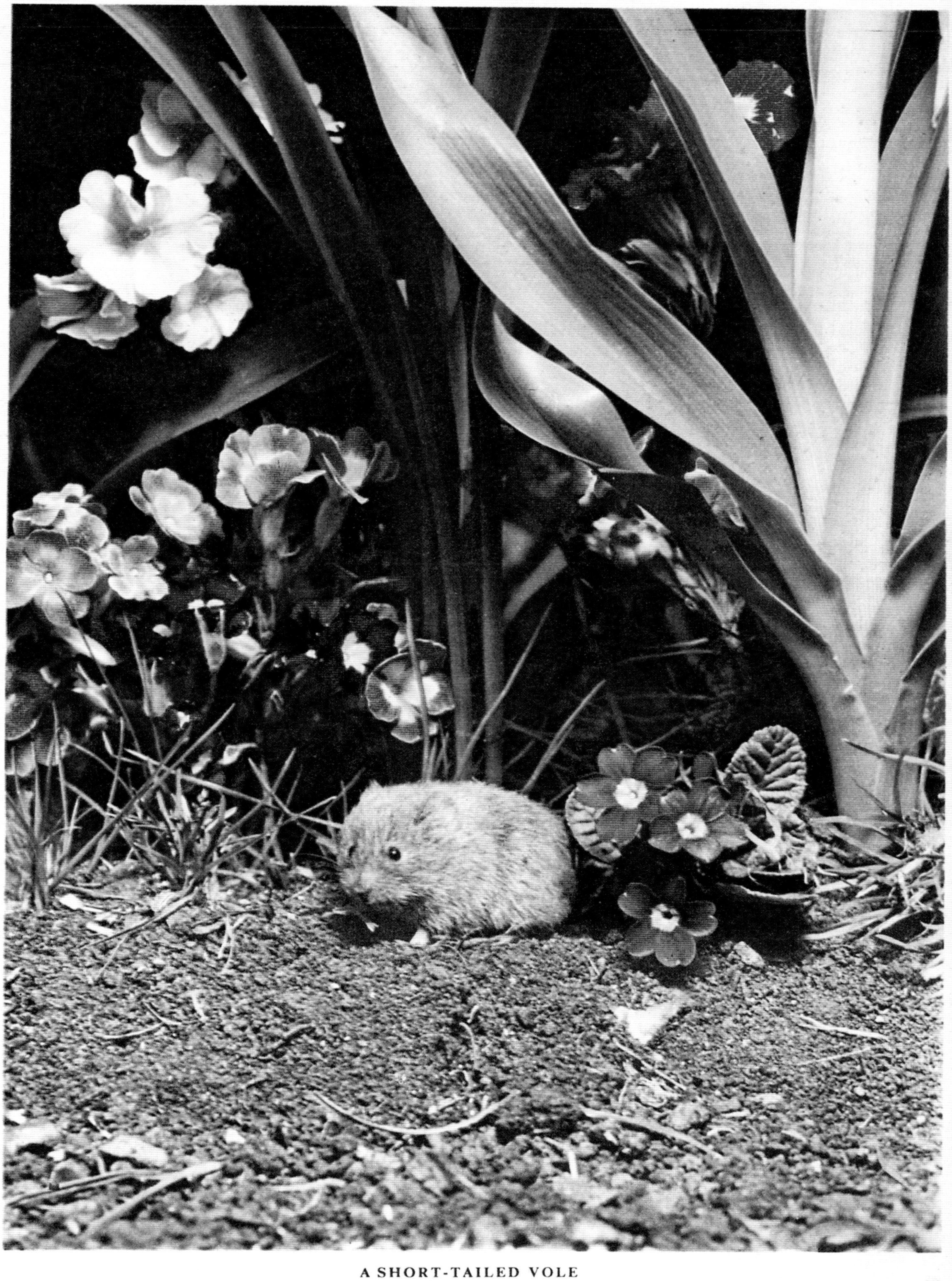

A SHORT-TAILED VOLE

by JOHN MARKHAM, F.R.P.S., F.S.Z.

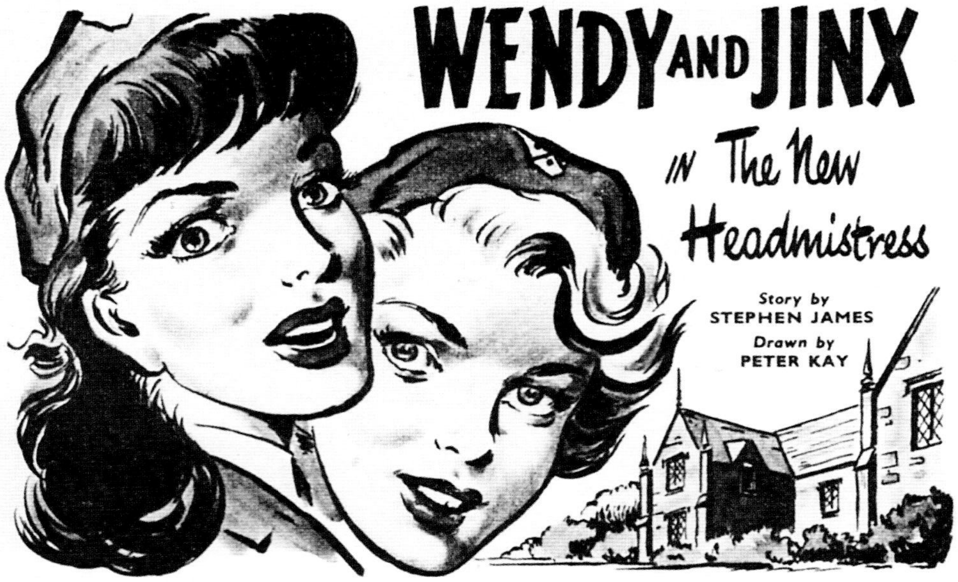

WENDY AND JINX
in The New Headmistress
Story by STEPHEN JAMES
Drawn by PETER KAY

Wendy and Jinx, inseparable friends of Manor School, return for the autumn term to learn that their headmistress has had an accident. Miss Kent, from Pine Ridge, a very strict school, has temporarily taken over. She makes several changes one of which is to separate Wendy and Jinx by putting Wendy into another dormitory. During tea, the girls decide to hold a meeting in the dorm after 'lights out' that night. At that moment Miss Kent sends for Wendy . . .

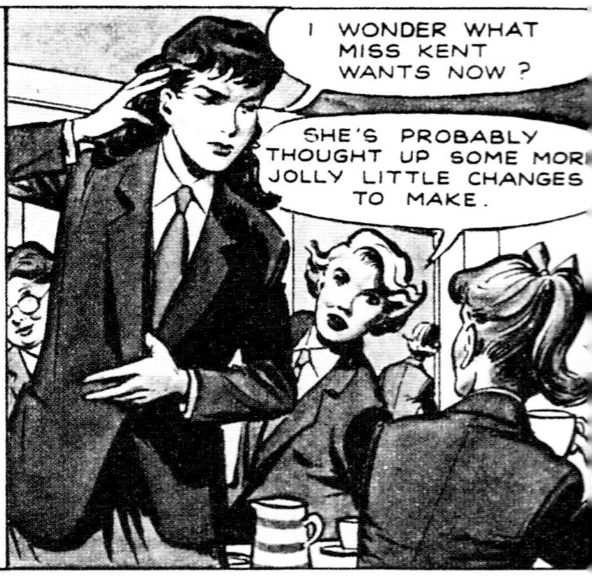

I WONDER WHAT MISS KENT WANTS NOW ?
SHE'S PROBABLY THOUGHT UP SOME MOR JOLLY LITTLE CHANGES TO MAKE.

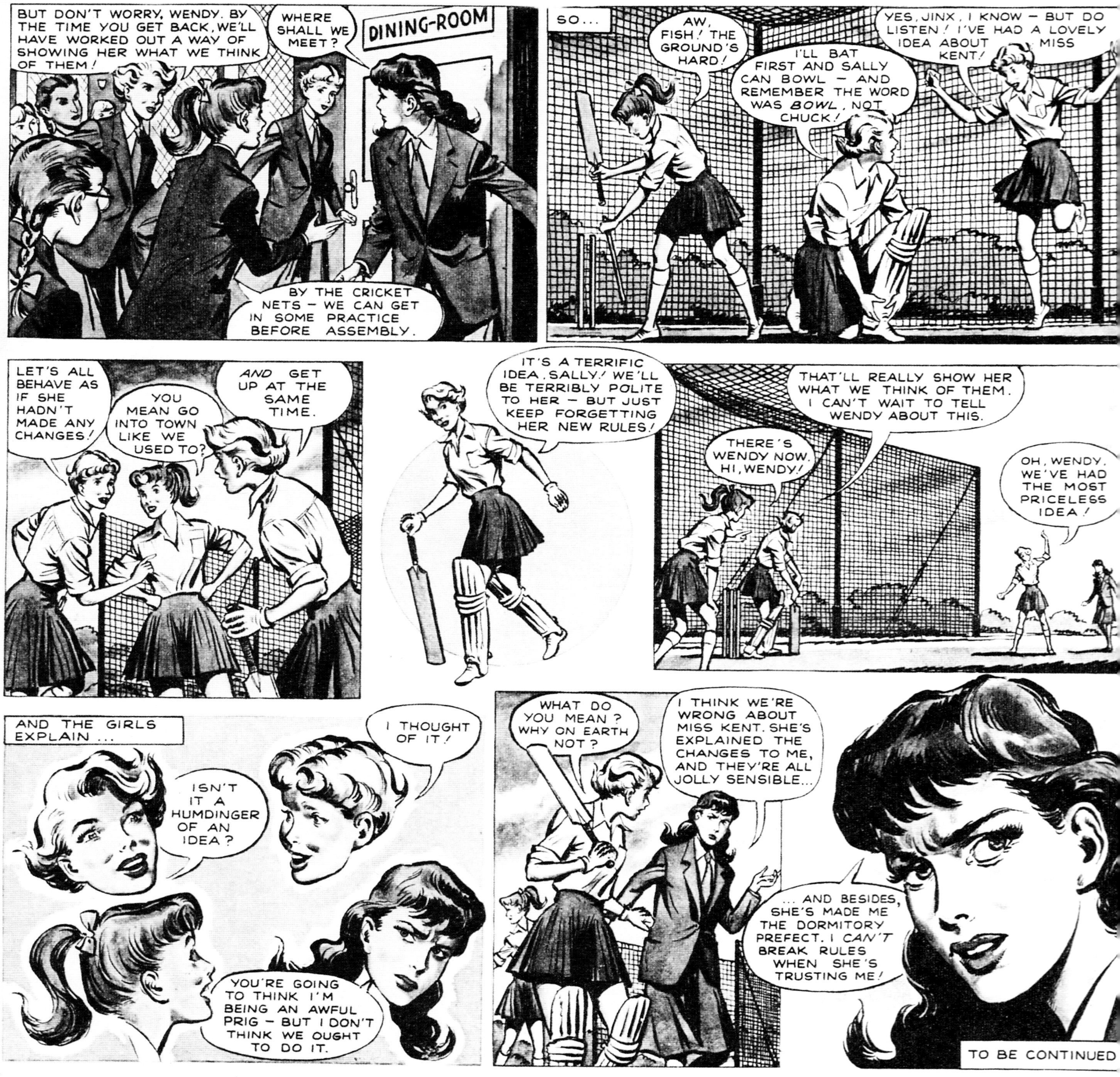

BUT DON'T WORRY, WENDY. BY THE TIME YOU GET BACK, WE'LL HAVE WORKED OUT A WAY OF SHOWING HER WHAT WE THINK OF THEM!
WHERE SHALL WE MEET?
DINING-ROOM
BY THE CRICKET NETS – WE CAN GET IN SOME PRACTICE BEFORE ASSEMBLY.
SO...
AW, FISH! THE GROUND'S HARD!
I'LL BAT FIRST AND SALLY CAN BOWL – AND REMEMBER THE WORD WAS BOWL, NOT CHUCK!
YES, JINX, I KNOW – BUT DO LISTEN! I'VE HAD A LOVELY IDEA ABOUT MISS KENT!
LET'S ALL BEHAVE AS IF SHE HADN'T MADE ANY CHANGES!
YOU MEAN GO INTO TOWN LIKE WE USED TO?
AND GET UP AT THE SAME TIME.
IT'S A TERRIFIC IDEA, SALLY! WE'LL BE TERRIBLY POLITE TO HER – BUT JUST KEEP FORGETTING HER NEW RULES!
THAT'LL REALLY SHOW HER WHAT WE THINK OF THEM. I CAN'T WAIT TO TELL WENDY ABOUT THIS.
THERE'S WENDY NOW. HI, WENDY!
OH, WENDY, WE'VE HAD THE MOST PRICELESS IDEA!
AND THE GIRLS EXPLAIN ...
ISN'T IT A HUMDINGER OF AN IDEA?
I THOUGHT OF IT!
YOU'RE GOING TO THINK I'M BEING AN AWFUL PRIG – BUT I DON'T THINK WE OUGHT TO DO IT.
WHAT DO YOU MEAN? WHY ON EARTH NOT?
I THINK WE'RE WRONG ABOUT MISS KENT. SHE'S EXPLAINED THE CHANGES TO ME, AND THEY'RE ALL JOLLY SENSIBLE...
... AND BESIDES, SHE'S MADE ME THE DORMITORY PREFECT. I CAN'T BREAK RULES WHEN SHE'S TRUSTING ME!
TO BE CONTINUED

continued on page 3

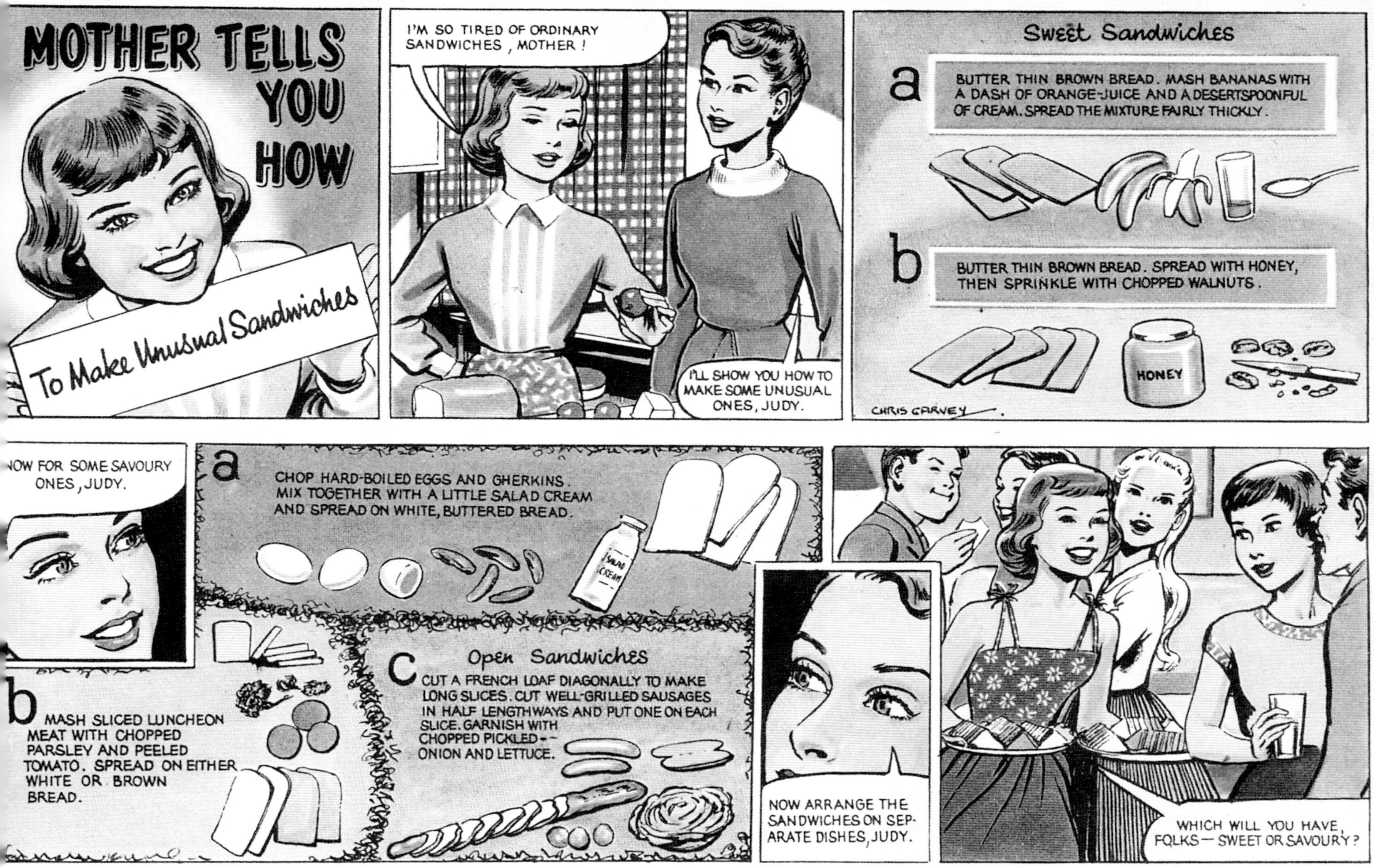
MOTHER TELLS YOU HOW
To Make Unusual Sandwiches
I'M SO TIRED OF ORDINARY SANDWICHES, MOTHER!
I'LL SHOW YOU HOW TO MAKE SOME UNUSUAL ONES, JUDY.
Sweet Sandwiches
a
BUTTER THIN BROWN BREAD. MASH BANANAS WITH A DASH OF ORANGE-JUICE AND A DESERTSPOONFUL OF CREAM. SPREAD THE MIXTURE FAIRLY THICKLY.
b
BUTTER THIN BROWN BREAD. SPREAD WITH HONEY, THEN SPRINKLE WITH CHOPPED WALNUTS.
HONEY
CHRIS GARVEY
NOW FOR SOME SAVOURY ONES, JUDY.
a
CHOP HARD-BOILED EGGS AND GHERKINS. MIX TOGETHER WITH A LITTLE SALAD CREAM AND SPREAD ON WHITE, BUTTERED BREAD.
SALAD CREAM
b
MASH SLICED LUNCHEON MEAT WITH CHOPPED PARSLEY AND PEELED TOMATO. SPREAD ON EITHER WHITE OR BROWN BREAD.
c
Open Sandwiches
CUT A FRENCH LOAF DIAGONALLY TO MAKE LONG SLICES. CUT WELL-GRILLED SAUSAGES IN HALF LENGTHWAYS AND PUT ONE ON EACH SLICE. GARNISH WITH CHOPPED PICKLED ONION AND LETTUCE.
NOW ARRANGE THE SANDWICHES ON SEPARATE DISHES, JUDY.
WHICH WILL YOU HAVE, FOLKS — SWEET OR SAVOURY?

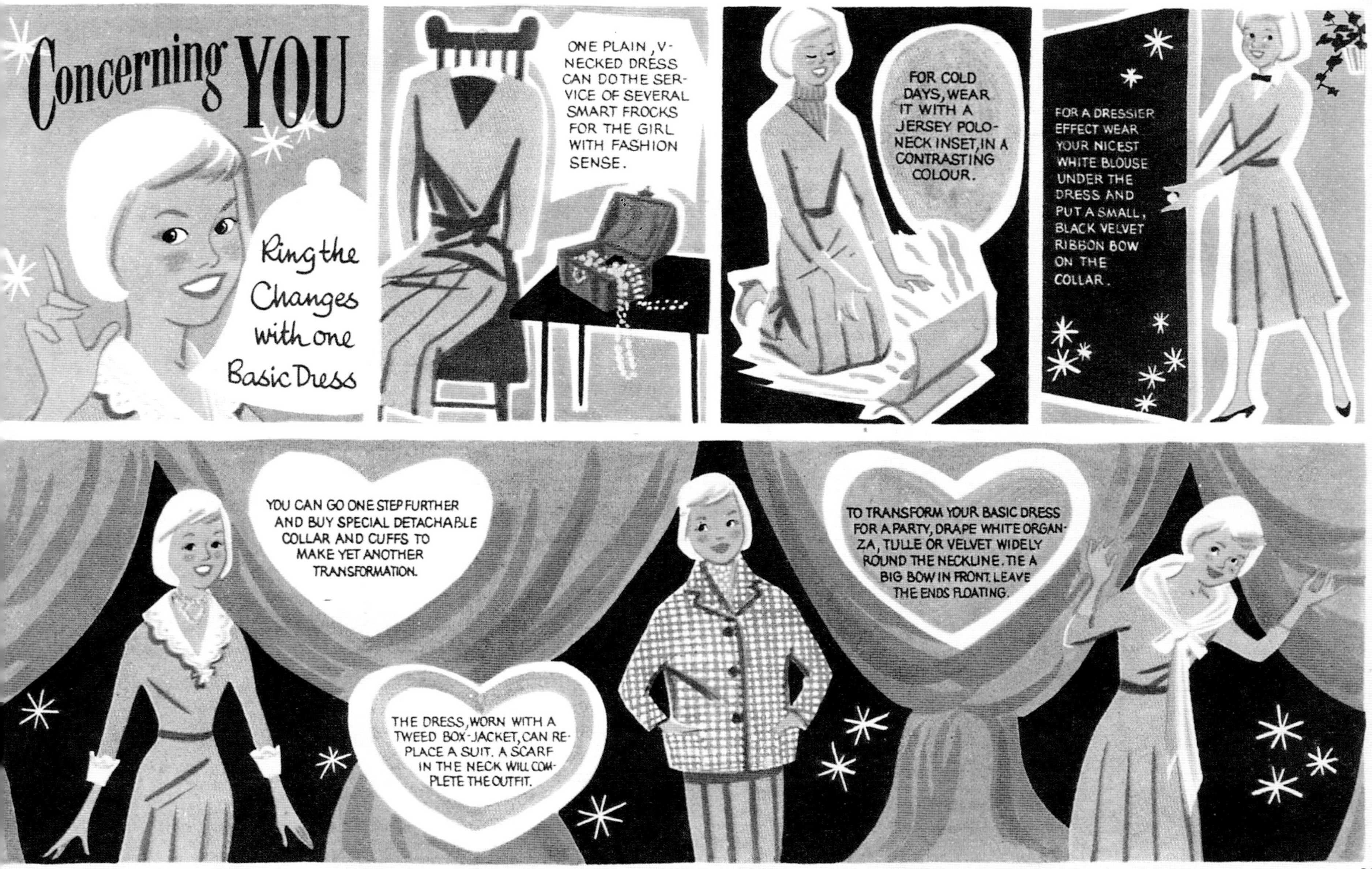
Concerning YOU
Ring the Changes with one Basic Dress
ONE PLAIN, V-NECKED DRESS CAN DO THE SERVICE OF SEVERAL SMART FROCKS FOR THE GIRL WITH FASHION SENSE.
FOR COLD DAYS, WEAR IT WITH A JERSEY POLO-NECK INSET, IN A CONTRASTING COLOUR.
FOR A DRESSIER EFFECT WEAR YOUR NICEST WHITE BLOUSE UNDER THE DRESS AND PUT A SMALL, BLACK VELVET RIBBON BOW ON THE COLLAR.
YOU CAN GO ONE STEP FURTHER AND BUY SPECIAL DETACHABLE COLLAR AND CUFFS TO MAKE YET ANOTHER TRANSFORMATION.
THE DRESS, WORN WITH A TWEED BOX-JACKET, CAN REPLACE A SUIT. A SCARF IN THE NECK WILL COMPLETE THE OUTFIT.
TO TRANSFORM YOUR BASIC DRESS FOR A PARTY, DRAPE WHITE ORGANZA, TULLE OR VELVET WIDELY ROUND THE NECKLINE. TIE A BIG BOW IN FRONT. LEAVE THE ENDS FLOATING.

A Letter from the Editor

GIRL OFFICE, 18 FURNIVAL ST., LONDON, E.C.4.

25th November, 1953

AMUSING things happen to all of us at some time or another. Perhaps they haven't seemed so funny at the time, but afterwards – how we've laughed over them! Well, this week's competition is an invitation to you to tell us *your* funniest experience – and there are six really lovely wrist watches for the six most amusing stories we receive. Hurry up with your entries and see if you can win one. By the way, we hope to publish the winning 'funnies' in GIRL later on.

At the bottom of this page you'll see another invitation – to come to either my Christmas party at Nottingham or the one at Plymouth. If you'd like to be there – and I can promise lots of fun – send in your application right away.

Yours sincerely,

Marcus Morris

Six wonderful wrist watches to be won this week!

TELL US YOUR FUNNIEST EXPERIENCE

. . . and a super prize may be yours

DID something amusing happen to you today – or yesterday, last week or last year? Think back and you're almost sure to remember something which made you laugh when you told your friends about it. Why not share the joke with us? – It may win you one of the six wonderful wrist watches we're offering as prizes!

HERE ARE THE RULES:

1. Write out your most amusing experience on a postcard in your best writing. It must be true and not longer than fifty words.

2. On the same postcard add your name, address and age last birthday.

3. Points will be given for neatness and good handwriting as well as for the funniest story.

4. Top age limit is sixteen.

5. All entries should be sent to: GIRL Watches-a-Week Competition No. 1, GIRL, Long Lane, Aintree, Liverpool 9, to arrive there not later than December 7th.

6. Send no money; this is FREE.

7. The decision of the Editor and judges is final and no correspondence will be entered into concerning any of the entries.

Special Christmas Carol Services

Write to us for your free tickets NOW

THIS year, just like last year, we are having magnificent Carol Services in several great cathedrals and churches throughout the country. They are specially for readers of GIRL, EAGLE and ROBIN, who will be able to join in singing all the best-known carols. Be sure to come – and bring your parents and friends too! Specially chosen readers will take part in the service with the Editor.

The Carol Services will be held on:
Sat. 19th December at **St. Paul's Cathedral**, London 2.15
Mon. 21st December at **Portsmouth Cathedral** 3.00
Tues. 22nd December at **Birmingham Parish Church** 2.30
Wed. 23rd December at **Manchester Cathedral** 2.30
Thur. 24th December at **Saint Giles' Cathedral**, Edinburgh 3.00

Make sure of getting your seat by writing at once to: Carol Services, GIRL, Long Lane, Aintree, Liverpool 9, enclosing a large envelope addressed to yourself bearing a 1½d stamp, asking for tickets for the service you want to attend. Tickets will be sent out in strict rotation.

Two younger brothers

Q. I am thirteen years of age and I have a bedroom of my own in which I keep my belongings. I have two brothers aged seven and five. Do you think it is fair that my mother should let them go into my bedroom to take the things out of my drawers?

A. *We think that your brothers should be given drawers and boxes of their own, and that you should not be allowed to go to them any more than they should be allowed to go to yours.*

Try to work out a system with your family which will give you all a fair share of privacy.

* * *

Wearing glasses

Q. I notice that in most of the girls' or boys' papers I read all the 'dopes' wear glasses. I, and many of my friends, wear glasses and we do not consider ourselves 'dopes'. What do you think?

A. *You are quite right. It is very old-fashioned to suppose that only 'dopes' wear glasses. Many very brilliant women wear them and look most attractive.*

READERS' LETTERS

5/- will be paid for every reader's letter printed on this page.

Rose's hair is two feet long

THIS IS A snapshot of my mother, my sister and myself. My mother's hair and my own is two feet long, my sister's one foot eleven and a half inches. We have had long hair all our lives – even mother – and it takes her a whole evening to wash our three heads! We enjoy this – but we dread having to comb it out before it is plaited. I take after my mother with dark hair. My sister Helen's is light brown. – *Rose Napper, Blandford, Dorset.*

* * *

Mystery voice!

I AM GOING to Ireland to a little cottage in the Mountains of Mourne. My cousin lives there with his mother and father. He has a budgie and one day, when my auntie was upstairs and the milkman came, the budgie shouted: "No milk today, thank you" – and the man went off without leaving any. It wasn't as funny as it sounds, because they live a long way from a village! – *Norma Gwynne, Upper Stratton, Swindon, Wiltshire.*

* * *

Gay's big family

IN MY FAMILY – besides Mummy, Daddy and my brother and sister – I have twenty cousins, eleven aunts, eleven uncles, one great-uncle, six great-aunts and two grannies. – *Gay Anne Brench, Aldershot, Hampshire.*

* * *

Secret signal

WHY DON'T GIRL Adventurers who hold meetings in a shed or a room have a special knock? G. A. in morse code would be G – dash, dash, dot; A – dot, dash. G.C. (GIRL Club) would be G – dash, dash, dot; C – dash, dot, dash, dot. – *Marjorie Lang, Kilbirnie, Ayrshire.*

Here comes the bride!

ON SATURDAY at our village church Rev White married Mr Black to Miss Brown. Have other readers heard of any 'coloured' weddings? – *Rosalind Peden, Epping, Essex.*

Come to our Christmas Party!

There are two to choose from – one in Nottingham and one in Plymouth.

THE Editor is holding two Christmas parties for the Club members of GIRL and its brother paper EAGLE. One is in Nottingham on December 29th and the other in Plymouth on December 30th. Both parties are from 3.30 until 6 o'clock. Would YOU like to come?

Those of you who live in or near either of these towns should write at once (on a postcard, please, giving your name, full address and Club number) to: GIRL Adventurers' Christmas Parties, GIRL, Long Lane, Aintree, Liverpool 9, stating which of the parties you would like to attend.

We haven't room for everybody, unfortunately, but the first 125 applicants for each town will be sent invitations. The Editor hopes to be at both parties and you'll be able to enjoy a huge tea, lots of games and fun. Hurry up and write in to us!

If your birth date's here we'll send you a present

IF you are a member of the GIRL Adventurers Club, and if you were born on any of the dates listed, we will give you a free present. Choose from:– a sewing kit, a stamp album, a ball-point pen, a stationery folder, a handbag badge, a propelling pencil, a birthday book, a bicycle bell, a gilt-framed miniature of the Queen, a Coronation brooch or a set of coloured pencils.

Make certain the day, the month and the year are all the same as your birthday, then write the date on a postcard – with your full name and address, your Club number and the present you would prefer from the list given – and send it to: GIRL Adventurers' Birthday Presents (36), GIRL Reader Services, Long Lane, Aintree, Liverpool 9.

Your postcard must reach us not later than Tuesday, December 1st, and *you must already be a member of the GIRL Adventurers Club* to claim a present.

Each week we will publish a list of dates in GIRL. The same birthday date may appear more than once, but no member can claim more than one present.

Feb. 16th 1941
April 24th 1937
Nov 3rd 1940
June 30th 1942
Aug 8th 1939
Dec 11th 1938

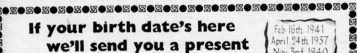

A holiday in the Austrian mountains is something most of us only dream about – but it came true for these girls and boys. They are a party of GIRL and EAGLE readers who went to Niedernsill, where they spent ten exciting days sightseeing.

She won a bike!

Here's Patricia Wilson (9) who won our Bike-a-Week Comp. No 14.

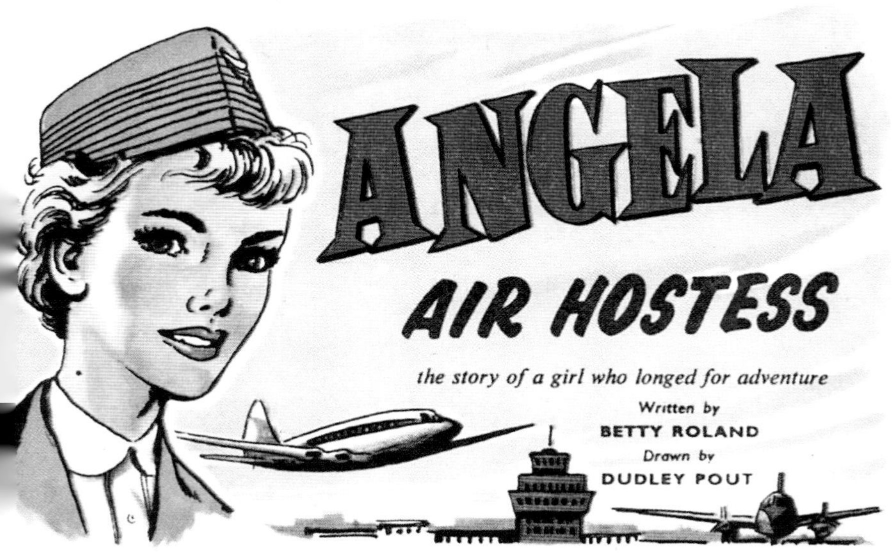

ANGELA
AIR HOSTESS

the story of a girl who longed for adventure

Written by
BETTY ROLAND
Drawn by
DUDLEY POUT

Angela Wells lives with her mother and brother Clive, who is studying – though not as hard as he might – for a medical degree. Angela works in an office and also helps her mother, who takes in paying guests. Angela's father, a flying ace, was killed during the war. She has inherited his love of flying and wants to be an Air Hostess, but her mother hates planes. When a rich old lady takes over Angela's room, Angela braves her mother's disapproval, applies for an interview with a big Airline and is asked to come before the Selection Board. When she visits London Airport, Angela asks a Senior Air Hostess for a few hints . . .

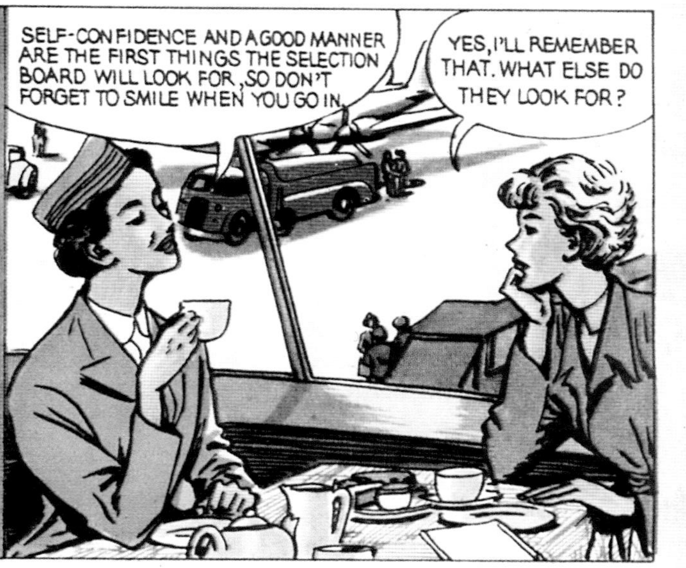
SELF-CONFIDENCE AND A GOOD MANNER ARE THE FIRST THINGS THE SELECTION BOARD WILL LOOK FOR, SO DON'T FORGET TO SMILE WHEN YOU GO IN.
YES, I'LL REMEMBER THAT. WHAT ELSE DO THEY LOOK FOR?

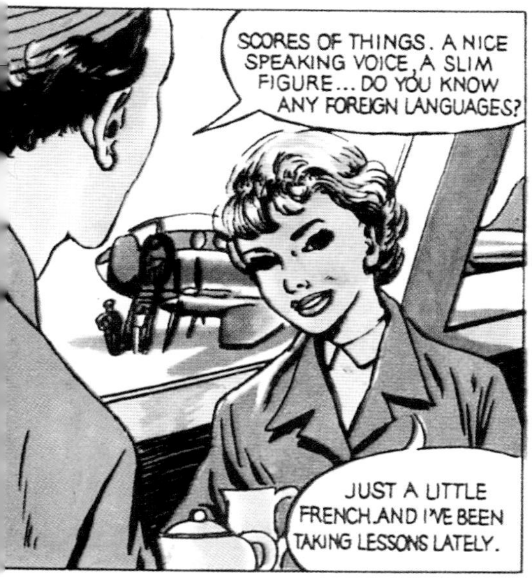
SCORES OF THINGS. A NICE SPEAKING VOICE, A SLIM FIGURE... DO YOU KNOW ANY FOREIGN LANGUAGES?
JUST A LITTLE FRENCH. AND I'VE BEEN TAKING LESSONS LATELY.

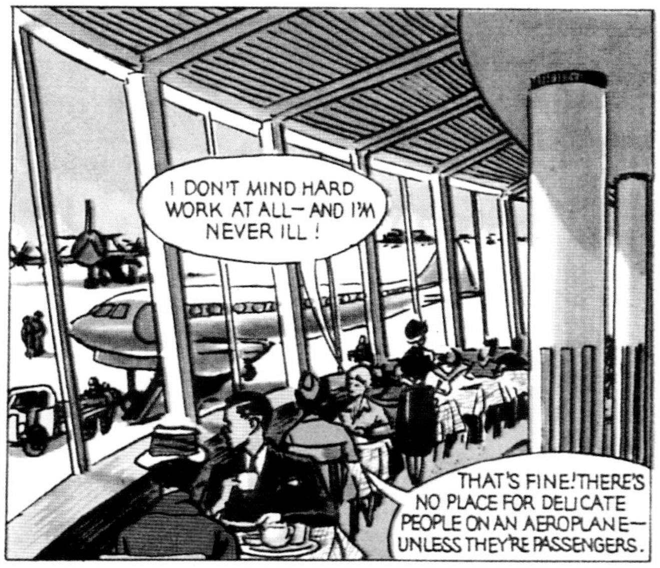
I DON'T MIND HARD WORK AT ALL – AND I'M NEVER ILL!
THAT'S FINE! THERE'S NO PLACE FOR DELICATE PEOPLE ON AN AEROPLANE – UNLESS THEY'RE PASSENGERS.

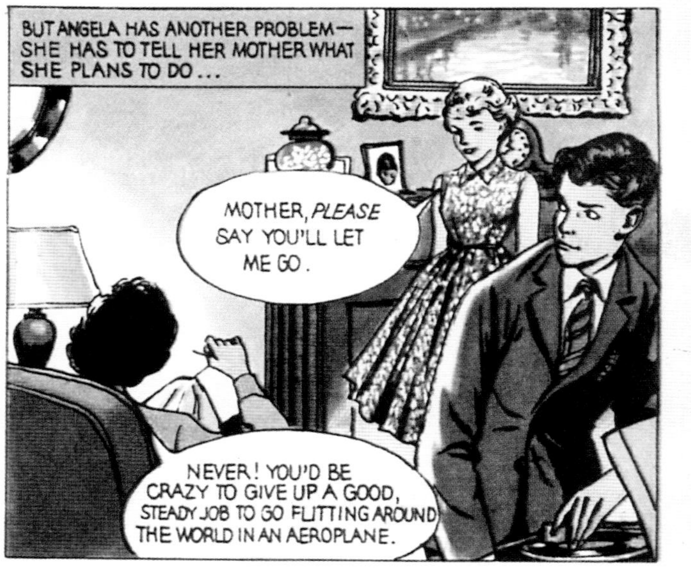
BUT ANGELA HAS ANOTHER PROBLEM – SHE HAS TO TELL HER MOTHER WHAT SHE PLANS TO DO...
MOTHER, PLEASE SAY YOU'LL LET ME GO.
NEVER! YOU'D BE CRAZY TO GIVE UP A GOOD, STEADY JOB TO GO FLITTING AROUND THE WORLD IN AN AEROPLANE.

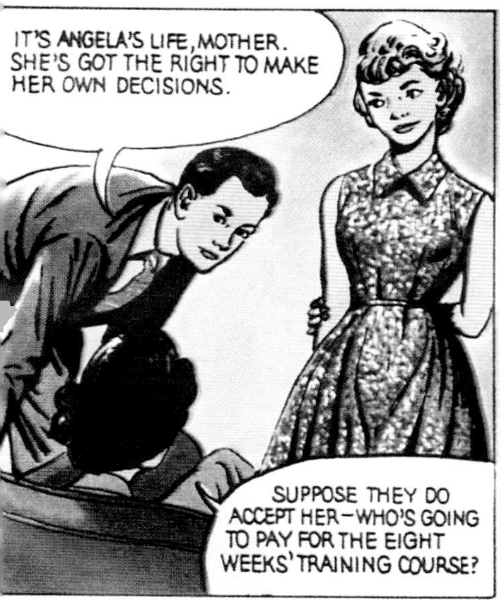
IT'S ANGELA'S LIFE, MOTHER. SHE'S GOT THE RIGHT TO MAKE HER OWN DECISIONS.
SUPPOSE THEY DO ACCEPT HER – WHO'S GOING TO PAY FOR THE EIGHT WEEKS' TRAINING COURSE?

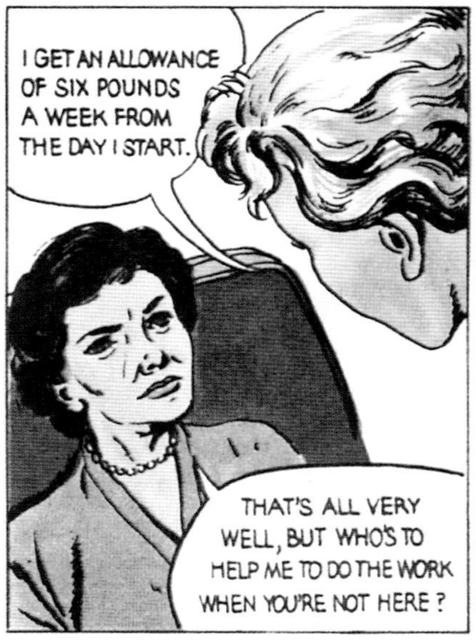
I GET AN ALLOWANCE OF SIX POUNDS A WEEK FROM THE DAY I START.
THAT'S ALL VERY WELL, BUT WHO'S TO HELP ME TO DO THE WORK WHEN YOU'RE NOT HERE?

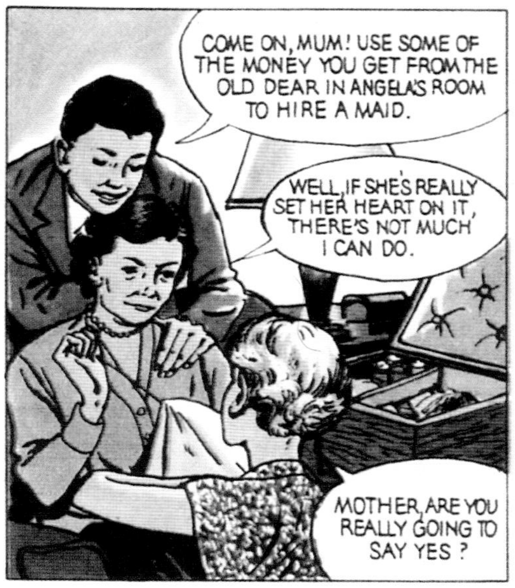
COME ON, MUM! USE SOME OF THE MONEY YOU GET FROM THE OLD DEAR IN ANGELA'S ROOM TO HIRE A MAID.
WELL, IF SHE'S REALLY SET HER HEART ON IT, THERE'S NOT MUCH I CAN DO.
MOTHER, ARE YOU REALLY GOING TO SAY YES?

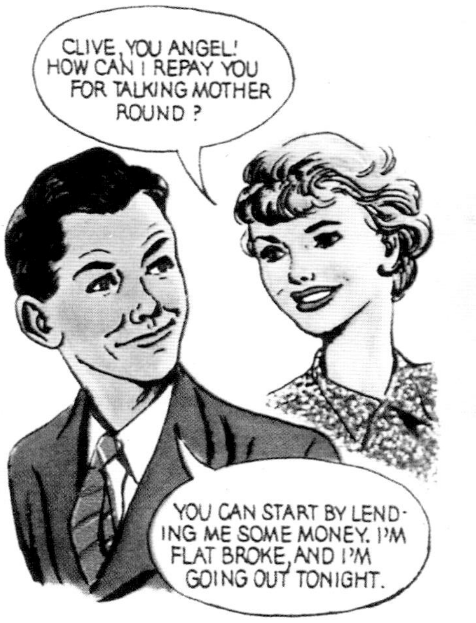
CLIVE, YOU ANGEL! HOW CAN I REPAY YOU FOR TALKING MOTHER ROUND?
YOU CAN START BY LENDING ME SOME MONEY. I'M FLAT BROKE, AND I'M GOING OUT TONIGHT.

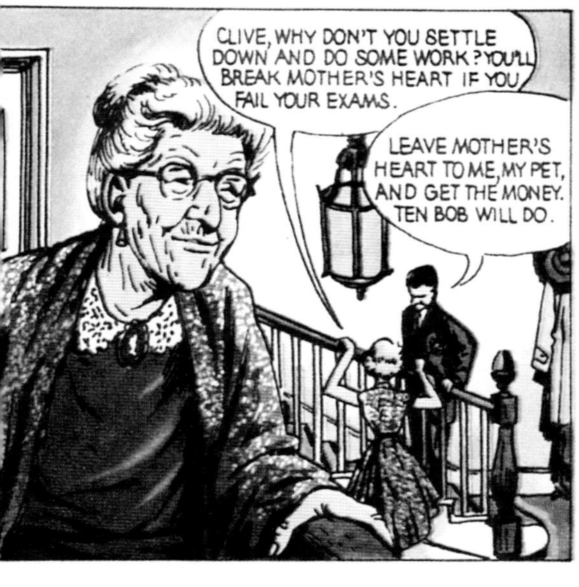
CLIVE, WHY DON'T YOU SETTLE DOWN AND DO SOME WORK? YOU'LL BREAK MOTHER'S HEART IF YOU FAIL YOUR EXAMS.
LEAVE MOTHER'S HEART TO ME, MY PET, AND GET THE MONEY. TEN BOB WILL DO.

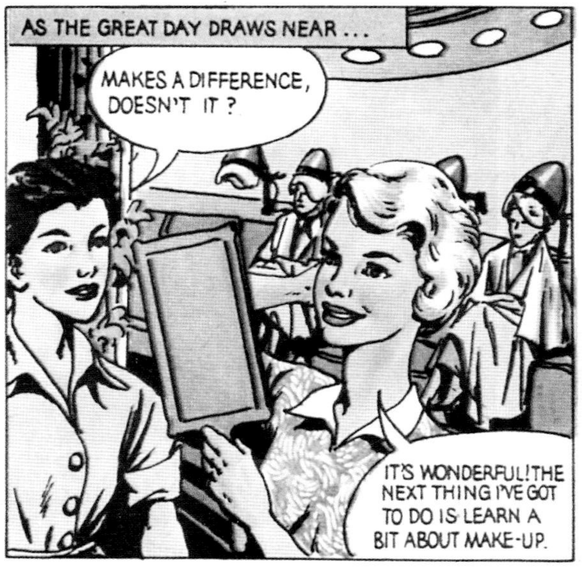
AS THE GREAT DAY DRAWS NEAR...
MAKES A DIFFERENCE, DOESN'T IT?
IT'S WONDERFUL! THE NEXT THING I'VE GOT TO DO IS LEARN A BIT ABOUT MAKE-UP.

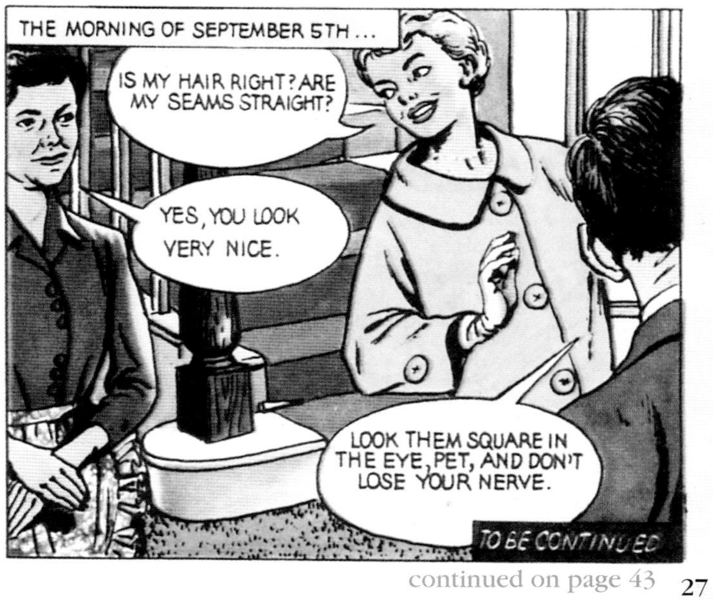
THE MORNING OF SEPTEMBER 5TH...
IS MY HAIR RIGHT? ARE MY SEAMS STRAIGHT?
YES, YOU LOOK VERY NICE.
LOOK THEM SQUARE IN THE EYE, PET, AND DON'T LOSE YOUR NERVE.
TO BE CONTINUED

continued on page 43

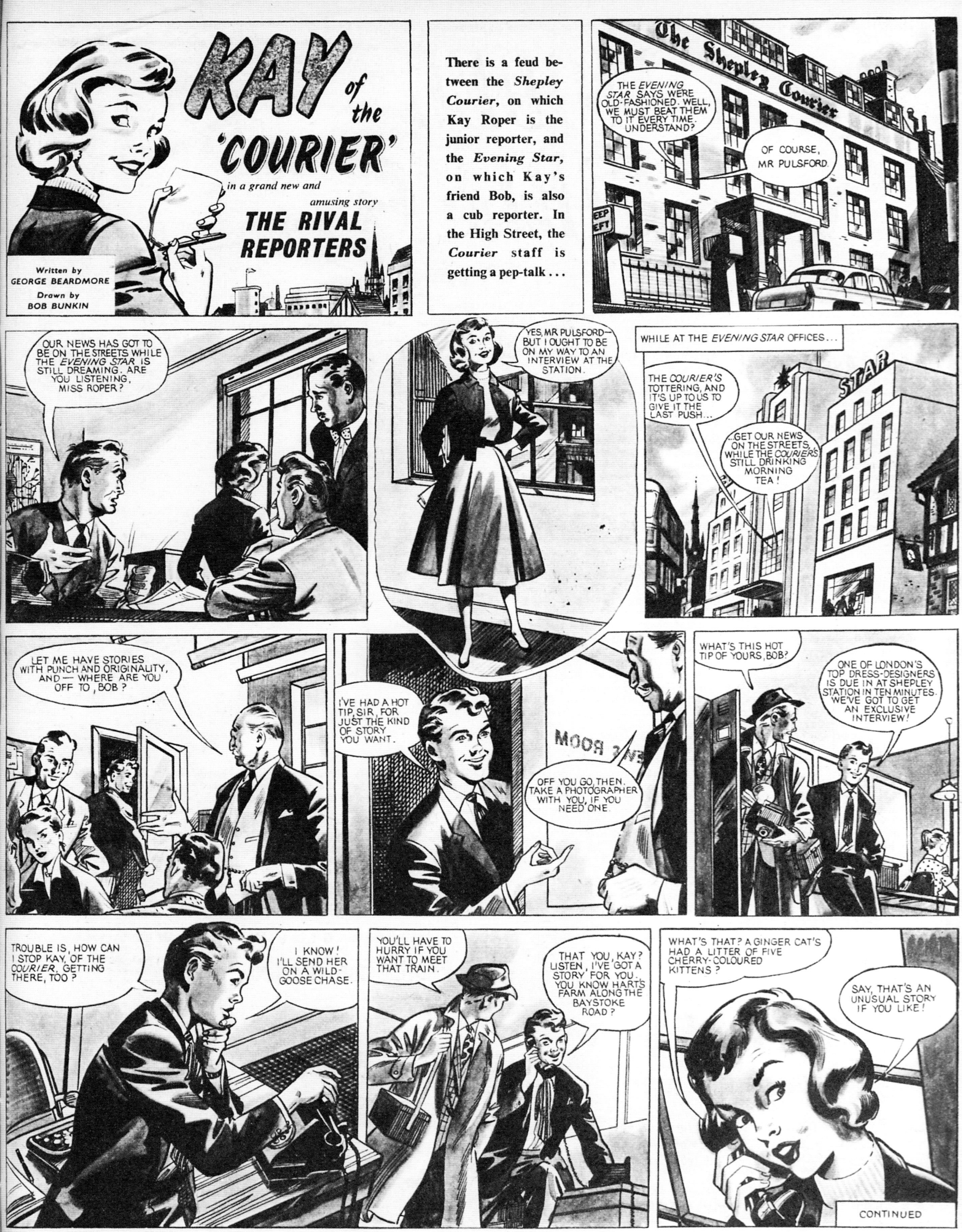
KAY of the 'COURIER'
in a grand new and amusing story
THE RIVAL REPORTERS
Written by GEORGE BEARDMORE
Drawn by BOB BUNKIN
There is a feud between the Shepley Courier, on which Kay Roper is the junior reporter, and the Evening Star, on which Kay's friend Bob, is also a cub reporter. In the High Street, the Courier staff is getting a pep-talk . . .
The Shepley Courier
THE EVENING STAR SAYS WE'RE OLD-FASHIONED. WELL, WE MUST BEAT THEM TO IT EVERY TIME. UNDERSTAND?
OF COURSE, MR PULSFORD.
OUR NEWS HAS GOT TO BE ON THE STREETS WHILE THE EVENING STAR IS STILL DREAMING. ARE YOU LISTENING, MISS ROPER?
YES, MR PULSFORD— BUT I OUGHT TO BE ON MY WAY TO AN INTERVIEW AT THE STATION.
WHILE AT THE EVENING STAR OFFICES...
STAR
THE COURIER'S TOTTERING, AND IT'S UP TO US TO GIVE IT THE LAST PUSH...
...GET OUR NEWS ON THE STREETS, WHILE THE COURIER'S STILL DRINKING MORNING TEA!
LET ME HAVE STORIES WITH PUNCH AND ORIGINALITY, AND — WHERE ARE YOU OFF TO, BOB?
I'VE HAD A HOT TIP, SIR, FOR JUST THE KIND OF STORY YOU WANT.
OFF YOU GO, THEN. TAKE A PHOTOGRAPHER WITH YOU, IF YOU NEED ONE.
WHAT'S THIS HOT TIP OF YOURS, BOB?
ONE OF LONDON'S TOP DRESS-DESIGNERS IS DUE IN AT SHEPLEY STATION IN TEN MINUTES. WE'VE GOT TO GET AN EXCLUSIVE INTERVIEW!
TROUBLE IS, HOW CAN I STOP KAY, OF THE COURIER, GETTING THERE, TOO?
I KNOW! I'LL SEND HER ON A WILD-GOOSE CHASE.
YOU'LL HAVE TO HURRY IF YOU WANT TO MEET THAT TRAIN.
THAT YOU, KAY? LISTEN, I'VE GOT A STORY FOR YOU. YOU KNOW HART'S FARM ALONG THE BAYSTOKE ROAD?
WHAT'S THAT? A GINGER CAT'S HAD A LITTER OF FIVE CHERRY-COLOURED KITTENS?
SAY, THAT'S AN UNUSUAL STORY IF YOU LIKE!
CONTINUED

continued on page 48

PEOPLE WITH MUSIC

This month's star:- ELVIS PRESLEY

Turn to Page 9 for a colour portrait of this famous record personality!

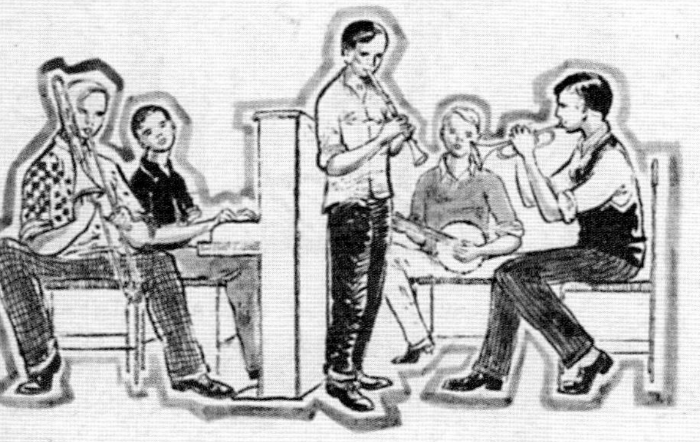

THEY call Louis Armstrong the Father of Jazz. If that's true, Elvis Presley is surely the Prince of Pops. Elvis was born on January 8th, 1935. "We had twins," his mother said, "Jesse Garon and Elvis Aron. But Jesse died young. Maybe that's why Elvis is so dear to us."

When Elvis was small his great joy was singing in church. His mother and father sang too. The three of them would sing "I Won't Have To Cross Jordan Alone" loud and strong each Sunday. The first person to appreciate the beauty of Elvis's voice was George Klein, who went to the same school as Elvis and edited the school magazine. "We were singing Christmas carols," Klein said, "and Elvis sang 'Cold, Cold, Icy Fingers'. I never forgot it. It was great." At that time, nobody else thought he was great – not even his mother.

So Elvis decided to make a record – "just to see what I sounded like!" He went to the offices of the Sun Record Company. His hair was long and shaggy: his clothes were rather worn. They told him it would cost four dollars to make a record. Elvis handed them his money. "Well, what do you want to sing?" they asked. "I can sing anything," said Elvis. The technicians groaned and switched on the microphones. But when Sam Phillips, who owned the record company, heard Elvis's disc he was impressed – so impressed that, when he discovered a ballad written by a convict in a Tennessee gaol, he asked Elvis to record it.

A few weeks later a disc-jockey played *That's All Right*, sung by Elvis, from Memphis radio station. "I played the record at 9.30 p.m.," the disc-jockey said, "and the 'phones rang all night asking who Elvis was, where he was, and how soon they could hear more of him."

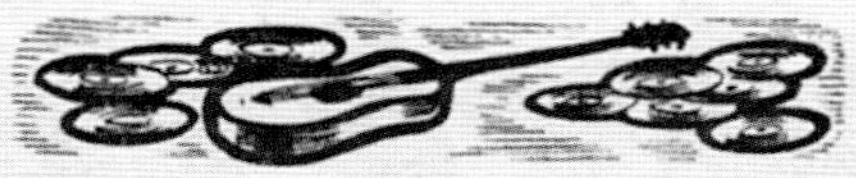

Today, we know who he is and where he is, *and* we want more of him. **The Best Of Elvis** (LP HMV DLP 1159) includes his top hits, **Heartbreak Hotel, Hound Dog,** and **Playin' For Keeps.** And if you liked **Teddy Bear,** try Elvis's new number, **Treat Me Nice** (RCA 1028), one of the hits from his latest film.

Jimmy Swing

Also worth hearing...

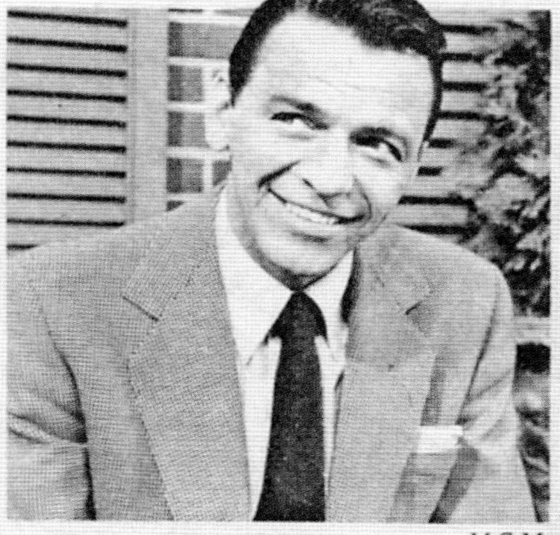

M.G.M.

Frank Sinatra is still a top favourite. Hear his recording of **All The Way** (Capitol CL 14800). Also look out for his long-player – **That Old Feeling** (LP Philips BBL 7180).

Johnny Ray singing **Texas Tambourine** (Philips PB 762); **Grand Encounter,** featuring John Lewis and Bill Perkins (LP Vogue LAE 12065); Skiffle – The Charles McDevitt Group, with Shirley Douglas in **Across the Bridge** (Oriole CB 1405).

JIMMY SWING WILL BE REVIEWING NEW RECORDS FROM TIME TO TIME

FOR GIRL ADVENTURERS

RIDING HOLIDAYS

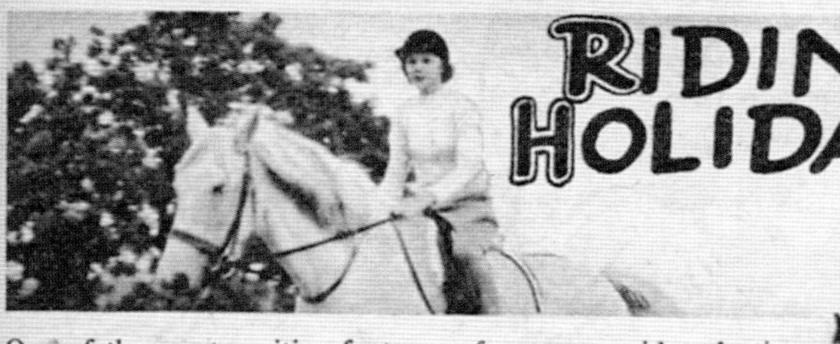

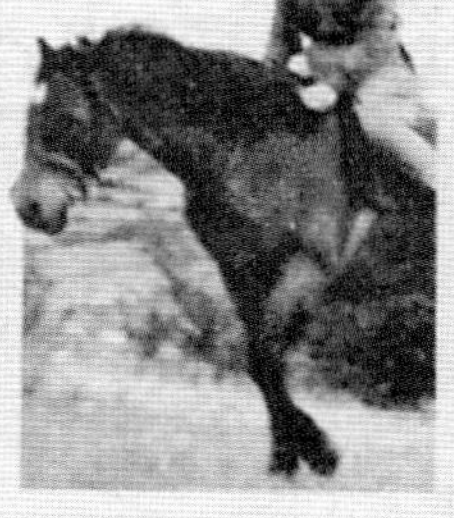

One of the most exciting features of our very wide selection of Summer Holidays is the Riding and Walking in Wales Tour. Always popular, it gives GIRL Adventurers the opportunity to explore, on foot and in the saddle, the beautiful Welsh countryside. Send for our special Holiday Brochure for full details of this and many more exciting tours open to Club Members between 12 and 16 years of age. Write now, to: – GIRL SUMMER HOLIDAYS, Long Lane, Aintree, Liverpool 9, enclosing a self-addressed, gummed label bearing a 2d. stamp. Please remember to state your Club Number.

⋆ Star Adventurer ⋆

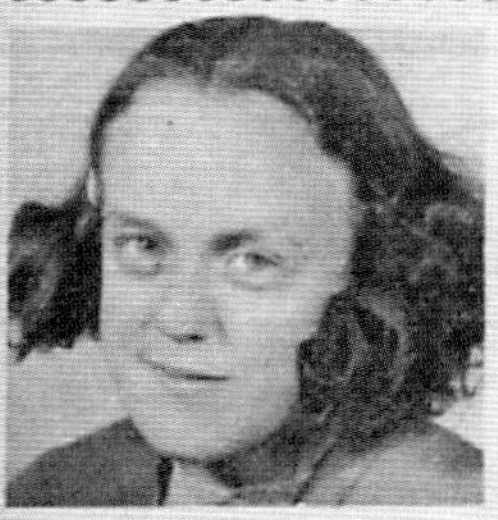

The Star Adventurer's Badge is the highest honour your club can award. It is given to club members who have outstanding records of courage, unselfishness and helpfulness. This week, we are pleased to announce that fourteen-year-old Eileen Moody of Boughton, Newark, Notts, has won her Star for courage and helpfulness.

Lucky Birthdates

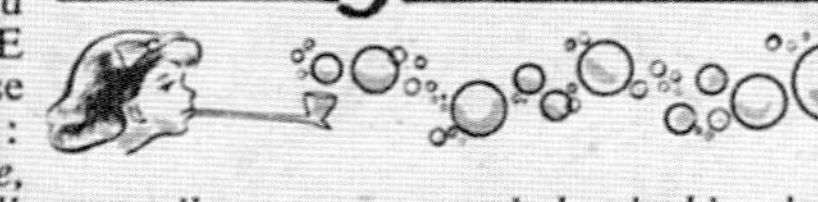

If you are a GIRL Adventurer and your birthdate appears in this week's list, you are entitled to a FREE birthday gift! Choose it from the following: – GIRL *handbag badge, stamp album, propelling pencil,* GIRL *autograph book, bicycle bell, ballpoint pen or coloured pencils.* State your choice on a postcard, giving us your name, address, Club Number and the date you were born. Send it to: – BIRTHDATES (11), GIRL Club, Long Lane, Aintree, Liverpool 9, to reach us by Thursday, 20th March. Overseas members whose birthdates appear here will automatically receive their presents.

7 FEB. 1944
29 APR. 1945
15 JUNE 1946
22 AUG. 1947
2 OCT. 1948
31 DEC. 1949

WHAT'S YOUR WORRY?

If you have a worry you'd like to share, and feel our experts can help, just write to: GIRL, 18 Furnival Street, London, E.C.4, and mark your letter WHAT'S YOUR WORRY? No names will be printed, but let us have a stamped, self-addressed envelope if you would like a personal reply by letter.

She's called 'fussy'

Q. At school they call me 'fussy', but I don't know what kind of fussy they mean by this. What should I do?

Try to develop some definite interest with the others in your class. This will help you not to pay too much attention to little things that go wrong. It is nothing to be ashamed of, or to worry about, and you will find that you will gradually grow out of the habit.

* * *

Getting too excited

Q. I get too excited at school, and this causes me to fail my tests. How can I learn to be more calm?

A. *You will grow calmer as you get older. Meanwhile, listen to all your lessons very carefully, and do your very best to remember what you hear.*

* * *

Blushing

Q. When the headmaster announces from the platform that someone has done wrong, I always blush. Can I do anything about it?

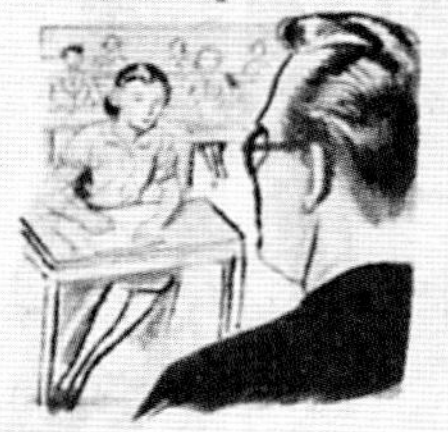

A. *No. You are a sensitive type of girl and that is why you respond as you do.*

Walking home

Q. There is a boy at school who always waits for me and wants to walk home with me. I do not like him. What can I do?

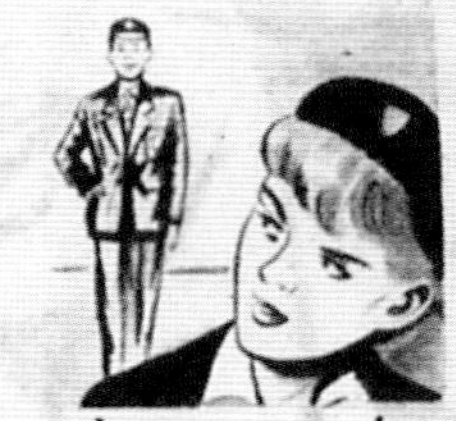

A. *Either tell him that you prefer to go home alone, or make sure you have picked your own friends to go home with before you leave the school.*

* * *

No longer friends

Q. A boy I have known a long time suddenly said he would never like me again because he had heard some tales about me. They weren't true. How can I make him be friends with me again?

A. *Don't try to. If he believes spiteful rumours rather than your word, we think that you would be well advised to forget all about your friendship.*

* * *

Her friend is cheeky

Q. I have a friend I like very much, but when I am with her she is often cheeky to other people. Why is this, and can I stop her from doing it?

A. *She is probably showing off because it makes her feel important to be rude at the expense of others. Tell her that she is far nicer when she does not show off. That may help to make her behave in a friendlier way to others.*

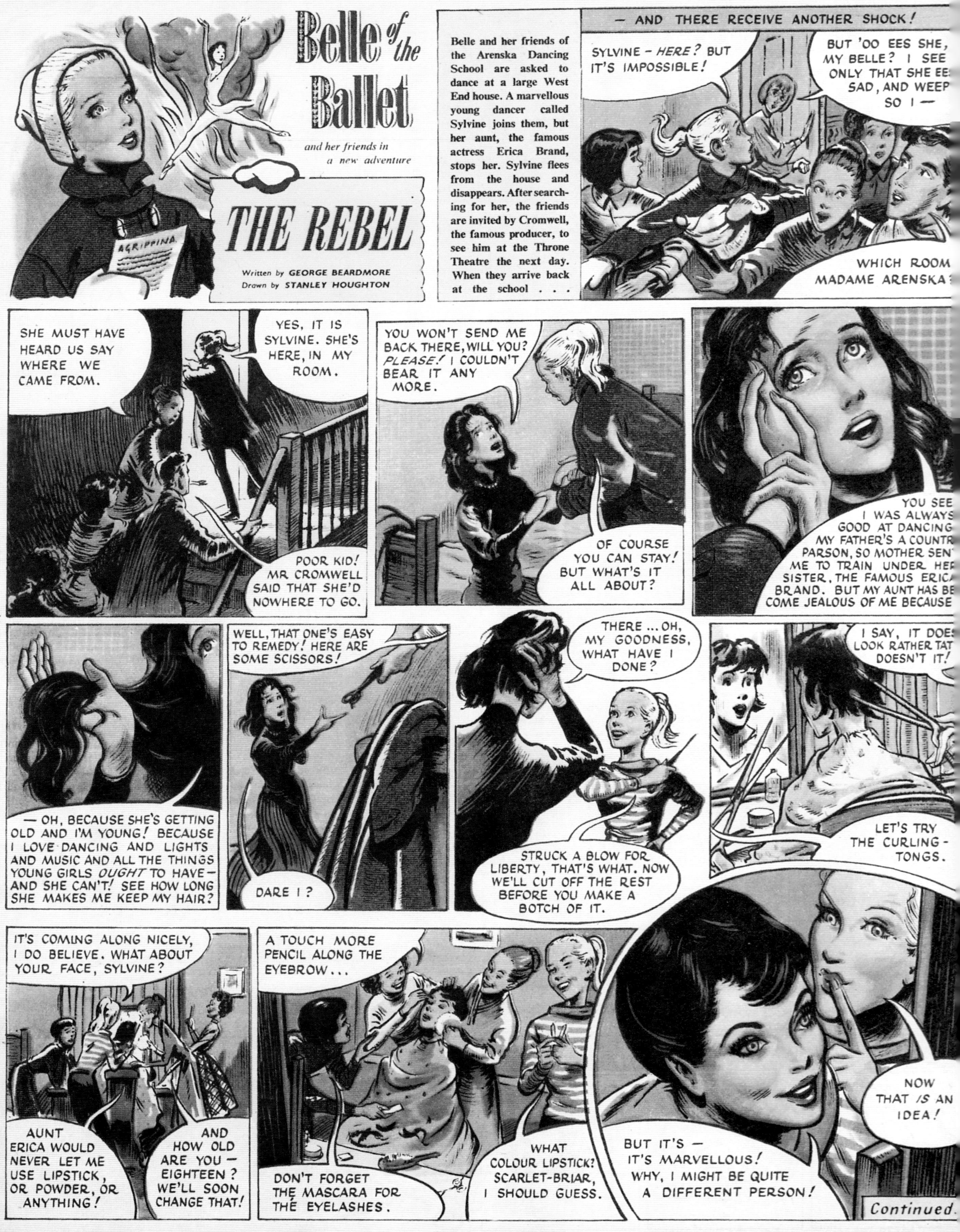
Belle of the Ballet
and her friends in a new adventure
THE REBEL
Written by GEORGE BEARDMORE
Drawn by STANLEY HOUGHTON
AGRIPPINA
Belle and her friends of the Arenska Dancing School are asked to dance at a large West End house. A marvellous young dancer called Sylvine joins them, but her aunt, the famous actress Erica Brand, stops her. Sylvine flees from the house and disappears. After searching for her, the friends are invited by Cromwell, the famous producer, to see him at the Throne Theatre the next day. When they arrive back at the school . . .
— AND THERE RECEIVE ANOTHER SHOCK!
SYLVINE – HERE? BUT IT'S IMPOSSIBLE!
BUT 'OO EES SHE, MY BELLE? I SEE ONLY THAT SHE EE SAD, AND WEEP SO I —
WHICH ROOM MADAME ARENSKA
SHE MUST HAVE HEARD US SAY WHERE WE CAME FROM.
YES, IT IS SYLVINE. SHE'S HERE, IN MY ROOM.
POOR KID! MR CROMWELL SAID THAT SHE'D NOWHERE TO GO.
YOU WON'T SEND ME BACK THERE, WILL YOU? PLEASE! I COULDN'T BEAR IT ANY MORE.
OF COURSE YOU CAN STAY! BUT WHAT'S IT ALL ABOUT?
YOU SEE I WAS ALWAYS GOOD AT DANCING MY FATHER'S A COUNTR PARSON, SO MOTHER SEN ME TO TRAIN UNDER HE SISTER, THE FAMOUS ERIC BRAND. BUT MY AUNT HAS BE COME JEALOUS OF ME BECAUSE
— OH, BECAUSE SHE'S GETTING OLD AND I'M YOUNG! BECAUSE I LOVE DANCING AND LIGHTS AND MUSIC AND ALL THE THINGS YOUNG GIRLS OUGHT TO HAVE— AND SHE CAN'T! SEE HOW LONG SHE MAKES ME KEEP MY HAIR?
WELL, THAT ONE'S EASY TO REMEDY! HERE ARE SOME SCISSORS!
DARE I?
THERE ... OH, MY GOODNESS, WHAT HAVE I DONE?
STRUCK A BLOW FOR LIBERTY, THAT'S WHAT. NOW WE'LL CUT OFF THE REST BEFORE YOU MAKE A BOTCH OF IT.
I SAY, IT DOES LOOK RATHER TAT DOESN'T IT!
LET'S TRY THE CURLING-TONGS.
IT'S COMING ALONG NICELY, I DO BELIEVE. WHAT ABOUT YOUR FACE, SYLVINE?
AUNT ERICA WOULD NEVER LET ME USE LIPSTICK, OR POWDER, OR ANYTHING!
AND HOW OLD ARE YOU— EIGHTEEN? WE'LL SOON CHANGE THAT!
A TOUCH MORE PENCIL ALONG THE EYEBROW...
DON'T FORGET THE MASCARA FOR THE EYELASHES.
WHAT COLOUR LIPSTICK? SCARLET-BRIAR, I SHOULD GUESS.
NOW THAT IS AN IDEA!
BUT IT'S — IT'S MARVELLOUS! WHY, I MIGHT BE QUITE A DIFFERENT PERSON!
Continued

continued on page 40

★ Jacky meets Joan Collins ★

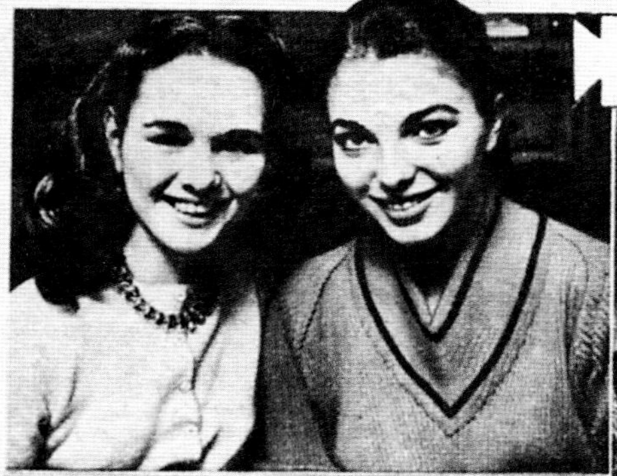

With best wishes to GIRL readers from Joan Collins

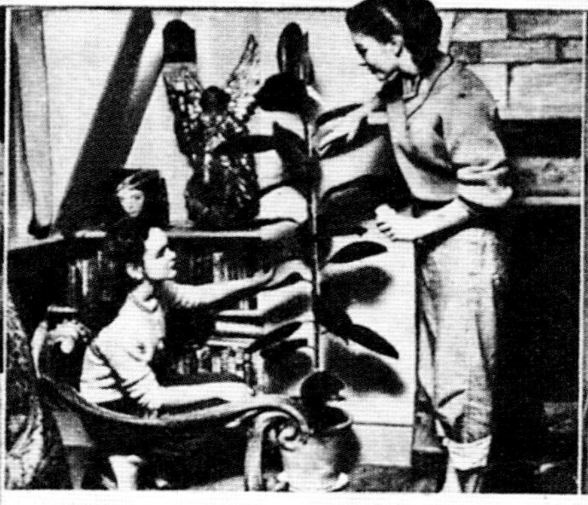

Film actress Joan Collins is the proud owner of a rubber plant. Know what she cleans it with? - Hair cream!

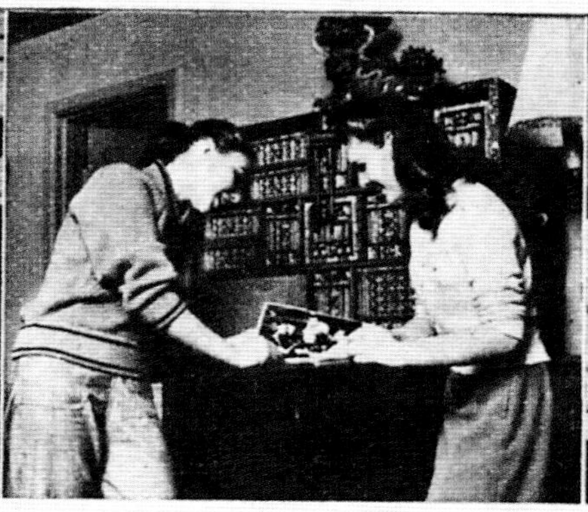

It's quite a climb to Joan's top-floor London flat, but it's worth the effort. She showed Jacky stills from her films.

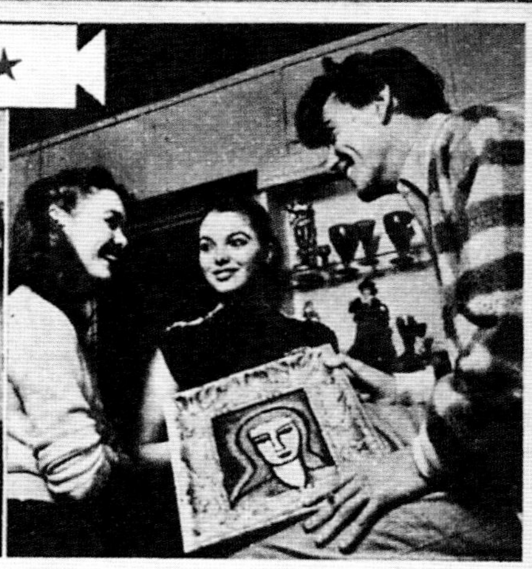

Joan is married to actor Maxwell Reed. Max is interested in modern art and has painted this portrait of his wife.

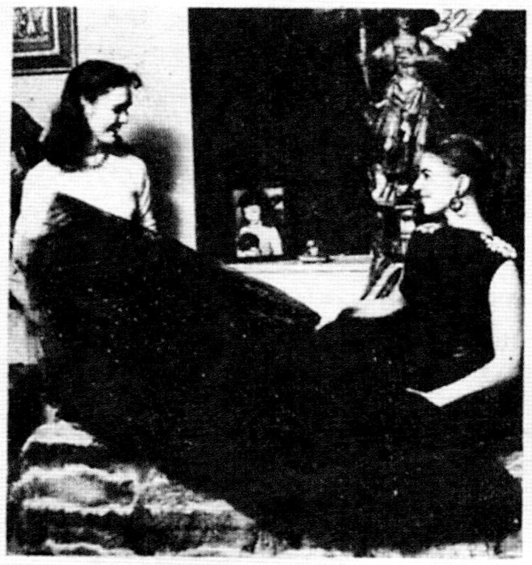

She loves pretty clothes. This beautiful black evening dress studded with gold stars is one that she designed herself.

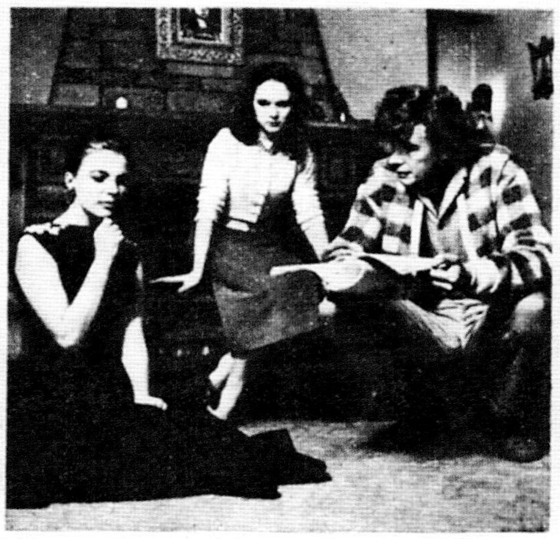

Max helped Joan rehearse for a new film. An actress's life isn't all glamour and a lot of time has to be spent learning scripts.

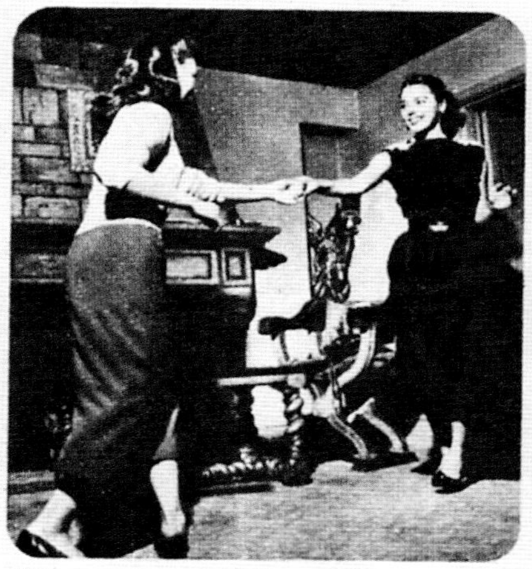

Discovering that Jacky is a jive fan too, Joan pushed back the furniture and they had their own private jive session.

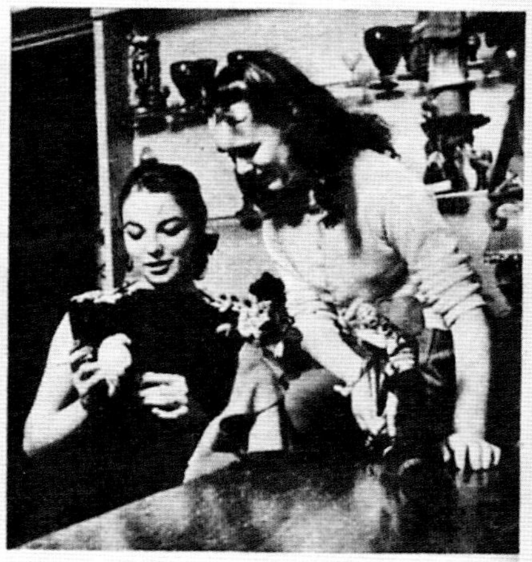

While in Spain, Joan collected these charming little dancers. Her hobbies are drawing, reading and dress-designing.

IMPROVE YOUR TENNIS

with LORNA CAWTHORN **No. 2**

(Twice Junior Champion of Great Britain – 1949 and 1950)

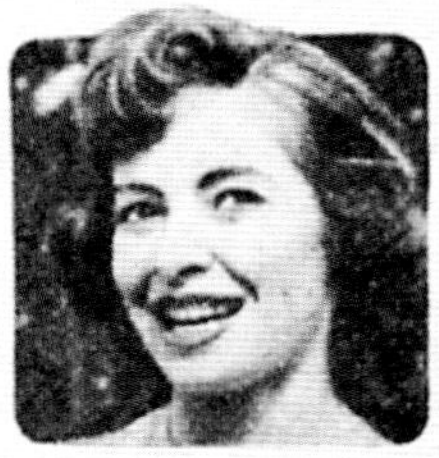

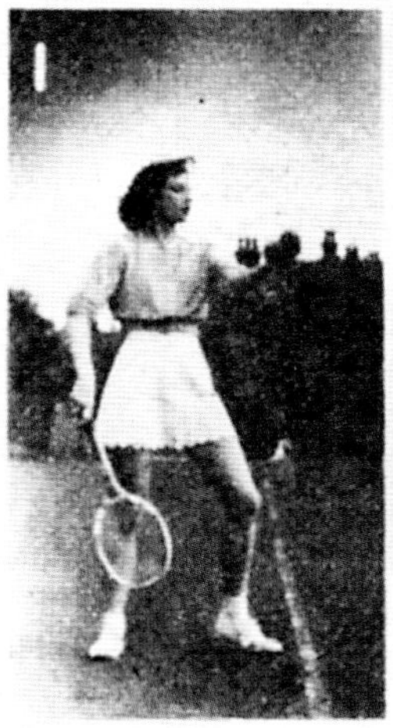
1

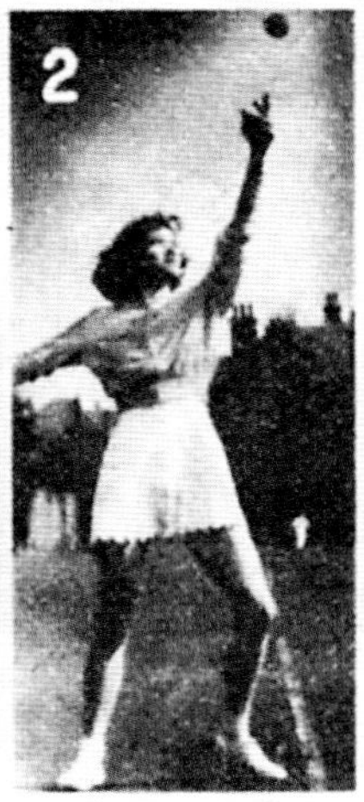
2

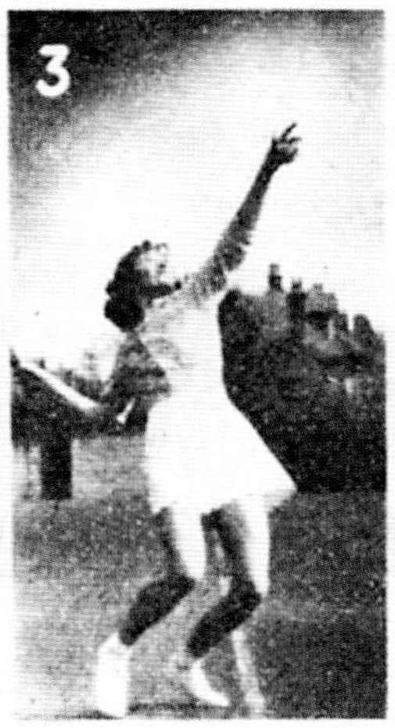
3

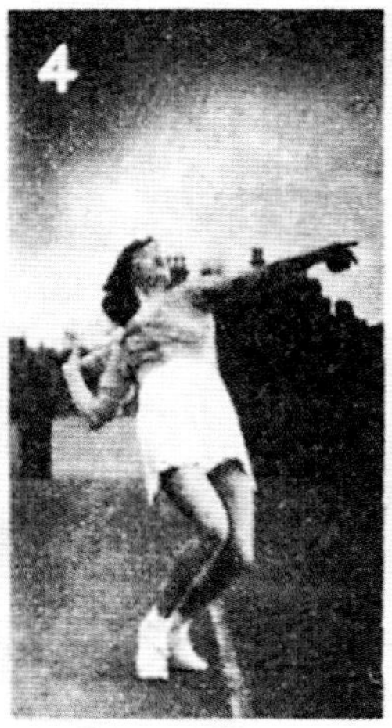
4

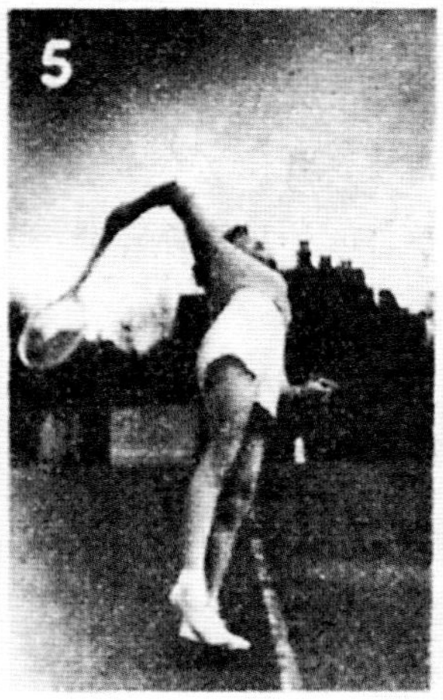
5

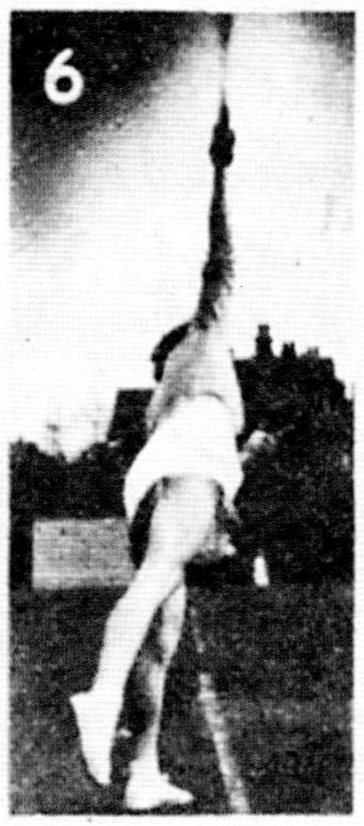
6

HOW TO SERVE

Start by learning a straightforward Flat Hit service upon which you can rely. The basic action is the same as you'd use to throw a stone high over your head. Once that's been grasped, it is a matter of practice to achieve good timing, synchronisation of ball and racquet, speed and accuracy.

1. Stand sideways to the net, with forward foot clear of the baseline and pointing in the direction you want the ball to go, and the other foot a comfortable distance from it. Hold the balls naturally in front of your body, and let the racquet head point downwards in your right hand. **2.** Throw the ball straight up in the air as if putting it upon a shelf about 18" above your head. Don't throw it so high that you lose control. Left arm and racquet arm move simultaneously. **3.** Getting ready to hit the ball, during which weight will be transferred to left leg. Left arm points upward to keep a line on the ball, and eyes are fixed firmly on the ball. **4.** Note arched back and bent knees as Lorna prepares to get her full weight behind the ball and plenty of zip into the service. **5.** Judging the right moment to hit, Lorna goes up on her toes – behind the baseline to avoid a foot fault – and her racquet arm starts to straighten and come through. **6.** Lorna makes contact with the ball, reaching upwards to make fullest use of her height. One foot maintains contact with the court and the leg is braced to take the weight. **7.** The follow-through. Lorna's right foot swings forward on to the court and her racquet swings through to the natural completion of its arc.

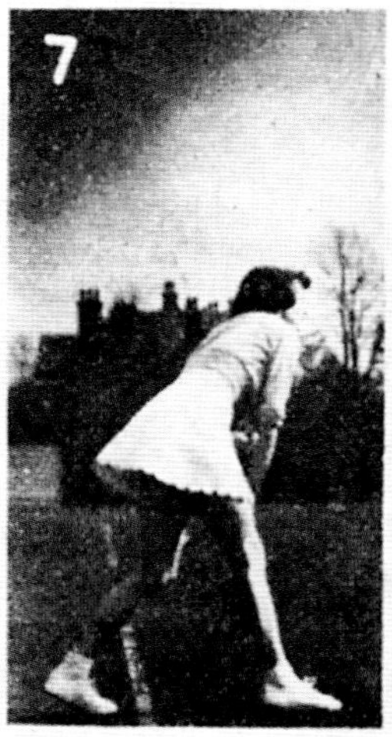
7

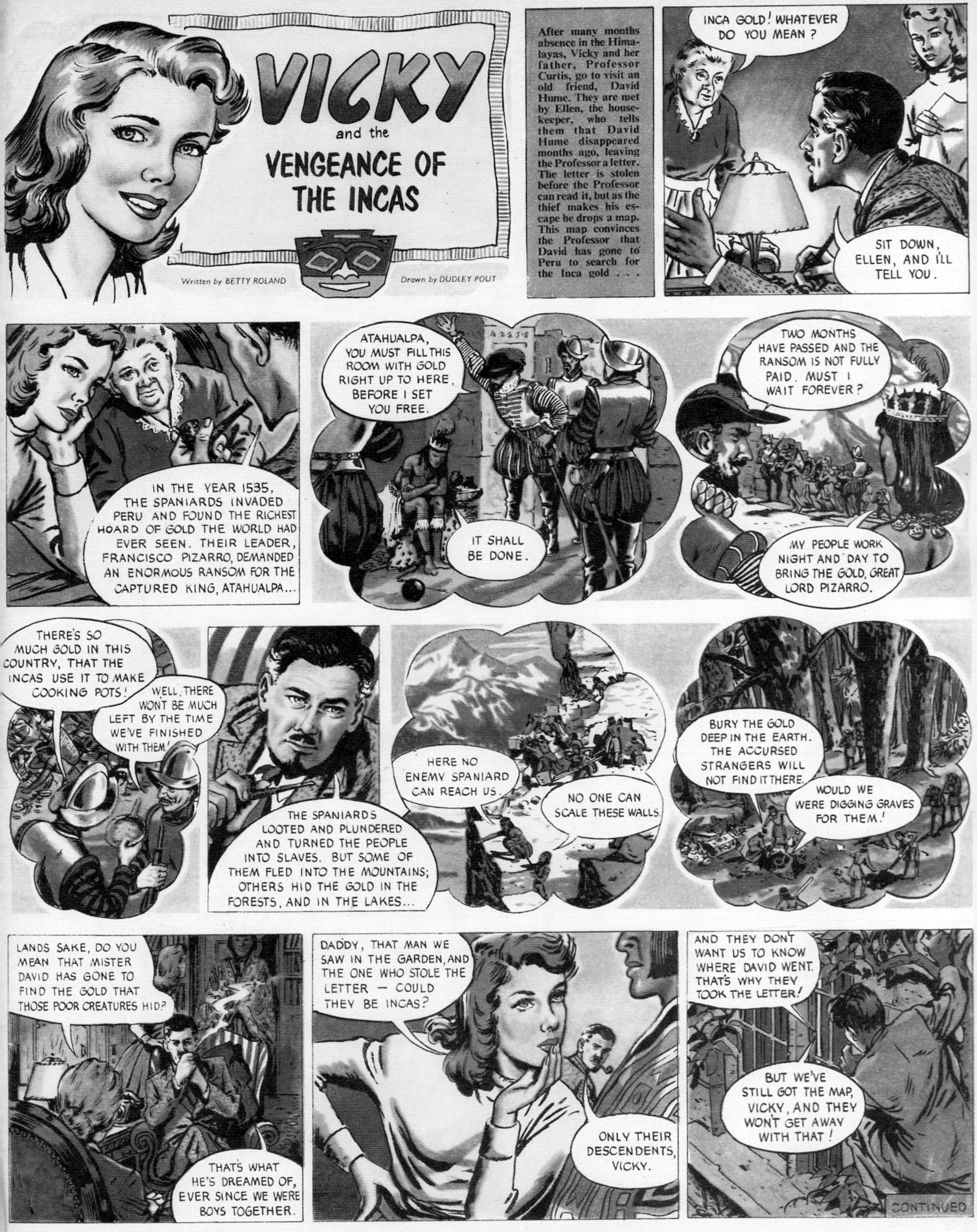
VICKY
and the
VENGEANCE OF THE INCAS
Written by BETTY ROLAND
Drawn by DUDLEY POUT
After many months absence in the Himalayas, Vicky and her father, Professor Curtis, go to visit an old friend, David Hume. They are met by Ellen, the housekeeper, who tells them that David Hume disappeared months ago, leaving the Professor a letter. The letter is stolen before the Professor can read it, but as the thief makes his escape he drops a map. This map convinces the Professor that David has gone to Peru to search for the Inca gold . . .
INCA GOLD! WHATEVER DO YOU MEAN?
SIT DOWN, ELLEN, AND I'LL TELL YOU.
IN THE YEAR 1535, THE SPANIARDS INVADED PERU AND FOUND THE RICHEST HOARD OF GOLD THE WORLD HAD EVER SEEN. THEIR LEADER, FRANCISCO PIZARRO, DEMANDED AN ENORMOUS RANSOM FOR THE CAPTURED KING, ATAHUALPA...
ATAHUALPA, YOU MUST FILL THIS ROOM WITH GOLD RIGHT UP TO HERE, BEFORE I SET YOU FREE.
IT SHALL BE DONE.
TWO MONTHS HAVE PASSED AND THE RANSOM IS NOT FULLY PAID. MUST I WAIT FOREVER?
MY PEOPLE WORK NIGHT AND DAY TO BRING THE GOLD, GREAT LORD PIZARRO.
THERE'S SO MUCH GOLD IN THIS COUNTRY, THAT THE INCAS USE IT TO MAKE COOKING POTS!
WELL, THERE WON'T BE MUCH LEFT BY THE TIME WE'VE FINISHED WITH THEM!
THE SPANIARDS LOOTED AND PLUNDERED AND TURNED THE PEOPLE INTO SLAVES. BUT SOME OF THEM FLED INTO THE MOUNTAINS; OTHERS HID THE GOLD IN THE FORESTS, AND IN THE LAKES...
HERE NO ENEMY SPANIARD CAN REACH US.
NO ONE CAN SCALE THESE WALLS.
BURY THE GOLD DEEP IN THE EARTH. THE ACCURSED STRANGERS WILL NOT FIND IT THERE.
WOULD WE WERE DIGGING GRAVES FOR THEM!
LANDS SAKE, DO YOU MEAN THAT MISTER DAVID HAS GONE TO FIND THE GOLD THAT THOSE POOR CREATURES HID?
THAT'S WHAT HE'S DREAMED OF, EVER SINCE WE WERE BOYS TOGETHER.
DADDY, THAT MAN WE SAW IN THE GARDEN, AND THE ONE WHO STOLE THE LETTER — COULD THEY BE INCAS?
ONLY THEIR DESCENDENTS, VICKY.
AND THEY DON'T WANT US TO KNOW WHERE DAVID WENT. THAT'S WHY THEY TOOK THE LETTER!
BUT WE'VE STILL GOT THE MAP, VICKY, AND THEY WON'T GET AWAY WITH THAT!
CONTINUED

continued on page 46

Photographs by BERT HARDY

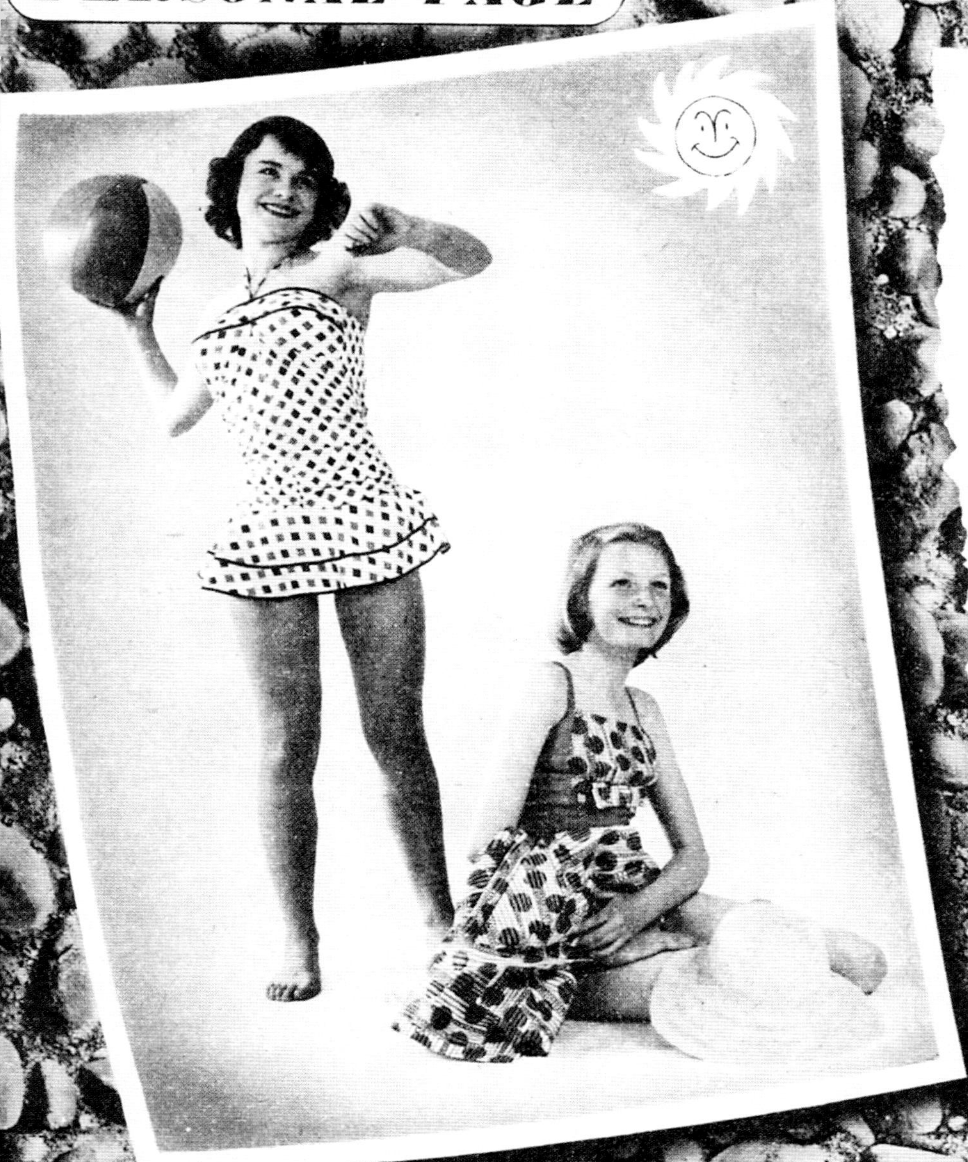

Focus on Beach Belles

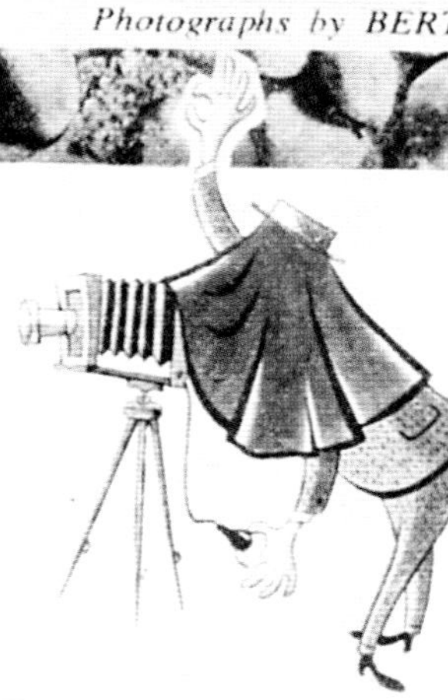

A HOLIDAY by the sea is the high spot of the year for most people, and an attractive beach outfit is part of the fun.

Elasticated swimsuits, like the two shown here, are comfortable to wear and 'stay put' in the water. Being made of cotton and rayon they dry quickly, too. Even if you still prefer the regulation-style suit for serious swimming, one of these would make an attractive alternative for sun-bathing.

Shorts, or jeans, and a sun-top are the best things to wear for beach games. The ones I have picked will wash easily and drip-dry, and will need little or no ironing. On a dull day a sweater can be worn on top, ready to be pulled off at the first gleam of sunshine. You'll find a list of prices and stockists on page 11.

Marjorie Elliott

The frilled swimsuit is by Slix and comes in many colours on a white ground. The charming jacket and bloomer-suit are designed by Renda.

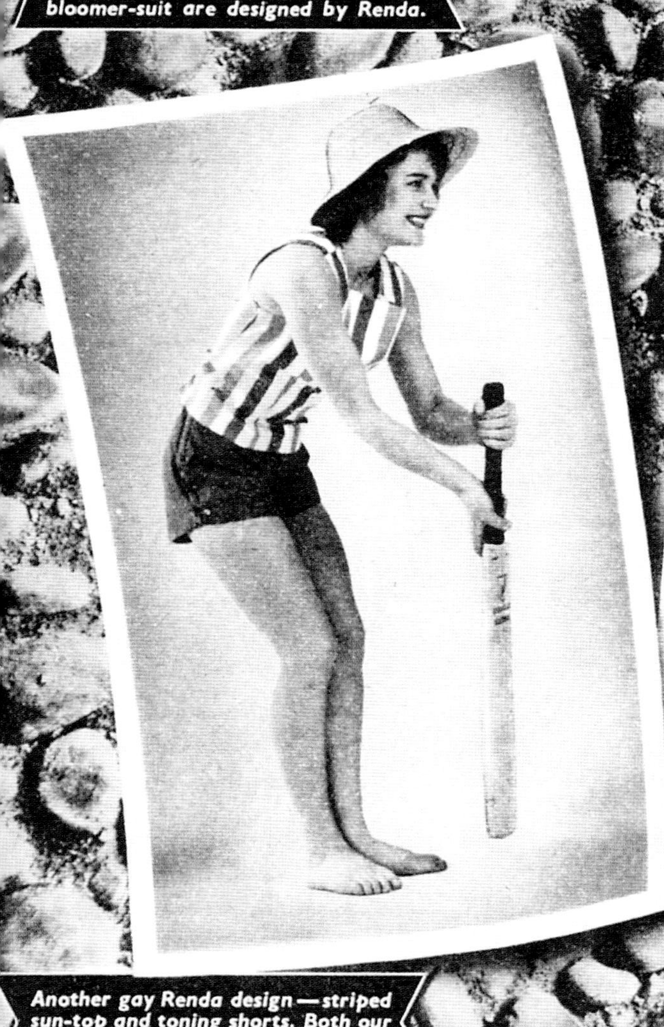

Another gay Renda design—striped sun-top and toning shorts. Both our hats are by the Eaton Bag Co.

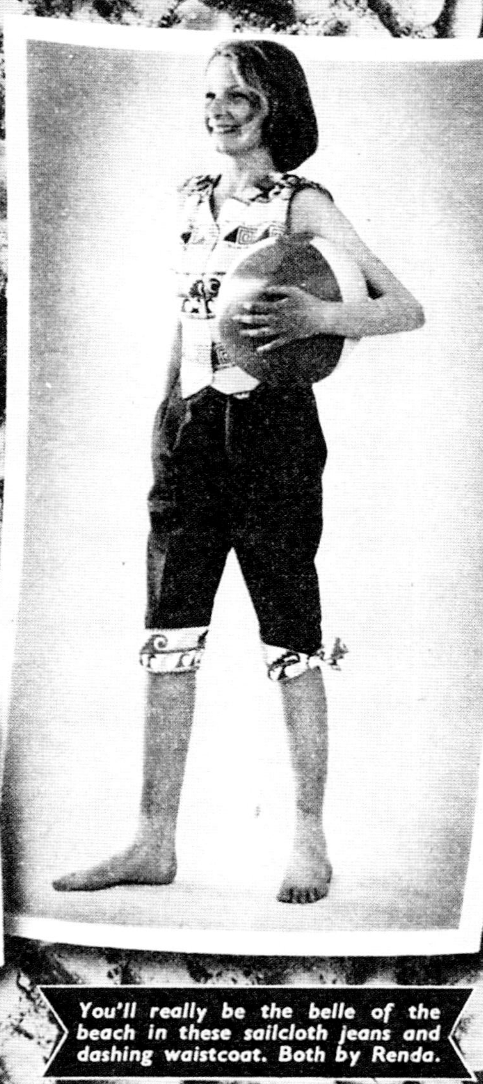

You'll really be the belle of the beach in these sailcloth jeans and dashing waistcoat. Both by Renda.

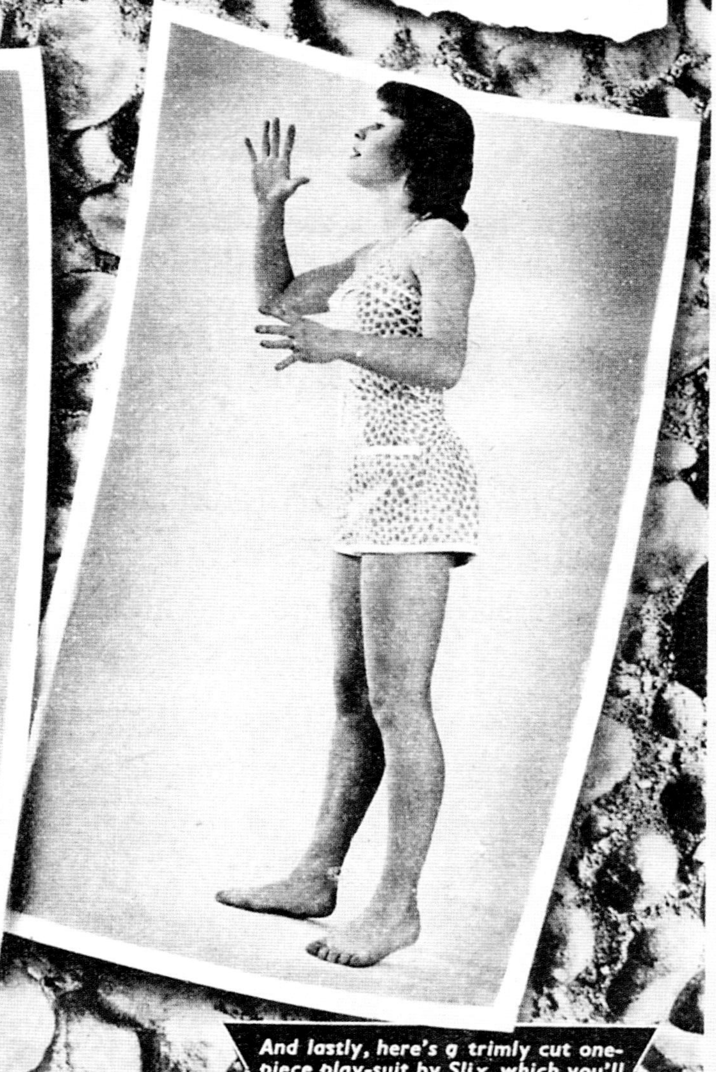

And lastly, here's a trimly cut one-piece play-suit by Slix, which you'll find flatters every kind of figure.

Registered at the G.P.O. for transmission by Magazine Post to Canada (including Newfoundland). GIRL printed in Great Britain by Eric Bemrose Ltd., Long Lane, Liverpool 9, for the Proprietors and Publishers, Hulton Press Ltd., 161/166 Fleet Street, London, E.C.4. Sole agents for Australia and New Zealand, Gordon & Gotch (A/sia) Ltd.; South Africa, Central News Agency Ltd. Subscription

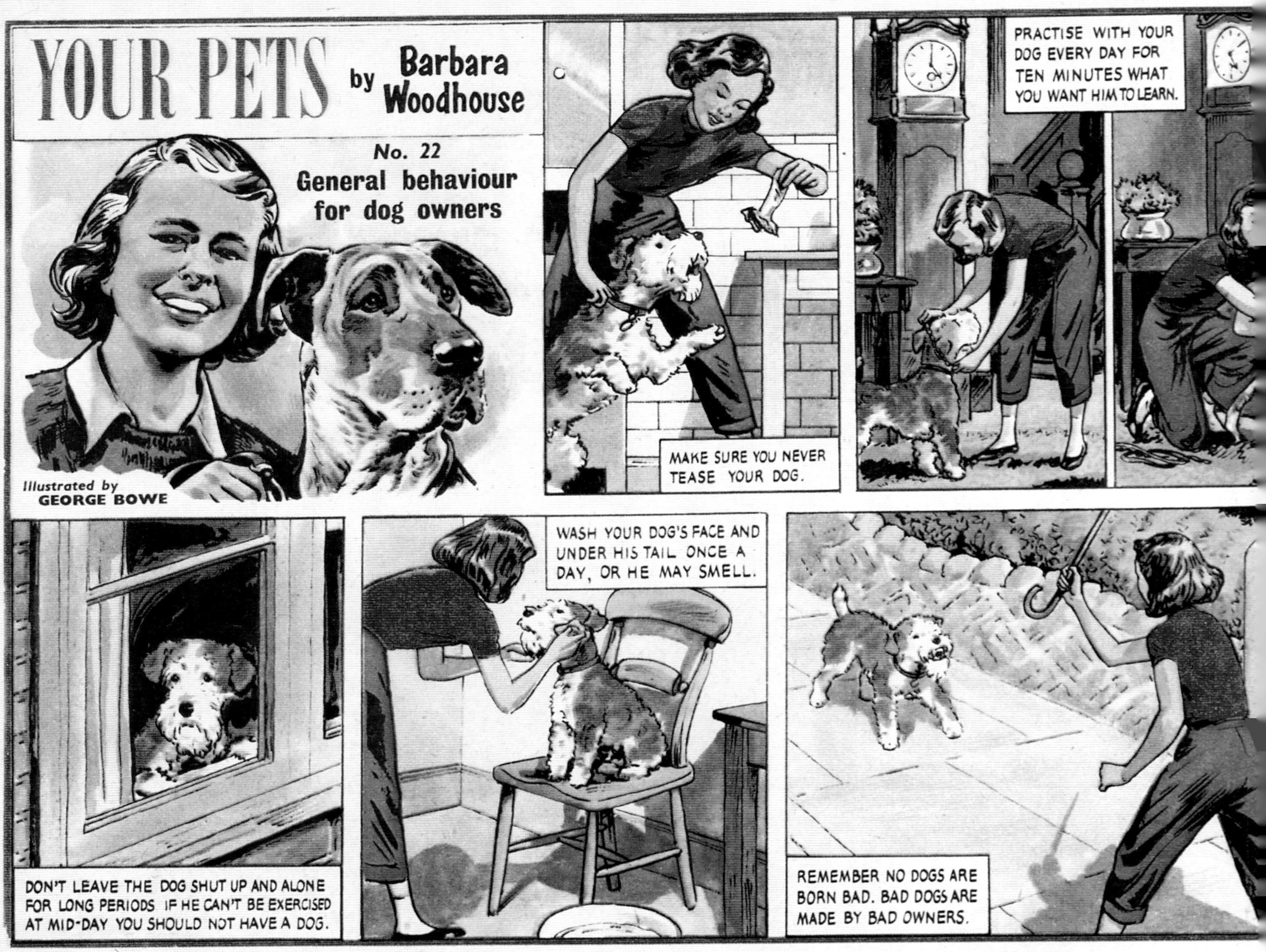

YOUR PETS by Barbara Woodhouse
No. 22
General behaviour for dog owners
Illustrated by GEORGE BOWE
MAKE SURE YOU NEVER TEASE YOUR DOG.
PRACTISE WITH YOUR DOG EVERY DAY FOR TEN MINUTES WHAT YOU WANT HIM TO LEARN.
DON'T LEAVE THE DOG SHUT UP AND ALONE FOR LONG PERIODS. IF HE CAN'T BE EXERCISED AT MID-DAY YOU SHOULD NOT HAVE A DOG.
WASH YOUR DOG'S FACE AND UNDER HIS TAIL ONCE A DAY, OR HE MAY SMELL.
REMEMBER NO DOGS ARE BORN BAD. BAD DOGS ARE MADE BY BAD OWNERS.

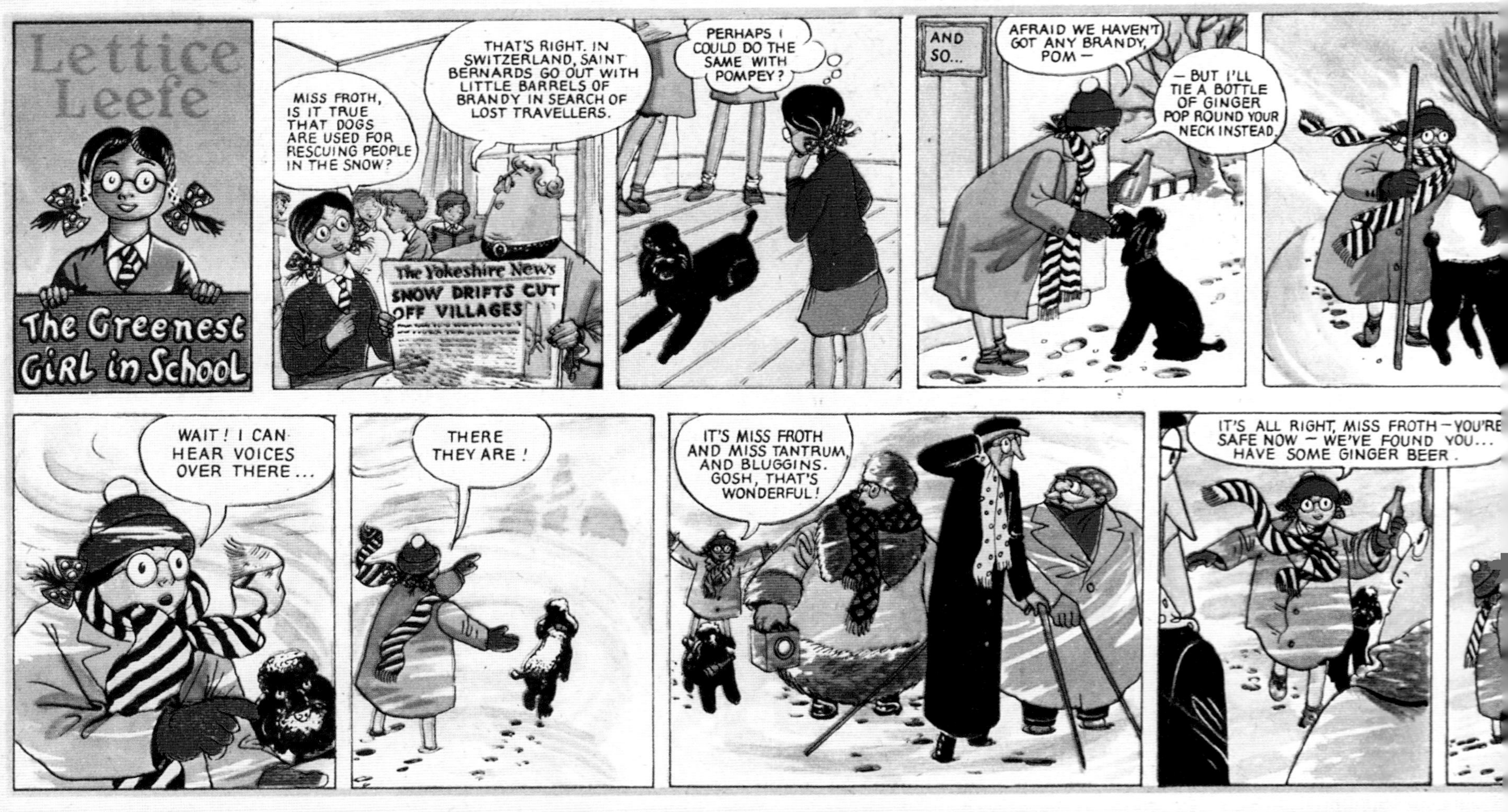

Lettice Leefe
The Greenest Girl in School
MISS FROTH, IS IT TRUE THAT DOGS ARE USED FOR RESCUING PEOPLE IN THE SNOW?
THAT'S RIGHT. IN SWITZERLAND, SAINT BERNARDS GO OUT WITH LITTLE BARRELS OF BRANDY IN SEARCH OF LOST TRAVELLERS.
The Yokeshire News
SNOW DRIFTS CUT OFF VILLAGES
PERHAPS I COULD DO THE SAME WITH POMPEY?
AND SO...
AFRAID WE HAVEN'T GOT ANY BRANDY, POM —
— BUT I'LL TIE A BOTTLE OF GINGER POP ROUND YOUR NECK INSTEAD.
WAIT! I CAN HEAR VOICES OVER THERE...
THERE THEY ARE!
IT'S MISS FROTH AND MISS TANTRUM, AND BLUGGINS. GOSH, THAT'S WONDERFUL!
IT'S ALL RIGHT, MISS FROTH — YOU'RE SAFE NOW — WE'VE FOUND YOU... HAVE SOME GINGER BEER.

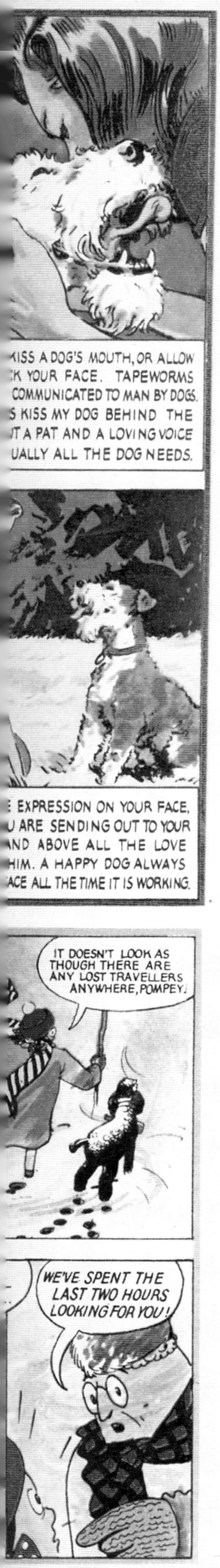
IT DOESN'T LOOK AS THOUGH THERE ARE ANY LOST TRAVELLERS ANYWHERE, POMPEY!
WE'VE SPENT THE LAST TWO HOURS LOOKING FOR YOU!

Girl Picture Gallery

No. 261

Here is a beautiful spring picture for your scrap-book, of a song thrush with a newly-hatched family.

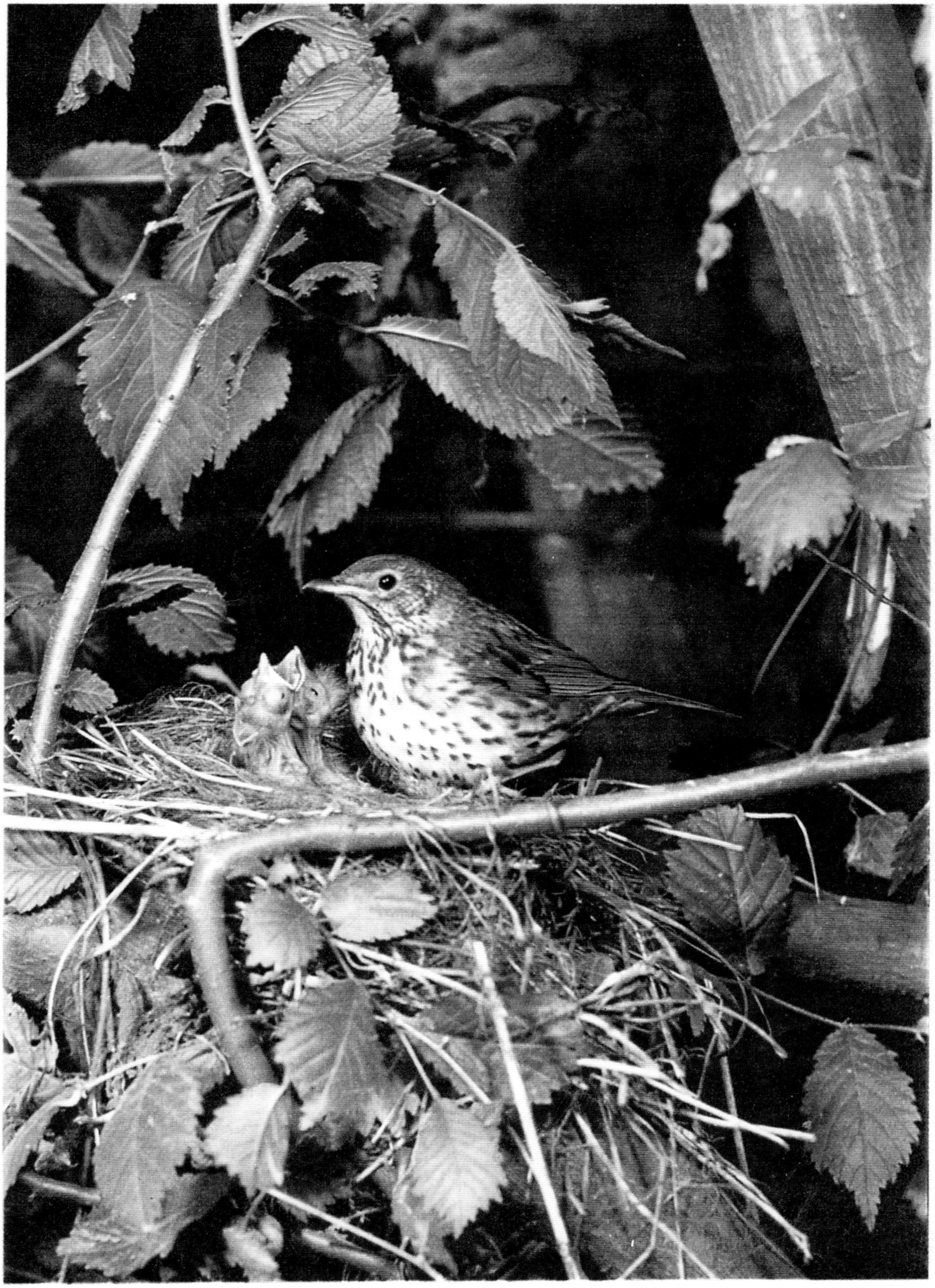

THE NEW ARRIVALS

by JOHN MARKHAM, F.R.P.S., F.Z.S.

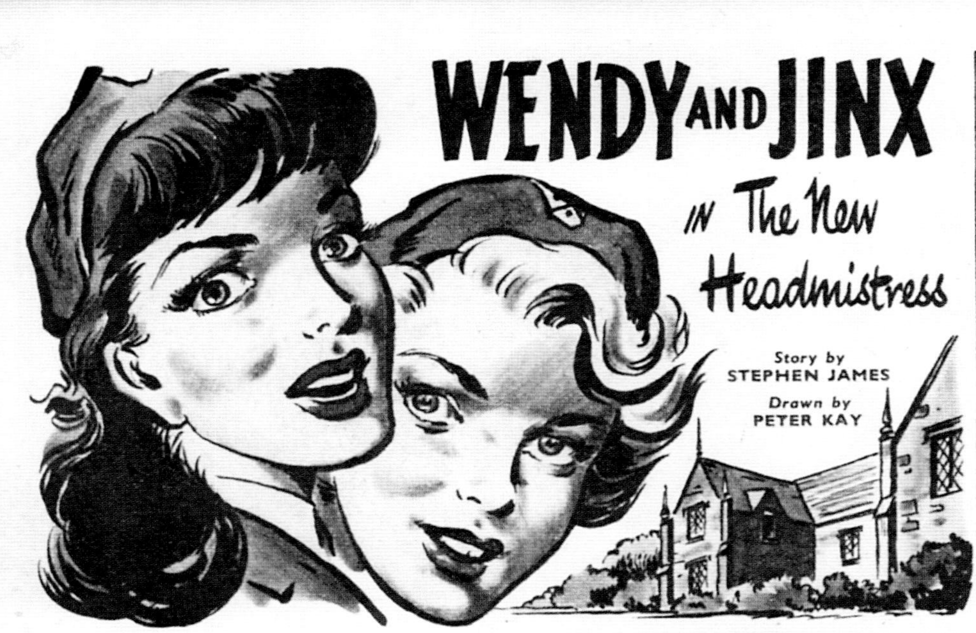
WENDY AND JINX
in The New Headmistress
Story by STEPHEN JAMES
Drawn by PETER KAY

Wendy and Jinx, inseparable friends of Manor School, return for the autumn term to learn that their headmistress has had an accident, and that Miss Kent is temporarily taking over. She separates Wendy and Jinx, and makes several other changes. Wendy is made dormitory prefect and, although she doesn't agree with the changes, she feels she must uphold the new Head. Jinx and Sally (a junior) are late for assembly. Jinx cannot tell Miss Kent that they were looking for Sally's escaped hamster, because Sally will lose her pet if it gets her into any more scrapes. So Miss Kent accuses them of deliberate disobedience . . .

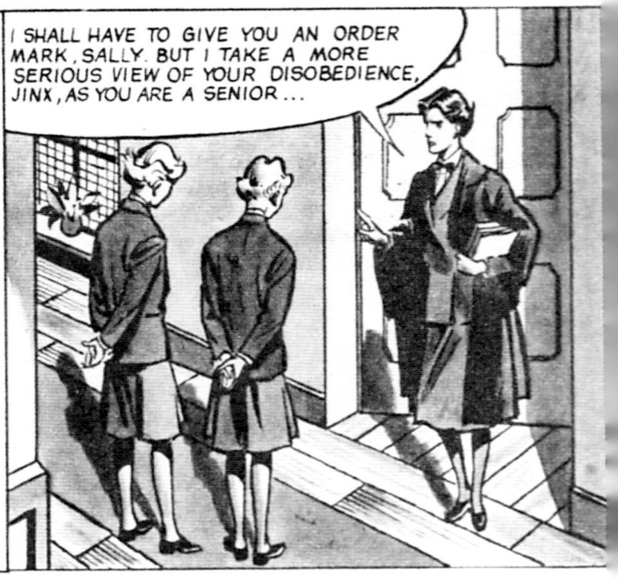
I SHALL HAVE TO GIVE YOU AN ORDER MARK, SALLY. BUT I TAKE A MORE SERIOUS VIEW OF YOUR DISOBEDIENCE, JINX, AS YOU ARE A SENIOR...

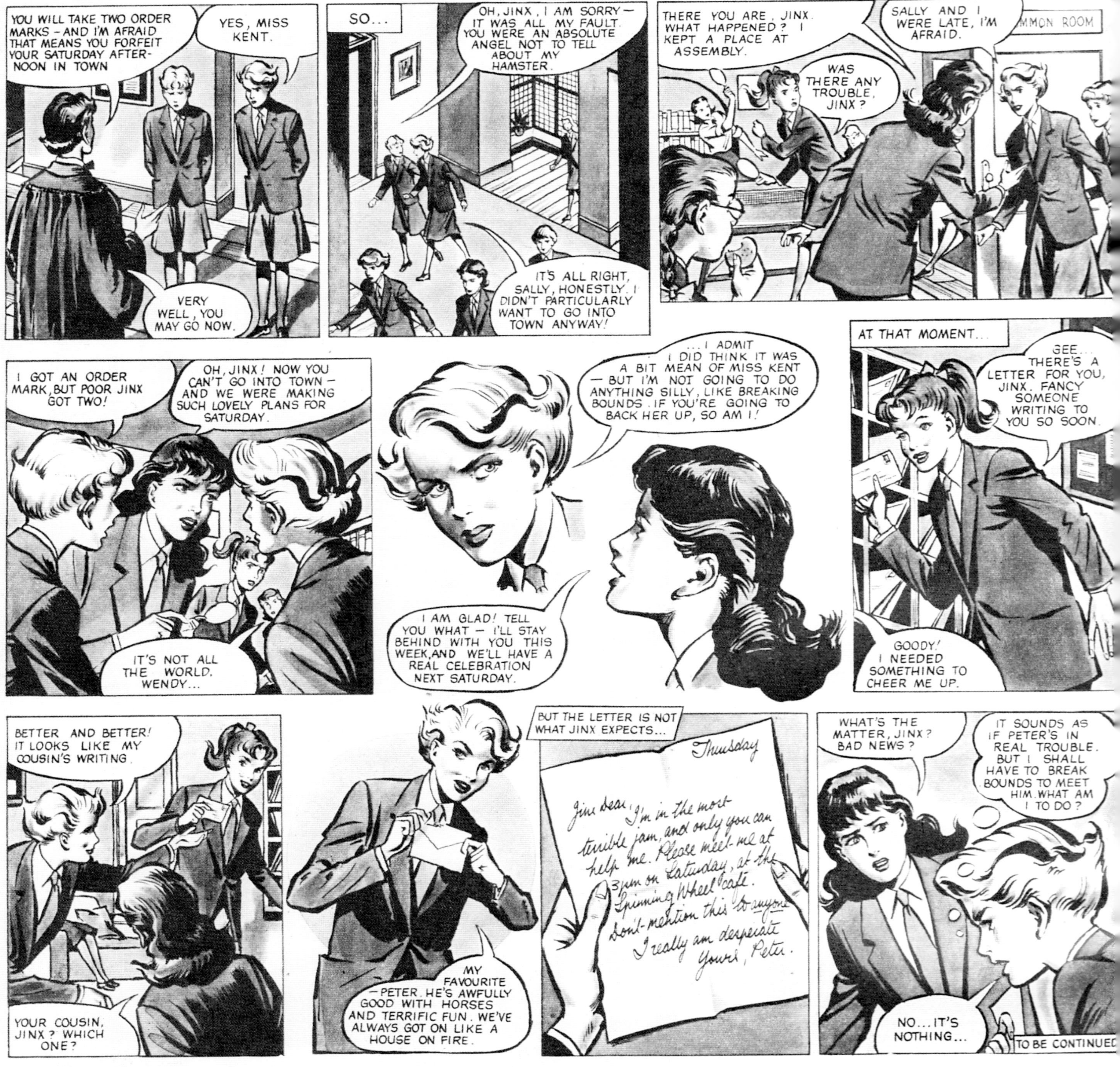
YOU WILL TAKE TWO ORDER MARKS – AND I'M AFRAID THAT MEANS YOU FORFEIT YOUR SATURDAY AFTERNOON IN TOWN
YES, MISS KENT.
VERY WELL, YOU MAY GO NOW.
SO...
OH, JINX, I AM SORRY – IT WAS ALL MY FAULT. YOU WERE AN ABSOLUTE ANGEL NOT TO TELL ABOUT MY HAMSTER.
IT'S ALL RIGHT, SALLY, HONESTLY. I DIDN'T PARTICULARLY WANT TO GO INTO TOWN ANYWAY!
THERE YOU ARE, JINX. WHAT HAPPENED? I KEPT A PLACE AT ASSEMBLY.
SALLY AND I WERE LATE, I'M AFRAID.
MMON ROOM
WAS THERE ANY TROUBLE, JINX?
I GOT AN ORDER MARK, BUT POOR JINX GOT TWO!
OH, JINX! NOW YOU CAN'T GO INTO TOWN – AND WE WERE MAKING SUCH LOVELY PLANS FOR SATURDAY.
IT'S NOT ALL THE WORLD, WENDY...
... I ADMIT I DID THINK IT WAS A BIT MEAN OF MISS KENT – BUT I'M NOT GOING TO DO ANYTHING SILLY, LIKE BREAKING BOUNDS. IF YOU'RE GOING TO BACK HER UP, SO AM I!
I AM GLAD! TELL YOU WHAT – I'LL STAY BEHIND WITH YOU THIS WEEK, AND WE'LL HAVE A REAL CELEBRATION NEXT SATURDAY.
AT THAT MOMENT...
GEE... THERE'S A LETTER FOR YOU, JINX. FANCY SOMEONE WRITING TO YOU SO SOON.
GOODY! I NEEDED SOMETHING TO CHEER ME UP.
BETTER AND BETTER! IT LOOKS LIKE MY COUSIN'S WRITING.
YOUR COUSIN, JINX? WHICH ONE?
MY FAVOURITE – PETER. HE'S AWFULLY GOOD WITH HORSES AND TERRIFIC FUN. WE'VE ALWAYS GOT ON LIKE A HOUSE ON FIRE.
BUT THE LETTER IS NOT WHAT JINX EXPECTS...
Thursday
Jinx dear, I'm in the most terrible jam, and only you can help me. Please meet me at 3pm on Saturday, at the Spinning Wheel café. Don't mention this to anyone. I really am desperate. Yours, Peter.
WHAT'S THE MATTER, JINX? BAD NEWS?
IT SOUNDS AS IF PETER'S IN REAL TROUBLE. BUT I SHALL HAVE TO BREAK BOUNDS TO MEET HIM. WHAT AM I TO DO?
NO... IT'S NOTHING...
TO BE CONTINUED

continued on page 5

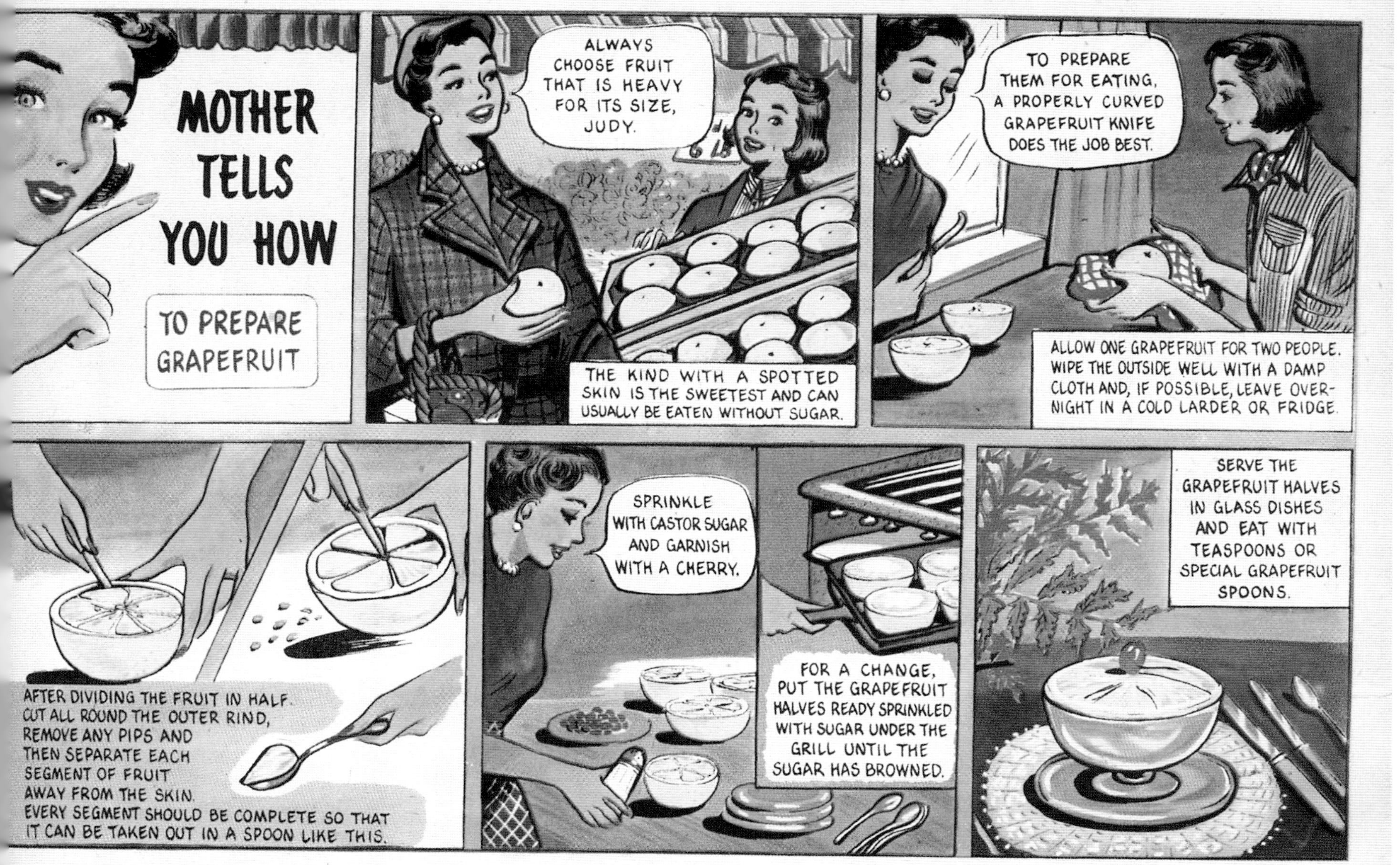
MOTHER TELLS YOU HOW
TO PREPARE GRAPEFRUIT
ALWAYS CHOOSE FRUIT THAT IS HEAVY FOR ITS SIZE, JUDY.
THE KIND WITH A SPOTTED SKIN IS THE SWEETEST AND CAN USUALLY BE EATEN WITHOUT SUGAR.
TO PREPARE THEM FOR EATING, A PROPERLY CURVED GRAPEFRUIT KNIFE DOES THE JOB BEST.
ALLOW ONE GRAPEFRUIT FOR TWO PEOPLE. WIPE THE OUTSIDE WELL WITH A DAMP CLOTH AND, IF POSSIBLE, LEAVE OVER-NIGHT IN A COLD LARDER OR FRIDGE.
AFTER DIVIDING THE FRUIT IN HALF CUT ALL ROUND THE OUTER RIND, REMOVE ANY PIPS AND THEN SEPARATE EACH SEGMENT OF FRUIT AWAY FROM THE SKIN. EVERY SEGMENT SHOULD BE COMPLETE SO THAT IT CAN BE TAKEN OUT IN A SPOON LIKE THIS.
SPRINKLE WITH CASTOR SUGAR AND GARNISH WITH A CHERRY.
FOR A CHANGE, PUT THE GRAPEFRUIT HALVES READY SPRINKLED WITH SUGAR UNDER THE GRILL UNTIL THE SUGAR HAS BROWNED.
SERVE THE GRAPEFRUIT HALVES IN GLASS DISHES AND EAT WITH TEASPOONS OR SPECIAL GRAPEFRUIT SPOONS.

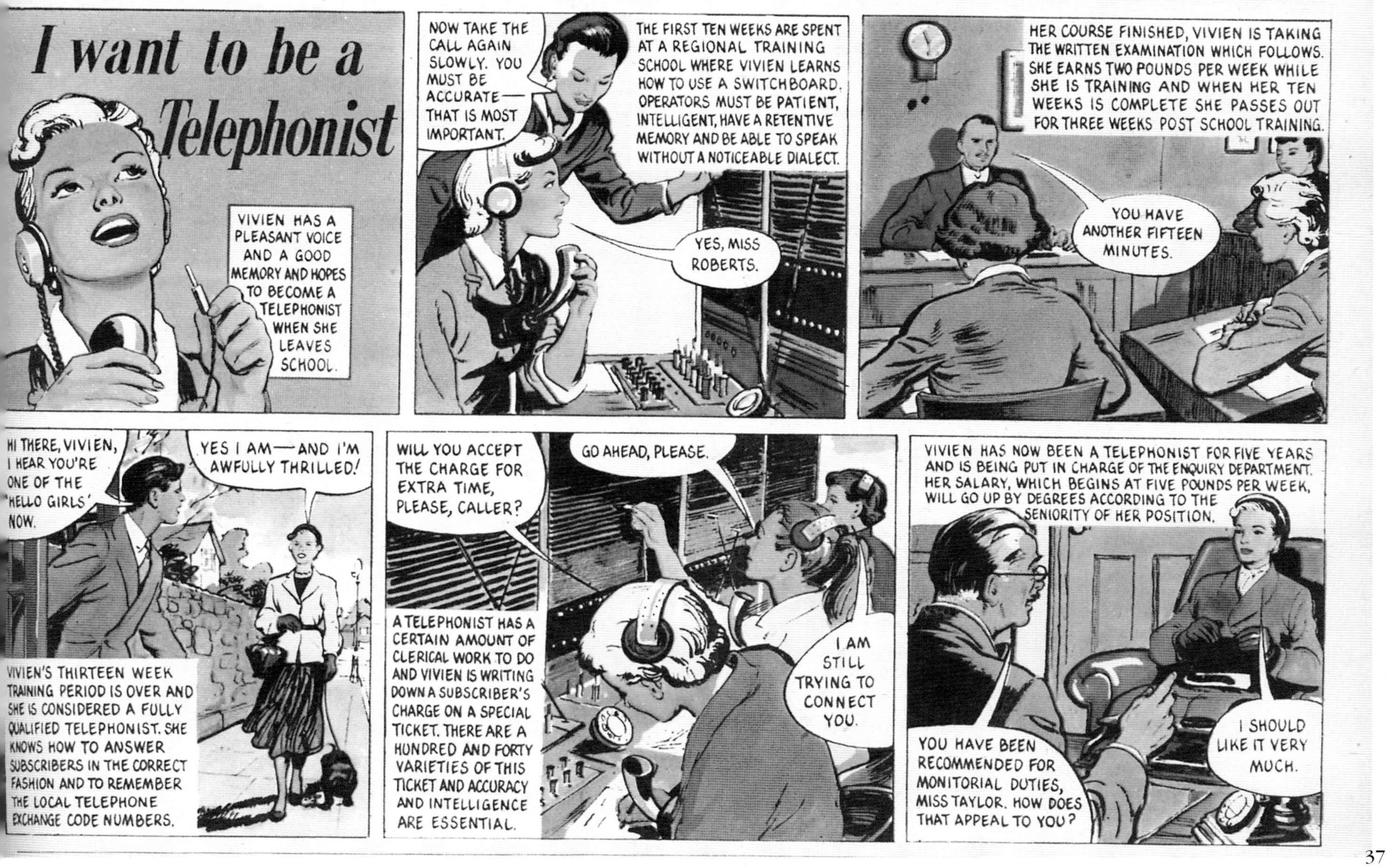
I want to be a Telephonist
VIVIEN HAS A PLEASANT VOICE AND A GOOD MEMORY AND HOPES TO BECOME A TELEPHONIST WHEN SHE LEAVES SCHOOL.
NOW TAKE THE CALL AGAIN SLOWLY. YOU MUST BE ACCURATE— THAT IS MOST IMPORTANT.
THE FIRST TEN WEEKS ARE SPENT AT A REGIONAL TRAINING SCHOOL WHERE VIVIEN LEARNS HOW TO USE A SWITCHBOARD. OPERATORS MUST BE PATIENT, INTELLIGENT, HAVE A RETENTIVE MEMORY AND BE ABLE TO SPEAK WITHOUT A NOTICEABLE DIALECT.
YES, MISS ROBERTS.
HER COURSE FINISHED, VIVIEN IS TAKING THE WRITTEN EXAMINATION WHICH FOLLOWS. SHE EARNS TWO POUNDS PER WEEK WHILE SHE IS TRAINING AND WHEN HER TEN WEEKS IS COMPLETE SHE PASSES OUT FOR THREE WEEKS POST SCHOOL TRAINING.
YOU HAVE ANOTHER FIFTEEN MINUTES.
HI THERE, VIVIEN, I HEAR YOU'RE ONE OF THE 'HELLO GIRLS' NOW.
YES I AM—AND I'M AWFULLY THRILLED!
VIVIEN'S THIRTEEN WEEK TRAINING PERIOD IS OVER AND SHE IS CONSIDERED A FULLY QUALIFIED TELEPHONIST. SHE KNOWS HOW TO ANSWER SUBSCRIBERS IN THE CORRECT FASHION AND TO REMEMBER THE LOCAL TELEPHONE EXCHANGE CODE NUMBERS.
WILL YOU ACCEPT THE CHARGE FOR EXTRA TIME, PLEASE, CALLER?
GO AHEAD, PLEASE.
A TELEPHONIST HAS A CERTAIN AMOUNT OF CLERICAL WORK TO DO AND VIVIEN IS WRITING DOWN A SUBSCRIBER'S CHARGE ON A SPECIAL TICKET. THERE ARE A HUNDRED AND FORTY VARIETIES OF THIS TICKET AND ACCURACY AND INTELLIGENCE ARE ESSENTIAL.
I AM STILL TRYING TO CONNECT YOU.
VIVIEN HAS NOW BEEN A TELEPHONIST FOR FIVE YEARS AND IS BEING PUT IN CHARGE OF THE ENQUIRY DEPARTMENT. HER SALARY, WHICH BEGINS AT FIVE POUNDS PER WEEK, WILL GO UP BY DEGREES ACCORDING TO THE SENIORITY OF HER POSITION.
YOU HAVE BEEN RECOMMENDED FOR MONITORIAL DUTIES, MISS TAYLOR. HOW DOES THAT APPEAL TO YOU?
I SHOULD LIKE IT VERY MUCH.

Dick was the proud escort of two beautiful models!

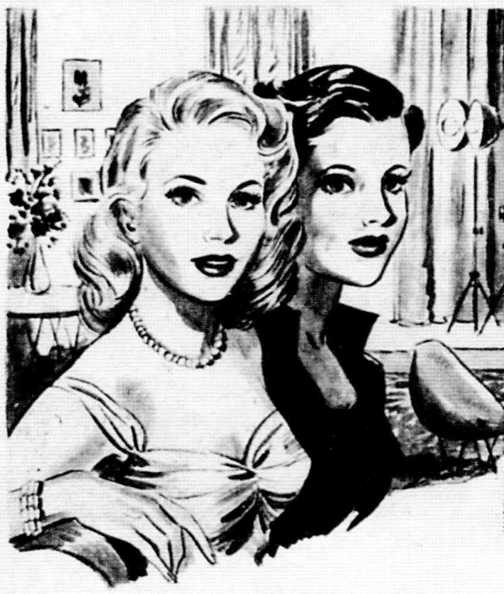

MODEL GIRLS

Written by **BOB KING**

The Belle of the Ball

JILL and Marie, the two young models, were dressing in the bedroom of the tiny flat they shared. The room was an untidy whirl of stiffened net petticoats, odd nylons, boxes of make-up and pairs of pretty dancing shoes.

"Oh, Jill!" Marie cried happily, as she threw a third waist petticoat like a cloud of foam over her head. "Wouldn't eet be stumendous if one of us won the Belle of the Ball contest tonight!"

"Stumendous!" agreed Jill, with a laugh. She was used to Marie's English by now.

"Of course," Marie added, with a pretty pout, "if eet is you that wins, perhaps I may be a leetle jalous, Jill."

"Jealous!" Jill corrected her. "But, Marie – why?"

"Oh, not that you have won the contest – but that you will get the prize, which is a week-end in Paris," Marie said, not too seriously. "How can I stay here in happiness, while you are having a holiday in my home-town?"

Jill laughed. "Well, let's not count our chickens before they're hatched." Then catching sight of Marie's puzzled face, added quickly: "It's an English expression. It means . . . um . . . we mustn't cross the bridge until we come to it."

Marie looked even more puzzled. "Ees very confusing, this English. Sometime I think I never learn it. Never!"

And with that she picked up the beautiful full-skirted dress with its layers and layers of net and sequins and its trim little tight-fitted bodice, and tying a silk scarf over her face, to protect her dress from her make-up, she tossed the dress over her head and wriggled into it. At the same time, Jill, on the other side of the room, was adding the finishing touches to her hair.

Suddenly a long string of French exclamations of dismay came from Marie.

Jill turned quickly towards her. "Whatever's the matter?" she said.

Tears of disappointment welled up in the French girl's eyes. "The quick-fastener on my dress!" she cried. "She is jammed and I pull her, and now all her teeth fall out. Oh, Jill, what can I do?"

Jill rushed to her friend's side to examine the fastener. Sure enough, there was a gap right in the middle, and nothing would hold the lovely frock tight to Marie's waist now but a new fastener. And, thought Jill, we haven't one in the flat – all the shops are shut – and even if we had one, there wouldn't be time to sew it in now.

In a flash, Jill had decided what to do. This was Marie's first Model Girl Ball, and nothing was going to spoil the occasion for her. Jill started to remove her own lovely dress of palest pink tulle.

Marie looked at her in surprise. "Why are you changing again, Jill? What good will zat do?"

"Now, Marie," Jill told her in a firm voice. "You're going to do as I tell you, and I won't take no for an answer. You are going to the Ball in my dress, and I shall wear my blue. It's very pretty."

"Oh, but – zat is not good," Marie cried. "Your blue is very pretty, yes. But if you wear it you will not stand a chance for the prize. It is in the rules that the dress the competitors wear cannot be designed or made by a professional. And your blue, it was made by Monsieur Rakko, yes?"

Indeed, it was because of this rule of entry to the Belle of the Ball contest, that Jill and Marie had spent days designing their own dresses, and planning and sewing for the Ball.

Jill nodded. "Yes, dear," she said. "I know, but there may be many years ahead for me to try my hand at winning the contest – while this may be your only chance. Next year you may be back in Paris again. Now, I insist – so we'll say no more about it."

Reluctantly, but with a warm, grateful smile for her friend, Marie took the cloud of pink tulle that Jill held out to her and put it on.

"Oh, Marie," said Jill. "It looks lovely – much prettier on you than me. That's just the right pink for a brunette. I felt it was a bit sugary on me."

Marie's eyes softened. "You just say thees to make me feel better!"

When Dick, the young photographer, who was escorting both the girls to the Model Girl Ball arrived half an hour later, he found them both ready.

"My goodness," he said, looking from one to the other. "I think I'll just slip back to the studio for my camera and some colour film – this is too good a chance to miss. You both look enchanting!"

The Model Girl Ball is the event of the year at the Chester Hotel. The entrance to the hotel had been choked for some hours by sightseers waiting for the celebrities to arrive. As Dick, Jill and Marie drew up in their taxi, there was a great flashing and popping of press-camera light bulbs.

"Well," said Dick, "what it is to be famous! I feel like a film star at a firs night – or would if I didn't know it wa you two attracting all the attention!"

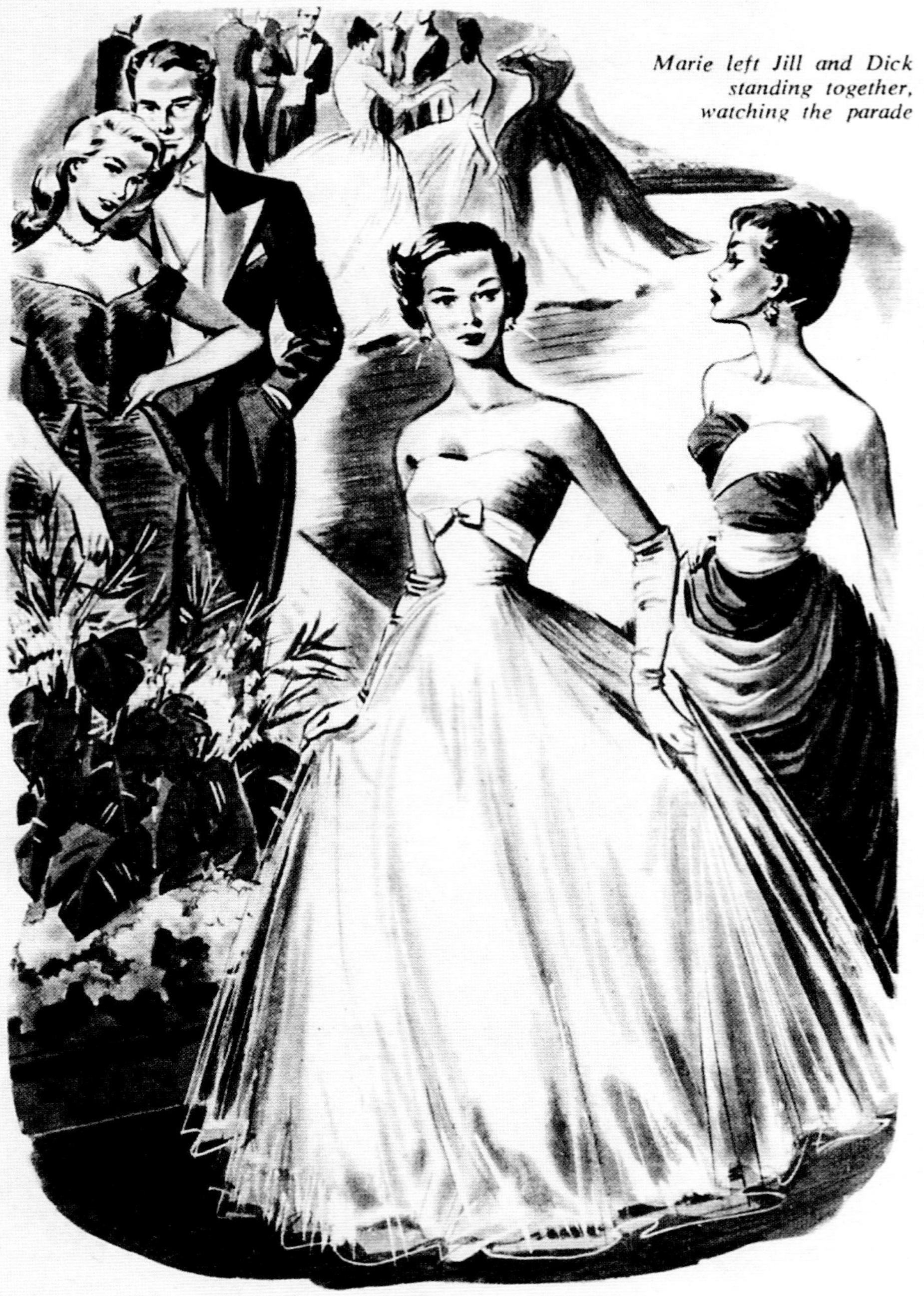

Marie left Jill and Dick standing together, watching the parade

The three of them pressed through th crowds into the great, sparkling ballroom

Jill held her breath. "Oh," she saic "Isn't it wonderful? Look at the lovel dresses!"

Marie shook her head. "I wonder, Jil whatever made us think we would stand chance. You were right about the he hatching bridges, yes?"

Dick looked from Marie to Jill in su prise. "Whatever is she talking abou now?" he asked, raising an eyebrow.

Jill just giggled.

They all had a wonderful evening. Ji and Marie danced every dance, and Dic bathed in the glory of being the escor to two of the prettiest girls in the roon Then came the announcement for the bi moment of the evening. All the girls wh were professional models, and who wer wearing a dress designed and made by a amateur, or by themselves, were asked t parade round the room and across th stage in front of the judges. From th parade the judges would choose the mod girl to be Belle of the Ball.

Jill gave Marie a gentle push. "Off yo go, honey," she said. "Good luck!"

"Oh, Jill," Marie protested. "I do n want to enter without you . . ."

"Nonsense. You *must*. Go on!"

With one more backward glance, Mari left Jill and Dick standing together, watch ing the parade.

A hundred or more of the most beaut ful girls in Britain walked, poised an graceful, past them and in a long line u to the stage. Dresses glittering and spark ling, and in every colour and ever material, swirled and swayed as the proud wearers filed past the judges.

Jill watched Marie, and thought tha none of the other girls matched up to he dark-haired, vivacious friend.

At last it was over. There was a sudde silence while the judges put their head together. Jill crossed her fingers.

Then the crowd held its breath as on of the judges rose from the group an walked – oh so slowly – to a microphon at the front of the stage. You could hav heard a pin drop from the other side c the ballroom, as he held up his hand fc attention.

"Ladies and gentlemen," he announce "This is the moment you have all bee waiting for. The name of this year's Bell of the Ball . . ." he paused for a momer to look down at a piece of paper in h hand. "She is *Miss Marie Dupont!"*

A great thunder of clapping bea through the ballroom and Jill rushed ove to where Marie was standing, surrounde by a crowd of admiring men and wome But before Jill could add her congratu lations to the others, the judge held up h hand once again for silence.

"And this year," he said, raising h voice to be heard over the noise, "w have a special surprise. The famou French dress designer, Monsieur Rakko who is one of our judges this evening has been so impressed with the Belle c the Ball's dress, that he has offered exactl the same prize – a week-end in Paris – t the designer of Marie Dupont's dress. understand that she, too, is a model, b an odd coincidence. So will Marie Dupor and Jill Lewis come up on the stag please, and receive their prizes fror Monsieur Rakko?"

Jill suddenly felt her mouth open an her feet freeze to the floor, but at tha moment Marie flung her arms about he

"Jill! Jill!" the French girl yelled abov the roar of the crowd. "The leetle chicken have hatched many bridges . . . and now can show you around my Paris and not b jalous."

"Jealous," corrected Jill, in a daze voice, as they both walked together t wards the stage.

Another complete story next wee

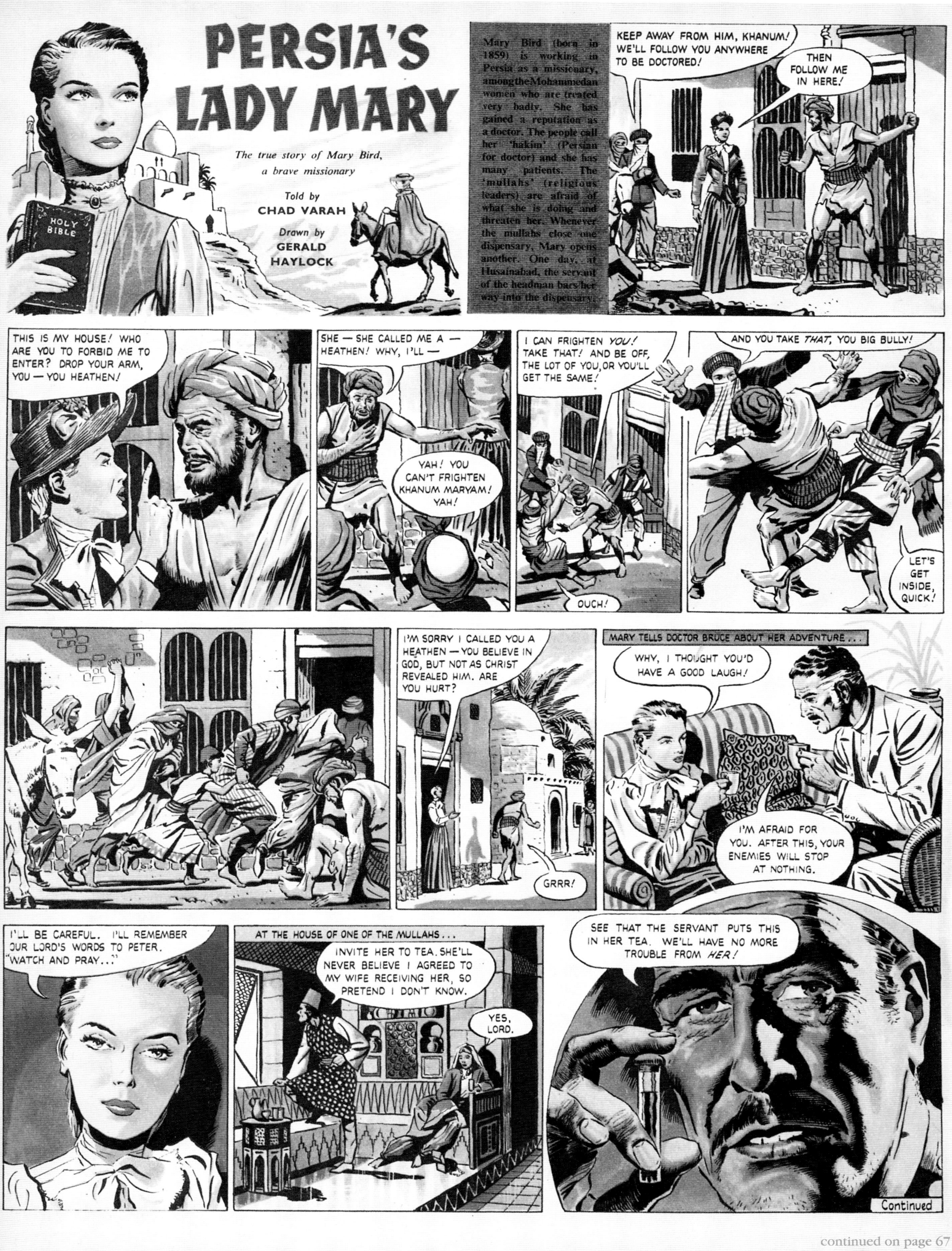
PERSIA'S LADY MARY
The true story of Mary Bird, a brave missionary
Told by CHAD VARAH
Drawn by GERALD HAYLOCK
HOLY BIBLE
Mary Bird (born in 1859) is working in Persia as a missionary, amongtheMohammedan women who are treated very badly. She has gained a reputation as a doctor. The people call her 'hakim' (Persian for doctor) and she has many patients. The 'mullahs' (religious leaders) are afraid of what she is doing and threaten her. Whenever the mullahs close one dispensary, Mary opens another. One day, at Husainabad, the servant of the headman bars her way into the dispensary.
KEEP AWAY FROM HIM, KHANUM! WE'LL FOLLOW YOU ANYWHERE TO BE DOCTORED!
THEN FOLLOW ME IN HERE!
THIS IS MY HOUSE! WHO ARE YOU TO FORBID ME TO ENTER? DROP YOUR ARM, YOU — YOU HEATHEN!
SHE — SHE CALLED ME A — HEATHEN! WHY, I'LL —
YAH! YOU CAN'T FRIGHTEN KHANUM MARYAM! YAH!
I CAN FRIGHTEN YOU! TAKE THAT! AND BE OFF, THE LOT OF YOU, OR YOU'LL GET THE SAME!
OUCH!
AND YOU TAKE THAT, YOU BIG BULLY!
LET'S GET INSIDE, QUICK!
I'M SORRY I CALLED YOU A HEATHEN — YOU BELIEVE IN GOD, BUT NOT AS CHRIST REVEALED HIM. ARE YOU HURT?
GRRR!
MARY TELLS DOCTOR BRUCE ABOUT HER ADVENTURE...
WHY, I THOUGHT YOU'D HAVE A GOOD LAUGH!
I'M AFRAID FOR YOU. AFTER THIS, YOUR ENEMIES WILL STOP AT NOTHING.
I'LL BE CAREFUL. I'LL REMEMBER OUR LORD'S WORDS TO PETER. "WATCH AND PRAY..."
AT THE HOUSE OF ONE OF THE MULLAHS...
INVITE HER TO TEA. SHE'LL NEVER BELIEVE I AGREED TO MY WIFE RECEIVING HER, SO PRETEND I DON'T KNOW.
YES, LORD.
SEE THAT THE SERVANT PUTS THIS IN HER TEA. WE'LL HAVE NO MORE TROUBLE FROM HER!
Continued

continued on page 67

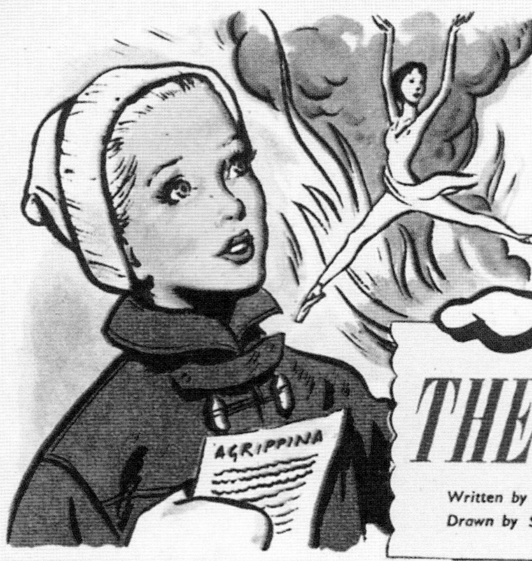
AGRIPPINA

Belle of the Ballet

and her friends in a grand adventure

THE REBEL

Written by GEORGE BEARDMORE
Drawn by STANLEY HOUGHTON

Belle and her friends of the Arenska Dancing School take pity on Sylvine, a marvellous dancer whose career is being ruined by her jealous aunt, the famous actress, Erica Brand. Erica takes Sylvine out of a ballet and sends her to a finishing school in Sussex. Belle has been asked by Sylvine's god-father to get her away, so Belle, Mamie, David and Felix, search for her. Eventually they find her taking riding lessons on the Downs . . .

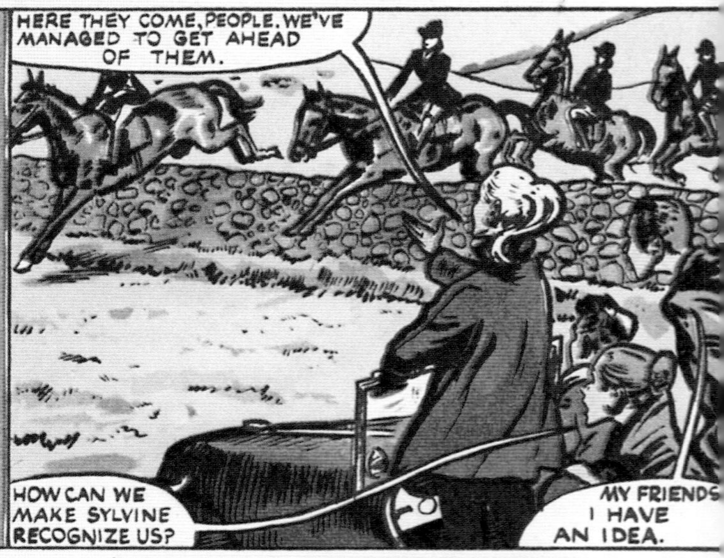
HERE THEY COME, PEOPLE. WE'VE MANAGED TO GET AHEAD OF THEM.
HOW CAN WE MAKE SYLVINE RECOGNIZE US?
MY FRIENDS I HAVE AN IDEA.

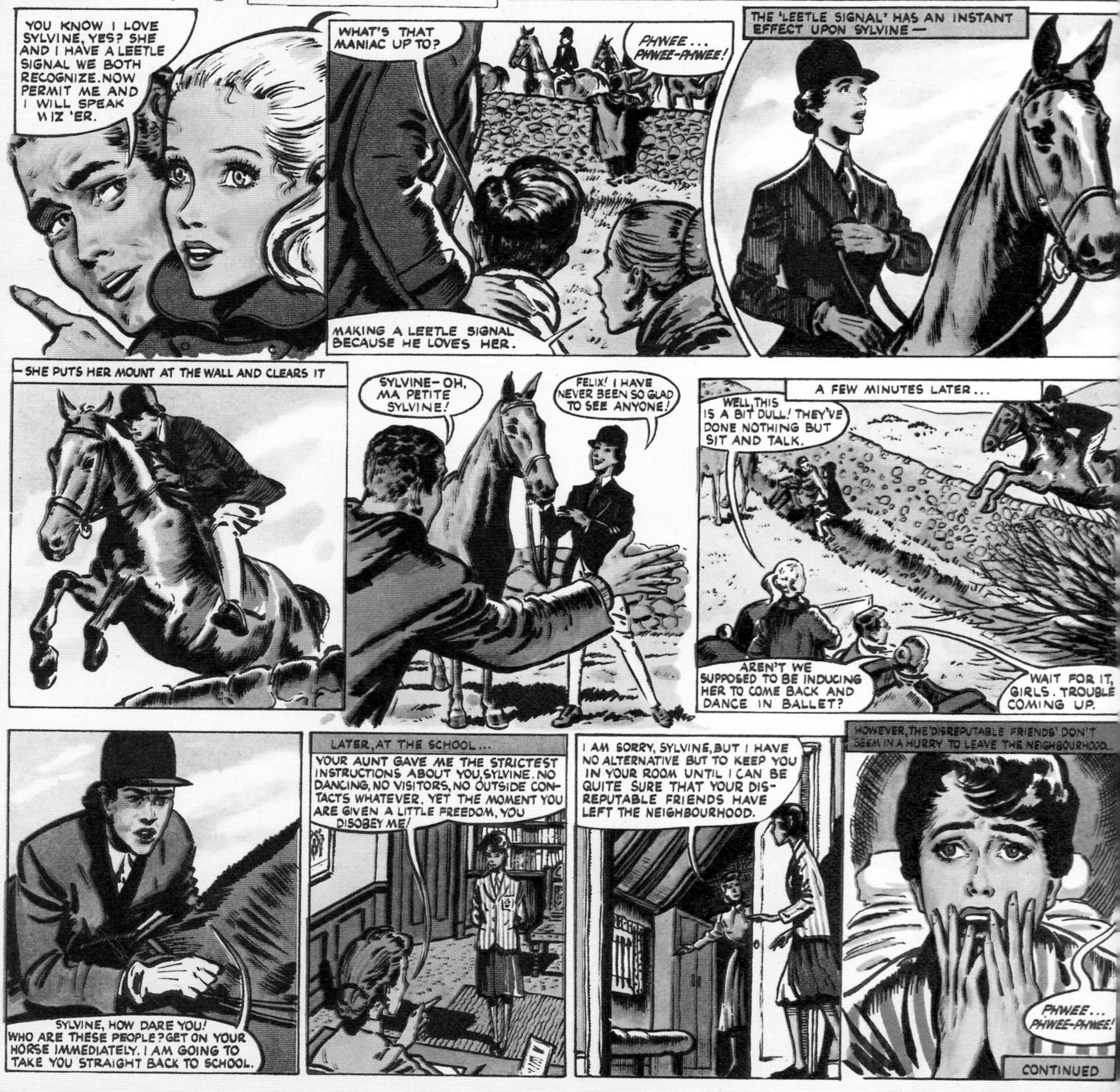
YOU KNOW I LOVE SYLVINE, YES? SHE AND I HAVE A LEETLE SIGNAL WE BOTH RECOGNIZE. NOW PERMIT ME AND I WILL SPEAK WIZ 'ER.
WHAT'S THAT MANIAC UP TO?
PHWEE... PHWEE-PHWEE!
MAKING A LEETLE SIGNAL BECAUSE HE LOVES HER.
THE 'LEETLE SIGNAL' HAS AN INSTANT EFFECT UPON SYLVINE—
—SHE PUTS HER MOUNT AT THE WALL AND CLEARS IT
SYLVINE—OH, MA PETITE SYLVINE!
FELIX! I HAVE NEVER BEEN SO GLAD TO SEE ANYONE!
A FEW MINUTES LATER...
WELL, THIS IS A BIT DULL! THEY'VE DONE NOTHING BUT SIT AND TALK.
AREN'T WE SUPPOSED TO BE INDUCING HER TO COME BACK AND DANCE IN BALLET?
WAIT FOR IT, GIRLS. TROUBLE COMING UP.
SYLVINE, HOW DARE YOU! WHO ARE THESE PEOPLE? GET ON YOUR HORSE IMMEDIATELY. I AM GOING TO TAKE YOU STRAIGHT BACK TO SCHOOL.
LATER, AT THE SCHOOL...
YOUR AUNT GAVE ME THE STRICTEST INSTRUCTIONS ABOUT YOU, SYLVINE. NO DANCING, NO VISITORS, NO OUTSIDE CONTACTS WHATEVER. YET THE MOMENT YOU ARE GIVEN A LITTLE FREEDOM, YOU DISOBEY ME!
I AM SORRY, SYLVINE, BUT I HAVE NO ALTERNATIVE BUT TO KEEP YOU IN YOUR ROOM UNTIL I CAN BE QUITE SURE THAT YOUR DISREPUTABLE FRIENDS HAVE LEFT THE NEIGHBOURHOOD.
HOWEVER, THE 'DISREPUTABLE FRIENDS' DON'T SEEM IN A HURRY TO LEAVE THE NEIGHBOURHOOD...
PHWEE... PHWEE-PHWEE!
CONTINUED

continued on page 54

★ Jacky meets Donald Sinden ★

With best wishes to GIRL readers from Donald Sinden

Donald Sinden, the actor, his wife Diana and Jeremy (aged 3) took Jacky for one of their favourite walks by the River Thames.

Jeremy loves watching the boats there. Maybe he inherits this from Donald, who was born by the sea, at Plymouth.

In Donald's Chelsea flat Jacky had fun playing native guitars. Donald got them in Africa while he was filming *Mogambo*.

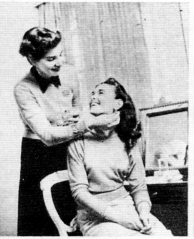

Known on the stage as Diana Mahony, Donald's wife told Jacky how they met while playing in *Romeo and Juliet*.

Jacky was enchanted by Jeremy's miniature aquarium. This is filled with tiny glass fish and strange little animals.

Playing with young Jeremy, reading and decorating (he wanted to be an architect when he was a boy) are Donald's hobbies.

Getting things ship-shape in the kitchen! A sailor in *The Cruel Sea*, Donald is a medical student in his new film – *Doctor in the House*.

A Letter from the Editor

GIRL OFFICE, 43 SHOE LANE, LONDON, E.C.4.

18th July, 1956

HAVE you seen the announcement about our great boys' and girls' Exhibition yet? We are all very busy with it now, choosing and arranging the stands. I must say, although it's hard work, it's enormously exciting watching an Exhibition come to life from scratch. I hope lots of you will manage to be there, with your parents and friends, too. You'll enjoy it!

One of the exhibits will be a space fleet review – that's to say, models of how we imagine a space fleet will look in not so very many years from now. And talking of space and star ships, I'm very pleased that so many of you are enjoying "Reach for a Star". Thank you very much for all your letters.

Yours sincerely,

Marcus Morris

READERS' LETTERS

5/- will be paid for every reader's letter printed on this page.

A letter from Southern Rhodesia

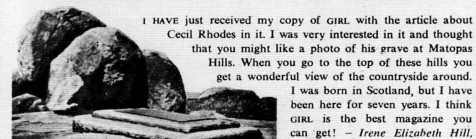

I HAVE just received my copy of GIRL with the article about Cecil Rhodes in it. I was very interested in it and thought that you might like a photo of his grave at Matopas Hills. When you go to the top of these hills you get a wonderful view of the countryside around.

I was born in Scotland, but I have been here for seven years. I think GIRL is the best magazine you can get! – *Irene Elizabeth Hill, S. Rhodesia.*

* * * * * *

Bribery !

I BUY GIRL every week, and like to read it without being disturbed. However, I get no peace, because my uncle likes to read it, too – so I buy him EAGLE to keep him quiet! – *Helen Cranstoun, nr. Horsham, Sussex.*

* * *

Judith's Chinese friends

I THOUGHT you might be interested to see this snapshot of myself with our Chinese servant's children when I was in Malaya. The dresses they are wearing are their best ones. They put them on specially for the photograph. While I was there I taught

them to sing 'Baa Baa Black Sheep', and every morning they used to sit on the steps of my bungalow and sing it to me before I got out of bed. The land you can see in the distance in the snap is Penang Island. The children's names are : – Tee, Heing, Yang, Sa-jong and Wah. – *Judith Linda Scoble, St. Judes, Plymouth.*

Ed.: Well, Judith, we feel that by now you should really know 'Baa Baa Black Sheep' pretty well!

WINNERS

There are fifteen main winners for GIRL Competition 19. They are : – Christine Law of Sheffield; Margaret Jones of Bedford; Maureen Penfold of Doncaster; Susan Lloyd of Chester; Christine Cubbin of Bromborough, Cheshire; Hilary Glynn of Chingford; Mary Wade of South Luffenham, Rutland; Rosemary Parker of Weeping Cross, Stafford; Jennifer Smith of Hemel Hempstead; Margaret Talbot of Ipswich; Veronica Green of Worcester; Annette Dow of Dundee; Yvonne Bowden of Palmers Green; Anne Atkinson of Northtown; and Isobel Bailey of Balby.

GIRL Personality Parade

Here are two more pictures for your Personality Parade album. Cut them out and stick them in the right spaces.

SIX GIRL TENNIS RACKETS to be won.

and there are boxes of GIRL soap for the runners-up!

If you'd like to be the proud possessor of one of these Slazenger GIRL tennis rackets, get busy on our competition right away. It's a competition designed to test your knowledge of British towns. Each illustration pairs up with one of the words to give the name of a well-known British town. Easy, isn't it? And perhaps it will be your lucky week!

1	– – – –	GUARD
2	– – – –	MOUTH
3	– – –	SEA
4	– – – –	DIFF
5	– – – –	AN
6	– – – –	ON

HERE ARE THE RULES:

1. Pair up the illustrations with the word endings to form the names of towns in the British Isles. When you have worked them out, write the names on a postcard.

2. In the top right-hand corner of the same postcard add your name, address and age last birthday.

3. Points will be given for neatness and handwriting as well as for the correct solutions. The ages of the entrants will also taken into consideration in the judging

4. This competition is open to all girls to and including the age of sixteen.

5. All entries should be sent to : – G Competition No. 29, GIRL Reader Servic Long Lane, Aintree, Liverpool 9, to arr there not later than 30th July.

6. Send no money; this is FREE.

7. The Editor's and judges' decision is fir No correspondence will be entered in

Star Adventurer

MARIANNE LITTLE, aged 15, of Corbridge, Northumberland, recently added to her record of service in a splendid way, by taking over the care of a young baby, and also looking after the home of which it was a member, when the mother was taken away to hospital. Marianne's claim is supported by the leader of The Girls' Friendly Society, to which she belongs.

SMALL SISTER by Fiddy

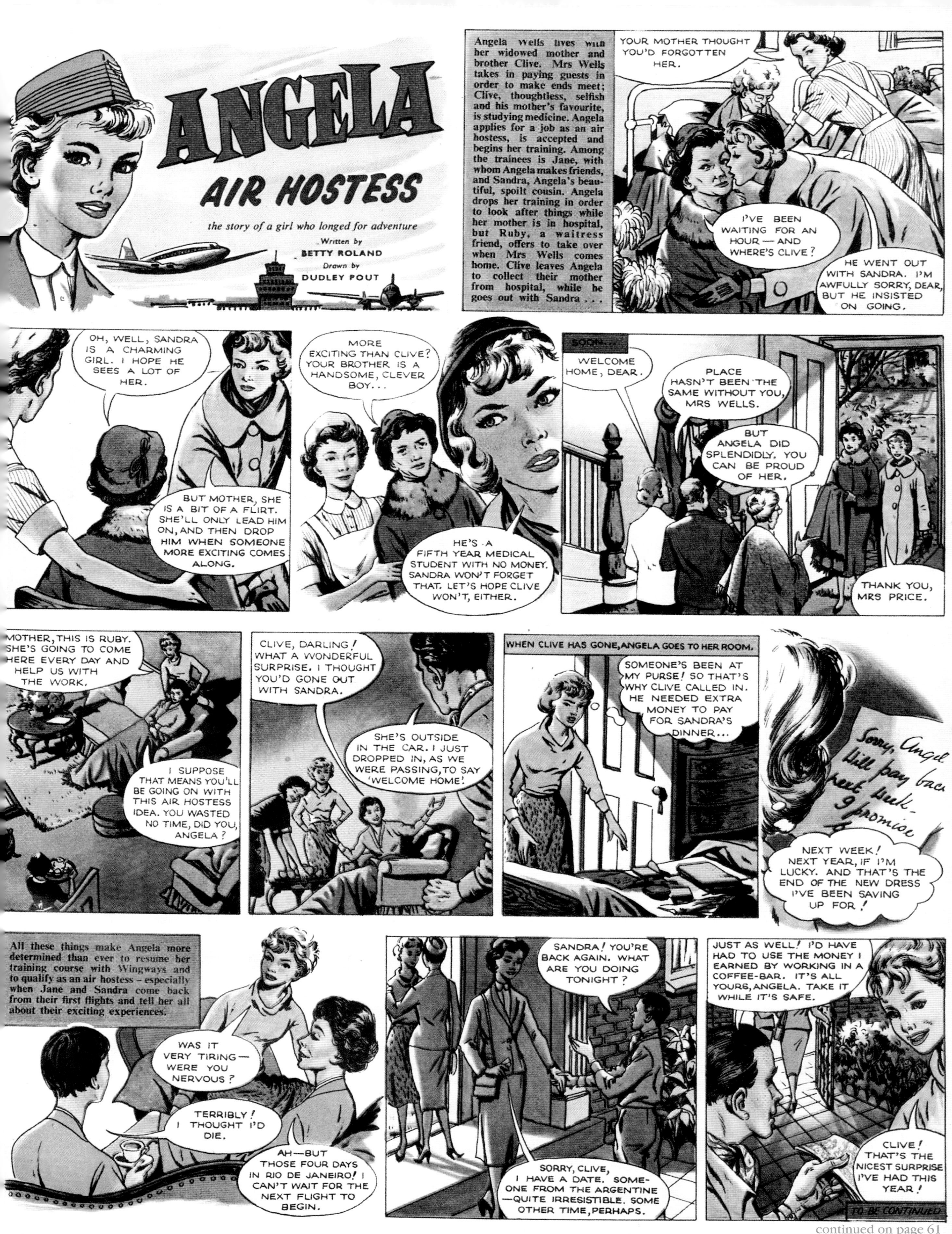
ANGELA
AIR HOSTESS
the story of a girl who longed for adventure
Written by BETTY ROLAND
Drawn by DUDLEY POUT
Angela Wells lives with her widowed mother and brother Clive. Mrs Wells takes in paying guests in order to make ends meet; Clive, thoughtless, selfish and his mother's favourite, is studying medicine. Angela applies for a job as an air hostess, is accepted and begins her training. Among the trainees is Jane, with whom Angela makes friends, and Sandra, Angela's beautiful, spoilt cousin. Angela drops her training in order to look after things while her mother is in hospital, but Ruby, a waitress friend, offers to take over when Mrs Wells comes home. Clive leaves Angela to collect their mother from hospital, while he goes out with Sandra . . .
YOUR MOTHER THOUGHT YOU'D FORGOTTEN HER.
I'VE BEEN WAITING FOR AN HOUR — AND WHERE'S CLIVE?
HE WENT OUT WITH SANDRA. I'M AWFULLY SORRY, DEAR, BUT HE INSISTED ON GOING.
OH, WELL, SANDRA IS A CHARMING GIRL. I HOPE HE SEES A LOT OF HER.
BUT MOTHER, SHE IS A BIT OF A FLIRT. SHE'LL ONLY LEAD HIM ON, AND THEN DROP HIM WHEN SOMEONE MORE EXCITING COMES ALONG.
MORE EXCITING THAN CLIVE? YOUR BROTHER IS A HANDSOME, CLEVER BOY...
HE'S A FIFTH YEAR MEDICAL STUDENT WITH NO MONEY. SANDRA WON'T FORGET THAT. LET'S HOPE CLIVE WON'T, EITHER.
SOON...
WELCOME HOME, DEAR.
PLACE HASN'T BEEN THE SAME WITHOUT YOU, MRS WELLS.
BUT ANGELA DID SPLENDIDLY. YOU CAN BE PROUD OF HER.
THANK YOU, MRS PRICE.
MOTHER, THIS IS RUBY. SHE'S GOING TO COME HERE EVERY DAY AND HELP US WITH THE WORK.
I SUPPOSE THAT MEANS YOU'LL BE GOING ON WITH THIS AIR HOSTESS IDEA. YOU WASTED NO TIME, DID YOU, ANGELA?
CLIVE, DARLING! WHAT A WONDERFUL SURPRISE. I THOUGHT YOU'D GONE OUT WITH SANDRA.
SHE'S OUTSIDE IN THE CAR. I JUST DROPPED IN, AS WE WERE PASSING, TO SAY 'WELCOME HOME'.
WHEN CLIVE HAS GONE, ANGELA GOES TO HER ROOM.
SOMEONE'S BEEN AT MY PURSE! SO THAT'S WHY CLIVE CALLED IN. HE NEEDED EXTRA MONEY TO PAY FOR SANDRA'S DINNER...
Sorry, Angel
I'll pay bac
next week -
I promise
NEXT WEEK! NEXT YEAR, IF I'M LUCKY. AND THAT'S THE END OF THE NEW DRESS I'VE BEEN SAVING UP FOR!
All these things make Angela more determined than ever to resume her training course with Wingways and to qualify as an air hostess – especially when Jane and Sandra come back from their first flights and tell her all about their exciting experiences.
WAS IT VERY TIRING — WERE YOU NERVOUS?
TERRIBLY! I THOUGHT I'D DIE.
AH—BUT THOSE FOUR DAYS IN RIO DE JANEIRO! I CAN'T WAIT FOR THE NEXT FLIGHT TO BEGIN.
SANDRA! YOU'RE BACK AGAIN. WHAT ARE YOU DOING TONIGHT?
SORRY, CLIVE, I HAVE A DATE. SOMEONE FROM THE ARGENTINE —QUITE IRRESISTIBLE. SOME OTHER TIME, PERHAPS.
JUST AS WELL! I'D HAVE HAD TO USE THE MONEY I EARNED BY WORKING IN A COFFEE-BAR. IT'S ALL YOURS, ANGELA. TAKE IT WHILE IT'S SAFE.
CLIVE! THAT'S THE NICEST SURPRISE I'VE HAD THIS YEAR!
TO BE CONTINUED

continued on page 61

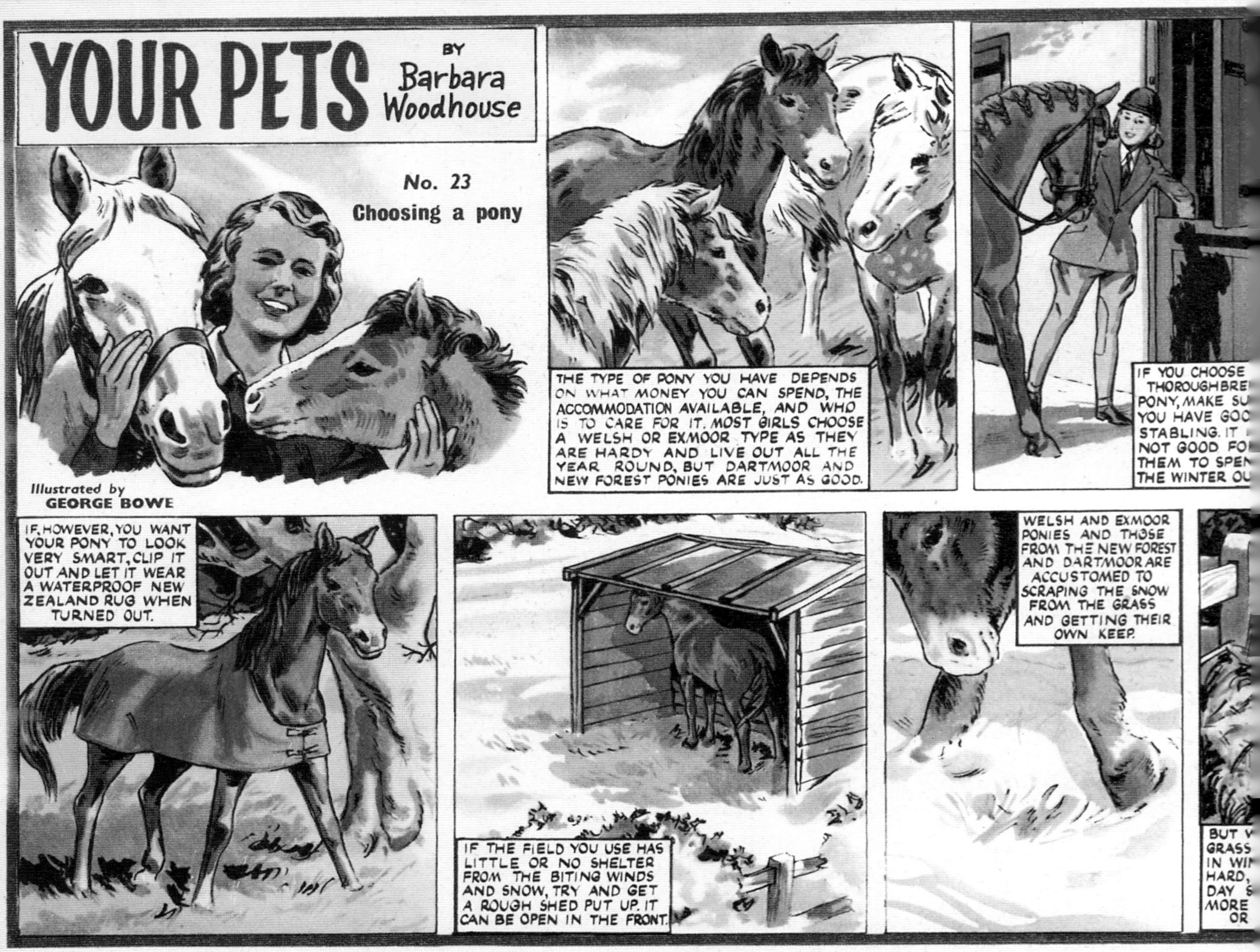
YOUR PETS
BY Barbara Woodhouse
No. 23
Choosing a pony
Illustrated by GEORGE BOWE
THE TYPE OF PONY YOU HAVE DEPENDS ON WHAT MONEY YOU CAN SPEND, THE ACCOMMODATION AVAILABLE, AND WHO IS TO CARE FOR IT. MOST GIRLS CHOOSE A WELSH OR EXMOOR TYPE AS THEY ARE HARDY AND LIVE OUT ALL THE YEAR ROUND, BUT DARTMOOR AND NEW FOREST PONIES ARE JUST AS GOOD.
IF YOU CHOOSE THOROUGHBRE PONY, MAKE SU YOU HAVE GOO STABLING. IT NOT GOOD FO THEM TO SPEN THE WINTER OU
IF, HOWEVER, YOU WANT YOUR PONY TO LOOK VERY SMART, CLIP IT OUT AND LET IT WEAR A WATERPROOF NEW ZEALAND RUG WHEN TURNED OUT.
IF THE FIELD YOU USE HAS LITTLE OR NO SHELTER FROM THE BITING WINDS AND SNOW, TRY AND GET A ROUGH SHED PUT UP. IT CAN BE OPEN IN THE FRONT.
WELSH AND EXMOOR PONIES AND THOSE FROM THE NEW FOREST AND DARTMOOR ARE ACCUSTOMED TO SCRAPING THE SNOW FROM THE GRASS AND GETTING THEIR OWN KEEP.
BUT W GRASS IN WI HARD, DAY MORE OR

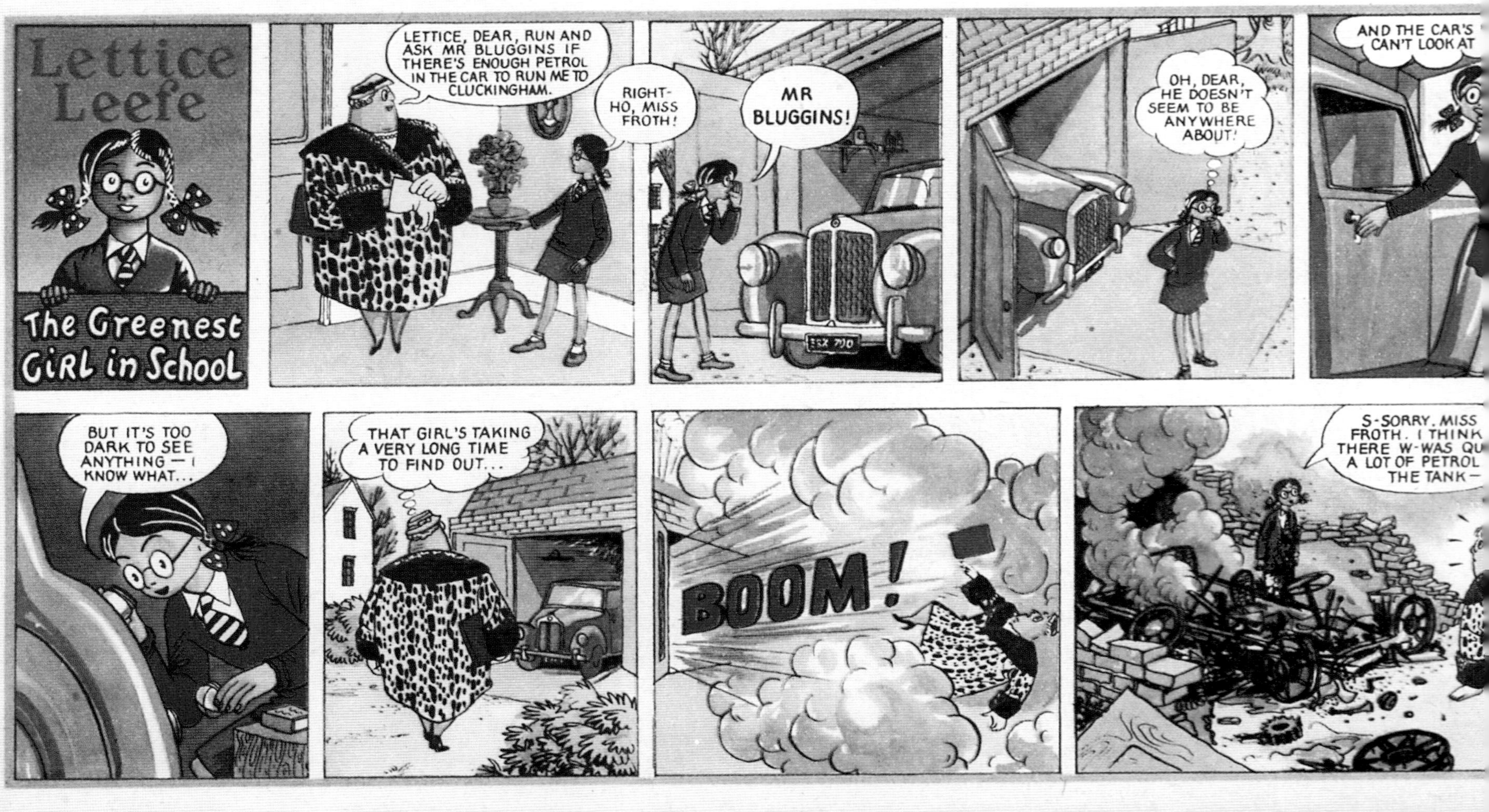
Lettice Leefe
The Greenest GIRL in School
LETTICE, DEAR, RUN AND ASK MR BLUGGINS IF THERE'S ENOUGH PETROL IN THE CAR TO RUN ME TO CLUCKINGHAM.
RIGHT-HO, MISS FROTH!
MR BLUGGINS!
OH, DEAR, HE DOESN'T SEEM TO BE ANYWHERE ABOUT!
AND THE CAR'S CAN'T LOOK AT
BUT IT'S TOO DARK TO SEE ANYTHING — I KNOW WHAT...
THAT GIRL'S TAKING A VERY LONG TIME TO FIND OUT...
BOOM!
S-SORRY, MISS FROTH. I THINK THERE W-WAS QU A LOT OF PETROL THE TANK—

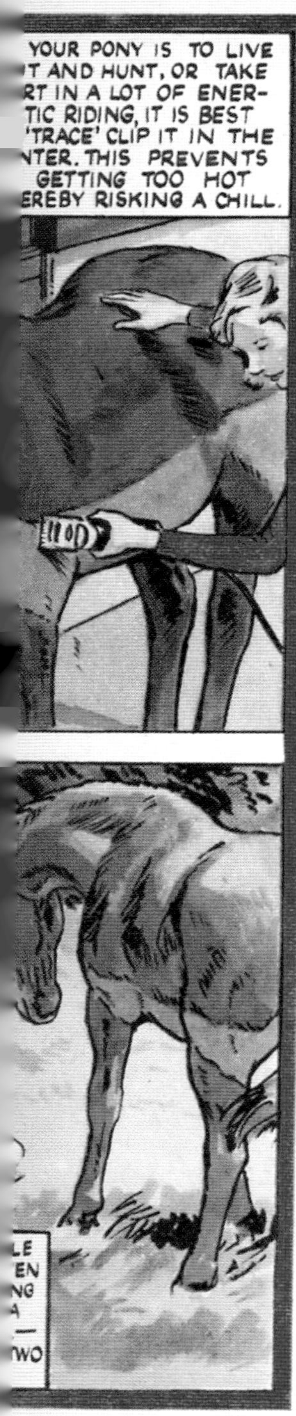
YOUR PONY IS TO LIVE
T AND HUNT, OR TAKE
RT IN A LOT OF ENER-
TIC RIDING, IT IS BEST
'TRACE' CLIP IT IN THE
NTER. THIS PREVENTS
GETTING TOO HOT
EREBY RISKING A CHILL.

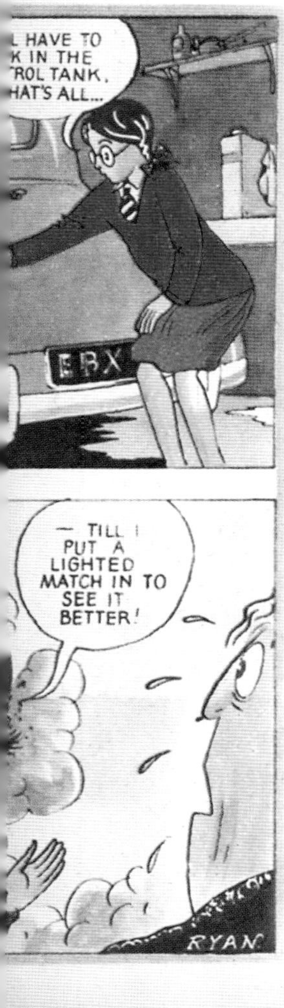
L HAVE TO
K IN THE
TROL TANK,
HAT'S ALL...
ERX
— TILL I
PUT A
LIGHTED
MATCH IN TO
SEE IT
BETTER!
RYAN

Girl Picture Gallery

No. 268

His Royal Highness the Duke of Edinburgh celebrated his birthday earlier this week, and here is a portrait of him to mark the occasion.

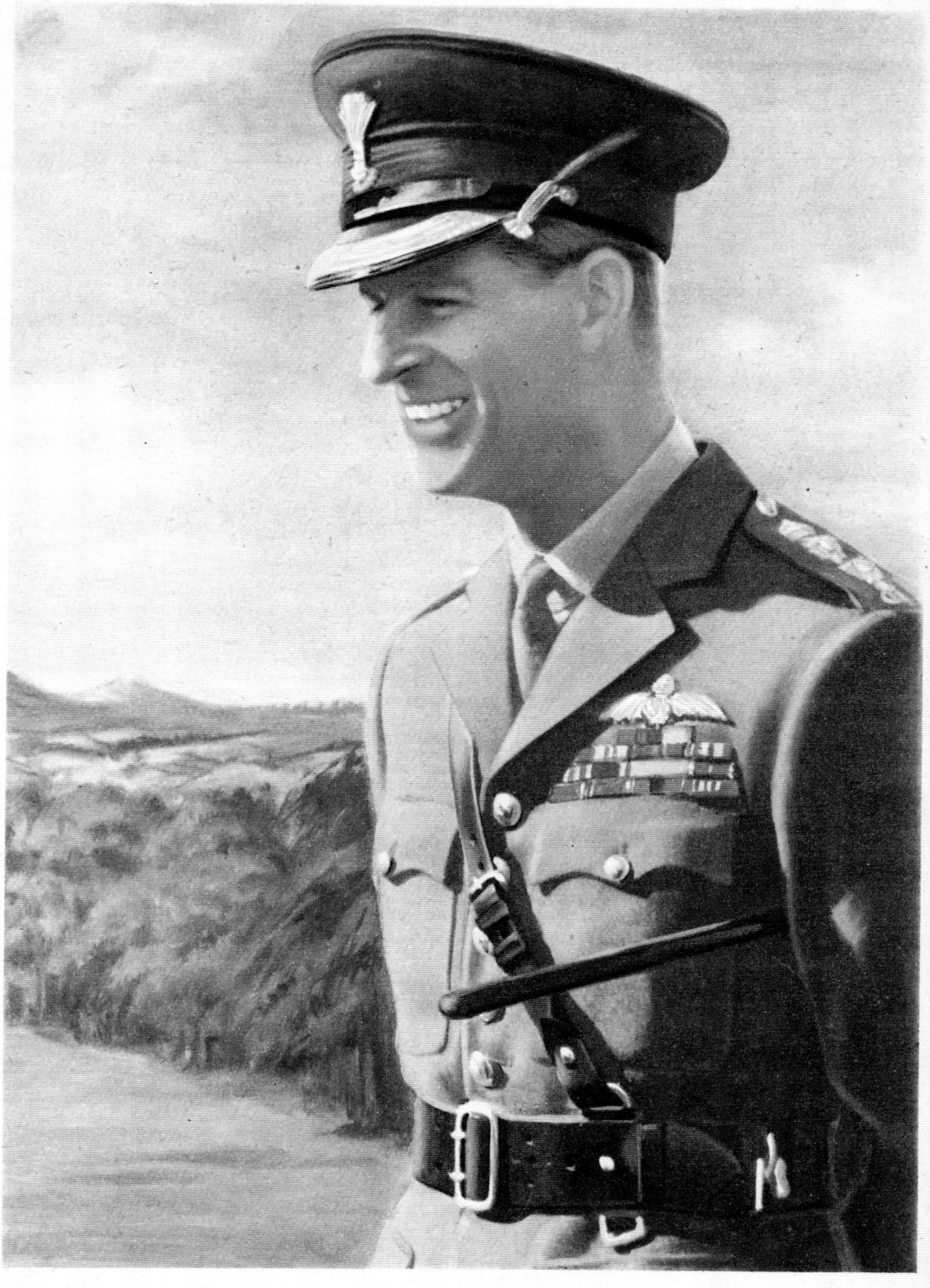

THE DUKE OF EDINBURGH

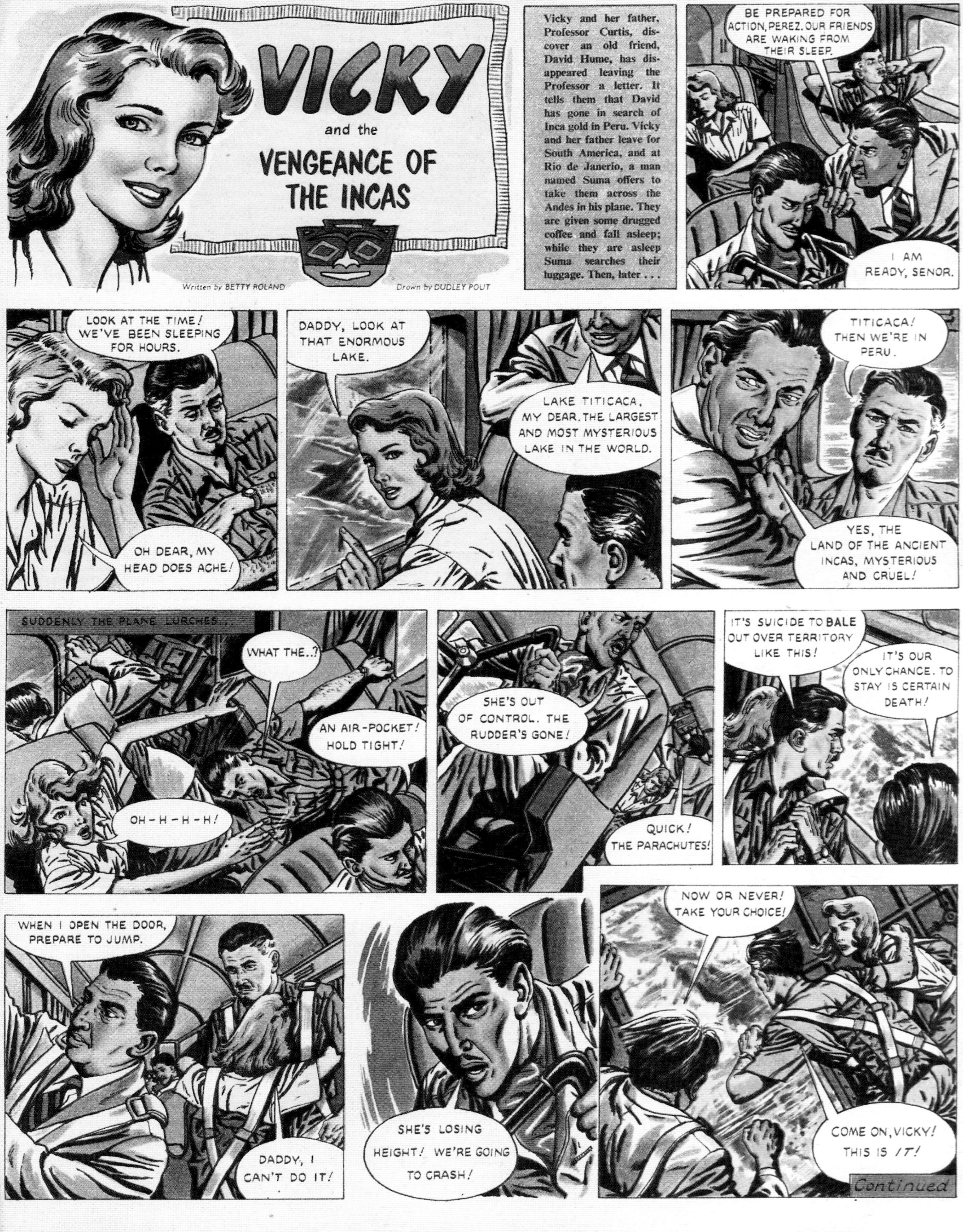
VICKY
and the
VENGEANCE OF THE INCAS
Written by BETTY ROLAND
Drawn by DUDLEY POUT
Vicky and her father, Professor Curtis, discover an old friend, David Hume, has disappeared leaving the Professor a letter. It tells them that David has gone in search of Inca gold in Peru. Vicky and her father leave for South America, and at Rio de Janerio, a man named Suma offers to take them across the Andes in his plane. They are given some drugged coffee and fall asleep; while they are asleep Suma searches their luggage. Then, later . . .
BE PREPARED FOR ACTION, PEREZ. OUR FRIENDS ARE WAKING FROM THEIR SLEEP.
I AM READY, SENOR.
LOOK AT THE TIME! WE'VE BEEN SLEEPING FOR HOURS.
OH DEAR, MY HEAD DOES ACHE!
DADDY, LOOK AT THAT ENORMOUS LAKE.
LAKE TITICACA, MY DEAR. THE LARGEST AND MOST MYSTERIOUS LAKE IN THE WORLD.
TITICACA! THEN WE'RE IN PERU.
YES, THE LAND OF THE ANCIENT INCAS, MYSTERIOUS AND CRUEL!
SUDDENLY THE PLANE LURCHES...
WHAT THE..?
AN AIR-POCKET! HOLD TIGHT!
OH-H-H-H!
SHE'S OUT OF CONTROL. THE RUDDER'S GONE!
QUICK! THE PARACHUTES!
IT'S SUICIDE TO BALE OUT OVER TERRITORY LIKE THIS!
IT'S OUR ONLY CHANCE. TO STAY IS CERTAIN DEATH!
WHEN I OPEN THE DOOR, PREPARE TO JUMP.
DADDY, I CAN'T DO IT!
SHE'S LOSING HEIGHT! WE'RE GOING TO CRASH!
NOW OR NEVER! TAKE YOUR CHOICE!
COME ON, VICKY! THIS IS IT!
Continued

continued on page 5

The Long and Short of Your Hair

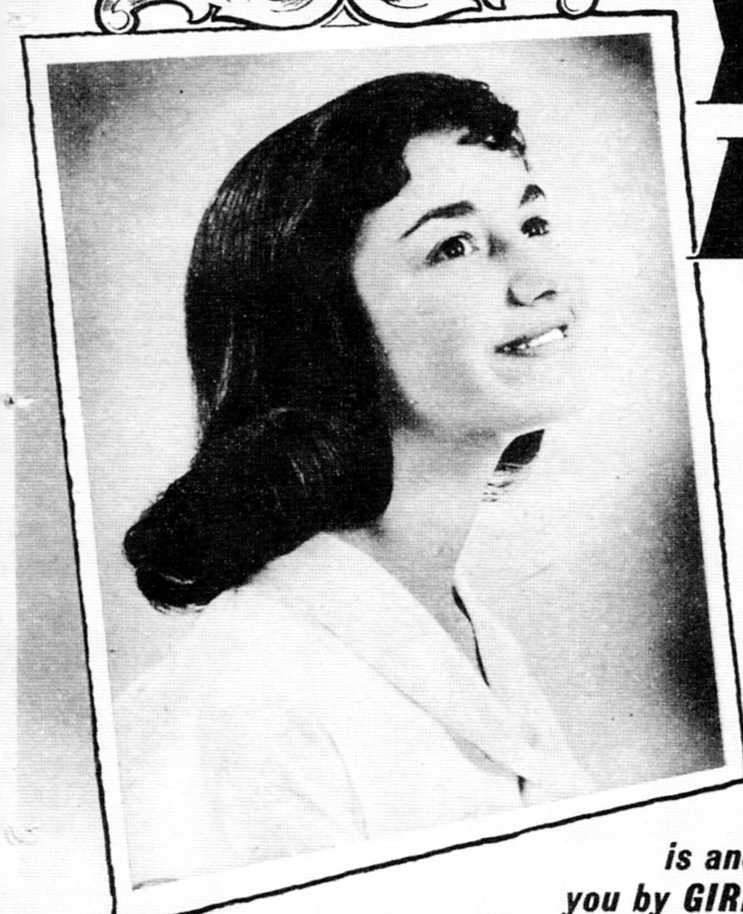

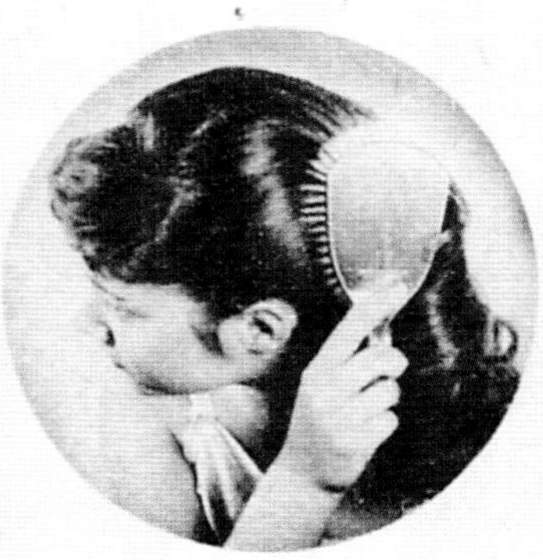

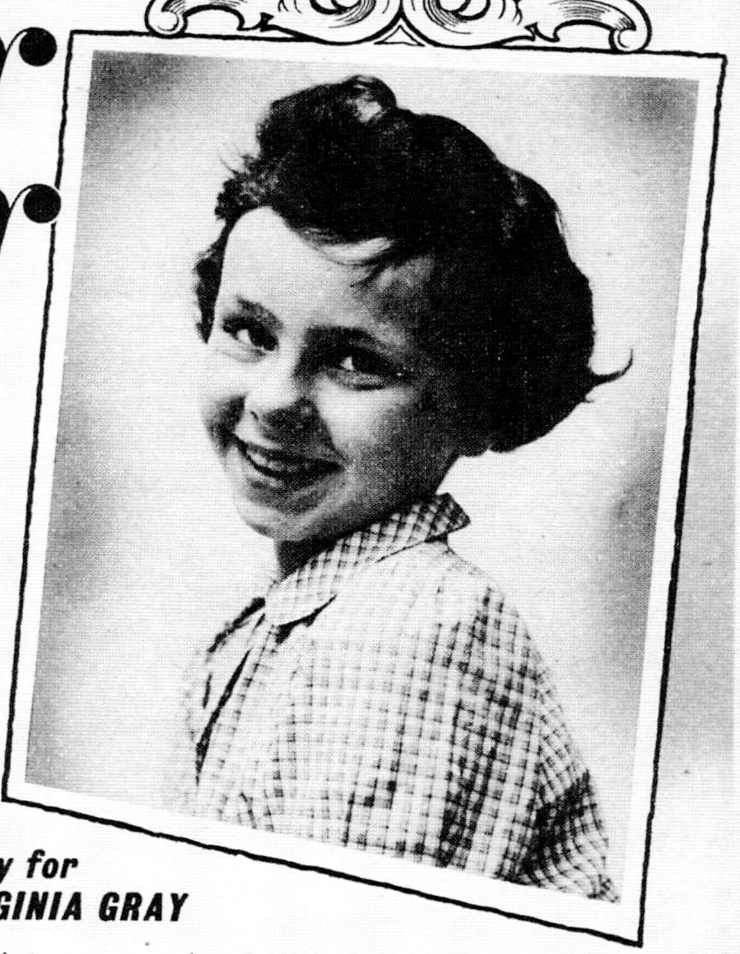

Photographed by BERT HARDY

Here, in answer to your many letters, is another feature especially for you by GIRL's Beauty Editor, VIRGINIA GRAY

THE first time you look at yourself in a mirror and think: 'my hair needs shampooing' – instead of waiting until mother moans, wrings her hands and gives up in despair – then you'll know you are becoming what fashion magazines call 'beauty conscious'.

At first it can be discouraging; there are so many shampoos, brilliantines and setting lotions to choose from, so much to learn. So let's start together with essentials.

How often should your hair be washed?

A good working average is once a week. Only girls who live in the clean atmosphere of country districts can leave it longer, while those with greasy hair will almost certainly find a weekly shampoo insufficient.

What shampoo should you use?

Here again, it depends very largely upon your type of hair. Boots, in their No. 7 preparations, have introduced two shampoos which state clearly and sensibly exactly what they are. Extra Rich is for dry, Tone-up for oily heads. There are plenty of others to choose from, and all are pretty reliable nowadays.

What should be done about dandruff?

If it is a mild form, wash as often as you can manage it. Some shampoos, such as Vosene and Loxene, help to combat the condition, though scrupulous cleanliness is the most important factor.

If your dandruff is severe you may need the advice of a Trichologist – some good hairdressers have one on their staff – but a course of Sebbix applications can do a great deal of good. Brushes and combs should be washed *daily*.

How can very oily hair be treated?

Besides frequent washing there are several ways to keep oiliness under control. Massaging the scalp with your finger tips – moving the skin firmly in small circles – is excellent, for it tones-up glands and muscles. Rubbing your head with hot, dry towels is a useful between-washing cleanser. Keep off brushing; it simply draws the grease down the hair-length.

What about dry hair?

Here, a good, medium-hard hair brush is your most useful ally. Brush for five minutes by the clock at bed-time every night and you'll see an astonishing difference within a week.

Your hair is fine and rat's taily?

This sort is frequently mistaken for greasy hair for it soon becomes lank, clogged with soot and grime. A short, clubbed cut is needed to give bulk, and possibly a light perm in the ends for the same purpose. After each shampoo the merest touch of 'Countess' will cut down static electricity and keep it in shape. *Never* use hard, rough brushing for this type of hair; it is far too fragile.

Is long or short hair easier to manage?

Here we plunge into styling. So much depends on personal taste. In general, I would advise long, pony-tail styles for girls who have thick hair and a pretty hairline, back and front. If the hairline is too high at the back of your neck, or if you have a long, thin neck, you'll tend to look 'scalped' if you scrape your hair upwards; instead I advise a short style or medium length page-boy. For those with a low or not-too-pretty forehead, a fringe brushed cross-wise is an excellent idea. Short styles are prettier if you have a long face which needs additional width or if your hair is thin and straggles easily. Round faces demand hair close to the ears and high above the forehead, while short necks appear longer when a brushed-up style is worn.

These are basic rules, but if you have any special hair problems, write to me at the address on the Editor's letter.

HAIR DOs AND DONTs

DOs

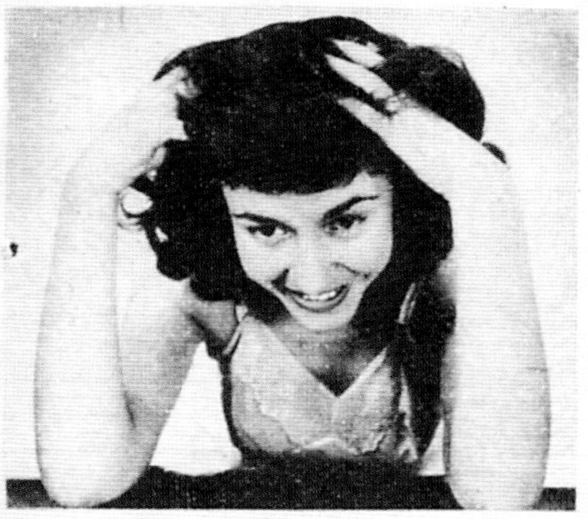

1. Do brush your hair regularly every day, and remember to massage your scalp once or twice a week.

2. Always have your hair professionally cut. Ask politely, but as firmly as you can, for an assistant who specializes in shaping.

3. Be sure to find out beforehand what the charge will be. Hairdressers vary a lot between trimming and re-shaping.

4. Mind you choose the right setting-lotion for YOUR sort of hair. A transparent one for fine or oily hair, the thicker sort for dry.

5. Do rinse very thoroughly between and after shampoo applications, or your set will emerge a sticky mess!

6. Brush your hair lightly while it is still damp – whether or not you intend to put it into pin-curls.

7. Try setting clips for anchoring your pin-curls – instead of metal curlers which can stretch and break your hair.

8. Use rollers if you wish your hair to stand high, or to make it look bulkier; they give a delightfully soft curl, too.

9. After sea-bathing, DO rinse your hair in clear water. There's nothing like salt-water and sun to make hair look and feel like straw.

10. Use a non-drying lacquer occasionally if you have fly-away hair which needs keeping in its place. Satin Spray is excellent.

DONTs

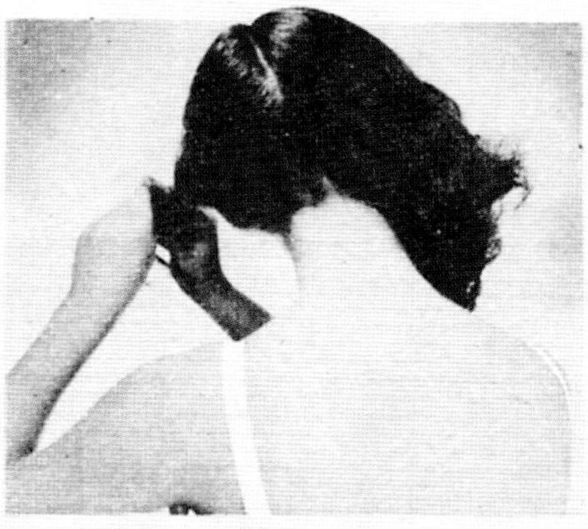

1. PLEASE don't part your hair at the centre back and pull into plaits. Sometimes it takes years to overcome the tendency to part here.

2. Never use a brush or comb that is sharp or harsh enough to scratch your scalp. Troublesome infections can start that way.

3. Don't cut or shave the tendrils of hair at the back of your neck or in front of your ears. You'll make an unsightly stubble.

4. Don't believe the people who tell you that curl can be cut out of your hair. Good tapering can encourage a wave, bad cutting can't destroy it.

5. Never neglect breaking, splitting ends. Have them trimmed off. Use your brush lightly and treat your hair to a conditioner after each shampoo.

6. Don't neglect to brush or massage because your hair falls more than usual. It needs the stimulus – but look to your health.

7. It's inadvisable to change your hairstyle just before a big date. Give yourself time to get used to it – and forget it!

8. Take care not to leave out of your diet foods that benefit hair. Vitamin B foods – yeast, wholemeal bread and liver.

9. Never believe that elastic bands to keep up a pony-tail will go unnoticed. It takes only a minute to cover them with a ribbon.

10. Don't be afraid to use hair-decorations for parties – but keep them small and neat. Daisies and rose buds can be charming on Alice bands.

Registered at the G.P.O. for transmission by Magazine Post to Canada (including Newfoundland). GIRL printed in Great Britain by Eric Bemrose Ltd., Long Lane, Liverpool 9, for the Proprietors and Publishers, Hulton Press Ltd., 161/166 Fleet Street, London, E.C.4. Sole agents for Australia and New Zealand, Gordon & Gotch (A/sia) Ltd.; South Africa, Central News Agency Ltd. Subscription Rate: Inland, 12 months 28/2; 6 months 14/1; abroad 12 months 26/-; 6 months 13/-. Postage for single copies: Inland 2d.; Foreign 1½d.; Canada 1d. You can have GIRL sent to any address in this

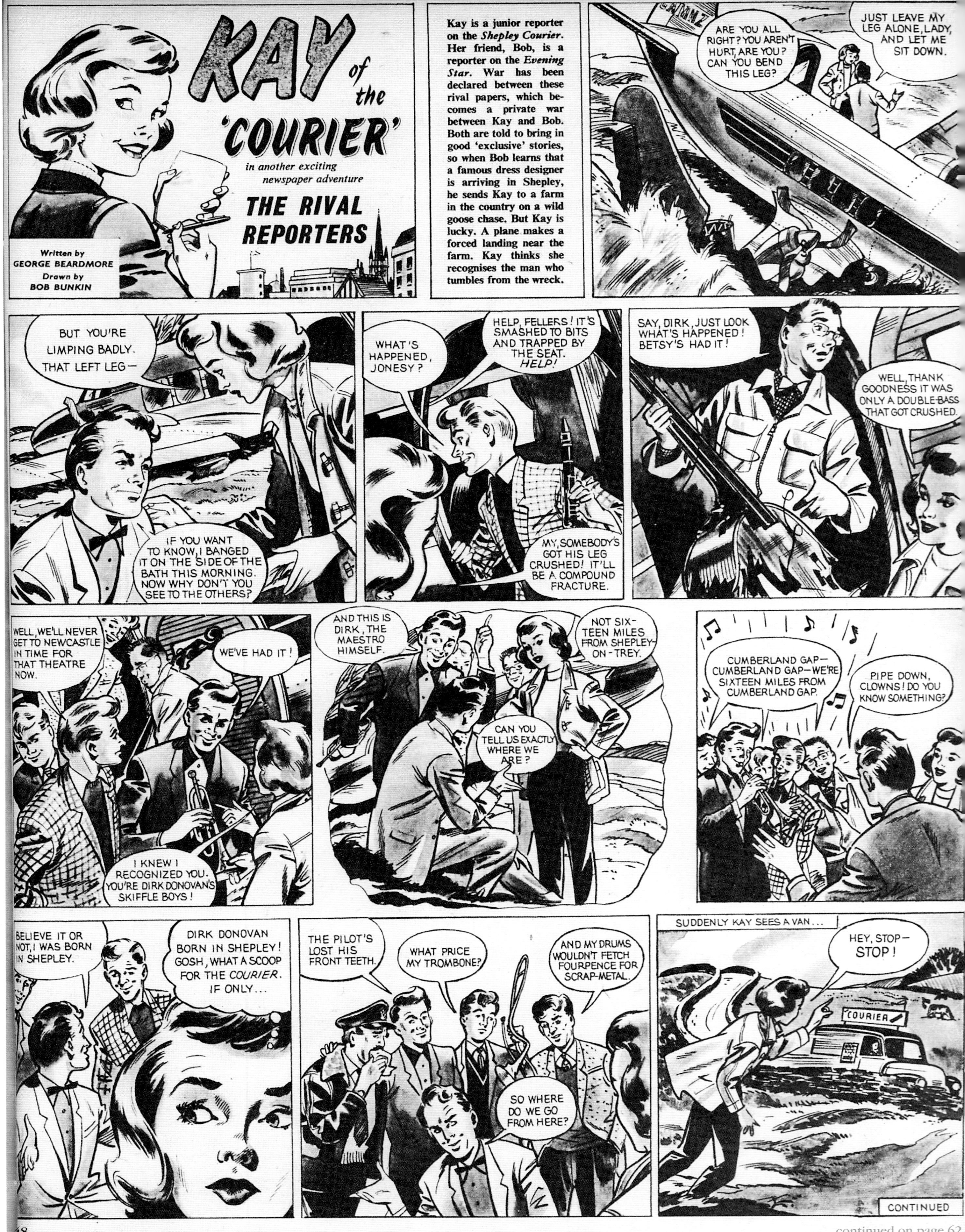

KAY of the 'COURIER'
in another exciting newspaper adventure
THE RIVAL REPORTERS
Written by GEORGE BEARDMORE
Drawn by BOB BUNKIN
Kay is a junior reporter on the *Shepley Courier*. Her friend, Bob, is a reporter on the *Evening Star*. War has been declared between these rival papers, which becomes a private war between Kay and Bob. Both are told to bring in good 'exclusive' stories, so when Bob learns that a famous dress designer is arriving in Shepley, he sends Kay to a farm in the country on a wild goose chase. But Kay is lucky. A plane makes a forced landing near the farm. Kay thinks she recognises the man who tumbles from the wreck.
ARE YOU ALL RIGHT? YOU AREN'T HURT, ARE YOU? CAN YOU BEND THIS LEG?
JUST LEAVE MY LEG ALONE, LADY, AND LET ME SIT DOWN.
BUT YOU'RE LIMPING BADLY. THAT LEFT LEG—
IF YOU WANT TO KNOW, I BANGED IT ON THE SIDE OF THE BATH THIS MORNING. NOW WHY DON'T YOU SEE TO THE OTHERS?
WHAT'S HAPPENED, JONESY?
HELP, FELLERS! IT'S SMASHED TO BITS AND TRAPPED BY THE SEAT. HELP!
MY, SOMEBODY'S GOT HIS LEG CRUSHED! IT'LL BE A COMPOUND FRACTURE.
SAY, DIRK, JUST LOOK WHAT'S HAPPENED! BETSY'S HAD IT!
WELL, THANK GOODNESS IT WAS ONLY A DOUBLE-BASS THAT GOT CRUSHED.
WELL, WE'LL NEVER GET TO NEWCASTLE IN TIME FOR THAT THEATRE NOW.
WE'VE HAD IT!
I KNEW I RECOGNIZED YOU. YOU'RE DIRK DONOVAN'S SKIFFLE BOYS!
AND THIS IS DIRK, THE MAESTRO HIMSELF.
NOT SIXTEEN MILES FROM SHEPLEY-ON-TREY.
CAN YOU TELL US EXACTLY WHERE WE ARE?
CUMBERLAND GAP—CUMBERLAND GAP—WE'RE SIXTEEN MILES FROM CUMBERLAND GAP.
PIPE DOWN, CLOWNS! DO YOU KNOW SOMETHING?
BELIEVE IT OR NOT, I WAS BORN IN SHEPLEY.
DIRK DONOVAN BORN IN SHEPLEY! GOSH, WHAT A SCOOP FOR THE COURIER. IF ONLY...
THE PILOT'S LOST HIS FRONT TEETH.
WHAT PRICE MY TROMBONE?
AND MY DRUMS WOULDN'T FETCH FOURPENCE FOR SCRAP-METAL.
SO WHERE DO WE GO FROM HERE?
SUDDENLY KAY SEES A VAN...
HEY, STOP—STOP!
COURIER
CONTINUED

continued on page 62

IF YOUR FACE IS LONG, TRY THE EFFECT OF A SLIGHTLY UPSWEPT FRAME TO GIVE WIDTH AT THE TEMPLES. CHOOSE IT IN SOLID COLOUR, WITH RATHER WIDE SIDE PIECES.
GIRLS WHO WEAR SPECTACLES ALL THE TIME OFTEN LIKE TO SAVE UP FOR AN EXTRA PAIR TO ALTERNATE WITH THEIR N.H.S GLASSES. LIKE HAIRSTYLES, THE FRAMES SHOULD BE CHOSEN TO FLATTER YOUR FEATURES.
Concerning YOU
SPECTACLES
DON'T CHOOSE RIMLESS GLASSES—THEY ARE TOO OLD FOR ANYONE STILL AT SCHOOL. DON'T GO FOR OVER-ORNAMENTED FRAMES EITHER, AS THEY ARE DIFFICULT TO CLEAN.
IF YOU CANNOT DECIDE WHAT SHAPE YOUR FACE IS, REMEMBER THAT A MODIFIED UPSWEPT SHAPE SUITS EVERYONE. SEE THAT THE TOP OF THE FRAME FOLLOWS THE CURVE OF THE EYEBROWS.
IF YOU HAVE A SQUARE JAW, DON'T CHOOSE ANYTHING TOO ANGULAR. SETTLE FOR A MORE ROUNDED SHAPE, WITH COLOUR CONCENTRATED ON THE OUTER CORNERS.
FOR A ROUND FACE TRY A MORE TIP-TILTED STYLE, WITH THE COLOUR CONFINED TO THE TOP OF THE FRAME. THIS WILL HELP TO GIVE AN ILLUSION OF LENGTH TO THE FACE.

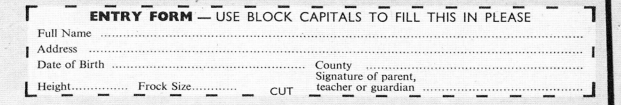

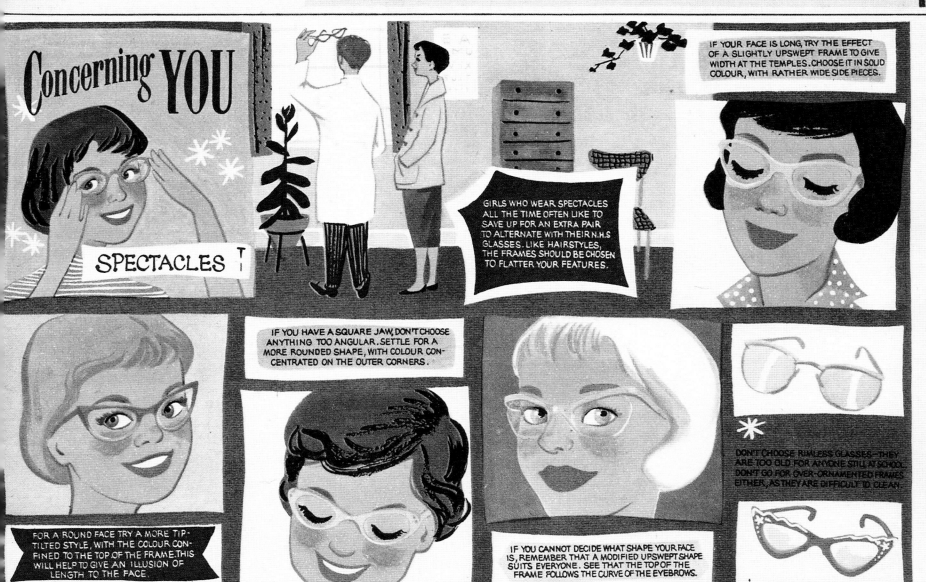

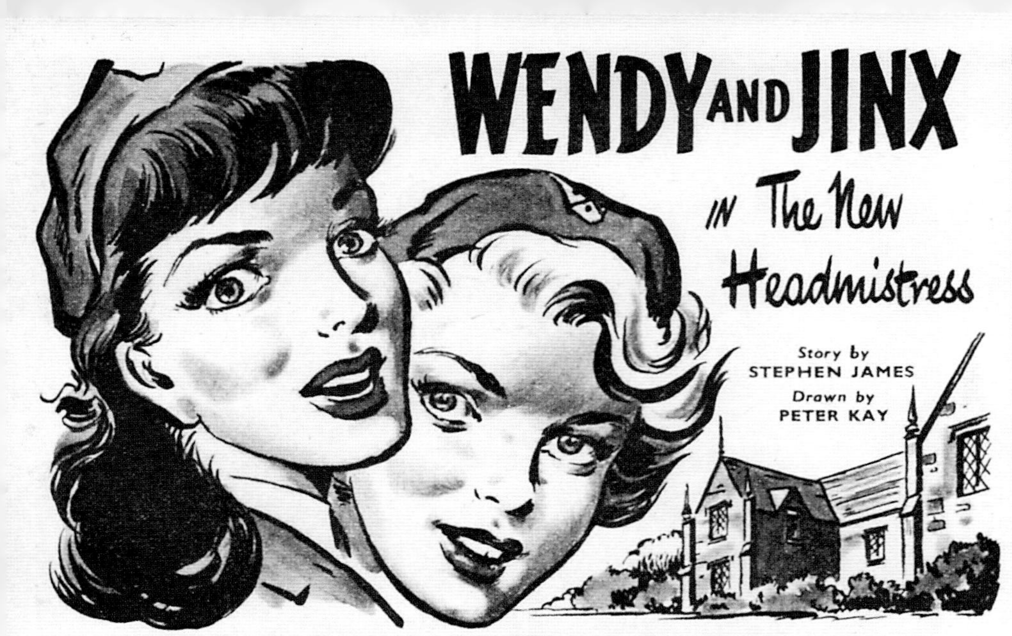
WENDY AND JINX
IN The New Headmistress
Story by STEPHEN JAMES
Drawn by PETER KAY

Wendy and Jinx, inseparable friends of Manor School, are angry when the strict new Headmistress, Miss Kent, separates them and makes many other unpopular changes. However, when Wendy is made dormitory prefect, the friends decide they must uphold the Head. Then Jinx receives a letter from her cousin Peter, asking her to meet him in town on Saturday, as he is in trouble. Jinx has been forbidden to go to town that day; but she decides she must go. She sees her friends off on the Town bus, then gets a lift there herself. But Wendy gets off the bus and returns to school to keep Jinx company.

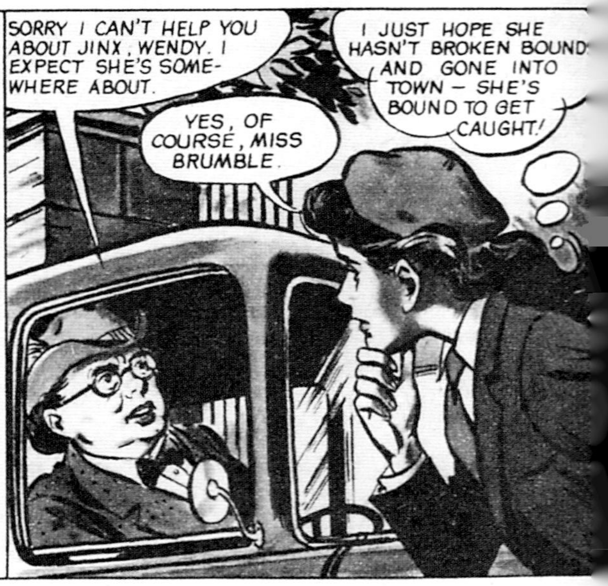
SORRY I CAN'T HELP YOU ABOUT JINX, WENDY. I EXPECT SHE'S SOMEWHERE ABOUT.
YES, OF COURSE, MISS BRUMBLE.
I JUST HOPE SHE HASN'T BROKEN BOUNDS AND GONE INTO TOWN – SHE'S BOUND TO GET CAUGHT!

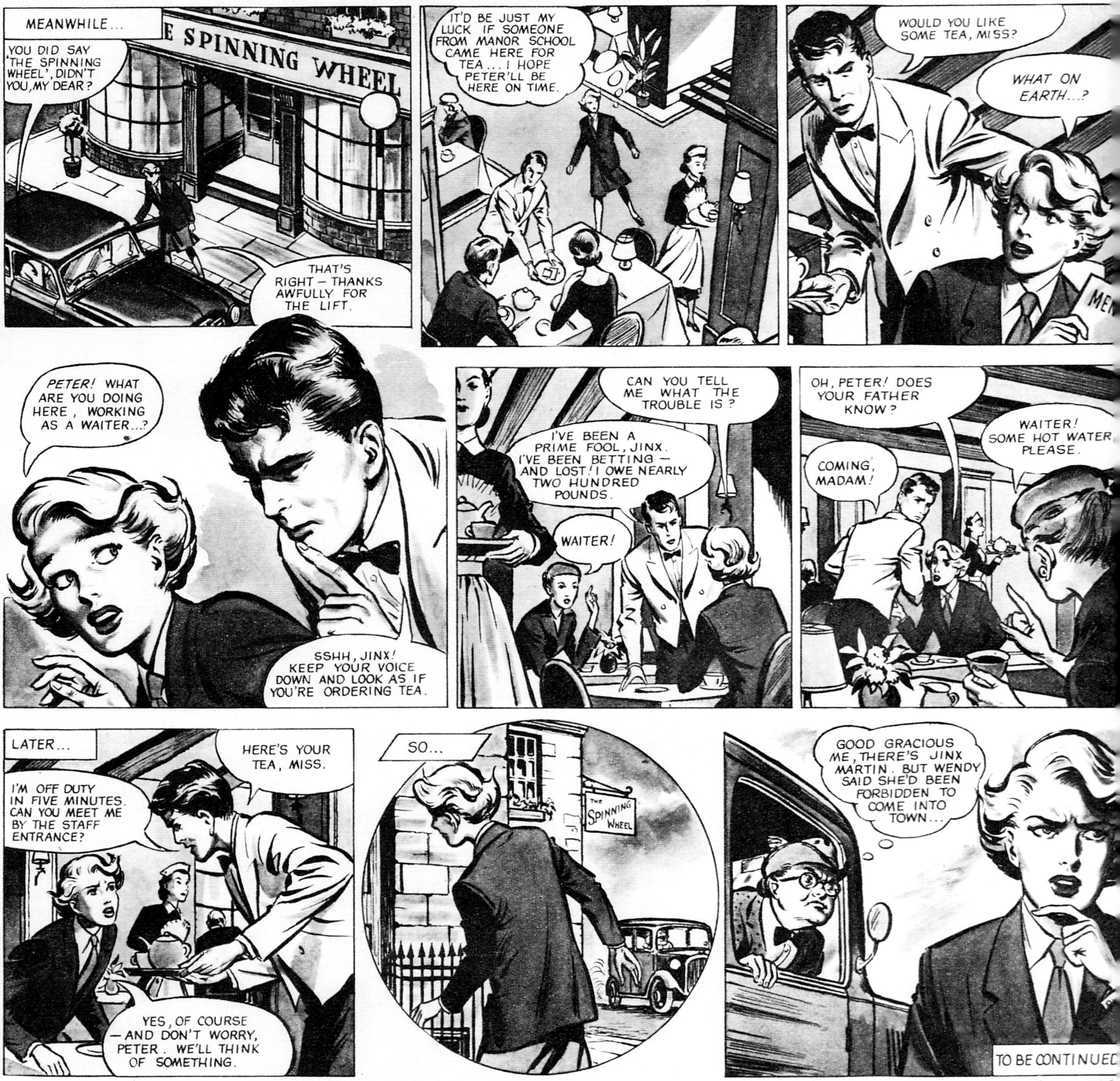
MEANWHILE...
YOU DID SAY 'THE SPINNING WHEEL', DIDN'T YOU, MY DEAR?
E SPINNING WHEEL
THAT'S RIGHT – THANKS AWFULLY FOR THE LIFT.
IT'D BE JUST MY LUCK IF SOMEONE FROM MANOR SCHOOL CAME HERE FOR TEA... I HOPE PETER'LL BE HERE ON TIME.
WOULD YOU LIKE SOME TEA, MISS?
WHAT ON EARTH...?
PETER! WHAT ARE YOU DOING HERE, WORKING AS A WAITER...?
SSHH, JINX! KEEP YOUR VOICE DOWN AND LOOK AS IF YOU'RE ORDERING TEA.
CAN YOU TELL ME WHAT THE TROUBLE IS?
I'VE BEEN A PRIME FOOL, JINX. I'VE BEEN BETTING – AND LOST! I OWE NEARLY TWO HUNDRED POUNDS.
WAITER!
OH, PETER! DOES YOUR FATHER KNOW?
WAITER! SOME HOT WATER PLEASE.
COMING, MADAM!
LATER...
I'M OFF DUTY IN FIVE MINUTES. CAN YOU MEET ME BY THE STAFF ENTRANCE?
HERE'S YOUR TEA, MISS.
YES, OF COURSE – AND DON'T WORRY, PETER. WE'LL THINK OF SOMETHING.
SO...
THE SPINNING WHEEL
GOOD GRACIOUS ME, THERE'S JINX MARTIN. BUT WENDY SAID SHE'D BEEN FORBIDDEN TO COME INTO TOWN...
TO BE CONTINUED

continued on page 6

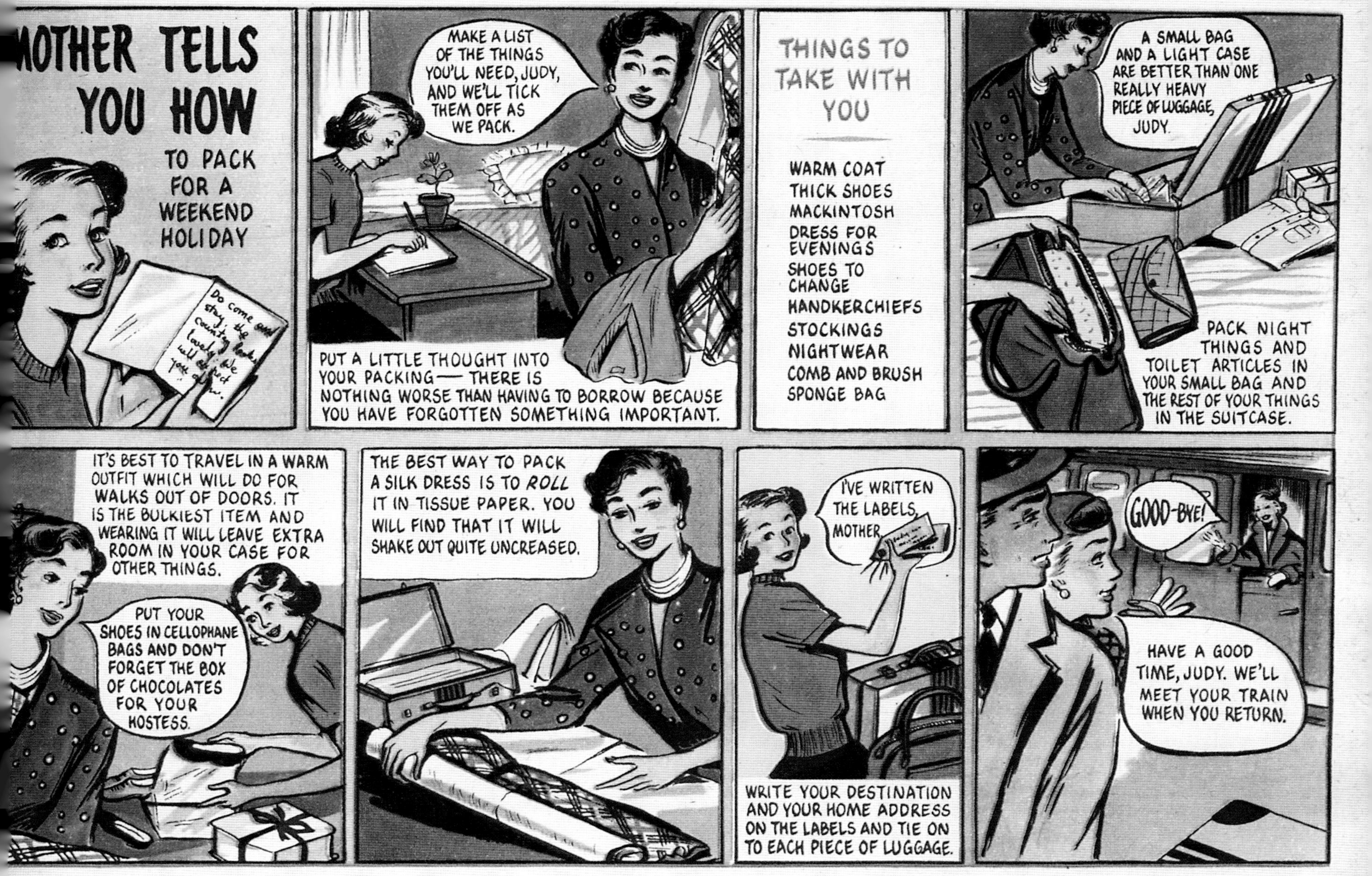
MOTHER TELLS YOU HOW
TO PACK FOR A WEEKEND HOLIDAY
MAKE A LIST OF THE THINGS YOU'LL NEED, JUDY, AND WE'LL TICK THEM OFF AS WE PACK.
PUT A LITTLE THOUGHT INTO YOUR PACKING — THERE IS NOTHING WORSE THAN HAVING TO BORROW BECAUSE YOU HAVE FORGOTTEN SOMETHING IMPORTANT.
THINGS TO TAKE WITH YOU
WARM COAT
THICK SHOES
MACKINTOSH
DRESS FOR EVENINGS
SHOES TO CHANGE
HANDKERCHIEFS
STOCKINGS
NIGHTWEAR
COMB AND BRUSH
SPONGE BAG
A SMALL BAG AND A LIGHT CASE ARE BETTER THAN ONE REALLY HEAVY PIECE OF LUGGAGE, JUDY.
PACK NIGHT THINGS AND TOILET ARTICLES IN YOUR SMALL BAG AND THE REST OF YOUR THINGS IN THE SUITCASE.
IT'S BEST TO TRAVEL IN A WARM OUTFIT WHICH WILL DO FOR WALKS OUT OF DOORS. IT IS THE BULKIEST ITEM AND WEARING IT WILL LEAVE EXTRA ROOM IN YOUR CASE FOR OTHER THINGS.
PUT YOUR SHOES IN CELLOPHANE BAGS AND DON'T FORGET THE BOX OF CHOCOLATES FOR YOUR HOSTESS.
THE BEST WAY TO PACK A SILK DRESS IS TO ROLL IT IN TISSUE PAPER. YOU WILL FIND THAT IT WILL SHAKE OUT QUITE UNCREASED.
I'VE WRITTEN THE LABELS, MOTHER.
WRITE YOUR DESTINATION AND YOUR HOME ADDRESS ON THE LABELS AND TIE ON TO EACH PIECE OF LUGGAGE.
GOOD-BYE!
HAVE A GOOD TIME, JUDY. WE'LL MEET YOUR TRAIN WHEN YOU RETURN.

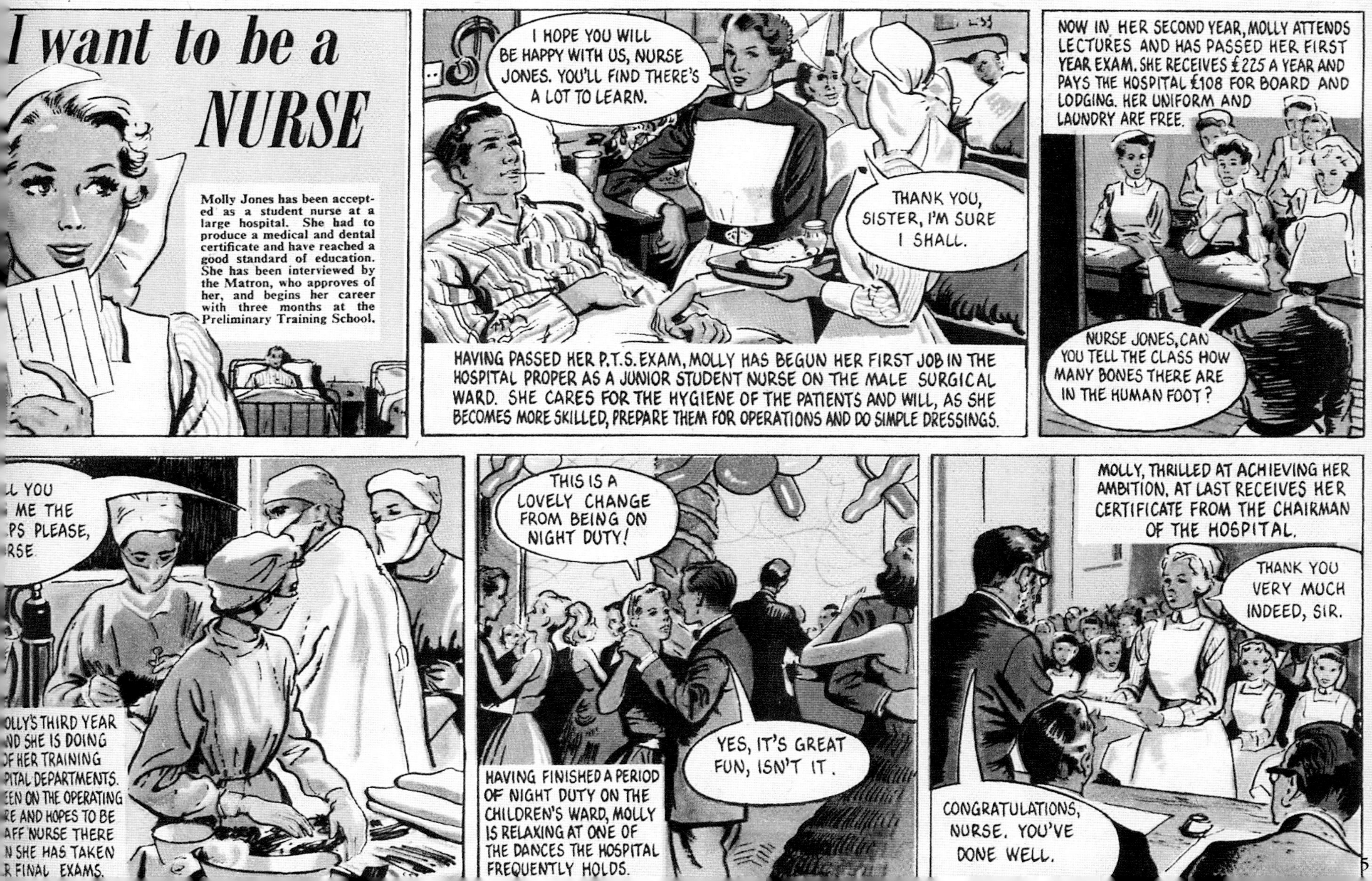
I want to be a NURSE
Molly Jones has been accepted as a student nurse at a large hospital. She had to produce a medical and dental certificate and have reached a good standard of education. She has been interviewed by the Matron, who approves of her, and begins her career with three months at the Preliminary Training School.
I HOPE YOU WILL BE HAPPY WITH US, NURSE JONES. YOU'LL FIND THERE'S A LOT TO LEARN.
THANK YOU, SISTER, I'M SURE I SHALL.
HAVING PASSED HER P.T.S. EXAM, MOLLY HAS BEGUN HER FIRST JOB IN THE HOSPITAL PROPER AS A JUNIOR STUDENT NURSE ON THE MALE SURGICAL WARD. SHE CARES FOR THE HYGIENE OF THE PATIENTS AND WILL, AS SHE BECOMES MORE SKILLED, PREPARE THEM FOR OPERATIONS AND DO SIMPLE DRESSINGS.
NOW IN HER SECOND YEAR, MOLLY ATTENDS LECTURES AND HAS PASSED HER FIRST YEAR EXAM. SHE RECEIVES £225 A YEAR AND PAYS THE HOSPITAL £108 FOR BOARD AND LODGING. HER UNIFORM AND LAUNDRY ARE FREE.
NURSE JONES, CAN YOU TELL THE CLASS HOW MANY BONES THERE ARE IN THE HUMAN FOOT?
LL YOU ME THE PS PLEASE, RSE.
OLLY'S THIRD YEAR ND SHE IS DOING F HER TRAINING PITAL DEPARTMENTS. EEN ON THE OPERATING RE AND HOPES TO BE AFF NURSE THERE N SHE HAS TAKEN R FINAL EXAMS.
THIS IS A LOVELY CHANGE FROM BEING ON NIGHT DUTY!
YES, IT'S GREAT FUN, ISN'T IT.
HAVING FINISHED A PERIOD OF NIGHT DUTY ON THE CHILDREN'S WARD, MOLLY IS RELAXING AT ONE OF THE DANCES THE HOSPITAL FREQUENTLY HOLDS.
MOLLY, THRILLED AT ACHIEVING HER AMBITION, AT LAST RECEIVES HER CERTIFICATE FROM THE CHAIRMAN OF THE HOSPITAL.
THANK YOU VERY MUCH INDEED, SIR.
CONGRATULATIONS, NURSE. YOU'VE DONE WELL.

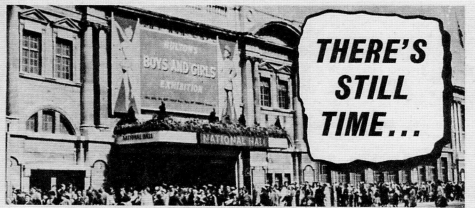

HULTON'S BOYS AND GIRLS EXHIBITION
NATIONAL HALL
THERE'S STILL TIME...

to visit the Boys & Girls Exhibition!

★★★★★★★ INTERESTED in fashion, or farming? Mining, or magic? Ballet, or beauty – or both? Then you must come to the Hulton's Boys and Girls Exhibition, which is open from 9.30 a.m. to 8 p.m. until Saturday, 23rd August. There's no room to tell you about the hundred and one things you can see and do – come along and see for yourself. A really exciting time awaits you in the National Hall, Olympia! ★★★★★★★

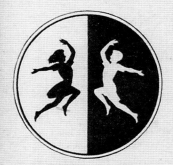

ADMISSION 1s. 9d.

How to get there

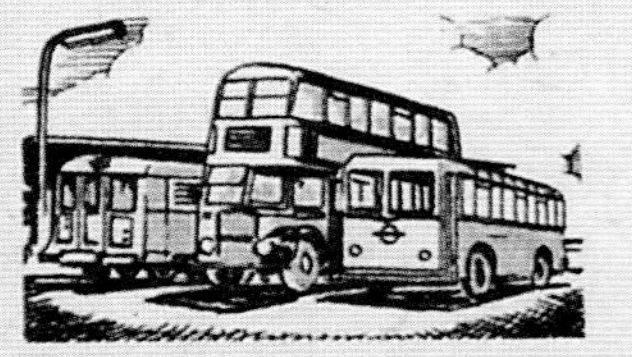

BUSES
9, 27, 28, 49, 73, 91 and 270.

TRAINS (Underground) There will be a special service running from Earl's Court.

GREEN LINE BUSES 701, 702, 704, 705, 714, 716 and 716A.

PHOTO CONTEST

FIRST PRIZE!

KODAK BROWNIE II
This easy-to-operate movie camera takes pictures in black and white and colour. It has an all-purpose exposure guide.

THE GIRL Snapshot Competition is running NOW and we want you to send us your snaps. You can enter pictures in any of these groups – or in all of them, for that matter! The groups are: **HUMOROUS** (anything that makes you laugh): **ACTION** (a picture that captures movement): **VIEW** (any scene, town or country): **NATURE** (birds, animals, flowers, etc.).

Every photograph must be at least postcard size, and a coupon cut from GIRL must accompany each one submitted.

You can win a record player! This competition is open to all readers under 17 years of age. Send your entry in an unsealed envelope bearing a 2d. stamp. Retain your negative. Closing date: Tuesday, September 2nd, 1958.

ENTRY FORM G4

GIRL Snapshot Contest
(Fill in using block letters)

NAME..

ADDRESS..

....

....

....

Paste this entry form securely on the back of your entry and send to: GIRL SNAPSHOT COMPETITION Long Lane, Aintree, Liverpool 9.

SIGNATURE.. AGE..........

Mark X on group in which entry is made

Humorous	
Action	
View	
Nature	

I accept the conditions of the competition, and agree that the Editor's decision shall be final. I confirm also that I took the attached photograph.

CLOSING DATE 2nd SEPTEMBER

The GIRL Stroller

just in time for Christmas!

Made specially for YOU – this up-to-the-minute GIRL Stroller Bag is perfect for holidays, week-ends or carrying your sports gear. It's ideal for cyclists and hikers, too! Duffle bags are the rage on the Continent, and now here they are for you! The material used is a hard-wearing and durable waterproof rayon in beautiful shades of Blue, Green and Tan. Edges are trimmed in contrasting colour piping. The base is strengthened and reinforced, and white draw-up cord is supplied for carrying purposes. The attractive Girl motif has been incorporated on the bag by a new manufacturing process. On sale at all good stores and leather shops. If you have difficulty in obtaining one, write to Sports Utilities Ltd., Grange Works, Glodwick Road, Oldham, Lancs.

PRICE 18/6

What wonderful dressing-up there'll be

EMERGENCY–WARD 10

NURSES' UNIFORM AND CAPE

15/11 *post free*

It's the official uniform worn by all the nurses in ITV's "Emergency — Ward 10". What glorious games there'll be — with the smart blue and white dress, the cap and apron with the red cross, the scarlet-lined blue cape.

Or this outfit in super quality, plus starched cuffs, a set of toy medical instruments, nurses' diploma, temperature charts — all in a strong carrying case for visiting 'patients'. *Post free* **24/11**

STATE DRESS LENGTH 28″ OR 32″

Make sure of this wonderful gift — send Cash / Cheque / P.O. today to

PROGRAMME GIFT COMPANY

Dept. 35, 86 Elm Park Avenue, London, N.15

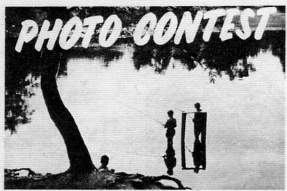

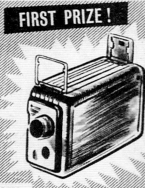

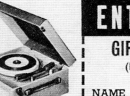

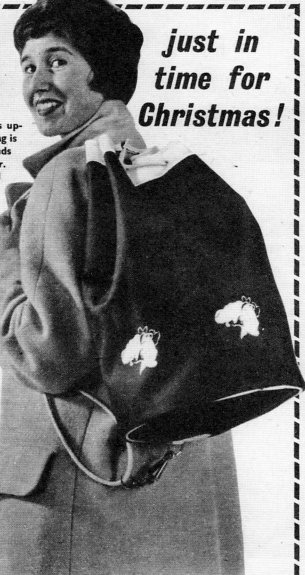

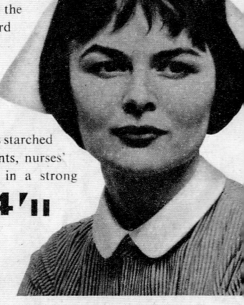

THIS IS WHAT YOU HAVE TO DO: Choose the coat you like best out of the eight styles pictured here and write a short essay of no more than thirty words saying why you like the style you have chosen. Age and neatness will be taken into account by the judges. Complete the form below and send it with your essay to Harlee, "Girl" Dept., Langham House, 302-308, Regent Street, London, W.1. Post before April 2nd, 1958.

ENTER FOR THE Harlee COMPETITION

Choose from these 8 lovely styles

WHICH DO YOU LIKE BEST?

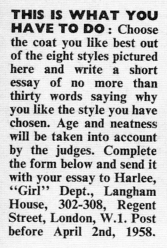

GAY Here's wonderful value and superb styling that only "Harlee" can give you. In a fine Blended Rayon with contrast Velvet collar and piped pockets. This fitted Suit for the smart teen-timer has two skirts – one is fully flared and the other is sunray pleated. Grey only.
FOR CHILDREN UP TO 15 YEARS.

PATRICIA A fitted Coat styled specially for the smart teen-timer in a Fine All Wool Tweed. There are half-moon pockets and two softly rolled pleats at back which create the splendid fully flared effect. Seven beautiful shades.
FOR CHILDREN UP TO 15 YEARS.

SALLY Tailored with inspiration in a fancy knobble Tweed mixture. A "Harlee" teen-ager with special interest on the back which has centre roll pleat falling from bow. Note the wide handsome collar.
Green, Pink, Turquoise, Lilac.
FOR CHILDREN UP TO 15 YEARS.

ROSEMARY A double-breasted beauty in All Wool Fancy Tweed with distinctive Moygashel trimmed collar. The flap pockets feature two buttons and the folded pleats from waist achieve that marvellous fully flared effect.
Natural, Turquoise, Gold, Tan.
FOR CHILDREN UP TO 12 YEARS.

£50 FOR THE BEST ESSAY

£20 FOR SECOND BEST

£10 FOR THIRD BEST

AND 30 CONSOLATION PRIZES OF £1 EACH

JENNIFER Styled for fashion flattery in a really attractive Double Texture Tweed. There's a rolled pleat each side back and front. The ideal choice for spring.
Blue, Turquoise, Pink, Gold.
FOR CHILDREN UP TO 12 YEARS.

MARILYN A Suit de-luxe in a Hop-sack design Pure Wool. Special fashion features are the gauging each side back, new shaped pockets and the charming bow at back. The skirt is fully flared.
Bright shades of Turquoise, Royal, Natural, Salmon, Blue.
FOR CHILDREN UP TO 12 YEARS.

PHILLIPPA Only "Harlee" could achieve this delightful styling for children. In 100% Plain Wool, with neat flap each side bodice and a small belt at back from which fall several graceful pleats. The crossover collar is finished with six neat spratheads. Seven bewitching shades.
FOR CHILDREN UP TO 12 YEARS.

CHRISTINE Fashioned to perfection in All Wool Knobble Tweed to create the utmost charm for children. This delightful Swagger features interesting flap pockets and the new button-over collar.
Pinky Tone, Blue, Honey, Turquoise.
FOR CHILDREN UP TO 12 YEARS.

Fill in this Competition Form and we hope you will be one of the lucky ones

Fill in this form in BLOCK LETTERS, cut neatly round dotted line, and post it together with your essay to HARLEE ('GIRL' DEPT.), LANGHAM HOUSE, 302-308, REGENT STREET, LONDON, W.1. in a sealed envelope using 3d. stamp.

I like...best and I am enclosing my essay saying why.

My full name is...

and I live at ....

....

My age is

If you have already received our Spring Brochure kindly put X here ☐

Closing Date APRIL 2nd. Results will be announced in GIRL, MAY 14th.

They're Heavenly – They're Harlee

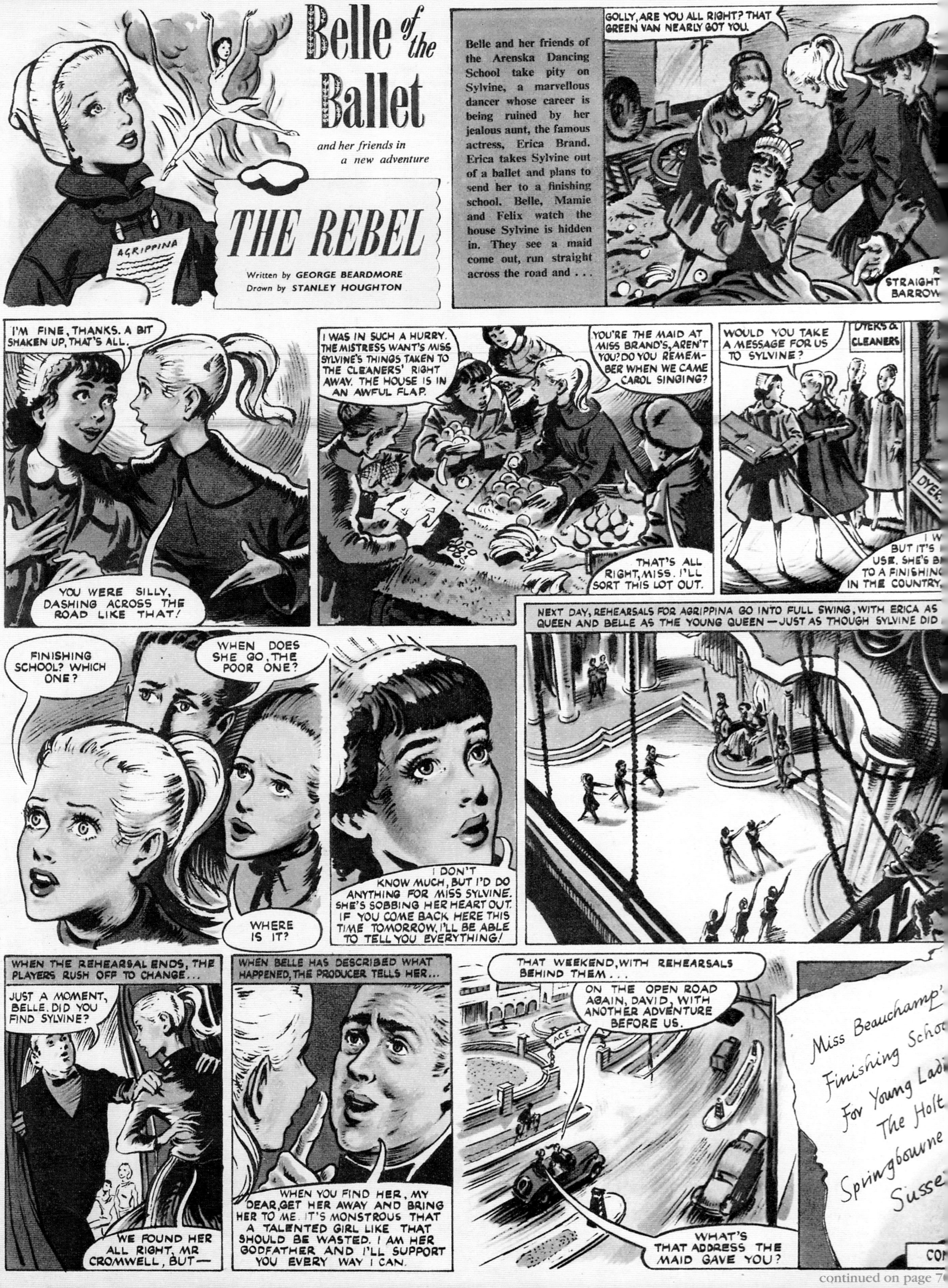

Belle of the Ballet
and her friends in a new adventure
THE REBEL
Written by GEORGE BEARDMORE
Drawn by STANLEY HOUGHTON
AGRIPPINA
Belle and her friends of the Arenska Dancing School take pity on Sylvine, a marvellous dancer whose career is being ruined by her jealous aunt, the famous actress, Erica Brand. Erica takes Sylvine out of a ballet and plans to send her to a finishing school. Belle, Mamie and Felix watch the house Sylvine is hidden in. They see a maid come out, run straight across the road and . . .
STRAIGHT
BARROW
GOLLY, ARE YOU ALL RIGHT? THAT GREEN VAN NEARLY GOT YOU.
I'M FINE, THANKS. A BIT SHAKEN UP, THAT'S ALL.
YOU WERE SILLY, DASHING ACROSS THE ROAD LIKE THAT!
I WAS IN SUCH A HURRY. THE MISTRESS WANT'S MISS SYLVINE'S THINGS TAKEN TO THE CLEANERS' RIGHT AWAY. THE HOUSE IS IN AN AWFUL FLAP.
YOU'RE THE MAID AT MISS BRAND'S, AREN'T YOU? DO YOU REMEMBER WHEN WE CAME CAROL SINGING?
THAT'S ALL RIGHT, MISS. I'LL SORT THIS LOT OUT.
WOULD YOU TAKE A MESSAGE FOR US TO SYLVINE?
CLEANERS
BUT IT'S
TO A FINISHING
IN THE COUNTRY.
FINISHING SCHOOL? WHICH ONE?
WHEN DOES SHE GO, THE POOR ONE?
WHERE IS IT?
I DON'T KNOW MUCH, BUT I'D DO ANYTHING FOR MISS SYLVINE. SHE'S SOBBING HER HEART OUT. IF YOU COME BACK HERE THIS TIME TOMORROW, I'LL BE ABLE TO TELL YOU EVERYTHING!
NEXT DAY, REHEARSALS FOR AGRIPPINA GO INTO FULL SWING, WITH ERICA AS
QUEEN AND BELLE AS THE YOUNG QUEEN — JUST AS THOUGH SYLVINE DID
WHEN THE REHEARSAL ENDS, THE PLAYERS RUSH OFF TO CHANGE...
JUST A MOMENT, BELLE. DID YOU FIND SYLVINE?
WE FOUND HER ALL RIGHT, MR CROMWELL, BUT—
WHEN BELLE HAS DESCRIBED WHAT HAPPENED, THE PRODUCER TELLS HER...
WHEN YOU FIND HER, MY DEAR, GET HER AWAY AND BRING HER TO ME. IT'S MONSTROUS THAT A TALENTED GIRL LIKE THAT SHOULD BE WASTED. I AM HER GODFATHER AND I'LL SUPPORT YOU EVERY WAY I CAN.
THAT WEEKEND, WITH REHEARSALS BEHIND THEM...
ON THE OPEN ROAD AGAIN, DAVID, WITH ANOTHER ADVENTURE BEFORE US.
WHAT'S THAT ADDRESS THE MAID GAVE YOU?
Miss Beauchamp's
Finishing
For Young
The Holt
Springbourne

continued on page 7

Jacky visits Éamonn Andrews

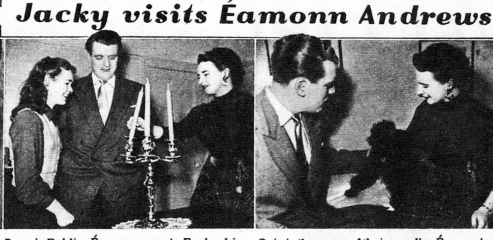

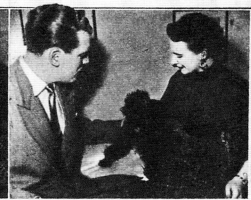

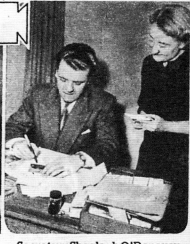

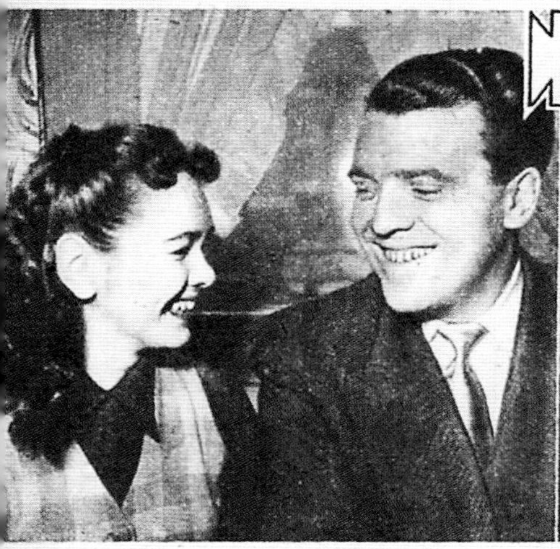

Éamonn Andrews' voice was familiar to Jacky because she'd heard it so often on the B.B.C. But she was delighted to meet him in person.

Born in Dublin, Éamonn came to England in 1950. He and his wife, Grainne, live in the West End of London near Broadcasting House.

Quiz is the name of their poodle. Éamonn's first broadcast was a boxing commentary in Ireland made after boxing in a match himself.

Secretary Sheelagh O'Donovan helps Éamonn answer all his correspondence and fan-mail.

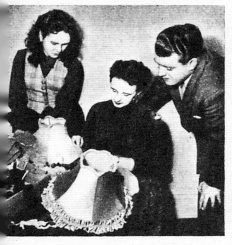

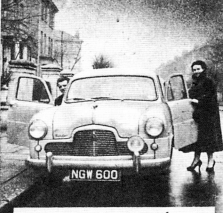

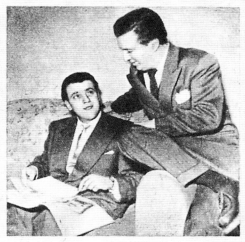

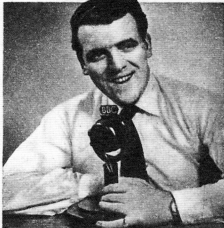

Jacky watched Grainne making lampshades, her favourite pastime. Éamonn's hobbies are photography, golf, squash.

NGW 600

"Coming for a drive?" Éamonn asked Jacky. T.V. and film commentaries are among his activities.

Jacky listened to Éamonn discussing his new radio programme 'Welcome to Britain' with his manager Mr Edward Sommerfield.

Saturday night Sports Report, in which Éamonn stars, is said to have a listening public of more than twelve million people.

NEW SPRING BOOKS

Here are some suggestions for your holiday reading

by Jill Russell

REBEL
BY

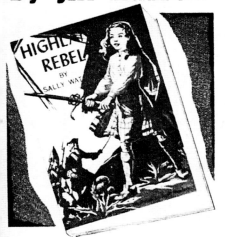

THE new book I've enjoyed reading most during the last few weeks is HIGHLAND REBEL, by Sally Watson (Hutchinson, 10/6). It's a historical novel, and the heroine, Lauren Cameron, is a devoted follower of Charles Edward Stuart, better known as Bonnie Prince Charlie. Now I've never been a great admirer of the Young Pretender, but I was fascinated by this story, which is really exceptionally exciting and well told. I can thoroughly recommend it to all girls under fourteen years old.

Books for older girls

DANCING SKATES by Constance M. White (Hutchinson, 8/6) is also extremely readable. The characters are well-drawn and the story is an interesting one. It will be of special interest to all those who are fond of ice-skating.

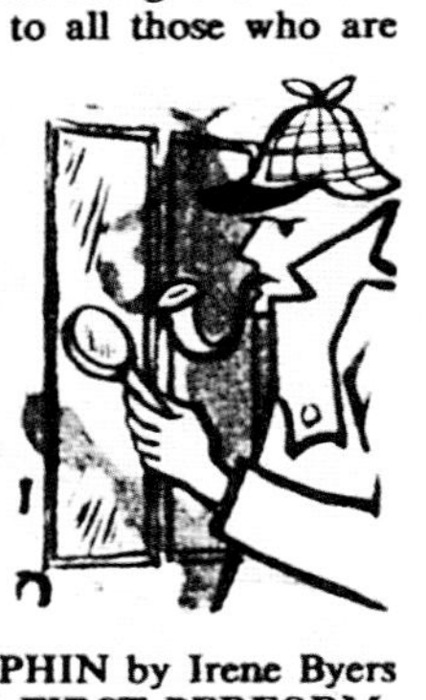

If you like detective stories, read NOREEN'S FIRST CASE by Helen Dawson (published by Dent at 10/6). It's about a young girl working as a detective's assistant and how she solves her first case. Two more entertaining mystery stories are THE SIGN OF THE DOLPHIN by Irene Byers (Hutchinson, 8/6) and FIRST PERFORMANCE by R. E. Masters (Macmillan, 10/6). These stories are about hunting for lost treasure – and in each case the treasure is something very unusual indeed. For those who prefer to read about everyday adventures, with a family background, I suggest FAMILY ON THE TIDE by Captain Frank Knight (Macmillan, 13/6) and ANN'S ALPINE ADVENTURE by Mabel Esther Allan (Hutchinson, 8/6). Both these stories are set in unusual places, but in each case the authors have been really concerned with how people get along together, and the way they deal with the stresses and strains that arise even in the most devoted families.

For younger readers

There are four books which I think the under twelves will enjoy, SUSAN AT SILBARTON by Cecily Sandbach (Hutchinson, 8/6), ALL BECAUSE OF POSY by Kathleen O'Farrell (Blackie, 6/-), STUDY NUMBER SIX by Nancy Breary (Blackie, 8/6), and LITTLE KARIN by Ebba Edskog (Epworth Press, 8/6). The first two are family stories and the third one, as the title suggests, a school story. The fourth book, LITTLE KARIN, is rather more unusual. It's a gentle and charming story about a little orphaned Swedish girl who goes to live with two elderly aunts. If you liked the Heidi stories, I think you will like LITTLE KARIN too.

Books for general interest

Some stories you can read again and again and never get tired of them – the Greek and Roman legends for instance. The same thing is true about our English legends of King Arthur and his Knights, and you will be pleased to hear that a collection of these, retold by Roger Lancelyn Green has just been published by Faber and Faber. KING ARTHUR AND HIS KNIGHTS OF THE ROUND TABLE costs 15/-, which is not expensive for a book you will always want to keep and reread.

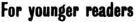

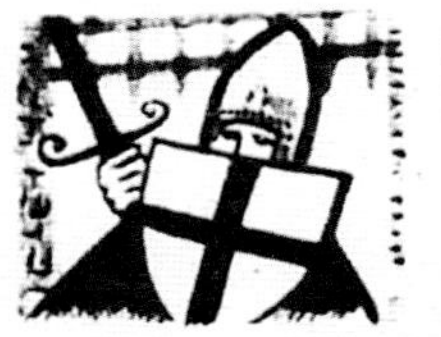

Those who like to collect the classics but have to watch their pocket-money, will be interested in the news that two new titles have been added to the list of Abbey classics (published by Murrays Sales and Service Co.). They are THE QUEEN'S NECKLACE by Alexandre Dumas and LES MISERABLES by Victor Hugo. These cost only 2/6 each.

Pet lovers of all ages should invest in a copy of FIRST AID FOR PETS by Dr. Leon F. Whitney (Faber & Faber, 12/6). It's full of important and up-to-date information about the care of domestic animals, all well set out and easy to follow. If you study it carefully, you need never suffer that dreadful feeling of helplessness when one of your pets falls ill.

The GIRL novels

TO LET
Belle of the Ballet's Gala Performance

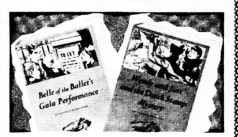

Finally, I'd like to remind you that copies of the GIRL novels (Hulton Press) are still available. The books are WENDY AND JINX IN THE DUTCH STAMP MYSTERY and BELLE OF THE BALLET'S GALA PERFORMANCE. They are both excellent value at 7/6. There is another GIRL book on sale at the moment —the GIRL BOOK OF MODERN ADVENTURES. Published by Hulton Press, this is full of really thrilling stories and only costs 6/-.

★ **(If you are interested in books, you should enter for the Brock Book Competition, which is being run by Brockhampton Press, between April 24th and May 11th. Your local newsagent will be able to give you all the details.)**

BEGINNING TODAY—A THRILLING NEW SERIAL!

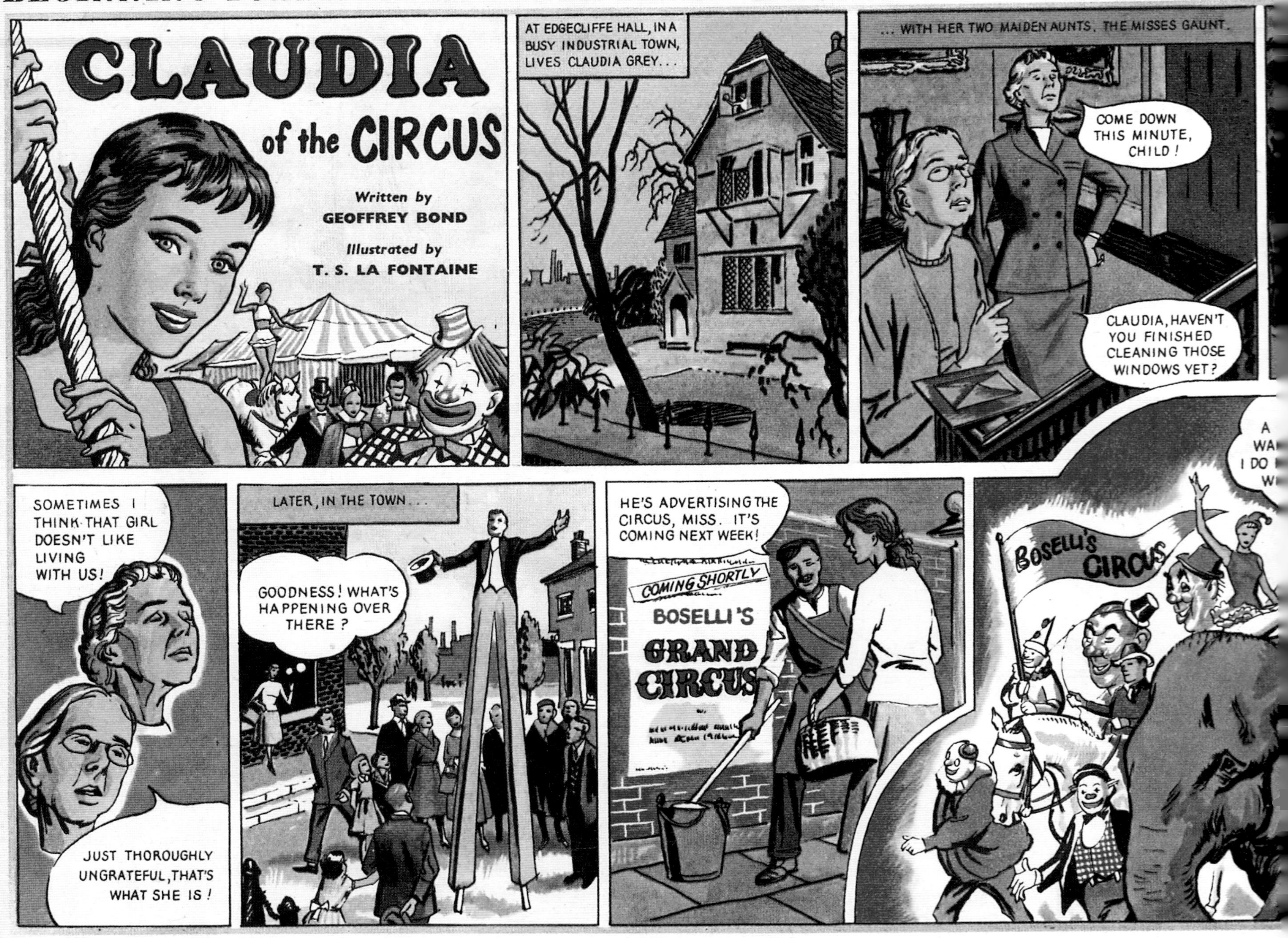

CLAUDIA of the CIRCUS
Written by GEOFFREY BOND
Illustrated by T. S. LA FONTAINE
AT EDGECLIFFE HALL, IN A BUSY INDUSTRIAL TOWN, LIVES CLAUDIA GREY...
... WITH HER TWO MAIDEN AUNTS, THE MISSES GAUNT.
COME DOWN THIS MINUTE, CHILD!
CLAUDIA, HAVEN'T YOU FINISHED CLEANING THOSE WINDOWS YET?
SOMETIMES I THINK THAT GIRL DOESN'T LIKE LIVING WITH US!
JUST THOROUGHLY UNGRATEFUL, THAT'S WHAT SHE IS!
LATER, IN THE TOWN...
GOODNESS! WHAT'S HAPPENING OVER THERE?
HE'S ADVERTISING THE CIRCUS, MISS. IT'S COMING NEXT WEEK!
COMING SHORTLY
BOSELLI'S
GRAND CIRCUS
BOSELLI'S CIRCUS

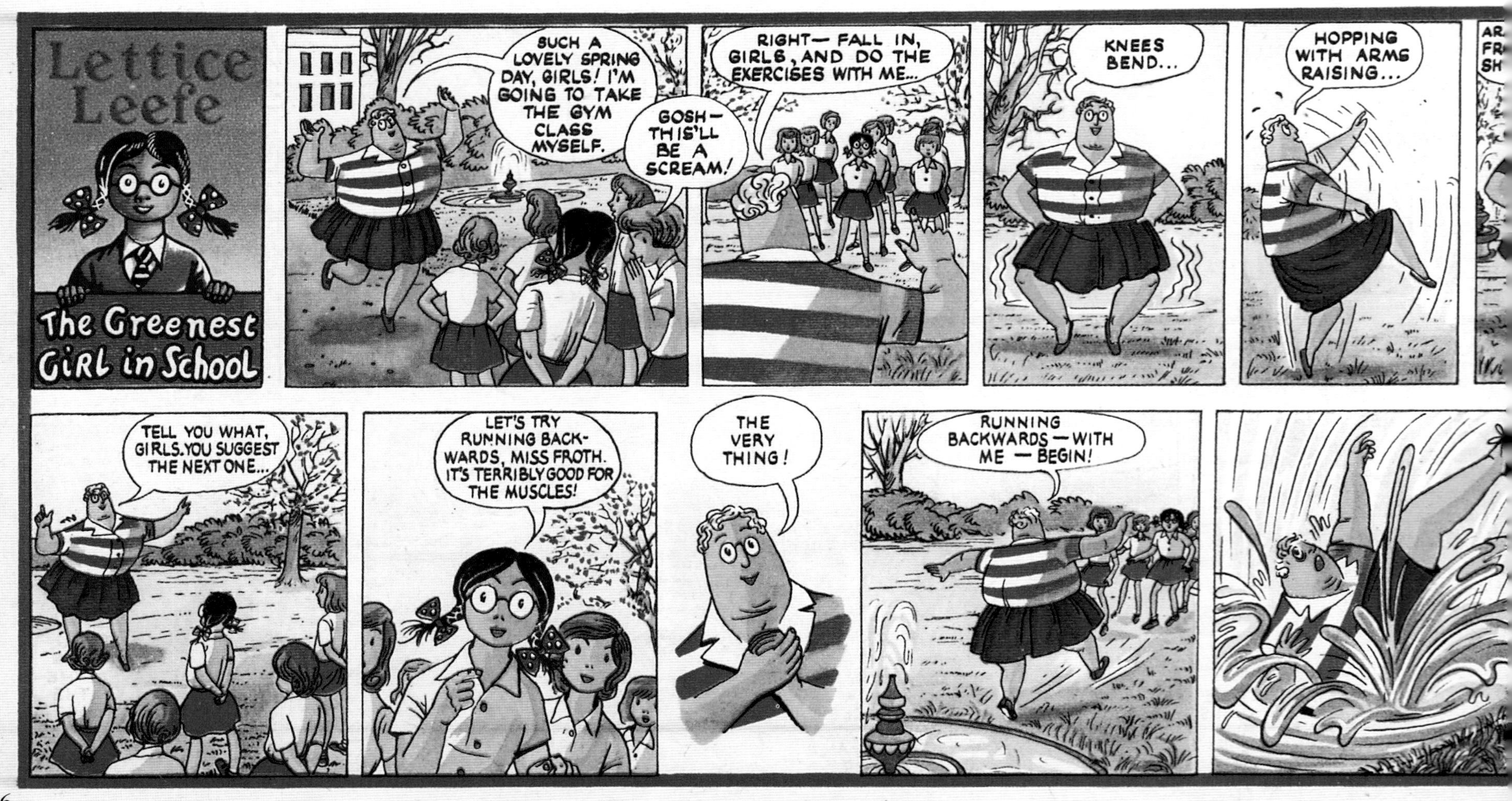

Lettice Leefe
The Greenest Girl in School
SUCH A LOVELY SPRING DAY, GIRLS! I'M GOING TO TAKE THE GYM CLASS MYSELF.
GOSH—THIS'LL BE A SCREAM!
RIGHT— FALL IN, GIRLS, AND DO THE EXERCISES WITH ME...
KNEES BEND...
HOPPING WITH ARMS RAISING...
TELL YOU WHAT, GIRLS. YOU SUGGEST THE NEXT ONE...
LET'S TRY RUNNING BACKWARDS, MISS FROTH. IT'S TERRIBLY GOOD FOR THE MUSCLES!
THE VERY THING!
RUNNING BACKWARDS—WITH ME—BEGIN!

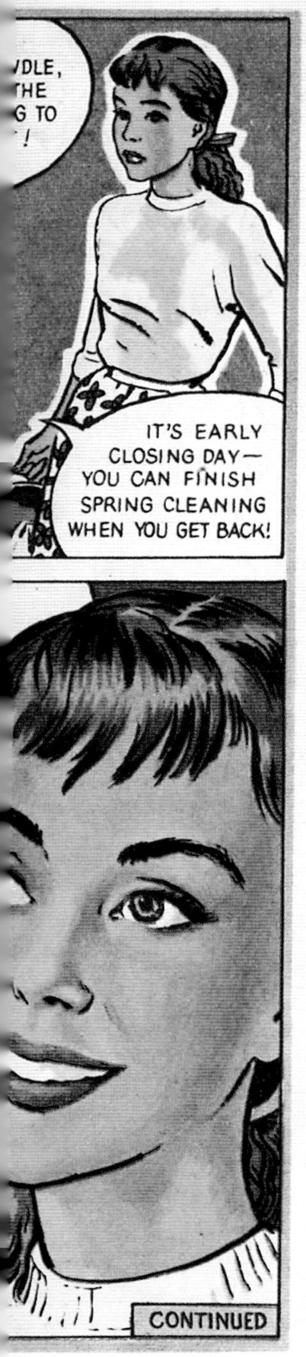
IT'S EARLY CLOSING DAY— YOU CAN FINISH SPRING CLEANING WHEN YOU GET BACK!
CONTINUED

continued on page 68

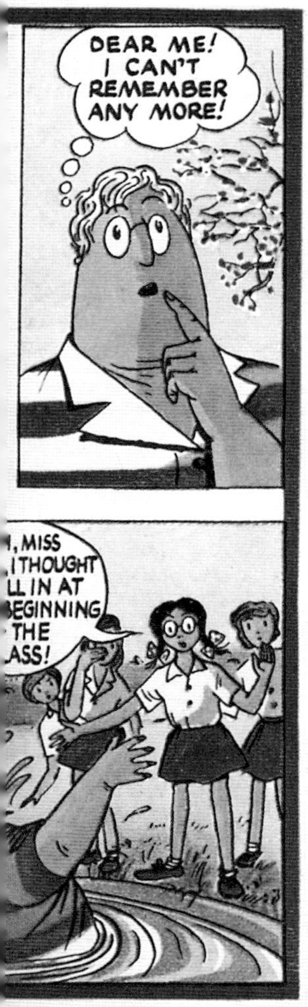
DEAR ME! I CAN'T REMEMBER ANY MORE!

Girl Picture Gallery

No. 259

Here is a portrait of a very popular star. You will soon be able to see him in 'Doctor at Large' at your local cinema.

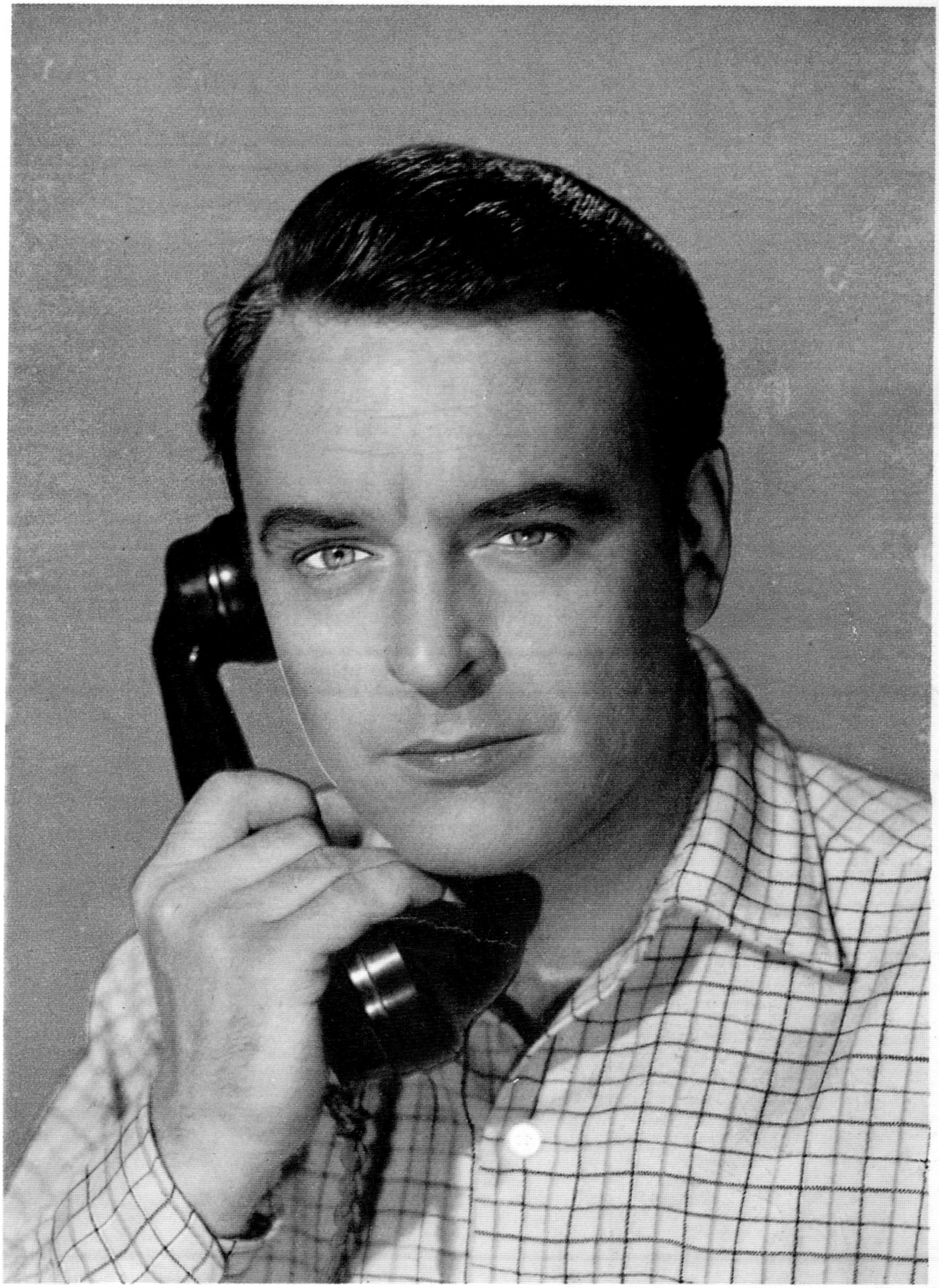

Rank Organisation

DONALD SINDEN

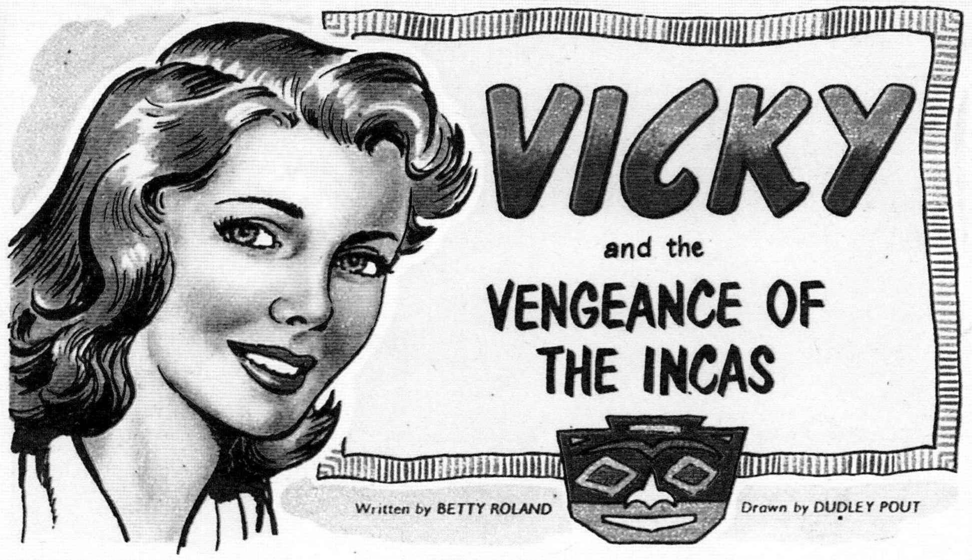
VICKY
and the
VENGEANCE OF THE INCAS
Written by BETTY ROLAND
Drawn by DUDLEY POUT

Vicky and her father, Professor Curtis, are on their way to find David Hume, who went in search of Inca gold. When they reach Rio de Janeiro they are offered a lift to Peru in a private plane. The plane gets out of control so Vicky and her father bale out. They land safely and, seeing the plane still airborne, realize it had been a plot to kill them. They find a village where everybody is ill with fever. Vicky and her father nurse everyone back to health, and the Indians bring gifts as tokens of their gratitude. Among them is an ancient Inca seal, and the Professor begs them to tell him where it came from. Eventually, they agree to take him there.

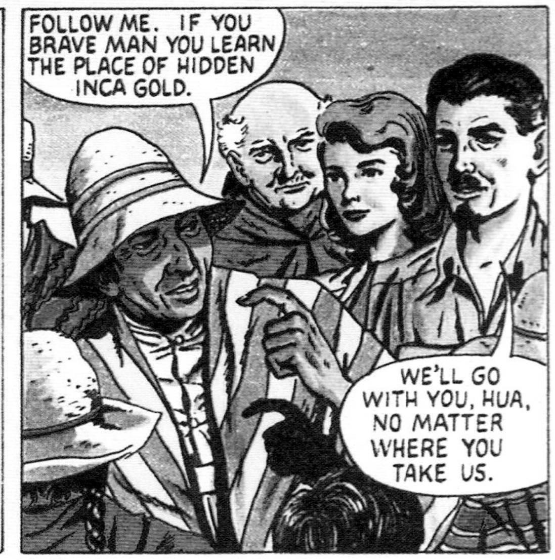
FOLLOW ME. IF YOU BRAVE MAN YOU LEARN THE PLACE OF HIDDEN INCA GOLD.
WE'LL GO WITH YOU, HUA, NO MATTER WHERE YOU TAKE US.

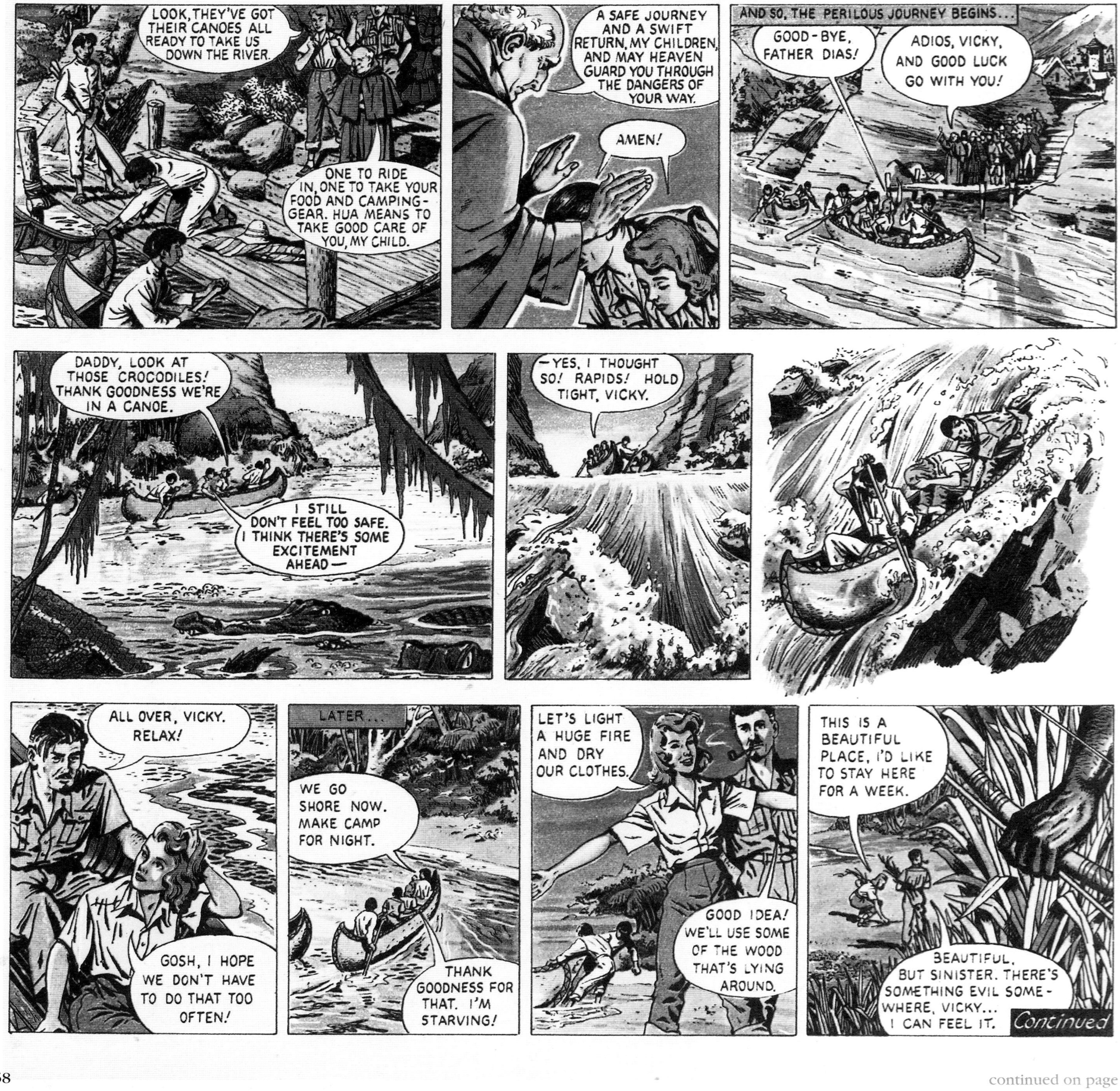
LOOK, THEY'VE GOT THEIR CANOES ALL READY TO TAKE US DOWN THE RIVER.
ONE TO RIDE IN, ONE TO TAKE YOUR FOOD AND CAMPING-GEAR. HUA MEANS TO TAKE GOOD CARE OF YOU, MY CHILD.
A SAFE JOURNEY AND A SWIFT RETURN, MY CHILDREN, AND MAY HEAVEN GUARD YOU THROUGH THE DANGERS OF YOUR WAY.
AMEN!
AND SO, THE PERILOUS JOURNEY BEGINS...
GOOD-BYE, FATHER DIAS!
ADIOS, VICKY, AND GOOD LUCK GO WITH YOU!
DADDY, LOOK AT THOSE CROCODILES! THANK GOODNESS WE'RE IN A CANOE.
I STILL DON'T FEEL TOO SAFE. I THINK THERE'S SOME EXCITEMENT AHEAD—
—YES, I THOUGHT SO! RAPIDS! HOLD TIGHT, VICKY.
ALL OVER, VICKY. RELAX!
GOSH, I HOPE WE DON'T HAVE TO DO THAT TOO OFTEN!
LATER...
WE GO SHORE NOW. MAKE CAMP FOR NIGHT.
THANK GOODNESS FOR THAT. I'M STARVING!
LET'S LIGHT A HUGE FIRE AND DRY OUR CLOTHES.
GOOD IDEA! WE'LL USE SOME OF THE WOOD THAT'S LYING AROUND.
THIS IS A BEAUTIFUL PLACE, I'D LIKE TO STAY HERE FOR A WEEK.
BEAUTIFUL, BUT SINISTER. THERE'S SOMETHING EVIL SOME-WHERE, VICKY... I CAN FEEL IT.
Continued

continued on page 7

GIRL POETRY COMPETITION

Here are a few of the poems composed by readers which were awarded prizes in our Spring Flower Poetry Competition.

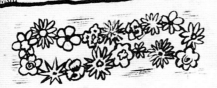

MY SPRING NECKLACE

by Julia Nepenthe Monro (age 8)

Goodbye, Heliotrope!
Spring is here!
With the blushing anemones
And the primroses dear.
Amaryllis dancing,
Cowslips prancing,
Gay polyanthus and narcissi clustering,
While the shy violets hide
And the rain comes peltering, peltering!

Snowdrops so delicate, green and white,
When the snow melts, then you are in sight!
I hope you like girls,
For you are my pearls,
Jewels of light,
Oh so bright!
With heads so graceful and stalks so thin,
Pretty and beautiful, I invite you in!

Aconites and celandines,
Vagabond or rare,
March to me in your golden lines
To match my golden hair!
Crocuses coming like coloured swords,
Up from the wet brown earth,
Fit for the sheaths of laughing lords.
To welcome the springtime's birth!

Violets, violets,
Come to the ball
From where you are sitting
In your dainty green hall!
Put on your purple dress
And your pretty green shawl
To dance with your partner
And be seen by all!

In between the moss
And in between the green,
Lilies of the valley
Are hardly to be seen.
Mummy comes to pick them,
So do I,
And because they're so beautiful,
We wish they wouldn't die!

Daffidowndillies,
Like the rays of the sun,
You must follow my lilies
And do what they've done!
Come into my necklace and fit in, please do,
Sweet Daffidowndillies,
Because I love you!

May-blossoms flowering
With their petals showering,
Dazzling me
So that I can't see!
Almond, blackthorn, pear, wild cherry;
And apple-blossoms with a chaffinch merry!
Tchi-tchirree tchi-tchee!

Tulips, and bluebells,
Music they make,
For springtime's beauty and my sake!
Tulips for gongs and bluebells' sweet chimes,
For wild dancing and happy times!

SPRING MORNING

by Susan Craggs (age 14)

The hoary grass blazes coldly with diamonds,
The pale, white rays of the dawn shiver
And dance among the shadows of the stirring
sycamore, new-leafed.
Ripples go scudding down the river,
Washing the reeds and reflecting the
pinky-pewter of the sky;
Three shelduck go whirling by
And dawn breaks.

• • •

Down by the old, cracked, paint-peeling
cucumber-frame.
Recumbent in the damp, earthy shade
Of the old wooden fence, bloom crocuses,
their gold and purple cups
Held stiff and straight, each little
leaf blade
A quivering variegated pennon, writhing like
wisps of smoke;
Crimped pistils, gold as egg yolk
Mouth like snakes.

Gold daffodils toss among the pink peach-
blossoms,
Nodding their yellow heads to the dawn.
The last late snowdrops, ruffled like a
lady's skirts and touched with green,
Prick pale frosted leaves around the lawn.
Clusters of grape hyacinths, blue as summer
skies, stately and proud;
Young narcissi, like a cloud,
Quiver and shake.

• • •

White and red cherry blossom petals bloom
and snow:
The hawthorn hedge, alive with young green
Hides in its shady banks and wealth of
scent; primroses and violets.
Nodding cowslips, gracious as a queen
Crown their goffered leaves with gold:
celandines look starlike by the ponds:
The willows droop new green fronds
Into the lake.

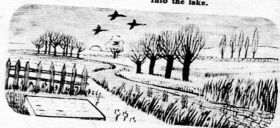

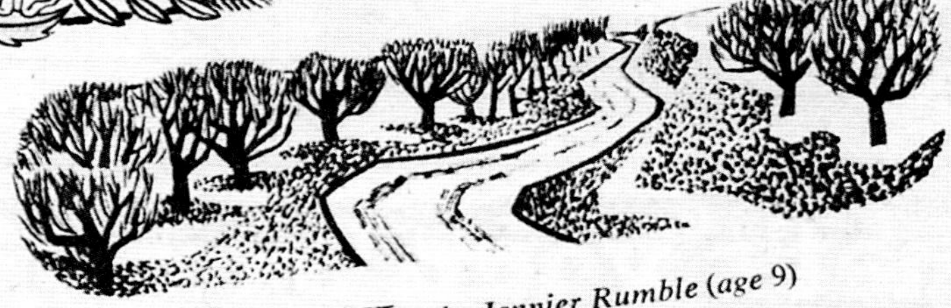

SORREL

by Jennier Rumble (age 9)

Like a gleaming silver carpet,
Up the bank the sorrel grows.
Through the woods and
o'er the mountain,
All the Spring the sorrel grows.

When darkness covers all
the mountain
Still I seem to see it glow.
Glowing like a silver fountain
Or a carpet of white snow.

WHAT'S YOUR WORRY?

A trouble shared is a trouble halved, so if there's something on your mind – anything at all – why not tell us about it and our experts will see what they can do to help. Just write to: GIRL, 18 Furnival St., London, E.C.4, and mark your letter WHAT'S YOUR WORRY? No names will be printed – but let us have a stamped, addressed envelope if you would like us to send you a reply by letter.

Eating food we don't like

Q. Do you think it is right that we should be made to eat things we don't like? I hate beans, but although my parents know this they always make me eat them.

A. *As a growing girl you need a good, varied, nourishing diet, but there is nothing in beans that you cannot get from other green vegetables. We think that, although too much faddiness about food is a bad thing, everyone has the right to dislike one or two items of diet and find a substitute.*

• • •

How much pocket money?

Q. Could you help my friend and myself with the question of pocket money? We are both fourteen and wonder how much we should be given each week. We know girls who get as much as five shillings and others who only get sixpence. Can you suggest a reasonable amount?

A. *Pocket money depends, to some extent, on the family income. These days the usual amount for girls of your age to receive is between 2/6 and 4/- a week. Younger girls should have less, of course.*

Trying to start a club

Q. Whenever I try to start a little club between my friends and myself it ends in a flop. If I *do* get one going and start giving directions to members some of them walk away saying: "Isn't she bossy, telling us to do this and that?" Is this because I tell them in the wrong way, or do you think it could be some other reason?

A. *People hate being bossed about. We are sure that you hate it yourself. So if you run a club don't give yourself all the responsibility, but be sure to make plans for it with the others. Perhaps you make the mistake of trying to run your club by telling others what to do. If you discuss plans together you can still take the lead (if you feel no one else will) without actually ordering them about and, at the same time, help the others to take an interest in the club.*

• • •

Going to a new school

Q. I shall soon be moving to a new school which is much bigger than the one I attend now. I know it's silly, but I feel very worried about going to it for the first time. Can you help me?

A. *You are almost bound to feel strange at first in your new school, but if you take a real interest in what is going on and try to be quietly friendly to all the other pupils you will soon feel at home.*

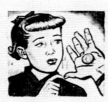

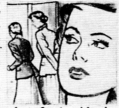

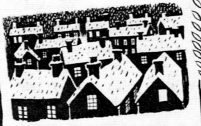

WAITING FOR SPRING

by Hilary Jane Brill (age 11)

Will it ever stop snowing?
Out of the grey-leaden sky,
Will we ever see scillas again?
Blue as the evening sky.

• • •

Will the buds ever open?
Will the birds ever sing?
When I see crocuses growing,
Then I shall know it is spring.

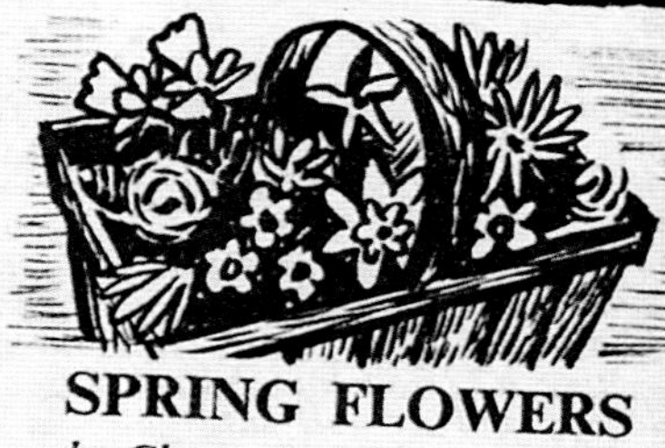

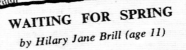

SPRING FLOWERS

by Cherry Burroughs (age 12)

Come with me to Covent Garden,
Just about the break of day
There to catch a glimpse of springtime,
Sending winter's gloom away
Box on box of shining treasure,
Every heart with gladness fills,
For the sunshine comes to London,
With the golden daffodils.

• • •

Flower bells ring from St. Mary's,
Filling all the frosty air,
Chiming out a joyful message,
Spreading glory everywhere,
Soon the trees will wear green dresses,
Lambs will skip on April hills,
But the springtime comes to London,
With the golden daffodils.

Registered at the G.P.O. for transmission by Magazine Post to Canada (including Newfoundland), GIRL printed in Great Britain by Eric Bemrose Ltd., Long Lane, Liverpool 9, for the Proprietors and Publishers, Hulton Press Ltd., 161/166 Fleet Street, London, E.C.4. Sole agents for Australia and New Zealand, Gordon & Gotch (A/sia) Ltd.; South Africa, Central News Agency Ltd. Subscription Rate: Inland, 12 months 28/2; 6 months 14/1: abroad, 12 months 26/-; 6 months 13/-. Postage for single copies: 2d.; Canada 1d. You can have GIRL sent to any address in this country for one year for 28/2, abroad for 26/-, and to Canada at a

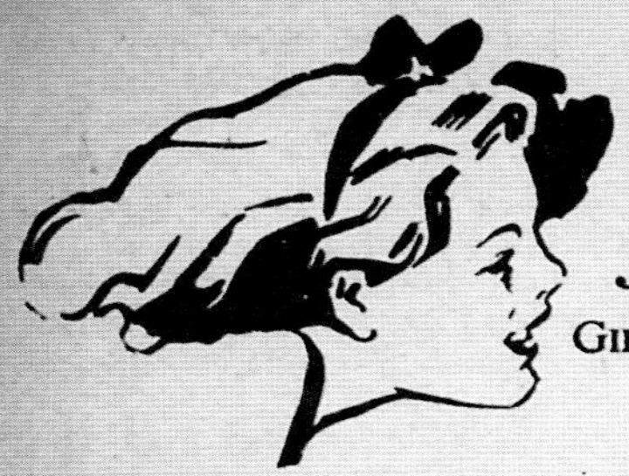

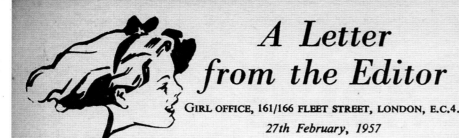

A Letter from the Editor

GIRL OFFICE, 161/166 FLEET STREET, LONDON, E.C.4.

27th February, 1957

THIS week, on page fourteen, we are publishing photographs of last year's painting competition winners, showing what a wonderful time they had in the beautiful city of Venice.

If you enjoy reading don't forget copies of the GIRL novels about your favourite characters are still obtainable at all booksellers. They are 'Belle of the Ballet's Gala Performance' and 'Wendy and Jinx and the Dutch Stamp Mystery'. I am sure you will find them exciting reading.

Also this week an exciting new serial starts on page twelve. It's about a girl who is a 'Junior Model'. I do hope you will enjoy it.

Yours sincerely,

Marcus Morris

SOLVE OUR PICTURE QUIZ

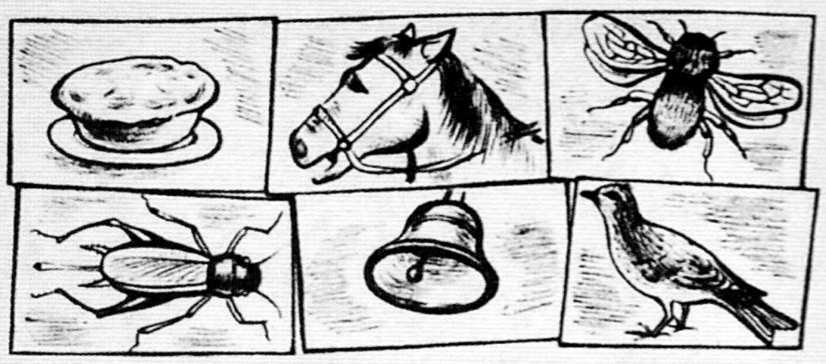

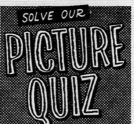

WONDERFUL PRIZES TO WIN!

On the right we have printed a list of common sayings, complete except for one word. Above you will see six drawings, each one represents the missing word in one of the sayings. All you have to do to win one of our grand prizes is to complete the sayings.

HERE ARE THE RULES:

All you have to do is complete the six sayings with the help of the illustrations above. When you have done this, write the solutions on a postcard and remember to use your very best handwriting. Points will be given for handwriting as well as for the correct answers. Send your postcard to: – Competition No. 9, GIRL, Long Lane, Aintree, Liverpool 9, to arrive there not later than 12th March. This competition is FREE! The Editor's and judges' decision is final. No correspondence will be entered into.

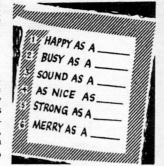

1. HAPPY AS A ______
2. BUSY AS A ______
3. SOUND AS A ______
4. AS NICE AS ______
5. STRONG AS A ______
6. MERRY AS A ______

FOR GIRL ADVENTURERS

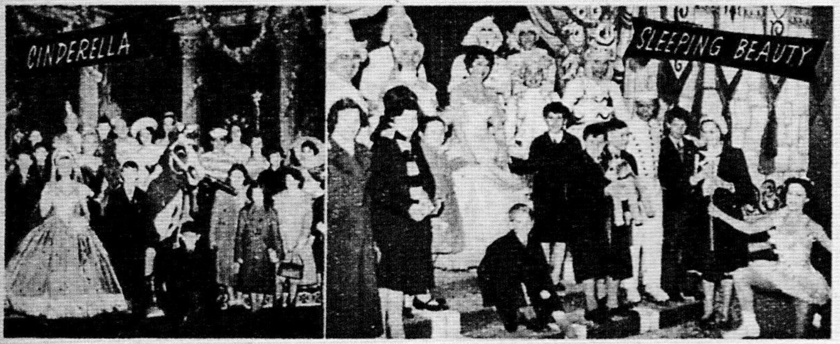
CINDERELLA
SLEEPING BEAUTY

Around and about with GIRL Club

THERE'S always something going on in GIRL Club! During the pantomime season members all over the country have been on similar trips such as these two groups here, seen in the first picture, backstage at 'Cinderella on Ice' at Shrewsbury, and in the second with the principals of 'Sleeping Beauty' at Leicester. Our club members certainly enjoy themselves.

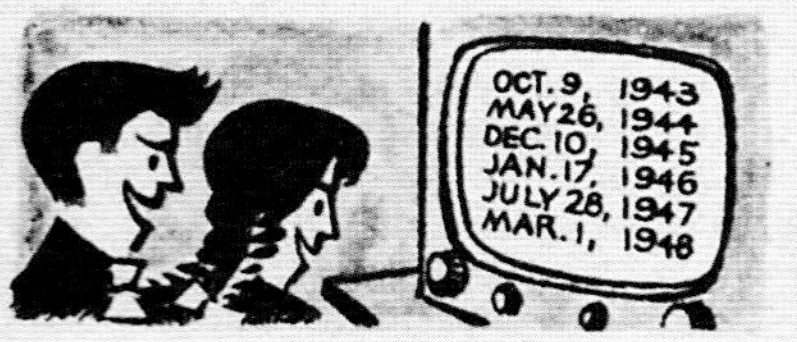
OCT. 9, 1943
MAY 26, 1944
DEC. 10, 1945
JAN. 17, 1946
JULY 28, 1947
MAR. 1, 1948

If you are a GIRL Adventurer and your birthdate appears in this week's list, you are entitled to a FREE birthday gift! Choose it from the following: stamp album, propelling pencil, stationery folder, bicycle bell, ball point pen, coloured pencils or GIRL handbag badge. Then state your choice on a postcard, giving us your name, address and club number and the date you were born and post it to: BIRTHDATES (24) GIRL Club, Long Lane, Aintree, Liverpool, 9. Your postcard must reach us by Thursday, 7th March. Overseas members whose birthdates appear above will receive their presents automatically.

READER'S LETTER

5/- will be paid for every reader's letter printed on this page.

★

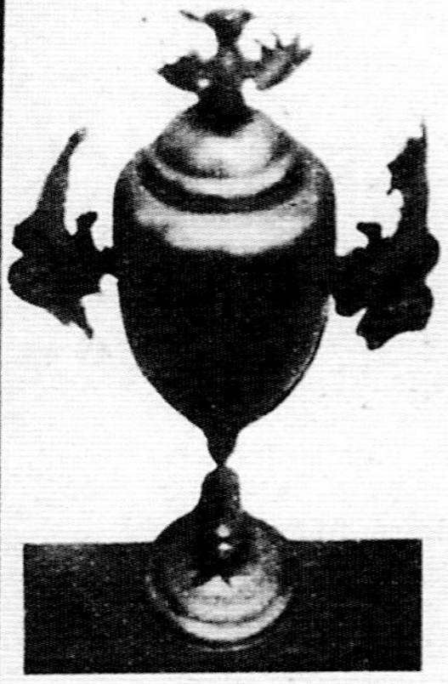

A much travelled Reader

I WAS born in Nairobi, and flew to Egypt at three weeks old. I continued to travel with my parents. One of the places we went to was Cha Kwo Ling (near Kowloon), where we were presented with the cup in the picture for being the first white people there.

We also travelled to Shanghai, Hong Kong, Lagos, Gold Coast and then back to England. Mummy and Daddy have come back to England for good, but my three brothers, my sister and myself intend to go back overseas. – *Pippa Moon, Leigh-on-Sea, Essex.*

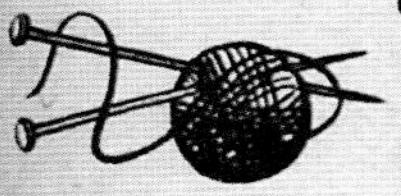

Your last Opportunity!

Our National Knitting Competition closes on 4th March, and this is the last entry coupon we shall be printing in GIRL. We hope you've all enjoyed the competition – we're very much looking forward to judging the entries.

Read the rules carefully

1. Entrants in group I must follow the pattern published last week and choose wool made by one of the firms on the list. Entrants in groups II and III must choose patterns produced by one of the firms on the same list and follow the instructions inside, using the wool specified.
2. The coupon on this page must be filled in by you and signed by a parent, guardian or teacher in the place marked. The label from the wool you used should be stuck firmly in the space provided and the whole coupon pinned carefully to your entry before it is sent to us. If you are in either group II or III enclose the pattern you used with your entry.
3. All entries should be sent to: **Girl Knitting Competition, GIRL Reader Services, Long Lane, Aintree, Liverpool, 9.** Final closing date of the competition is 4th March, 1957, but we would welcome entries as soon as possible.
4. Entries must be carefully packed. They should be sent in in plain manila envelopes, and the age group of the sender should be marked in capitals on the outside of the envelope. We accept no responsibility for those lost or damaged in transit.
5. Each parcel must contain stamps for the return postage and a self-addressed label.
6. The competition is open to all girls under the age of seventeen on the closing date. It will be judged by our panel of experts in three different age groups.
   (I) up to and including eleven.
   (II) twelve and thirteen.
   (III) fourteen, fifteen and sixteen.
7. No entries from overseas are eligible.
8. The decision of the Editor and judges is final, and we regret that no correspondence can be entered into regarding any of the entries.

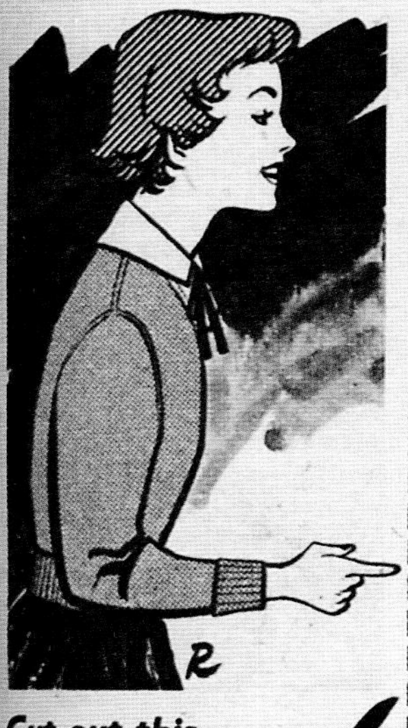

Cut out this coupon and send it with your entry

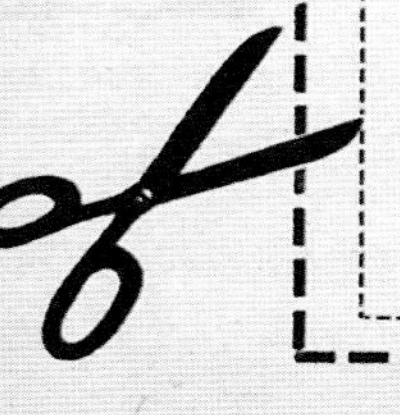

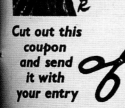

The GIRL Knitting Competition

(Please write in BLOCK capital letters)

This is to certify that this is the original work of: F

Name .... Age ....

Address ....

....

....

Description of entry ....

....

Stick a label here from the wool you use.

Group ....

* **Signature of parent, teacher or guardian**
(* Cross out those which do not apply)

WINNERS

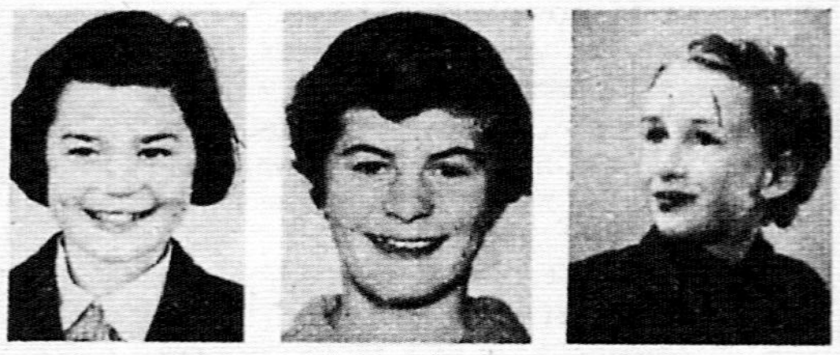

Hilda Murray **Veronica Hurst** **Gillian Jowitt**

In GIRL Competition No. 52 the lucky radio winner was Gillian Jowitt, of New Earswick, Yorkshire, and Veronica Hurst of Southwold, Suffolk, won a rug-making set. Unfortunately, we have no room to print the names of the other winners who won Pik-Paks and GIRL novels, but a full list can be obtained on request from our Liverpool address.

SMALL SISTER by Fiddy

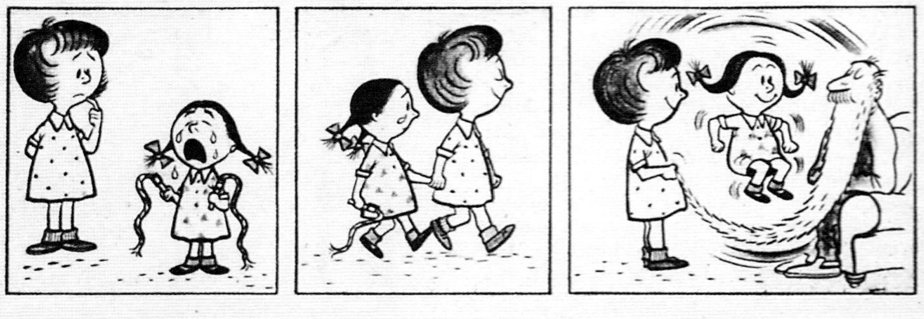

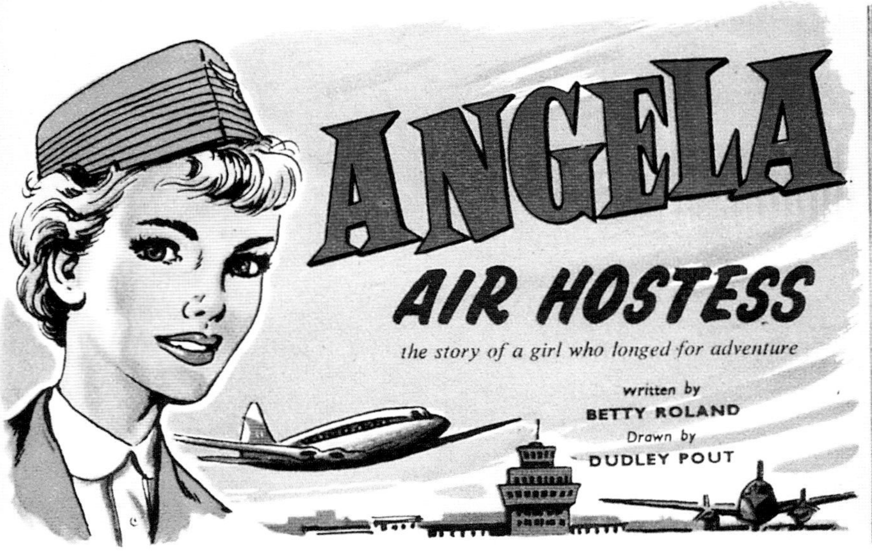
ANGELA
AIR HOSTESS
the story of a girl who longed for adventure
written by
BETTY ROLAND
Drawn by
DUDLEY POUT

Angela Wells lives with her widowed mother and brother Clive. Mrs Wells takes in paying guests in order to make ends meet: Clive, thoughtless, selfish and his mother's favourite, is studying medicine. Angela, training to be an Air Hostess, oversleeps on the morning of her final exams and misses the bus to the Training School. Luckily, one of the senior pilots gives her a lift in his car and, although Angela does not know his name, he makes a terrific impression on her. After qualifying, Angela and her friends go into the Air Crew Club to celebrate, and there Angela again sees the senior pilot. He is talking to her beautiful, spoilt cousin, Sandra. As he leaves . . .

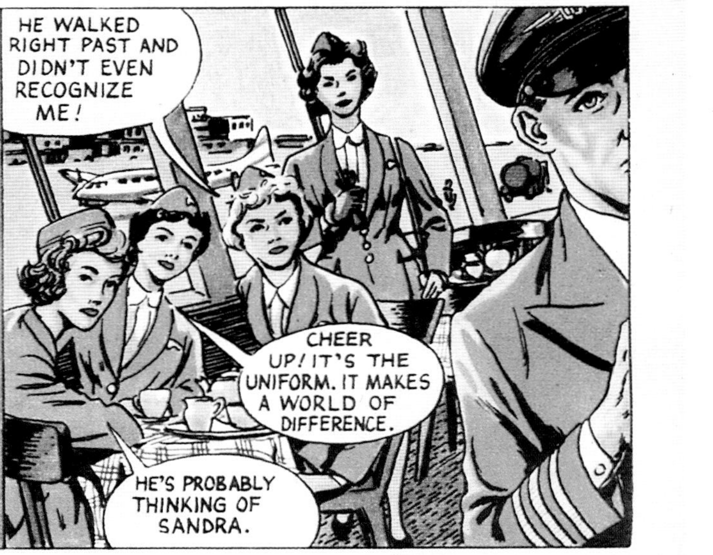
HE WALKED RIGHT PAST AND DIDN'T EVEN RECOGNIZE ME!
CHEER UP! IT'S THE UNIFORM. IT MAKES A WORLD OF DIFFERENCE.
HE'S PROBABLY THINKING OF SANDRA.

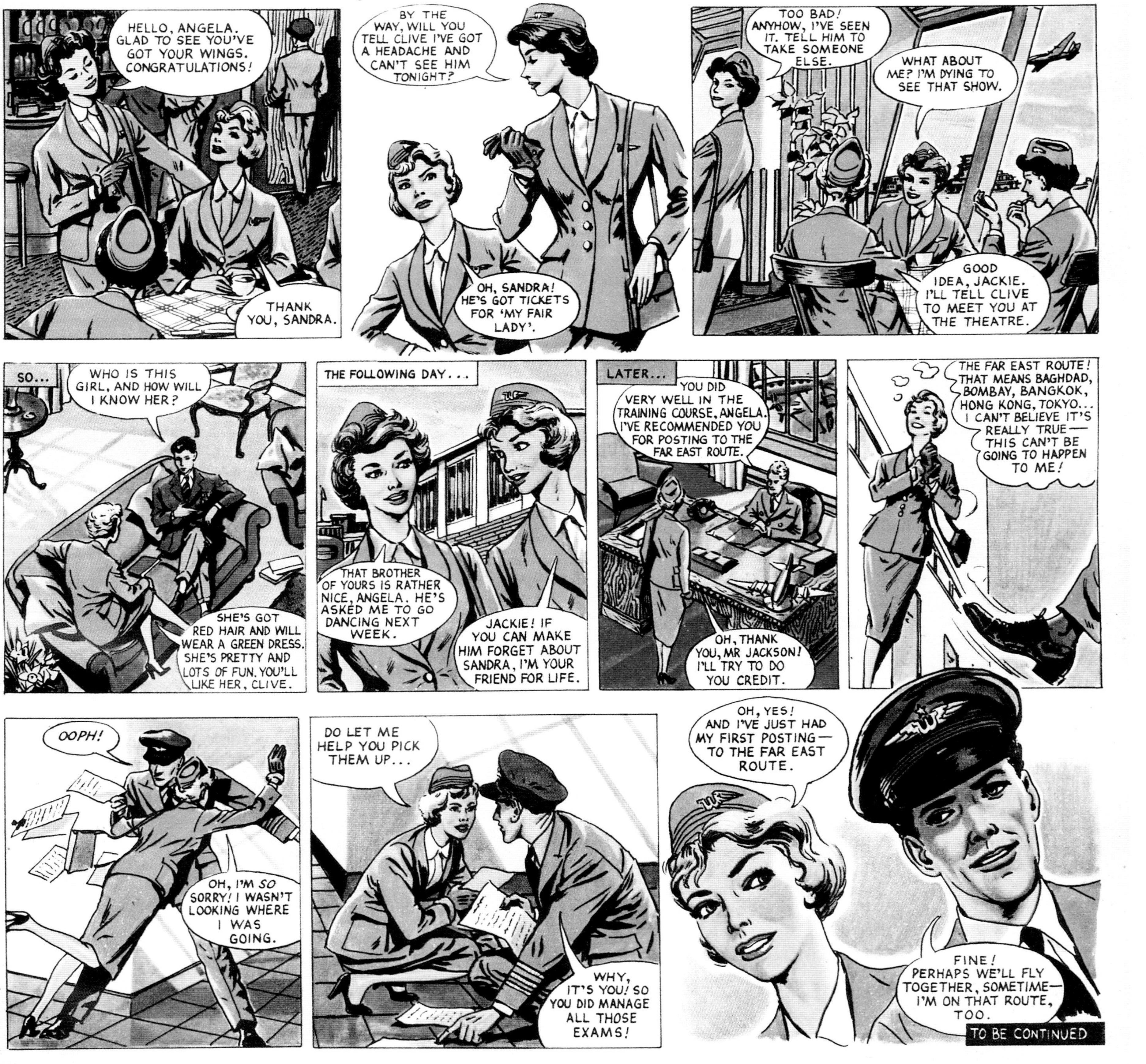
HELLO, ANGELA. GLAD TO SEE YOU'VE GOT YOUR WINGS. CONGRATULATIONS!
THANK YOU, SANDRA.
BY THE WAY, WILL YOU TELL CLIVE I'VE GOT A HEADACHE AND CAN'T SEE HIM TONIGHT?
OH, SANDRA! HE'S GOT TICKETS FOR 'MY FAIR LADY'.
TOO BAD! ANYHOW, I'VE SEEN IT. TELL HIM TO TAKE SOMEONE ELSE.
WHAT ABOUT ME? I'M DYING TO SEE THAT SHOW.
GOOD IDEA, JACKIE. I'LL TELL CLIVE TO MEET YOU AT THE THEATRE.
SO...
WHO IS THIS GIRL, AND HOW WILL I KNOW HER?
SHE'S GOT RED HAIR AND WILL WEAR A GREEN DRESS. SHE'S PRETTY AND LOTS OF FUN. YOU'LL LIKE HER, CLIVE.
THE FOLLOWING DAY...
THAT BROTHER OF YOURS IS RATHER NICE, ANGELA. HE'S ASKED ME TO GO DANCING NEXT WEEK.
JACKIE! IF YOU CAN MAKE HIM FORGET ABOUT SANDRA, I'M YOUR FRIEND FOR LIFE.
LATER...
YOU DID VERY WELL IN THE TRAINING COURSE, ANGELA. I'VE RECOMMENDED YOU FOR POSTING TO THE FAR EAST ROUTE.
OH, THANK YOU, MR JACKSON! I'LL TRY TO DO YOU CREDIT.
THE FAR EAST ROUTE! THAT MEANS BAGHDAD, BOMBAY, BANGKOK, HONG KONG, TOKYO... I CAN'T BELIEVE IT'S REALLY TRUE— THIS CAN'T BE HAPPEN GOING TO HAPPEN TO ME!
OOPH!
OH, I'M SO SORRY! I WASN'T LOOKING WHERE I WAS GOING.
DO LET ME HELP YOU PICK THEM UP...
WHY, IT'S YOU! SO YOU DID MANAGE ALL THOSE EXAMS!
OH, YES! AND I'VE JUST HAD MY FIRST POSTING— TO THE FAR EAST ROUTE.
FINE! PERHAPS WE'LL FLY TOGETHER, SOMETIME— I'M ON THAT ROUTE, TOO.
TO BE CONTINUED

continued on page 79

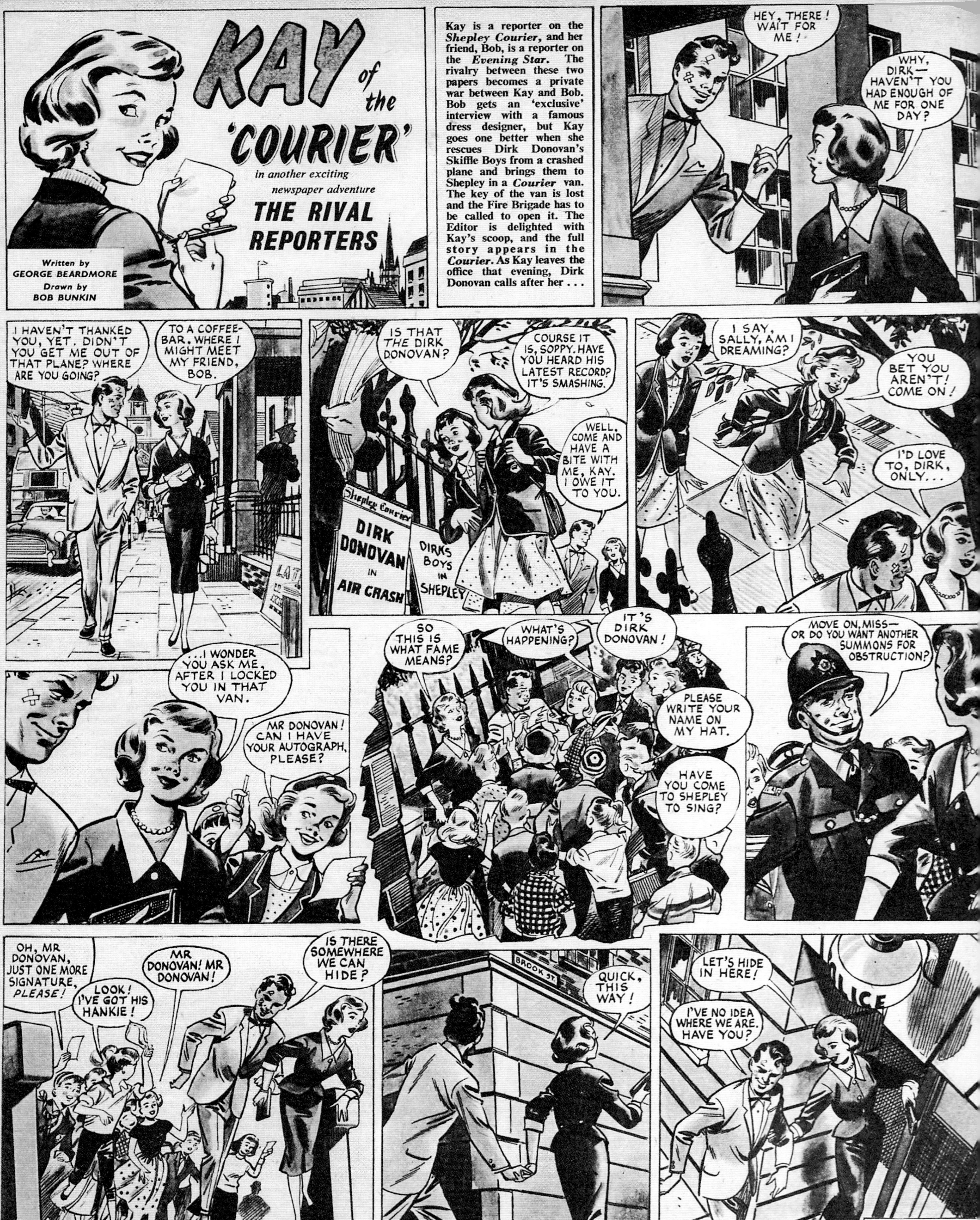
KAY of the 'COURIER'
in another exciting newspaper adventure
THE RIVAL REPORTERS
Written by GEORGE BEARDMORE
Drawn by BOB BUNKIN
Kay is a reporter on the *Shepley Courier*, and her friend, Bob, is a reporter on the *Evening Star*. The rivalry between these two papers becomes a private war between Kay and Bob. Bob gets an 'exclusive' interview with a famous dress designer, but Kay goes one better when she rescues Dirk Donovan's Skiffle Boys from a crashed plane and brings them to Shepley in a *Courier* van. The key of the van is lost and the Fire Brigade has to be called to open it. The Editor is delighted with Kay's scoop, and the full story appears in the *Courier*. As Kay leaves the office that evening, Dirk Donovan calls after her . . .
HEY, THERE! WAIT FOR ME!
WHY, DIRK— HAVEN'T YOU HAD ENOUGH OF ME FOR ONE DAY?
I HAVEN'T THANKED YOU, YET. DIDN'T YOU GET ME OUT OF THAT PLANE? WHERE ARE YOU GOING?
TO A COFFEE-BAR. WHERE I MIGHT MEET MY FRIEND, BOB.
IS THAT *THE* DIRK DONOVAN?
COURSE IT IS, SOPPY. HAVE YOU HEARD HIS LATEST RECORD? IT'S SMASHING.
WELL, COME AND HAVE A BITE WITH ME, KAY. I OWE IT TO YOU.
Shepley Courier
DIRK DONOVAN IN AIR CRASH
DIRKS BOYS IN SHEPLEY
I SAY, SALLY, AM I DREAMING?
YOU BET YOU AREN'T! COME ON!
I'D LOVE TO, DIRK, ONLY...
...I WONDER YOU ASK ME, AFTER I LOCKED YOU IN THAT VAN.
MR DONOVAN! CAN I HAVE YOUR AUTOGRAPH, PLEASE?
SO THIS IS WHAT FAME MEANS?
WHAT'S HAPPENING?
IT'S DIRK DONOVAN!
PLEASE WRITE YOUR NAME ON MY HAT.
HAVE YOU COME TO SHEPLEY TO SING?
MOVE ON, MISS— OR DO YOU WANT ANOTHER SUMMONS FOR OBSTRUCTION?
OH, MR DONOVAN, JUST ONE MORE SIGNATURE, *PLEASE*!
LOOK! I'VE GOT HIS HANKIE!
MR DONOVAN! MR DONOVAN!
IS THERE SOMEWHERE WE CAN HIDE?
BROOK ST.
QUICK, THIS WAY!
LET'S HIDE IN HERE!
I'VE NO IDEA WHERE WE ARE. HAVE YOU?
TO BE CONTINUED.

continued on page 9

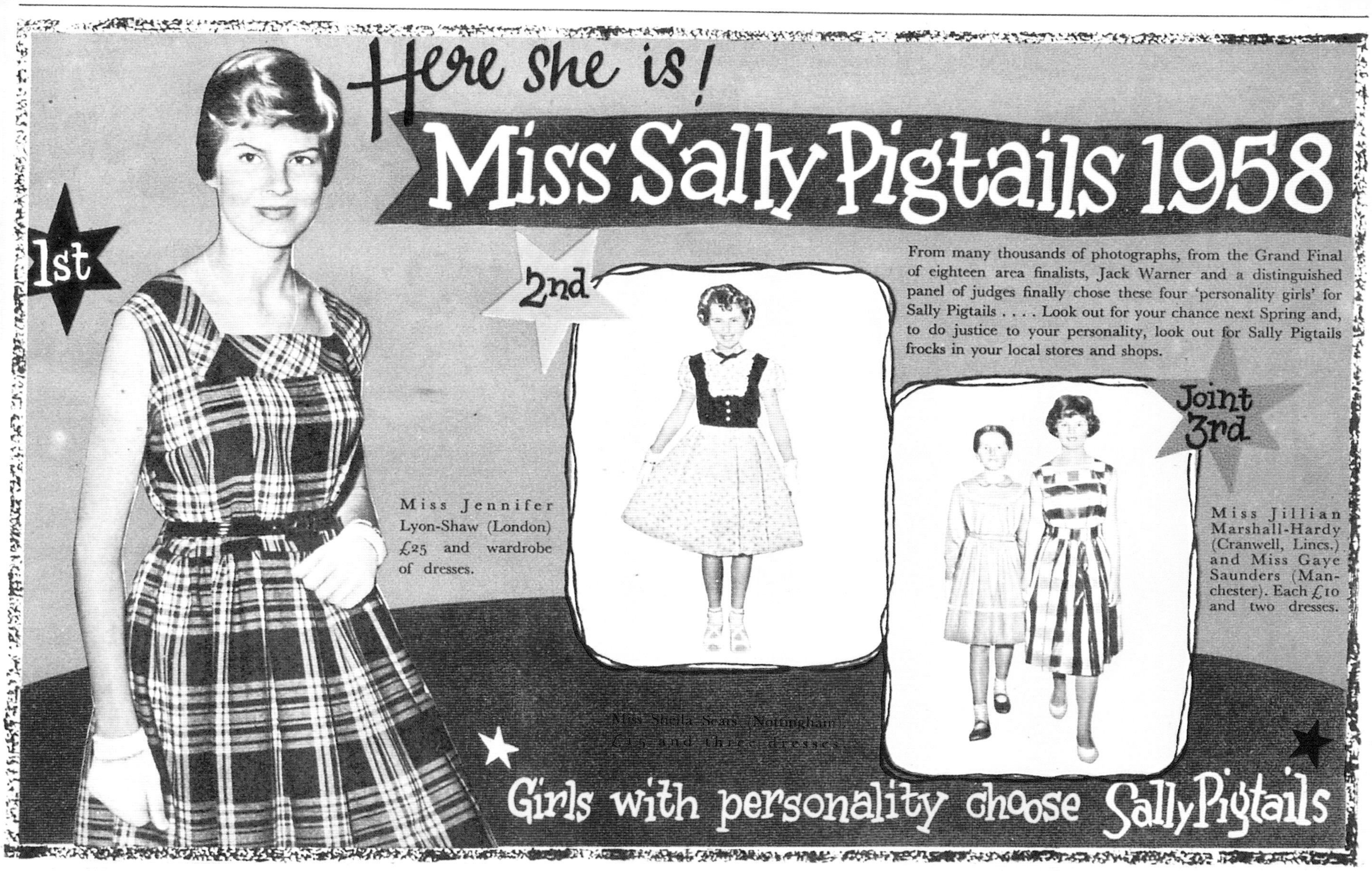
Here she is!
Miss Sally Pigtails 1958
1st
2nd
From many thousands of photographs, from the Grand Final of eighteen area finalists, Jack Warner and a distinguished panel of judges finally chose these four 'personality girls' for Sally Pigtails . . . . Look out for your chance next Spring and, to do justice to your personality, look out for Sally Pigtails frocks in your local stores and shops.
Joint 3rd.
Miss Jennifer Lyon-Shaw (London) £25 and wardrobe of dresses.
Miss Jillian Marshall-Hardy (Cranwell, Lincs.) and Miss Gaye Saunders (Manchester). Each £10 and two dresses.
Miss Sheila Sears (Nottingham) £15 and three dresses.
Girls with personality choose Sally Pigtails

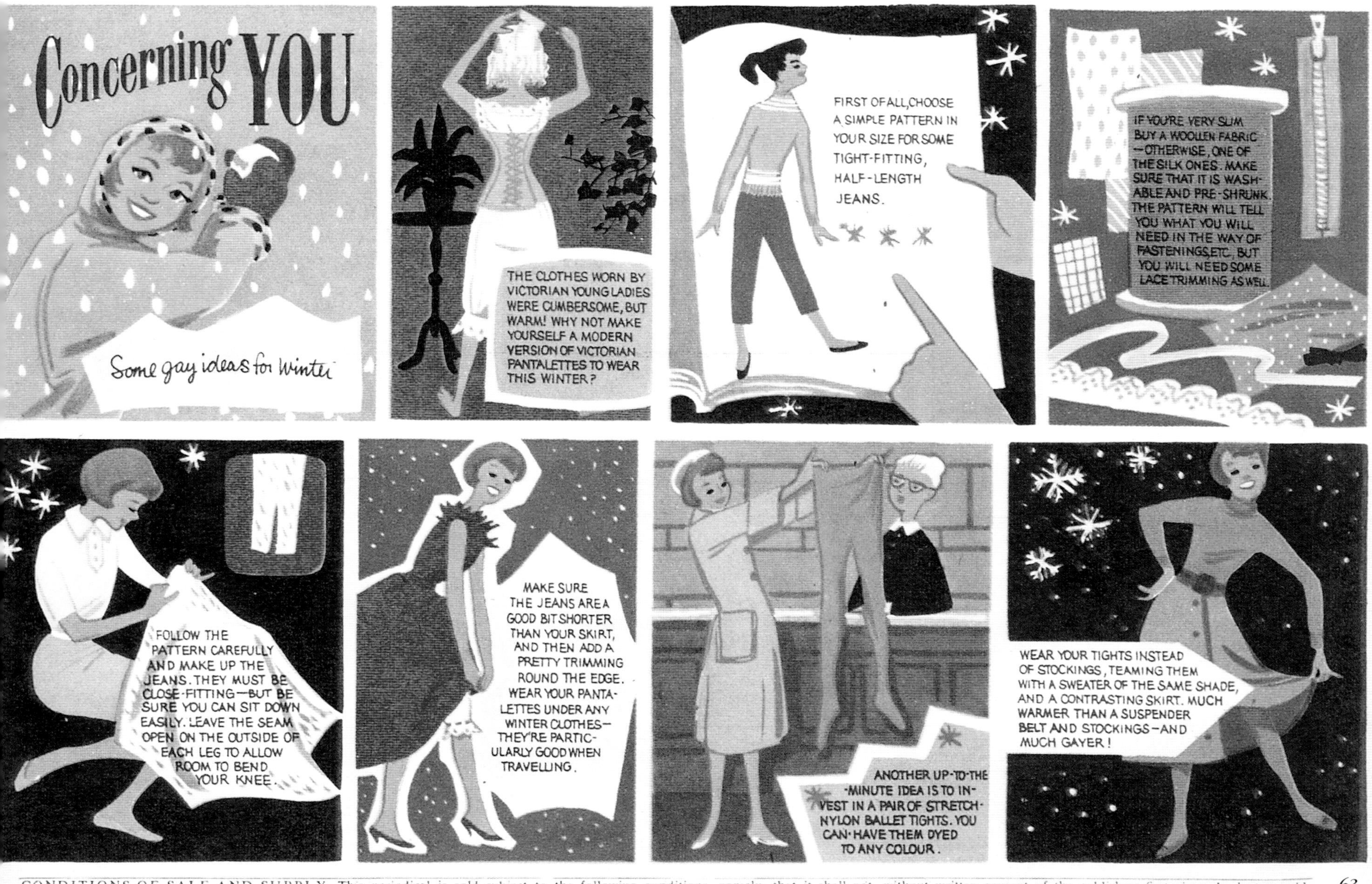
Concerning YOU
Some gay ideas for winter
THE CLOTHES WORN BY VICTORIAN YOUNG LADIES WERE CUMBERSOME, BUT WARM! WHY NOT MAKE YOURSELF A MODERN VERSION OF VICTORIAN PANTALETTES TO WEAR THIS WINTER?
FIRST OF ALL, CHOOSE A SIMPLE PATTERN IN YOUR SIZE FOR SOME TIGHT-FITTING, HALF-LENGTH JEANS.
IF YOU'RE VERY SLIM BUY A WOOLLEN FABRIC —OTHERWISE, ONE OF THE SILK ONES. MAKE SURE THAT IT IS WASHABLE AND PRE-SHRUNK. THE PATTERN WILL TELL YOU WHAT YOU WILL NEED IN THE WAY OF FASTENINGS, ETC, BUT YOU WILL NEED SOME LACE TRIMMING AS WELL.
FOLLOW THE PATTERN CAREFULLY AND MAKE UP THE JEANS. THEY MUST BE CLOSE-FITTING—BUT BE SURE YOU CAN SIT DOWN EASILY. LEAVE THE SEAM OPEN ON THE OUTSIDE OF EACH LEG TO ALLOW ROOM TO BEND YOUR KNEE.
MAKE SURE THE JEANS ARE A GOOD BIT SHORTER THAN YOUR SKIRT, AND THEN ADD A PRETTY TRIMMING ROUND THE EDGE. WEAR YOUR PANTALETTES UNDER ANY WINTER CLOTHES—THEY'RE PARTICULARLY GOOD WHEN TRAVELLING.
ANOTHER UP-TO-THE-MINUTE IDEA IS TO INVEST IN A PAIR OF STRETCH-NYLON BALLET TIGHTS. YOU CAN HAVE THEM DYED TO ANY COLOUR.
WEAR YOUR TIGHTS INSTEAD OF STOCKINGS, TEAMING THEM WITH A SWEATER OF THE SAME SHADE, AND A CONTRASTING SKIRT. MUCH WARMER THAN A SUSPENDER BELT AND STOCKINGS—AND MUCH GAYER!

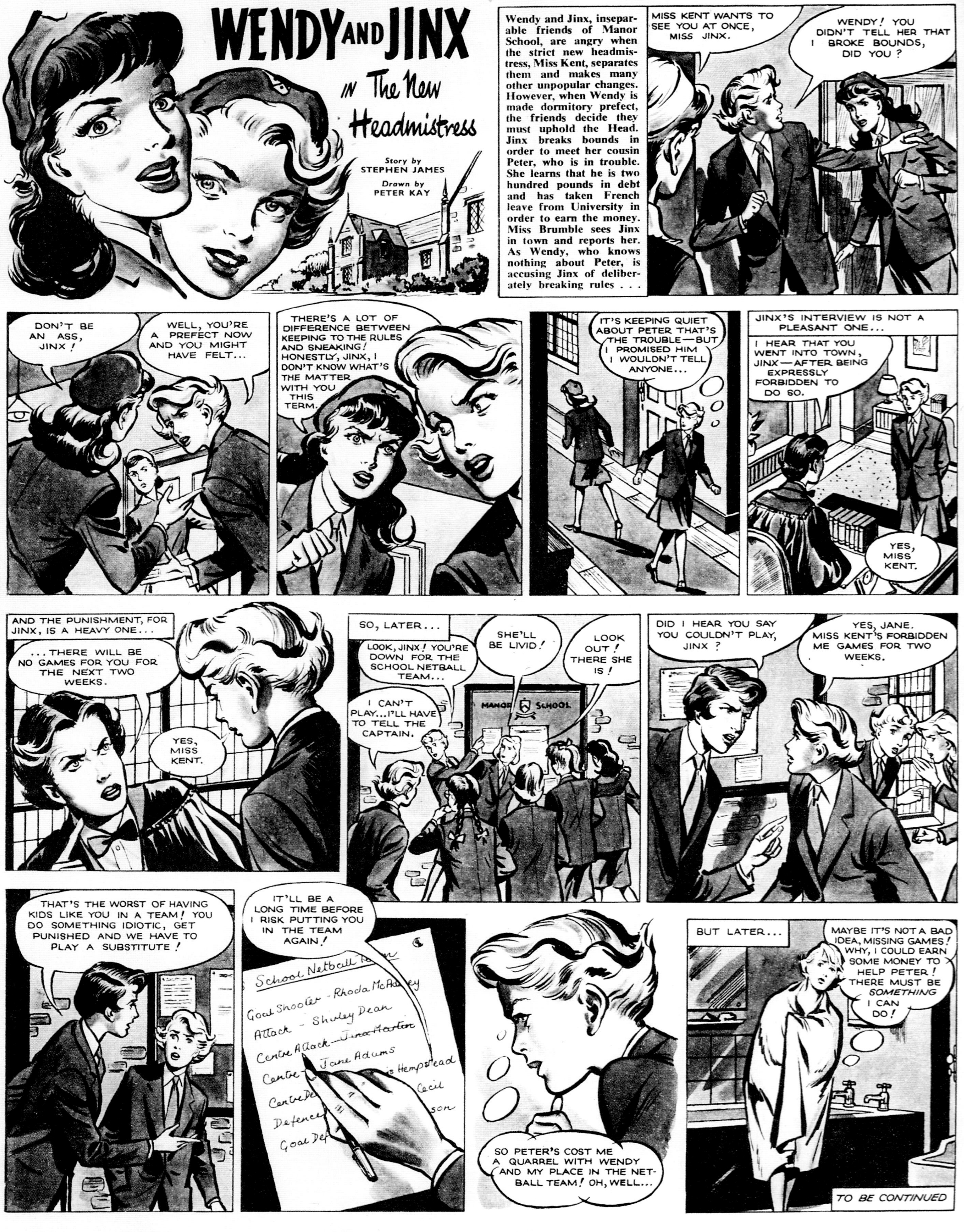

WENDY AND JINX
in The New Headmistress
Story by STEPHEN JAMES
Drawn by PETER KAY
Wendy and Jinx, inseparable friends of Manor School, are angry when the strict new headmistress, Miss Kent, separates them and makes many other unpopular changes. However, when Wendy is made dormitory prefect, the friends decide they must uphold the Head. Jinx breaks bounds in order to meet her cousin Peter, who is in trouble. She learns that he is two hundred pounds in debt and has taken French leave from University in order to earn the money. Miss Brumble sees Jinx in town and reports her. As Wendy, who knows nothing about Peter, is accusing Jinx of deliberately breaking rules . . .
MISS KENT WANTS TO SEE YOU AT ONCE, MISS JINX.
WENDY! YOU DIDN'T TELL HER THAT I BROKE BOUNDS, DID YOU?
DON'T BE AN ASS, JINX!
WELL, YOU'RE A PREFECT NOW AND YOU MIGHT HAVE FELT...
THERE'S A LOT OF DIFFERENCE BETWEEN KEEPING TO THE RULES AND SNEAKING! HONESTLY, JINX, I DON'T KNOW WHAT'S THE MATTER WITH YOU THIS TERM.
IT'S KEEPING QUIET ABOUT PETER THAT'S THE TROUBLE—BUT I PROMISED HIM I WOULDN'T TELL ANYONE...
JINX'S INTERVIEW IS NOT A PLEASANT ONE...
I HEAR THAT YOU WENT INTO TOWN, JINX—AFTER BEING EXPRESSLY FORBIDDEN TO DO SO.
YES, MISS KENT.
AND THE PUNISHMENT, FOR JINX, IS A HEAVY ONE...
...THERE WILL BE NO GAMES FOR YOU FOR THE NEXT TWO WEEKS.
YES, MISS KENT.
SO, LATER...
LOOK, JINX! YOU'RE DOWN FOR THE SCHOOL NETBALL TEAM...
SHE'LL BE LIVID!
LOOK OUT! THERE SHE IS!
I CAN'T PLAY...I'LL HAVE TO TELL THE CAPTAIN.
MANOR SCHOOL
DID I HEAR YOU SAY YOU COULDN'T PLAY, JINX?
YES, JANE. MISS KENT'S FORBIDDEN ME GAMES FOR TWO WEEKS.
THAT'S THE WORST OF HAVING KIDS LIKE YOU IN A TEAM! YOU DO SOMETHING IDIOTIC, GET PUNISHED AND WE HAVE TO PLAY A SUBSTITUTE!
IT'LL BE A LONG TIME BEFORE I RISK PUTTING YOU IN THE TEAM AGAIN!
Attack - Shirley Dean
Jane Adams
SO PETER'S COST ME A QUARREL WITH WENDY AND MY PLACE IN THE NETBALL TEAM! OH, WELL...
BUT LATER...
MAYBE IT'S NOT A BAD IDEA, MISSING GAMES! WHY, I COULD EARN SOME MONEY TO HELP PETER! THERE MUST BE *SOMETHING* I CAN DO!
TO BE CONTINUED

continued on page 80

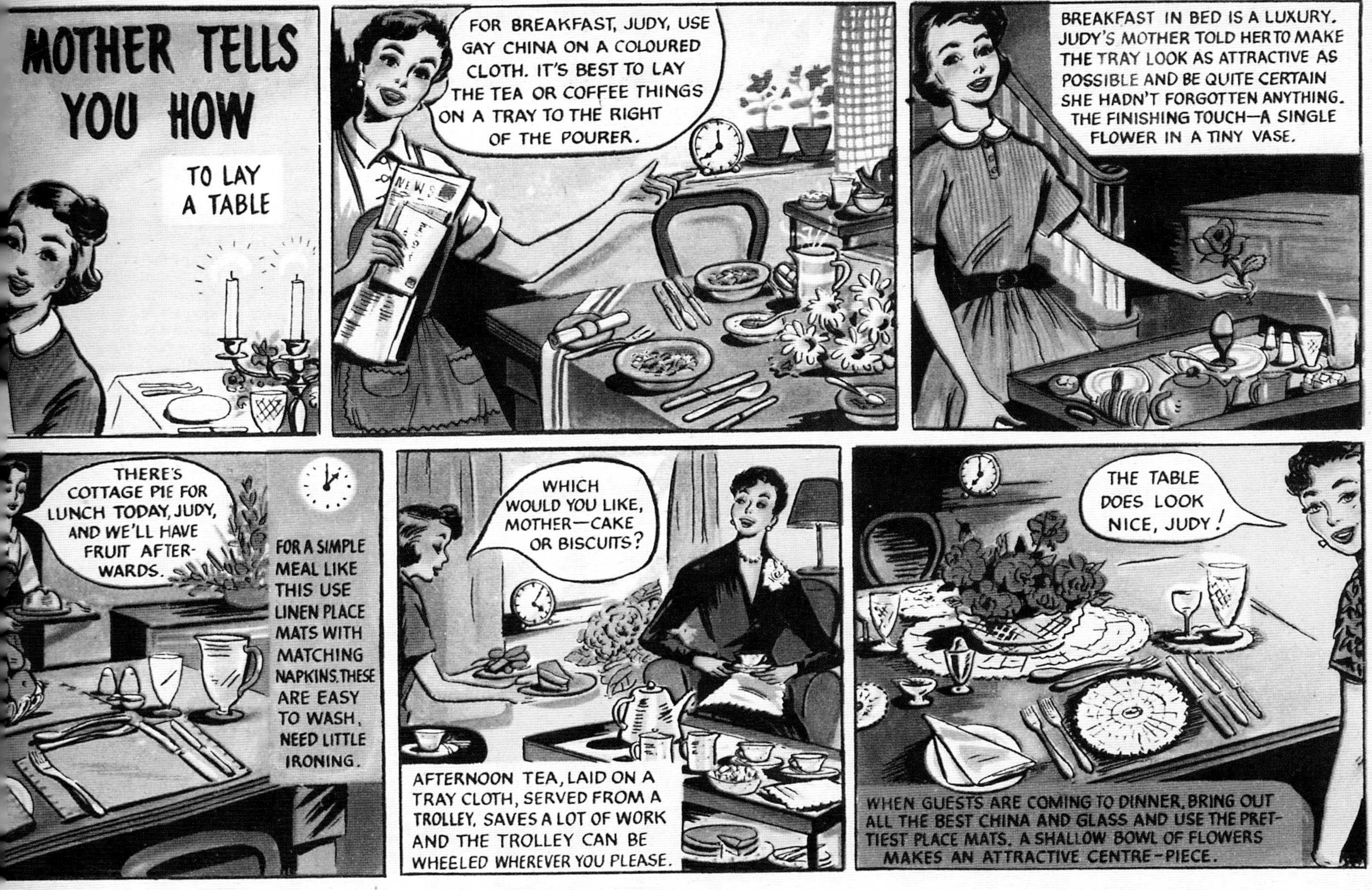
MOTHER TELLS YOU HOW
TO LAY A TABLE
FOR BREAKFAST, JUDY, USE GAY CHINA ON A COLOURED CLOTH. IT'S BEST TO LAY THE TEA OR COFFEE THINGS ON A TRAY TO THE RIGHT OF THE POURER.
BREAKFAST IN BED IS A LUXURY. JUDY'S MOTHER TOLD HER TO MAKE THE TRAY LOOK AS ATTRACTIVE AS POSSIBLE AND BE QUITE CERTAIN SHE HADN'T FORGOTTEN ANYTHING. THE FINISHING TOUCH—A SINGLE FLOWER IN A TINY VASE.
THERE'S COTTAGE PIE FOR LUNCH TODAY, JUDY, AND WE'LL HAVE FRUIT AFTERWARDS.
FOR A SIMPLE MEAL LIKE THIS USE LINEN PLACE MATS WITH MATCHING NAPKINS. THESE ARE EASY TO WASH, NEED LITTLE IRONING.
WHICH WOULD YOU LIKE, MOTHER—CAKE OR BISCUITS?
AFTERNOON TEA, LAID ON A TRAY CLOTH, SERVED FROM A TROLLEY, SAVES A LOT OF WORK AND THE TROLLEY CAN BE WHEELED WHEREVER YOU PLEASE.
THE TABLE DOES LOOK NICE, JUDY!
WHEN GUESTS ARE COMING TO DINNER, BRING OUT ALL THE BEST CHINA AND GLASS AND USE THE PRETTIEST PLACE MATS. A SHALLOW BOWL OF FLOWERS MAKES AN ATTRACTIVE CENTRE-PIECE.

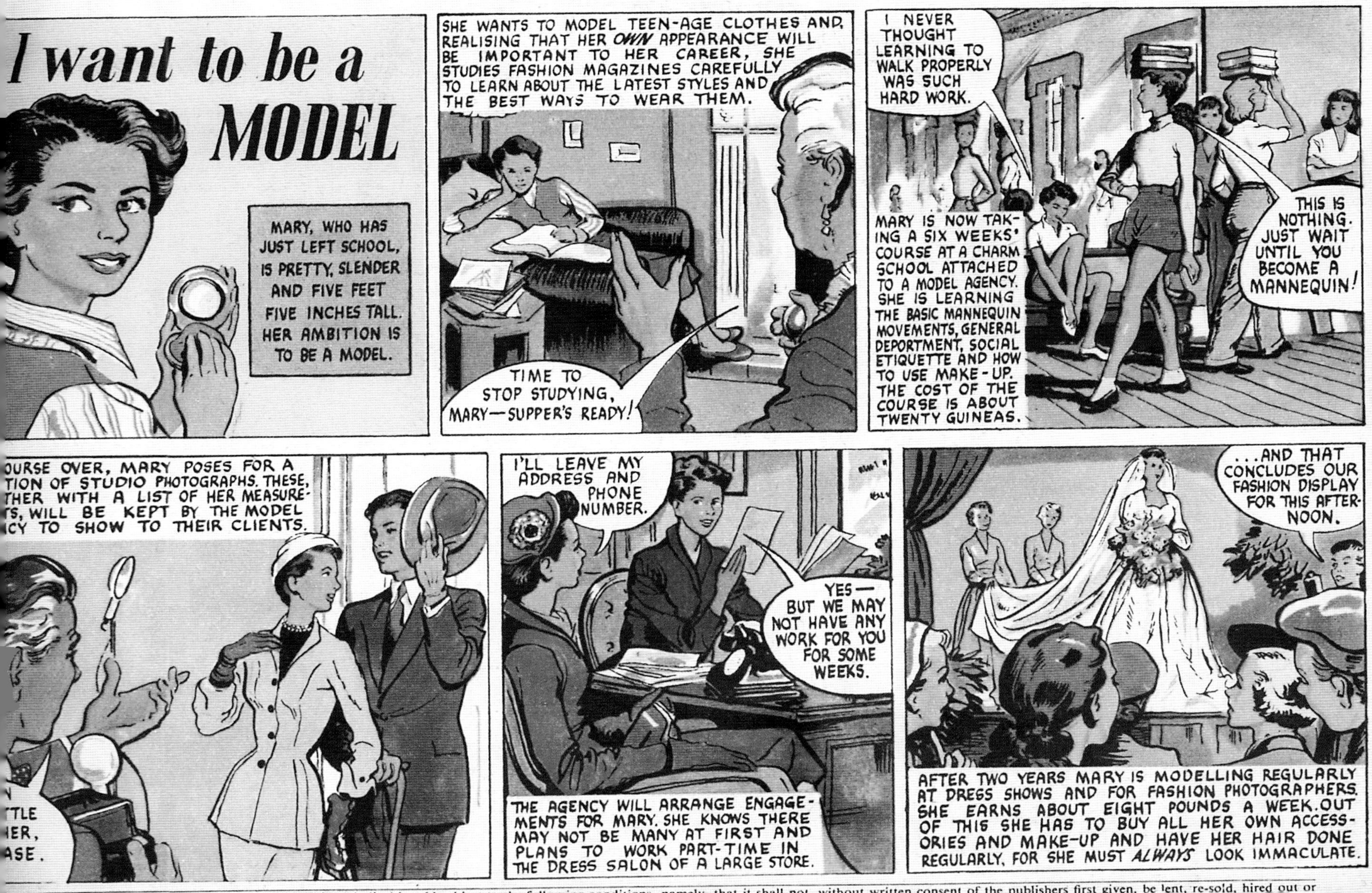
I want to be a MODEL
MARY, WHO HAS JUST LEFT SCHOOL, IS PRETTY, SLENDER AND FIVE FEET FIVE INCHES TALL. HER AMBITION IS TO BE A MODEL.
SHE WANTS TO MODEL TEEN-AGE CLOTHES AND, REALISING THAT HER OWN APPEARANCE WILL BE IMPORTANT TO HER CAREER, SHE STUDIES FASHION MAGAZINES CAREFULLY TO LEARN ABOUT THE LATEST STYLES AND THE BEST WAYS TO WEAR THEM.
TIME TO STOP STUDYING, MARY—SUPPER'S READY!
I NEVER THOUGHT LEARNING TO WALK PROPERLY WAS SUCH HARD WORK.
THIS IS NOTHING. JUST WAIT UNTIL YOU BECOME A MANNEQUIN!
MARY IS NOW TAKING A SIX WEEKS' COURSE AT A CHARM SCHOOL ATTACHED TO A MODEL AGENCY. SHE IS LEARNING THE BASIC MANNEQUIN MOVEMENTS, GENERAL DEPORTMENT, SOCIAL ETIQUETTE AND HOW TO USE MAKE-UP. THE COST OF THE COURSE IS ABOUT TWENTY GUINEAS.
OURSE OVER, MARY POSES FOR A TION OF STUDIO PHOTOGRAPHS. THESE, THER WITH A LIST OF HER MEASURE- TS, WILL BE KEPT BY THE MODEL CY TO SHOW TO THEIR CLIENTS.
N TTLE HER, ASE.
I'LL LEAVE MY ADDRESS AND PHONE NUMBER.
YES—BUT WE MAY NOT HAVE ANY WORK FOR YOU FOR SOME WEEKS.
THE AGENCY WILL ARRANGE ENGAGEMENTS FOR MARY. SHE KNOWS THERE MAY NOT BE MANY AT FIRST AND PLANS TO WORK PART-TIME IN THE DRESS SALON OF A LARGE STORE.
...AND THAT CONCLUDES OUR FASHION DISPLAY FOR THIS AFTERNOON.
AFTER TWO YEARS MARY IS MODELLING REGULARLY AT DRESS SHOWS AND FOR FASHION PHOTOGRAPHERS. SHE EARNS ABOUT EIGHT POUNDS A WEEK. OUT OF THIS SHE HAS TO BUY ALL HER OWN ACCESSORIES AND MAKE-UP AND HAVE HER HAIR DONE REGULARLY, FOR SHE MUST ALWAYS LOOK IMMACULATE.

ADVENTURE CORNER

Each week we are publishing the stories of GIR readers who lead interesting lives. If you d write in to 'Adventure Corner' and tell us all about i

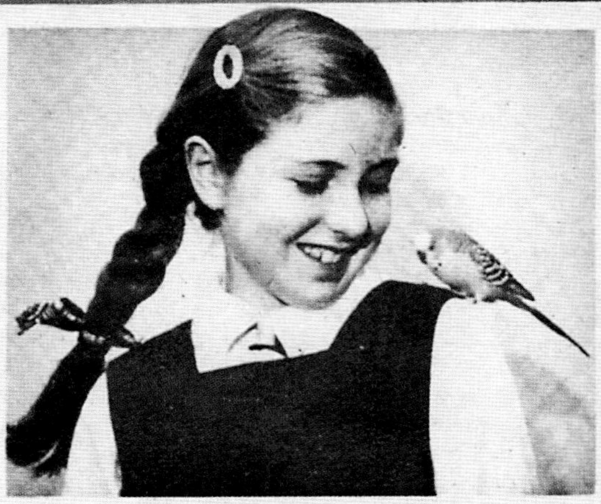

This week's adventure is about Jennifer Stannard of Islington, London, who although she adores animals has got only one budgerigar.

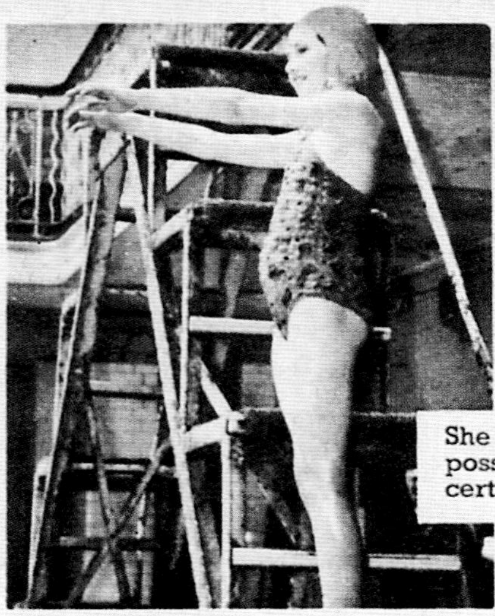

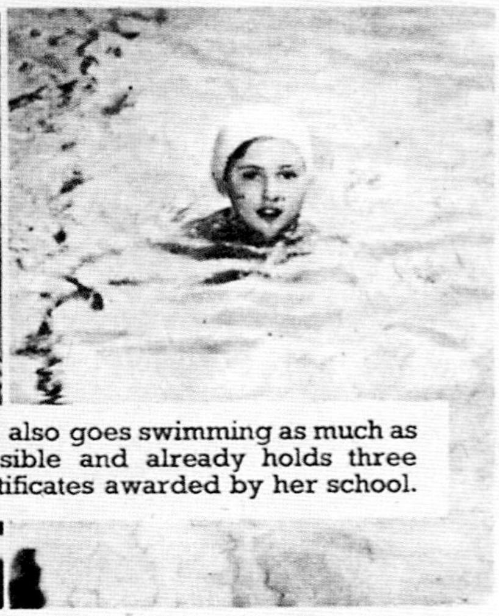

She also goes swimming as much as possible and already holds three certificates awarded by her school.

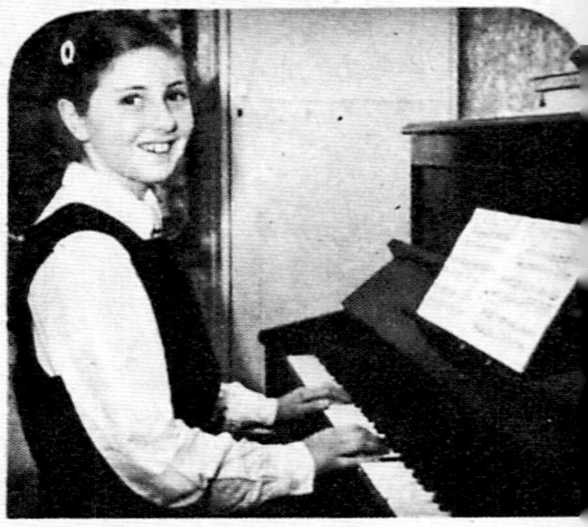

Jennifer loves to play the piano and has thre certificates – one for practical and two fo theory. She is now practising hard for a fourth

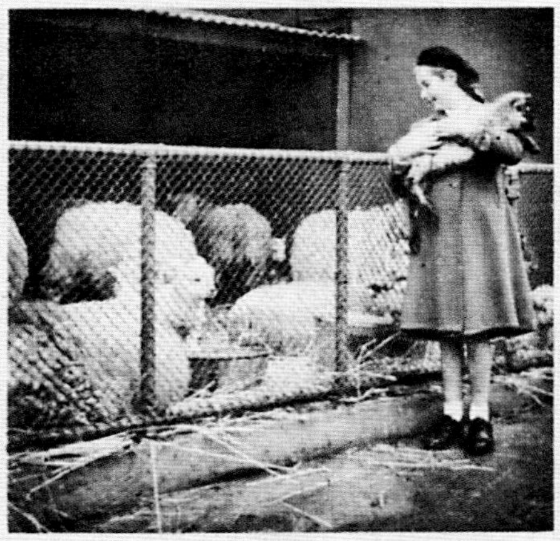

Jennifer likes nothing better than to visit the zoo. Here you see her cuddling an adorable week-old mottled lamb.

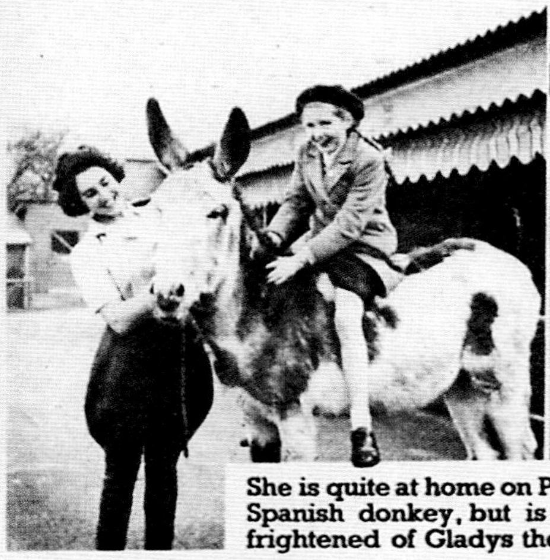

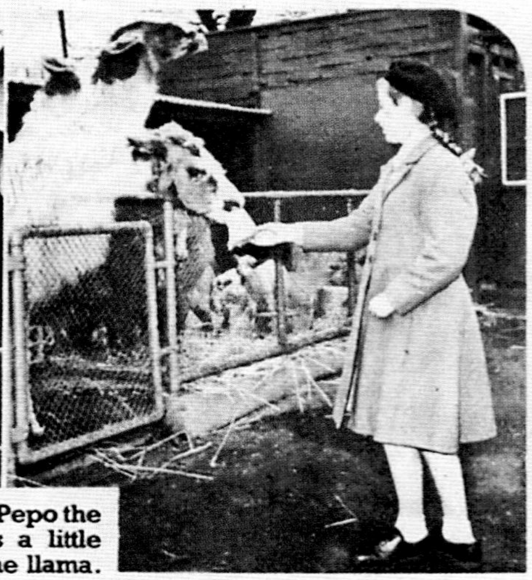

She is quite at home on Pepo the Spanish donkey, but is a little frightened of Gladys the llama.

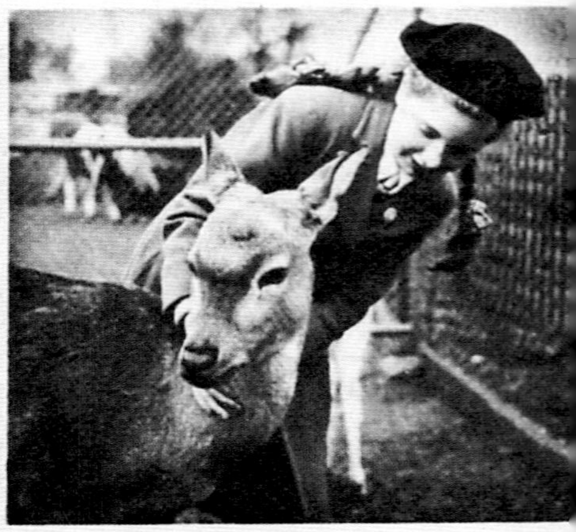

After visiting the Children's Zoo many times Jennifer has decided that her favourit animal there is Patsy, a very friendly dee

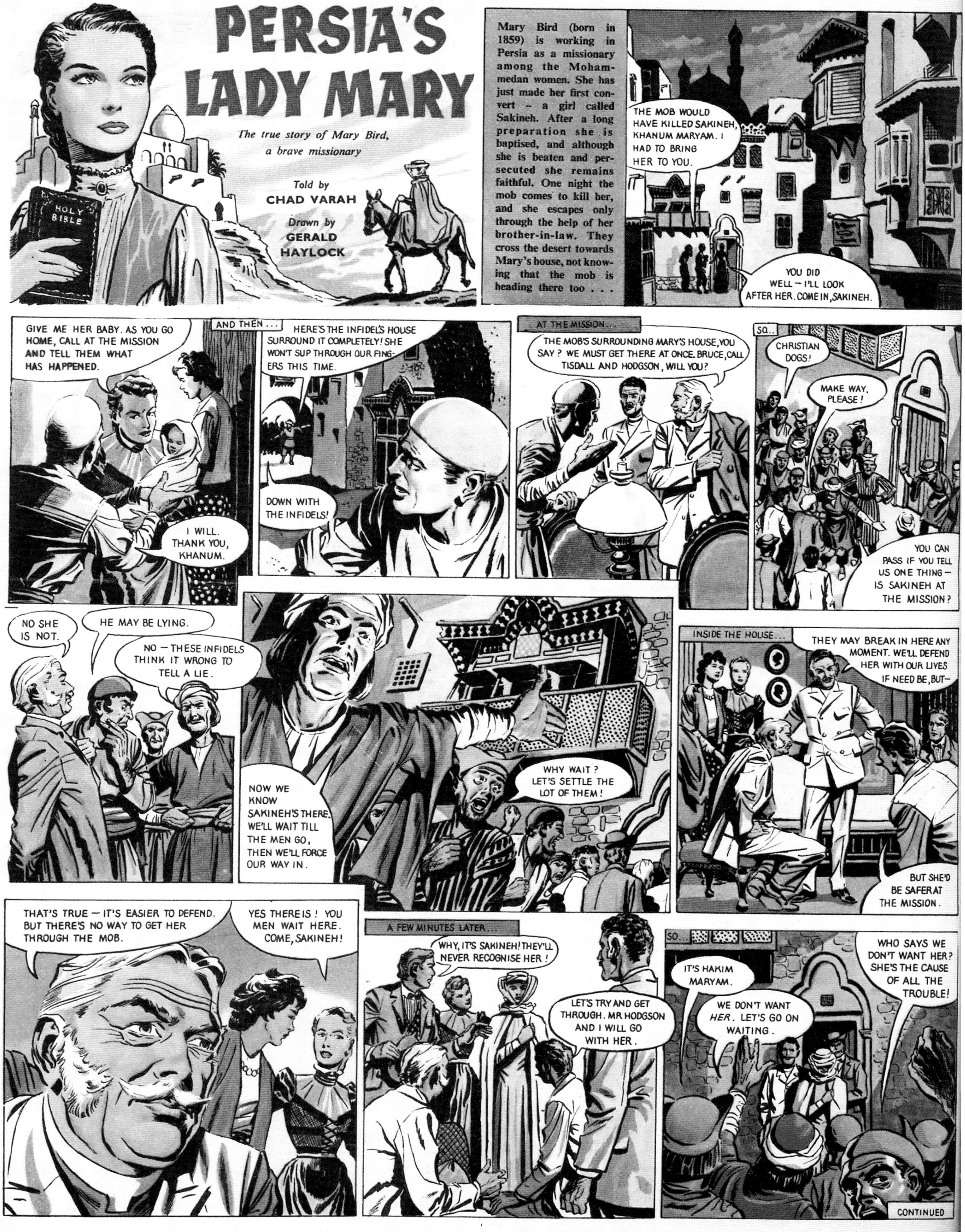
PERSIA'S LADY MARY
The true story of Mary Bird, a brave missionary
Told by CHAD VARAH
Drawn by GERALD HAYLOCK
HOLY BIBLE
Mary Bird (born in 1859) is working in Persia as a missionary among the Mohammedan women. She has just made her first convert – a girl called Sakineh. After a long preparation she is baptised, and although she is beaten and persecuted she remains faithful. One night the mob comes to kill her, and she escapes only through the help of her brother-in-law. They cross the desert towards Mary's house, not knowing that the mob is heading there too . . .
THE MOB WOULD HAVE KILLED SAKINEH, KHANUM MARYAM. I HAD TO BRING HER TO YOU.
YOU DID WELL – I'LL LOOK AFTER HER. COME IN, SAKINEH.
GIVE ME HER BABY. AS YOU GO HOME, CALL AT THE MISSION AND TELL THEM WHAT HAS HAPPENED.
I WILL. THANK YOU, KHANUM.
AND THEN . . .
HERE'S THE INFIDEL'S HOUSE SURROUND IT COMPLETELY! SHE WON'T SLIP THROUGH OUR FINGERS THIS TIME.
DOWN WITH THE INFIDELS!
AT THE MISSION . . .
THE MOB'S SURROUNDING MARY'S HOUSE, YOU SAY? WE MUST GET THERE AT ONCE. BRUCE, CALL TISDALL AND HODGSON, WILL YOU?
SO . .
CHRISTIAN DOGS!
MAKE WAY, PLEASE!
YOU CAN PASS IF YOU TELL US ONE THING – IS SAKINEH AT THE MISSION?
NO SHE IS NOT.
HE MAY BE LYING.
NO – THESE INFIDELS THINK IT WRONG TO TELL A LIE.
NOW WE KNOW SAKINEH'S THERE. WE'LL WAIT TILL THE MEN GO, THEN WE'LL FORCE OUR WAY IN.
WHY WAIT? LET'S SETTLE THE LOT OF THEM!
INSIDE THE HOUSE . . .
THEY MAY BREAK IN HERE ANY MOMENT. WE'LL DEFEND HER WITH OUR LIVES IF NEED BE, BUT–
BUT SHE'D BE SAFER AT THE MISSION.
THAT'S TRUE – IT'S EASIER TO DEFEND. BUT THERE'S NO WAY TO GET HER THROUGH THE MOB.
YES THERE IS! YOU MEN WAIT HERE. COME, SAKINEH!
A FEW MINUTES LATER . . .
WHY, IT'S SAKINEH! THEY'LL NEVER RECOGNISE HER!
LET'S TRY AND GET THROUGH. MR HODGSON AND I WILL GO WITH HER.
SO . . .
IT'S HAKIM MARYAM.
WE DON'T WANT HER. LET'S GO ON WAITING.
WHO SAYS WE DON'T WANT HER? SHE'S THE CAUSE OF ALL THE TROUBLE!
CONTINUED

continued on page 121

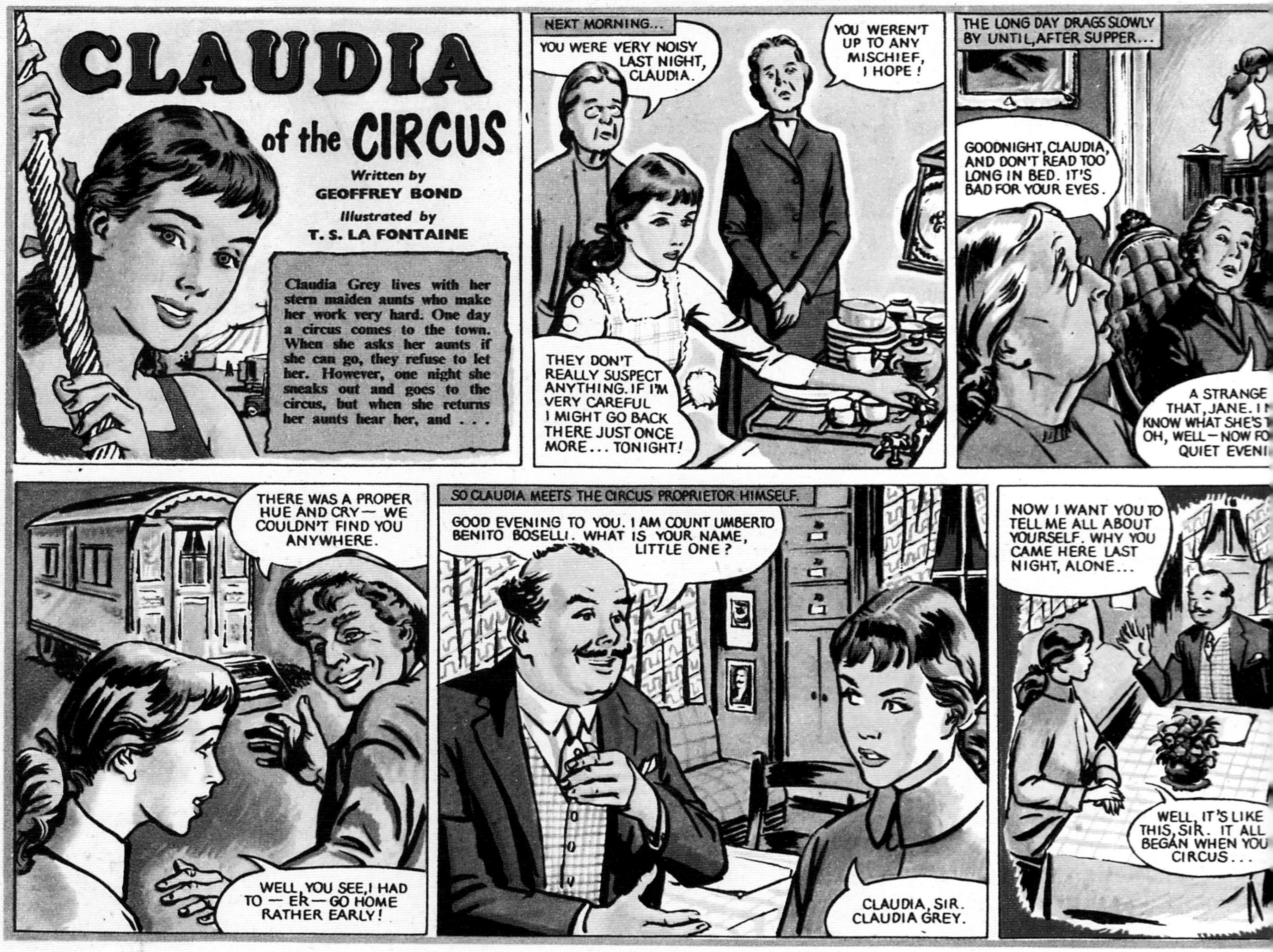
CLAUDIA of the CIRCUS
Written by GEOFFREY BOND
Illustrated by T. S. LA FONTAINE
Claudia Grey lives with her stern maiden aunts who make her work very hard. One day a circus comes to the town. When she asks her aunts if she can go, they refuse to let her. However, one night she sneaks out and goes to the circus, but when she returns her aunts hear her, and . . .
NEXT MORNING...
YOU WERE VERY NOISY LAST NIGHT, CLAUDIA.
YOU WEREN'T UP TO ANY MISCHIEF, I HOPE!
THEY DON'T REALLY SUSPECT ANYTHING. IF I'M VERY CAREFUL I MIGHT GO BACK THERE JUST ONCE MORE... TONIGHT!
THE LONG DAY DRAGS SLOWLY BY UNTIL, AFTER SUPPER...
GOODNIGHT, CLAUDIA, AND DON'T READ TOO LONG IN BED. IT'S BAD FOR YOUR EYES.
A STRANGE THAT, JANE. I KNOW WHAT SHE'S OH, WELL — NOW FO QUIET EVENI
THERE WAS A PROPER HUE AND CRY — WE COULDN'T FIND YOU ANYWHERE.
WELL, YOU SEE, I HAD TO — ER — GO HOME RATHER EARLY!
SO CLAUDIA MEETS THE CIRCUS PROPRIETOR HIMSELF.
GOOD EVENING TO YOU. I AM COUNT UMBERTO BENITO BOSELLI. WHAT IS YOUR NAME, LITTLE ONE?
CLAUDIA, SIR. CLAUDIA GREY.
NOW I WANT YOU TO TELL ME ALL ABOUT YOURSELF. WHY YOU CAME HERE LAST NIGHT, ALONE...
WELL, IT'S LIKE THIS, SIR. IT ALL BEGAN WHEN YOU CIRCUS...

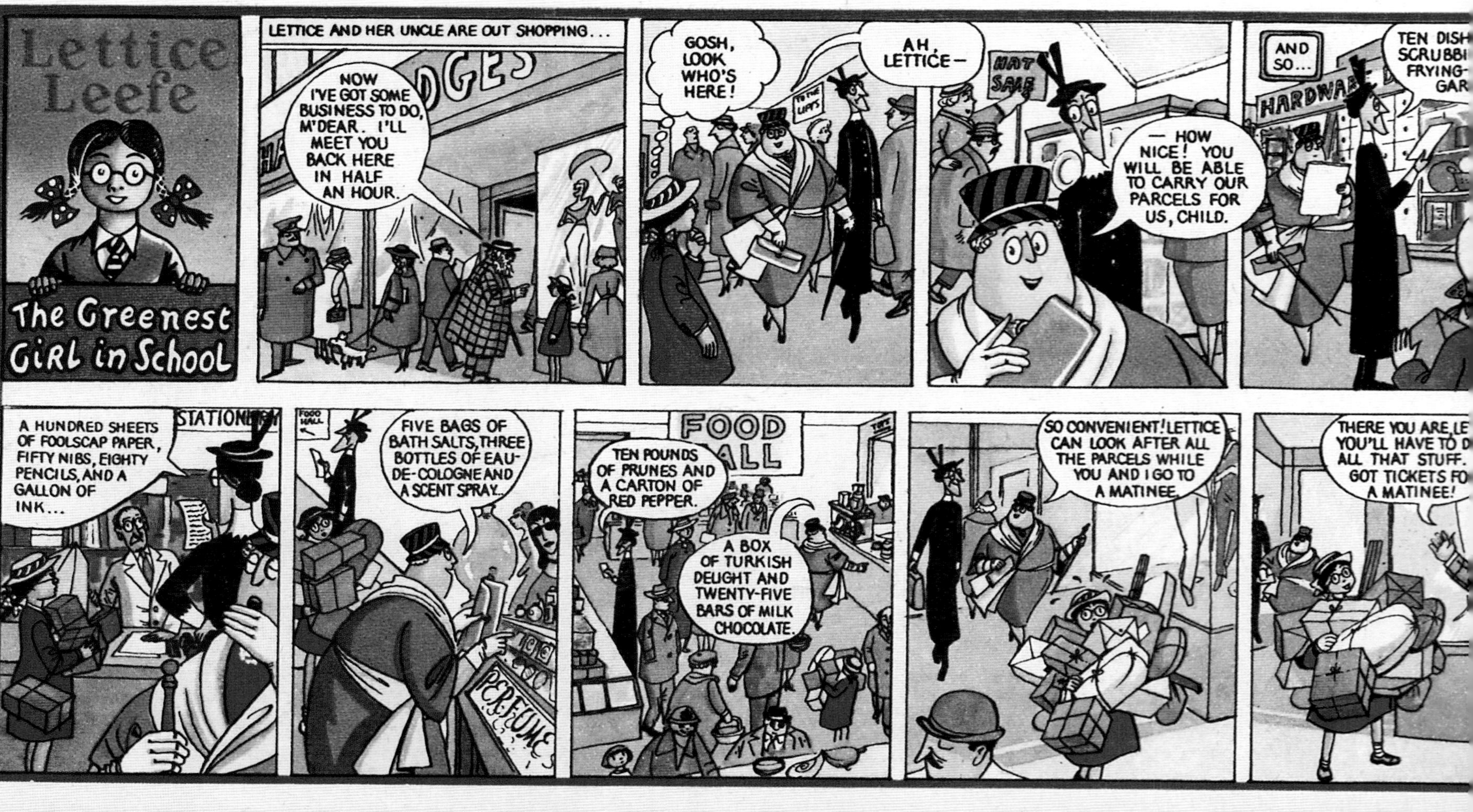
Lettice Leefe
The Greenest Girl in School
LETTICE AND HER UNCLE ARE OUT SHOPPING...
NOW I'VE GOT SOME BUSINESS TO DO, M'DEAR. I'LL MEET YOU BACK HERE IN HALF AN HOUR.
GOSH, LOOK WHO'S HERE!
AH, LETTICE —
HAT SALE
— HOW NICE! YOU WILL BE ABLE TO CARRY OUR PARCELS FOR US, CHILD.
AND SO...
TEN DISH SCRUBBI FRYING- GAR
HARDWA
A HUNDRED SHEETS OF FOOLSCAP PAPER, FIFTY NIBS, EIGHTY PENCILS, AND A GALLON OF INK...
STATIONERY
FIVE BAGS OF BATH SALTS, THREE BOTTLES OF EAU-DE-COLOGNE AND A SCENT SPRAY...
PERFUMES
FOOD HALL
TEN POUNDS OF PRUNES AND A CARTON OF RED PEPPER.
A BOX OF TURKISH DELIGHT AND TWENTY-FIVE BARS OF MILK CHOCOLATE.
SO CONVENIENT! LETTICE CAN LOOK AFTER ALL THE PARCELS WHILE YOU AND I GO TO A MATINEE.
THERE YOU ARE, LE YOU'LL HAVE TO D ALL THAT STUFF. GOT TICKETS FO A MATINEE!

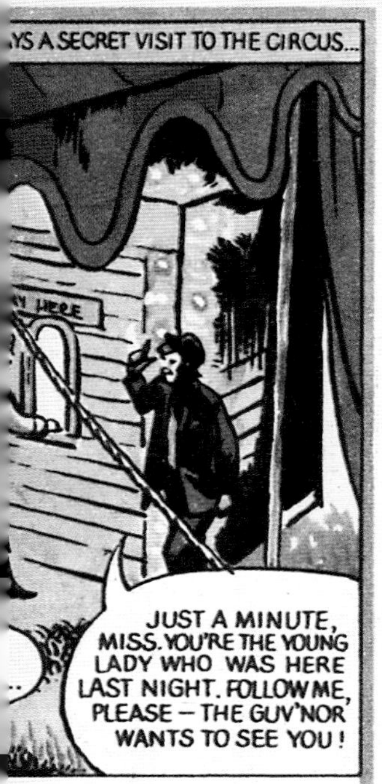
A SECRET VISIT TO THE CIRCUS...
JUST A MINUTE, MISS. YOU'RE THE YOUNG LADY WHO WAS HERE LAST NIGHT. FOLLOW ME, PLEASE – THE GUV'NOR WANTS TO SEE YOU!

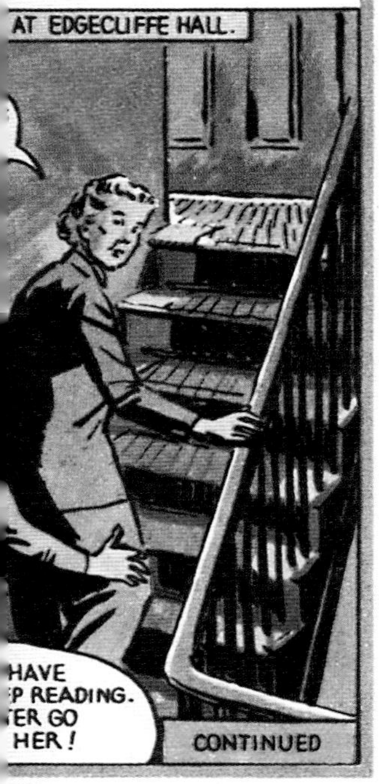
AT EDGECLIFFE HALL.
CONTINUED

continued on page 82

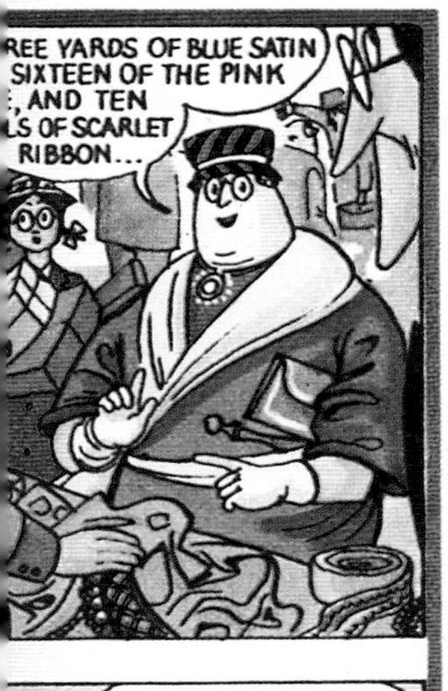
SIXTEEN OF THE PINK
AND TEN
RIBBON...

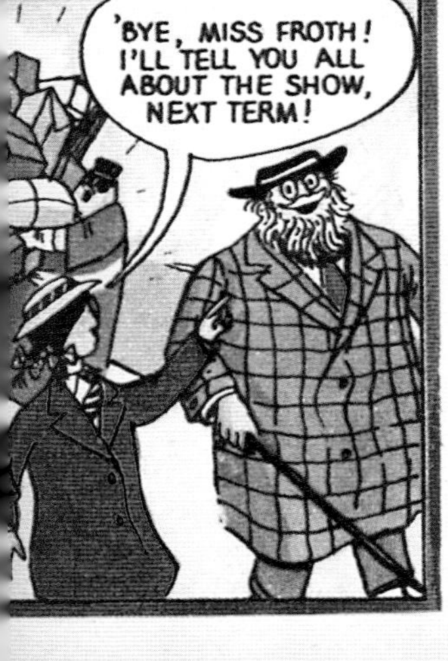
'BYE, MISS FROTH! I'LL TELL YOU ALL ABOUT THE SHOW, NEXT TERM!

Girl Picture Gallery

No. 320

When this well-known T.V. performer paid us a visit recently, we persuaded him to pose for this splendid new portrait.

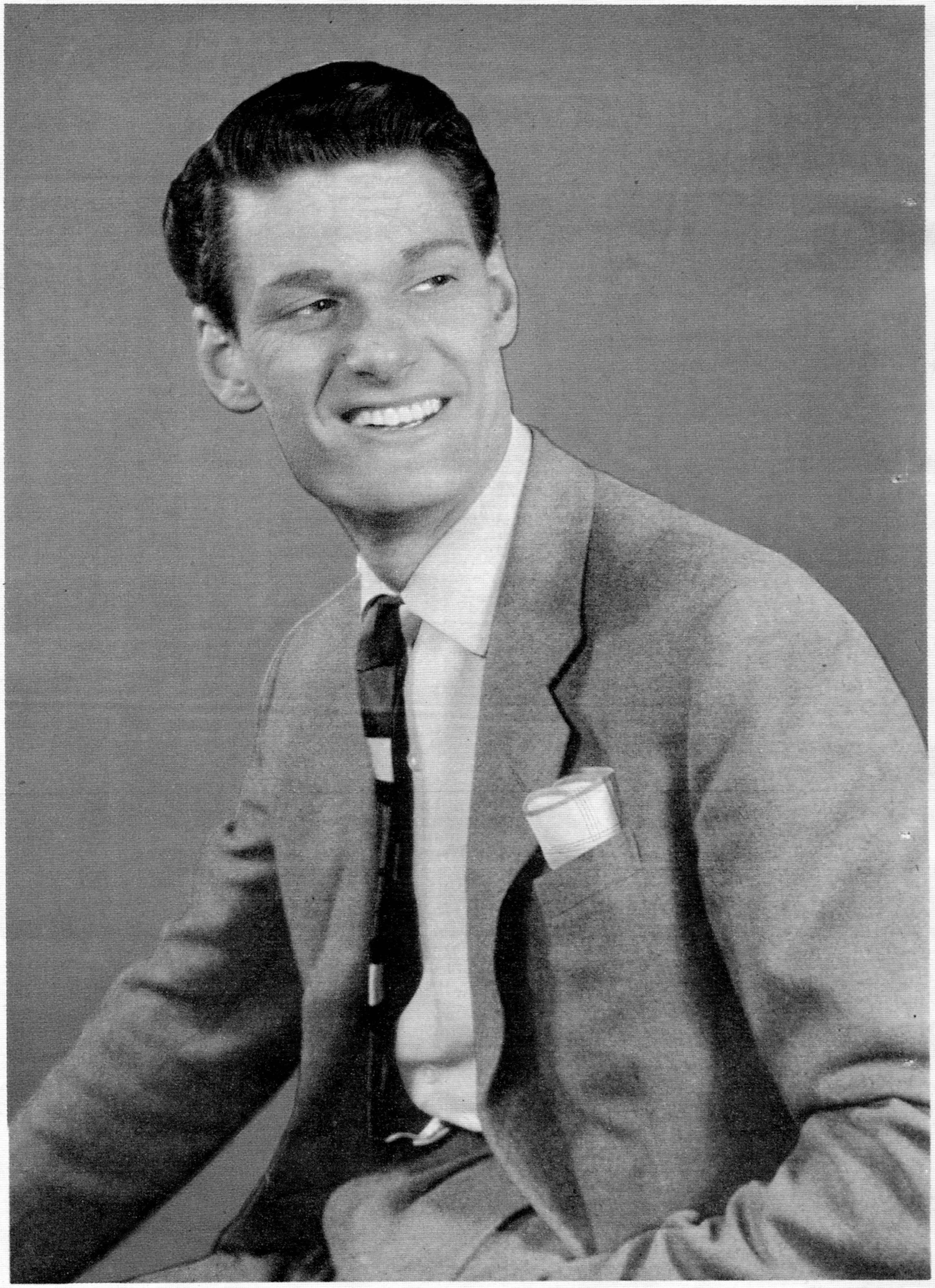

PETE MURRAY

Specially photographed for GIRL by Bert Hardy.

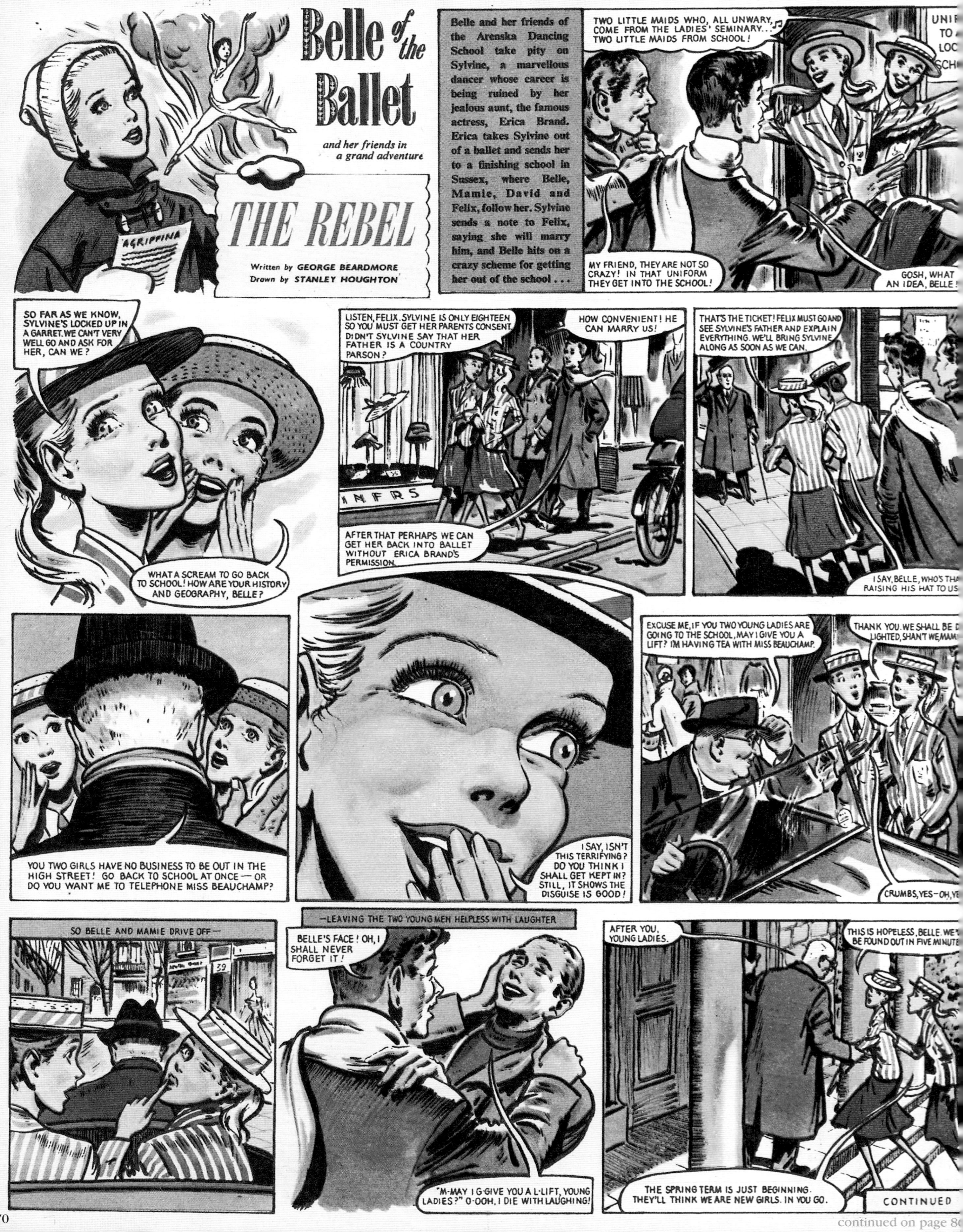

Belle of the Ballet
and her friends in a grand adventure
THE REBEL
Written by GEORGE BEARDMORE
Drawn by STANLEY HOUGHTON
'AGRIPPINA'
Belle and her friends of the Arenska Dancing School take pity on Sylvine, a marvellous dancer whose career is being ruined by her jealous aunt, the famous actress, Erica Brand. Erica takes Sylvine out of a ballet and sends her to a finishing school in Sussex, where Belle, Mamie, David and Felix, follow her. Sylvine sends a note to Felix, saying she will marry him, and Belle hits on a crazy scheme for getting her out of the school . . .
TWO LITTLE MAIDS WHO, ALL UNWARY, COME FROM THE LADIES' SEMINARY... TWO LITTLE MAIDS FROM SCHOOL!
MY FRIEND, THEY ARE NOT SO CRAZY! IN THAT UNIFORM THEY GET INTO THE SCHOOL!
GOSH, WHAT AN IDEA, BELLE!
SO FAR AS WE KNOW, SYLVINE'S LOCKED UP IN A GARRET. WE CAN'T VERY WELL GO AND ASK FOR HER, CAN WE?
WHAT A SCREAM TO GO BACK TO SCHOOL! HOW ARE YOUR HISTORY AND GEOGRAPHY, BELLE?
LISTEN, FELIX. SYLVINE IS ONLY EIGHTEEN SO YOU MUST GET HER PARENTS CONSENT. DIDN'T SYLVINE SAY THAT HER FATHER IS A COUNTRY PARSON?
HOW CONVENIENT! HE CAN MARRY US!
INFRS
AFTER THAT PERHAPS WE CAN GET HER BACK INTO BALLET WITHOUT ERICA BRAND'S PERMISSION.
THAT'S THE TICKET! FELIX MUST GO AND SEE SYLVINE'S FATHER AND EXPLAIN EVERYTHING. WE'LL BRING SYLVINE ALONG AS SOON AS WE CAN.
I SAY, BELLE, WHO'S THA RAISING HIS HAT TO US
YOU TWO GIRLS HAVE NO BUSINESS TO BE OUT IN THE HIGH STREET! GO BACK TO SCHOOL AT ONCE — OR DO YOU WANT ME TO TELEPHONE MISS BEAUCHAMP?
I SAY, ISN'T THIS TERRIFYING? DO YOU THINK I SHALL GET KEPT IN? STILL, IT SHOWS THE DISGUISE IS GOOD!
EXCUSE ME, IF YOU TWO YOUNG LADIES ARE GOING TO THE SCHOOL, MAY I GIVE YOU A LIFT? I'M HAVING TEA WITH MISS BEAUCHAMP.
THANK YOU. WE SHALL BE D LIGHTED, SHAN'T WE, MAM
CRUMBS, YES—OH, YE
SO BELLE AND MAMIE DRIVE OFF—
—LEAVING THE TWO YOUNG MEN HELPLESS WITH LAUGHTER
BELLE'S FACE! OH, I SHALL NEVER FORGET IT!
"M-MAY I G-GIVE YOU A L-LIFT, YOUNG LADIES?" O-OOH, I DIE WITH LAUGHING!
AFTER YOU, YOUNG LADIES.
THIS IS HOPELESS, BELLE. WE' BE FOUND OUT IN FIVE MINUTE
THE SPRING TERM IS JUST BEGINNING. THEY'LL THINK WE ARE NEW GIRLS. IN YOU GO.
CONTINUED

continued on page 80

★ Jacky sees GIRL printed ★

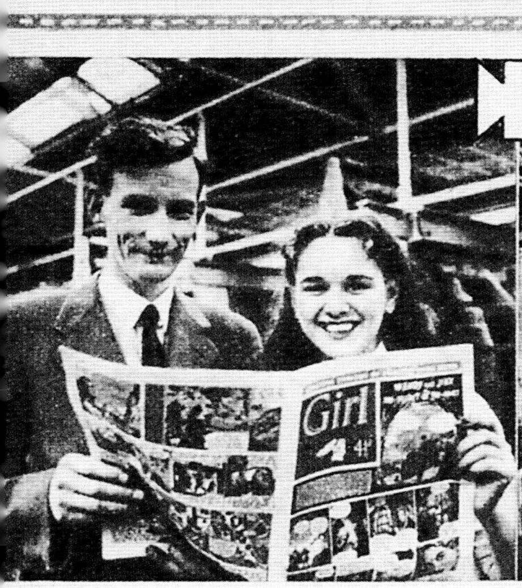
Girl

ky met Mr Michael Bemrose, Production nager of our Liverpool printers. He gave a copy of GIRL – just off the presses.

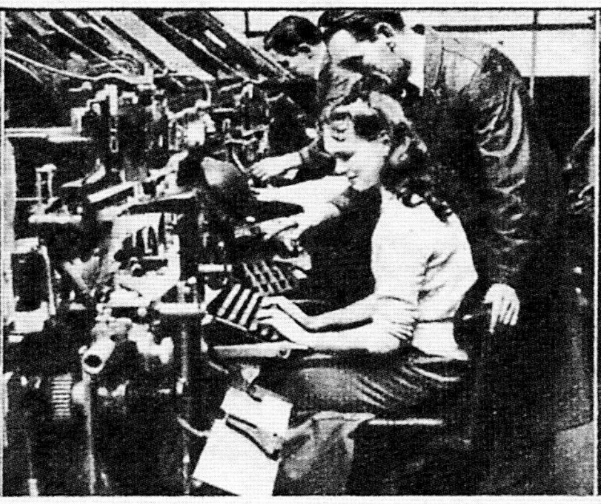

Then she saw the words being set in metal as the operator typed – 7 lines a minute. Much too fast for one-finger typist Jacky!

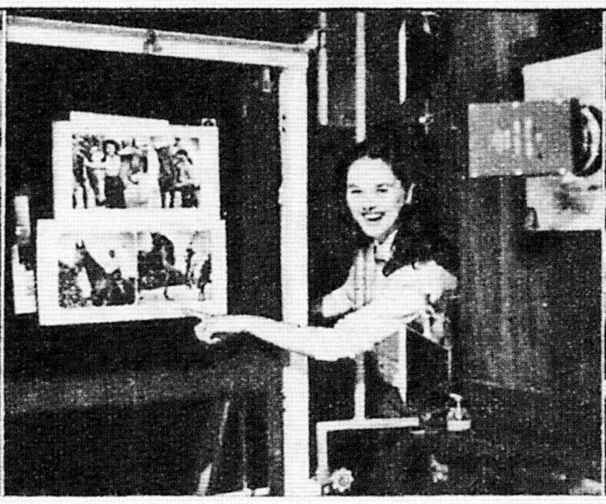

This giant camera 'copies' every part of a page, reduces it to the correct size. All strips must be photographed five times.

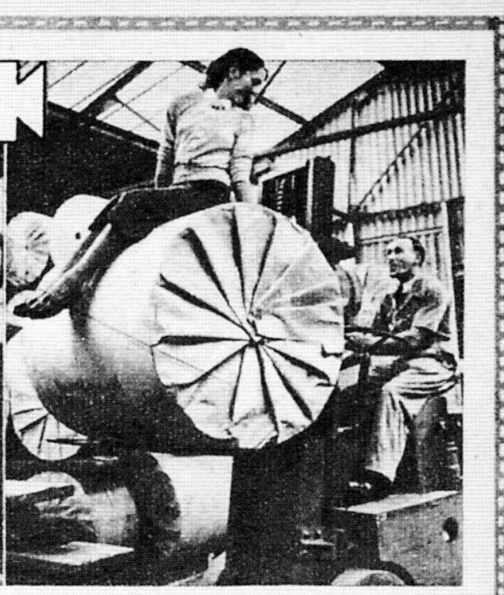

"Where to?" laughed Jacky, on top of a reel of newsprint. The hydraulic truck stacks the reel ready for use.

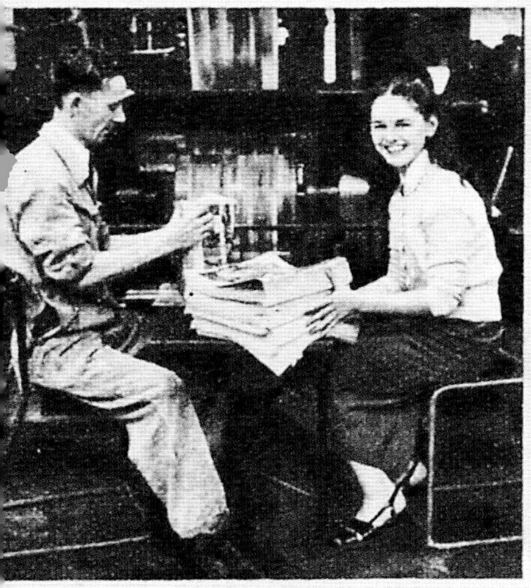

wn they go – 333 complete copies of GIRL ery minute. Our highly efficient press nts both sides at once, cuts and folds.

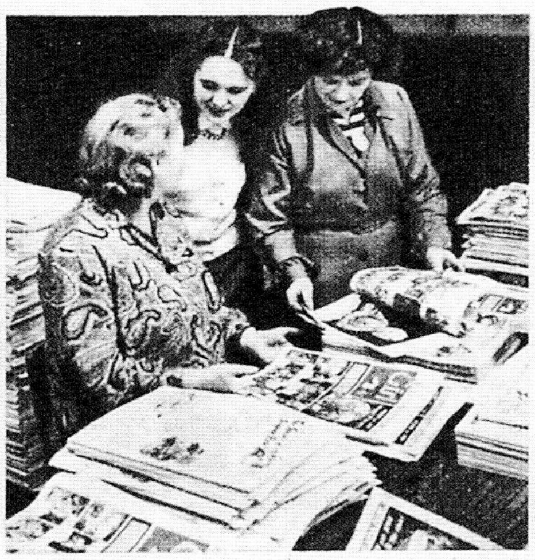

Women sorting pages stopped work for a chat with Jacky to tell her how their own daughters read about her every week.

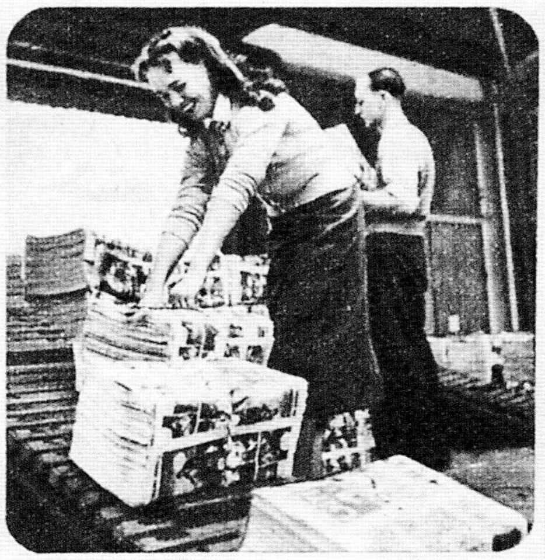

When roped bundles on the 'caterpillar' reached the top, Jacky put them on to a truck for distribution all over England.

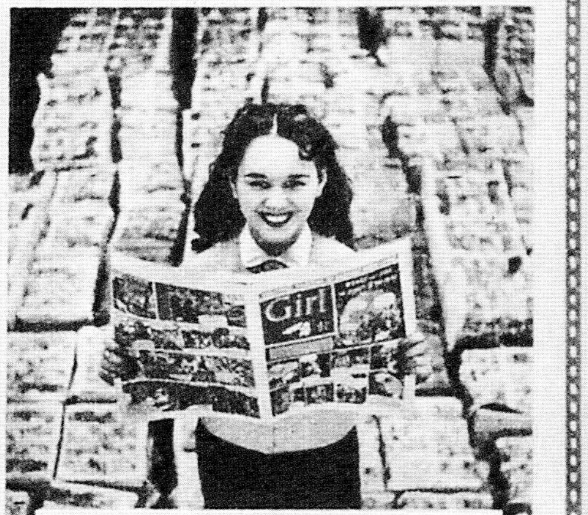
Girl

All GIRL's together! Some of the thousands of copies to be seen by GIRL readers everywhere.

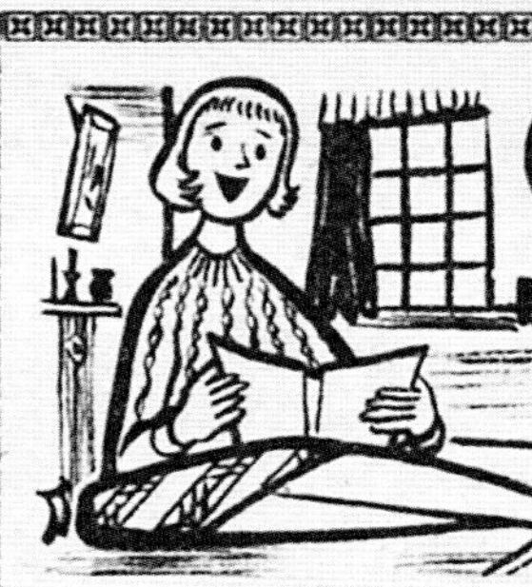

Girl BOOK LIST

by JILL RUSSELL

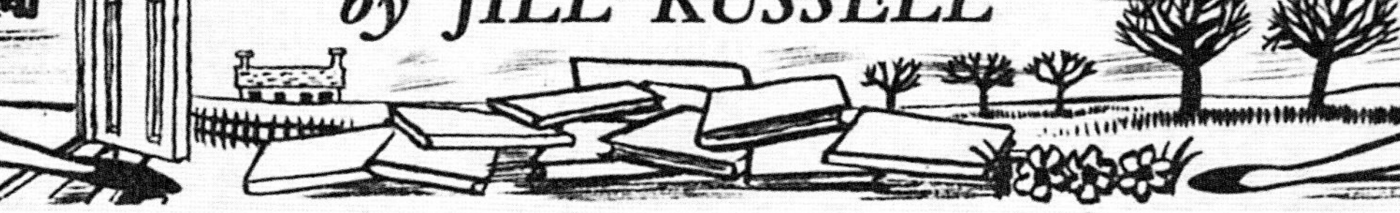
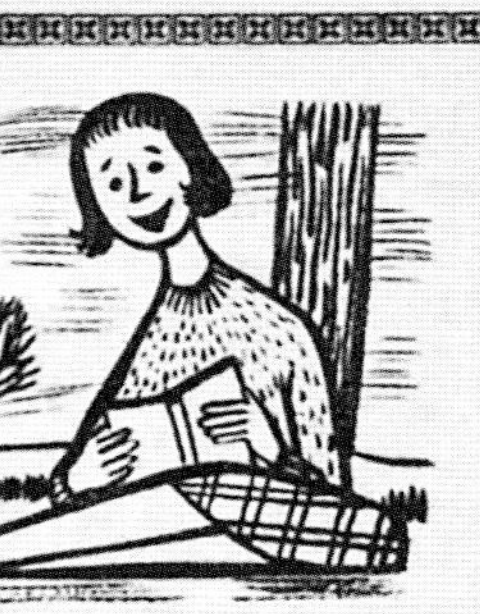

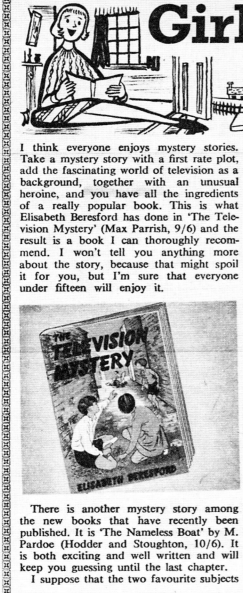

I think everyone enjoys mystery stories. Take a mystery story with a first rate plot, add the fascinating world of television as a background, together with an unusual heroine, and you have all the ingredients of a really popular book. This is what Elisabeth Beresford has done in 'The Television Mystery' (Max Parrish, 9/6) and the result is a book I can thoroughly recommend. I won't tell you anything more about the story, because that might spoil it for you, but I'm sure that everyone under fifteen will enjoy it.

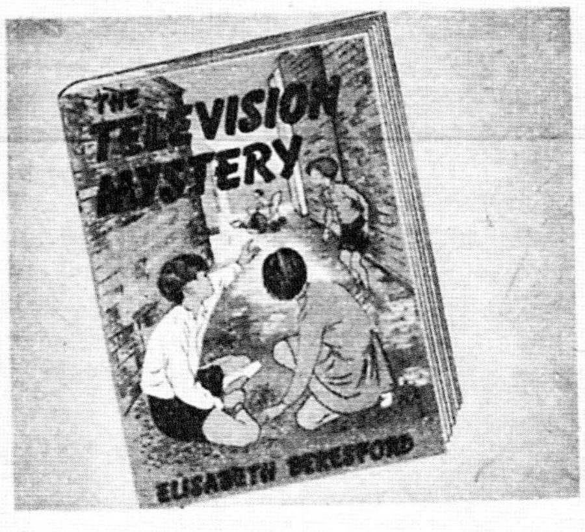
The Television Mystery
Elisabeth Beresford

There is another mystery story among the new books that have recently been published. It is 'The Nameless Boat' by M. Pardoe (Hodder and Stoughton, 10/6). It is both exciting and well written and will keep you guessing until the last chapter.

I suppose that the two favourite subjects for girls' books are still dancing and riding, and no book list would be complete without a horse story and a ballet story. I'd like to recommend one of each – 'The Second Mount' by Christine Pullein-Thompson (Burke, 8/6) and 'Ballet for Drina' by Jean Estoril (Hodder and Stoughton, 10/6). 'The Second Mount' is a sequel to 'The First Rosette' which I expect many of you have read. It's about the adventures of David and Pat when they start their own riding school. 'Ballet for Drina' tells how Drina managed to start her ballet career in spite of obstacles and strong opposition from her family. I enjoyed both these stories very much.

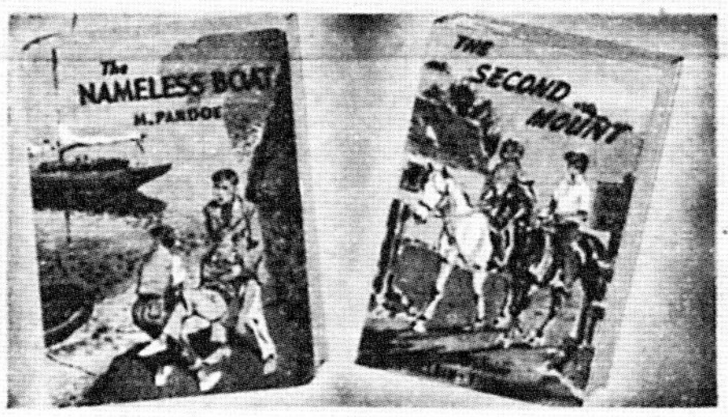
The Nameless Boat
M. Pardoe
The Second Mount

Next I'd like to recommend 'The Secret Journey' by Rosemary Weir (Max Parrish, 9/6). Four children, whose parents are in Burma, go to spend their holidays with an uncle. But their uncle is just off on an expedition to Tibet. It seems as if the children will have nowhere to go, but by chance they are made a present of a horse and cart. So they pack their belongings into it and set off across England. The problems they have to cope with and the adventures they have on the way make very exciting reading.

★ ★ ★

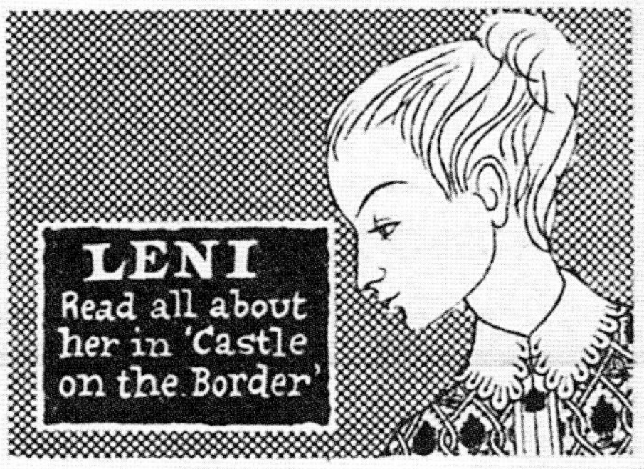
LENI
Read all about her in 'Castle on the Border'

I've left the most unusual of the new books until last. It is called 'Castle on the Border' and is by a German author, Margot Benary (Macmillan, 13/6). It is primarily a book for teenagers, but I think many younger girls will like reading it. The story is set in post-war Germany and the heroine, Leni, is an orphan whose ambition is to be a great actress like her mother. She succeeds, but 'Castle on the Border' is by no means just a story about a young unknown actress making good. It's a book about real people which you will think about and remember long after you've finished reading it. In my opinion it's a very good book indeed.

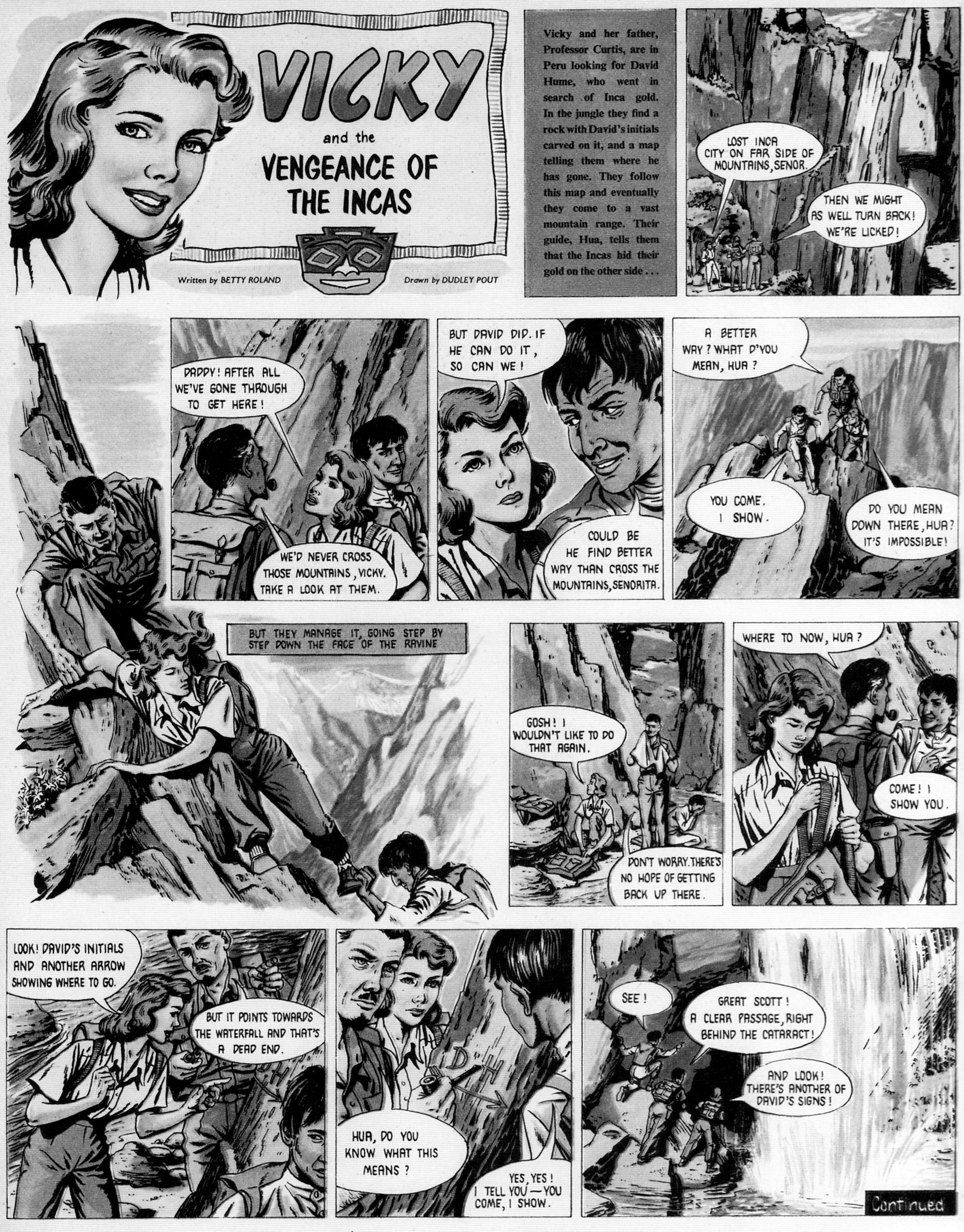
VICKY
and the
VENGEANCE OF THE INCAS
Written by BETTY ROLAND
Drawn by DUDLEY POUT
Vicky and her father, Professor Curtis, are in Peru looking for David Hume, who went in search of Inca gold. In the jungle they find a rock with David's initials carved on it, and a map telling them where he has gone. They follow this map and eventually they come to a vast mountain range. Their guide, Hua, tells them that the Incas hid their gold on the other side . . .
LOST INCA CITY ON FAR SIDE OF MOUNTAINS, SENOR.
THEN WE MIGHT AS WELL TURN BACK! WE'RE LICKED!
DADDY! AFTER ALL WE'VE GONE THROUGH TO GET HERE!
WE'D NEVER CROSS THOSE MOUNTAINS, VICKY. TAKE A LOOK AT THEM.
BUT DAVID DID. IF HE CAN DO IT, SO CAN WE!
COULD BE HE FIND BETTER WAY THAN CROSS THE MOUNTAINS, SENORITA.
A BETTER WAY? WHAT D'YOU MEAN, HUA?
YOU COME. I SHOW.
DO YOU MEAN DOWN THERE, HUA? IT'S IMPOSSIBLE!
BUT THEY MANAGE IT, GOING STEP BY STEP DOWN THE FACE OF THE RAVINE
GOSH! I WOULDN'T LIKE TO DO THAT AGAIN.
DON'T WORRY. THERE'S NO HOPE OF GETTING BACK UP THERE.
WHERE TO NOW, HUA?
COME! I SHOW YOU.
LOOK! DAVID'S INITIALS AND ANOTHER ARROW SHOWING WHERE TO GO.
BUT IT POINTS TOWARDS THE WATERFALL AND THAT'S A DEAD END.
HUA, DO YOU KNOW WHAT THIS MEANS?
YES, YES! I TELL YOU—YOU COME, I SHOW.
SEE!
GREAT SCOTT! A CLEAR PASSAGE, RIGHT BEHIND THE CATARACT!
AND LOOK! THERE'S ANOTHER OF DAVID'S SIGNS!
Continued

continued on page 8

*[T]his week **JUNE PAUL** joins the valiant [o]utlaws in Sherwood Forest*

Try anything once!

Pictures by
BERT HARDY

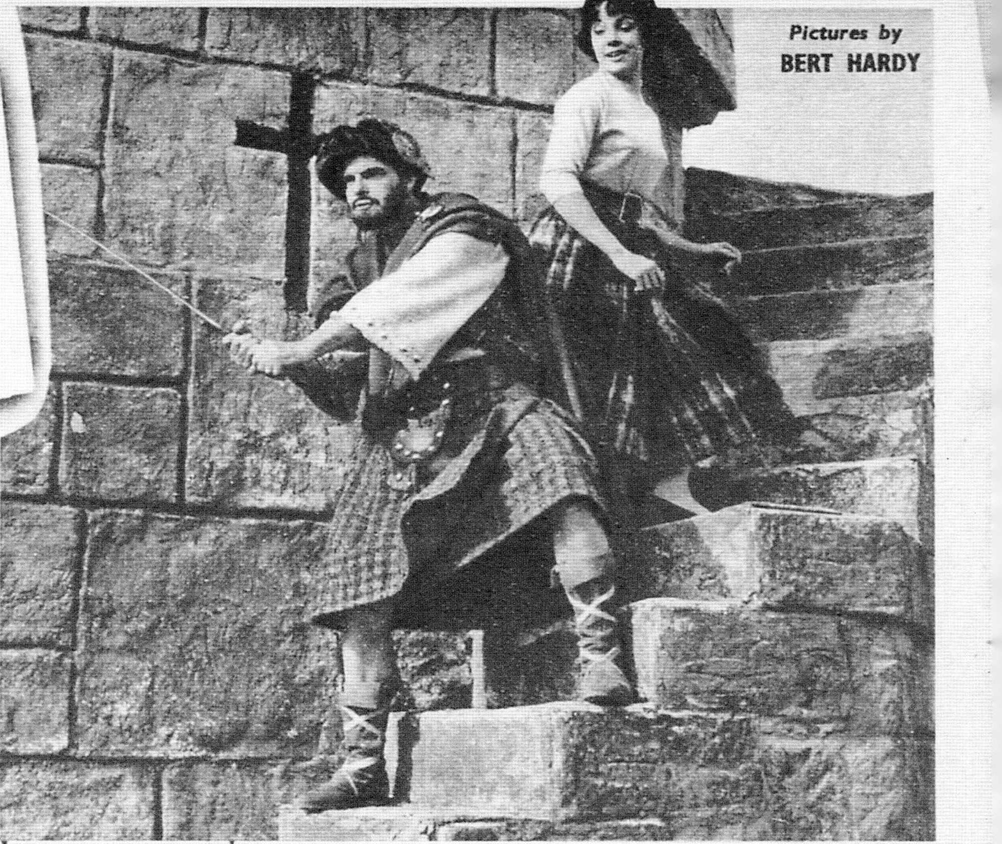

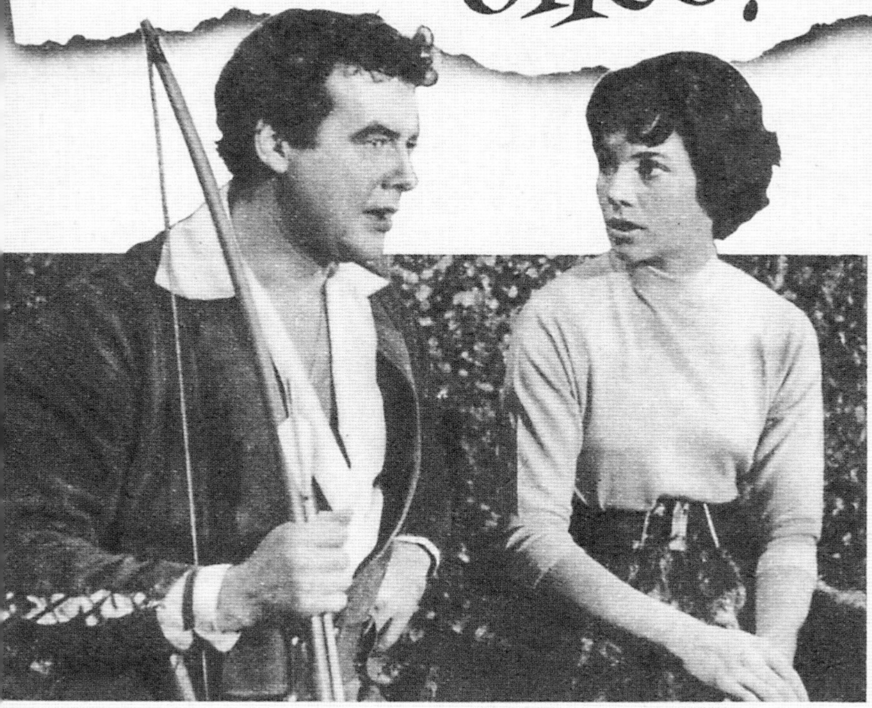

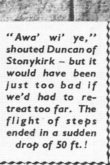

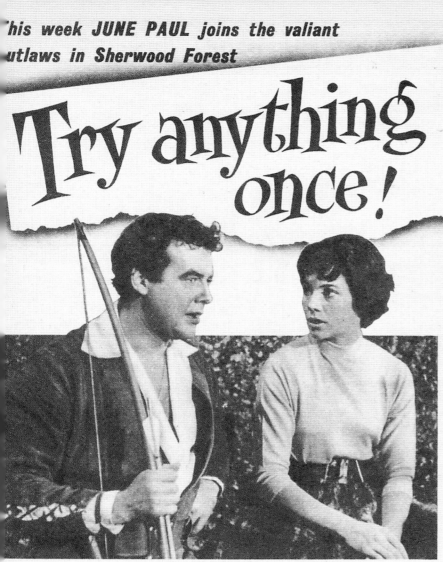

I sat overawed as Robin Hood talked. I think he's wonderful.

"Awa' wi' ye," shouted Duncan of Stonykirk – but it would have been just too bad if we'd had to retreat too far. The flight of steps ended in a sudden drop of 50 ft.!

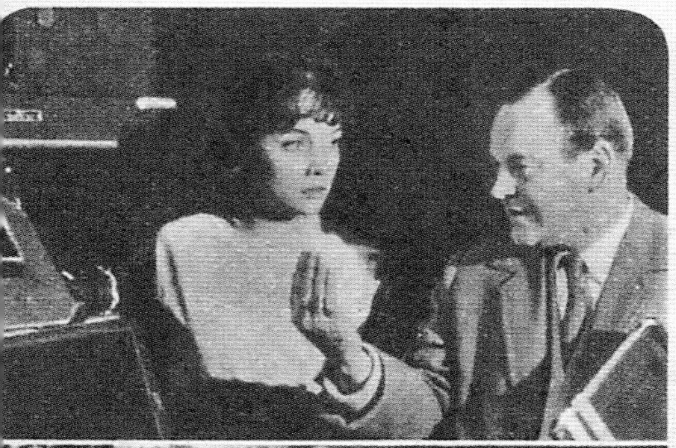

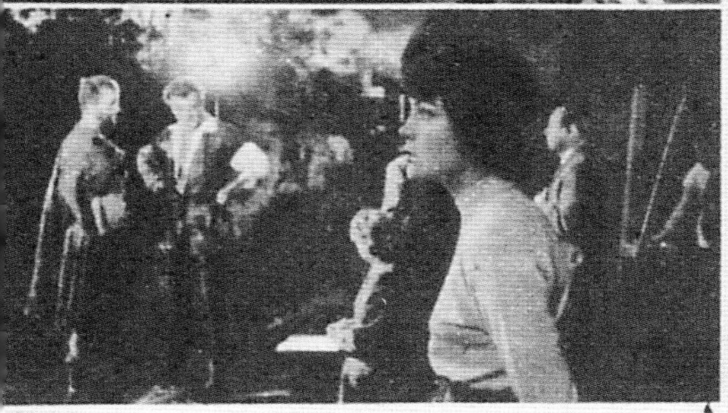

Filming is a serious matter either side of the camera. Director Terry Bishop explains mechanics while Robin Hood prepares the next scene

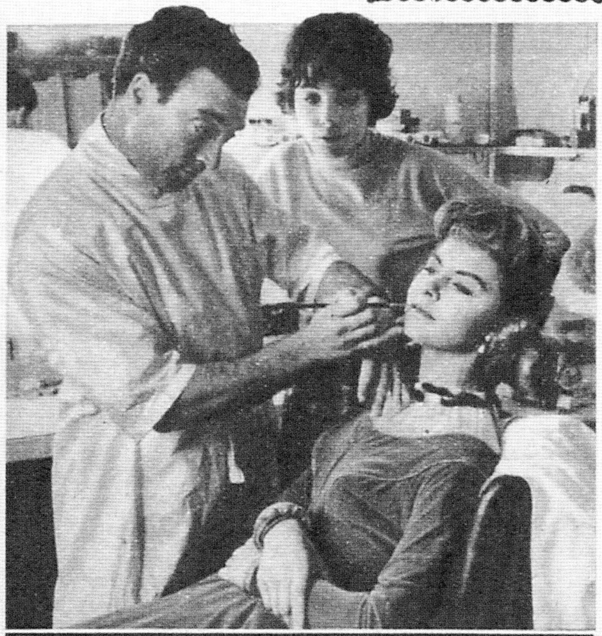

Beautiful Pat Driscoll isn't at the dentist's. She's having the finishing touches put to her make-up. Even Robin's glade needs glamour

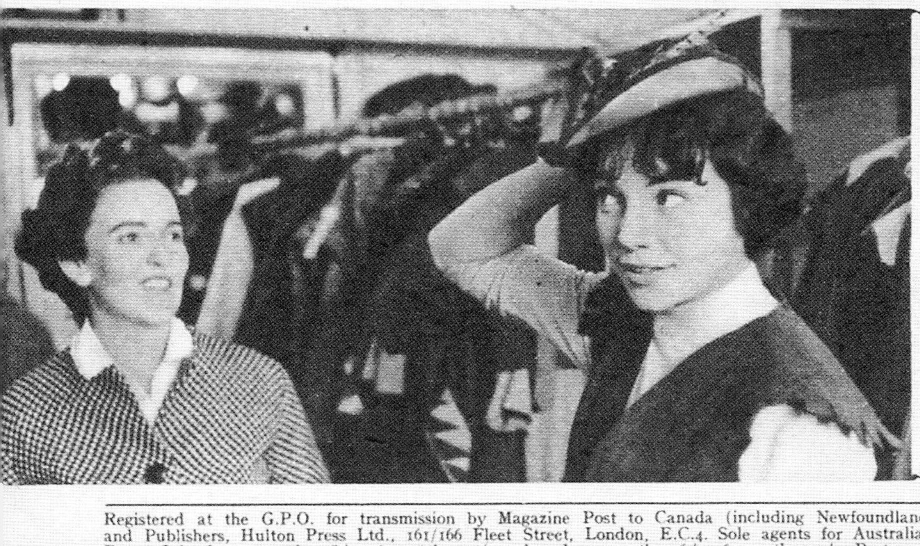

Brenda Gardner designs and makes the costumes herself. I couldn't help feeling that Robin might have risked capture even for me in this little hat

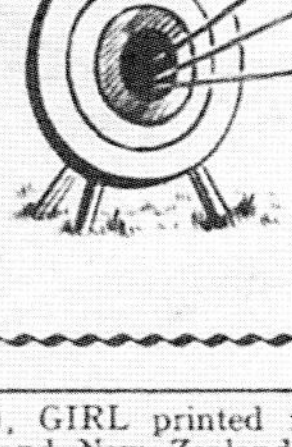

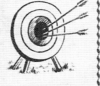

IT all felt rather like a dream. There I was, standing in the darkness, gazing into a beautiful sunlit glade, watching a tall, richly robed man who was about to launch an arrow into a cowering peasant. Suddenly, from the undergrowth, came a menacing voice: "Throw down that bow." Dropping his weapon, the man slowly turned and said: "Must you always interfere with my plans, Robin Hood?"

But that's where my dream ended. " Cut ! " shouted the director – and another few feet of film were 'in the can', ready to make up another thrilling adventure of Robin Hood.

The scene was no less dream-like even when the lights clicked on in the vast studio at Walton-on-Thames, which is the indoor home of so many television film serials. Maid Marion was sitting reading a newspaper; helmeted soldiers sat around smoking cigarettes as Little John strode by complete with tights, leather jerkin – and brown brogue shoes. Ranged around the indoor 'glen' three enormous film cameras pointed their blind eyes at the now empty scene of a woodland path – it was not until you looked upwards that you saw that the apparently giant trees had been unceremoniously lopped off just above camera level.

"Pretty fantastic, isn't it?" said the director, Terry Bishop. "It may be cheating, but we found it very difficult to shoot long scenes outdoors – so we made an exact replica of Robin's camp here in the studio. When you see the outlaws in their camp on your television screen, you can be almost certain that it was shot in here. All the long-distance shots are made on location only a few miles from here, though."

"I suppose, that's where the castle lies?" I asked hopefully, hanging on to the last few shreds of my dream.

"Hey, Duncan, will you show our guest around our castle?" said the director, grinning, as a terrifyingly fierce Highlander swept by with his kilt swirling.

"Och, lassie, it's noo castle but a couple o' plaster walls," growled my bearded guide, "but weel, come on."

Sure enough, walls which looked as sturdy as Stonehenge were mere wood and plaster.

"Here, lassie!" said Duncan of Stonykirk, alias Hugh McDermott, drawing his two-handed claymore. "I'll show ye how we fought seven hundred years ago." He then proceeded to cut madly at thin air, forcing me behind him and backing slowly up the pseudo - stone stairway. "I won't let 'em at ye, lassie," he panted, still retreating from our invisible assailants.

Inside the studio the scene was being changed, ready for the next 'take'. One half-hour film per week throughout the winter means a pretty tight schedule, and hard work by everyone from the wardrobe mistress to Richard Greene himself.

Maid Marion wore a sack!

I asked Brenda Gardner, who is in charge of producing everything, from Robin's Lincoln green to the feather in Maid Marion's cap, where she finds so many varied costumes. "I do a lot of research into clothes worn around the year 1200, and then I design and make most of the costumes myself – but the women's dresses are a problem. A real Maid Marion would have worn a dress more resembling a long nightshirt, so we had to do something about that."

"Robin's on set," I heard being called from the studio, so, excusing myself from the 'wardrobe', I rushed over to see Richard Greene in action.

Robin was standing in the studio glade talking to Little John, and as I watched him, I realized just why the series of films is so popular both in America and over here. He fits the part of the legendary outlaw to perfection. His bright blue eyes twinkled merrily under black curly hair, and I sat enthralled as he explained the technicalities of archery.

I'm jolly glad that I've been given a chance of re-living mediaeval Britain through the eyes of Robin Hood and his Merry Men – and each time I sit in front of the TV screen, I'll remember just what a lucky girl Maid Marion is!

Registered at the G.P.O. for transmission by Magazine Post to Canada (including Newfoundland), GIRL printed in Great Britain by Eric Bemrose Ltd., Long Lane, Liverpool 9, for the Proprietors and Publishers, Hulton Press Ltd., 161/166 Fleet Street, London, E.C.4. Sole agents for Australia and New Zealand, Gordon & Gotch (A/sia) Ltd.; South Africa, Central News Agency Ltd. Subscription Rate: Inland, 12 months 28/2; 6 months 14/1; abroad 12 months 26/-; 6 months 13/-. Postage for single copies: Inland 2d; Foreign 1½d; Canada 1d. You can have GIRL sent to any address in this

'GIRL' PARTY AT PINEWOOD!

A special party to mark a special occasion – GIRL'S fifth birthday !

ON Friday, we celebrate the fifth birthday of GIRL. Our first issue came out on November 2nd, 1951. Happy anniversary to all our readers, and especially to those who remember the first issue. As we told you earlier, we decided to celebrate with a party at Pinewood film studios where so many of the great J. Arthur Rank films have been made. We do wish all our readers could have been there! As that was impossible, we picked twenty Club members at random, and asked them to come along to the studio with us. It was a really wonderful day, and on this page you can see some of the pictures we took. Our first stop was Windsor, where we looked round the castle. After that we then had tea (with a magnificent birthday cake) and met some of Britain's leading stars. We were lucky enough, too, to see two films in the making—"True as a Turtle", starring John Gregson and June Thorburn, and "Up in the World", starring that great comedian Norman Wisdom. We all had a very happy birthday party and we hope you will enjoy reading about it!

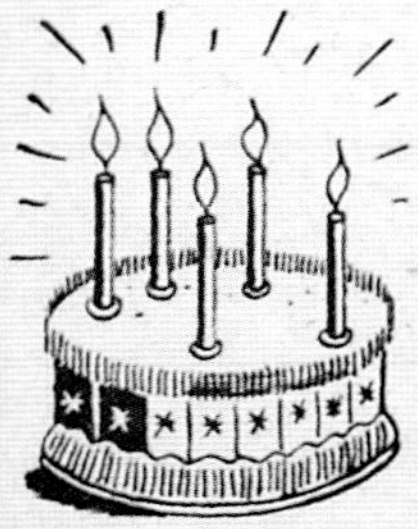

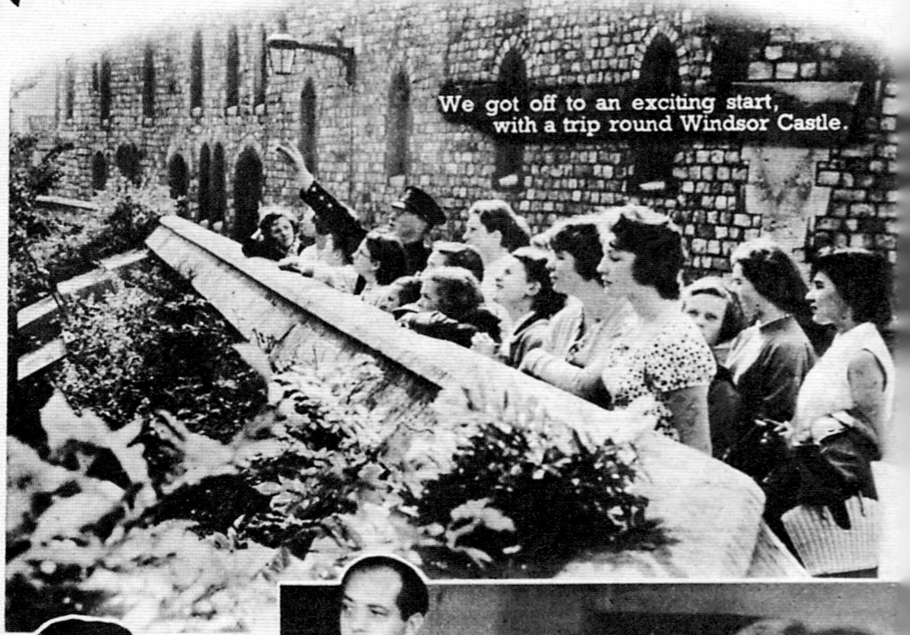

We got off to an exciting start, with a trip round Windsor Castle.

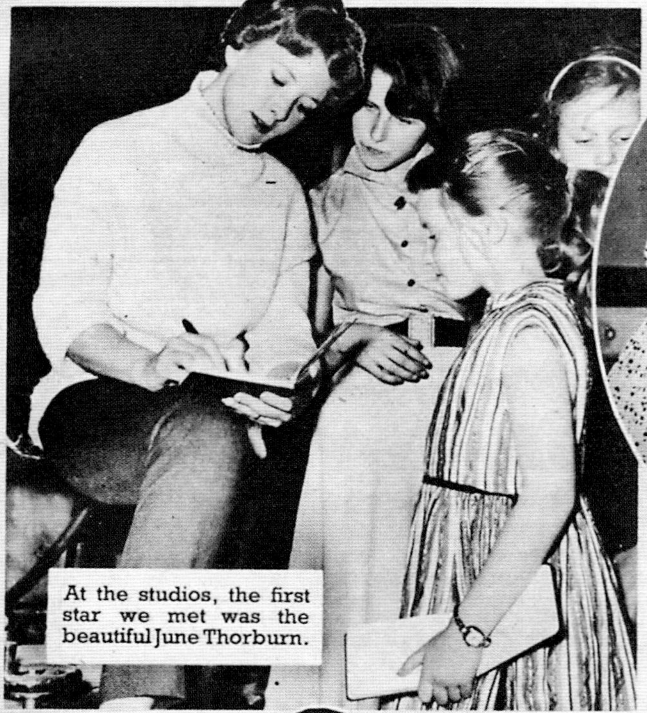

At the studios, the first star we met was the beautiful June Thorburn.

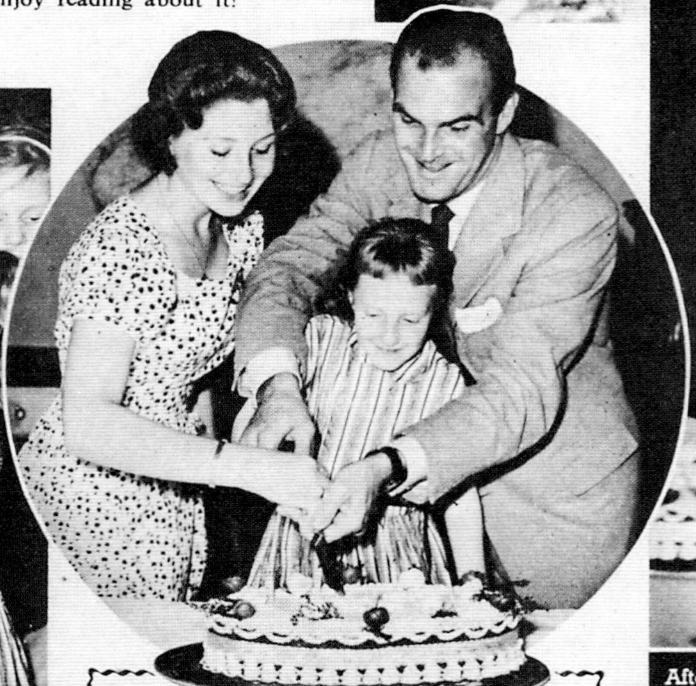

Tea time next – and time to cut the cake!

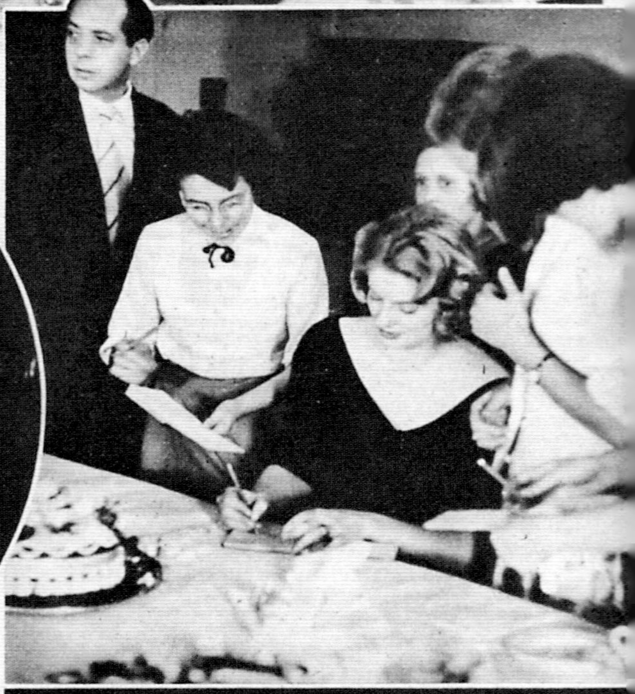

After Stanley Baker had helped cut the cake, Miss Jean Crouch, the Assistant Editor, was soon signing autographs.

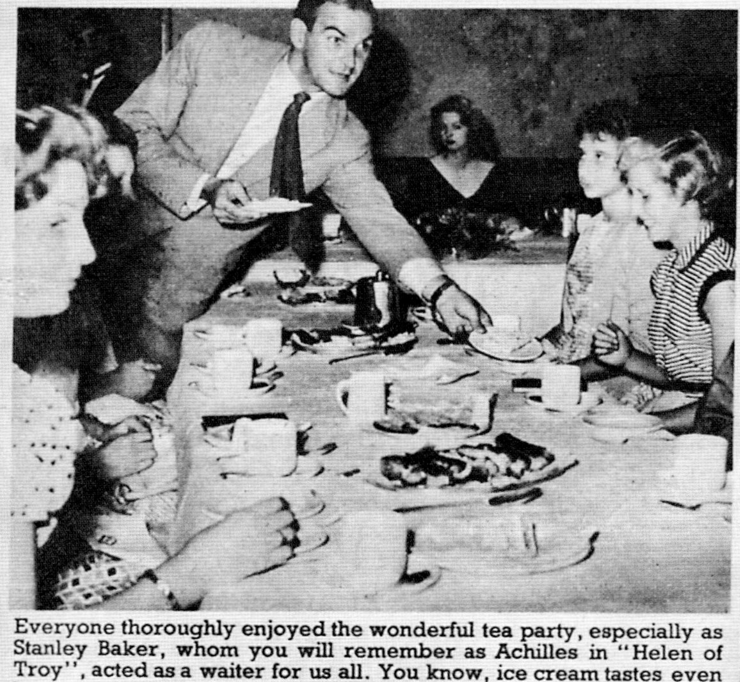

Everyone thoroughly enjoyed the wonderful tea party, especially as Stanley Baker, whom you will remember as Achilles in "Helen of Troy", acted as a waiter for us all. You know, ice cream tastes even better than usual when your favourite film star fetches it for you!

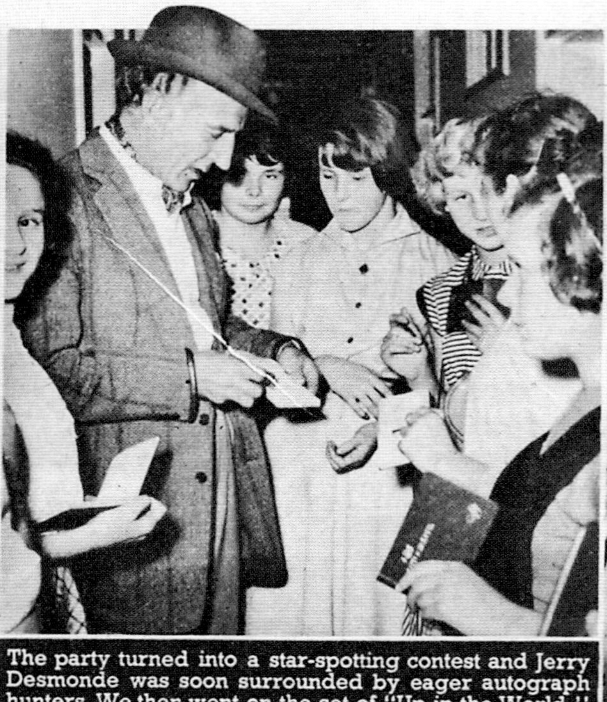

The party turned into a star-spotting contest and Jerry Desmonde was soon surrounded by eager autograph hunters. We then went on the set of "Up in the World."

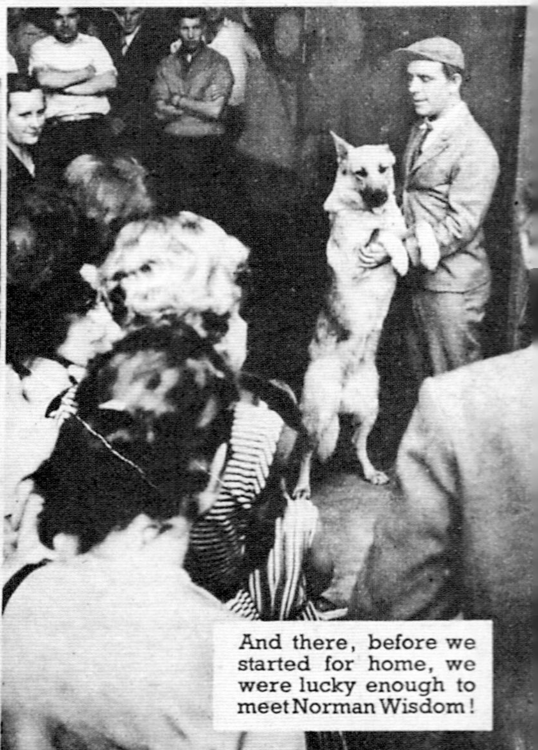

And there, before we started for home, we were lucky enough to meet Norman Wisdom!

Registered at the G.P.O. for transmission by Magazine Post to Canada (including Newfoundland). GIRL printed in Great Britain by Eric Bemrose Ltd., Long Lane, Liverpool 9, for the Proprietors and Publishers

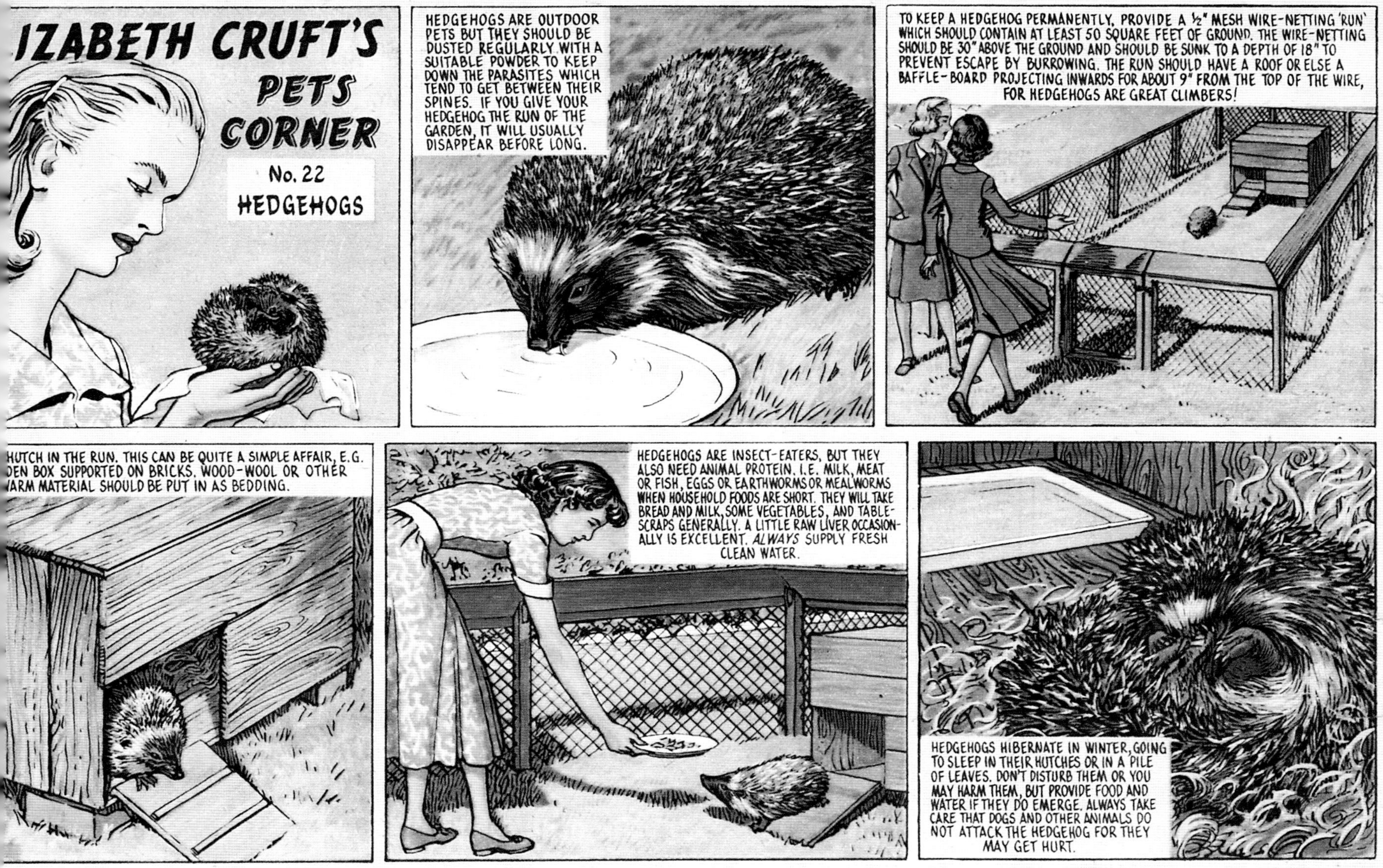
IZABETH CRUFT'S PETS CORNER
No. 22 HEDGEHOGS
HEDGEHOGS ARE OUTDOOR PETS BUT THEY SHOULD BE DUSTED REGULARLY WITH A SUITABLE POWDER TO KEEP DOWN THE PARASITES WHICH TEND TO GET BETWEEN THEIR SPINES. IF YOU GIVE YOUR HEDGEHOG THE RUN OF THE GARDEN, IT WILL USUALLY DISAPPEAR BEFORE LONG.
TO KEEP A HEDGEHOG PERMANENTLY, PROVIDE A ½" MESH WIRE-NETTING 'RUN' WHICH SHOULD CONTAIN AT LEAST 50 SQUARE FEET OF GROUND. THE WIRE-NETTING SHOULD BE 30" ABOVE THE GROUND AND SHOULD BE SUNK TO A DEPTH OF 18" TO PREVENT ESCAPE BY BURROWING. THE RUN SHOULD HAVE A ROOF OR ELSE A BAFFLE-BOARD PROJECTING INWARDS FOR ABOUT 9" FROM THE TOP OF THE WIRE, FOR HEDGEHOGS ARE GREAT CLIMBERS!
HUTCH IN THE RUN. THIS CAN BE QUITE A SIMPLE AFFAIR, E.G. DEN BOX SUPPORTED ON BRICKS. WOOD-WOOL OR OTHER VARM MATERIAL SHOULD BE PUT IN AS BEDDING.
HEDGEHOGS ARE INSECT-EATERS, BUT THEY ALSO NEED ANIMAL PROTEIN, I.E. MILK, MEAT OR FISH, EGGS OR EARTHWORMS OR MEALWORMS WHEN HOUSEHOLD FOODS ARE SHORT. THEY WILL TAKE BREAD AND MILK, SOME VEGETABLES, AND TABLE-SCRAPS GENERALLY. A LITTLE RAW LIVER OCCASIONALLY IS EXCELLENT. ALWAYS SUPPLY FRESH CLEAN WATER.
HEDGEHOGS HIBERNATE IN WINTER, GOING TO SLEEP IN THEIR HUTCHES OR IN A PILE OF LEAVES. DON'T DISTURB THEM OR YOU MAY HARM THEM, BUT PROVIDE FOOD AND WATER IF THEY DO EMERGE. ALWAYS TAKE CARE THAT DOGS AND OTHER ANIMALS DO NOT ATTACK THE HEDGEHOG FOR THEY MAY GET HURT.

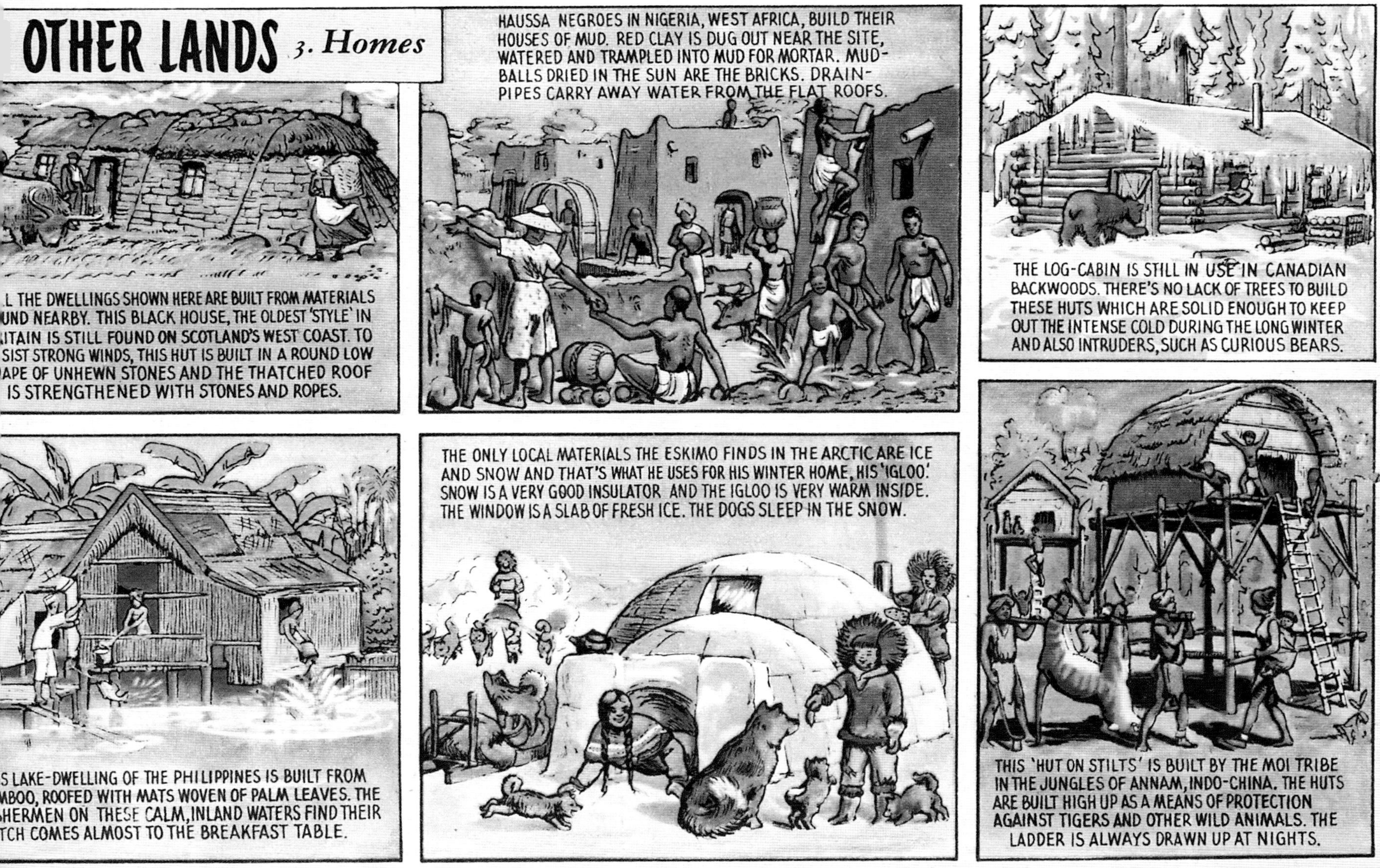
OTHER LANDS 3. Homes
L THE DWELLINGS SHOWN HERE ARE BUILT FROM MATERIALS UND NEARBY. THIS BLACK HOUSE, THE OLDEST 'STYLE' IN ITAIN IS STILL FOUND ON SCOTLAND'S WEST COAST. TO SIST STRONG WINDS, THIS HUT IS BUILT IN A ROUND LOW APE OF UNHEWN STONES AND THE THATCHED ROOF IS STRENGTHENED WITH STONES AND ROPES.
HAUSSA NEGROES IN NIGERIA, WEST AFRICA, BUILD THEIR HOUSES OF MUD. RED CLAY IS DUG OUT NEAR THE SITE, WATERED AND TRAMPLED INTO MUD FOR MORTAR. MUD-BALLS DRIED IN THE SUN ARE THE BRICKS. DRAIN-PIPES CARRY AWAY WATER FROM THE FLAT ROOFS.
THE LOG-CABIN IS STILL IN USE IN CANADIAN BACKWOODS. THERE'S NO LACK OF TREES TO BUILD THESE HUTS WHICH ARE SOLID ENOUGH TO KEEP OUT THE INTENSE COLD DURING THE LONG WINTER AND ALSO INTRUDERS, SUCH AS CURIOUS BEARS.
S LAKE-DWELLING OF THE PHILIPPINES IS BUILT FROM MBOO, ROOFED WITH MATS WOVEN OF PALM LEAVES. THE HERMEN ON THESE CALM, INLAND WATERS FIND THEIR TCH COMES ALMOST TO THE BREAKFAST TABLE.
THE ONLY LOCAL MATERIALS THE ESKIMO FINDS IN THE ARCTIC ARE ICE AND SNOW AND THAT'S WHAT HE USES FOR HIS WINTER HOME, HIS 'IGLOO.' SNOW IS A VERY GOOD INSULATOR AND THE IGLOO IS VERY WARM INSIDE. THE WINDOW IS A SLAB OF FRESH ICE. THE DOGS SLEEP IN THE SNOW.
THIS 'HUT ON STILTS' IS BUILT BY THE MOI TRIBE IN THE JUNGLES OF ANNAM, INDO-CHINA. THE HUTS ARE BUILT HIGH UP AS A MEANS OF PROTECTION AGAINST TIGERS AND OTHER WILD ANIMALS. THE LADDER IS ALWAYS DRAWN UP AT NIGHTS.

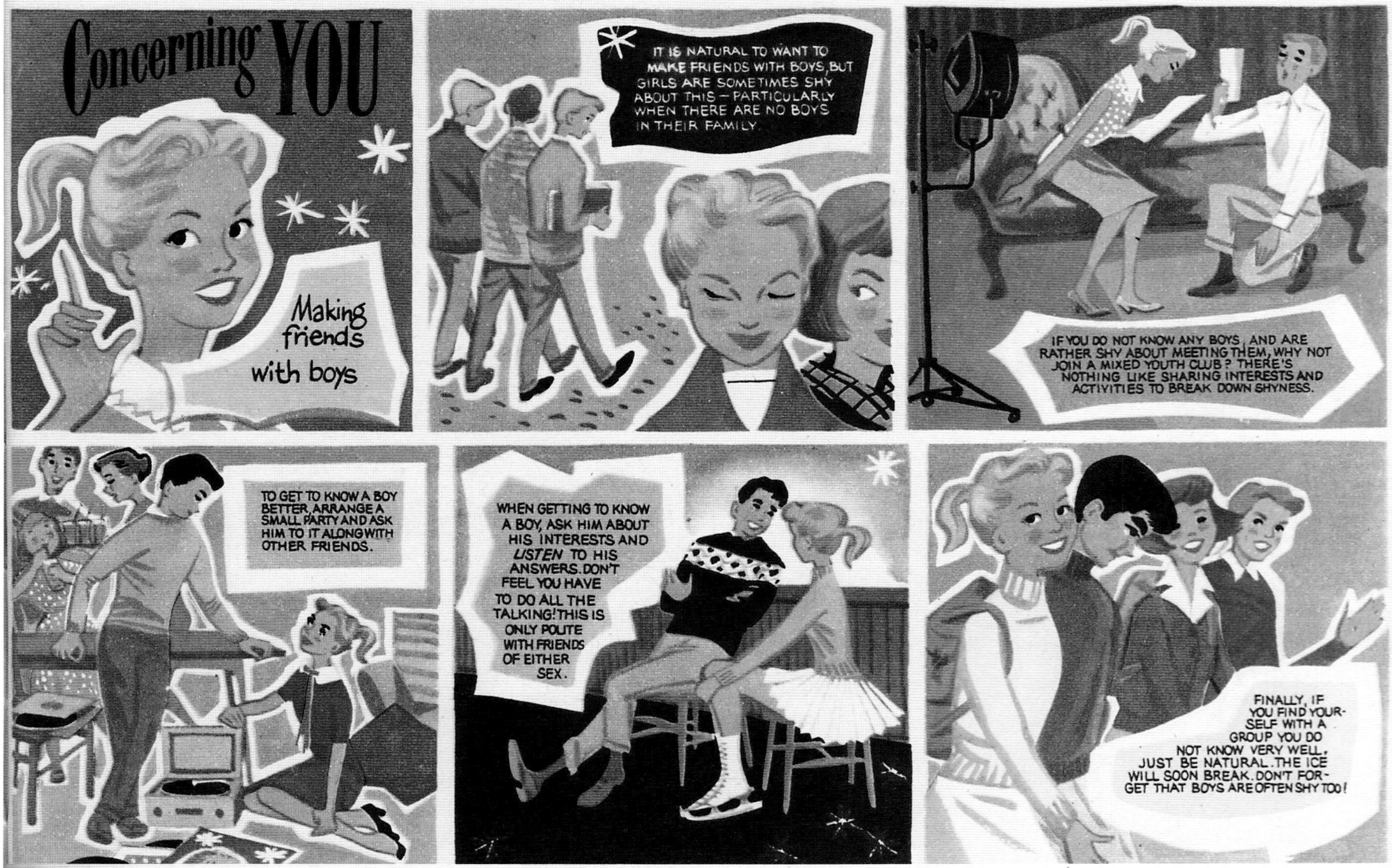
Concerning YOU
Making friends with boys
IT IS NATURAL TO WANT TO MAKE FRIENDS WITH BOYS, BUT GIRLS ARE SOMETIMES SHY ABOUT THIS – PARTICULARLY WHEN THERE ARE NO BOYS IN THEIR FAMILY.
IF YOU DO NOT KNOW ANY BOYS, AND ARE RATHER SHY ABOUT MEETING THEM, WHY NOT JOIN A MIXED YOUTH CLUB? THERE'S NOTHING LIKE SHARING INTERESTS AND ACTIVITIES TO BREAK DOWN SHYNESS.
TO GET TO KNOW A BOY BETTER, ARRANGE A SMALL PARTY AND ASK HIM TO IT ALONG WITH OTHER FRIENDS.
WHEN GETTING TO KNOW A BOY, ASK HIM ABOUT HIS INTERESTS AND LISTEN TO HIS ANSWERS. DON'T FEEL YOU HAVE TO DO ALL THE TALKING! THIS IS ONLY POLITE WITH FRIENDS OF EITHER SEX.
FINALLY, IF YOU FIND YOURSELF WITH A GROUP YOU DO NOT KNOW VERY WELL, JUST BE NATURAL. THE ICE WILL SOON BREAK. DON'T FORGET THAT BOYS ARE OFTEN SHY TOO!

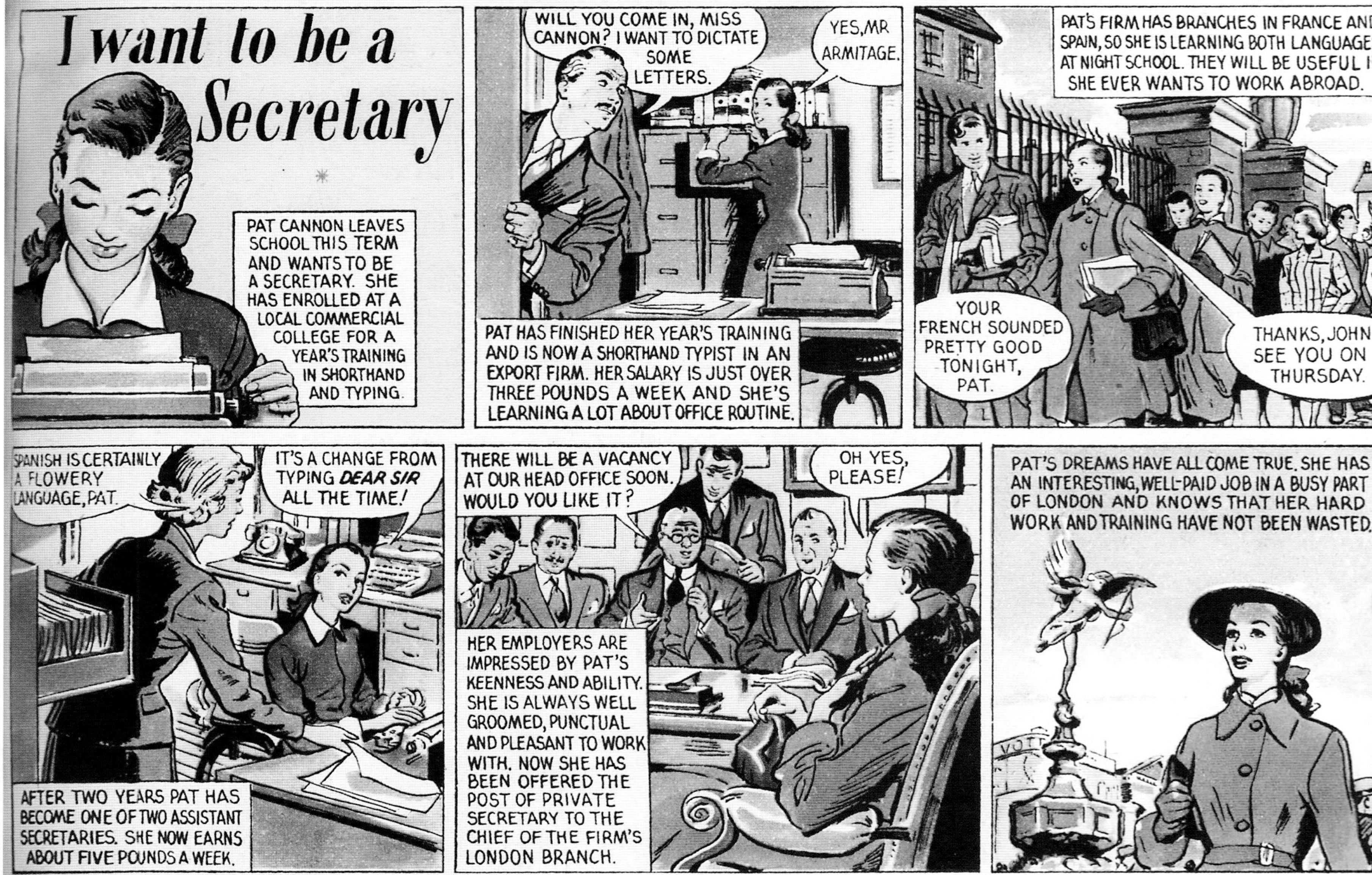
I want to be a Secretary
PAT CANNON LEAVES SCHOOL THIS TERM AND WANTS TO BE A SECRETARY. SHE HAS ENROLLED AT A LOCAL COMMERCIAL COLLEGE FOR A YEAR'S TRAINING IN SHORTHAND AND TYPING.
WILL YOU COME IN, MISS CANNON? I WANT TO DICTATE SOME LETTERS.
YES, MR ARMITAGE.
PAT HAS FINISHED HER YEAR'S TRAINING AND IS NOW A SHORTHAND TYPIST IN AN EXPORT FIRM. HER SALARY IS JUST OVER THREE POUNDS A WEEK AND SHE'S LEARNING A LOT ABOUT OFFICE ROUTINE.
PAT'S FIRM HAS BRANCHES IN FRANCE AND SPAIN, SO SHE IS LEARNING BOTH LANGUAGES AT NIGHT SCHOOL. THEY WILL BE USEFUL IF SHE EVER WANTS TO WORK ABROAD.
YOUR FRENCH SOUNDED PRETTY GOOD TONIGHT, PAT.
THANKS, JOHN! SEE YOU ON THURSDAY.
SPANISH IS CERTAINLY A FLOWERY LANGUAGE, PAT.
IT'S A CHANGE FROM TYPING DEAR SIR ALL THE TIME!
AFTER TWO YEARS PAT HAS BECOME ONE OF TWO ASSISTANT SECRETARIES. SHE NOW EARNS ABOUT FIVE POUNDS A WEEK.
THERE WILL BE A VACANCY AT OUR HEAD OFFICE SOON. WOULD YOU LIKE IT?
OH YES, PLEASE!
HER EMPLOYERS ARE IMPRESSED BY PAT'S KEENNESS AND ABILITY. SHE IS ALWAYS WELL GROOMED, PUNCTUAL AND PLEASANT TO WORK WITH. NOW SHE HAS BEEN OFFERED THE POST OF PRIVATE SECRETARY TO THE CHIEF OF THE FIRM'S LONDON BRANCH.
PAT'S DREAMS HAVE ALL COME TRUE. SHE HAS AN INTERESTING, WELL-PAID JOB IN A BUSY PART OF LONDON AND KNOWS THAT HER HARD WORK AND TRAINING HAVE NOT BEEN WASTED.

ADVENTURE CORNER

If you lead an interesting life write in to 'Adventure Corner' and tell us all about it.

Frances Candfield

★

Twelve-year-old Frances Candfield has recently returned to England after living in Cyprus. She made a great many friends there, and thoroughly enjoyed every minute of the lovely climate.

While she was in Nicosia, Frances had a dog called Sally whom she adored. She found time to carry on with her piano lessons, but these always had to be during the cool of the evenings.

Here is Frances at a farm near Kyrenia — a favourite call for travellers — and riding at the Saddle Club at Athalassa.

At last Frances and her family returned to England. Here she is homeward bound on the "Maltese Prince" and at Cromer just after she had arrived.

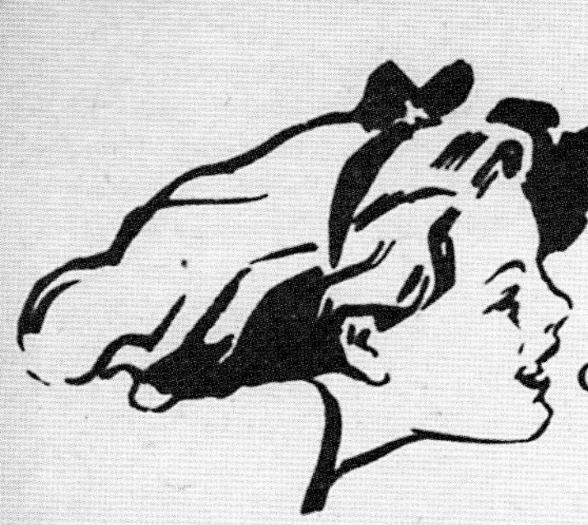

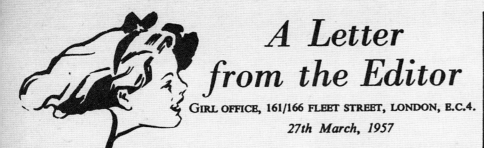

A Letter from the Editor

GIRL OFFICE, 161/166 FLEET STREET, LONDON, E.C.4.

27th March, 1957

I WOULD like to say thank you to everyone who entered for the Poetry Competition in January. The judges and myself have really enjoyed reading your poems and we were all very much impressed by the high standard of your work. It has been very difficult indeed to pick fifty prizewinners out of the several thousand entries sent in, because all of them were so good. We have come to a final decision at last, however, and the results of the competition will be announced in two weeks' time.

I'm sure you will all be pleased to know that Valerie Loeb, one of the main winners of the 1955 GIRL Painting Competition, has been awarded a place at the Slade School of Art. Many other past prizewinners are doing very well too.

Yours sincerely,

Marcus Morris

WINNERS

The top winner of GIRL Competition No. 6 is Pauline Jones of Hockley, near Tamworth, Staffordshire. Congratulations, Pauline! We would also like to send our congratulations to the twenty-five runners-up. We have no room to print all their names, but if anyone would like a complete list of winners, they can always obtain one from our Liverpool office, but please remember to enclose a stamped, self-addressed envelope.

NEWS FOR ALL BALLET LOVERS!

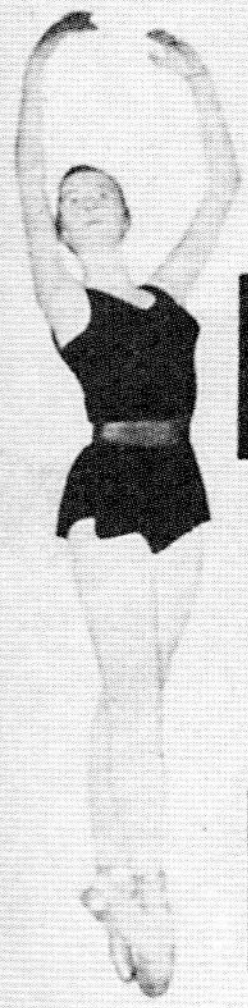

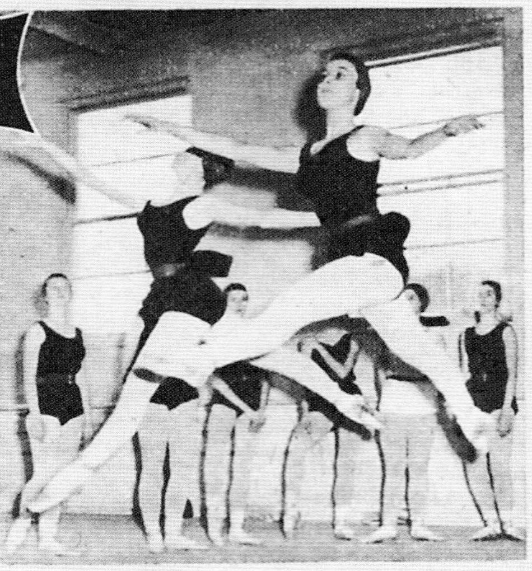

AS you know, the Royal Academy of Dancing's children's examinations are the first step towards a GIRL Ballet Scholarship. The grade examinations are being held in May and June and the closing dates for entries are as follows: –

Wednesday, 3rd April, 1957 – for those living in Scotland, North Wales, North of England and the Midlands.

Wednesday, 1st May, 1957 – for those living in the South of England, East Anglia and South Wales.

If you wish to enter, you should get in touch with your ballet teacher immediately. Anyone between the ages of 7 and 17 is eligible to try for a Grade Examination – remember though, that our Scholarship scheme only applies to those over 9 and under 13. Entry forms for the R.A.D. grade examinations should be obtained from your local R.A.D. organiser, unless you live in the greater London area, when you should apply direct to: – Royal Academy of Dancing, 15, Holland Park Gardens, London, W.14. Please mark your envelope "Children's Examinations".

There isn't much time, so write off quickly!

30 Oil-Painting Sets to be won this week!

All you have to do is solve this simple word-and-picture puzzle

Here is a nice spring puzzle for you. We want you to work out the names of six flowers, by adding the names of the objects in the picture to letters already given you. There are thirty wonderful oil-painting sets for the winners.

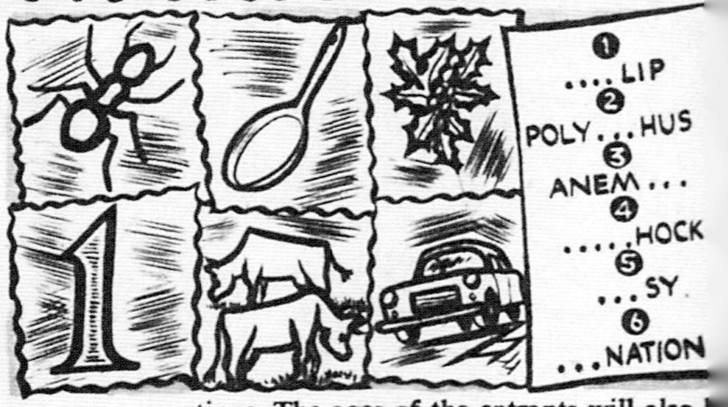
1 ....LIP
2 POLY....HUS
3 ANEM....
4 .....HOCK
5 ...SY
6 ...NATION

THE RULES

1. Each object in the illustration fits in with one of the words on the right to form the name of a flower. Pair up the words and pictures, then write the flower names on a postcard.

2. In the top right-hand corner of the same postcard add your name, address and age last birthday.

3. Points will be given for neatness and handwriting as well as for the correct solutions. The ages of the entrants will also be taken into consideration in the judging.

4. This competition is open to all gi[rls] up to and including the age of sixteen.

5. All entries should be sent to: – GI[RL] Competition No. 13, GIRL Reader Service[s], Long Lane, Aintree, Liverpool, 9, to arriv[e] there not later than 8th April, 1957.

6. Send no money; this is FREE.

7. The Editor's and judges' decision [is] final. No correspondence will be entere[d] into about any entry.

READERS' LETTERS

5/– *will be paid for every reader['s] letter printed on this pag[e]*

A LAMB WITH A BIG APPETITE

MY AUNT had a lamb she bought at market when it was only three days old and reared it on a bottle. When it was old enough to wander about the farm, it found that it could get its food straight from the cow. But in the end, it ate so much that my aunt was forced to sell it! – *E. M. Parkin, Hailsham, Sussex.*

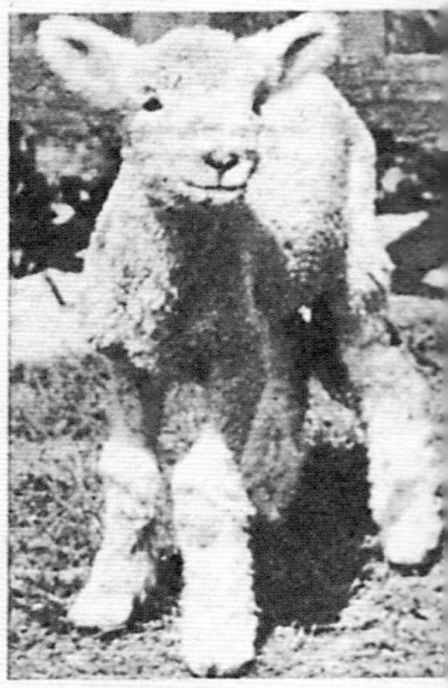

GIRL goes to Africa

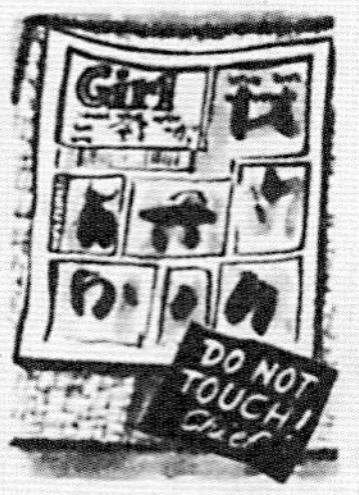
Girl
DO NOT TOUCH!

I HAVE recently come back from Sierra Leone, West Africa. I was three hundred miles out in the Bush. The biggest village consisted of five huts and one large hut for the chief. In the chief's hut I noticed a copy of GIRL lying on a fur rug, which was its own sacred place. Although it was quite battered, my father told me that they had found it in an uninhabited European bungalow. – *Christine Rayner, Walton-on-Thames, Surrey.*

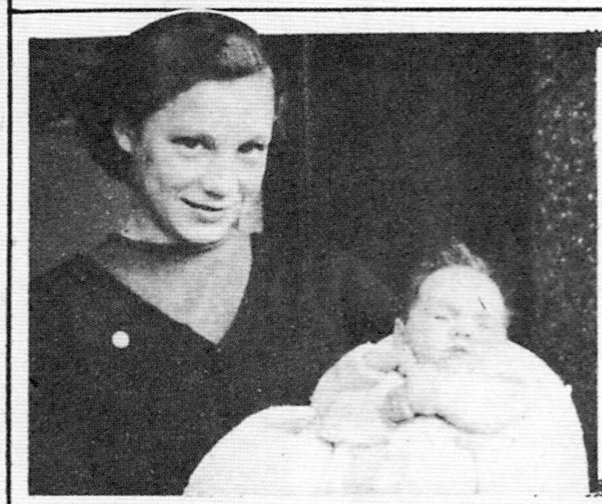

Star Adventurer

For an exceptional record of helpfulness in the home.

Josephine Westgate, aged 15, of Hayes, Middlesex.

COUPON G6

USE BLOCK LETTERS TO FILL THIS IN, PLEASE

This painting is the original work of:

FULL NAME ....

ADDRESS ....

....

....

AGE .... DATE OF BIRTH ....

SCHOOL ....

TITLE OF PAINTING ....

Signature of parent, teacher or guardian ....

(Maximum size of entry 3ft. x 2ft.).

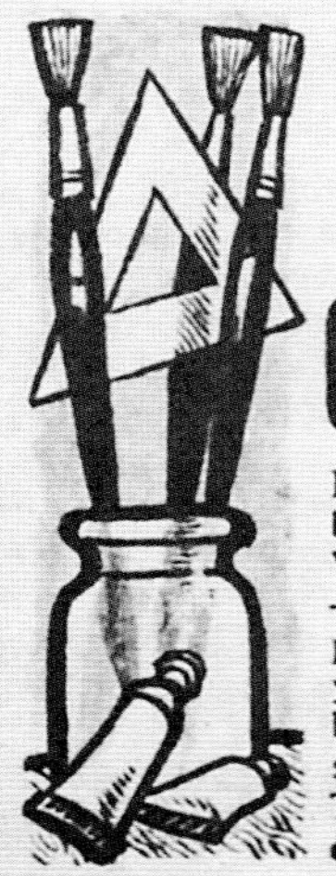

THE FOURTH GIRL PAINTING COMPETITION

Here is a competition to interest everybody – because everybody enjoys painting. We want you to paint something you enjoy – anything you like, a landscape, a portrait, or something you have made up yourself. Use the colour medium you like best, or if you would rather not paint, send us a sketch in pencil, charcoal or ink. The choice is yours, but remember the **closing date is 29th April, 1957.**

PLEASE READ THESE RULES VERY CAREFULLY

1. Paintings may be done in any colour medium. They may be on any subject, but must be original and not copied from other pictures or paintings. Entries must not exceed 3 ft. x 2 ft. and those measuring more than 2 ft. x 1 ft. should be mounted on stiff cardboard.
2. The coupon on this page must be filled in by you and signed by a parent, guardian or teacher in the place marked. It must then be glued firmly to the back of your painting before the painting is sent to us.
3. You may send in as many entries as you like, but each one must be accompanied by a coupon cut from GIRL. These coupons will be appearing each week.
4. All entries should be sent to: Art Council, GIRL Reader Services, Long Lane, Aintree, Liverpool, 9. Final closing date of the competition is 29th April, 1957, but we would welcome entries as soon as possible.
5. To prevent damage, paintings must be carefully packed. They should be sent in flat, unframed and witho[ut] glass. We accept no responsibility f[or] those lost or damaged in transit.
6. Each parcel must contain stamp[s] for postage and a self-addressed lab[el] if you want your painting returne[d]. Those paintings chosen for exhibitio[n] or reproduction become the pro[perty] of GIRL for the period require[d].
7. The competition is open to a[ll] girls up to the age of seventeen. [It] will be judged by our panel of a[rt] experts in four different age group[s]:
   (a) nine and under
   (b) ten and eleven
   (c) twelve and thirteen
   (d) fourteen, fifteen and sixteen.
   The age groups apply as on 29th April, 1957.
8. No entries sent in from oversea[s] are eligible.
9. The decision of the Editor in a[ll] matters relating to this competition [is] final, and we regret that no corre[spondence] can be entered into regard[ing] any of the entries submitted.

ANGELA
AIR HOSTESS

the story of a girl who longed for adventure

Written by
BETTY ROLAND

Drawn by
DUDLEY POUT

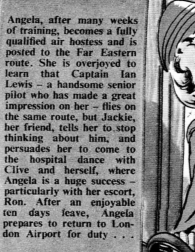

Angela, after many weeks of training, becomes a fully qualified air hostess and is posted to the Far Eastern route. She is overjoyed to learn that Captain Ian Lewis – a handsome senior pilot who has made a great impression on her – flies on the same route, but Jackie, her friend, tells her to stop thinking about him, and persuades her to come to the hospital dance with Clive and herself, where Angela is a huge success – particularly with her escort, Ron. After an enjoyable ten days leave, Angela prepares to return to London Airport for duty . . .

ANGELA, HAVE YOU GOT EVERYTHING? TOOTHPASTE, MONEY, PASSPORT?

YES, MOTHER DEAR, THE LOT!

DON'T THINK I'M SILLY. IT'S SAINT CHRISTOPHER — THE PATRON SAINT OF TRAVELLERS. WEAR IT ROUND YOUR NECK.

RUBY DEAR, HOW SWEET OF YOU!

GOOD-BYE, DARLING. GOOD LUCK!

LOCK YOUR DOOR AT NIGHT AND DON'T GO OUT WITH STRANGE MEN, ANGELA!

DON'T WORRY, MRS PRICE, SHE'LL BE TOO TIRED TO GO OUT WITH ANYONE!

Clive spoke jokingly, but Angela was soon to learn the truth of what he said. The ordeal of that first flight was something she would long remember as a nightmare of anxiety and tired feet! But, unaware of this, an excited girl arrives at the office of Mr Brooks, Chief of Catering Services . . .

ANGELA WELLS, SIR. REPORTING FOR DUTY, LONDON-TOKYO FLIGHT.

GLAD TO SEE YOU'RE HERE ON TIME, MISS WELLS. COME AND MEET THE OTHER MEMBERS OF THE CREW.

MR ALLEN, YOUR CHIEF STEWARD. MR YOUNG AND MR BARBER, HIS ASSISTANTS.

FIRST TIME UP, MISS WELLS?

DON'T WORRY, WE'LL LOOK AFTER YOU.

THE CABIN CREW IS BRIEFED ABOUT THE COMING FLIGHT.

THERE'LL BE SOME SPECIAL DIETS. TWO BRAHMIN PRIESTS AS FAR AS CALCUTTA, AND A DIABETIC GOING TO HONG KONG.

NO MEAT FOR THE BRAHMINS — NO STARCH OR SUGAR FOR THE DIABETIC. RIGHT! I'LL SEE TO THAT, SIR.

MISS WELLS, THERE ARE TWO YOUNG CHILDREN AND A MOTHER WITH A BABY. SEE YOU HAVE A GOOD SUPPLY OF TOYS, COMICS, PICTURE-BOOKS AND PUZZLES. NOT FORGETTING BABY FOOD AND SAFETY-PINS!

HERE'S THE PASSENGER-LIST. SOME V.I.P.s ON BOARD...A COUPLE OF FOREIGN DIPLOMATS ...AND ELSA CAVENDISH, THE FILM STAR.

SMELLING SALTS AND ASPIRIN FOR *HER*, MISS WELLS.

WE'RE SENDING OUT A SENIOR GIRL WITH YOU THIS TIME, MISS WELLS. SHE'S OVER AT THE CUSTOMS. MEANWHILE, YOU CAN GO TO AMENITIES AND CHECK THROUGH THIS LIST.

OH DEAR, WHAT A RELIEF! I THOUGHT I'D HAVE TO MANAGE ON MY OWN.

AMENITIES DEPARTMENT

BOOKS, PAPERS, MAGAZINES...RAZOR-BLADES, COSMETICS, SHAVING-SOAP...WRITING-PAPER, INK AND PENCILS... TOYS, PLAYING-CARDS, JIG-SAW PUZZLES.... HEAVENS, WHAT A LIST! I'LL NEVER GET IT DONE IN TIME. I WISH THAT OTHER GIRL WAS HERE TO HELP ME.

BUT WHEN SHE DOES ARRIVE...

SANDRA!

YOU TWO KNOW EACH OTHER? WELL, THAT'S FINE.

YES, WE KNOW EACH OTHER. ALMOST *TOO* WELL, DON'T WE, ANGELA DARLING?

TO BE CONTINUED

continued on page 97 79

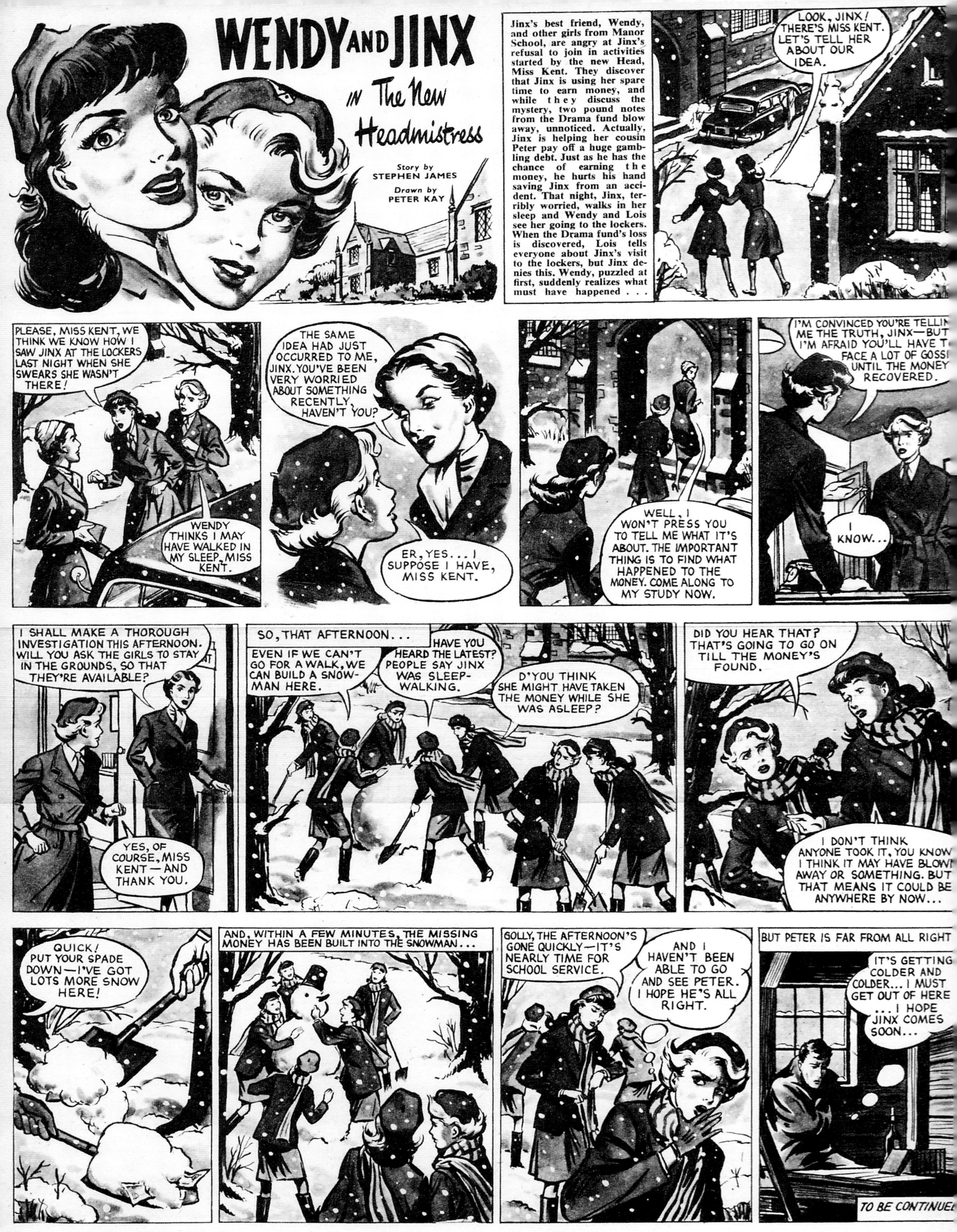
WENDY AND JINX
in The New Headmistress
Story by STEPHEN JAMES
Drawn by PETER KAY
Jinx's best friend, Wendy, and other girls from Manor School, are angry at Jinx's refusal to join in activities started by the new Head, Miss Kent. They discover that Jinx is using her spare time to earn money, and while they discuss the mystery, two pound notes from the Drama fund blow away, unnoticed. Actually, Jinx is helping her cousin Peter pay off a huge gambling debt. Just as he has the chance of earning the money, he hurts his hand saving Jinx from an accident. That night, Jinx, terribly worried, walks in her sleep and Wendy and Lois see her going to the lockers. When the Drama fund's loss is discovered, Lois tells everyone about Jinx's visit to the lockers, but Jinx denies this. Wendy, puzzled at first, suddenly realizes what must have happened . . .
LOOK, JINX! THERE'S MISS KENT. LET'S TELL HER ABOUT OUR IDEA.
PLEASE, MISS KENT, WE THINK WE KNOW HOW I SAW JINX AT THE LOCKERS LAST NIGHT WHEN SHE SWEARS SHE WASN'T THERE!
WENDY THINKS I MAY HAVE WALKED IN MY SLEEP, MISS KENT.
THE SAME IDEA HAD JUST OCCURRED TO ME, JINX. YOU'VE BEEN VERY WORRIED ABOUT SOMETHING RECENTLY, HAVEN'T YOU?
ER, YES... I SUPPOSE I HAVE, MISS KENT.
WELL, I WON'T PRESS YOU TO TELL ME WHAT IT'S ABOUT. THE IMPORTANT THING IS TO FIND WHAT HAPPENED TO THE MONEY. COME ALONG TO MY STUDY NOW.
I'M CONVINCED YOU'RE TELLIN ME THE TRUTH, JINX—BUT I'M AFRAID YOU'LL HAVE T FACE A LOT OF GOSSI UNTIL THE MONEY RECOVERED.
I KNOW...
I SHALL MAKE A THOROUGH INVESTIGATION THIS AFTERNOON. WILL YOU ASK THE GIRLS TO STAY IN THE GROUNDS, SO THAT THEY'RE AVAILABLE?
YES, OF COURSE, MISS KENT—AND THANK YOU.
SO, THAT AFTERNOON...
EVEN IF WE CAN'T GO FOR A WALK, WE CAN BUILD A SNOWMAN HERE.
HAVE YOU HEARD THE LATEST? PEOPLE SAY JINX WAS SLEEP-WALKING.
D'YOU THINK SHE MIGHT HAVE TAKEN THE MONEY WHILE SHE WAS ASLEEP?
DID YOU HEAR THAT? THAT'S GOING TO GO ON TILL THE MONEY'S FOUND.
I DON'T THINK ANYONE TOOK IT, YOU KNOW I THINK IT MAY HAVE BLOWN AWAY OR SOMETHING. BUT THAT MEANS IT COULD BE ANYWHERE BY NOW...
QUICK! PUT YOUR SPADE DOWN—I'VE GOT LOTS MORE SNOW HERE!
AND, WITHIN A FEW MINUTES, THE MISSING MONEY HAS BEEN BUILT INTO THE SNOWMAN...
GOLLY, THE AFTERNOON'S GONE QUICKLY—IT'S NEARLY TIME FOR SCHOOL SERVICE.
AND I HAVEN'T BEEN ABLE TO GO AND SEE PETER. I HOPE HE'S ALL RIGHT.
BUT PETER IS FAR FROM ALL RIGHT
IT'S GETTING COLDER AND COLDER... I MUST GET OUT OF HERE ... I HOPE JINX COMES SOON...
TO BE CONTINUE

continued on page

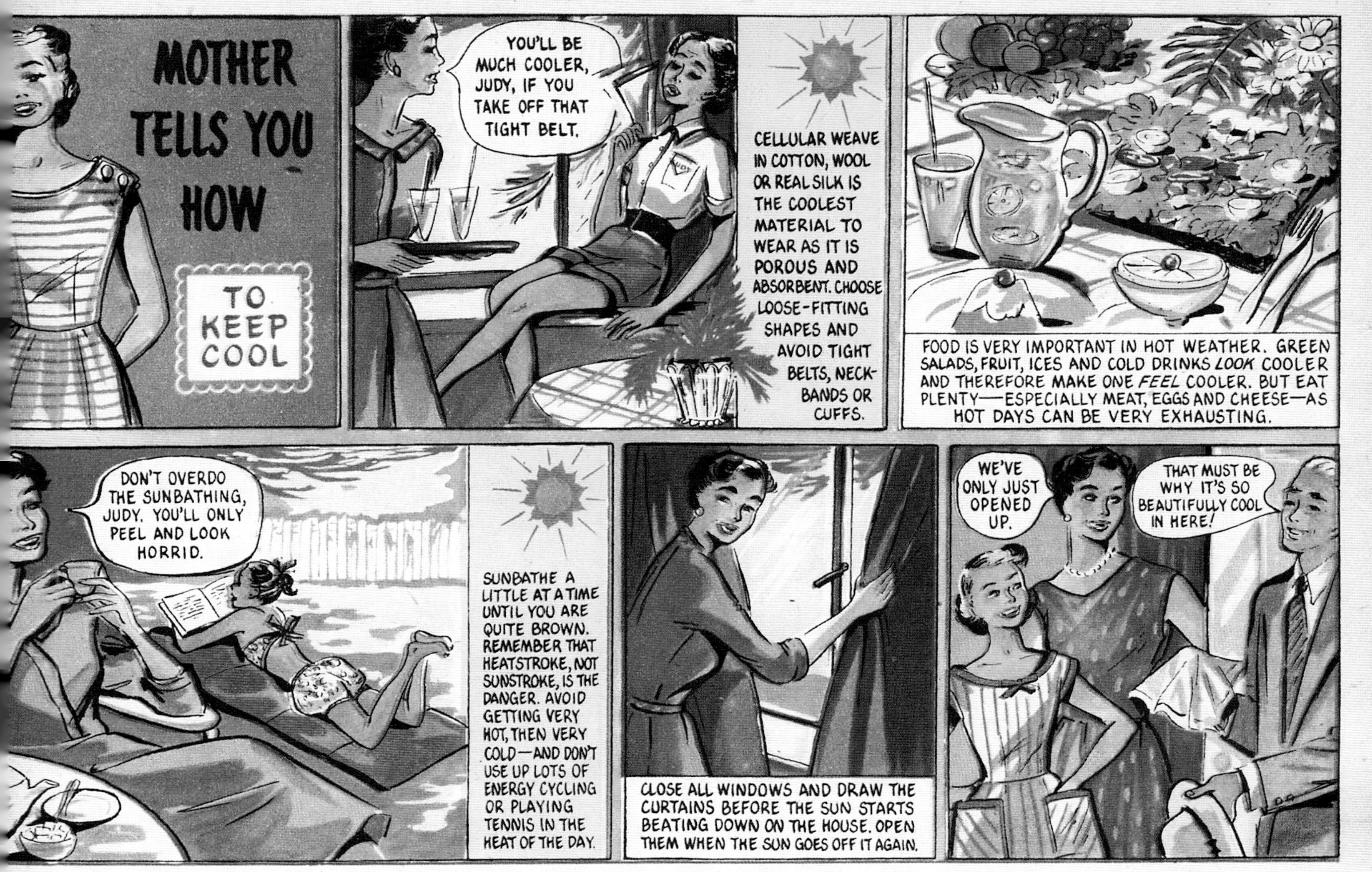

MOTHER TELLS YOU HOW
TO KEEP COOL
YOU'LL BE MUCH COOLER, JUDY, IF YOU TAKE OFF THAT TIGHT BELT.
CELLULAR WEAVE IN COTTON, WOOL OR REAL SILK IS THE COOLEST MATERIAL TO WEAR AS IT IS POROUS AND ABSORBENT. CHOOSE LOOSE-FITTING SHAPES AND AVOID TIGHT BELTS, NECK-BANDS OR CUFFS.
FOOD IS VERY IMPORTANT IN HOT WEATHER. GREEN SALADS, FRUIT, ICES AND COLD DRINKS *LOOK* COOLER AND THEREFORE MAKE ONE *FEEL* COOLER. BUT EAT PLENTY—ESPECIALLY MEAT, EGGS AND CHEESE—AS HOT DAYS CAN BE VERY EXHAUSTING.
DON'T OVERDO THE SUNBATHING, JUDY. YOU'LL ONLY PEEL AND LOOK HORRID.
SUNBATHE A LITTLE AT A TIME UNTIL YOU ARE QUITE BROWN. REMEMBER THAT HEATSTROKE, NOT SUNSTROKE, IS THE DANGER. AVOID GETTING VERY HOT, THEN VERY COLD—AND DON'T USE UP LOTS OF ENERGY CYCLING OR PLAYING TENNIS IN THE HEAT OF THE DAY.
CLOSE ALL WINDOWS AND DRAW THE CURTAINS BEFORE THE SUN STARTS BEATING DOWN ON THE HOUSE. OPEN THEM WHEN THE SUN GOES OFF IT AGAIN.
WE'VE ONLY JUST OPENED UP.
THAT MUST BE WHY IT'S SO BEAUTIFULLY COOL IN HERE!

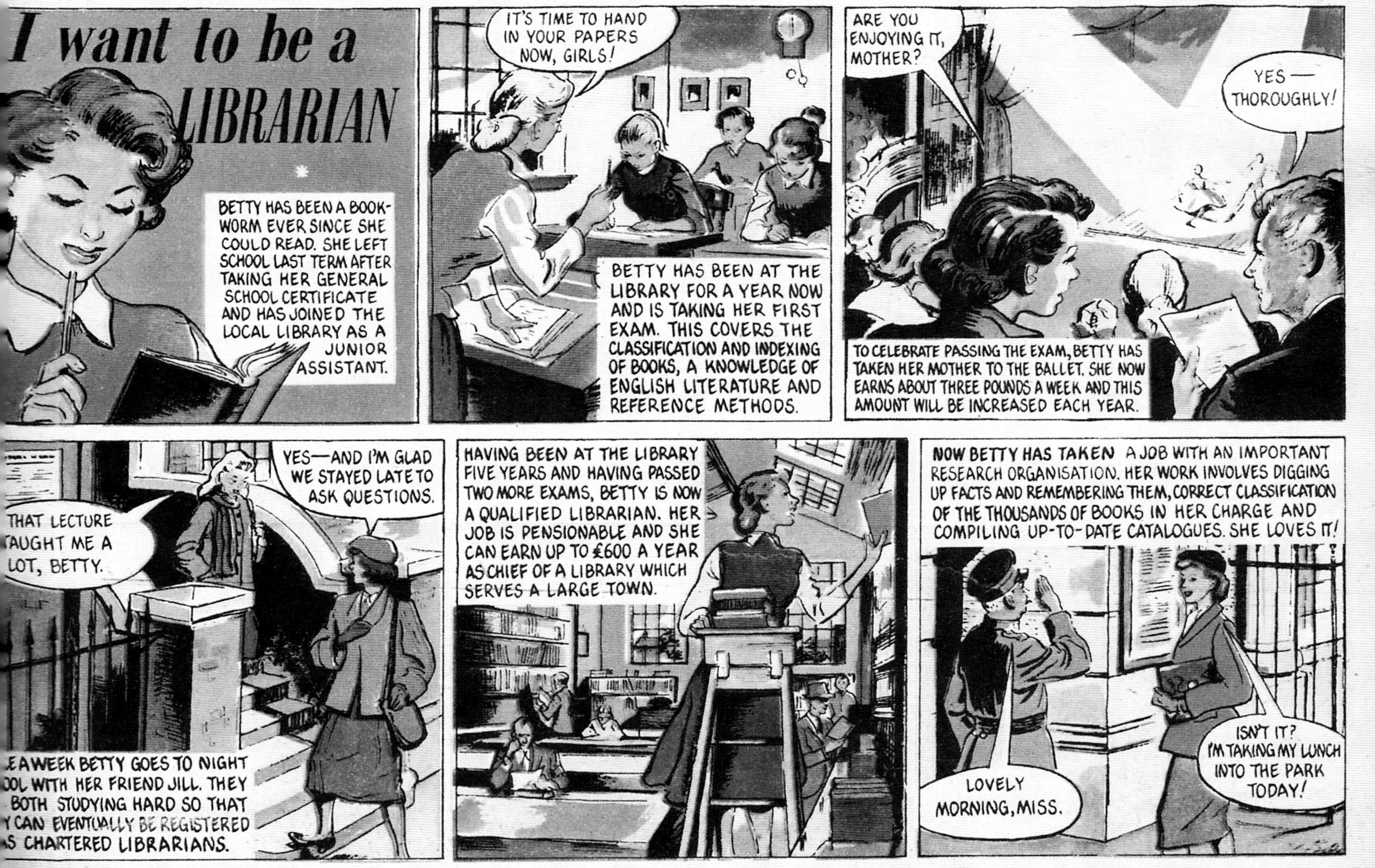

I want to be a LIBRARIAN
BETTY HAS BEEN A BOOK-WORM EVER SINCE SHE COULD READ. SHE LEFT SCHOOL LAST TERM AFTER TAKING HER GENERAL SCHOOL CERTIFICATE AND HAS JOINED THE LOCAL LIBRARY AS A JUNIOR ASSISTANT.
IT'S TIME TO HAND IN YOUR PAPERS NOW, GIRLS!
BETTY HAS BEEN AT THE LIBRARY FOR A YEAR NOW AND IS TAKING HER FIRST EXAM. THIS COVERS THE CLASSIFICATION AND INDEXING OF BOOKS, A KNOWLEDGE OF ENGLISH LITERATURE AND REFERENCE METHODS.
ARE YOU ENJOYING IT, MOTHER?
YES—THOROUGHLY!
TO CELEBRATE PASSING THE EXAM, BETTY HAS TAKEN HER MOTHER TO THE BALLET. SHE NOW EARNS ABOUT THREE POUNDS A WEEK AND THIS AMOUNT WILL BE INCREASED EACH YEAR.
THAT LECTURE TAUGHT ME A LOT, BETTY.
YES—AND I'M GLAD WE STAYED LATE TO ASK QUESTIONS.
E A WEEK BETTY GOES TO NIGHT OOL WITH HER FRIEND JILL. THEY BOTH STUDYING HARD SO THAT Y CAN EVENTUALLY BE REGISTERED S CHARTERED LIBRARIANS.
HAVING BEEN AT THE LIBRARY FIVE YEARS AND HAVING PASSED TWO MORE EXAMS, BETTY IS NOW A QUALIFIED LIBRARIAN. HER JOB IS PENSIONABLE AND SHE CAN EARN UP TO £600 A YEAR AS CHIEF OF A LIBRARY WHICH SERVES A LARGE TOWN.
NOW BETTY HAS TAKEN A JOB WITH AN IMPORTANT RESEARCH ORGANISATION. HER WORK INVOLVES DIGGING UP FACTS AND REMEMBERING THEM, CORRECT CLASSIFICATION OF THE THOUSANDS OF BOOKS IN HER CHARGE AND COMPILING UP-TO-DATE CATALOGUES. SHE LOVES IT!
LOVELY MORNING, MISS.
ISN'T IT? I'M TAKING MY LUNCH INTO THE PARK TODAY!

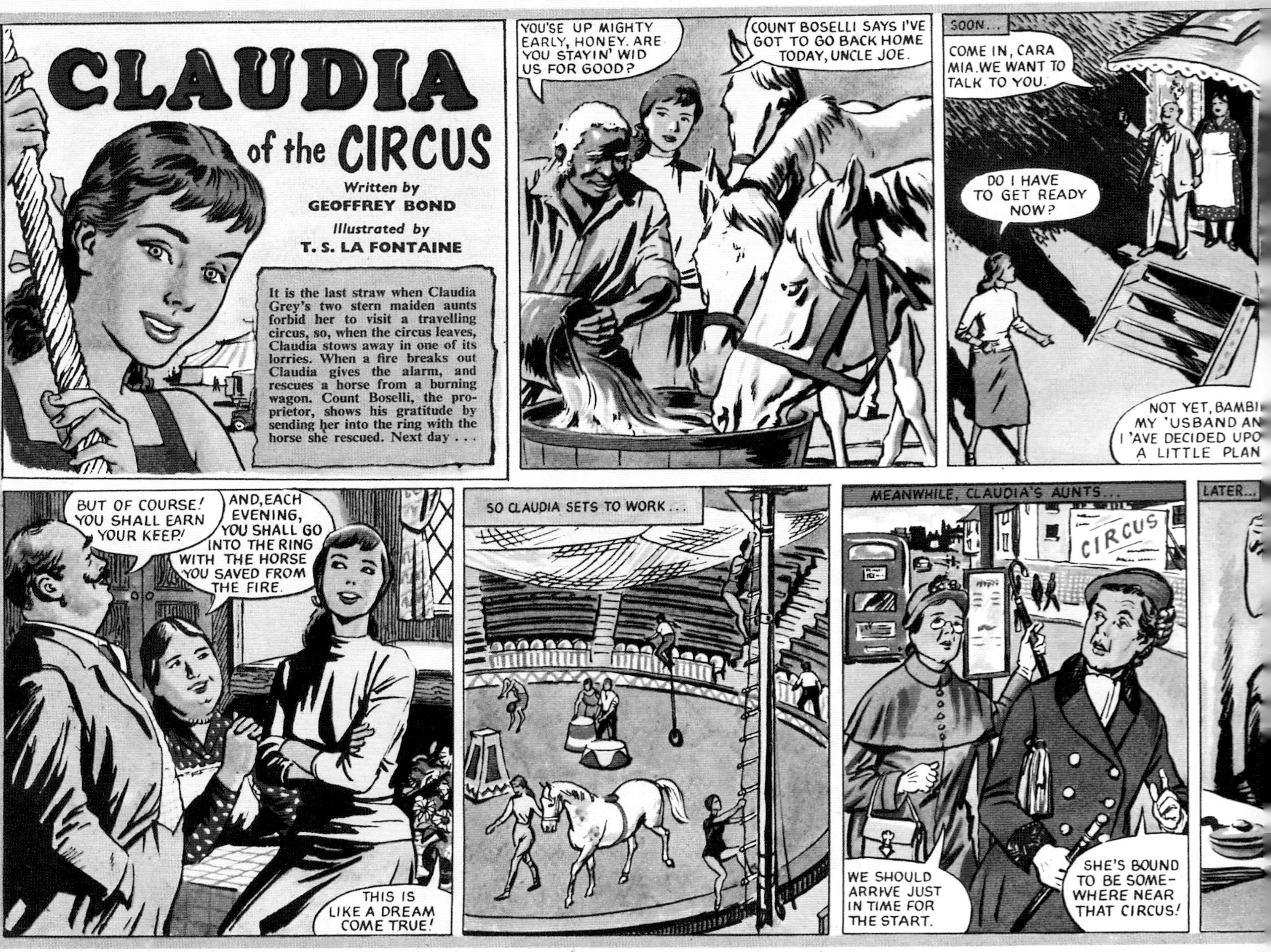
CLAUDIA of the CIRCUS
Written by GEOFFREY BOND
Illustrated by T. S. LA FONTAINE
It is the last straw when Claudia Grey's two stern maiden aunts forbid her to visit a travelling circus, so, when the circus leaves, Claudia stows away in one of its lorries. When a fire breaks out Claudia gives the alarm, and rescues a horse from a burning wagon. Count Boselli, the proprietor, shows his gratitude by sending her into the ring with the horse she rescued. Next day . . .
YOU'SE UP MIGHTY EARLY, HONEY. ARE YOU STAYIN' WID US FOR GOOD?
COUNT BOSELLI SAYS I'VE GOT TO GO BACK HOME TODAY, UNCLE JOE.
SOON...
COME IN, CARA MIA. WE WANT TO TALK TO YOU.
DO I HAVE TO GET READY NOW?
NOT YET, BAMBI MY 'USBAND AN I 'AVE DECIDED UPO A LITTLE PLAN
BUT OF COURSE! YOU SHALL EARN YOUR KEEP!
AND, EACH EVENING, YOU SHALL GO INTO THE RING WITH THE HORSE YOU SAVED FROM THE FIRE.
THIS IS LIKE A DREAM COME TRUE!
SO CLAUDIA SETS TO WORK...
MEANWHILE, CLAUDIA'S AUNTS...
CIRCUS
WE SHOULD ARRIVE JUST IN TIME FOR THE START.
SHE'S BOUND TO BE SOME-WHERE NEAR THAT CIRCUS!
LATER...

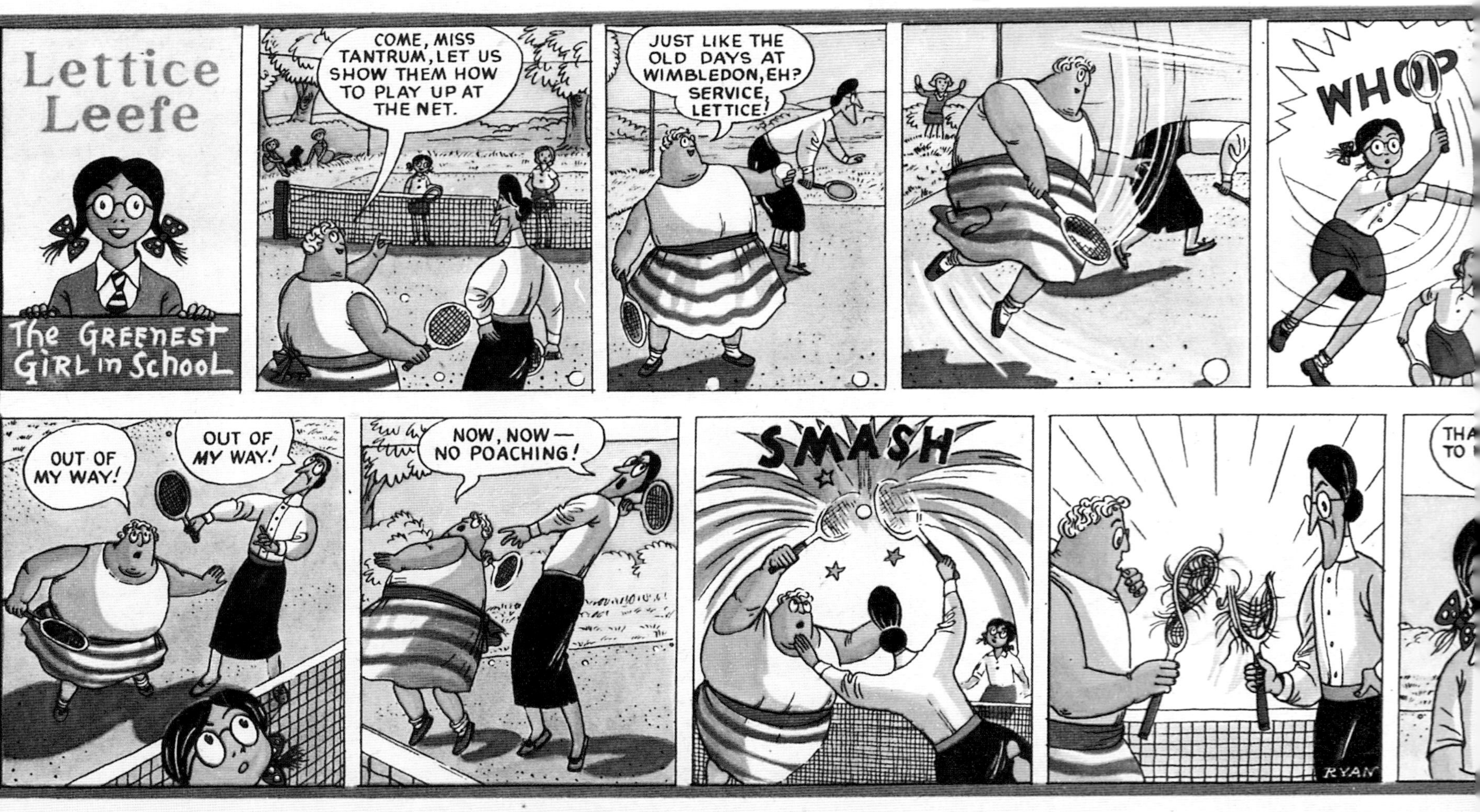
Lettice Leefe
The GREENEST GIRL in SchooL
COME, MISS TANTRUM, LET US SHOW THEM HOW TO PLAY UP AT THE NET.
JUST LIKE THE OLD DAYS AT WIMBLEDON, EH? SERVICE, LETTICE!
WHOP
OUT OF MY WAY!
OUT OF MY WAY!
NOW, NOW — NO POACHING!
SMASH
RYAN

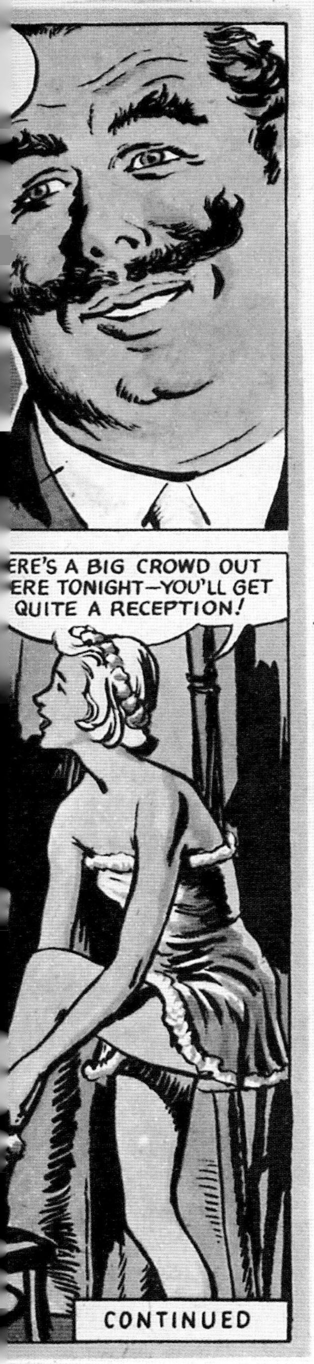
ERE'S A BIG CROWD OUT ERE TONIGHT—YOU'LL GET QUITE A RECEPTION!
CONTINUED

continued on page 98

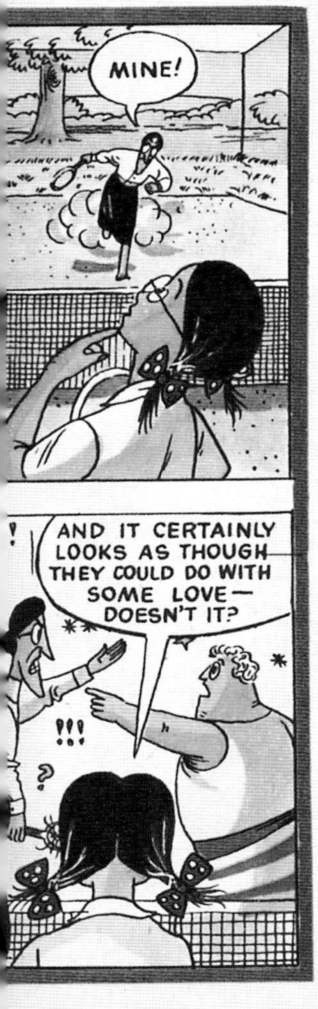
MINE!
AND IT CERTAINLY LOOKS AS THOUGH THEY COULD DO WITH SOME LOVE— DOESN'T IT?
!!!

Girl Picture Gallery

No. 264

Today we are publishing another picture in our popular nature series – a wonderful study of a young tawny owl.

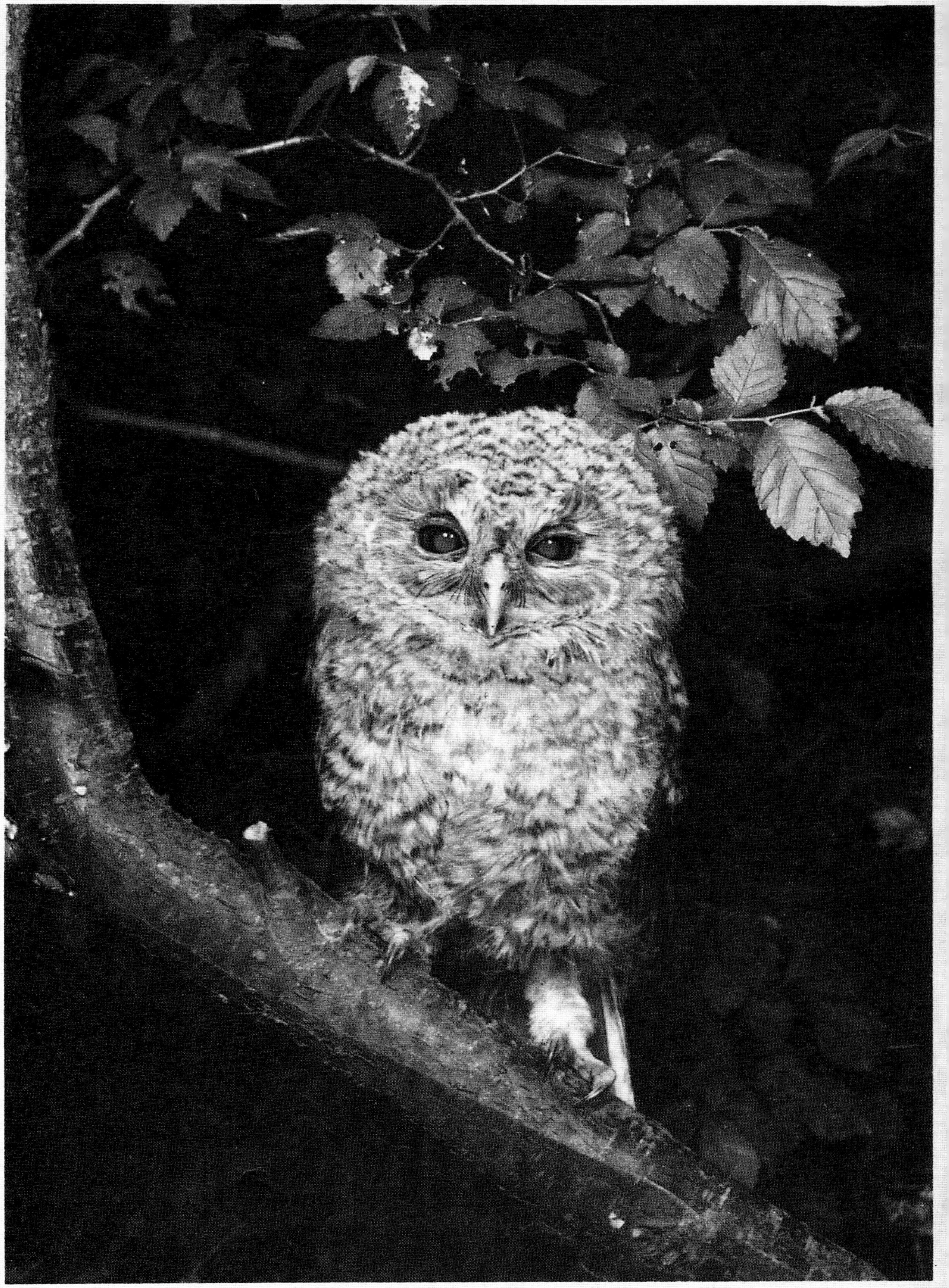

A YOUNG TAWNY OWL
by JOHN MARKHAM, F.R.P.S., F.Z.S.

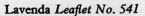

The Knitting Competition

FOR THE Girl UNDER 14

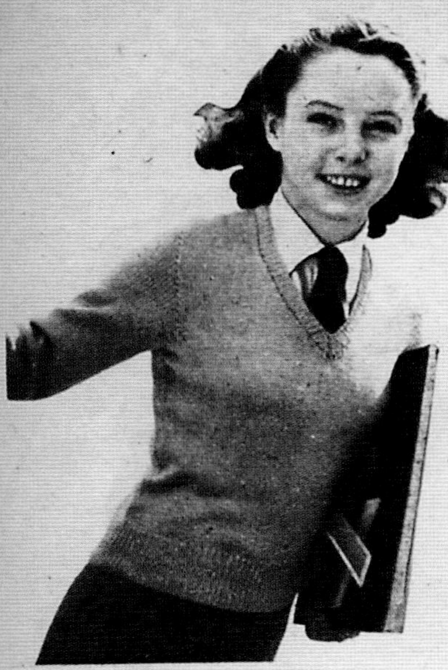

Sirdar *Leaflet No. 519*

If you're over twelve and not fourteen by the closing date of the competition, this is the section for you! All you have to do – after you've read the rules on the first page of this supplement – is visit your local woolshop and choose a pattern of a simple jumper. Look inside the pattern and see how much, and what kind of wool it says you need, and don't forget to buy it all at once, as you mayn't be able to get the same shade later. While you're there, check that you've got the right needles, too. Try Milwards "Disc" knitting needles, they show you the size very clearly, and produce nice smooth knitting. Now please, after you've taken lots of care about the actual knitting, don't spoil it by bad sewing up. Look for the instructions in your pattern, and remember the jumper should be pressed to give it the finished look.

These six are *examples* of patterns you could choose; you may choose another, but remember it must be issued by one of the makers listed on page one of this supplement. Good luck.

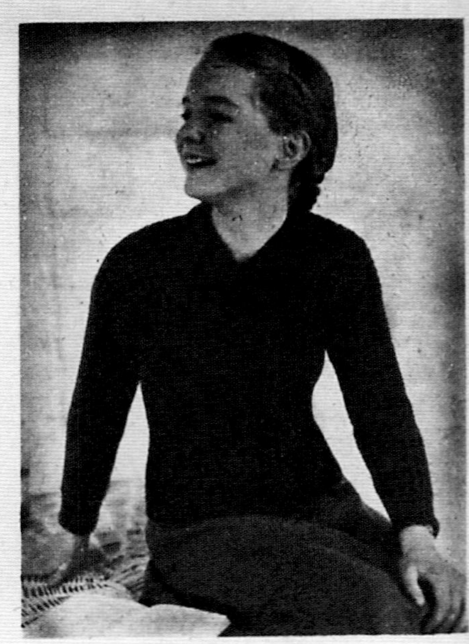

Patons & Baldwins *Leaflet No. 428*

Marriner *Leaflet No. 200*

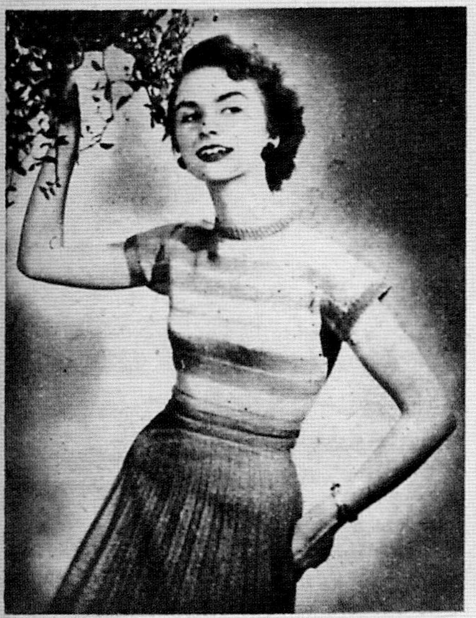

Lavenda *Leaflet No. 541*

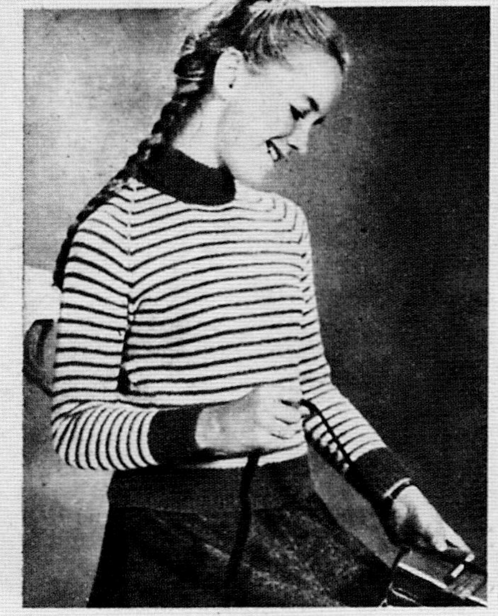

Copley's *Leaflet No. 1923*

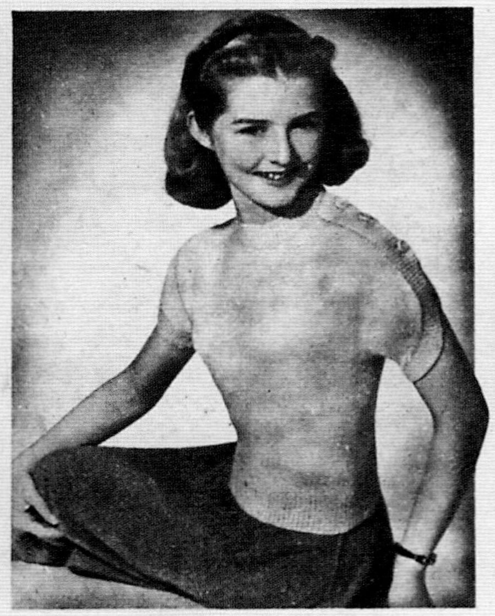

Lee Target *Leaflet No. 1277*

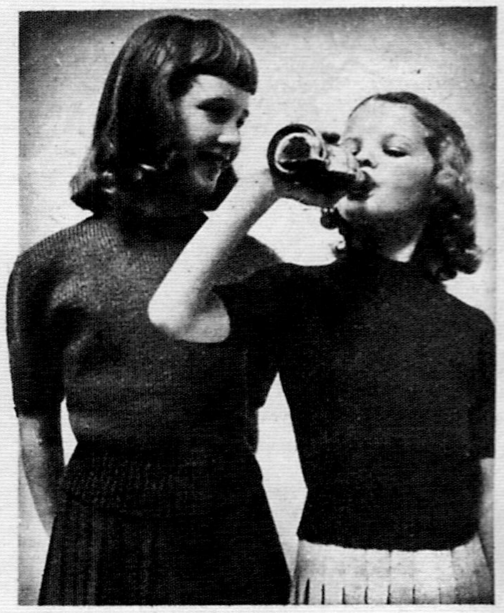

Increasing

You will be told in the instructions given for your jersey to "increase" at various places. The drawings show you the best way of doing this, so that the edges are kept very neat.

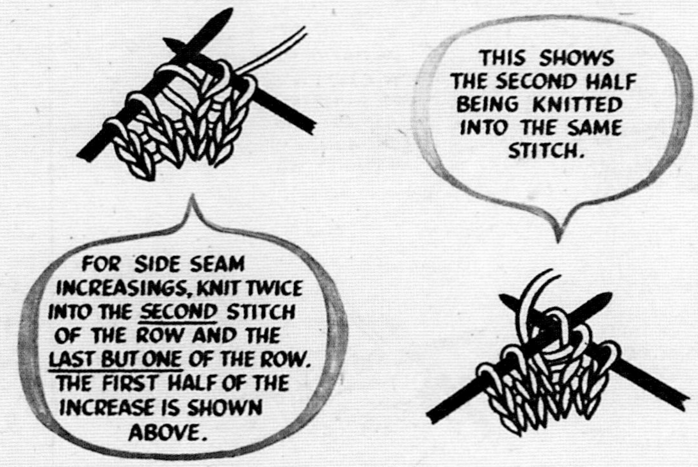
THIS SHOWS THE SECOND HALF BEING KNITTED INTO THE SAME STITCH.
FOR SIDE SEAM INCREASINGS, KNIT TWICE INTO THE SECOND STITCH OF THE ROW AND THE LAST BUT ONE OF THE ROW. THE FIRST HALF OF THE INCREASE IS SHOWN ABOVE.

Decreasing

When the instructions say "knit two together" this is how the work should look.

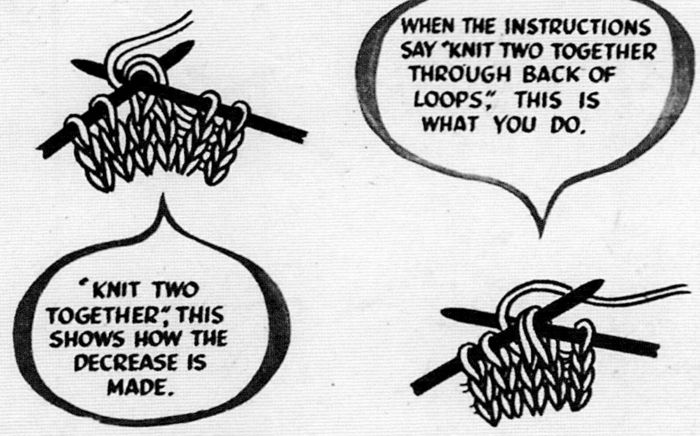
WHEN THE INSTRUCTIONS SAY "KNIT TWO TOGETHER THROUGH BACK OF LOOPS," THIS IS WHAT YOU DO.
"KNIT TWO TOGETHER," THIS SHOWS HOW THE DECREASE IS MADE.

Washing Hints

And remember, 'If it's safe in water, it's safe in ***LUX!****'*

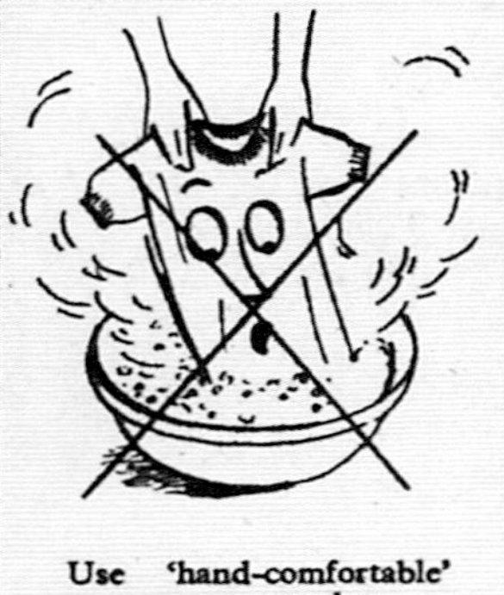

Use 'hand-comfortable' water – not too hot nor yet very cool.

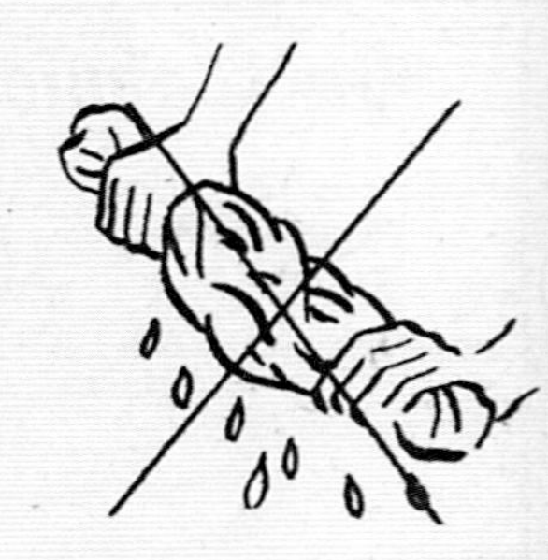

Squeeze as much water out as possible but *don't wring* the garment out of shape.

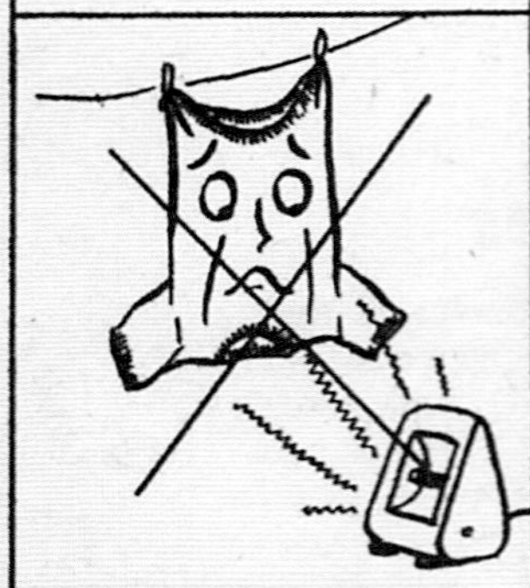

Dry in the open air if possible never before direct heat. Support the garment while drying.

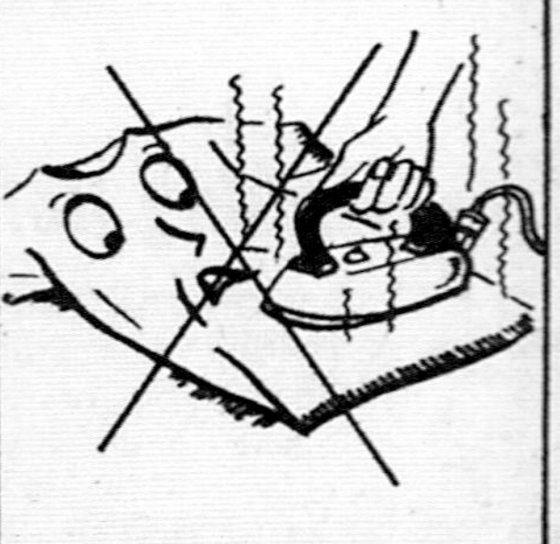

Press when nearly dry under a damp cloth with a hot iron.

The Knitting Competition

FOR THE Girl OVER 14

Wakefield Greenwood *Leaflet No. 146*

Good luck for **Girls** over fourteen and under seventeen! Here's a chance to knit a cardigan in just the colours you want, in the style of your choice, *and* win a handsome prize as well.

Make sure you've read carefully the rules on the first page of this supplement, then choose your pattern either from the six examples shown here or from amongst those issued by the makers listed on the front page. When visiting your woolshop make sure you buy the wool mentioned in the pattern. It's a very good plan to buy it all at once too, because shades are very difficult to match later. The only other item you need is knitting needles – if you have some, make sure they're the right size. For telling sizes easily, as well as smooth knitting, you should see Milwards DISC knitting needles – they're good.

When you have finished your cardigan, please take trouble over sewing the pieces together. It will make so much difference to the final look of all your careful knitting. Look for the instructions on your pattern and when all is complete give your fine work a 'pressing', using a warm iron and a clean, damp cloth.

Emu *Leaflet No. 619*

Wendywear *Leaflet No. 734*

Bairns-Wear *Leaflet No. 670*

Ladyship *Leaflet No. 3177*

Munrospun *Leaflet No. 6819*

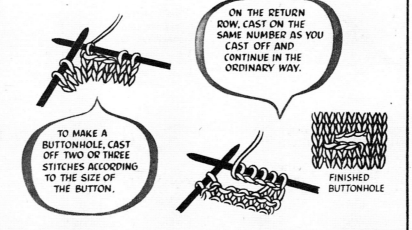

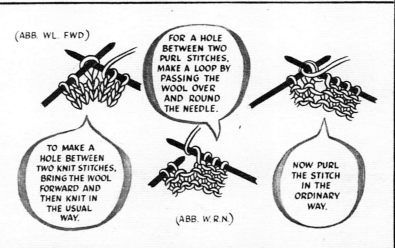

Buttonholes

A well knitted garment can be ruined by bad finishing. Take particular trouble with your buttonholes as shown right.

ON THE RETURN ROW, CAST ON THE SAME NUMBER AS YOU CAST OFF AND CONTINUE IN THE ORDINARY WAY.
TO MAKE A BUTTONHOLE, CAST OFF TWO OR THREE STITCHES ACCORDING TO THE SIZE OF THE BUTTON.
FINISHED BUTTONHOLE

Making Holes

For very small buttonholes all that is needed is a hole between two stitches. The drawing will show you how to do this.

(ABB. WL. FWD)
FOR A HOLE BETWEEN TWO PURL STITCHES, MAKE A LOOP BY PASSING THE WOOL OVER AND ROUND THE NEEDLE.
TO MAKE A HOLE BETWEEN TWO KNIT STITCHES, BRING THE WOOL FORWARD AND THEN KNIT IN THE USUAL WAY.
NOW PURL THE STITCH IN THE ORDINARY WAY.
(ABB. W.R.N.)

Have You Remembered the Golden Rules of KNITTING?

1	*First choose a pattern you really like.*
2	*Always buy the brand of wool named in the pattern.*
3	*Always buy enough wool to finish your garment.*
4	*Make sure you have the right size needles (the pattern tells you which size).*
5	*Always join your new ball of wool at the beginning of a row and never in the middle.*

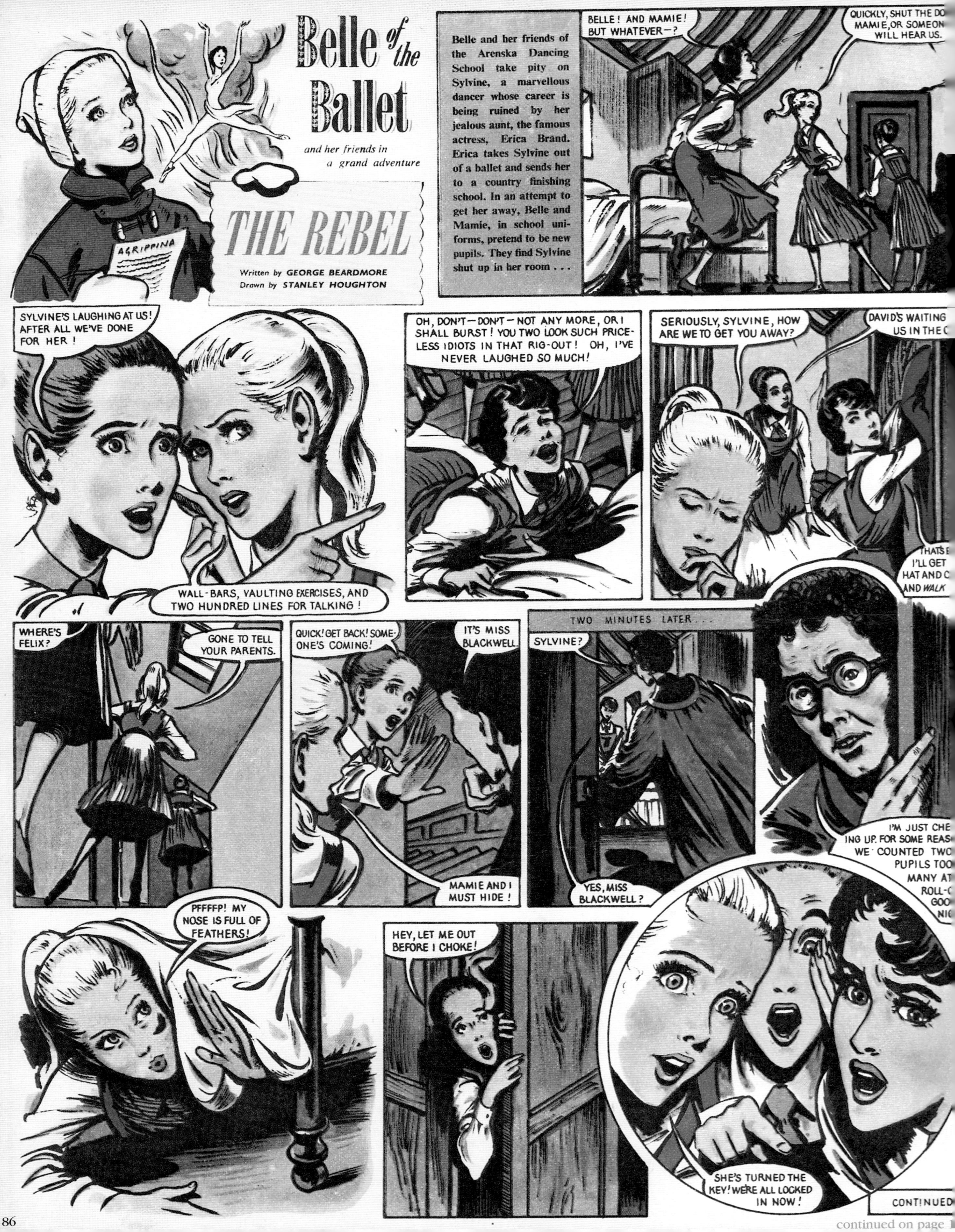
Belle of the Ballet
and her friends in a grand adventure
AGRIPPINA
THE REBEL
Written by GEORGE BEARDMORE
Drawn by STANLEY HOUGHTON
Belle and her friends of the Arenska Dancing School take pity on Sylvine, a marvellous dancer whose career is being ruined by her jealous aunt, the famous actress, Erica Brand. Erica takes Sylvine out of a ballet and sends her to a country finishing school. In an attempt to get her away, Belle and Mamie, in school uniforms, pretend to be new pupils. They find Sylvine shut up in her room . . .
BELLE! AND MAMIE! BUT WHATEVER—?
QUICKLY, SHUT THE DO MAMIE, OR SOMEON WILL HEAR US.
SYLVINE'S LAUGHING AT US! AFTER ALL WE'VE DONE FOR HER!
WALL-BARS, VAULTING EXERCISES, AND TWO HUNDRED LINES FOR TALKING!
OH, DON'T—DON'T—NOT ANY MORE, OR I SHALL BURST! YOU TWO LOOK SUCH PRICELESS IDIOTS IN THAT RIG-OUT! OH, I'VE NEVER LAUGHED SO MUCH!
SERIOUSLY, SYLVINE, HOW ARE WE TO GET YOU AWAY?
DAVID'S WAITING US IN THE C
THAT'S E I'LL GET HAT AND C AND WALK
WHERE'S FELIX?
GONE TO TELL YOUR PARENTS.
QUICK! GET BACK! SOMEONE'S COMING!
IT'S MISS BLACKWELL.
MAMIE AND I MUST HIDE!
TWO MINUTES LATER . . .
SYLVINE?
YES, MISS BLACKWELL?
I'M JUST CHE ING UP. FOR SOME REAS WE COUNTED TWO PUPILS TOO MANY AT ROLL-C GOO NI
PFFFFP! MY NOSE IS FULL OF FEATHERS!
HEY, LET ME OUT BEFORE I CHOKE!
SHE'S TURNED THE KEY! WE'RE ALL LOCKED IN NOW!
CONTINUED

continued on page

Jacky visits Leytonstone County High School for Girls

When Jacky visited the Leytonstone County High School for Girls in London, a group of fourth formers came to welcome her.

In the hall Jacky met members of the school orchestra. They love music and gave a performance in Jacky's honour.

Jacky was interested in a rabbit's skeleton, which lower fifth form girls were studying with the help of the biology mistress.

Next Jacky went along to the gymnasium. There she watched a fine display of rope climbing by these second form pupils.

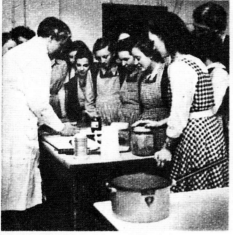

Cookery is one of the most popular subjects and in the Domestic Science room these girls were learning how to bake raspberry buns.

The school has its own swimming pool and most of the girls are good swimmers. Jacky saw a life-saving demonstration.

Attractive gardens surround the school and down by the lily pond Jacky posed for three senior girls in the art class.

Jacky enjoyed her visit to Leytonstone and before she left she had coffee in the Prefects' study.

What's Your Worry?

If you have a worry you'd like to share, and feel our experts can help, just write to: – GIRL, 161/166 Fleet Street, London, E.C.4, and mark your letter 'WHAT'S YOUR WORRY?'. No names will be printed, but let us have a stamped, self-addressed envelope if you would like a personal reply by letter. A published reply will always involve a few weeks' delay.

ROCK LEWIS
IN
THE SHIPWRECK

She admires film stars

Q. I get very excited about film stars. Is this wrong?

A. *Certainly not, but it is a great mistake to spend too much of your time dreaming about film stars, instead of making friends amongst those who live round you, and entering into activities and interests with your companions.*

* * *

She would like a boy friend

Q. All my friends have boy friends, but I don't seem to be able to get one. How can I make myself more attractive?

A. *We think you may be TOO self-absorbed. It is vitality and interest in things, not merely looks, which makes a person attractive. If you can really get into the way of enjoying life without being too self-conscious, you will soon find that friendships come along.*

* * *

Can she join the Brownies?

Q. I am Jewish and would like to join the Brownies. The only troop in our district is a Church group. Do you think that they would let me join them?

A. *We do! The teachings of Jesus tell us that we should welcome all peoples, and that all we human beings should be friendly with one another. We advise you to go and have a talk with the person in charge of the Church troop.*

Her friend always boasts

Q. My friend is a fearful boaster. This embarrasses me. I wish you would tell me how I can stop her boasting so much.

A. *You must ask yourself WHY your friend boasts so much. We think she does so in order to make herself feel more important. What you must do is try to show her that the fact of her boasting does not make her liked any more in the eyes of her friends, but makes her liked less. Once she realises this, she will probably be more prepared to give her attention to using her energies in a useful way, instead of on boasting.*

* * *

She is a tomboy

Q. I seem to play with boys all the time, and I have my hair cut short. I like aeroplanes and football. Is it wrong to be like a boy?

A. *It is a good thing to enjoy the interests of boys, and their company, but you should develop interests with girl friends as well.*

* * *

Friendship

Q. How can I get to know a boy at my Youth Club who interests me very much?

A. *The best way to develop a friendship in a Youth Club is to join in the activities of the Club which you can share together.*

* * *

Nursing

Q. I want to be a nurse when I leave school, but I am afraid the training will be a bit expensive. Is it?

A. *No, you will get paid a small sum while you are training.*

* * *

Her friend shows-off

Q. My friend is a show-off. How can I make her behave properly?

A. *Are you sure that YOU do not go to the other extreme and hang back a little too much? We think that perhaps she is too forthcoming and you are not forthcoming enough. Why don't you discuss the problem along these lines?*

For GIRL Adventurers

Your chance to see "Toad of Toad Hall"

FOR GIRL Adventurers living in or near London we have 30 FREE tickets for A. A. Milne's play "Toad of Toad Hall" performed by a company from the Shakespeare Memorial Theatre. The tickets are for the matinée performance at the Princes Theatre, London, on Saturday 22nd January. We know you will all enjoy this wonderful play, and from the picture above you can get some idea of the enchanting scenery and costumes. If *YOU* would like tickets write to:–"TOAD OF TOAD HALL", GIRL Reader Services, Long Lane, Aintree, Liverpool 9. The writers of the first 30 letters opened will be the lucky ones. Don't forget to tell us your name, address, club number and age when you send us your application.

Our Christmas Party at LIVERPOOL

LIVERPOOL GIRL adventurers had a wonderful time during the Christmas Party at Reece's Restaurant on Saturday, 11th December. Besides having a lovely tea, they were able to meet Mr Morris, the Editor, with other members of his staff. Everyone enjoyed the conjuror's tricks and then joined in community singing led by the Editor. At the end each GIRL Adventurer received a small gift.

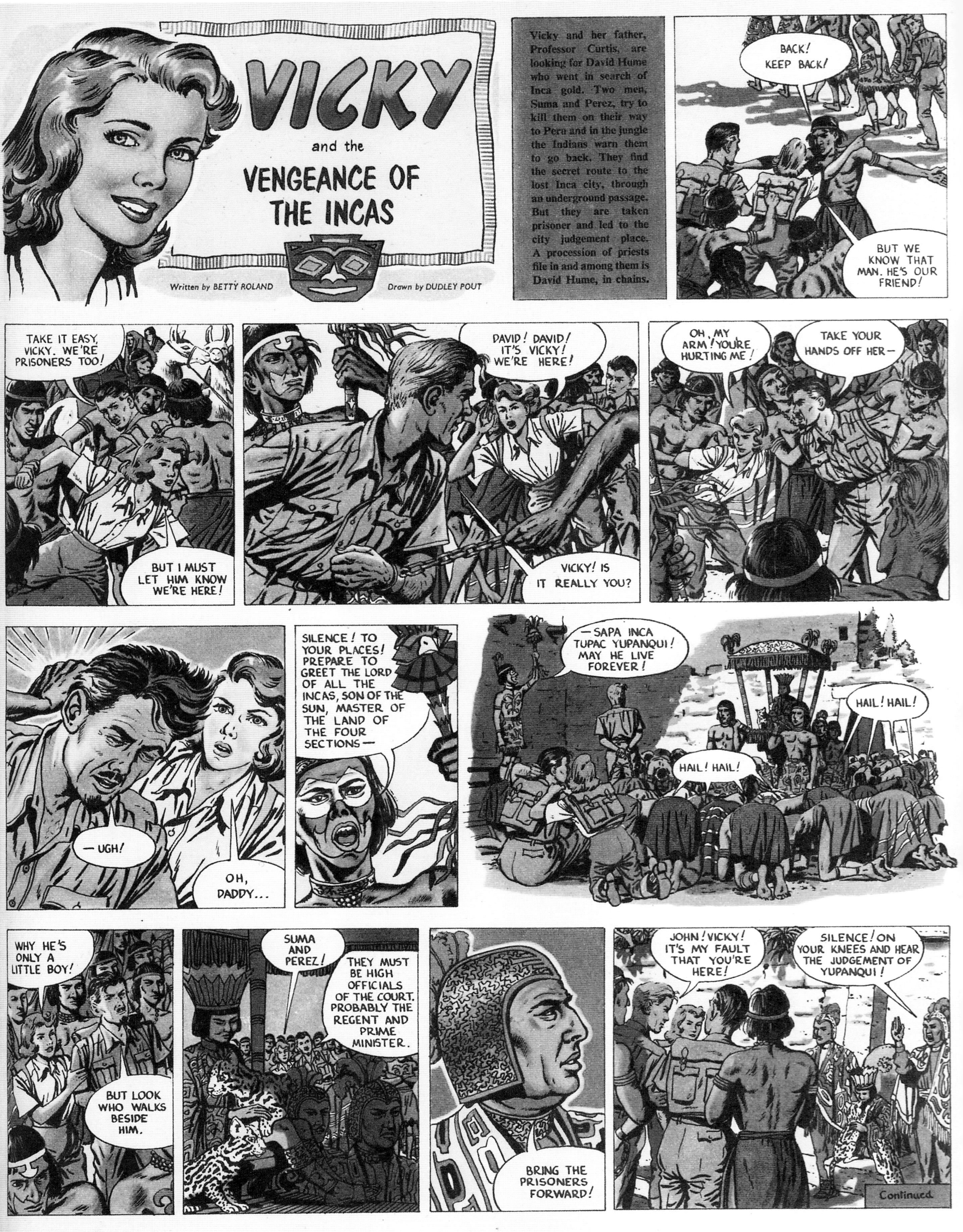
VICKY
and the
VENGEANCE OF THE INCAS
Written by BETTY ROLAND
Drawn by DUDLEY POUT
Vicky and her father, Professor Curtis, are looking for David Hume who went in search of Inca gold. Two men, Suma and Perez, try to kill them on their way to Peru and in the jungle the Indians warn them to go back. They find the secret route to the lost Inca city, through an underground passage. But they are taken prisoner and led to the city judgement place. A procession of priests file in and among them is David Hume, in chains.
BACK! KEEP BACK!
BUT WE KNOW THAT MAN. HE'S OUR FRIEND!
TAKE IT EASY, VICKY. WE'RE PRISONERS TOO!
BUT I MUST LET HIM KNOW WE'RE HERE!
DAVID! DAVID! IT'S VICKY! WE'RE HERE!
VICKY! IS IT REALLY YOU?
OH, MY ARM! YOU'RE HURTING ME!
TAKE YOUR HANDS OFF HER—
—UGH!
OH, DADDY...
SILENCE! TO YOUR PLACES! PREPARE TO GREET THE LORD OF ALL THE INCAS, SON OF THE SUN, MASTER OF THE LAND OF THE FOUR SECTIONS—
—SAPA INCA TUPAC YUPANQUI! MAY HE LIVE FOREVER!
HAIL! HAIL!
HAIL! HAIL!
WHY HE'S ONLY A LITTLE BOY!
BUT LOOK WHO WALKS BESIDE HIM.
SUMA AND PEREZ!
THEY MUST BE HIGH OFFICIALS OF THE COURT. PROBABLY THE REGENT AND PRIME MINISTER.
BRING THE PRISONERS FORWARD!
JOHN! VICKY! IT'S MY FAULT THAT YOU'RE HERE!
SILENCE! ON YOUR KNEES AND HEAR THE JUDGEMENT OF YUPANQUI!
Continued

continued on page 1

Summer Time

WE couldn't have chosen a better time to launch our first fashion feature, for teenage clothes have never been prettier than now. Here are some of the prettiest. They are not expensive and are wonderfully versatile. For those who like full-skirted dresses we have picked two romantic cottons, crisp enough to work in, and pretty enough for parties. For those who like suits, here's a gem of a jersey suit which won't crease whatever you do to it. And for those who like separates, here's a dashing blazer and skirt. You'll find a list of stockists and prices on page 11.

All these clothes are good quality and hard-wearing – and they will never, never date. But clothes as good-looking as these can speak for themselves!

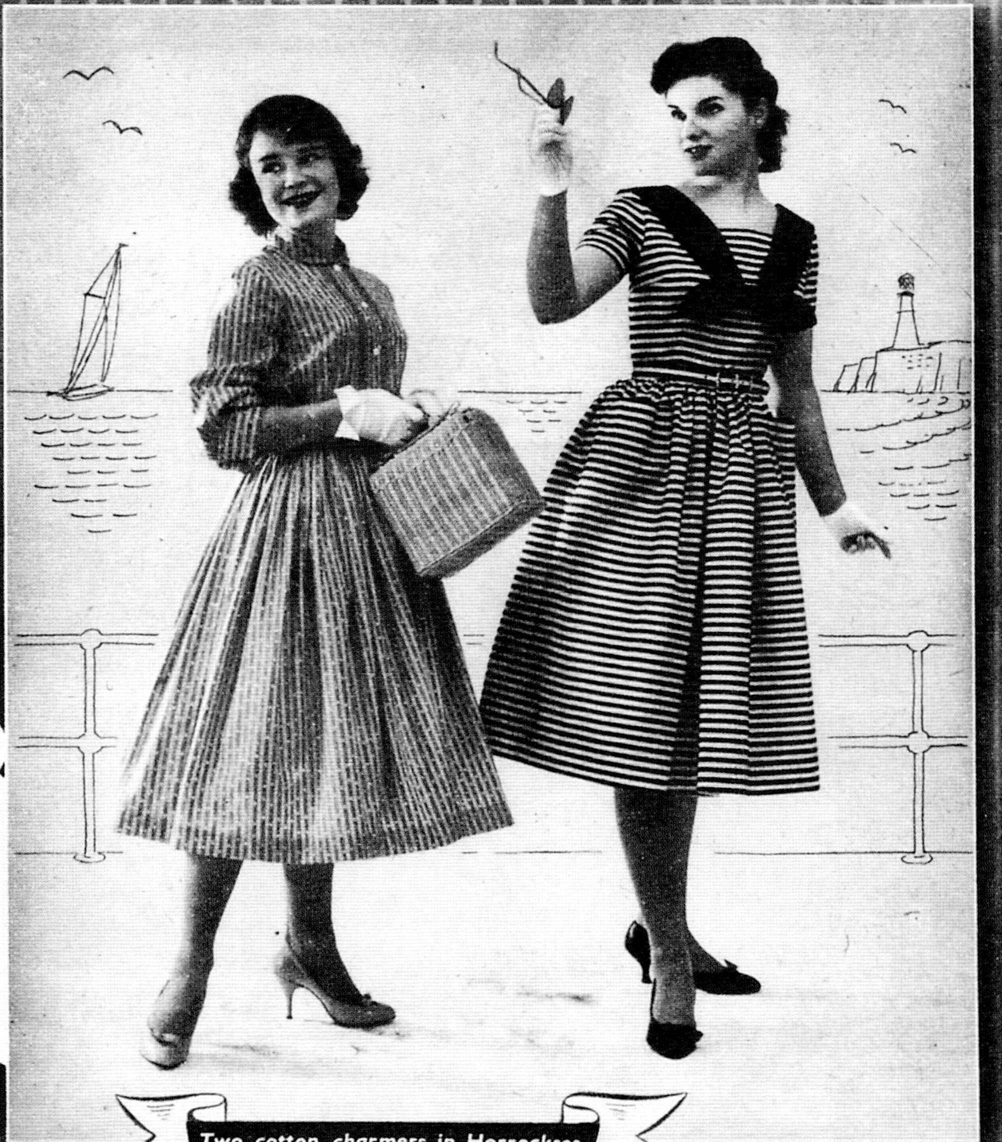

Two cotton charmers in Horrockses Younger Set range. Both of them come in several gay colours, on a white ground. They cost about four guineas

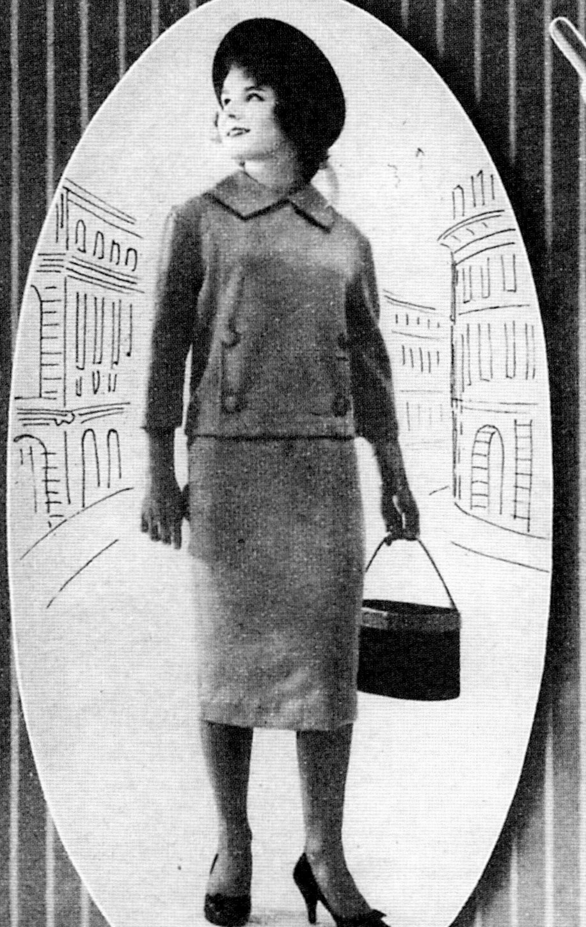

A wool jersey suit with an easy line by Estrava. You can buy it in pretty pastel shades and also in black

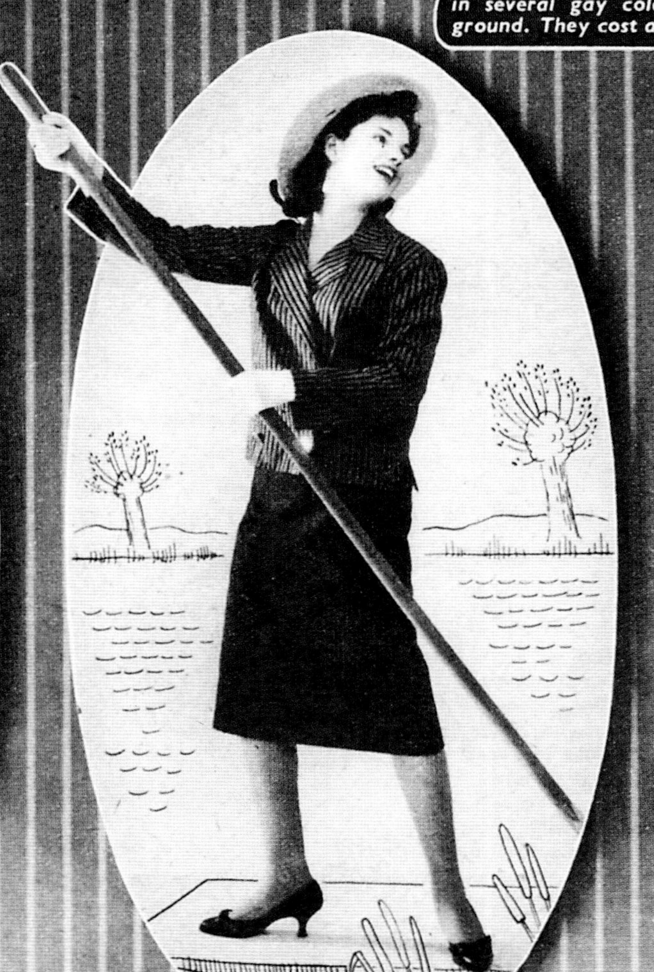

This striped blazer and cotton Adapta skirt are also by Estrava. The skirt adapts to fit a 24"-28" waist

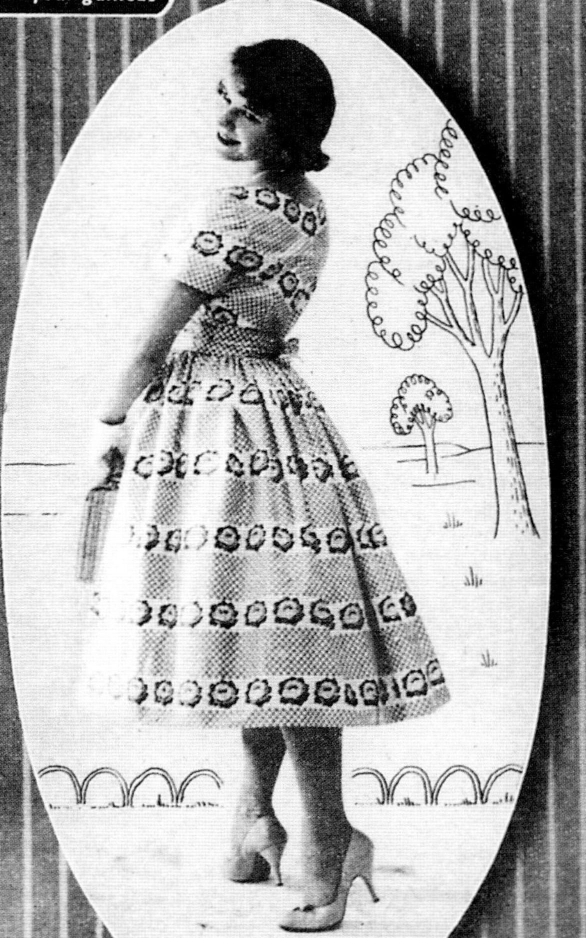

A romantic rose-printed dress by Horrockses. Notice the fashionable V-neckline and the very full skirt

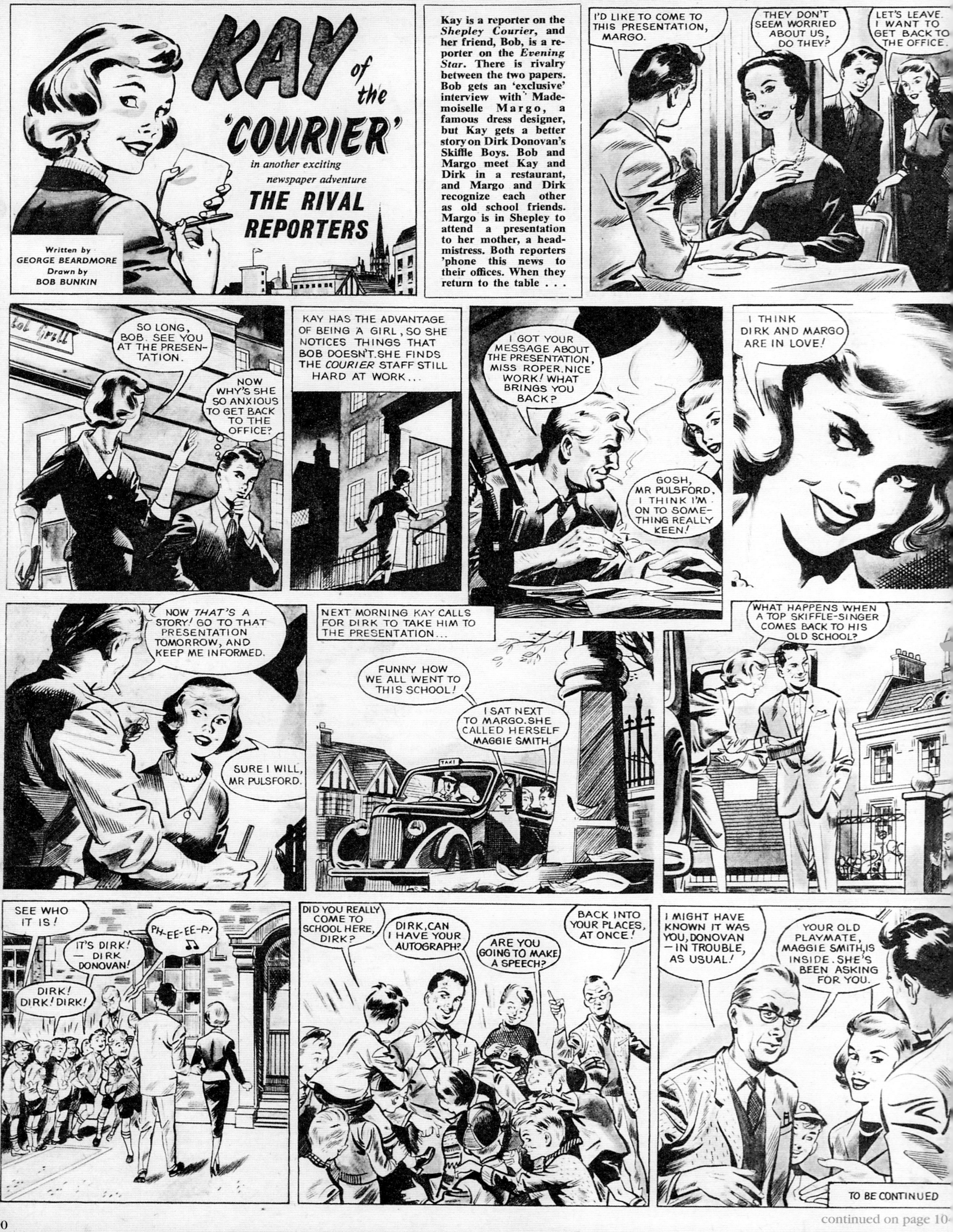
KAY of the 'COURIER'
in another exciting newspaper adventure
THE RIVAL REPORTERS
Written by GEORGE BEARDMORE
Drawn by BOB BUNKIN
Kay is a reporter on the Shepley Courier, and her friend, Bob, is a reporter on the Evening Star. There is rivalry between the two papers. Bob gets an 'exclusive' interview with Mademoiselle Margo, a famous dress designer, but Kay gets a better story on Dirk Donovan's Skiffle Boys. Bob and Margo meet Kay and Dirk in a restaurant, and Margo and Dirk recognize each other as old school friends. Margo is in Shepley to attend a presentation to her mother, a headmistress. Both reporters 'phone this news to their offices. When they return to the table . . .
I'D LIKE TO COME TO THIS PRESENTATION, MARGO.
THEY DON'T SEEM WORRIED ABOUT US, DO THEY?
LET'S LEAVE. I WANT TO GET BACK TO THE OFFICE.
SO LONG, BOB. SEE YOU AT THE PRESENTATION.
NOW WHY'S SHE SO ANXIOUS TO GET BACK TO THE OFFICE?
KAY HAS THE ADVANTAGE OF BEING A GIRL, SO SHE NOTICES THINGS THAT BOB DOESN'T. SHE FINDS THE COURIER STAFF STILL HARD AT WORK...
I GOT YOUR MESSAGE ABOUT THE PRESENTATION, MISS ROPER. NICE WORK! WHAT BRINGS YOU BACK?
GOSH, MR PULSFORD, I THINK I'M ON TO SOMETHING REALLY KEEN!
I THINK DIRK AND MARGO ARE IN LOVE!
NOW THAT'S A STORY! GO TO THAT PRESENTATION TOMORROW, AND KEEP ME INFORMED.
SURE I WILL, MR PULSFORD.
NEXT MORNING KAY CALLS FOR DIRK TO TAKE HIM TO THE PRESENTATION...
FUNNY HOW WE ALL WENT TO THIS SCHOOL!
I SAT NEXT TO MARGO. SHE CALLED HERSELF MAGGIE SMITH.
TAXI
WHAT HAPPENS WHEN A TOP SKIFFLE-SINGER COMES BACK TO HIS OLD SCHOOL?
SEE WHO IT IS!
IT'S DIRK! — DIRK DONOVAN!
PH-EE-EE-P!
DIRK! DIRK! DIRK!
DID YOU REALLY COME TO SCHOOL HERE, DIRK?
DIRK, CAN I HAVE YOUR AUTOGRAPH?
ARE YOU GOING TO MAKE A SPEECH?
BACK INTO YOUR PLACES, AT ONCE!
I MIGHT HAVE KNOWN IT WAS YOU, DONOVAN — IN TROUBLE, AS USUAL!
YOUR OLD PLAYMATE, MAGGIE SMITH, IS INSIDE. SHE'S BEEN ASKING FOR YOU.
TO BE CONTINUED

continued on page 10

ere are the results

you've been waiting for!

GIRL Snapshot Competition

HERE are the main winners in each section, together with a report by ace photographer Bert Hardy. The top prize-
ınner was Andrea Taylor of Sheffield, who on a ciné camera. Runners-up were: **Humour;** arol Dempster-Jones of Buckley, Flintshire. **ature;** Pamela Page of Liskeard, Cornwall. **iew;** Elisabeth Baker of Reading, Berks. **ction;** J. Pendlebury of Bolton, Lancs. They ch won a record player.

I thought that GIRL readers sent in a first-class tch of entries again this year. Considered as group, the pictures entered in the Nature ction were far and away the best, while the umorous ones came off worst. This was be- use they all looked too 'posed'. Mind you, isn't easy to take pictures which are really nny. I find that the best ones happen almost accident – you see a funny situation and u manage to snap it. When you set the scene st, the pictures rarely come off.

There was another fault common to all groups d that was a failure to consider the composi- n of the picture and the lighting. When com- titors considered these two points the results re striking – and were, in fact, the winners.

nsolation prizewinners

m afraid we haven't room here to mention the many solation-prizewinners, who each received a manicure set a photograph album. However, if you would like a plete list of these, write to: GIRL Reader Services, g Lane, Liverpool 9 – and do remember to enclose amped, addressed envelope, won't you?

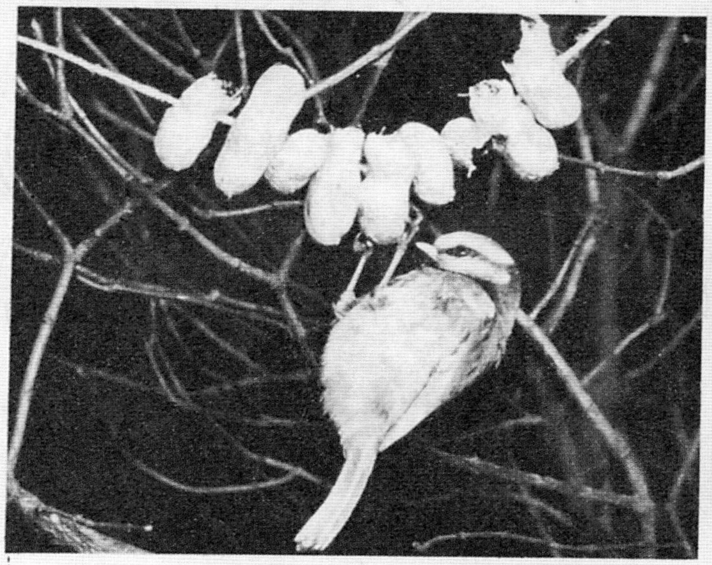

This is a first-class picture which I'd have been pleased to have taken myself! Andrea Taylor clearly has a quality which is essential for all nature photographers – the patience to wait for exactly the right moment.

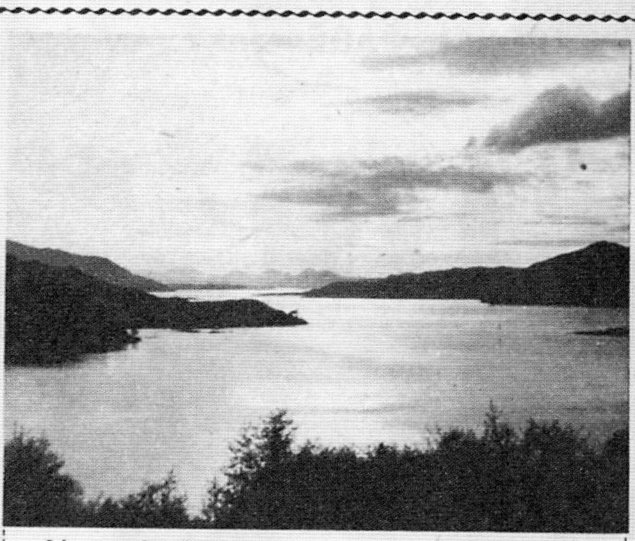

It's not always easy to take a really interesting landscape picture. But here, by making imaginative use of lighting and cloud, Elisabeth Baker manages to achieve a most impressive effect of peace and tranquillity.

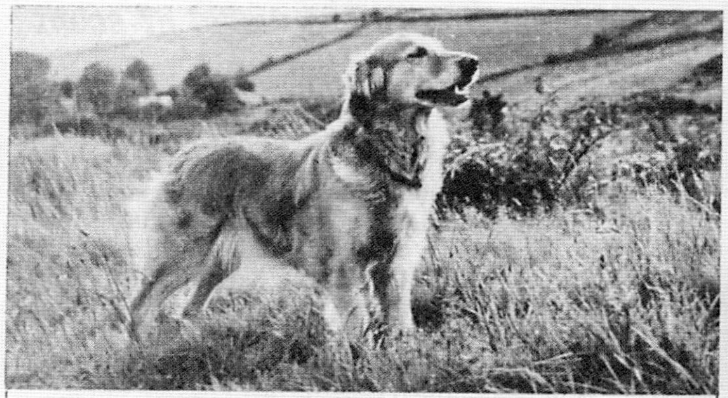

I have rarely seen background composition and lighting used to better effect than here, and I'd like to congratulate Pamela Page on a picture of excellent quality.

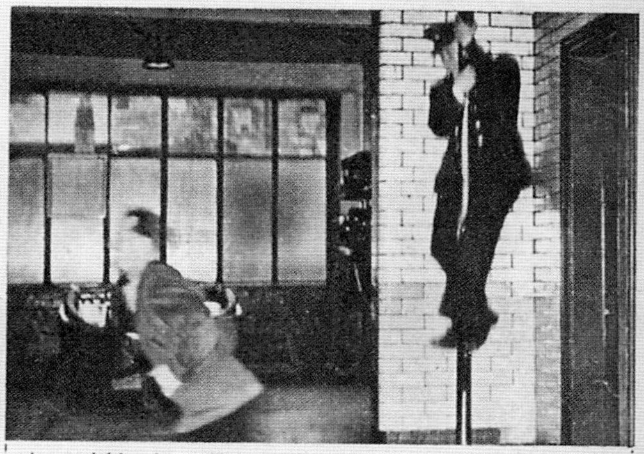

A good idea here. This picture of J. Pendlebury's conveys a real quality of urgency, due to the movement of the subjects.

WHAT'S YOUR WORRY?

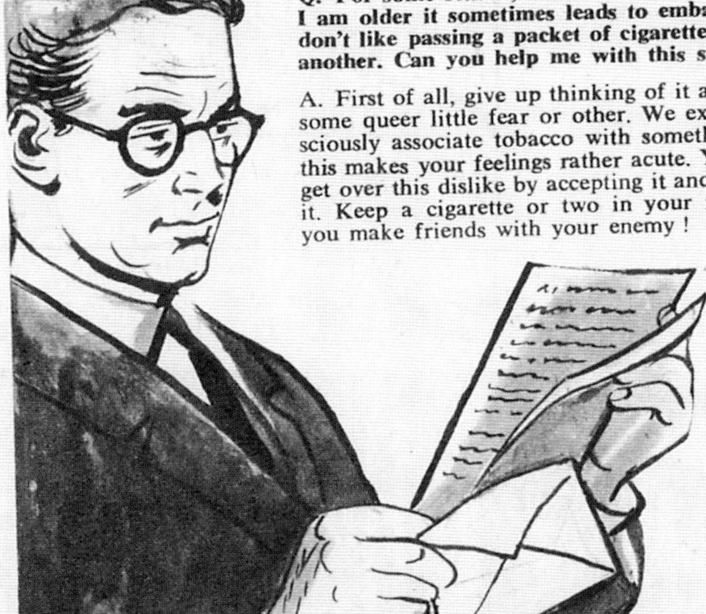

If you have a worry you'd like to share, and feel our experts can help, just write to: – GIRL, 161/166 Fleet Street, London, E.C.4., and mark your letter 'WHAT'S YOUR WORRY?' No names will be printed, but let us have a stamped, self-addressed envelope if you would like a personal reply by letter. A published reply will always involve a few weeks' delay.

For some reason, I hate tobacco . . .

Q. For some reason, I hate tobacco and always have. Now I am older it sometimes leads to embarrassment, because I don't like passing a packet of cigarettes from one person to another. Can you help me with this stupid habit?

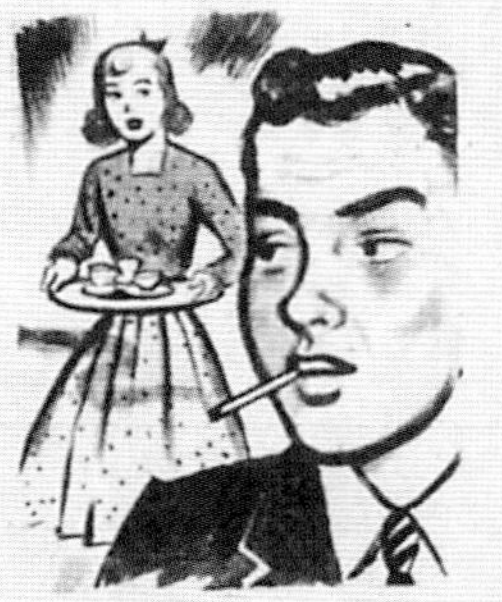

A. First of all, give up thinking of it as stupid. We all have some queer little fear or other. We expect that you unconsciously associate tobacco with something you dislike, and this makes your feelings rather acute. You can help yourself get over this dislike by accepting it and learning to live with it. Keep a cigarette or two in your room. This will help you make friends with your enemy!

My mother passes remarks

Q. How can I stop my mother passing rude remarks about my boy friend? She does not know how it hurts me.

A. Your mother is treating in a rather light-hearted way something about which you feel deeply. If you point this out to her, we think she will understand. We feel sure that she felt just the same as you when she was first interested in boys.

* * * * *

Which one likes me best?

Q. I am 14 years old, and I know two boys and like them both – but I don't know which one likes me best. If I knew, I would like to make him a special friend. How can I tell?

A. We think you are in too much of a hurry to pair yourself off with a particular boy. We advise you to get to know plenty of boys of about your own age. Sooner or later one will turn up whom you will be quite sure you want as a special friend.

* * * *

I am bothered with sties

Q. I get sties every now and then, and this makes my friends laugh at me. What can I do?

A. When you meet a friend, get in first with some such remark as "Sorry about my sty. It started last night" – or something of that kind.

* * * *

Do you think I should tell him?

Q. I am 15 years old. I like a boy of 20 very much, but I don't know if he likes me. We have been to each other's homes, and we are all friendly. Do you think I should tell him I like him, or should I just be friendly as at present?

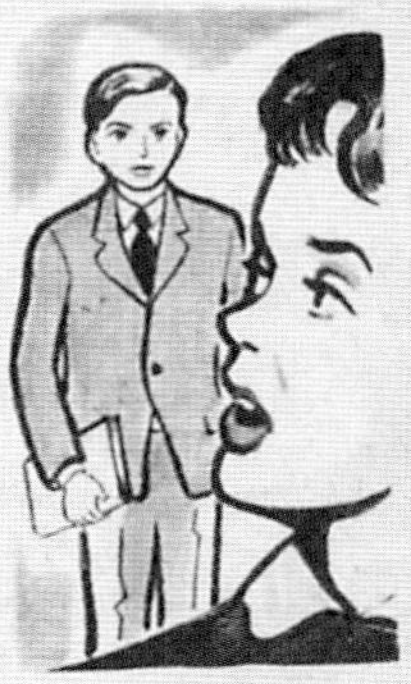

A. Go on as you are. You may feel very much that you want to tell him you like him, but this would very likely embarrass him, and might make your relationship strained and awkward.

GAY WEAR... PLAY WEAR... EVERYDAY WEAR

MY NEW COAT FEELS SUPER!

BOYS GO TO C&A TOO!

MY DRESS HAS THE NEW PINAFORE LOOK!

C&A MODES LIMITED

Personal Shoppers Only

MUMMY WILL LOVE C&A'S PRICES WHICH MAKE HER MONEY GO ROUND!

Cardigan neck line In whipcord or tweed. Turq., grey, tan, gold, red. 38″ 69/11, each size rising 2/6. **69/11**

All wool whipcord, detailed with velvet. Pink, green, mimosa, turq., powder blue 18″-22″. **49/11**

Tier-skirted, with epaulette frills, and bright contrast bodice. Royal, pink, tangerine. 20″, 16/11 22″, 17/11; 24″, 18/11. **16/11**

Waffle cotton with button-in yoke of crisp white pique Blue, pink, turq. 36″, 32/6; 38″-40″, 35/- ; 42″, 37/6. **32/6**

Back-button dress with jacket. In honeycomb waffle cotton flat for ironing. 24″-26″, 27/6; 28″-30″, 29/11; 32″-34″, 32/6. Pastels. **27/6**

Spruce little suit in smooth tweed, with knife-pleated skirt. Natural, green, 24″-30″, 69/11; 32″-36″, 72/6. **69/**

OBTAINABLE AT ALL C&A BRANCHES

shut your eyes!

open your mouth!

No mistaking Penguin flavours.

Golly-it's good!

A meal in itself,

sensibly wrapped

for picnics or seaside.

chocolate **Penguin**

ONLY 3½ᵈ

TRUST MACDONALDS TO BAKE THE BEST BISCUITS

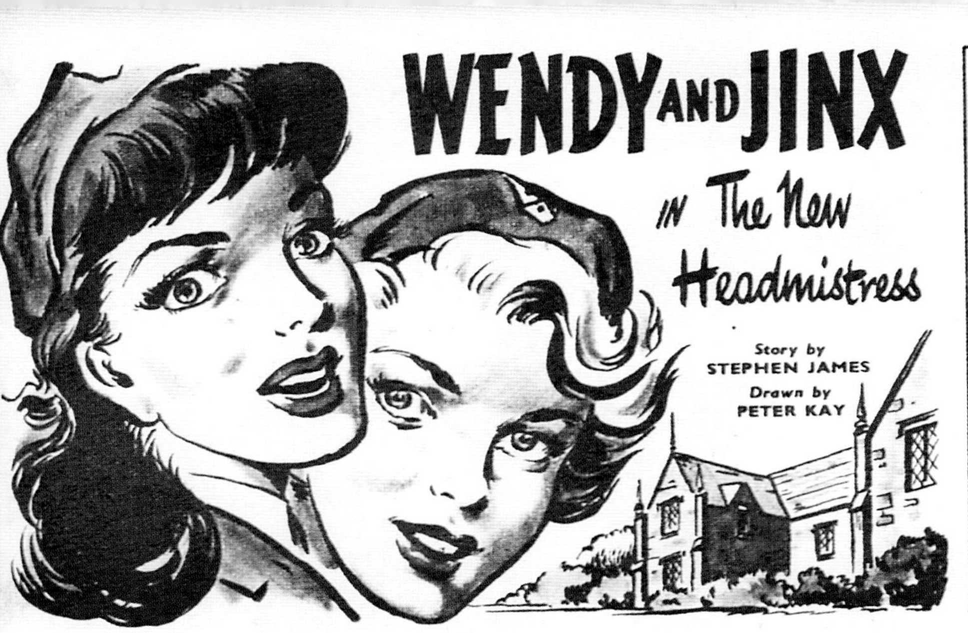
WENDY AND JINX
IN The New Headmistress
Story by STEPHEN JAMES
Drawn by PETER KAY

Wendy and Jinx, inseparable friends of Manor School, become estranged when Jinx refuses to join in the House activities started by the new Headmistress, Miss Kent. The reason is that Jinx is helping her cousin Peter pay off a huge gambling debt and is using her spare time to earn money. Peter himself earns money by writing – until he breaks his wrist saving Jinx from an accident. Time is running short, so Jinx suggests that Peter enters a talent contest as a last resort – but on the day of the contest, Jinx finds Peter very ill. She is desperate, but Wendy, who has followed her, persuades her to tell Miss Kent. While Miss Kent drives Peter to hospital, Wendy goes to enter the talent contest in Peter's place. The clerk tells her that she is too late . . .

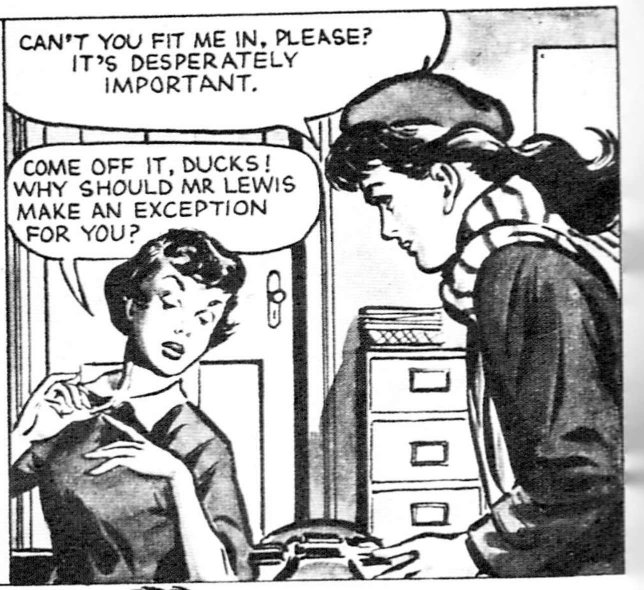
CAN'T YOU FIT ME IN, PLEASE? IT'S DESPERATELY IMPORTANT.
COME OFF IT, DUCKS! WHY SHOULD MR LEWIS MAKE AN EXCEPTION FOR YOU?

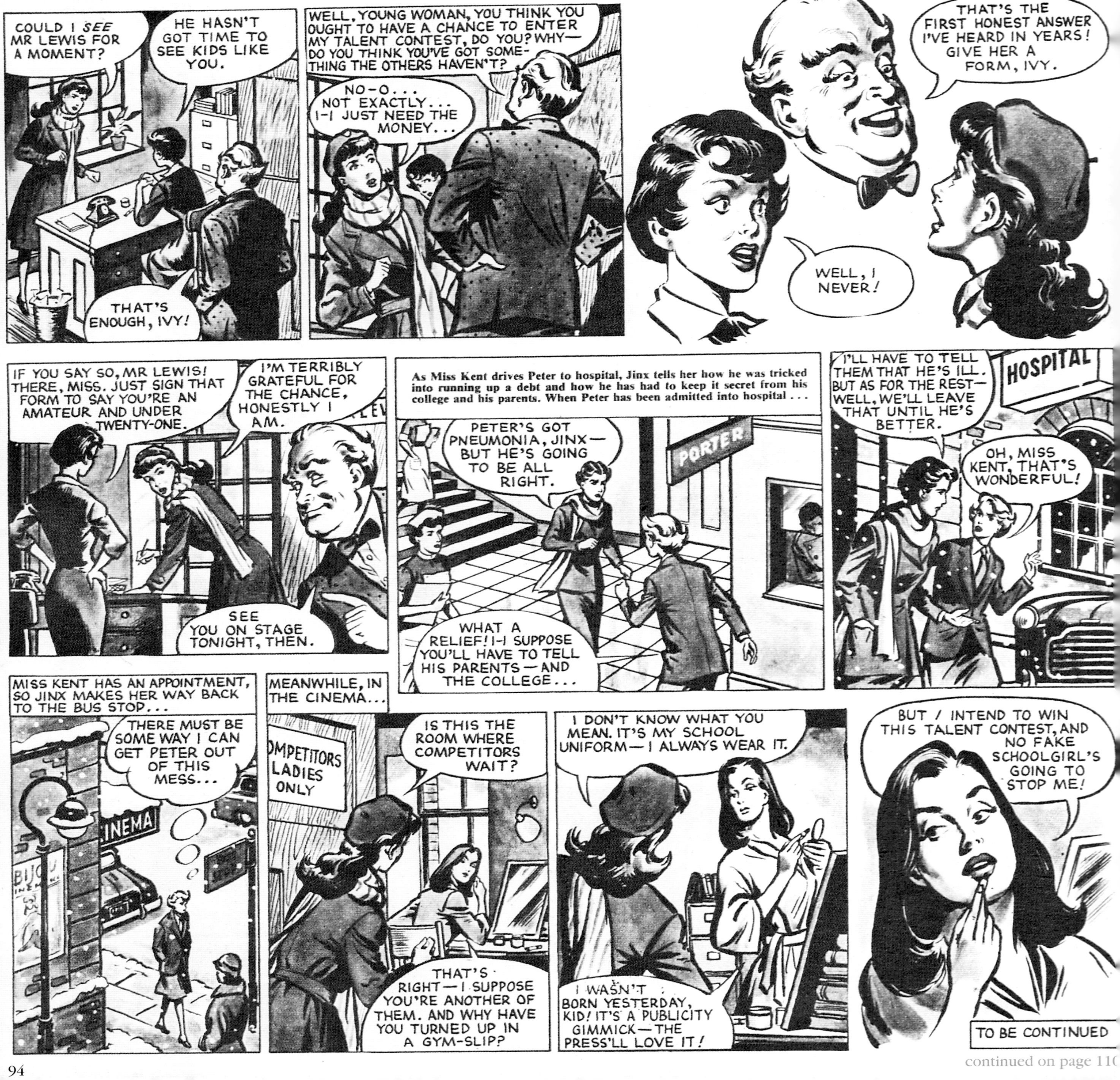
COULD I SEE MR LEWIS FOR A MOMENT?
HE HASN'T GOT TIME TO SEE KIDS LIKE YOU.
THAT'S ENOUGH, IVY!
WELL, YOUNG WOMAN, YOU THINK YOU OUGHT TO HAVE A CHANCE TO ENTER MY TALENT CONTEST, DO YOU? WHY— DO YOU THINK YOU'VE GOT SOMETHING THE OTHERS HAVEN'T?
NO-O... NOT EXACTLY... I-I JUST NEED THE MONEY...
THAT'S THE FIRST HONEST ANSWER I'VE HEARD IN YEARS! GIVE HER A FORM, IVY.
WELL, I NEVER!
IF YOU SAY SO, MR LEWIS! THERE, MISS. JUST SIGN THAT FORM TO SAY YOU'RE AN AMATEUR AND UNDER TWENTY-ONE.
I'M TERRIBLY GRATEFUL FOR THE CHANCE, HONESTLY I AM.
SEE YOU ON STAGE TONIGHT, THEN.
As Miss Kent drives Peter to hospital, Jinx tells her how he was tricked into running up a debt and how he has had to keep it secret from his college and his parents. When Peter has been admitted into hospital . . .
PETER'S GOT PNEUMONIA, JINX— BUT HE'S GOING TO BE ALL RIGHT.
PORTER
WHAT A RELIEF! I-I SUPPOSE YOU'LL HAVE TO TELL HIS PARENTS—AND THE COLLEGE...
HOSPITAL
I'LL HAVE TO TELL THEM THAT HE'S ILL. BUT AS FOR THE REST— WELL, WE'LL LEAVE THAT UNTIL HE'S BETTER.
OH, MISS KENT, THAT'S WONDERFUL!
MISS KENT HAS AN APPOINTMENT, SO JINX MAKES HER WAY BACK TO THE BUS STOP...
THERE MUST BE SOME WAY I CAN GET PETER OUT OF THIS MESS...
CINEMA
MEANWHILE, IN THE CINEMA...
OMPETITORS LADIES ONLY
IS THIS THE ROOM WHERE COMPETITORS WAIT?
THAT'S RIGHT—I SUPPOSE YOU'RE ANOTHER OF THEM. AND WHY HAVE YOU TURNED UP IN A GYM-SLIP?
I DON'T KNOW WHAT YOU MEAN. IT'S MY SCHOOL UNIFORM—I ALWAYS WEAR IT.
I WASN'T BORN YESTERDAY, KID! IT'S A PUBLICITY GIMMICK—THE PRESS'LL LOVE IT!
BUT I INTEND TO WIN THIS TALENT CONTEST, AND NO FAKE SCHOOLGIRL'S GOING TO STOP ME!
TO BE CONTINUED

continued on page 110

MOTHER TELLS YOU HOW

TO ENJOY A COUNTRY WALK

TAKE YOUR LIGHT-WEIGHT MAC, JUDY. IT WILL GO IN YOUR RUCKSACK.

WEAR STRONG SHOES AND LIGHT, ABSORBENT CLOTHES. TAKE A WOOLLIE TOO IN CASE THE WEATHER GETS COLD.

KEEP THE DISTANCE YOU PLAN TO WALK ON THE SHORT SIDE, THEN IF IT TURNS VERY HOT OR RAINS HARD YOU WON'T HAVE TO WORRY MUCH ABOUT GETTING BACK HOME.

PHEW, IT'S HOT! LET'S REST FOR A COUPLE OF HOURS UNDER THIS TREE.

AVOID WALKING IN THE HEAT. YOU WILL BE ABLE TO MAKE UP THE DELAY WHEN IT GETS COOLER AGAIN

STORM COMES UP SHELTER BARN OR UNDER A HEDGE U CAN. *NEVER* STAND UNDER S AS THEY ARE LIABLE TO TRUCK BY LIGHTNING.

SHUT THE GATE PROPERLY, BOB!

GATES LEFT OPEN CAN CAUSE FARMERS A LOT OF TROUBLE THROUGH CATTLE STRAYING. ANOTHER THING—SEE THAT ANY FIRES YOU MAKE ARE PUT OUT THOROUGHLY BEFORE YOU LEAVE.

SINGLE FILE HERE. WE MUSTN'T TRAMPLE THE CORN DOWN.

DID YOU ALL HAVE A GOOD TIME?

A WONDERFUL TIME, THANK YOU.

LOVELY, MOTHER. GOODNIGHT, EVERYONE!

I want to be an AIR STEWARDESS

PAULINE wants to be an air stewardess and, although she knows how difficult it is, has made a good start by passing her general certificate with a distinction in French.

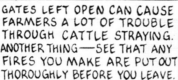

DOES THAT FEEL MORE COMFORTABLE, MRS SAUVEY?

MUCH BETTER, NURSE.

A MEMBER OF THE RED CROSS, PAULINE IS DOING FULL-TIME WORK IN HER LOCAL HOSPITAL. AIR STEWARDESSES NEED TO KNOW HOW TO CARE FOR SICK PASSENGERS AND PAULINE WILL DO TWO YEARS NURSING TO HELP REALISE HER CHERISHED AMBITION.

I DO HOPE MY APPLICATION HAS BEEN SUCCESSFUL.

WE'LL LET YOU KNOW OUR DECISION IN A FEW DAYS, MISS NICHOLS.

PAULINE'S GREAT DAY HAS ARRIVED AND SHE HAS BEEN GRANTED AN INTERVIEW WITH THE AIRLINE AUTHORITIES. SHE IS NOW TWENTY-ONE, WITH A SOUND KNOWLEDGE OF NURSING AND FRENCH, TOGETHER WITH HER FRIENDLY PERSONALITY AND GOOD GROOMING SHE HOPES HER APPLICATION WILL BE SUCCESSFUL.

THIS DIAGRAM MAKES IT CLEAR.

YES, I UNDERSTAND NOW.

TED, PAULINE HAS STARTED ELEVEN WEEKS HARD TRAINING. TENDS CLASSES TO LEARN ABOUT CATERING, HOW TO ATTEND CK PASSENGERS, FASTEN SAFELY BELTS, MAKE PEOPLE RTABLE AND BE CALM AND FRIENDLY UNDER ANY CIRCUMSTANCES.

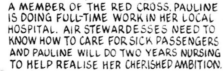

HERE IS YOUR LUNCH, MADAM.

PART OF PAULINE'S TRAINING IS IN AN AIRCRAFT ON THE GROUND WHERE OTHER TRAINEES ACT AS PASSENGERS. HERE SHE LEARNS HOW TO BALANCE TRAYS OF FOOD AND DRINKS AND SERVE THE PASSENGERS WITHOUT STUMBLING.

GOOD-BYE, MARY. I HOPE YOU'LL COME ON MY PLANE AGAIN ONE DAY.

THANK YOU FOR LOOKING AFTER ME.

PAULINE HAS NOW COMPLETED HER FIRST FLIGHT AND IS SAYING FAREWELL TO HER PASSENGERS. HER JOB IS EXACTING AS WELL AS EXCITING, AND VERY DIFFICULT TO OBTAIN. IF *YOU* FEEL YOU WOULD QUALIFY FOR THIS SPECIALISED WORK, WE HOPE YOU'LL BE EVERY BIT AS HAPPY AS PAULINE.

A Letter from the Editor

GIRL OFFICE, 161/166 FLEET STREET, LONDON, E.C.4.
3rd April, 1957.

A NEW serial is starting on page four this week. It is called 'Showboat Summer' and it's been written specially for GIRL by the well-known authoress Miss Pamela Brown. I expect that many of you are already keen readers of Miss Brown's books, but I wonder if you know that she wrote her first book when she was only fourteen!

Some of the winning entries of our Oral Hygiene Poster Competition are going to be exhibited at Selfridges in Oxford Street, London, from 17th to 27th April. Do visit it if you can – it's a most interesting exhibition.

Yours sincerely,

Marcus Morris

READER'S LETTER

5/– *will be paid for every reader's letter printed on this page.*

Jennifer and Jaunty

I THOUGHT you might be interested to see a photograph of our Keeshond, as one of this breed was Supreme Champion at Cruft's Dog Show this year. His name is Jaunty, and he is very fond of children. He is a very good watch-dog

The Keeshond, or Dutch barge-dog as he is also known, is the national dog of Holland and is used for guarding barges on the canals. – *Jennifer Birse, Gosport, Hants.*

Winners

Congratulations to the fifty winners of GIRL Competition No. 7. We wish we could print all their names, but as usual we are unfortunately rather cramped for space. However, we send them our very best wishes and congratulations just the same. A full list of the prizewinners' names can always be obtained on request from our Liverpool office. Please remember to enclose a stamped, self-addressed envelope.

PAINTING IN OILS

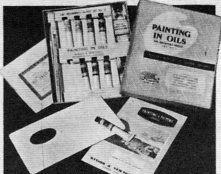

YOU can wi this superb Painting Set

There are THIRTY of these wonderful prizes to be won!

Have you ever tried painting in oils? It's great fun – and here's your chance to win a set of oil-paints. All you have to do is sort these objects into rhyming pairs, so set to work right away.

11b

HERE ARE THE RULES

1. The name of each object in the illustration rhymes with one of the others. Sort the objects into rhyming pairs and write the pairs down on a postcard.
2. In the top right-hand corner of the same postcard add your name, address and age last birthday.
3. Points will be given for neatness and handwriting as well as for the correct solutions. The ages of the entrants will also be taken into consideration in the judgi
4. This competition is open to all g up to and including the age of sixte
5. All entries should be sent to :– G Reader Services, GIRL Competition No. Long Lane, Aintree, Liverpool, 9, to arr there not later than 15th April.
6. Send no money; this is FREE.
7. The Editor's and judges' decision final. No correspondence will be ente into about any entry.

FOR GIRL ADVENTURERS

Happy Club Members consult the map for the next stage of their walking holiday. We have a brochure for YOU which gives all particulars of these inexpensive tours. If you are between 12 and 16, write at once for the GIRL/Y.H.A. booklet to: – SUMMER HOLIDAYS, Long Lane, Aintree, Liverpool, 9, enclosing a stamped, self-addressed label, and stating your club number.

★ **DON'T DELAY—WRITE TODAY**

STAR ADVENTURER

For an exceptional record of helpfulness in the home.

PATRICIA CARLING,
aged 10, of London, N.W.1.

AUGUST 5th 1948
APRIL 1st 1943
JUNE 19th 1944
SEPT. 27. 1945
NOV. 17. 1946
FEBRUARY 25th 1947

Birthdates

If you are a GIRL Adventurer and your birthdate appears in this week's list, you are entitled to a FREE birthday gift! Choose it from the following: **stamp album, propelling pencil, stationery folder, bicycle bell, ball point pen, coloured pencils or GIRL handbag badge.** Then state your choice on a postcard, giving your name, address and club number, and the date you were born and post it to: BIRTHDATES (29), GIRL Club, Long Lane, Aintree, Liverpool, 9. Your postcard must reach us by Thursday, April 11th.

Overseas members whose birthdates appear above will receive their presents automatically.

COUPON G7

USE BLOCK LETTERS TO FILL THIS IN, PLEASE

This painting is the original work of:

FULL NAME ....
ADDRESS ....
....
....
AGE .... DATE OF BIRTH ....
SCHOOL ....
TITLE OF PAINTING
Signature of parent, teacher or guardian ....
(Maximum size of entry 3ft. x 2ft.).

GIRL PAINTING COMPETITION

CLOSING DATE APRIL 29

Have you entered for our Painting Competition yet? We want you to paint something you like and then send it to us. Your entries will be judged by a panel of art experts, who will be looking for imagination and promise and not just for technical skill. The full rules appeared in last week's GIRL. Start on your entry now!

HERE ARE THE TABLE TENNIS RESULTS

CONGRATULATIONS *to Janet Roberts, winner of the Girls' Junior Final.*

MOMENTOUS MOMENT *w Mr Marcus Morris, Editor GIRL presents Mary Shan with her cup, when she the Girls' Senior Final.*

A few weeks ago, the finals of the GIRL Tal Tennis Competitions were held in London.

The outstanding player was undoubtedly Ma Shannon, from Worcester Park, who won the Gir Senior title by beating Betty Kinsley, of Hull, 22-2 21-16. Last year, Mary Shannon was the Juni Champion and, by age, still eligible for that eve However, by a new rule, she had to compete agai the older girls this year and her play was so br liant that she beat them all! The Girls' Junior Fin was so closely contested that there was scarcely point between the finalists, Lynda Gordon of Ma chester and Janet Roberts of Birminghar Eventually Janet Roberts won (22-20, 18-21, 22-2 making Lynda the runner-up for the second ye in succession.

During the morning Diane Rowe and Hel Elliot, two world champion players, selected pa ners from among the unlucky losers, and gave special exhibition match in the afternoon.

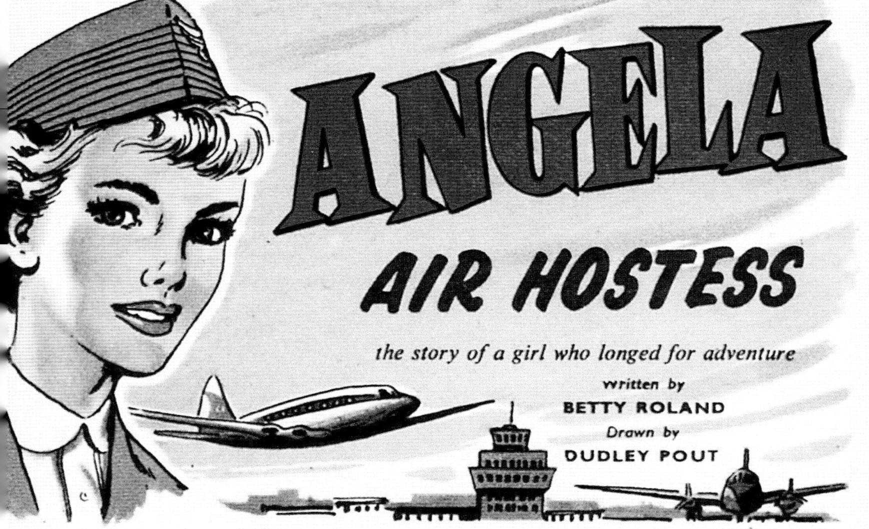

ANGELA AIR HOSTESS

the story of a girl who longed for adventure

written by BETTY ROLAND

Drawn by DUDLEY POUT

Angela Wells, an air hostess for Wingways, is furious when her beautiful, selfish, cousin Sandra, also an air hostess, comes to live at her mother's guest-house. Both girls are keen on Captain Ian Lewis – a handsome senior pilot – and Sandra has decided to keep an eye on her rival. Angela is posted to the Cairo flight, together with Ian and Sandra, but on the very first morning, Angela, deliberately made late by her unscrupulous cousin, is reprimanded by Ian. To Angela's surprise, Sandra lets her have the First Class passengers – but she soon discovers why. She has a temperamental passenger to deal with – the wife of a wealthy oil magnate . . .

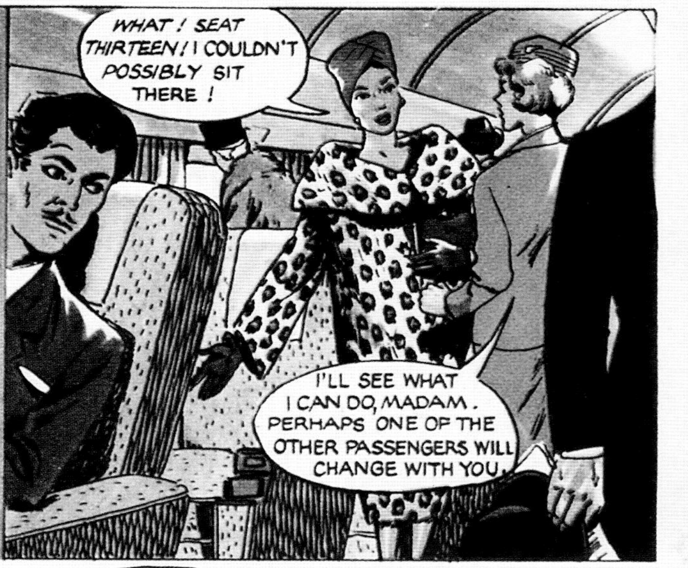
WHAT! SEAT THIRTEEN! I COULDN'T POSSIBLY SIT THERE!
I'LL SEE WHAT I CAN DO, MADAM. PERHAPS ONE OF THE OTHER PASSENGERS WILL CHANGE WITH YOU.

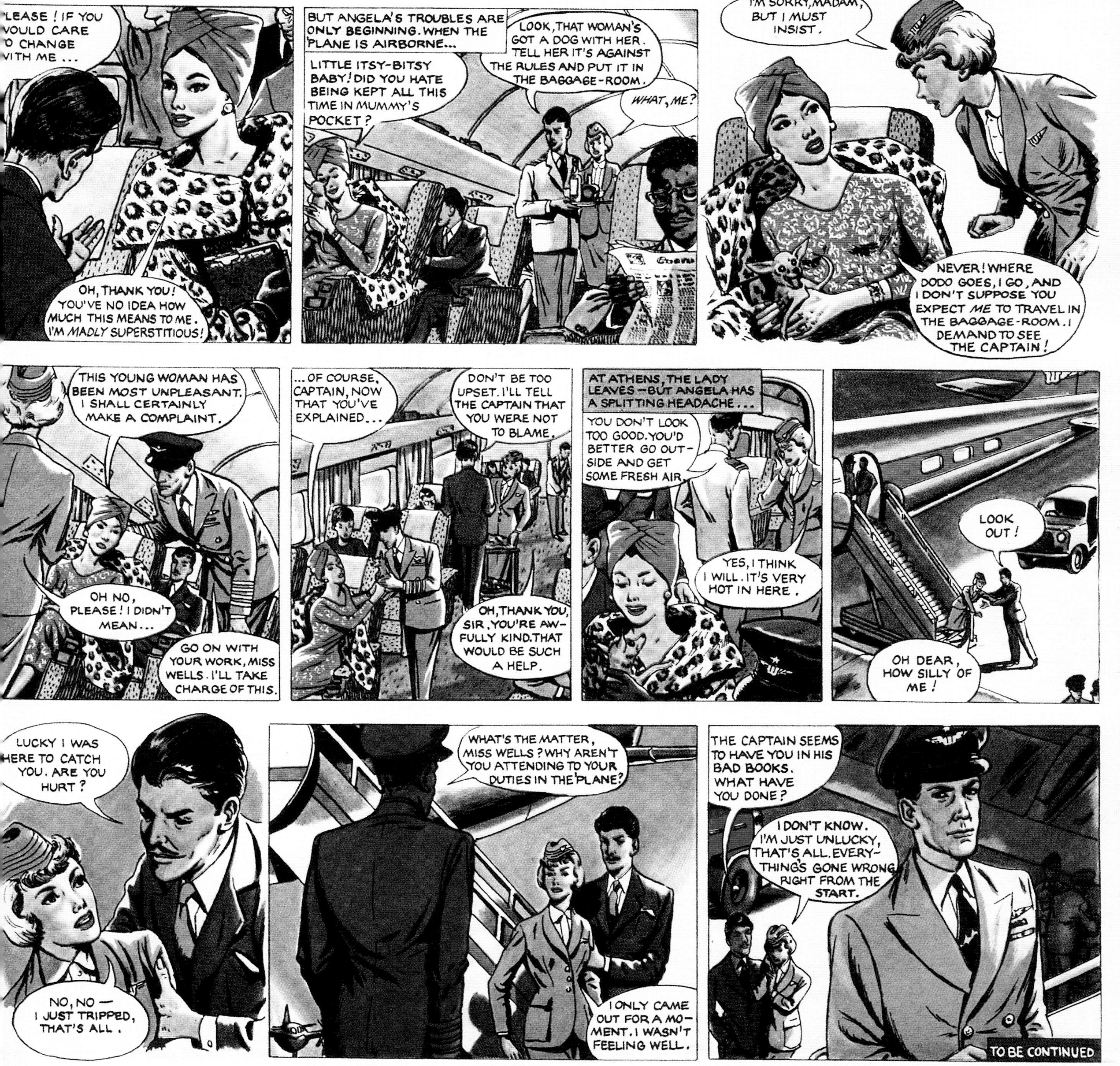
LEASE! IF YOU VOULD CARE O CHANGE VITH ME...
OH, THANK YOU! YOU'VE NO IDEA HOW MUCH THIS MEANS TO ME. I'M MADLY SUPERSTITIOUS!
BUT ANGELA'S TROUBLES ARE ONLY BEGINNING. WHEN THE PLANE IS AIRBORNE...
LITTLE ITSY-BITSY BABY! DID YOU HATE BEING KEPT ALL THIS TIME IN MUMMY'S POCKET?
LOOK, THAT WOMAN'S GOT A DOG WITH HER. TELL HER IT'S AGAINST THE RULES AND PUT IT IN THE BAGGAGE-ROOM.
WHAT, ME?
I'M SORRY, MADAM, BUT I MUST INSIST.
NEVER! WHERE DODO GOES, I GO, AND I DON'T SUPPOSE YOU EXPECT ME TO TRAVEL IN THE BAGGAGE-ROOM. I DEMAND TO SEE THE CAPTAIN!
THIS YOUNG WOMAN HAS BEEN MOST UNPLEASANT. I SHALL CERTAINLY MAKE A COMPLAINT.
OH NO, PLEASE! I DIDN'T MEAN...
GO ON WITH YOUR WORK, MISS WELLS. I'LL TAKE CHARGE OF THIS.
...OF COURSE, CAPTAIN, NOW THAT YOU'VE EXPLAINED...
DON'T BE TOO UPSET. I'LL TELL THE CAPTAIN THAT YOU WERE NOT TO BLAME.
OH, THANK YOU, SIR, YOU'RE AW-FULLY KIND. THAT WOULD BE SUCH A HELP.
AT ATHENS, THE LADY LEAVES—BUT ANGELA HAS A SPLITTING HEADACHE...
YOU DON'T LOOK TOO GOOD. YOU'D BETTER GO OUT-SIDE AND GET SOME FRESH AIR.
YES, I THINK I WILL. IT'S VERY HOT IN HERE.
LOOK OUT!
OH DEAR, HOW SILLY OF ME!
LUCKY I WAS HERE TO CATCH YOU. ARE YOU HURT?
NO, NO — I JUST TRIPPED, THAT'S ALL.
WHAT'S THE MATTER, MISS WELLS? WHY AREN'T YOU ATTENDING TO YOUR DUTIES IN THE PLANE?
I ONLY CAME OUT FOR A MO-MENT. I WASN'T FEELING WELL.
THE CAPTAIN SEEMS TO HAVE YOU IN HIS BAD BOOKS. WHAT HAVE YOU DONE?
I DON'T KNOW. I'M JUST UNLUCKY, THAT'S ALL. EVERY-THING'S GONE WRONG RIGHT FROM THE START.
TO BE CONTINUED

continued on page 115

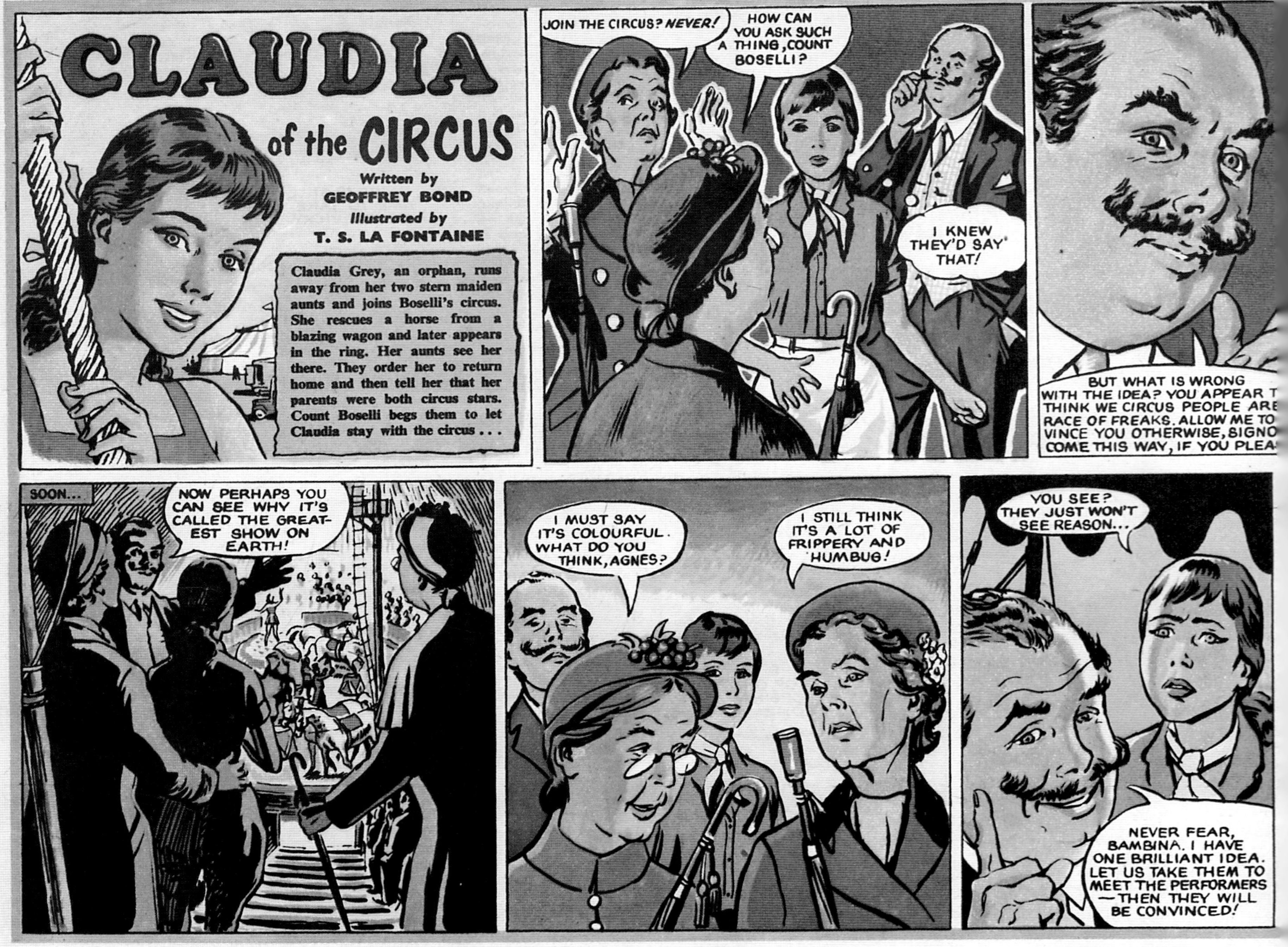
CLAUDIA
of the CIRCUS
Written by
GEOFFREY BOND
Illustrated by
T. S. LA FONTAINE
Claudia Grey, an orphan, runs away from her two stern maiden aunts and joins Boselli's circus. She rescues a horse from a blazing wagon and later appears in the ring. Her aunts see her there. They order her to return home and then tell her that her parents were both circus stars. Count Boselli begs them to let Claudia stay with the circus . . .
JOIN THE CIRCUS? NEVER!
HOW CAN YOU ASK SUCH A THING, COUNT BOSELLI?
I KNEW THEY'D SAY THAT!
BUT WHAT IS WRONG WITH THE IDEA? YOU APPEAR T THINK WE CIRCUS PEOPLE ARE RACE OF FREAKS. ALLOW ME TO VINCE YOU OTHERWISE, SIGNO COME THIS WAY, IF YOU PLEA
SOON...
NOW PERHAPS YOU CAN SEE WHY IT'S CALLED THE GREATEST SHOW ON EARTH!
I MUST SAY IT'S COLOURFUL. WHAT DO YOU THINK, AGNES?
I STILL THINK IT'S A LOT OF FRIPPERY AND 'HUMBUG'!
YOU SEE? THEY JUST WON'T SEE REASON...
NEVER FEAR, BAMBINA. I HAVE ONE BRILLIANT IDEA. LET US TAKE THEM TO MEET THE PERFORMERS —THEN THEY WILL BE CONVINCED!

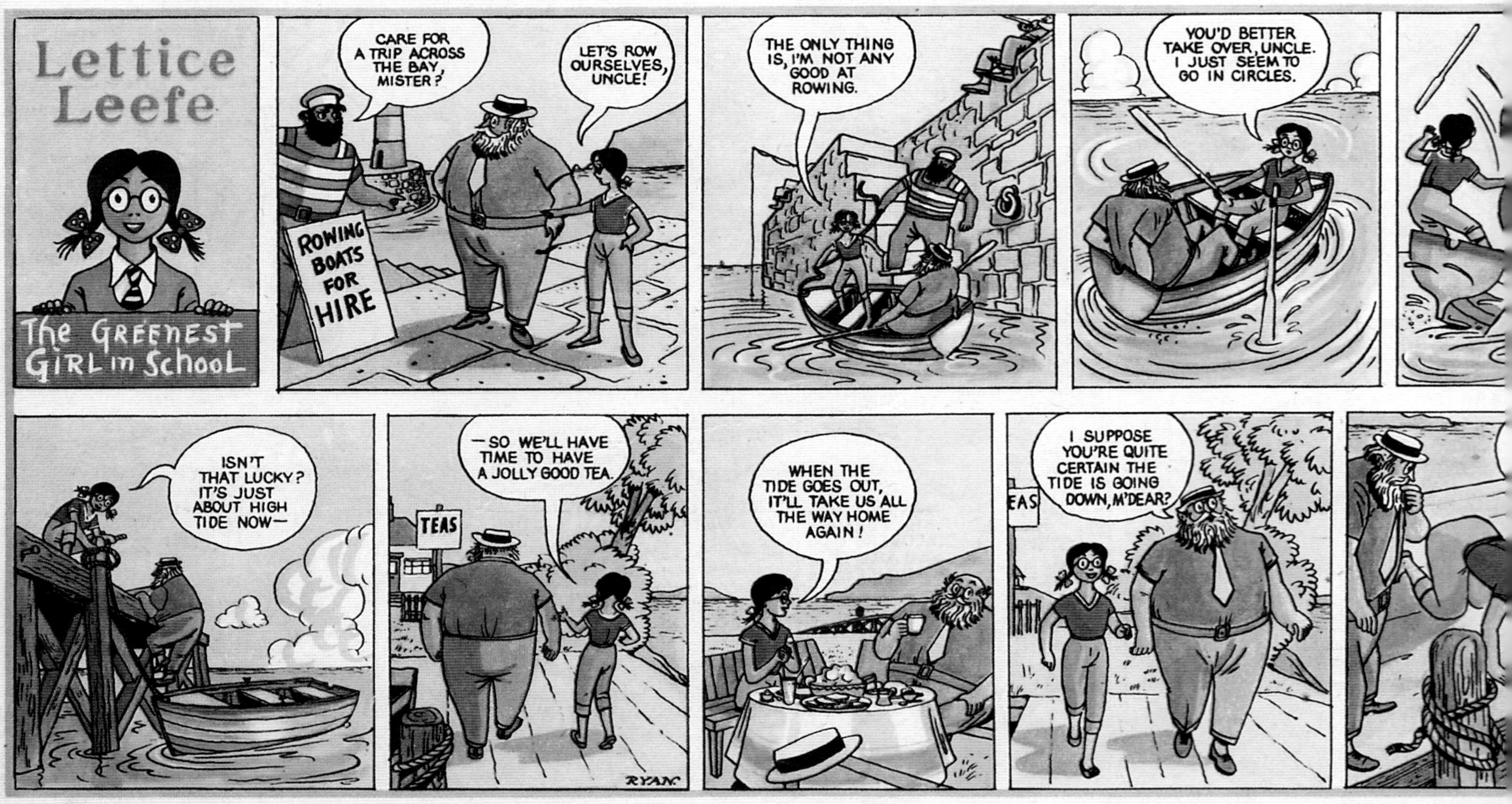
Lettice Leefe
The GREENEST GIRL in SchooL
CARE FOR A TRIP ACROSS THE BAY, MISTER?
LET'S ROW OURSELVES, UNCLE!
ROWING BOATS FOR HIRE
THE ONLY THING IS, I'M NOT ANY GOOD AT ROWING.
YOU'D BETTER TAKE OVER, UNCLE. I JUST SEEM TO GO IN CIRCLES.
ISN'T THAT LUCKY? IT'S JUST ABOUT HIGH TIDE NOW—
—SO WE'LL HAVE TIME TO HAVE A JOLLY GOOD TEA.
TEAS
WHEN THE TIDE GOES OUT, IT'LL TAKE US ALL THE WAY HOME AGAIN!
EAS
I SUPPOSE YOU'RE QUITE CERTAIN THE TIDE IS GOING DOWN, M'DEAR?
RYAN.

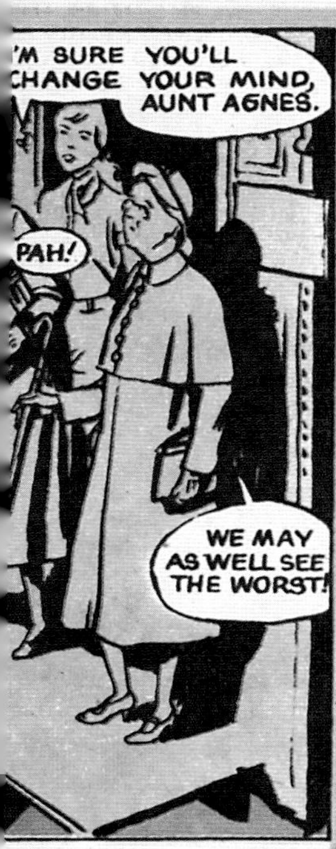
I'M SURE YOU'LL CHANGE YOUR MIND, AUNT AGNES.
PAH!
WE MAY AS WELL SEE THE WORST!

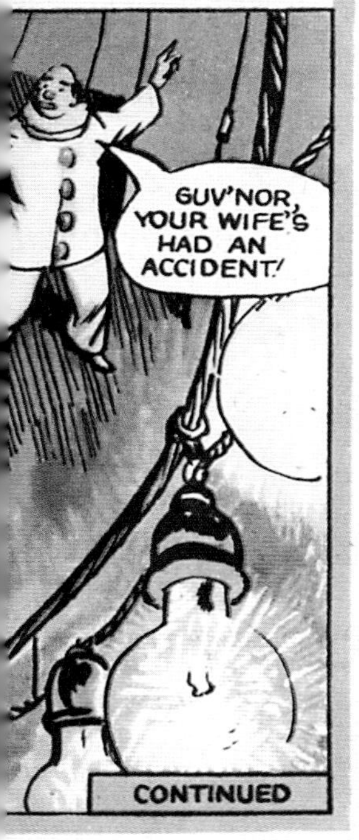
GUV'NOR, YOUR WIFE'S HAD AN ACCIDENT!
CONTINUED

continued on page 112

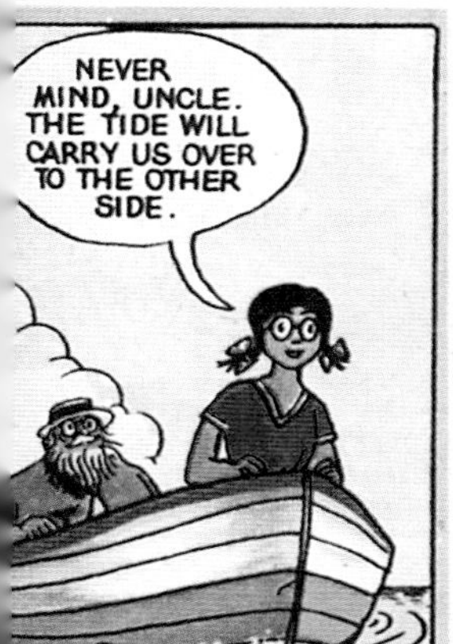
NEVER MIND, UNCLE. THE TIDE WILL CARRY US OVER TO THE OTHER SIDE.

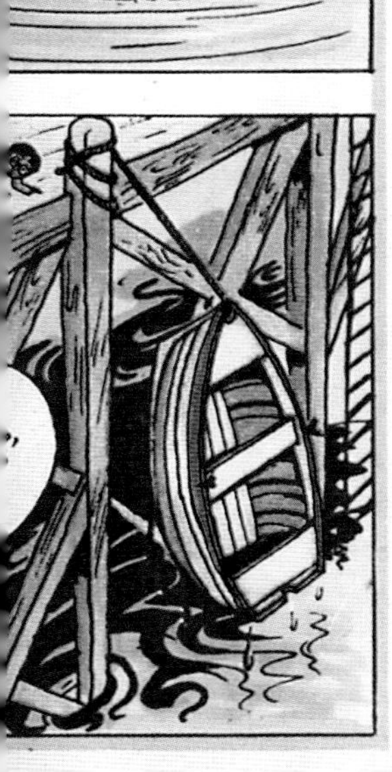

Girl Picture Gallery

No. 306

We hardly need to tell you who this is! Be sure that you don't miss his latest film, 'Jailhouse Rock'.

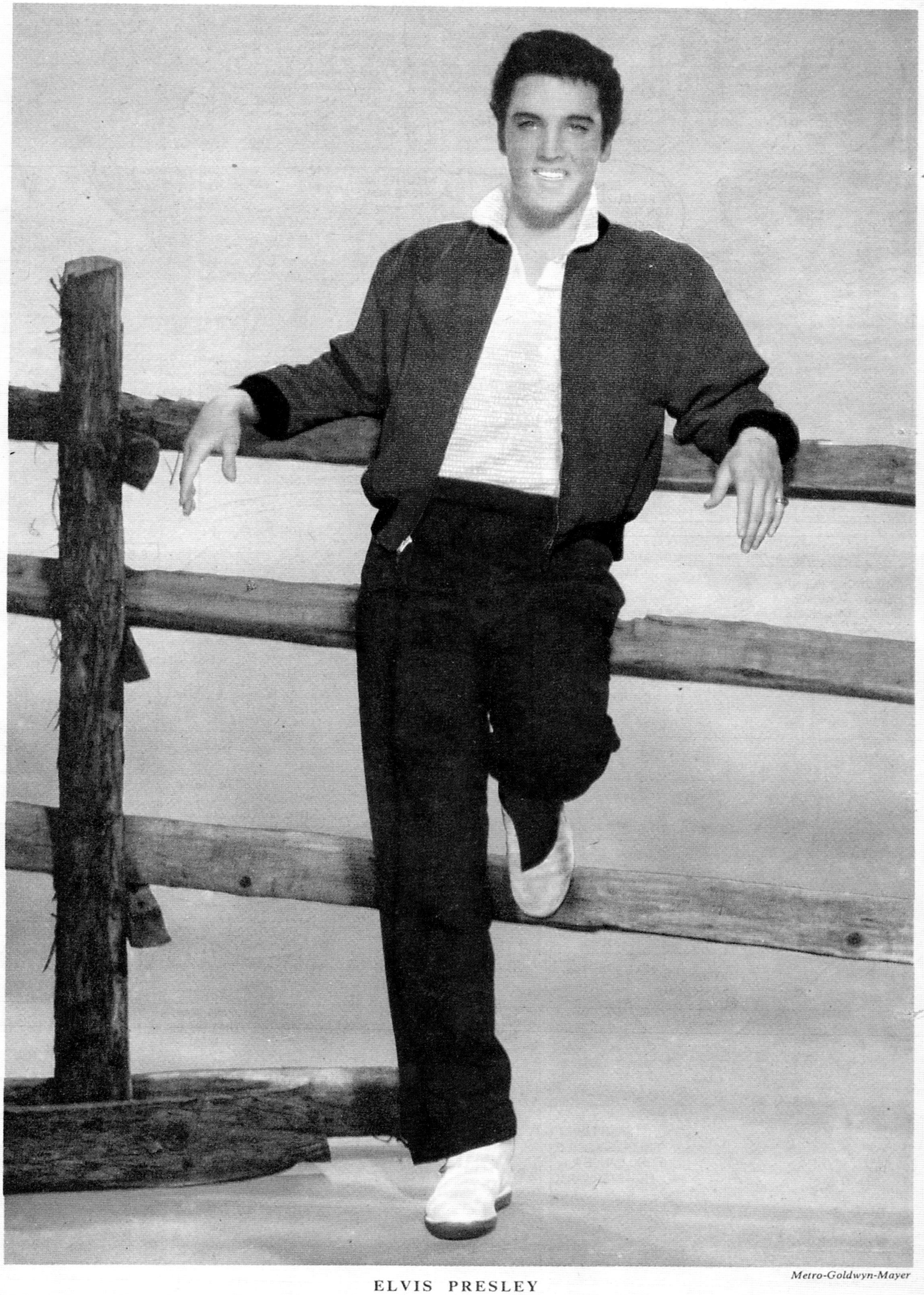

Metro-Goldwyn-Mayer

ELVIS PRESLEY

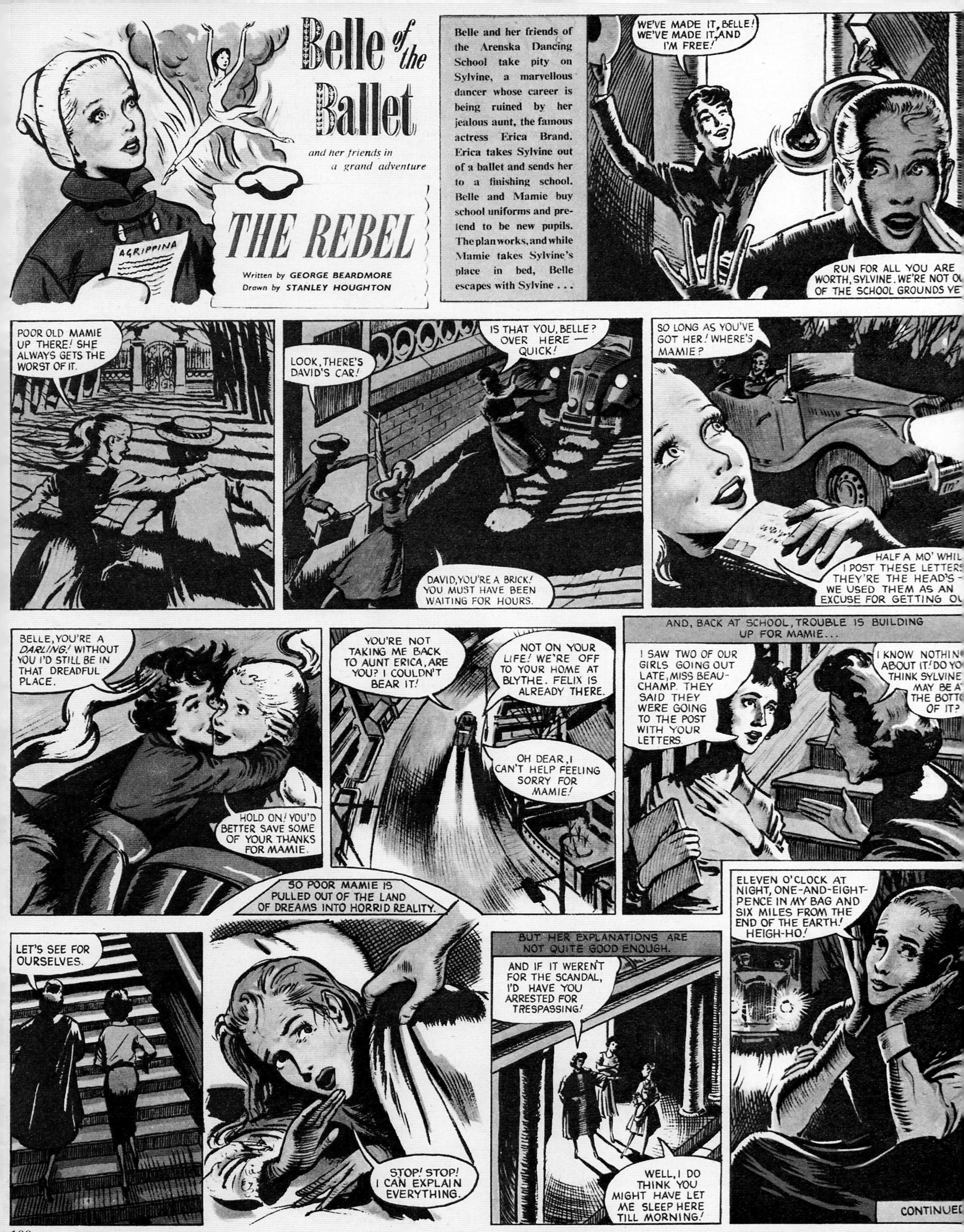
Belle of the Ballet
and her friends in a grand adventure
THE REBEL
Written by GEORGE BEARDMORE
Drawn by STANLEY HOUGHTON
AGRIPPINA
Belle and her friends of the Arenska Dancing School take pity on Sylvine, a marvellous dancer whose career is being ruined by her jealous aunt, the famous actress Erica Brand. Erica takes Sylvine out of a ballet and sends her to a finishing school. Belle and Mamie buy school uniforms and pretend to be new pupils. The plan works, and while Mamie takes Sylvine's place in bed, Belle escapes with Sylvine . . .
WE'VE MADE IT, BELLE! WE'VE MADE IT, AND I'M FREE!
RUN FOR ALL YOU ARE WORTH, SYLVINE. WE'RE NOT OU OF THE SCHOOL GROUNDS YET
POOR OLD MAMIE UP THERE! SHE ALWAYS GETS THE WORST OF IT.
LOOK, THERE'S DAVID'S CAR!
IS THAT YOU, BELLE? OVER HERE — QUICK!
DAVID, YOU'RE A BRICK! YOU MUST HAVE BEEN WAITING FOR HOURS.
SO LONG AS YOU'VE GOT HER! WHERE'S MAMIE?
HALF A MO' WHIL I POST THESE LETTERS THEY'RE THE HEAD'S — WE USED THEM AS AN EXCUSE FOR GETTING OU
BELLE, YOU'RE A DARLING! WITHOUT YOU I'D STILL BE IN THAT DREADFUL PLACE.
HOLD ON! YOU'D BETTER SAVE SOME OF YOUR THANKS FOR MAMIE.
YOU'RE NOT TAKING ME BACK TO AUNT ERICA, ARE YOU? I COULDN'T BEAR IT!
NOT ON YOUR LIFE! WE'RE OFF TO YOUR HOME AT BLYTHE. FELIX IS ALREADY THERE.
OH DEAR, I CAN'T HELP FEELING SORRY FOR MAMIE!
AND, BACK AT SCHOOL, TROUBLE IS BUILDING UP FOR MAMIE...
I SAW TWO OF OUR GIRLS GOING OUT LATE, MISS BEAUCHAMP. THEY SAID THEY WERE GOING TO THE POST WITH YOUR LETTERS.
I KNOW NOTHIN ABOUT IT! DO YO THINK SYLVINE MAY BE A THE BOTTO OF IT?
SO POOR MAMIE IS PULLED OUT OF THE LAND OF DREAMS INTO HORRID REALITY.
LET'S SEE FOR OURSELVES.
STOP! STOP! I CAN EXPLAIN EVERYTHING.
BUT HER EXPLANATIONS ARE NOT QUITE GOOD ENOUGH.
AND IF IT WEREN'T FOR THE SCANDAL, I'D HAVE YOU ARRESTED FOR TRESPASSING!
WELL, I DO THINK YOU MIGHT HAVE LET ME SLEEP HERE TILL MORNING!
ELEVEN O'CLOCK AT NIGHT, ONE-AND-EIGHTPENCE IN MY BAG AND SIX MILES FROM THE END OF THE EARTH! HEIGH-HO!
CONTINUED

continued on page 11

A GIRL Expert gives some hints on

FRIENDSHIP

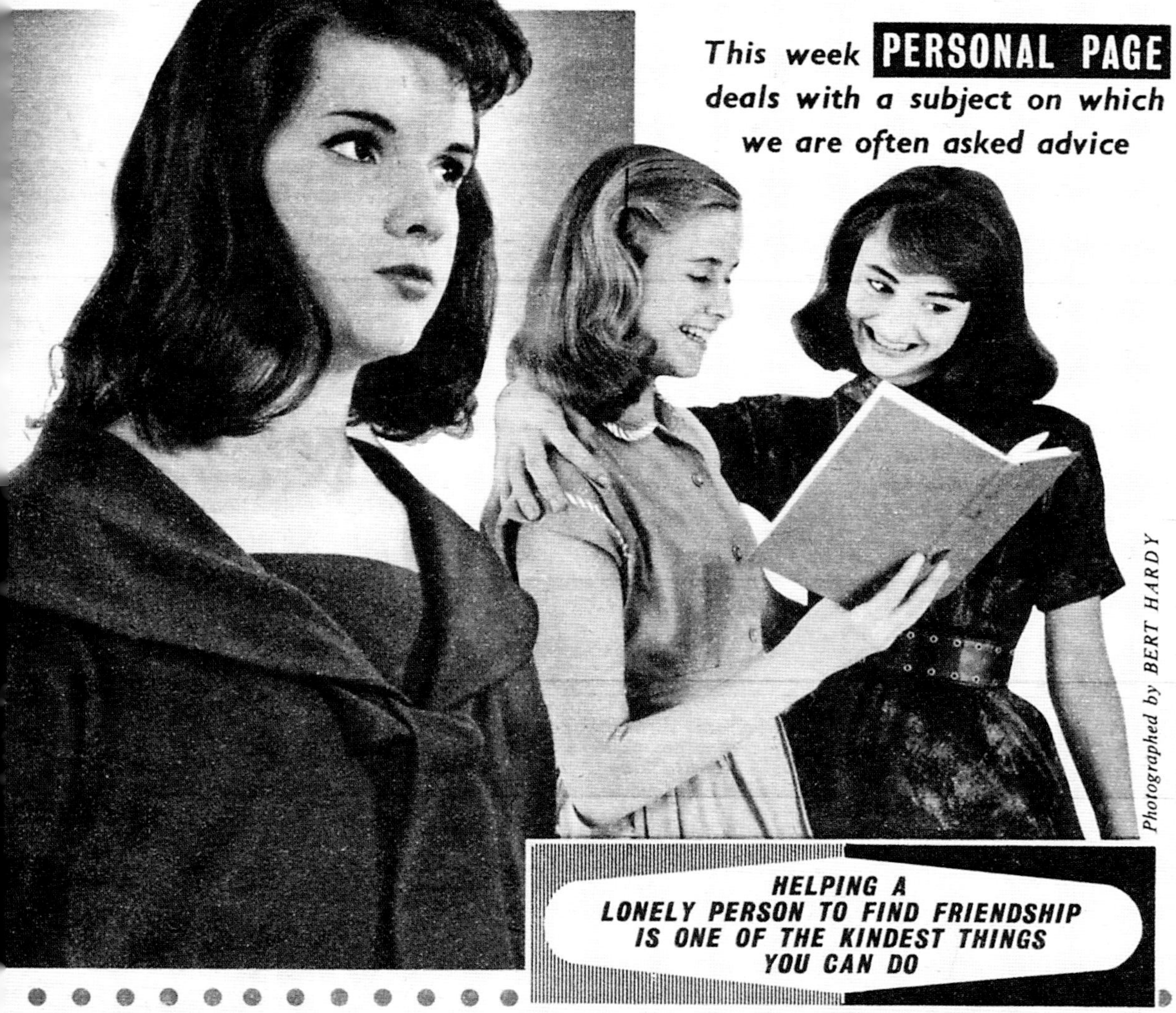

This week **PERSONAL PAGE** deals with a subject on which we are often asked advice

Photographed by BERT HARDY

HELPING A LONELY PERSON TO FIND FRIENDSHIP IS ONE OF THE KINDEST THINGS YOU CAN DO

How can we make friends with the people we like? How can we keep the friends we want? Everyone is interested in these questions because we all need friends and appreciate friendship.

It isn't luck. People do not make and keep friends because they are pretty, or have good figures, or are rich, or happen to live in a certain part of the town. People who make friends without difficulty have one thing only to thank for it – they know how to be friendly.

That sounds simple – but it is not as easy as it sounds, because friendship must be genuine if it is to find a response. It must not be gushing or artificial or too demanding.

You can't be very successful as a friend if you are too wrapped up in yourself. Friendship comes from sharing interests. If you want to make plenty of friends, you need to have interests of your own, and you must be prepared to share other people's interests.

Friendship is based on honesty

Trying to sell yourself too hard never works. Some people have such a poor opinion of themselves that they feel no one will want to be friends with them unless they make themselves more impressive in some way. This is a great mistake. Friendship is based on honesty in our feelings and behaviour. People want to get to know *us*, not a dramatized version of ourselves.

The best way to make friends is to be simple, natural and – well – friendly. Show you are glad to see people when you happen to meet them. Smile. Say hello. Ask a few questions. Show interest.

It's no good hanging back and waiting for other people to make the first move. They will think you are stand-offish and will ignore you. You must be welcoming to others if you want to make friends.

The right number of friends

What is the ideal number of friends? People vary. Some get on splendidly with throngs of friends; others prefer to belong to a small group of special friends. Almost everybody likes to have one or two extra-special friends, apart from friends in general.

A word on special friends. It doesn't work too well if two friends spend *all* their time with each other. This limits friendship too much and may make friends rather snappy towards each other. Plenty of friends as well as a special friend is the best idea.

Last and most important of all. If you make friends easily, give a hand to those who are not so fortunate. They need your help to get started. There is no kinder action on earth than to help a lonely person to find friendship.

WHAT'S YOUR WORRY?

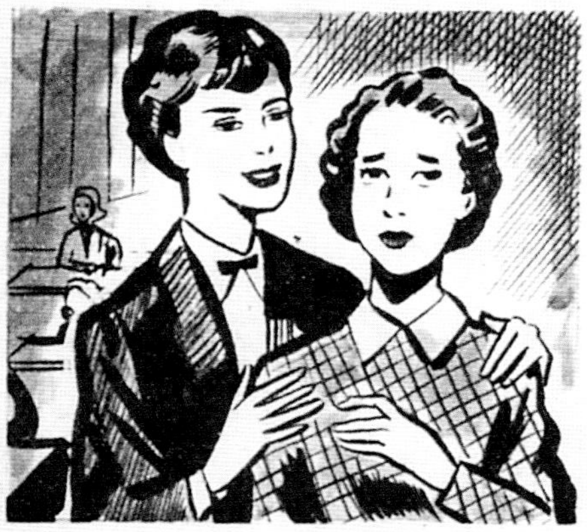

The form mistress' pet

Q. It worries me because I am the form-mistress' pet. Can you tell me what to do?

A. You must take special care not to put on airs of any kind where the other girls are concerned. Take a full interest in the life of the form and the interests of the other girls. Your friends will only object to your favoured position if you appear to take advantage of it.

★ ★ ★

Is my friend a tell-tale?

Q. My friend tells her mother everything. I think she's rather a tell-tale-tit. What do you think?

A. It depends *why* your friend tells her mother everything. Perhaps she is on excellent terms with her mother and talks to her about everything. If that is so, there is no element of sneaking in what she says to her mother. But if your friend tells her mother things with the intention of getting someone into trouble, then we agree that is most unpleasant.

★ ★ ★

Should I write to him?

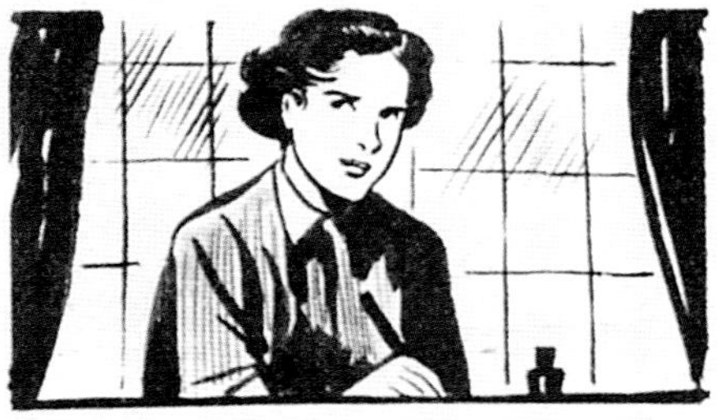

Q. Do you think it is wrong for a girl of 13 to write to a boy of 16?

A. Certainly it isn't wrong, so long as there is nothing underhand and secretive about the correspondence.

★ ★ ★

Who does he like best?

Q. My friend and I are both friendly with a boy who we see quite often. How can we find out which one he likes best?

A. How do you know he prefers either of you? He may enjoy meeting you both without giving another thought to which of you he likes best. We don't have to arrange all our friends in order of merit, you know.

★ ★ ★

She just won't be friendly

Q. There is a girl in our school with whom we would all like to be friendly but she just won't be friendly. What can we do?

A. (1) Find out what she can do towards some such occasion as a party or school play and get her to lend a hand doing it. (2) Find out what interests her, and bring her into the conversation by talking about her interests when opportunities offer themselves.

★ ★ ★

I cannot keep my friends

Q. How can I keep my friends? As soon as I find a new friend I seem to get aggravated with her and then I lose her.

A. You are forgetting that friendship depends on give and take. The moment your friend's behaviour doesn't suit you, you give her up. If you want the fun and satisfaction of friendship, you must be prepared to accept the point of view of other people and sometimes to give way to them.

How can I get my friend back?

Q. Last year I had a boy friend but I gave him up. Now I haven't a boy friend so I want him back again. How can I get him back again?

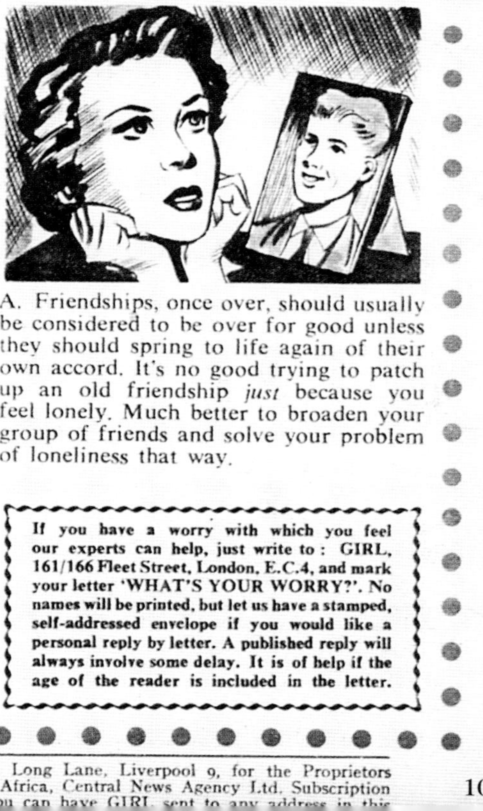

A. Friendships, once over, should usually be considered to be over for good unless they should spring to life again of their own accord. It's no good trying to patch up an old friendship *just* because you feel lonely. Much better to broaden your group of friends and solve your problem of loneliness that way.

If you have a worry with which you feel our experts can help, just write to: GIRL, 161/166 Fleet Street, London, E.C.4, and mark your letter 'WHAT'S YOUR WORRY?'. No names will be printed, but let us have a stamped, self-addressed envelope if you would like a personal reply by letter. A published reply will always involve some delay. It is of help if the age of the reader is included in the letter.

Registered at the G.P.O. for transmission by Magazine Post to Canada (including Newfoundland), GIRL printed in Great Britain by Eric Bemrose Ltd., Long Lane, Liverpool 9, for the Proprietors and Publishers, Hulton Press Ltd., 161/166 Fleet Street, London, E.C.4. Sole agents for Australia and New Zealand, Gordon & Gotch (A/sia) Ltd.; South Africa, Central News Agency Ltd. Subscription Rate: Inland, 12 months 28/2; 6 months 14/1; abroad 12 months 26/-; 6 months 13/-. Postage for single copies: Inland 2d.; Foreign 1½d.; Canada 1d. You can have GIRL sent to any address in this

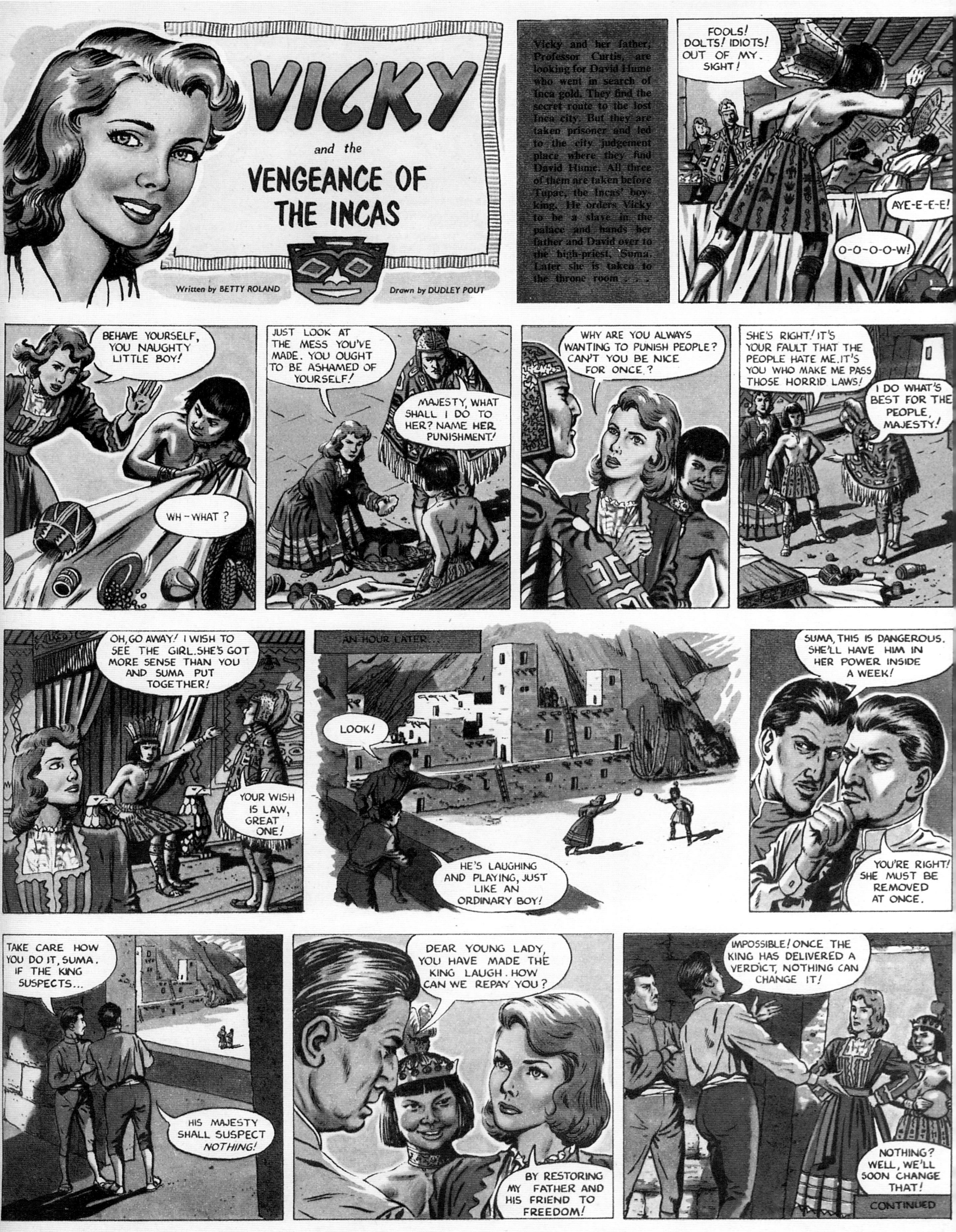
VICKY
and the
VENGEANCE OF THE INCAS
Written by BETTY ROLAND
Drawn by DUDLEY POUT
Vicky and her father, Professor Curtis, are looking for David Hume who went in search of Inca gold. They find the secret route to the lost Inca city. But they are taken prisoner and led to the city judgement place where they find David Hume. All three of them are taken before Tupac, the Incas' boy-king. He orders Vicky to be a slave in the palace and hands her father and David over to the high-priest, Suma. Later she is taken to the throne room . . .
FOOLS! DOLTS! IDIOTS! OUT OF MY SIGHT!
AYE-E-E-E!
O-O-O-O-W!
BEHAVE YOURSELF, YOU NAUGHTY LITTLE BOY!
WH-WHAT?
JUST LOOK AT THE MESS YOU'VE MADE. YOU OUGHT TO BE ASHAMED OF YOURSELF!
MAJESTY, WHAT SHALL I DO TO HER? NAME HER PUNISHMENT!
WHY ARE YOU ALWAYS WANTING TO PUNISH PEOPLE? CAN'T YOU BE NICE FOR ONCE?
SHE'S RIGHT! IT'S YOUR FAULT THAT THE PEOPLE HATE ME. IT'S YOU WHO MAKE ME PASS THOSE HORRID LAWS!
I DO WHAT'S BEST FOR THE PEOPLE, MAJESTY!
OH, GO AWAY! I WISH TO SEE THE GIRL. SHE'S GOT MORE SENSE THAN YOU AND SUMA PUT TOGETHER!
YOUR WISH IS LAW, GREAT ONE!
AN HOUR LATER...
LOOK!
HE'S LAUGHING AND PLAYING, JUST LIKE AN ORDINARY BOY!
SUMA, THIS IS DANGEROUS. SHE'LL HAVE HIM IN HER POWER INSIDE A WEEK!
YOU'RE RIGHT! SHE MUST BE REMOVED AT ONCE.
TAKE CARE HOW YOU DO IT, SUMA. IF THE KING SUSPECTS...
HIS MAJESTY SHALL SUSPECT NOTHING!
DEAR YOUNG LADY, YOU HAVE MADE THE KING LAUGH. HOW CAN WE REPAY YOU?
BY RESTORING MY FATHER AND HIS FRIEND TO FREEDOM!
IMPOSSIBLE! ONCE THE KING HAS DELIVERED A VERDICT, NOTHING CAN CHANGE IT!
NOTHING? WELL, WE'LL SOON CHANGE THAT!
CONTINUED

continued on page 1

Our Painting Competition

The winners' trip to VENICE

Our four winners spent seven days in this famous art centre.

VENICE is probably the most remarkable city in the world. Built on sand, with canals for streets, it should have tumbled down years ago according to the rules; but there it stands quiet and beautiful, a wonderful city for artists. Four young artists visited it last year, Pauline Knowles, Brigid Peppin, Douglas Boyd and Jeremy Annett. They had shared the first award in the 1956 GIRL, EAGLE and SWIFT Painting Competition and this holiday was their prize. They visited the Biennale, the great Venetian Art Exhibition. They visited the Cenedesa glass blowing factory at Murano where they drew their own designs which the Maestri (the master glass blowers) blew in glass. They learnt how to punt a gondola – but you can see how they enjoy themselves, the pictures tell their own story.

This year we are offering sixteen continental holidays. Eight for girls and eight for boys for the top winners in our Painting Competition. Turn to page 5 where you can read all the details.

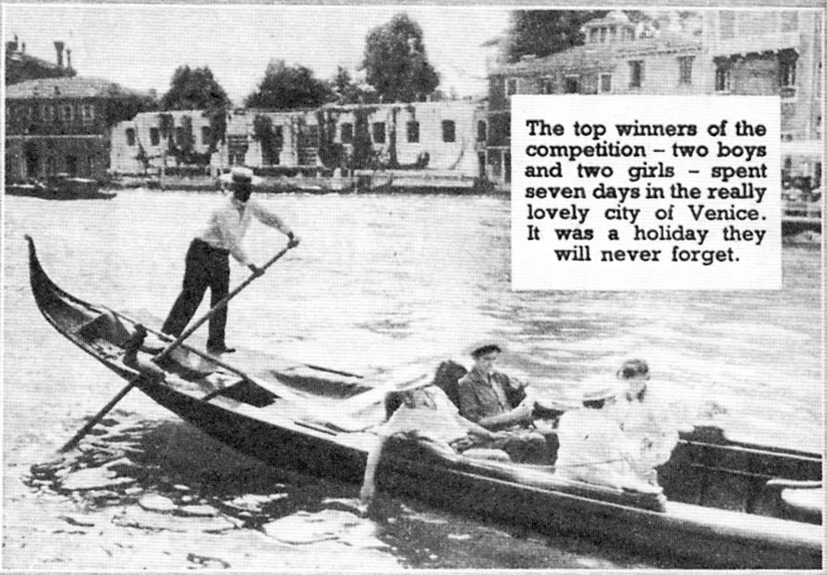

The top winners of the competition – two boys and two girls – spent seven days in the really lovely city of Venice. It was a holiday they will never forget.

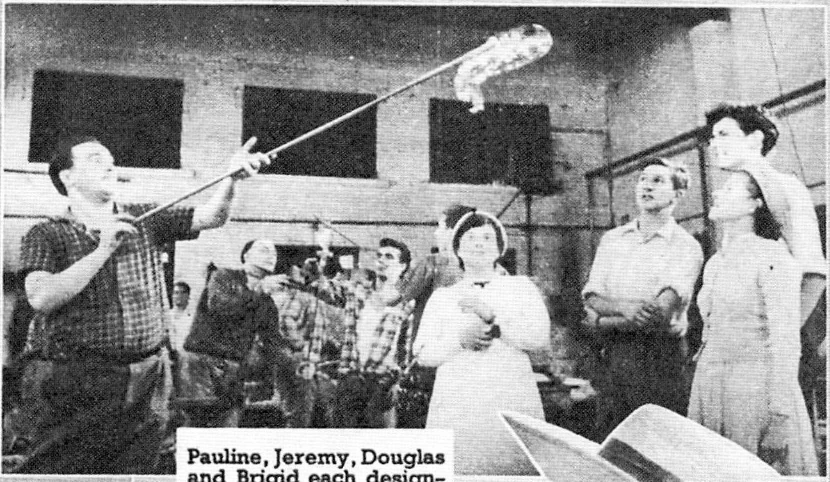

Pauline, Jeremy, Douglas and Brigid each designed an ornament when they visited the Cenedese Glass Factory. They were blown by the Maestri and here Brigid admires the lovely jug she designed.

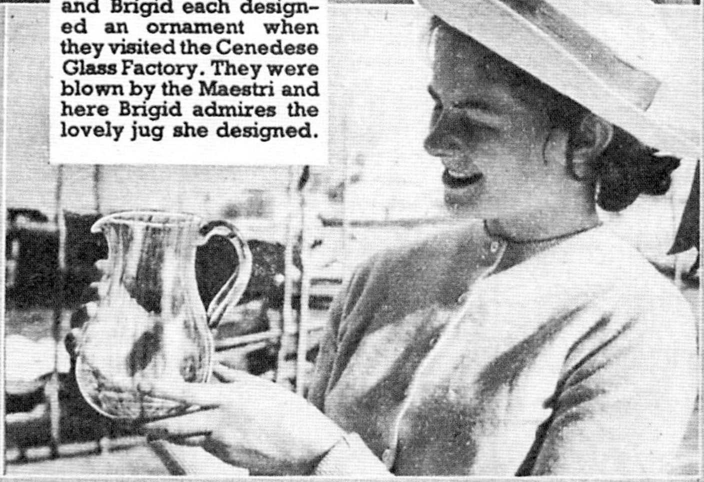

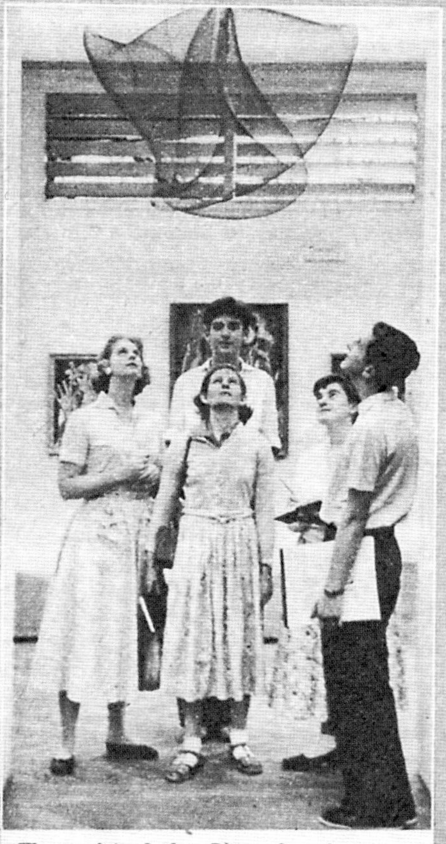

They visited the Biennale, the great Art Exhibition held every two years.

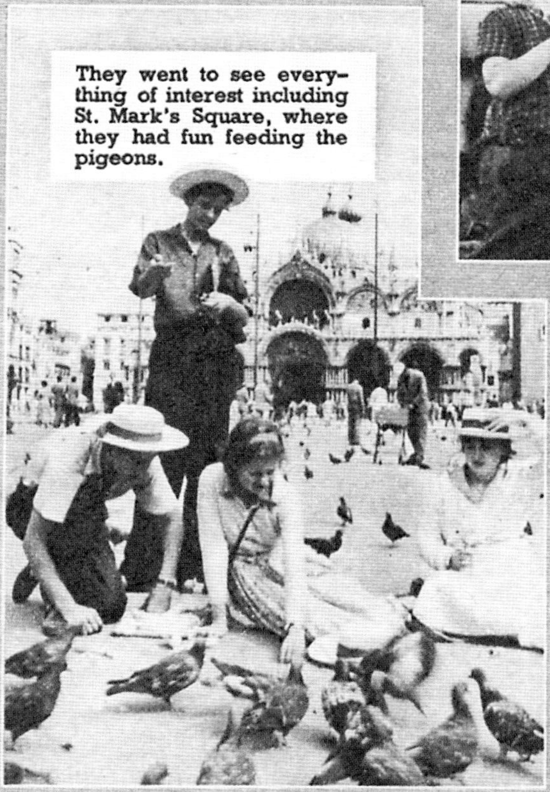

They went to see everything of interest including St. Mark's Square, where they had fun feeding the pigeons.

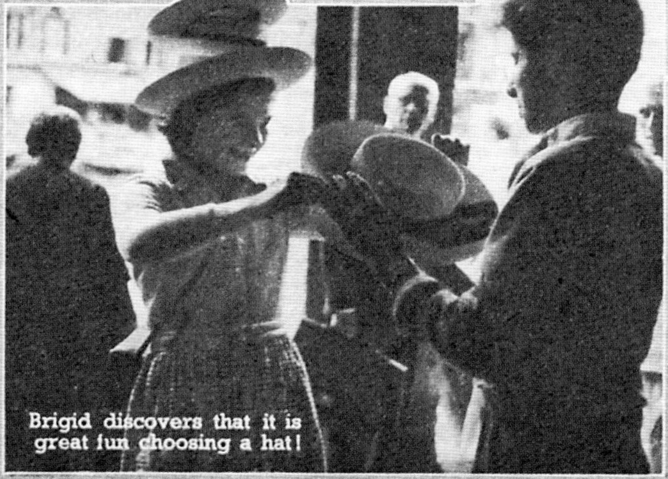

Brigid discovers that it is great fun choosing a hat!

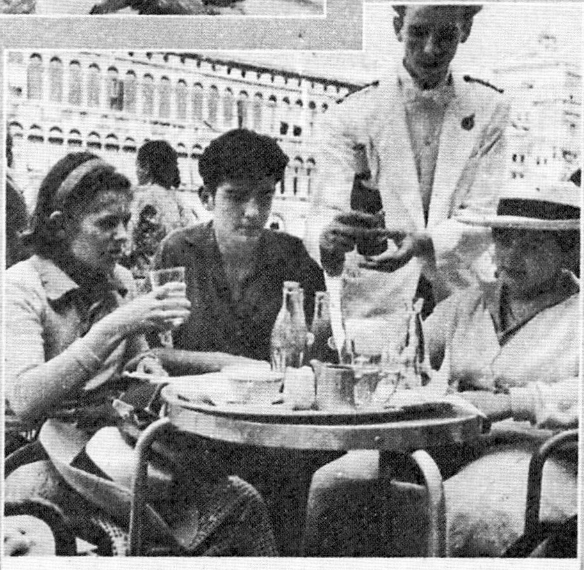

Cold drinks are a 'must' when you have been sight-seeing.

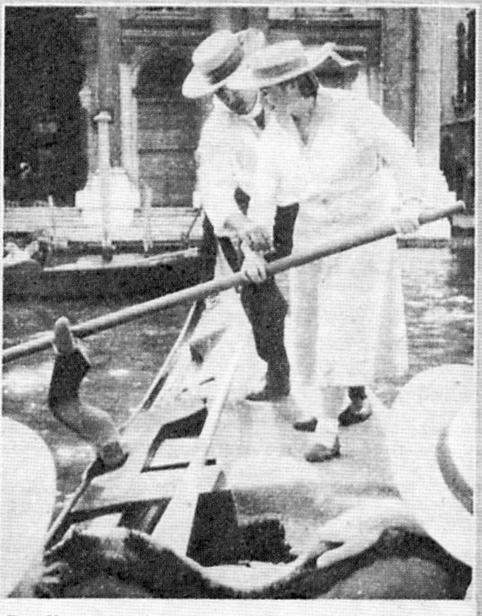

Pauline was determined to 'punt' a gondola before she left Venice – and succeeded!

Registered at the G.P.O. for transmission by Magazine Post to Canada (including Newfoundland). GIRL printed in Great Britain by Eric Bemrose Ltd., Long Lane, Liverpool 9, for the Proprietors and Publishers,

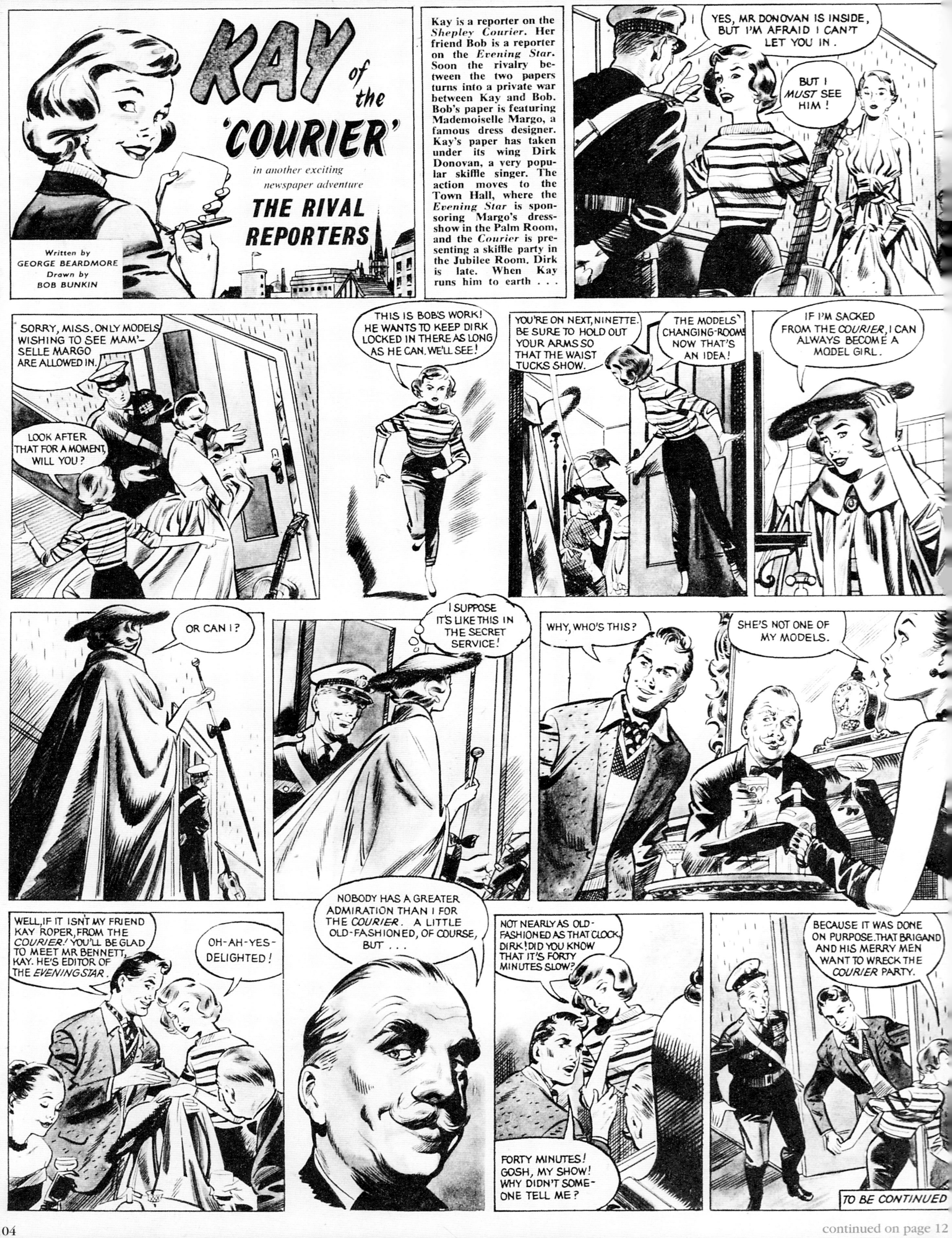
KAY of the 'COURIER'
in another exciting newspaper adventure
THE RIVAL REPORTERS
Written by GEORGE BEARDMORE Drawn by BOB BUNKIN
Kay is a reporter on the Shepley Courier. Her friend Bob is a reporter on the Evening Star. Soon the rivalry between the two papers turns into a private war between Kay and Bob. Bob's paper is featuring Mademoiselle Margo, a famous dress designer. Kay's paper has taken under its wing Dirk Donovan, a very popular skiffle singer. The action moves to the Town Hall, where the Evening Star is sponsoring Margo's dress-show in the Palm Room, and the Courier is presenting a skiffle party in the Jubilee Room. Dirk is late. When Kay runs him to earth . . .
YES, MR DONOVAN IS INSIDE, BUT I'M AFRAID I CAN'T LET YOU IN.
BUT I MUST SEE HIM!
SORRY, MISS. ONLY MODELS WISHING TO SEE MAM'-SELLE MARGO ARE ALLOWED IN.
LOOK AFTER THAT FOR A MOMENT, WILL YOU?
THIS IS BOB'S WORK! HE WANTS TO KEEP DIRK LOCKED IN THERE AS LONG AS HE CAN. WE'LL SEE!
YOU'RE ON NEXT, NINETTE. BE SURE TO HOLD OUT YOUR ARMS SO THAT THE WAIST TUCKS SHOW.
THE MODELS' CHANGING-ROOM! NOW THAT'S AN IDEA!
IF I'M SACKED FROM THE COURIER, I CAN ALWAYS BECOME A MODEL GIRL.
OR CAN I?
I SUPPOSE IT'S LIKE THIS IN THE SECRET SERVICE!
WHY, WHO'S THIS?
SHE'S NOT ONE OF MY MODELS.
WELL, IF IT ISN'T MY FRIEND KAY ROPER, FROM THE COURIER! YOU'LL BE GLAD TO MEET MR BENNETT, KAY. HE'S EDITOR OF THE EVENING STAR.
OH-AH-YES-DELIGHTED!
NOBODY HAS A GREATER ADMIRATION THAN I FOR THE COURIER. A LITTLE OLD-FASHIONED, OF COURSE, BUT . . .
NOT NEARLY AS OLD-FASHIONED AS THAT CLOCK, DIRK! DID YOU KNOW THAT IT'S FORTY MINUTES SLOW?
FORTY MINUTES! GOSH, MY SHOW! WHY DIDN'T SOME-ONE TELL ME?
BECAUSE IT WAS DONE ON PURPOSE. THAT BRIGAND AND HIS MERRY MEN WANT TO WRECK THE COURIER PARTY.
TO BE CONTINUED

continued on page 12

MOTHER TELLS YOU HOW

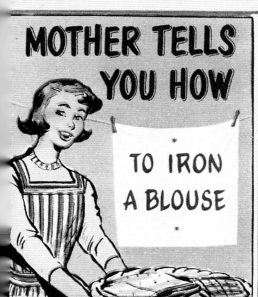

TO IRON A BLOUSE

"I WISH I COULD IRON MY BLOUSES SO THAT THEY LOOKED LIKE NEW, MOTHER."

"I'LL SHOW YOU THE RIGHT WAY, JUDY, AND THEN THEY WILL!"

"FIRST, SPRINKLE WATER ALL OVER THE BLOUSE TO BE IRONED."

"IT'S NO USE TRYING TO IRON A GARMENT UNLESS IT HAS BEEN THOROUGHLY DAMPENED."

NOW FOLD THE GARMENT, PULLING COLLARS AND CUFFS INTO SHAPE, THEN ROLL IT UP TIGHTLY IN A CLEAN TOWEL SO THAT IT BECOMES EVENLY DAMP ALL OVER.

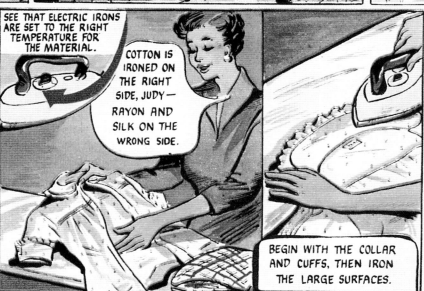

"SEE THAT ELECTRIC IRONS ARE SET TO THE RIGHT TEMPERATURE FOR THE MATERIAL."

"COTTON IS IRONED ON THE RIGHT SIDE, JUDY — RAYON AND SILK ON THE WRONG SIDE."

BEGIN WITH THE COLLAR AND CUFFS, THEN IRON THE LARGE SURFACES.

"THIS BLOUSE LOOKS AS CRISP AND NEAT AS A NEW ONE NOW, MOTHER!"

Concerning YOU

TO Gain Weight

IF YOU ARE TOO THIN FOR YOUR LIKING, DON'T MAKE THE MISTAKE OF EATING HEAVY MEALS. THESE WON'T ADD WEIGHT — THEY WILL SIMPLY GIVE YOU INDIGESTION.

EAT OFTEN BUT LIGHTLY. TRY AND INCLUDE SOME BUTTER, AND MILK, AT MOST MEALS. REMEMBER, TOO MUCH STARCHY FOOD IS AS BAD FOR YOU AS FOR A PLUMP PERSON, AND SALADS ARE JUST AS NECESSARY.

THIN PEOPLE USE UP THEIR RESERVES OF ENERGY VERY QUICKLY, SO DON'T FORGET YOUR 'ELEVENSES'. MALTED MILK OR A CHOCOLATE DRINK ARE EXCELLENT.

RELAX WHENEVER YOU CAN. IF YOU FEEL TIRED DON'T FORCE YOURSELF TO COMPLETE A TASK AT ONCE. IF POSSIBLE, RELAX IN AN ARMCHAIR WITH A BOOK FOR TEN MINUTES BEFORE GOING ON.

SLEEP IS MOST IMPORTANT, SO GET TO BED AS EARLY AS POSSIBLE. EXERCISE IN THE FRESH AIR WILL MAKE YOU HEALTHILY TIRED AND HELP YOU TO SLEEP, BUT DON'T OVER DO IT.

THIN PEOPLE ARE OFTEN WORRIERS. IF YOU HAVE ANY PROBLEMS, TALK THEM OVER WITH YOUR PARENTS, OR A FRIEND. YOU WILL BE SURPRISED HOW MUCH THIS HELPS!

Autumn is here, and Personal Page presents a preview of new fashions

Photographed by BERT HARI

PRETTY AS A PICTURE

Look and feel your best in these easy-to-wear fashions, designed to carry you through all the changing moods of an English autumn

NOW that the leaves are beginning to fall and colder weather isn't so far away, we all begin to think of warmer clothes. I have been busy looking at the autumn fashions and have picked some styles that could serve as a guide for your shopping.

If your age is about eleven, like our younger model, Sally, then a wool dress is certain to be your choice. Both the dresses she is wearing are warm without being bulky or heavy, and both have the full skirts that you all love. Too much trimming gives a cluttered-up look, and you can see from the photographs how effective the right amount can be.

The casual look

If you are older, then you are likely to be looking for a suit. I would recommend a loose jacket, rather than a fitted suit, for these reasons. They are becoming to all figures; they are very comfortable; and, while nobody wants to be a slave to fashion, the casual look *is* becoming much more popular.

Both the Harella suits which Rosemary is wearing are examples of this line. The tweed suit, which has slight fullness at the back of the jacket and fastens with large, plain buttons in front, is especially good. With an orlon sweater now, and a husky woollen one for colder weather, this would see you through the winter.

Chic—and practical

Another reason why I advise a loose-jacket suit is because it simplifies the problem of alterations. To alter a fitted jacket, which may not have its waistline in quite the same place as yours, is a tricky (and expensive) business, whereas this doesn't arise with a loose one. Then, too, if you are still growing, the unfitted jacket doesn't become useless as your measurements change. The sleeves can be cut to three-quarter length, the hem let down an inch, and the suit continues to give you good service.

Light-weight warmth

If something a little softer, and lighter in weight, would fit into your scheme better, why not an outfit in double-knit jersey? Both the Highlight Sports suits shown here have unlined tops, but the skirts are half-lined to prevent 'seating'. The jumper suit is the perfect background for accessories. Rosemary has added a white scarf and a simple gilt brooch, but it would have looked quite different (and just as attractive) if she had worn a necklace of plain beads and a fluffy angora beret, or short gloves and a shoulder bag.

Marjorie Elliott

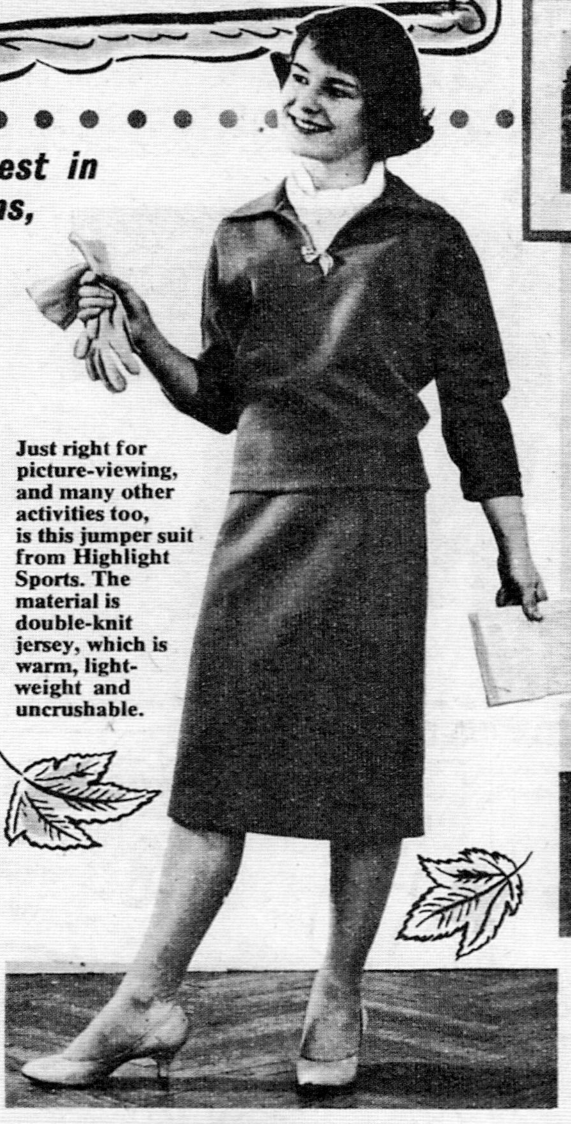

Just right for picture-viewing, and many other activities too, is this jumper suit from Highlight Sports. The material is double-knit jersey, which is warm, light-weight and uncrushable.

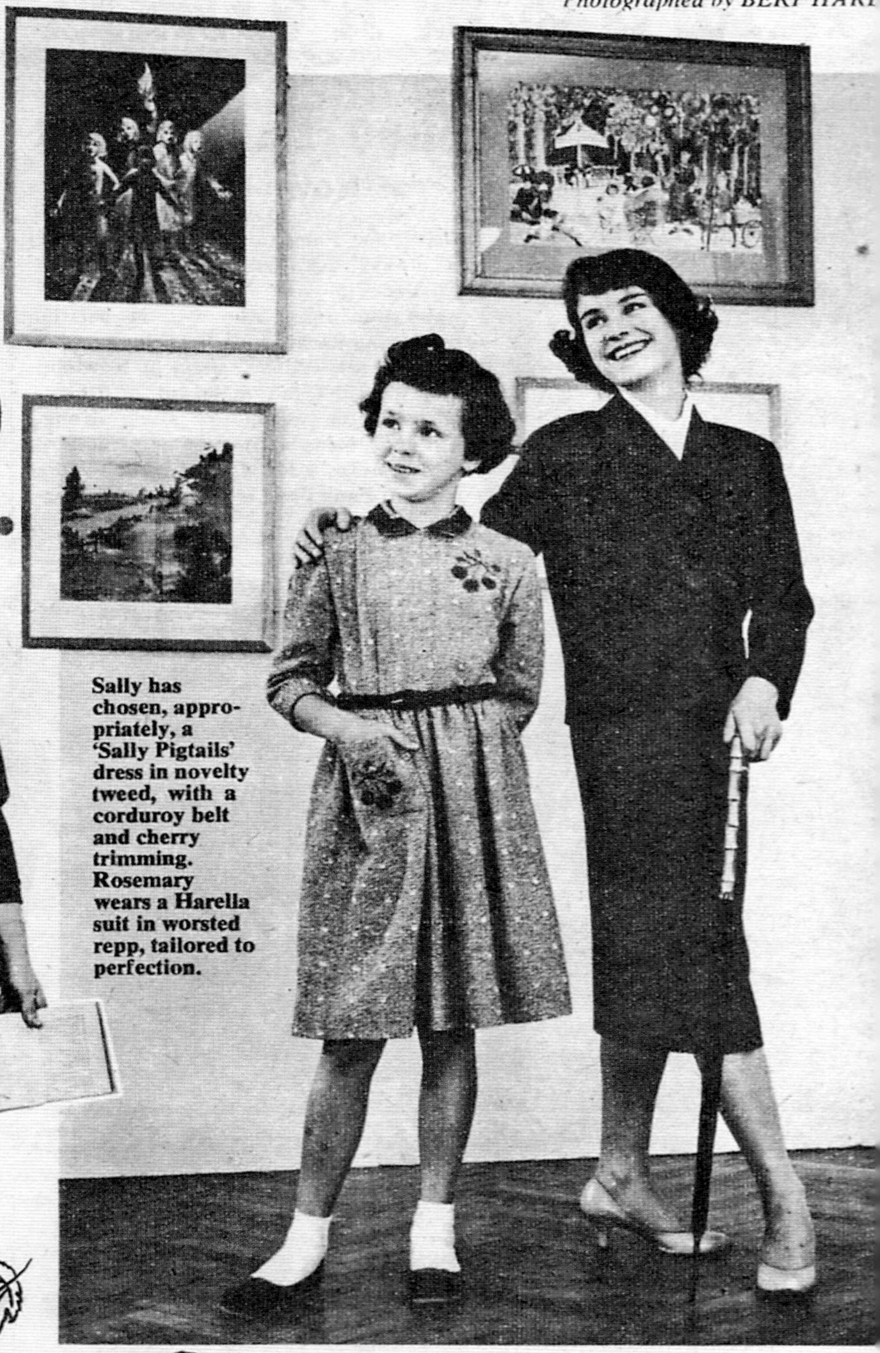

Sally has chosen, appropriately, a 'Sally Pigtails' dress in novelty tweed, with a corduroy belt and cherry trimming. Rosemary wears a Harella suit in worsted repp, tailored to perfection.

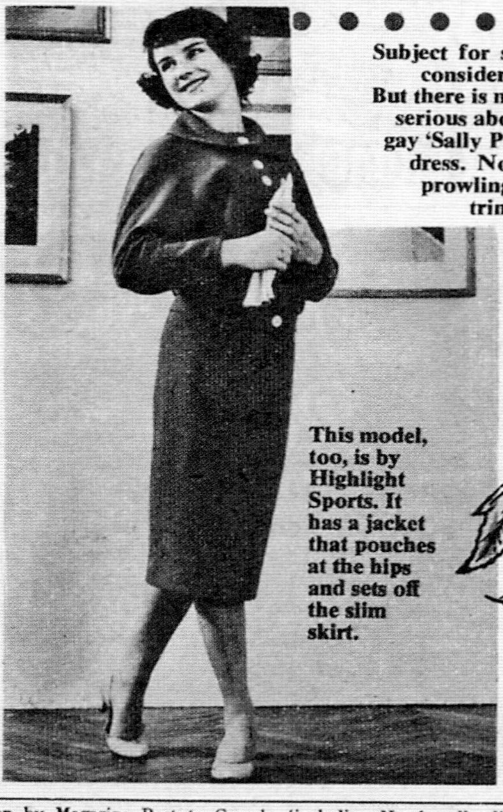

This model, too, is by Highlight Sports. It has a jacket that pouches at the hips and sets off the slim skirt.

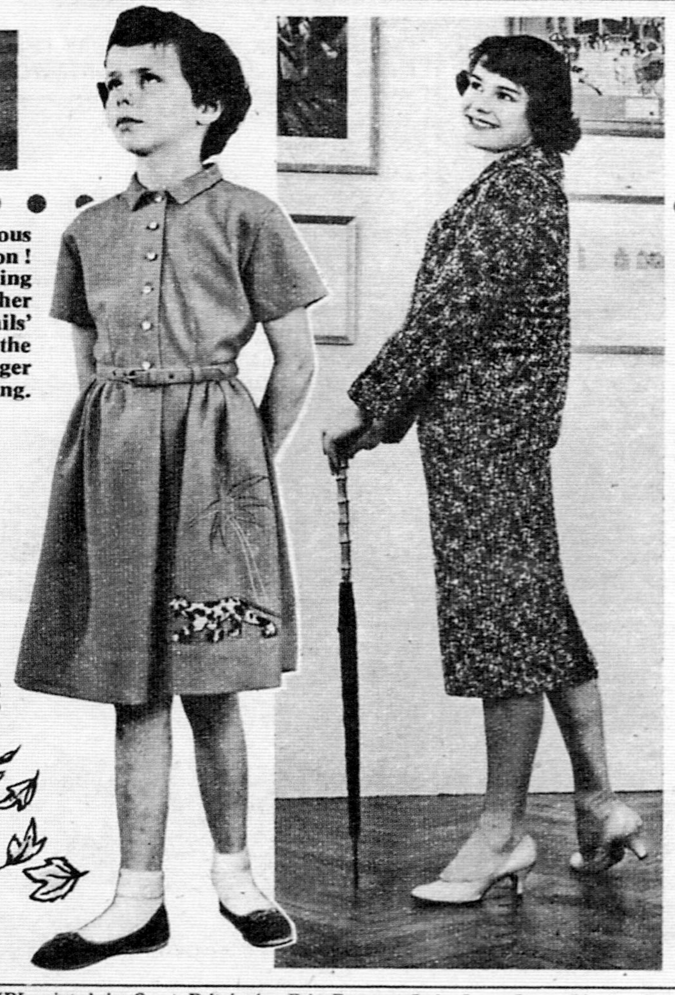

Subject for serious consideration! But there is nothing serious about her gay 'Sally Pigtails' dress. Note the prowling tiger trimming.

Rosemary loo pleased, and so would you, this tweed suit from the Hare range. It has all the fashion points and would be usef from now unti next Spring.

Registered at the G.P.O. for transmission by Magazine Post to Canada (including Newfoundland), GIRL printed in Great Britain by Eric Bemrose Ltd., Long Lane, Liverpool 9, for the Proprietors and Publishers, Hulton Press Ltd., 161/166 Fleet Street, London, E.C.4. Sole agents for Australia and New Zealand, Gordon & Gotch (A/sia) Ltd.; South Africa, Central News Agency Ltd. Subscriptio

THE ART OF CONVERSATION

However shy and diffident you may be, conversation is an art that you can learn

Photographed by BERT HARDY

NOTHING to say? That's a common complaint. A girl longs to be with someone she likes, imagines herself chatting gaily but, when the opportunity comes, she is tongue-[tied] and feels a fool just when she wants to make [a] good impression.

[W]hy *does* it have to happen like this? Is there any [cure]? That's what dozens of girls write in to ask.

[F]ortunately there *is* a cure. Conversation is an art [we] can all learn enough about to make a success [of it].

[L]et's first look at why the difficulty arises. Anxiety [saps] up our conversational powers. When we are [with] someone we like, but do not know very well, [we] are particularly anxious to make a good impression and are anxious in case we don't. That is what [cau]ses the trouble. We start apprehensive, lose our [tong]ues because of it, get embarrassed by the silence, [get] more apprehensive still because things are not [goin]g well – and so on.

[G]et rid of the starting anxiety and all will be well. [Her]e's how to do it. Don't waste time trying to think [of w]hat you can say, *make it your aim not to talk [your]self but to get the person you are with talking.*

[T]hat means two things. First, you must have some [que]stions ready to ask and, second, you must know [abo]ut the interests of your friend so that you can ask [que]stions that your friend will enjoy answering.

[A] conversation is like a bonfire; you may have to

light it two or three times but, once it is well alight, off it goes. Asking the right questions is the way to start the conversation. *About four good questions will get any conversation started.*

Now for another very important point. It's harder to listen when we are anxious than when we are at our ease. So, when starting up a difficult conversation, an extra effort *must* be made to listen carefully to what the other person is saying.

By listening carefully, we feed ideas from the person we are talking to into our minds, and this will often trigger off other ideas or questions in our minds. *That's how conversations keep going.* Anyone who learns to

ask good questions and to listen carefully can be a good conversationalist.

This is, then, the way to get a conversation launched. (1) Exchange greetings. (2) Ask a question you think will encourage the other person to talk. (3) Listen to the answer carefully. (4) Ask a question or make a remark about what has just been said or (5) ask a new question entirely – and so on.

Of course, if you are not an easy talker, you will not become brilliant all at once. You will need some practice. But if you practise along the right lines, you will be surprised how quickly you find yourself enjoying conversations instead of dreading them.

WHAT'S YOUR WORRY?

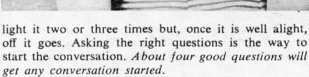

A lullaby at bedtime

Q. My uncle has given me a portable radio, but my mother won't let me have it on for more than half an hour after I go to bed. Do you think this is fair?

A. Of course it is very tempting to go on listening, but it is much more important that you should have ample sleep.

★　　★　　★

A loud, irritating voice

Q. I have a loud, piercing voice which seems to irritate people. How can I cure it?

A. You must relax more when you speak. Don't rush into speech quite so eagerly. Pause before you start and you will find it easier to moderate your voice.

★　　★　　★

Classical music or jazz?

Q. We are four friends, all 14. One of us likes classical music only. We like classical music and jazz. She says we have no minds of our own. What do you think?

A. We think the appreciation of music is a very personal matter. We should all respect each other's likes and dislikes, without feeling superior or inferior about our particular choice. Our view is that it is a good idea to have broad musical interests.

★　　★　　★

The friendly foursome

Q. My friend and I know two boys with whom we are friendly, and sometimes we go about together as a foursome. My parents don't mind, but I am afraid other people might see us together and criticize us. What do you think?

A. We cannot see any reason why other people should criticize you, and we think you should go on enjoying your friendship together.

Making a friend

Q. There is a coloured girl who has come to live in our street. She seems afraid of us and hardly says anything but 'yes' and 'no' when we speak to her. Would it be best to leave her alone?

A. No, don't leave her to be lonely. It is natural that she should feel rather shy and out of things at first. Invite her to your home and also ask one or two friends who would be particularly interested in making friends with her.

Registered at the G.P.O. for transmission by Magazine Post to Canada (including Newfoundland). GIRL printed in Great Britain by Eric Bemrose Ltd., Long Lane, Liverpool 9, for the Proprietors and Publishers Hulton Press Ltd., 161/166 Fleet Street, London, E.C.4. Sole agents for Australia and New Zealand Gordon & Gotch (A/sia) Ltd.; South Africa, Central News Agency Ltd.

I want to be a HOTEL RECEPTIONIST

*

DIANA IS VERY KEEN ON MEETING PEOPLE AND FOR TWO YEARS NOW, EVER SINCE SHE LEFT SCHOOL, HAS BEEN ASSISTANT RECEPTIONIST IN A LARGE HOTEL

SHE CONSULTS MRS SIMS, THE HOUSEKEEPER, ABOUT THE NUMBER OF EMPTY ROOMS. SOME MAY BE 'OFF' FOR SPRING-CLEANING AND DIANA HAS TO SEE THAT THE HOTEL IS NEITHER UNDER NOR OVER-BOOKED.

HOW LONG WILL IT TAKE TO SPRING-CLEAN THOSE TWO ROOMS, MRS SIMS?

OH, NOT MORE THAN A WEEK, MISS.

TRÈS BIEN, MONSIEUR.

DIANA ALSO HAS TO DEAL WITH MANY FOREIGN VISITORS AND THE FRENCH SHE LEARNED AT NIGHT SCHOOL IS A GREAT ASSET TO HER. HER SALARY IS ABOUT THREE POUNDS A WEEK, PLUS FREE BOARD AND LODGING, AND IT WILL BE INCREASED GRADUALLY.

DO YOU MIND DOING AN EXTRA HOUR'S DUTY FOR ME TODAY, JOAN?

NOT A BIT, DIANA. I'LL SEE YOU AT SIX INSTEAD OF FIVE THEN.

AFTER FOUR YEARS DIANA IS NOW SENIOR RECEPTIONIST AND HAS HER MEALS WITH THE OTHER SENIOR MEMBERS OF THE HOTEL STAFF. SHE SHARES HER DUTIES WITH THE OTHER RECEPTIONIST.

WE'RE DELIGHTED TO SEE YOU AGAIN, SIR.

THANK YOU. IT'S NICE TO BE BACK!

MAKING A LIST OF REGULAR VISITORS TO THE HOTEL AND REMEMBERING THEIR LIKES AND DISLIKES IS ONE OF DIANA'S MAIN DUTIES. SHE HAS BEEN IN HER JOB TEN YEARS NOW AND HER SMARTNESS, EFFICIENCY AND GOOD MANNERS HAVE MADE HER A GREAT FAVOURITE WITH THE GUESTS.

DIANA IS DRESSING FOR THE ANNUAL STAFF BALL HELD AT THE HOTEL. SHE IS VERY HAPPY IN HER JOB — NOT ONLY BECAUSE SHE LIKES THE WORK BUT BECAUSE SHE HAS MADE MANY FIRM FRIENDS.

GIRL BALLET SCHOLARSHIP SCHEME

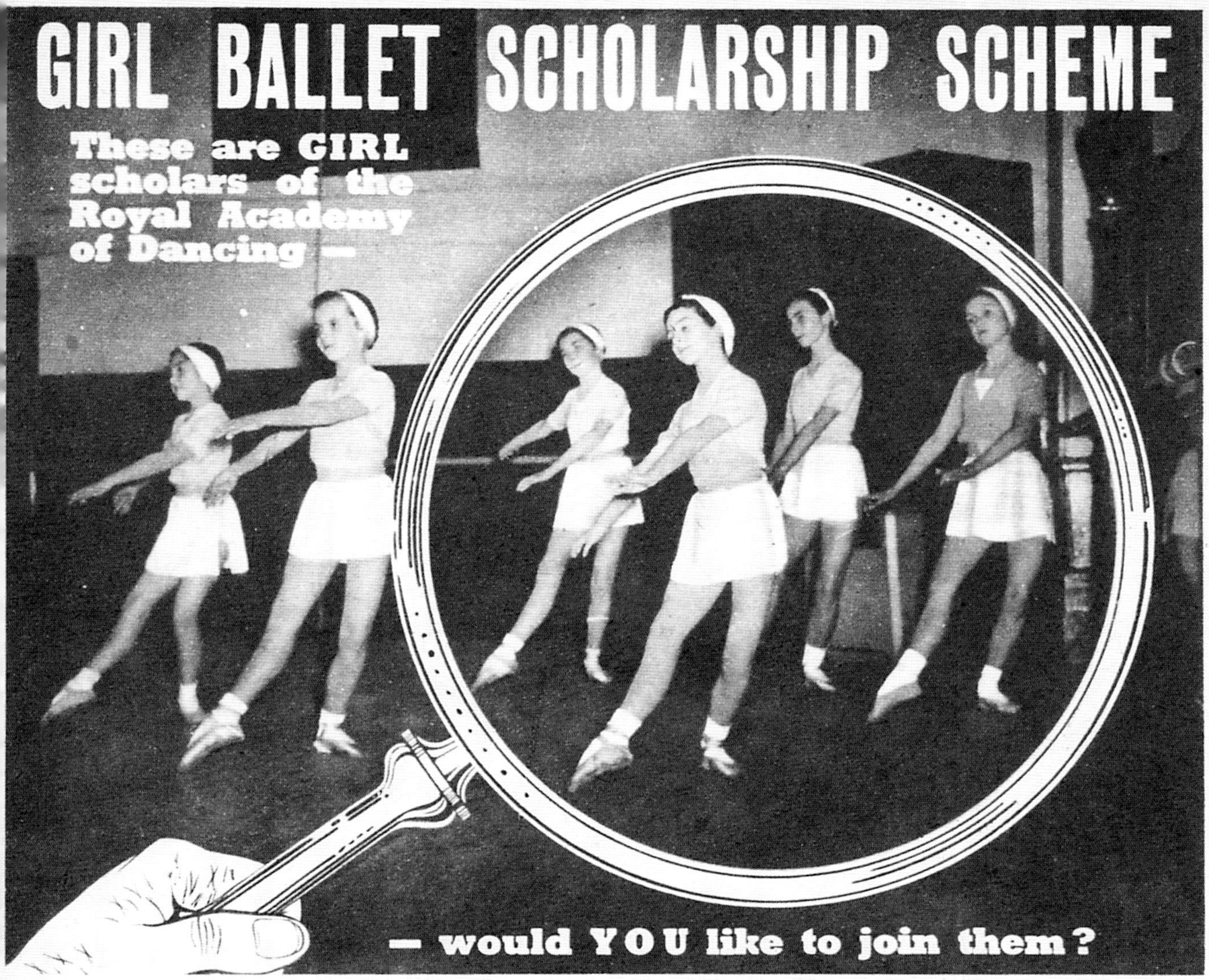

These are GIRL scholars of the Royal Academy of Dancing –

– would YOU like to join them?

IF you want to be a dancer, read this announcement carefully. GIRL, in co-operation with the Royal Academy of Dancing, has organised a special ballet scholarship scheme, which aims to give more and more girls the chance of ballet training, with the best teachers. The auditions for the GIRL R.A.D. Scholarships will be held this month. You may be eligible for one, if you hold the following qualifications.

1. **You are between 9 and 13 on 1st April, 1958.**
2. **You have passed at least Grade 1 of the R.A.D. Ballet in education children's examinations.**
3. **Your teacher is a member of the R.A.D.**
4. **You are a member of the GIRL Adventurers Club.**

The fee for an audition is normally a guinea, but to all GIRL club members, it is FREE. If the examiners award you a scholarship, you become a GIRL scholar of the Royal Academy of Dancing, and you are entitled to two free ballet lessons a week at the nearest R.A.D. Scholarship Centre for a period of up to five years. Best of all, one full-time GIRL Scholarship to the Royal Ballet School is awarded every year, and the candidates for this award are chosen from among the first year GIRL scholars of the R.A.D. This scholarship is for a period of 5 years, but it is only awarded if the judges consider that the standard is high enough.

★ ★ ★

If you think you may be eligible for a scholarship, write for full details to: GIRL Ballet Scholarship Scheme, Hulton House, 161/166, Fleet St., London, E.C.4. The closing date for this year's auditions is 17th January for girls living in London, and 31st January for girls in the provinces.

, and burst out laughing. Marie, who s as fit as a fiddle, had a lovely figure. 'Don't laugh!" said Marie. "I weigh self. I weigh . . ." Her voice sank to a gic whisper, "nearly twelve of what you l in Engleesh zese stones."

"What rubbish!" said Jill. "You couldn't ssibly! You would look enormous! You igh eight stone. We settled all that long o. That's about 51 kilos in French stem, and that's about right. Where on rth did you get the idea you weighed elve stone?"

"Eleven stone two," said Marie. "On ze w scales Dick get in ze studio."

"On the scales . . . ? The new ones?" id Jill. "But, just a minute." She tried to some mental arithmetic, failed, and ally scribbled with an eyebrow-pencil a box of paper tissues. "Oh, good ief!" she exclaimed. "I thought so! ght stone, which is what you weigh, is 2 pounds, and the new scales Dick got, igh in pounds, not stones and pounds. ou're the same weight you always were, u chump!"

A new light of hope glittered in Marie's es. "You are sure?" she said.

"Of course I am!"

"Oh, zis system!" said Marie, swinging rself off the bed with new and unsuscted vigour. "All ze pounds and shilgs, and rods, and poles, and furlongs, d zen dollars, and cents, and zis . . . s . . . *Oh, so stupid system!*"

Jill rocked with silent laughter. "I'm rry, Marie, but I can't help laughing. Vhere are you going?"

"I must 'phone Gaston," said Marie.

"You can't possibly go out after that ot bath," said Jill. "Tell him to come ound at eight, and he can eat with us."

"He can come round at eight," agreed Iarie. "But he eat by heemself. I can't ait anuzzer minute!"

When Jill passed her in the hall, on her ay to the kitchenette, Marie looked as if ne was ready to eat the telephone.

nother complete story next week

BIRTHDATES

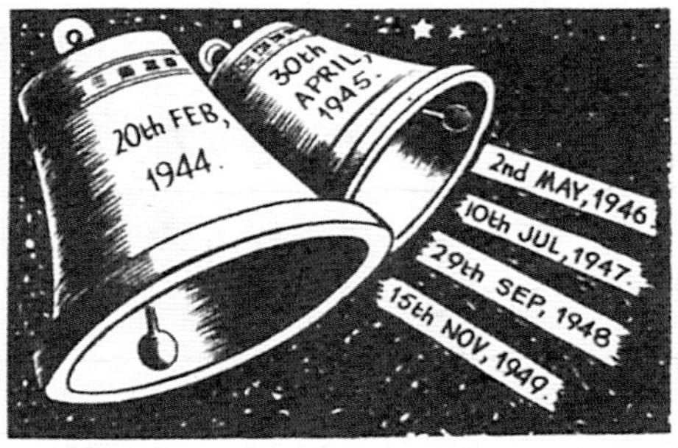
20th FEB, 1944.
30th APRIL, 1945.
2nd MAY, 1946.
10th JUL, 1947.
29th SEP, 1948.
15th NOV, 1949.

IF you are a GIRL Adventurer, and your birthdate appears in this week's list, you are entitled to a FREE birthday gift! Choose it from the following: – **GIRL handbag badge, stamp album, propelling pencil, stationery folder, bicycle bell, ball point pen or coloured pencils.** State your choice on a postcard, giving us your name, address and Club Number and the date you were born. Send it to BIRTHDATES (1), GIRL Club, Long Lane, Aintree, Liverpool, 9, to reach us by Thursday, 9th January. Overseas members whose birthdates appear here will automatically be sent their presents.

Star Adventurer of the Year

"If ever a more deserving case for a Star Adventurer's award is found, I hope I shall have the pleasure of assessing it." That is how our representative began his report on the claim sent in on behalf of Eileen Hawes for a Star Adventurer's Badge. Eileen's record is indeed a splendid one. Her mother is seriously handicapped by arthritis, and her younger sister is also often in need of help. Week in, week out, shopping, housework and nursing are undertaken cheerfully and completely by Eileen. By her untiring hard work, love, loyalty and devotion the home is kept going happily and in splendid order. Eileen's school is three miles from her home, and she walks there and back every day with her sister. She often feels tired; but she never gives up. Her record at school is just as exceptional as her record at home. We congratulate Eileen on having been selected as the 1957 Star Adventurer of the Year.

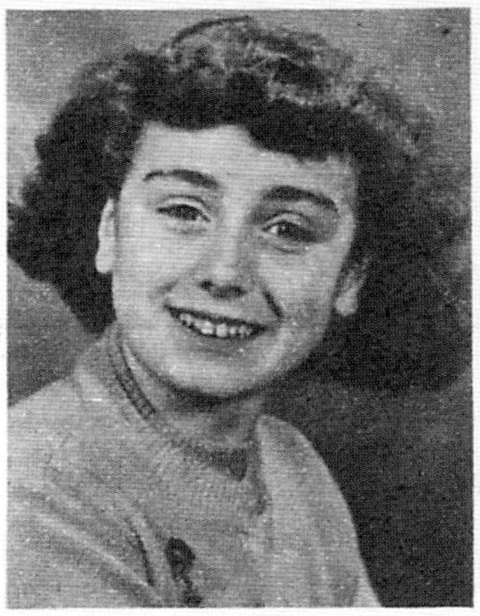

Eileen Hawes

NEW YEAR MESSAGE

★ ★ ★

Happy New Year to all you thousands of GIRL Adventurers wherever you may be! We would like to wish you every success and happiness for the coming year. Of course, this is the time of year for making good resolutions – ours is to organize more and more club activities, and to encourage more and more club members to get to know one another. If you have any ideas, please write and tell us. We are always grateful to have suggestions – and criticisms too – because this is *your* club, and that means we need your help in running it.

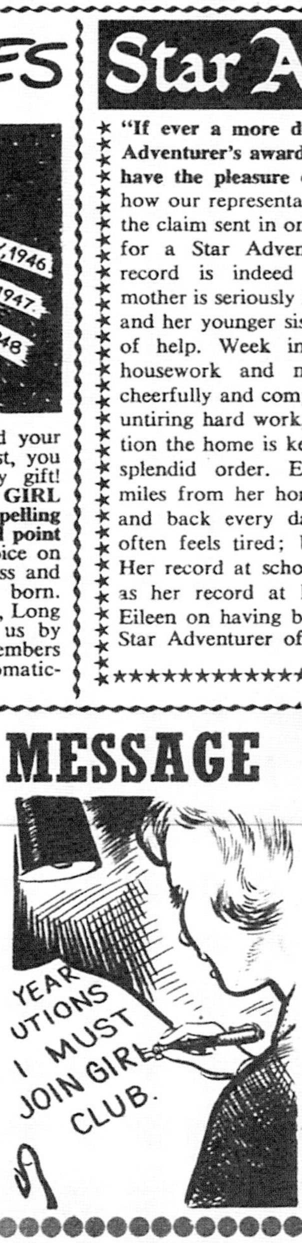
YEAR
UTIONS
I MUST
JOIN GIRL
CLUB.

How to join the GIRL Club

Fill in this coupon in block capitals, taking great care to put your full address. Then send it, with a postal order for 2/- made payable to Hulton Press Ltd., crossed '& Co.', to:- GIRL Club, Long Lane, Aintree, Liverpool, 9.

NAME ....

ADDRESS ....

....

DATE OF BIRTH..............**Month**..............**Year**........

I have placed a regular order for GIRL with: –

NEWSAGENT'S NAME ....

ADDRESS ....

....

Address this label to yourself, using block capitals.

NAME ....

ADDRESS ....

....

GM

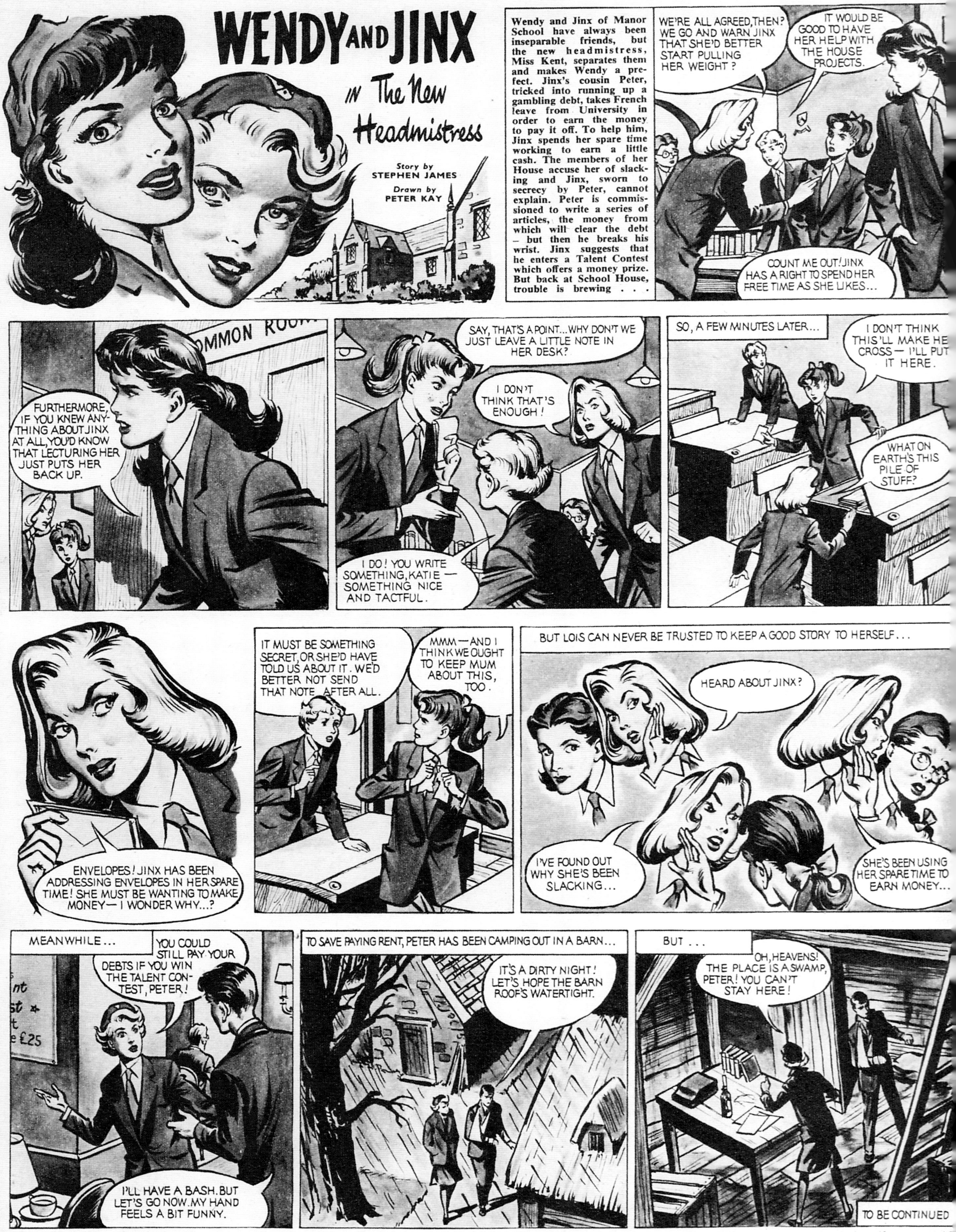
WENDY AND JINX
IN The New Headmistress
Story by STEPHEN JAMES
Drawn by PETER KAY
Wendy and Jinx of Manor School have always been inseparable friends, but the new headmistress, Miss Kent, separates them and makes Wendy a prefect. Jinx's cousin Peter, tricked into running up a gambling debt, takes French leave from University in order to earn the money to pay it off. To help him, Jinx spends her spare time working to earn a little cash. The members of her House accuse her of slacking and Jinx, sworn to secrecy by Peter, cannot explain. Peter is commissioned to write a series of articles, the money from which will clear the debt – but then he breaks his wrist. Jinx suggests that he enters a Talent Contest which offers a money prize. But back at School House, trouble is brewing . . .
WE'RE ALL AGREED, THEN? WE GO AND WARN JINX THAT SHE'D BETTER START PULLING HER WEIGHT?
IT WOULD BE GOOD TO HAVE HER HELP WITH THE HOUSE PROJECTS.
COUNT ME OUT! JINX HAS A RIGHT TO SPEND HER FREE TIME AS SHE LIKES...
COMMON ROOM
FURTHERMORE, IF YOU KNEW ANYTHING ABOUT JINX AT ALL, YOU'D KNOW THAT LECTURING HER JUST PUTS HER BACK UP.
SAY, THAT'S A POINT... WHY DON'T WE JUST LEAVE A LITTLE NOTE IN HER DESK?
I DON'T THINK THAT'S ENOUGH!
I DO! YOU WRITE SOMETHING, KATIE — SOMETHING NICE AND TACTFUL.
SO, A FEW MINUTES LATER...
I DON'T THINK THIS'LL MAKE HE CROSS — I'LL PUT IT HERE.
WHAT ON EARTH'S THIS PILE OF STUFF?
ENVELOPES! JINX HAS BEEN ADDRESSING ENVELOPES IN HER SPARE TIME! SHE MUST BE WANTING TO MAKE MONEY — I WONDER WHY...?
IT MUST BE SOMETHING SECRET, OR SHE'D HAVE TOLD US ABOUT IT. WE'D BETTER NOT SEND THAT NOTE AFTER ALL.
MMM — AND I THINK WE OUGHT TO KEEP MUM ABOUT THIS, TOO.
BUT LOIS CAN NEVER BE TRUSTED TO KEEP A GOOD STORY TO HERSELF...
HEARD ABOUT JINX?
I'VE FOUND OUT WHY SHE'S BEEN SLACKING...
SHE'S BEEN USING HER SPARE TIME TO EARN MONEY...
MEANWHILE...
YOU COULD STILL PAY YOUR DEBTS IF YOU WIN THE TALENT CONTEST, PETER!
I'LL HAVE A BASH. BUT LET'S GO NOW. MY HAND FEELS A BIT FUNNY.
TO SAVE PAYING RENT, PETER HAS BEEN CAMPING OUT IN A BARN...
IT'S A DIRTY NIGHT! LET'S HOPE THE BARN ROOF'S WATERTIGHT.
BUT . . .
OH, HEAVENS! THE PLACE IS A SWAMP, PETER! YOU CAN'T STAY HERE!
TO BE CONTINUED

continued on page 12

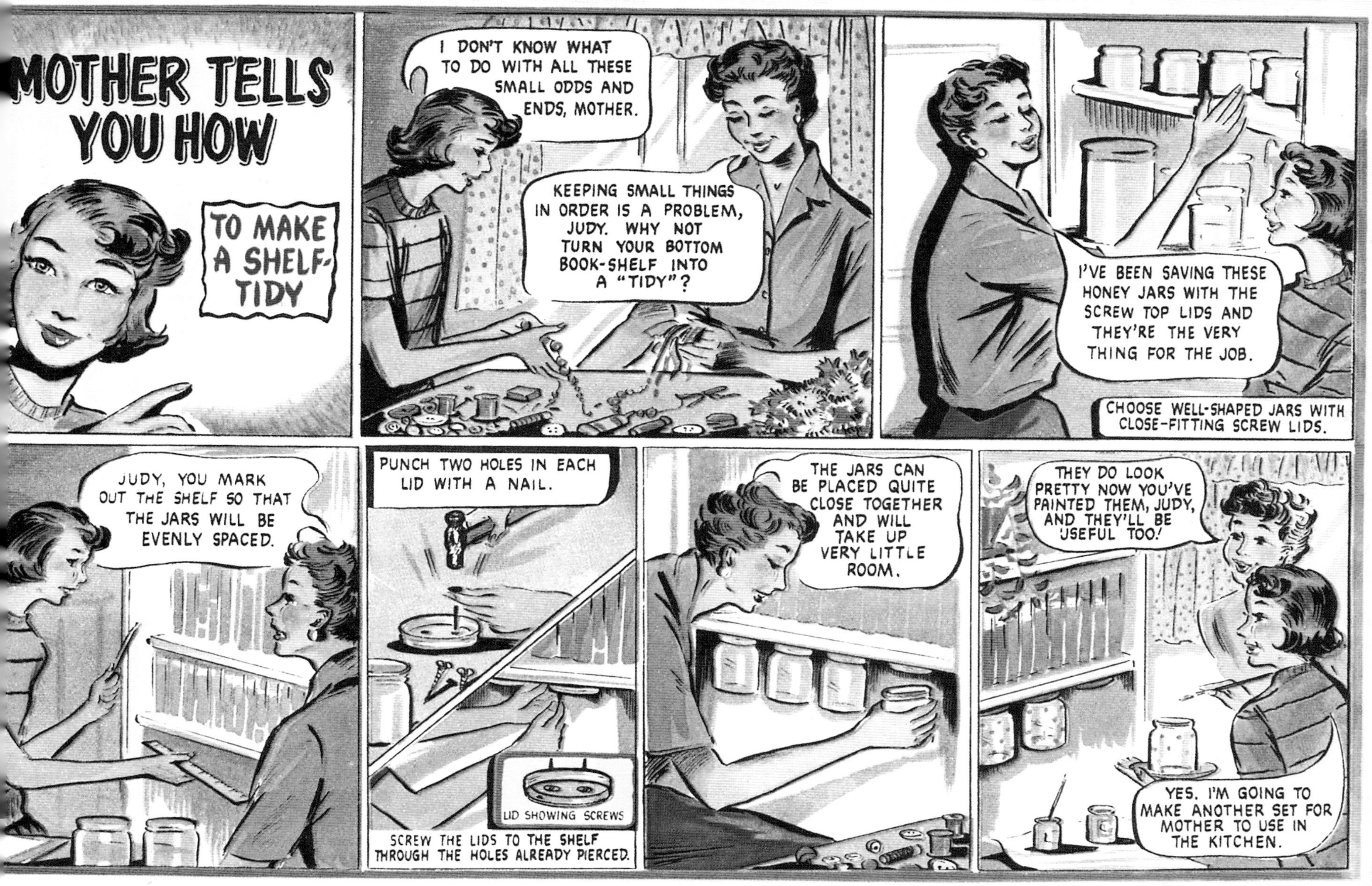
MOTHER TELLS YOU HOW
TO MAKE A SHELF-TIDY
I DON'T KNOW WHAT TO DO WITH ALL THESE SMALL ODDS AND ENDS, MOTHER.
KEEPING SMALL THINGS IN ORDER IS A PROBLEM, JUDY. WHY NOT TURN YOUR BOTTOM BOOK-SHELF INTO A "TIDY"?
I'VE BEEN SAVING THESE HONEY JARS WITH THE SCREW TOP LIDS AND THEY'RE THE VERY THING FOR THE JOB.
CHOOSE WELL-SHAPED JARS WITH CLOSE-FITTING SCREW LIDS.
JUDY, YOU MARK OUT THE SHELF SO THAT THE JARS WILL BE EVENLY SPACED.
PUNCH TWO HOLES IN EACH LID WITH A NAIL.
LID SHOWING SCREWS
SCREW THE LIDS TO THE SHELF THROUGH THE HOLES ALREADY PIERCED.
THE JARS CAN BE PLACED QUITE CLOSE TOGETHER AND WILL TAKE UP VERY LITTLE ROOM.
THEY DO LOOK PRETTY NOW YOU'VE PAINTED THEM, JUDY, AND THEY'LL BE USEFUL TOO!
YES. I'M GOING TO MAKE ANOTHER SET FOR MOTHER TO USE IN THE KITCHEN.

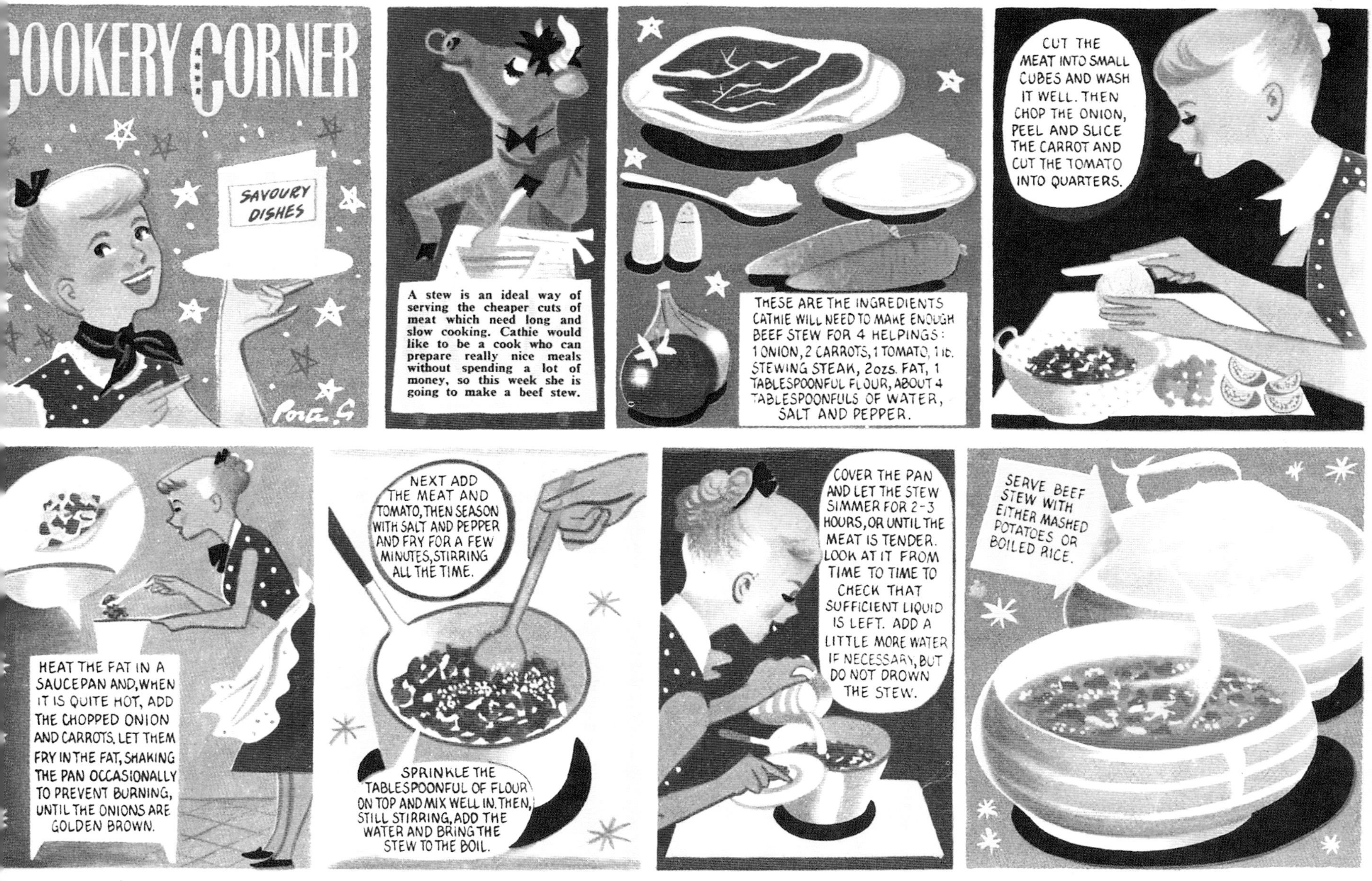
COOKERY CORNER
SAVOURY DISHES
A stew is an ideal way of serving the cheaper cuts of meat which need long and slow cooking. Cathie would like to be a cook who can prepare really nice meals without spending a lot of money, so this week she is going to make a beef stew.
THESE ARE THE INGREDIENTS CATHIE WILL NEED TO MAKE ENOUGH BEEF STEW FOR 4 HELPINGS: 1 ONION, 2 CARROTS, 1 TOMATO, 1 lb. STEWING STEAK, 2ozs. FAT, 1 TABLESPOONFUL FLOUR, ABOUT 4 TABLESPOONFULS OF WATER, SALT AND PEPPER.
CUT THE MEAT INTO SMALL CUBES AND WASH IT WELL. THEN CHOP THE ONION, PEEL AND SLICE THE CARROT AND CUT THE TOMATO INTO QUARTERS.
HEAT THE FAT IN A SAUCEPAN AND, WHEN IT IS QUITE HOT, ADD THE CHOPPED ONION AND CARROTS. LET THEM FRY IN THE FAT, SHAKING THE PAN OCCASIONALLY TO PREVENT BURNING, UNTIL THE ONIONS ARE GOLDEN BROWN.
NEXT ADD THE MEAT AND TOMATO, THEN SEASON WITH SALT AND PEPPER AND FRY FOR A FEW MINUTES, STIRRING ALL THE TIME.
SPRINKLE THE TABLESPOONFUL OF FLOUR ON TOP AND MIX WELL IN. THEN, STILL STIRRING, ADD THE WATER AND BRING THE STEW TO THE BOIL.
COVER THE PAN AND LET THE STEW SIMMER FOR 2-3 HOURS, OR UNTIL THE MEAT IS TENDER. LOOK AT IT FROM TIME TO TIME TO CHECK THAT SUFFICIENT LIQUID IS LEFT. ADD A LITTLE MORE WATER IF NECESSARY, BUT DO NOT DROWN THE STEW.
SERVE BEEF STEW WITH EITHER MASHED POTATOES OR BOILED RICE.

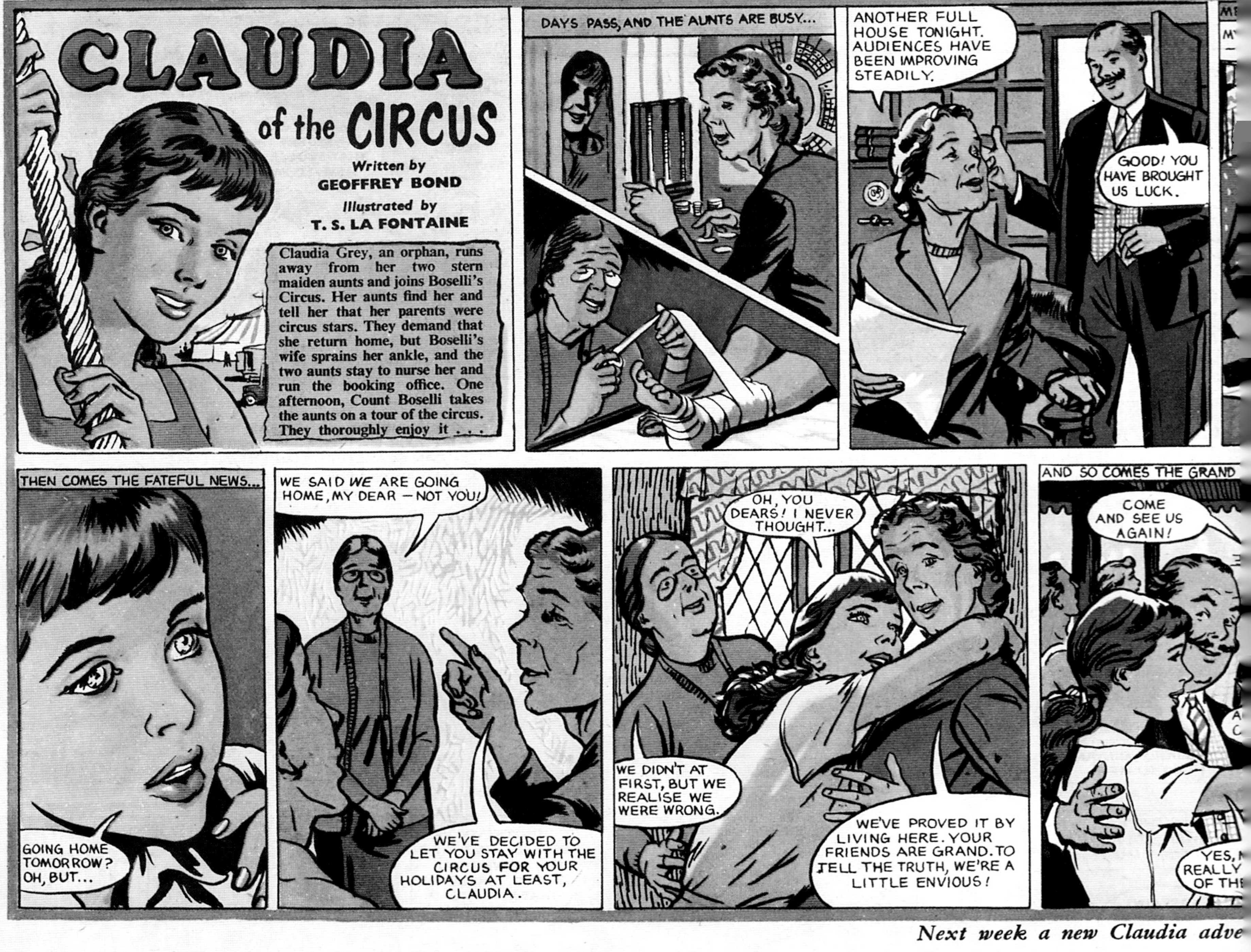
CLAUDIA of the CIRCUS
Written by GEOFFREY BOND
Illustrated by T. S. LA FONTAINE
Claudia Grey, an orphan, runs away from her two stern maiden aunts and joins Boselli's Circus. Her aunts find her and tell her that her parents were circus stars. They demand that she return home, but Boselli's wife sprains her ankle, and the two aunts stay to nurse her and run the booking office. One afternoon, Count Boselli takes the aunts on a tour of the circus. They thoroughly enjoy it . . .
DAYS PASS, AND THE AUNTS ARE BUSY...
ANOTHER FULL HOUSE TONIGHT. AUDIENCES HAVE BEEN IMPROVING STEADILY.
GOOD! YOU HAVE BROUGHT US LUCK.
THEN COMES THE FATEFUL NEWS...
GOING HOME TOMORROW? OH, BUT...
WE SAID WE ARE GOING HOME, MY DEAR — NOT YOU!
WE'VE DECIDED TO LET YOU STAY WITH THE CIRCUS FOR YOUR HOLIDAYS AT LEAST, CLAUDIA.
OH, YOU DEARS! I NEVER THOUGHT...
WE DIDN'T AT FIRST, BUT WE REALISE WE WERE WRONG.
WE'VE PROVED IT BY LIVING HERE. YOUR FRIENDS ARE GRAND. TO TELL THE TRUTH, WE'RE A LITTLE ENVIOUS!
AND SO COMES THE GRAND
COME AND SEE US AGAIN!

Next week a new Claudia adve

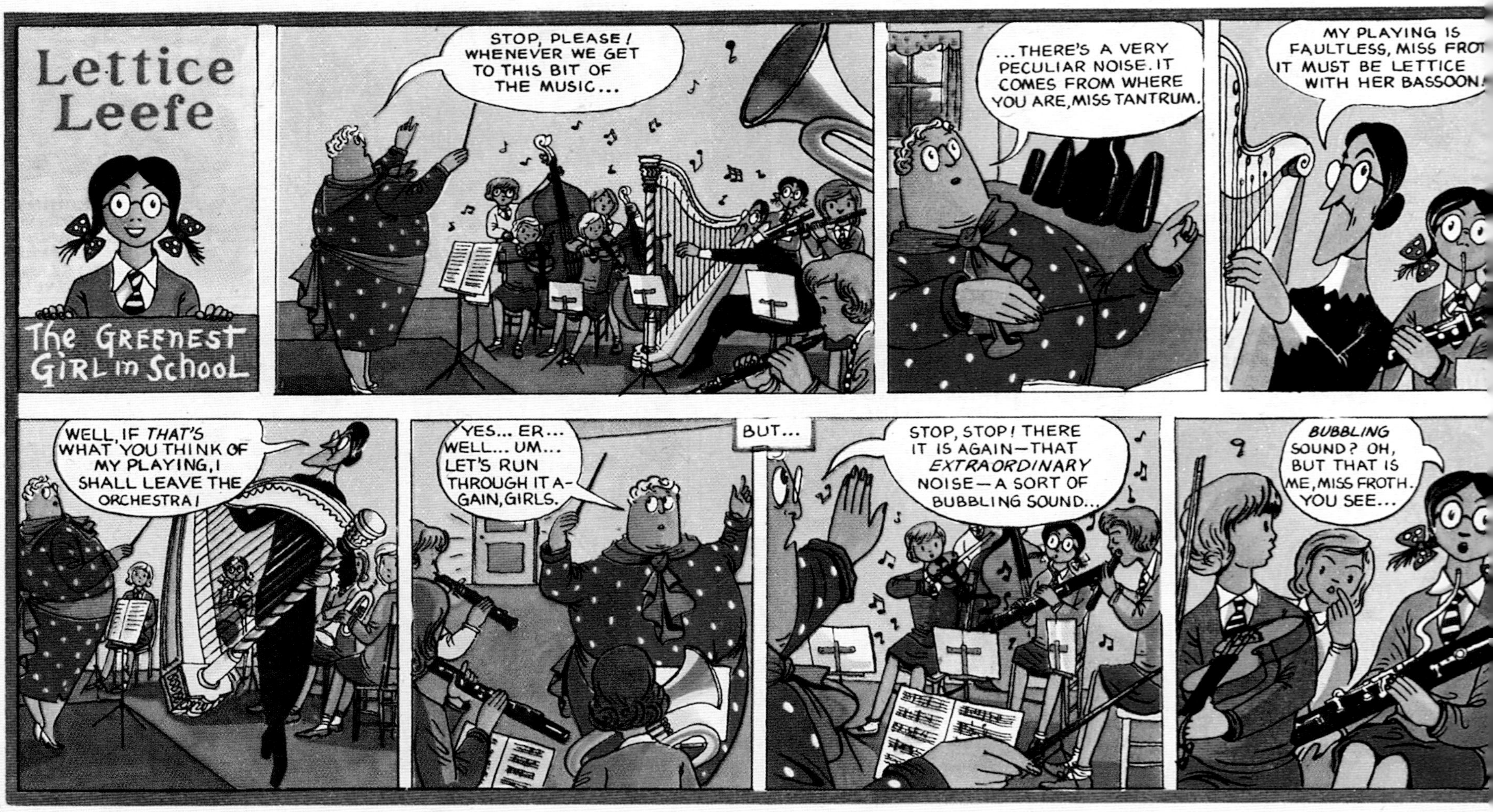
Lettice Leefe
The GREENEST GIRL in SchooL
STOP, PLEASE! WHENEVER WE GET TO THIS BIT OF THE MUSIC...
...THERE'S A VERY PECULIAR NOISE. IT COMES FROM WHERE YOU ARE, MISS TANTRUM.
MY PLAYING IS FAULTLESS, MISS FROT IT MUST BE LETTICE WITH HER BASSOON.
WELL, IF THAT'S WHAT YOU THINK OF MY PLAYING, I SHALL LEAVE THE ORCHESTRA!
YES... ER... WELL... UM... LET'S RUN THROUGH IT AGAIN, GIRLS.
BUT...
STOP, STOP! THERE IT IS AGAIN—THAT EXTRAORDINARY NOISE—A SORT OF BUBBLING SOUND...
BUBBLING SOUND? OH, BUT THAT IS ME, MISS FROTH. YOU SEE...

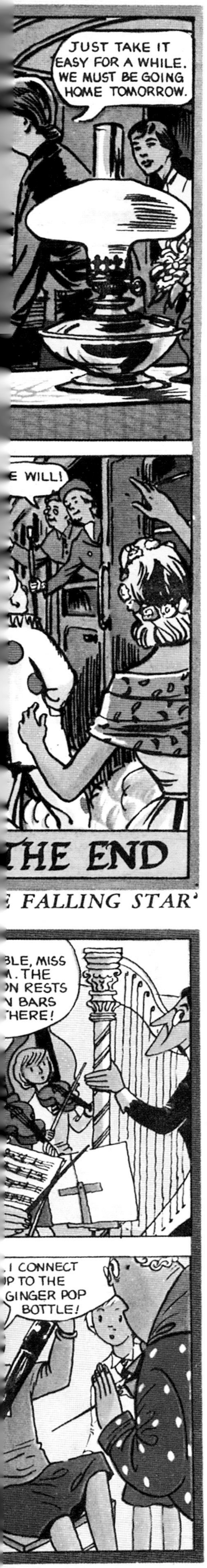
JUST TAKE IT EASY FOR A WHILE. WE MUST BE GOING HOME TOMORROW.
E WILL!
THE END
FALLING STAR'
BLE, MISS A. THE ON RESTS N BARS HERE!
I CONNECT P TO THE GINGER POP BOTTLE!

Girl Picture Gallery

No. 42

This painting will make a lovely addition to your album of pictures of the Royal Family.

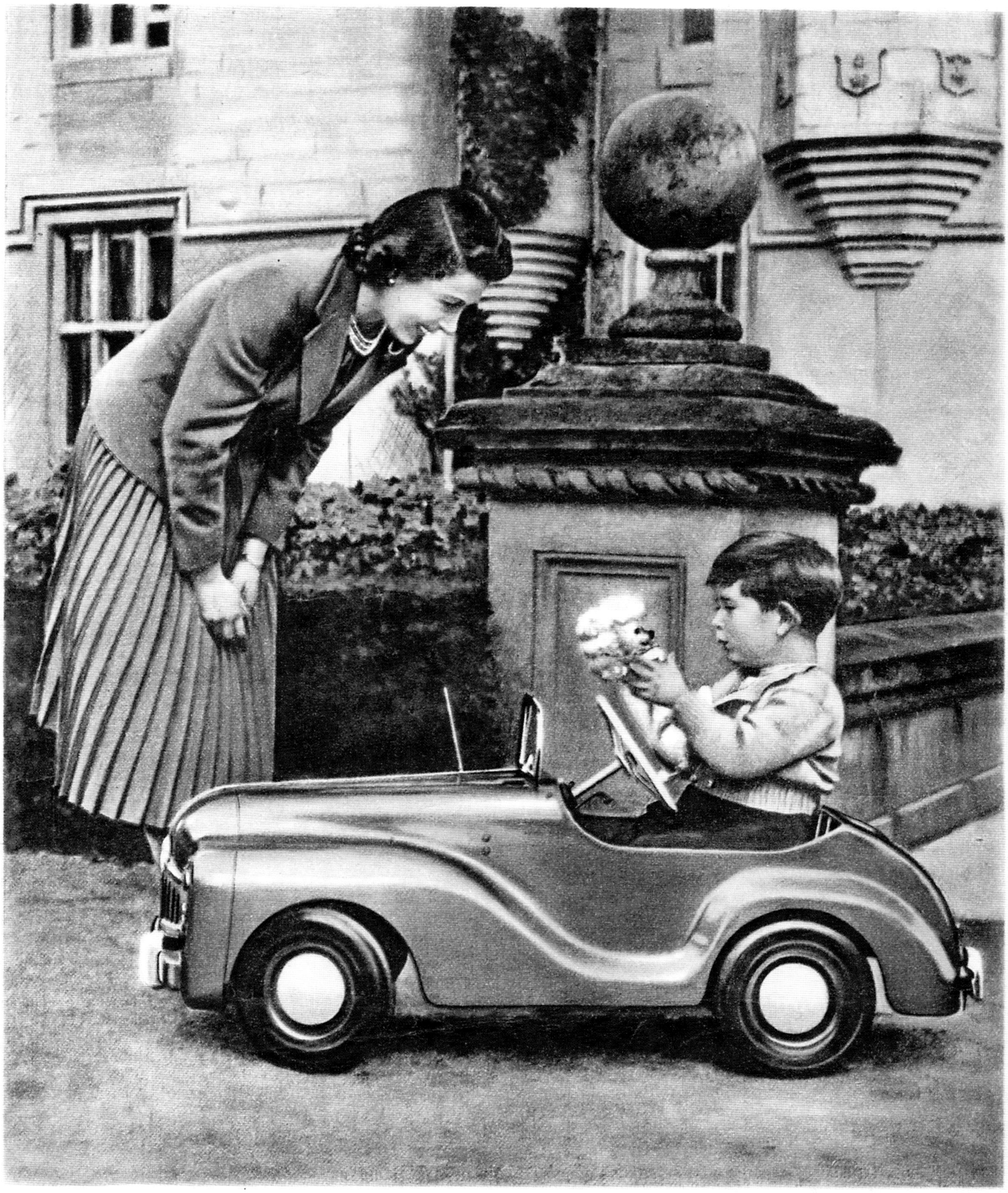

HER MAJESTY THE QUEEN WITH HER SON, PRINCE CHARLES

This charmingly informal picture of Her Majesty the Queen and her son, Prince Charles, is an oil painting made especially for GIRL from a photograph taken by Lisa Sheridan. Taking pictures of Royalty is not new to Lisa Sheridan as she has photographed the Queen ever since she was the same age as Prince Charles is now! The toy motor-car Prince Charles is driving is his favourite toy and was given to him by his grandparents last Christmas. He takes after his father in his interest in mechanical things and shows promise of becoming as good a driver.

A Letter from the Editor

GIRL OFFICE, 161/166 FLEET STREET, LONDON, E.C.4.

19th June, 1957

YOU'LL see some news about Show Jumping Championships on page 14 this week. GIRL and EAGLE are sponsoring the Junior Championships again this year, and we know that all the competitors will be very glad of the support of GIRL readers. If you live near any of the places where the qualifying rounds are being held, do go along and cheer your team!

This week our competition is open to both home and overseas readers – you can read the rules on this page. Do remember, home readers, that you have to send off your entry within twelve days as usual – the extended period of entry is only for readers living abroad.

Yours sincerely,

Marcus Morris

READERS' LETTERS

5/- *will be paid for every reader's letter printed on this page.*

Pat and her stray pets

HOW IS this for a record of stray pets? During the last four months my mother, sister and I have found, in various places, four motherless hedge-sparrows, one thrush with two broken legs, three stray dogs, one kitten and a hen. All of which we have nursed back to health, where possible.

I have enclosed a photo of Major, our labrador, who has been very puzzled by the various pets we have had. – *Pat Bootiman, Whitehaven, Cumberland.*

Pen friends for four years— thanks to GIRL

A picnic by the river

ONE DAY we went down to the river to have a picnic, and we caught some minnows. We took them home and put them into a bowl with river weed and some gravel at the bottom and now they are swimming about. – *Valerie Poole, Hereford.*

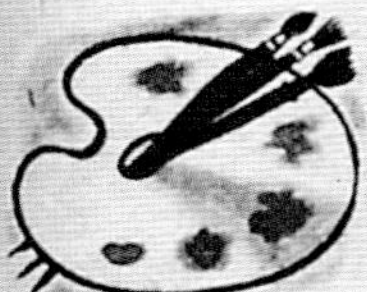

HERE IS a photograph of ourselves spending a holiday together, after writing to each other as pen-friends for four years. We thank GIRL for helping to form this wonderful friendship, as it was GIRL which brought us together.

We hope that many other members of our club will form friendships in this way. – *Jeanne Swain, Overton, Hants.*

PRESENTING THE PRIZEWINNERS

Congratulations to the winners of GIRL Competition No. 15: Marian Archer of Walsall; Marian Andrews of Plymouth; Margaret Banyard of Coventry; Pat Bielby of Llandudno; Terry Britton of Wickon Bonhunt, Nr. Newport; Barbara Champ of Birmingham 24; Wendy Churchyard of Twickenham; Deidre Cannon of St. Annes-on-Sea; Wendy Douglas of Petts Wood; Carole Dupury of Letchworth; P. Davidson of Newport; Alvyn Edgington of Harrow; Patricia Eastwood of Huddersfield; Annabel Ferriman of London, N.6; Hilary Groves of Preston; Maureen Hart of Farnham; Patricia Herbert of Headington; Eileen Holyoak of Keighley; Judith Jacques of Acomb, Yorkshire; Heather Jones of Rotherham; Judith Kendall of New Mills, Nr. Stockport; Emily Ryan of Cheshire; Sandra Rodwell of Manchester 23; Sonia Turner of East Cowes; Valerie Stephenson of Sandown; Gwen Taylor of Harwich; Muriel Westgate of Sittingbourne; Ann Weatherley of Edgware; Susan Ward of Birmingham 28 and Pauline West of Stanmore.

GIRL WINDOW No. 86

CANTEEN SET

Another aid to perfect camping is this canteen set designed specially for GIRL readers.

In frosted-finish, heavy aluminium throughout, this set consists of a frying-pan with fixed handle, serving pan, boiling pot with lid and handle, half-pint mug with black japanned handle. There is also a knife-fork-and-spoon compactum – complete at 22/-.

This set is ideal also for picnics and open-air holidays. Obtainable direct from the makers, The Belton Camping Equipment Co. Ltd., Amwell House, Hoddesdon, Herts; post-free delivery.

Calling Readers all over the world!

LETTICE LEEFE HAS HOLIDAY TROUBLE!

If you can help her out you may win a grand prize

There are 100 copies of the GIRL BOOK OF MODERN ADVENTURERS waiting to be won!

There's some sorting out here for Home and Abroad readers. This special competition, which is open to readers EVERYWHERE, offers these splendid prizes to the winners who can help Lettice Leefe pack for her holiday. At present she is unable to lock her trunk – can you, with the help of the following anagrams, sort out some of the most essential items and help her repack?

What you have to do:

Readers living in the British Isles. When you have discovered the 12 objects, write them on a postcard. Remember to add your name, age and address (using block letters) in the top right-hand corner. Send your card to GIRL Competition No. 25, GIRL Reader Services, Long Lane, Liverpool 9, to reach us not later than 1st July. Neatness and age will be taken into account when judging entries and the top age limit is 16. The Editor's decision is final and no correspondence can be entered into.

ALL OVERSEAS readers. Write the 12 objects on a postcard in the same way as home readers, and send your card to the same address. But mark your entry GIRL (Overseas) Comp. No. 25. Conditions are the same as for our home readers – the only difference being that CLOSING DATE is 25th October 1957. Your entries must be sent by SURFACE MAIL only (not airmail), and prizes will be sent to winners also by surface mail.

| HIGETIN |
| ITNUSSU |
| RAGCANDI |
| PRESSLIP |
| TIPTOECAT |
| HOTSHOTRUB |
| CANSOMISC |
| RAPALOS |
| MOSTCUE |
| BUSELOS |
| DASSNAL |
| STORSH |

PRIZES WILL BE DISTRIBUTED EVENLY BETWEEN HOME AND OVERSEAS WINNERS — 50 to each group.

ON HOLIDAY IN AUGUST?

Lucky you! For these are some of the places where you will find GIRL HOLIDAY PLAYTIME! Full details of all resorts where this FREE seaside fun will be in 1957 are coming soon. Also names of other resorts where you will be able to enter for the GIRL Treasure Hunts.

(Hold this up to a mirror – and discover the names)

LITTLEHAMPTON ● BOGNOR REGIS
WALTON-ON-NAZE ● WEYMOUTH ● GT. YARMOUTH
WESTON-SUPER-MARE ● GORLESTON-ON-SEA

ANGELA
AIR HOSTESS

the story of a girl who longed for adventure

Written by BETTY ROLAND
Drawn by DUDLEY POUT

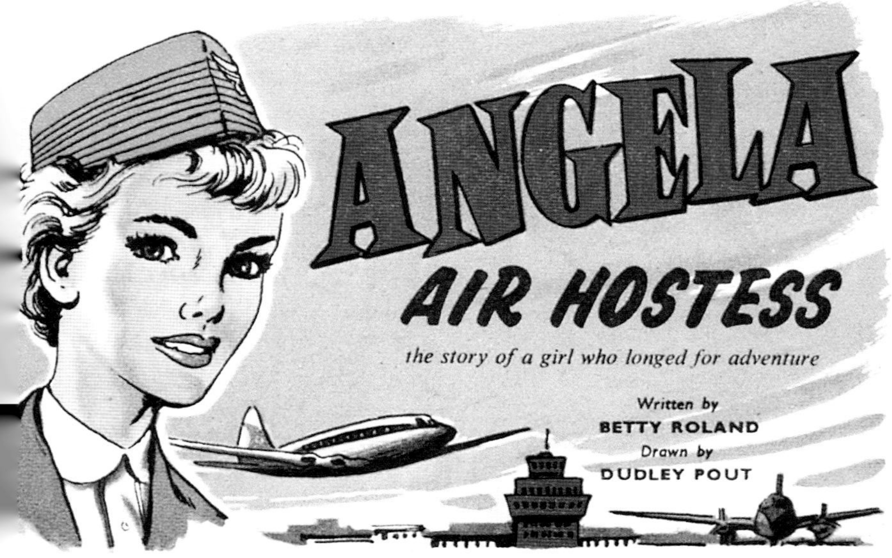

Air Hostess Angela Wells is posted to the Cairo flight with her spoilt cousin, Sandra, and Captain Ian Lewis, on whom the girls are both keen. Sandra gets Angela into Ian's bad books, and after that everything seems to go wrong. At Cairo, Mr Salem Hassid, a wealthy Egyptian passenger, takes Angela to visit his mother and small son, Ahmed. Owing to a car accident she arrives back at her hotel very late, and Ian is furious. Angela promises to take care of Ahmed, who is travelling to London on the return flight – but Sandra insists on looking after the little boy herself. When the 'plane stops at Athens to refuel, Ahmed disappears . . .

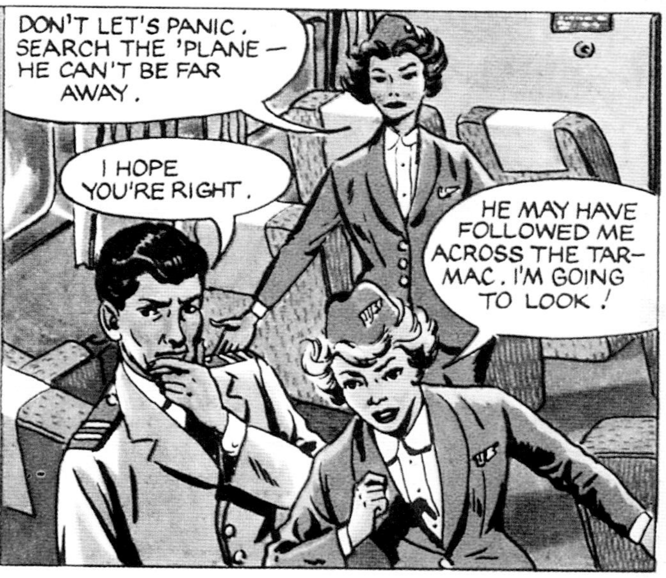
DON'T LET'S PANIC. SEARCH THE 'PLANE – HE CAN'T BE FAR AWAY.
I HOPE YOU'RE RIGHT.
HE MAY HAVE FOLLOWED ME ACROSS THE TAR-MAC. I'M GOING TO LOOK!

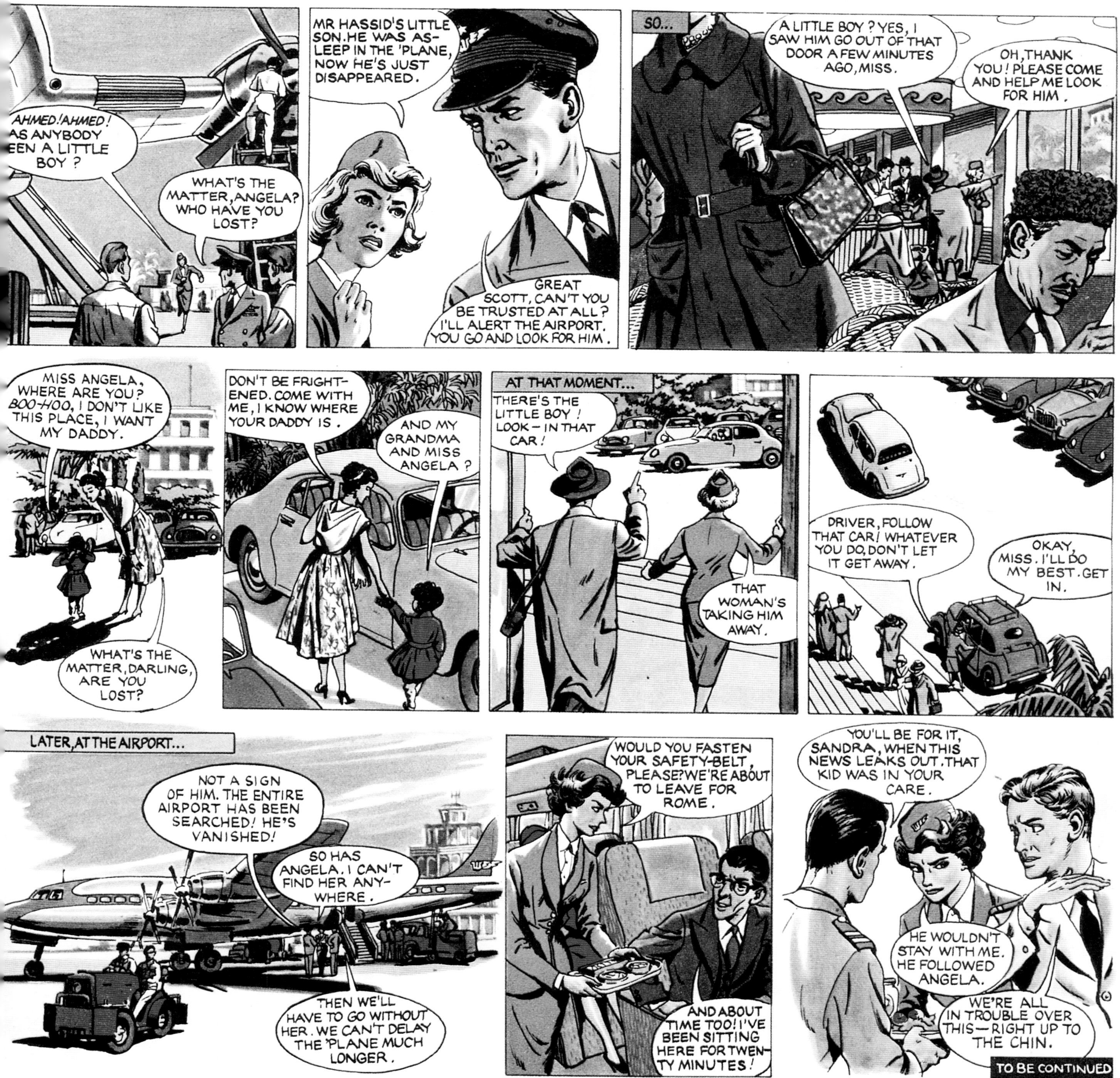
AHMED! AHMED! AS ANYBODY EEN A LITTLE BOY?
WHAT'S THE MATTER, ANGELA? WHO HAVE YOU LOST?
MR HASSID'S LITTLE SON. HE WAS AS-LEEP IN THE 'PLANE, NOW HE'S JUST DISAPPEARED.
GREAT SCOTT, CAN'T YOU BE TRUSTED AT ALL? I'LL ALERT THE AIRPORT. YOU GO AND LOOK FOR HIM.
SO...
A LITTLE BOY? YES, I SAW HIM GO OUT OF THAT DOOR A FEW MINUTES AGO, MISS.
OH, THANK YOU! PLEASE COME AND HELP ME LOOK FOR HIM.
MISS ANGELA, WHERE ARE YOU? BOO-HOO, I DON'T LIKE THIS PLACE, I WANT MY DADDY.
WHAT'S THE MATTER, DARLING, ARE YOU LOST?
DON'T BE FRIGHT-ENED. COME WITH ME, I KNOW WHERE YOUR DADDY IS.
AND MY GRANDMA AND MISS ANGELA?
AT THAT MOMENT...
THERE'S THE LITTLE BOY! LOOK – IN THAT CAR!
THAT WOMAN'S TAKING HIM AWAY.
DRIVER, FOLLOW THAT CAR! WHATEVER YOU DO, DON'T LET IT GET AWAY.
OKAY, MISS. I'LL DO MY BEST. GET IN.
LATER, AT THE AIRPORT...
NOT A SIGN OF HIM. THE ENTIRE AIRPORT HAS BEEN SEARCHED! HE'S VANISHED!
SO HAS ANGELA. I CAN'T FIND HER ANY-WHERE.
THEN WE'LL HAVE TO GO WITHOUT HER. WE CAN'T DELAY THE 'PLANE MUCH LONGER.
WOULD YOU FASTEN YOUR SAFETY-BELT, PLEASE? WE'RE ABOUT TO LEAVE FOR ROME.
AND ABOUT TIME TOO! I'VE BEEN SITTING HERE FOR TWEN-TY MINUTES!
YOU'LL BE FOR IT, SANDRA, WHEN THIS NEWS LEAKS OUT. THAT KID WAS IN YOUR CARE.
HE WOULDN'T STAY WITH ME. HE FOLLOWED ANGELA.
WE'RE ALL IN TROUBLE OVER THIS – RIGHT UP TO THE CHIN.
TO BE CONTINUED

continued on page 133

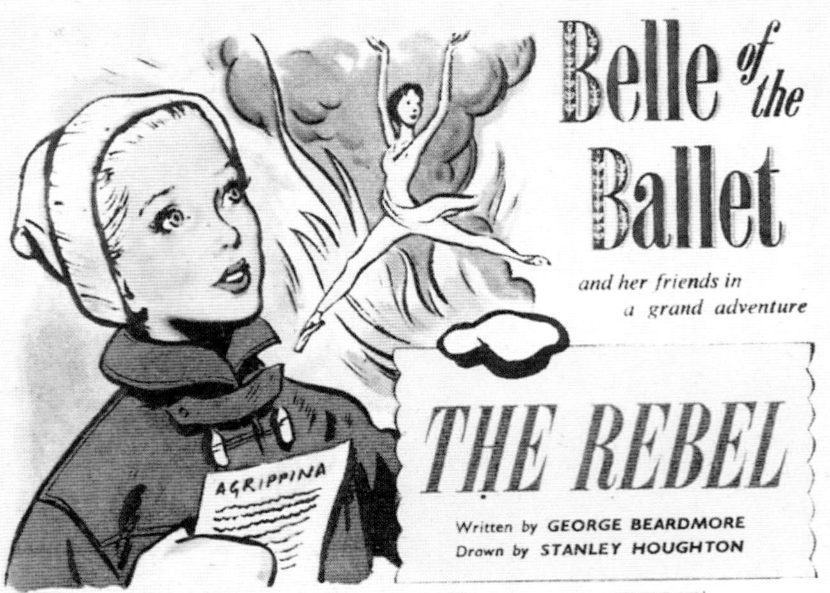
Belle of the Ballet
and her friends in a grand adventure
THE REBEL
Written by GEORGE BEARDMORE
Drawn by STANLEY HOUGHTON
AGRIPPINA

Belle Auburn and her friends, pupils of the Arenska Dancing School, take pity on Sylvine, a marvellous dancer whose career is being ruined by her jealous aunt, famous actress, Erica Brand. Belle rescues Sylvine from the Finishing School to which Erica has sent her, and now plans for Sylvine to dance in the ballet *Agrippina*. But first, a very important ceremony takes place – Sylvine's marriage to a young musician, Felix. Sylvine is given away by Abe Cromwell, her god-father, and the Service is taken by her father . . .

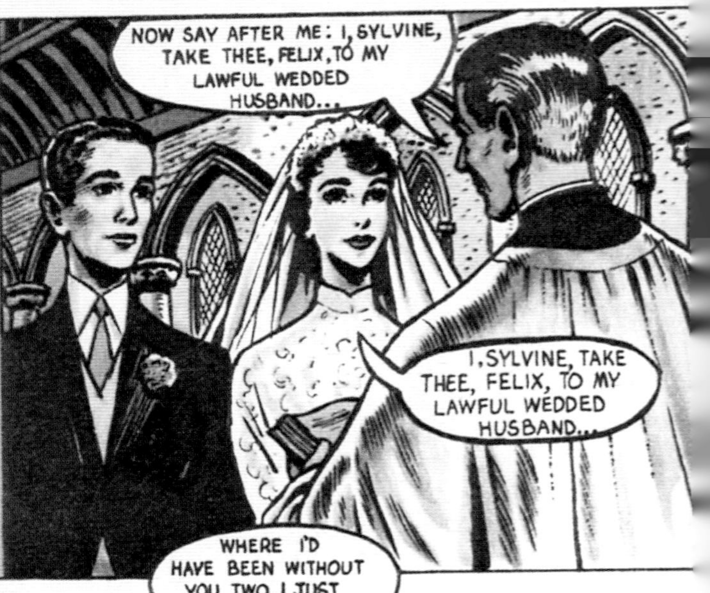
NOW SAY AFTER ME: I, SYLVINE, TAKE THEE, FELIX, TO MY LAWFUL WEDDED HUSBAND...
I, SYLVINE, TAKE THEE, FELIX, TO MY LAWFUL WEDDED HUSBAND...

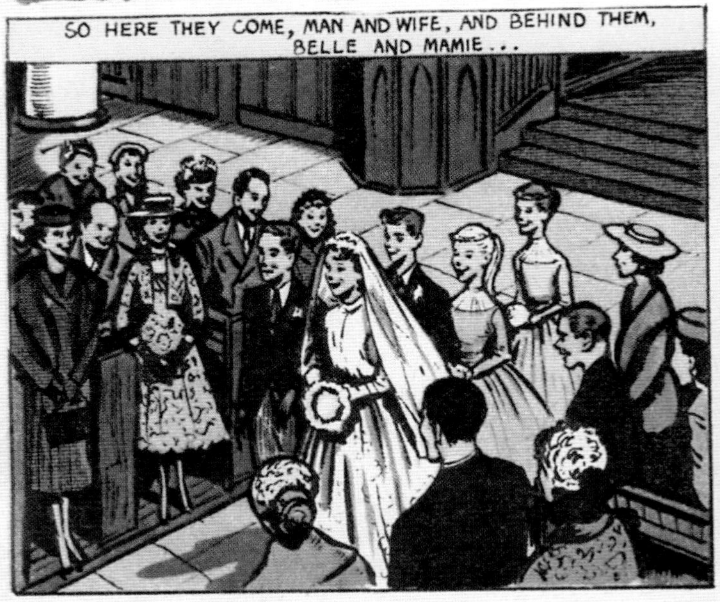
SO HERE THEY COME, MAN AND WIFE, AND BEHIND THEM, BELLE AND MAMIE . . .

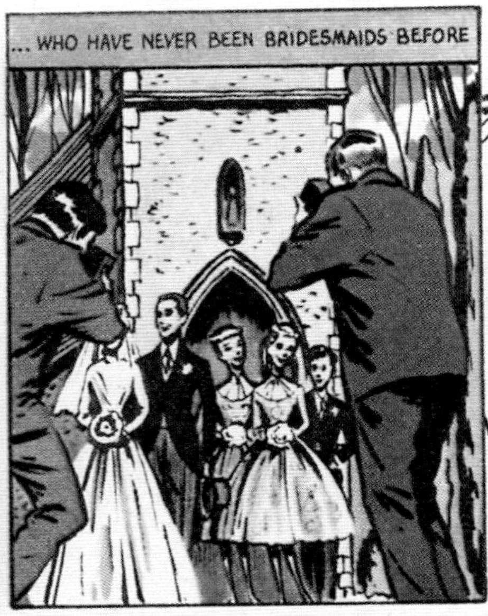
. . . WHO HAVE NEVER BEEN BRIDESMAIDS BEFORE

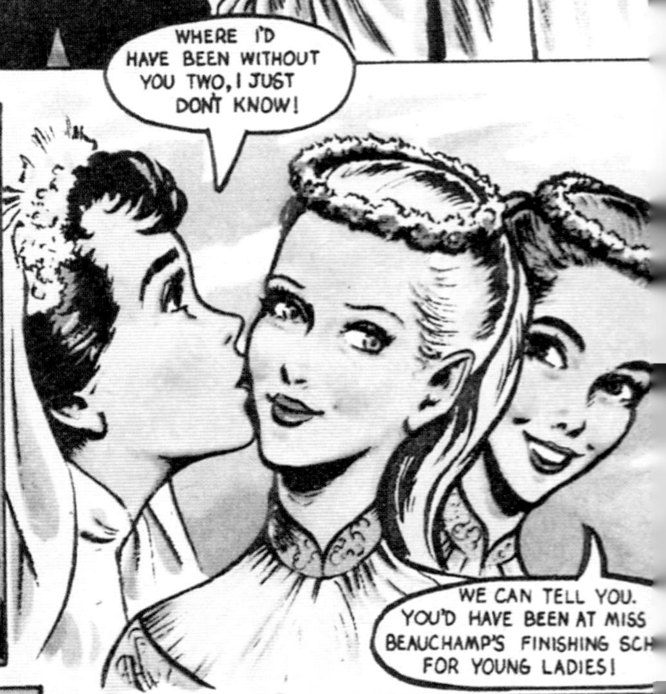
WHERE I'D HAVE BEEN WITHOUT YOU TWO, I JUST DON'T KNOW!
WE CAN TELL YOU. YOU'D HAVE BEEN AT MISS BEAUCHAMP'S FINISHING SCH FOR YOUNG LADIES!

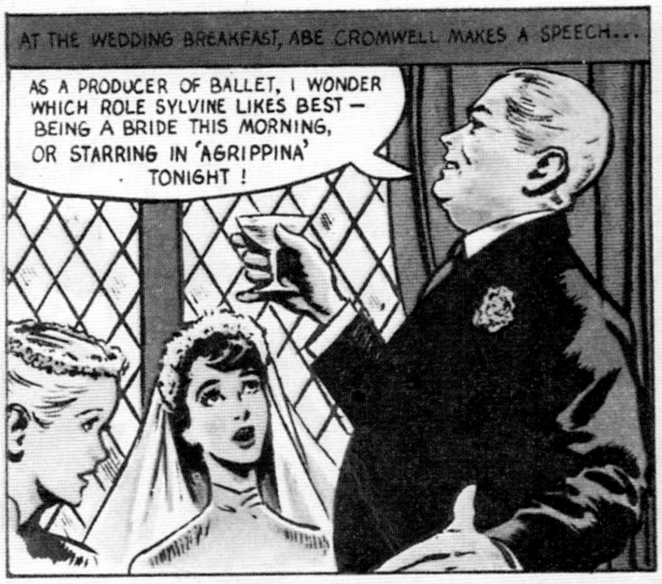
AT THE WEDDING BREAKFAST, ABE CROMWELL MAKES A SPEECH . . .
AS A PRODUCER OF BALLET, I WONDER WHICH ROLE SYLVINE LIKES BEST – BEING A BRIDE THIS MORNING, OR STARRING IN 'AGRIPPINA' TONIGHT!

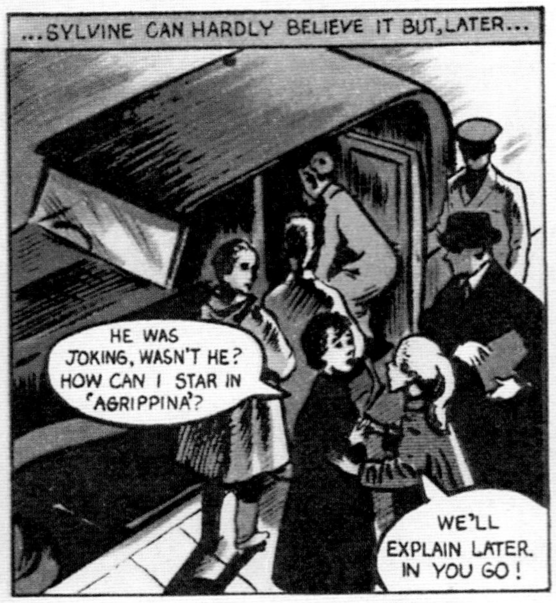
. . . SYLVINE CAN HARDLY BELIEVE IT BUT, LATER . . .
HE WAS JOKING, WASN'T HE? HOW CAN I STAR IN 'AGRIPPINA'?
WE'LL EXPLAIN LATER. IN YOU GO!

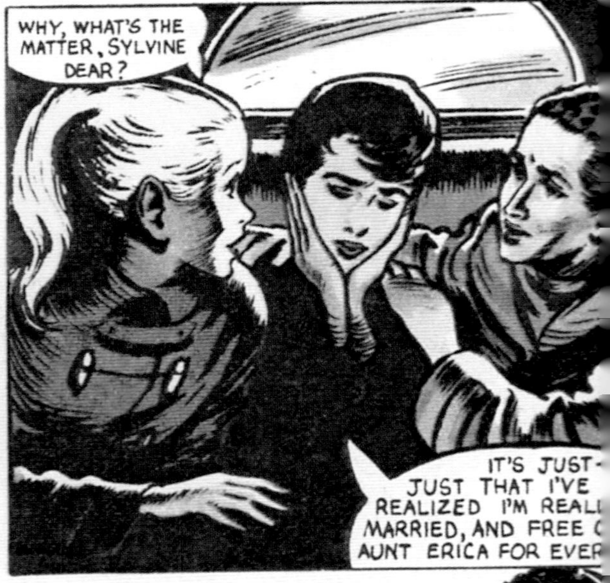
WHY, WHAT'S THE MATTER, SYLVINE DEAR?
IT'S JUST- JUST THAT I'VE REALIZED I'M REALI MARRIED, AND FREE O AUNT ERICA FOR EVER

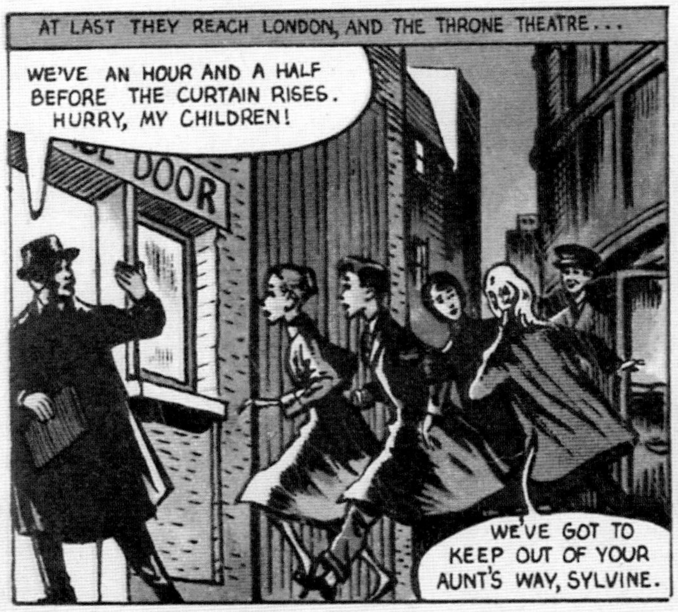
AT LAST THEY REACH LONDON, AND THE THRONE THEATRE . . .
WE'VE AN HOUR AND A HALF BEFORE THE CURTAIN RISES. HURRY, MY CHILDREN!
DOOR
WE'VE GOT TO KEEP OUT OF YOUR AUNT'S WAY, SYLVINE.

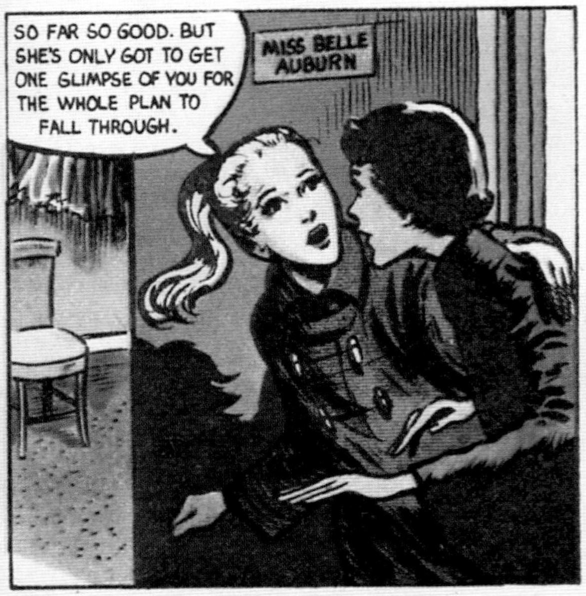
SO FAR SO GOOD. BUT SHE'S ONLY GOT TO GET ONE GLIMPSE OF YOU FOR THE WHOLE PLAN TO FALL THROUGH.
MISS BELLE AUBURN

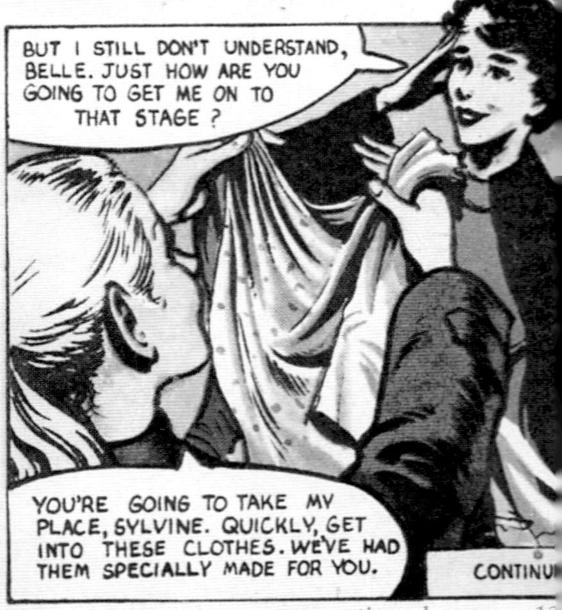
BUT I STILL DON'T UNDERSTAND, BELLE. JUST HOW ARE YOU GOING TO GET ME ON TO THAT STAGE?
YOU'RE GOING TO TAKE MY PLACE, SYLVINE. QUICKLY, GET INTO THESE CLOTHES. WE'VE HAD THEM SPECIALLY MADE FOR YOU.
CONTINU

continued on page 13

Gwenyth Clark writes many books and demonstrates handicraft on TV.

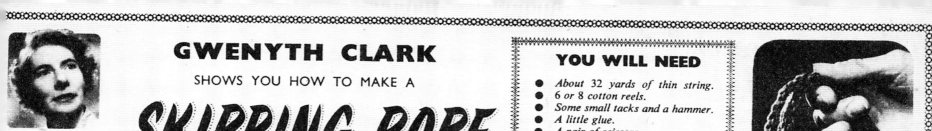

GWENYTH CLARK

SHOWS YOU HOW TO MAKE A

SKIPPING ROPE

YOU WILL NEED

- *About 32 yards of thin string.*
- *6 or 8 cotton reels.*
- *Some small tacks and a hammer.*
- *A little glue.*
- *A pair of scissors.*
- *A piece of wire about 10″ long.*

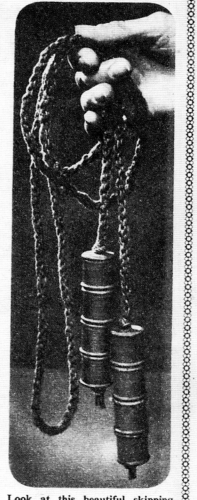

THE spring weather makes us all feel we could skip for joy, so why not make your own skipping rope? To measure the completed rope for your own height, hold the two ends in your hands and put your foot on the middle of the rope. The ends in your hands should nearly reach your ears.

1

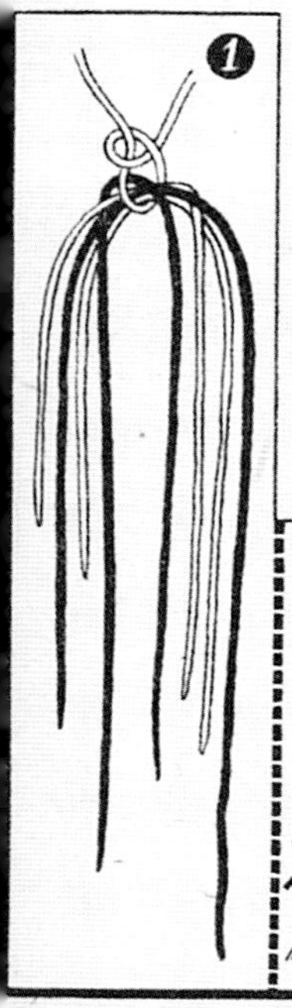

Making the cord

Diagram 1. Take 4 long pieces of thin string, fold them over and tie them together with string so that all the ends hang at different levels.

Diagram 2. With the string tying your cord strings together, attach them to the back rail of a chair. Spread the ends out with one pair out to each side (see a & b) and the other pair up and down (see x & y).

Diagram 3. To tie the knots to make the cord you take the four side strings a & b and tie them together in a single knot, pulling the ends sideways so that a & b change places. Then you take x & y pieces and tie them together in a single knot over the one just tied. Pull these ends up and down so that y now goes over the back of the chair and x hangs down. Continue knotting the strings alternately in this way.

Diagram 4 shows you how to join on a new piece of string when one end is nearly used up. Make the join when the end has just been used to make a knot, tie the new piece on close to this knot and cut the end close so that when the next pair of strings are tied, the join will be hidden underneath their knot.

2
x
b
a
y
3
4
5
6
7
GLUE

Making the handles

Diagram 5. This shows one end of the rope attached to one handle made from 4 small cotton or silk reels. These are glued together after scraping off the labels. To make the join stronger see:–

Diagrams 6 & 7. A tack is partly hammered into one reel and the end left standing up is filed to a point. The surface of the reel is then glued and the next reel hammered on to the tack. Each reel is attached to the others in the same way.

When the glue has set the handle can be painted with some hard-surfaced paint. Let it dry thoroughly before:–

Attaching the handle

Tie a knot in the finishing end of your cord leaving long ends. Fold a piece of wire in half, like a large hair pin (this should be longer than your handles), thread the ends of string into the bent end, push the ends of wire through the handle and draw the ends of string through. Remove the wire and tie the ends in a firm knot close to the handle and cut off the spare pieces leaving a small tassel of ends.

At the end of your cord (the starting end) you only have two ends of string from the piece used to tie the cord strings together. Thread 2 or 3 more through the same loop and attach these ends to the second handle as before, using the wire to thread them.

Look at this beautiful skipping rope! If you follow the instructions given here you will be able to make yourself one just like it – and in no time, too.

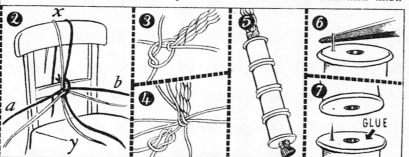

WHAT'S YOUR WORRY?

A trouble shared is a trouble halved, so if there's something on your mind – anything at all – why not tell us about it and our experts will see what they can do to help. Just write to: GIRL, 18 Furnival St., London E.C.4, and mark your letter WHAT'S YOUR WORRY? No names will be printed – but let us have a stamped, addressed envelope if you would like us to send you a reply by letter

Wrong to love an aunt and uncle?

Q. I love my mother and father very much, but I have an aunt and an uncle whom I love also. I feel that this is wrong. What do you think?

A. *Love is not something which can be limited, and it is certainly not wrong to love other members of the family dearly, as well as your parents; nor will you be blamed for doing so.*

* * *

Friendship with a boy

Q. I go to a co-ed school and have made friends with a boy there. We like each other very much, but do you think we are too young to take our friendship seriously at thirteen years old?

A. *Yes, we do. Boys and girls of thirteen should be doing their best to develop many different interests and friendships. It is too soon for a boy and a girl to start concentrating just on each other. In fact, happy relationships in boy and girl friendships later on are considerably helped by a variety of companionships in early years.*

She's very shy

Q. I am shy of helping people in public. Can you suggest a remedy?

A. *Pick on a particular day – and be determined on that day to take every opportunity of helping people that you can.*

* * *

A stray cat

Q. A very bedraggled and ugly street cat lives near us. What do you think we should do about it?

A. *Ring up your local branch of the R.S.P.C.A. and ask for their advice on the matter.*

* * *

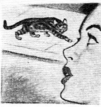

Disliked because she's a monitor

Q. At school I am a monitor in charge of the stairs. All the girls hate me because they are not monitors too and are jealous. Please can you help me?

A. *It sounds as if you may be a bit too bossy. Try doing your duties more cheerfully, and be careful not to order the others about in a haughty way. Just say what you have to say in a quiet and polite manner.*

* * *

What shall she call her?

Q. What should I call the young lady who lives next door? She is twenty-five. Should I use her Christian name?

A. *Call her by her surname to begin with. When you are friends she'll probably invite you to use her Christian name.*

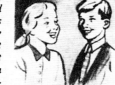

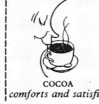

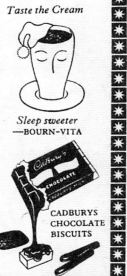

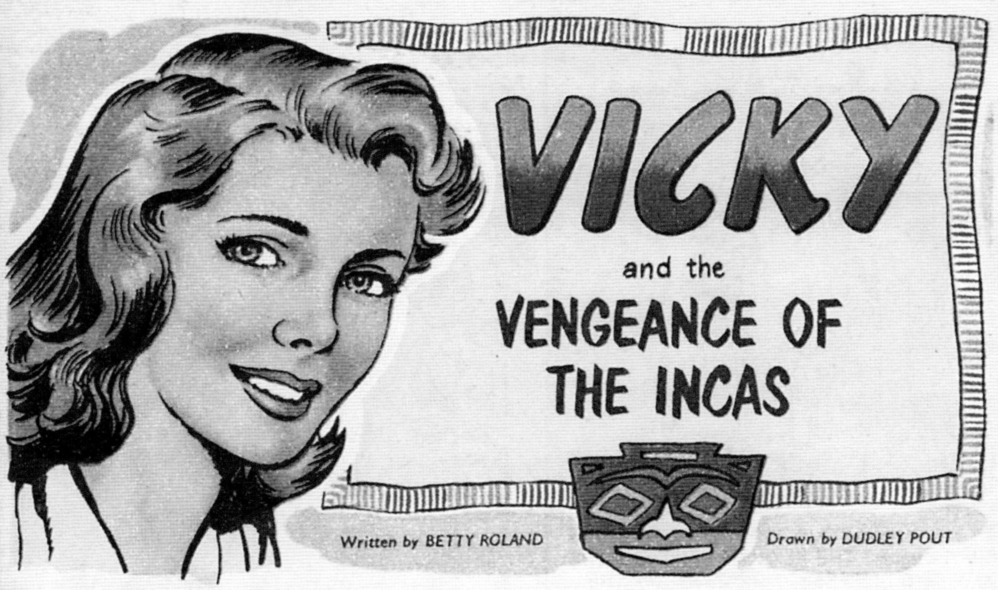
VICKY
and the
VENGEANCE OF THE INCAS
Written by BETTY ROLAND
Drawn by DUDLEY POUT

Vicky and her father, Professor Curtis, have found David Hume in the lost Inca city but they are taken prisoner. Hua, their guide, goes for help. Tupac, the Incas' boy-king, orders Vicky to be a slave in his palace and her father and David are to be put to death. The execution is to take place in the Temple of the Sun God. Vicky makes a desperate attempt to save their lives and . . .

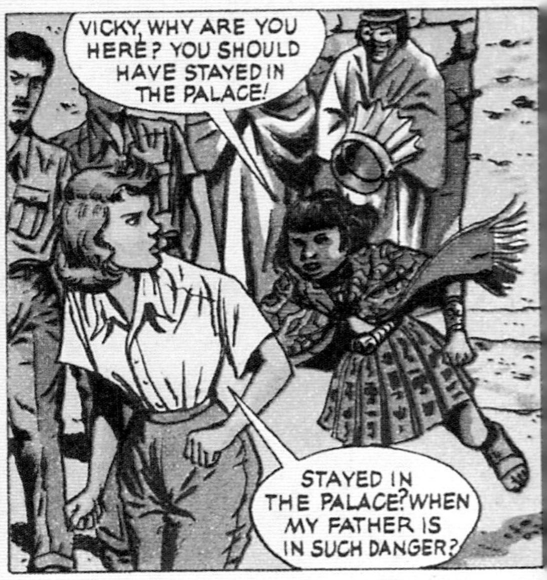
VICKY, WHY ARE YOU HERE? YOU SHOULD HAVE STAYED IN THE PALACE!
STAYED IN THE PALACE? WHEN MY FATHER IS IN SUCH DANGER?

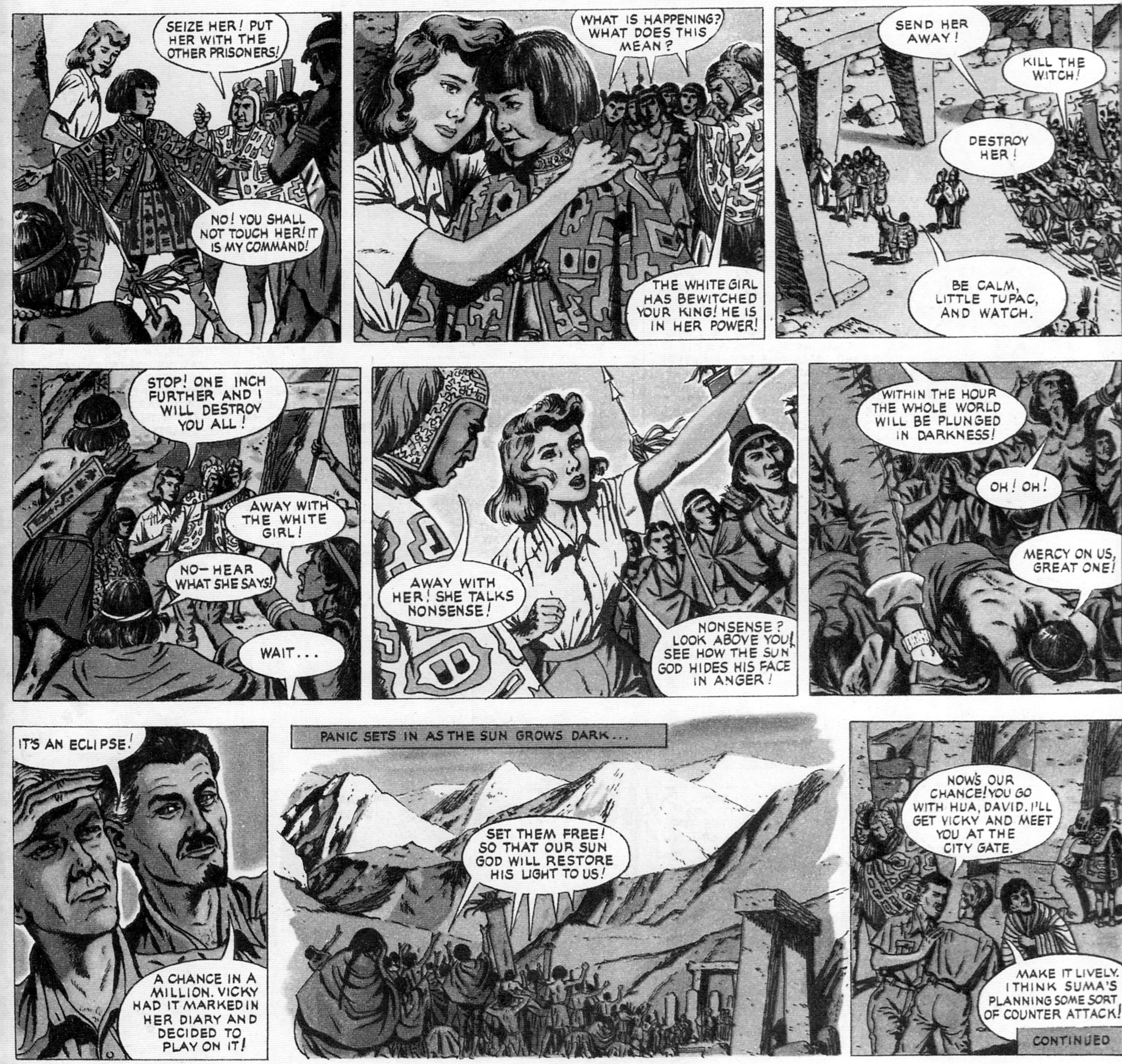
SEIZE HER! PUT HER WITH THE OTHER PRISONERS!
NO! YOU SHALL NOT TOUCH HER! IT IS MY COMMAND!
WHAT IS HAPPENING? WHAT DOES THIS MEAN?
THE WHITE GIRL HAS BEWITCHED YOUR KING! HE IS IN HER POWER!
SEND HER AWAY!
KILL THE WITCH!
DESTROY HER!
BE CALM, LITTLE TUPAC, AND WATCH.
STOP! ONE INCH FURTHER AND I WILL DESTROY YOU ALL!
AWAY WITH THE WHITE GIRL!
NO—HEAR WHAT SHE SAYS!
WAIT...
AWAY WITH HER! SHE TALKS NONSENSE!
NONSENSE? LOOK ABOVE YOU! SEE HOW THE SUN GOD HIDES HIS FACE IN ANGER!
WITHIN THE HOUR THE WHOLE WORLD WILL BE PLUNGED IN DARKNESS!
OH! OH!
MERCY ON US, GREAT ONE!
IT'S AN ECLIPSE!
A CHANCE IN A MILLION. VICKY HAD IT MARKED IN HER DIARY AND DECIDED TO PLAY ON IT!
PANIC SETS IN AS THE SUN GROWS DARK...
SET THEM FREE! SO THAT OUR SUN GOD WILL RESTORE HIS LIGHT TO US!
NOW'S OUR CHANCE! YOU GO WITH HUA, DAVID. I'LL GET VICKY AND MEET YOU AT THE CITY GATE.
MAKE IT LIVELY. I THINK SUMA'S PLANNING SOME SORT OF COUNTER ATTACK!
CONTINUED

continued on page 138

Fashion News FOR NOVEMBER

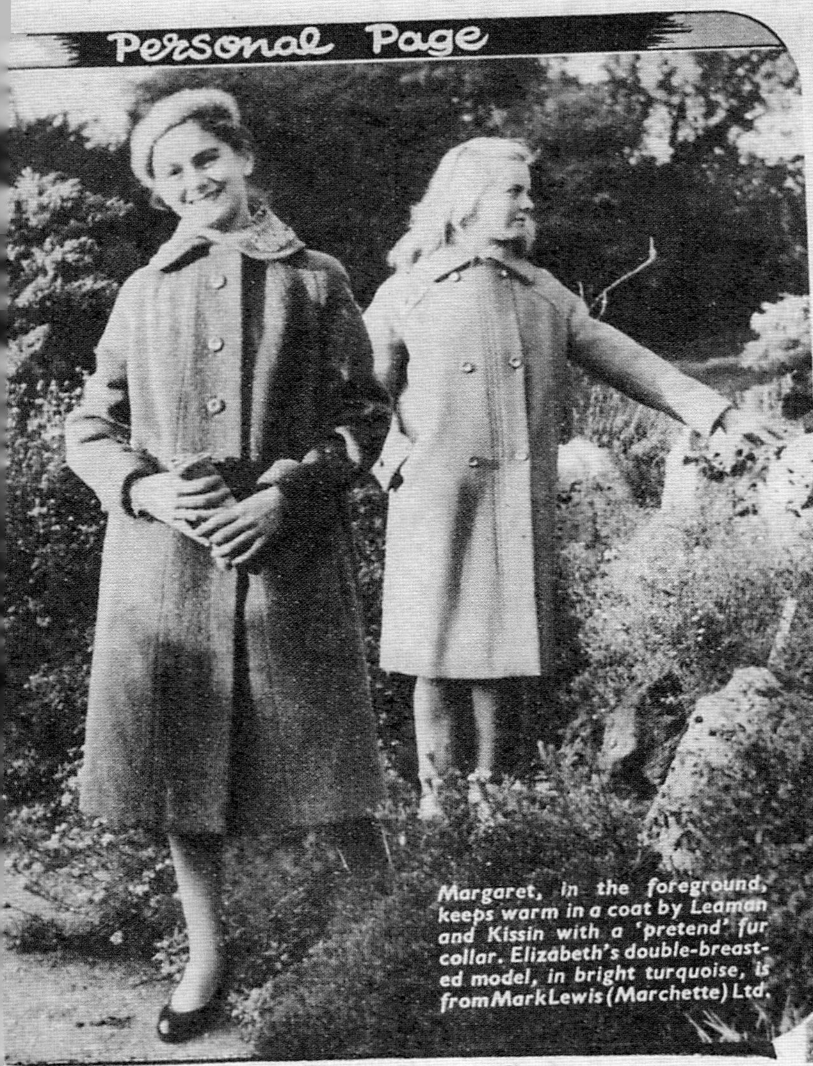

Margaret, in the foreground, keeps warm in a coat by Leaman and Kissin with a 'pretend' fur collar. Elizabeth's double-breasted model, in bright turquoise, is from Mark Lewis (Marchette) Ltd.

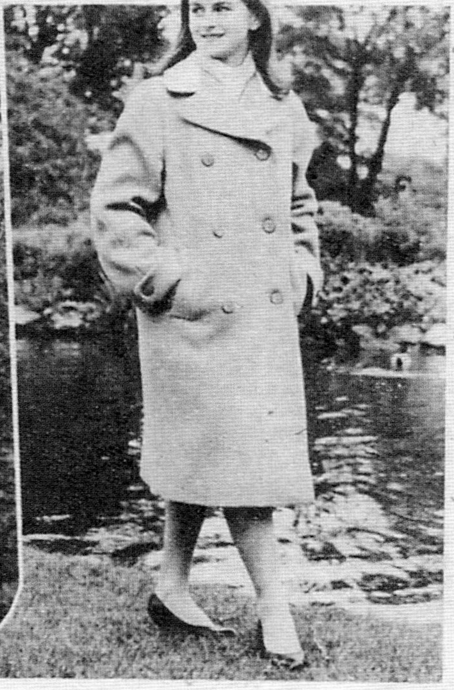

Now's the time to plan your winter wardrobe — and it's best to start with a coat

A warm, camel-coloured classic from Mark Lewis (Marchette) Ltd., to wear over everything. The collar is cut from the off-white reverse side of the cloth.

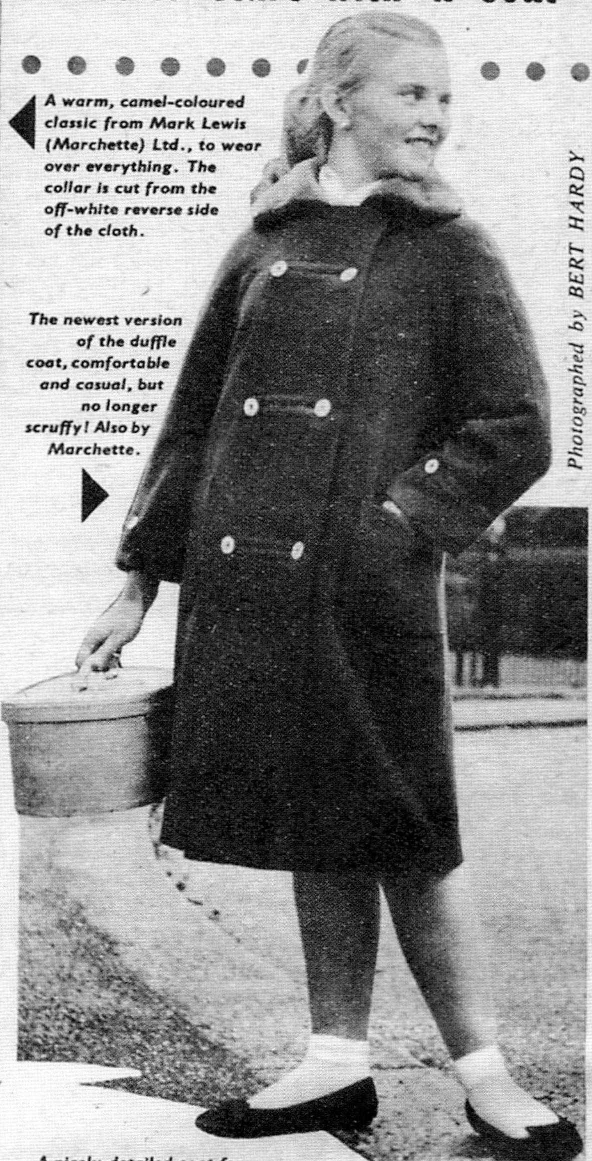

The newest version of the duffle coat, comfortable and casual, but no longer scruffy! Also by Marchette.

Photographed by BERT HARDY

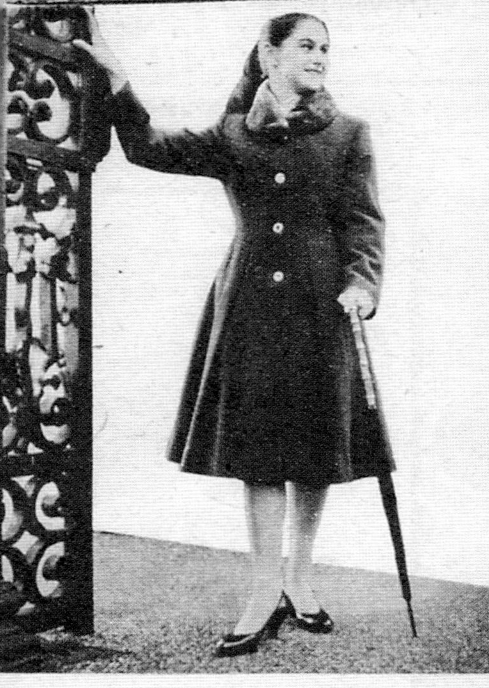

...arming coat ...he girl with a ... waist. Warm ...ur, in lovely ...urs, with a nylon ...collar. Also by ...chette.

A NEW winter coat, like a new suit, is one of the 'basic buys' and needs careful choosing. It must be warm and hard-wearing, of course, and since you are all becoming so fashion-conscious, thank goodness, it should also be stylish so that you get a 'lift' out of wearing it.

I chose a good assortment of new coats and had them photographed in Regents Park, so that you can see how attractive they look in the open-air.

Which should it be, a fitted or an unfitted coat? As in suits, my money goes on unfitted styles every time. Many girls live in 'separates' in the winter, and an unfitted coat slips on over the chunkiest sweater without giving you a bundled-up feeling or making you look like a pudding done up for the pot.

However, since fitted coats are still favourites with many people, I have found two which avoid the fussiness which sometimes spoils this line. Elizabeth, our younger model, wears a coat by Leaman and Kissin; and Margaret, a model by Mark Lewis (Marchette) Ltd. Both coats are super-neat in design and the details are scaled to match the sizes. Beware of over-large collars and cuffs or a too nipped-in waistline if you are choosing a fitted coat.

Loose coats nowadays incorporate many fashion points. The Minimode model that Elizabeth wears as she watches the ducks couldn't be more up-to-date. This is the Trapeze line, stiffened to hold its shape and wide enough round the hem to go comfortably over a full-skirted party dress. The front is just as attractive, but I had it photographed from the back so that you could see the line of buttons and the square-cut collar which are really new.

Less formal coats are just as carefully styled. The camel-coloured classic that Margaret models is so designed that, if you found yourself too tall for it next year, it could easily be cut to three-quarter length.

Elizabeth's 'fur'-collared coat is our old friend the duffle coat in a new guise. Now full-length, it has been streamlined and given a new elegance which makes it suitable wear for many more occasions. Incidentally, nylon fur collars are seen everywhere nowadays. They are just as cosy as natural fur but are lighter and harder wearing.

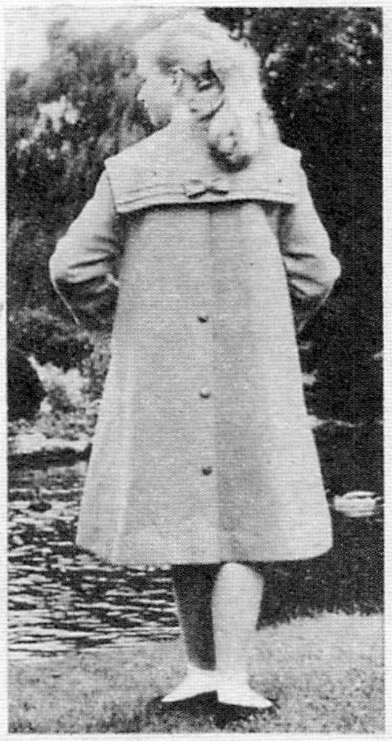

In this smart coat the ducks should be watching Elizabeth! In soft coral wool, by Minimode.

WHERE TO BUY THEM

MARCHETTE COATS

Fitted coat in six colours including Red, Green, Royal: £6-£8, according to size. Camel-coloured classic: £8-£9, according to size. Both from **Lewis's Ltd.** of Leeds, Liverpool, Manchester, and **Nursery Land,** 180 Kilburn High Road, London, N.W.6.

Double-breasted coat in Royal, Rose and Turquoise: £5-£6.10.0, according to size. Duffle-style coat in six shades, including Blue Grotto, Red, Green: £6-£8.10.0, according to size. Both from **Nursery Land** (address as above).

Minimode coat in Coral, Royal, and Blue Grotto: from £5.19.6. From Minimode stockists throughout the country.

Leaman and Kissin fitted coat: 6 gns., all sizes. Colours – Kingfisher, Mink, Moss Green, Cherry, Royal: **Derry and Toms,** London. Swagger coat: 6 gns., all sizes. Colours – as above. **Fisher's** of Wood Green, London. Both coats also stocked by **Barbara Britten Ltd.,** Newcastle-on-Tyne.

***Note:* This information is correct at time of going to press, but you are advised to check with the stockists.**

A nicely-detailed coat for the younger teenager. A Leaman and Kissin model.

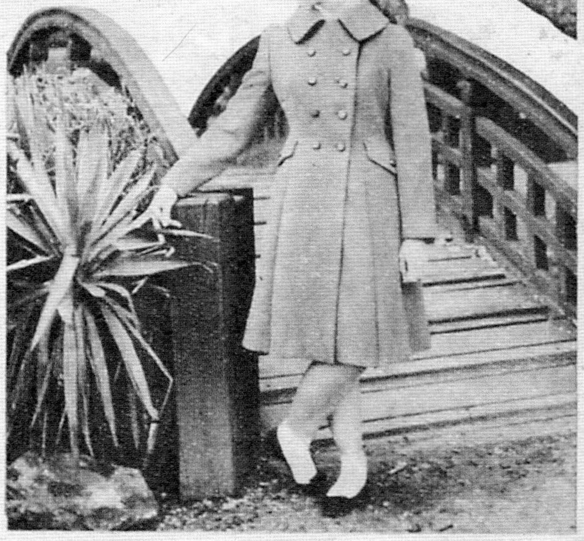

Penny saves the show, and teaches Jeremy Seymour a lesson!

PENNY STARR

The story of a television make-up girl

Written by PETER LING and SHEILAH WARD

Illustrated by ROY NEWBY

Penny in Wonderland

"I SHALL be late . . . I shall be late," muttered an irritable voice. Penny Starr, the newest make-up girl at the National Television Studios, looked round in surprise. The play they were working on was 'Alice in Wonderland', but the actor playing the part of the White Rabbit didn't seem to be rehearsing his opening lines.

"Can I help you, Mr Seymour?" she enquired pleasantly.

"I doubt it," he snapped. "I can't find my head!"

Penny couldn't help smiling. He looked odd, wearing yellow fur feet, and yellow paws, which didn't match his own red, angry face.

"Of course . . . you're meant to have a mask like the other animal characters . . ." she began.

"Not in the least like the others. Mine was ordered specially," Jeremy Seymour corrected her fretfully. "It's a very important part!"

"Please don't worry," Penny tried to reassure him. "I'll find it."

Taking advantage of a brief lull in the rehearsal, she slipped away to begin her search.

Costumes always came from the Wardrobe, but Penny had kept her eyes and ears open during her short time at the studios, and realized that the mask might have been made in the Property Department. The lordly Mr Seymour had probably not enquired about that.

Below ground, in a great cavern lined with row upon row of shelves, lit dimly by electric bulbs that cast long shadows, Penny stood and listened. It was very quiet, far from the bustle of the studios and offices upstairs.

"I feel like Alice at the bottom of the rabbit-hole," she said aloud, and was rather startled by the echoes round her.

She glanced along the nearest shelves. One was devoted to food; huge joints of meat and piles of fruit, so real that she had to touch them to make sure that they were only papier mâché. Further along there was a gleam of white teeth among the shadows. Penny shuddered, then smiled as she recognized a rather battered old tiger, curled up in a comradely fashion next to an equally harmless crocodile.

Then the keen-eyed guardian of this treasure house appeared.

"Mr Seymour's mask? Let me see now," he began, in answer to her query. "Oh, yes, I know. There was something about that. There was a misunderstanding, and it was made with white fur."

"But he is the White Rabbit," said Penny, bewildered.

"I know that," said her new acquaintance. "Not been here long, have you?"

"Not very," Penny admitted.

"Then you've not seen what happens when somebody wears something white in front of the cameras. Well, I'll tell you; first it flares as if someone had put a match to it, then it goes black. Of course, a lot of funny things have happened like that . . . remember the white ponies that we had in 'Cinderella'? . . . Oh, no, that'd be before your time."

"White ponies? And did they 'flare'?"

"All over the screen. A proper firework display, that was. You see, if you have to put a white tablecloth in a play, or a white apron, or anything like that, we supply a pale blue one usually – but you can't order pale blue ponies!"

"So what did you do?"

"After the first rehearsal, we had to darken them down with powder . . . just the same as I'm going to do with this rabbit's head. Come on we can't stay here all day, gossiping about powdering ponies."

"I'd love to hear another time," said Penny.

"Well, pop down for a chat some day," replied the Property Master. "But we'd better take Mr Seymour's head up to the studio, and darken it down with a spot of brown powder. There's quite a knack to it – I'll show you, if you're interested . . ."

Jeremy Seymour wasn't very pleased to see Penny return.

"You've been a long time," he remarked accusingly, and put out a hand to snatch the mask. The Property Master attempted to explain that it could not be worn until it had been darkened.

"Give it to me then," Jeremy Seymour interrupted rudely. "I'll do it myself. After the way I've been messed about today, I can't trust anyone here to do anything properly!"

The Property Master drew himself up to his full height – thereby reaching very nearly up to Jeremy Seymour's chin.

"I've been in charge of properties, man and boy, for thirty-five years – and for better actors than you'll ever be, Mr Seymour. If you think you can do the job, you're very welcome to try."

Penny retreated to a safe distance from Jeremy Seymour, who looked as if he might explode at any moment, and began to take notes about Alice, and the other characters who needed make-up.

Occasionally, she glanced back at Mr Seymour, perched on an upturned bucket, dabbing away at the mask with the tin of brown powder. He achieved a pale creamy shade on one side, and tried to do the other. When it was finished he stepped back to admire the result, and found that the second side was slightly darker. He went back to retouch the first side . . .

In the final rehearsal, when the White Rabbit rushed past Alice in the meadow, the producer called down to the studio:

"Hold it there . . . !"

He had to. Everyone in the cast was rocking with laughter.

At some time during his powder activities, Jeremy Seymour must have [sus]pected that he had gone too far, beca[use] he had tried to remove some of the p[ow]der with a wet sponge. Unfortunately, [no]body had a chance to tell him that [the] brownish powder he had been applying [so] liberally was nothing more nor less t[han] common-or-garden cocoa!

The result was that, when mixed w[ith] water, it had gone darker still, and [the] White Rabbit now looked indescriba[bly] funny – as Penny described it afterwa[rds] he was a cross between a drowned rat [and] a chocolate pudding!

One thing was certain. He was no lo[nger] the White Rabbit.

The producer came down from the gl[ass-] panelled control box, obviously struggl[ing] between amusement and anger.

"It's all very well," he said, wiping [the] tears from his eyes, "but we've got an h[our] to go . . . and we can't have you wear[ing] that thing, Jerry. Even Props couldn't m[ake] it look right now."

Penny came forward rather shyly.

"I think I could do something with cr[êpe] hair and greasepaint," she offered.

"I'll give you ten minutes," said [the] producer.

Penny flew for her make-up kit, sat [Mr] Seymour down in a quiet corner beh[ind] the scenes and set to work.

She took out some lengths of crepe [hair] – a pale cream colour; not white! Quic[kly]

"I think I can do something," Penny offered.

she teased out half a dozen plaits, th[en] took her scissors and a bottle of spi[rit] gum, and inch by inch began snipping a[nd] sticking, painting every scrap of his f[ace] with the strong-smelling gum, and de[ftly] fixing each little patch of hair in pla[ce.] It was a long job, but she worked w[ith] amazing speed, and under her hands a c[on-] vincing animal face soon appeared, co[m-] pletely blotting out the rather subd[ued] Jeremy Seymour underneath.

To finish off, she widened his eyes w[ith] greasepaint, and then stood back.

"There! Lewis Carroll would be pro[ud] of you, after all!" she smiled.

But Mr Seymour made no apologies [to] Penny, and gave her no thanks.

"I think Props might have told me it w[as] cocoa," was his one resentful remark.

Penny turned to Anna Farrell, who w[as] her colleague on the show.

"I think he'll let Props have a free ha[nd] in future," she remarked, laughing.

"I don't know," Anna replied. "He [got] off very lightly."

"So far . . . But just you wait!" Pen[ny] grinned. "It'll be no fun peeling off th[at] hair. Somehow I think Mr Seymour's go[ing] to learn his lesson – the hard way!"

Another Penny Starr story next week[.]

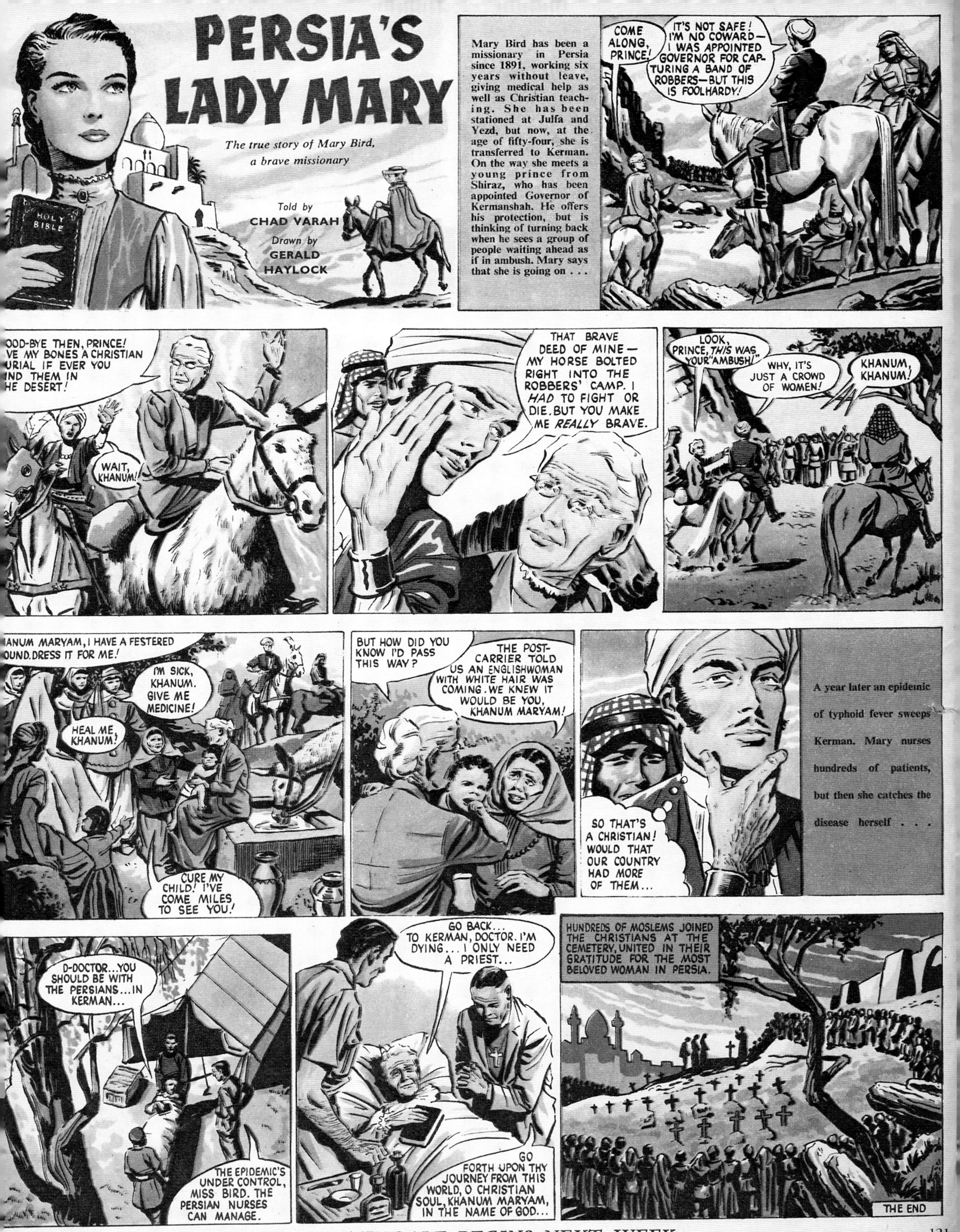
PERSIA'S LADY MARY
The true story of Mary Bird, a brave missionary
Told by CHAD VARAH
Drawn by GERALD HAYLOCK
HOLY BIBLE
Mary Bird has been a missionary in Persia since 1891, working six years without leave, giving medical help as well as Christian teaching. She has been stationed at Julfa and Yezd, but now, at the age of fifty-four, she is transferred to Kerman. On the way she meets a young prince from Shiraz, who has been appointed Governor of Kermanshah. He offers his protection, but is thinking of turning back when he sees a group of people waiting ahead as if in ambush. Mary says that she is going on . . .
COME ALONG, PRINCE!
IT'S NOT SAFE! I'M NO COWARD— I WAS APPOINTED GOVERNOR FOR CAPTURING A BAND OF ROBBERS—BUT THIS IS FOOLHARDY!
OOD-BYE THEN, PRINCE! VE MY BONES A CHRISTIAN URIAL IF EVER YOU IND THEM IN HE DESERT!
WAIT, KHANUM!
THAT BRAVE DEED OF MINE— MY HORSE BOLTED RIGHT INTO THE ROBBERS' CAMP. I HAD TO FIGHT OR DIE. BUT YOU MAKE ME REALLY BRAVE.
LOOK, PRINCE, THIS WAS YOUR "AMBUSH!"
WHY, IT'S JUST A CROWD OF WOMEN!
KHANUM, KHANUM!
HANUM MARYAM, I HAVE A FESTERED OUND. DRESS IT FOR ME!
I'M SICK, KHANUM. GIVE ME MEDICINE!
HEAL ME, KHANUM!
CURE MY CHILD! I'VE COME MILES TO SEE YOU!
BUT HOW DID YOU KNOW I'D PASS THIS WAY?
THE POST-CARRIER TOLD US AN ENGLISHWOMAN WITH WHITE HAIR WAS COMING. WE KNEW IT WOULD BE YOU, KHANUM MARYAM!
SO THAT'S A CHRISTIAN! WOULD THAT OUR COUNTRY HAD MORE OF THEM...
A year later an epidemic of typhoid fever sweeps Kerman. Mary nurses hundreds of patients, but then she catches the disease herself . . .
D-DOCTOR...YOU SHOULD BE WITH THE PERSIANS...IN KERMAN...
THE EPIDEMIC'S UNDER CONTROL, MISS BIRD. THE PERSIAN NURSES CAN MANAGE.
GO BACK... TO KERMAN, DOCTOR. I'M DYING... I ONLY NEED A PRIEST...
GO FORTH UPON THY JOURNEY FROM THIS WORLD, O CHRISTIAN SOUL, KHANUM MARYAM, IN THE NAME OF GOD...
HUNDREDS OF MOSLEMS JOINED THE CHRISTIANS AT THE CEMETERY, UNITED IN THEIR GRATITUDE FOR THE MOST BELOVED WOMAN IN PERSIA.
THE END

THE STORY OF FLORENCE NIGHTINGALE BEGINS NEXT WEEK

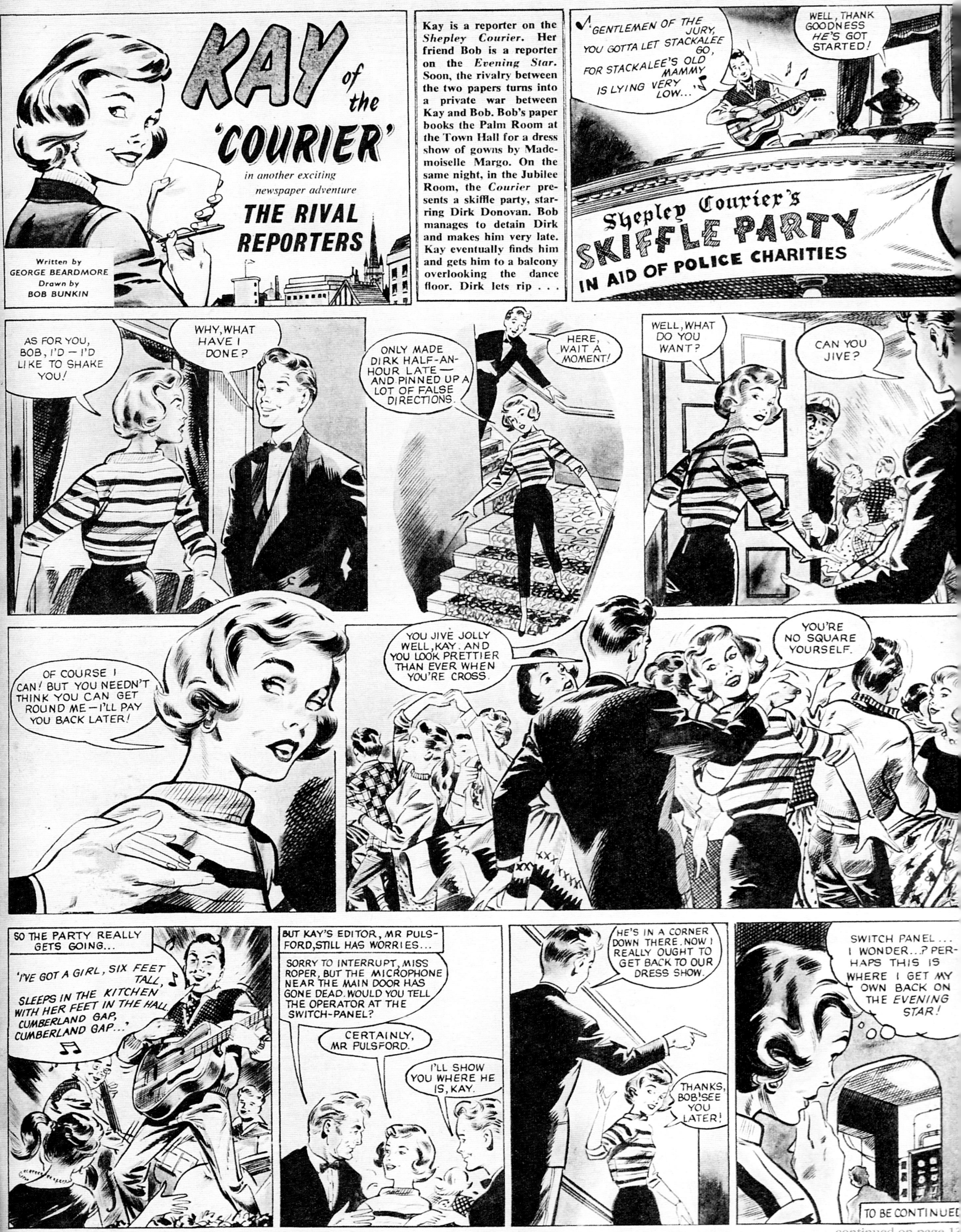
KAY of the 'COURIER'
in another exciting newspaper adventure
THE RIVAL REPORTERS
Written by GEORGE BEARDMORE Drawn by BOB BUNKIN
Kay is a reporter on the Shepley Courier. Her friend Bob is a reporter on the Evening Star. Soon, the rivalry between the two papers turns into a private war between Kay and Bob. Bob's paper books the Palm Room at the Town Hall for a dress show of gowns by Mademoiselle Margo. On the same night, in the Jubilee Room, the Courier presents a skiffle party, starring Dirk Donovan. Bob manages to detain Dirk and makes him very late. Kay eventually finds him and gets him to a balcony overlooking the dance floor. Dirk lets rip . . .
GENTLEMEN OF THE JURY, YOU GOTTA LET STACKALEE GO, FOR STACKALEE'S OLD MAMMY IS LYING VERY LOW...
WELL, THANK GOODNESS HE'S GOT STARTED!
Shepley Courier's SKIFFLE PARTY IN AID OF POLICE CHARITIES
AS FOR YOU, BOB, I'D — I'D LIKE TO SHAKE YOU!
WHY, WHAT HAVE I DONE?
ONLY MADE DIRK HALF-AN-HOUR LATE — AND PINNED UP A LOT OF FALSE DIRECTIONS.
HERE, WAIT A MOMENT!
WELL, WHAT DO YOU WANT?
CAN YOU JIVE?
OF COURSE I CAN! BUT YOU NEEDN'T THINK YOU CAN GET ROUND ME — I'LL PAY YOU BACK LATER!
YOU JIVE JOLLY WELL, KAY. AND YOU LOOK PRETTIER THAN EVER WHEN YOU'RE CROSS.
YOU'RE NO SQUARE YOURSELF.
SO THE PARTY REALLY GETS GOING...
'I'VE GOT A GIRL, SIX FEET TALL, SLEEPS IN THE KITCHEN WITH HER FEET IN THE HALL. CUMBERLAND GAP, CUMBERLAND GAP...'
BUT KAY'S EDITOR, MR PULSFORD, STILL HAS WORRIES...
SORRY TO INTERRUPT, MISS ROPER, BUT THE MICROPHONE NEAR THE MAIN DOOR HAS GONE DEAD. WOULD YOU TELL THE OPERATOR AT THE SWITCH-PANEL?
CERTAINLY, MR PULSFORD.
I'LL SHOW YOU WHERE HE IS, KAY.
HE'S IN A CORNER DOWN THERE. NOW I REALLY OUGHT TO GET BACK TO OUR DRESS SHOW.
THANKS, BOB! SEE YOU LATER!
SWITCH PANEL... I WONDER...? PERHAPS THIS IS WHERE I GET MY OWN BACK ON THE EVENING STAR!
TO BE CONTINUED

continued on page 13

Simply Lovely

This week, VIRGINIA GRAY is writing specially for girls who are just starting to use make-up.

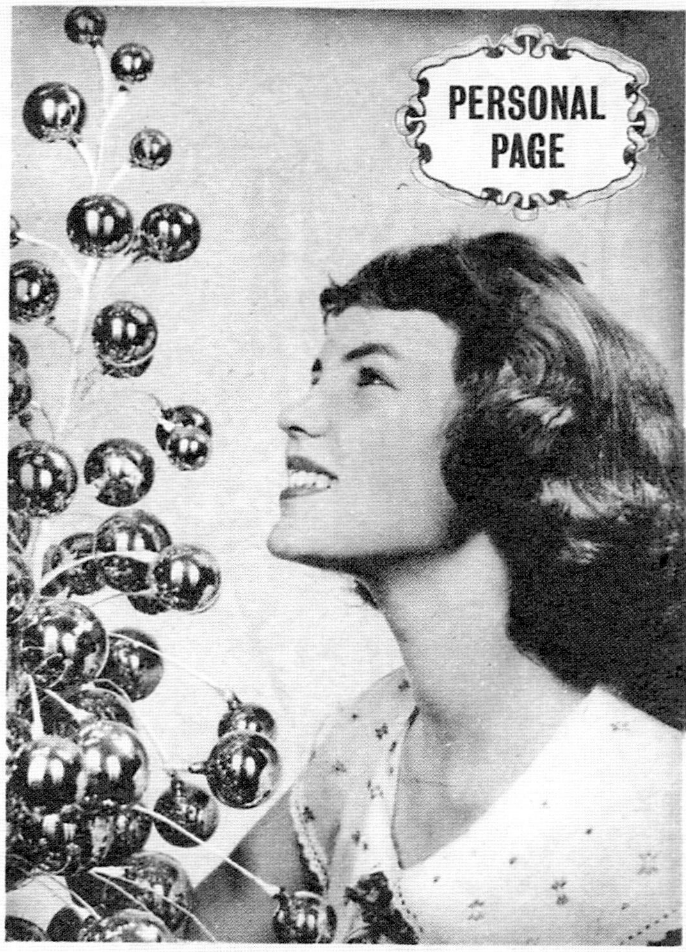

PERSONAL PAGE

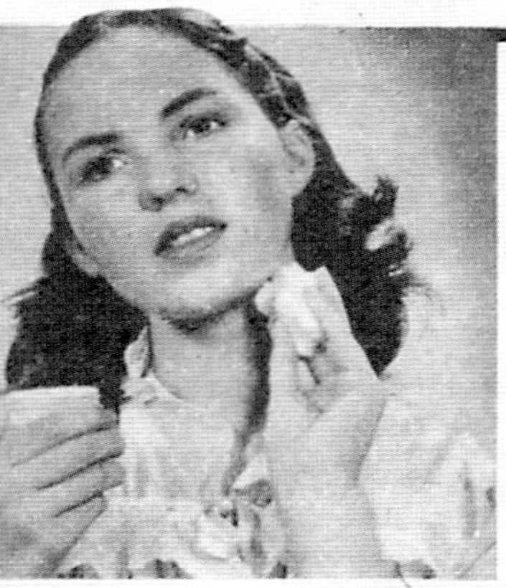

First of all Beverly uses Pond's cold cream twice over, to clean her face and neck thoroughly, after one lathering with a mild soap. Her skin is dry, otherwise I would have advised creaming first, soap afterwards. The cream can be removed with face tissues or with cotton-wool dipped in cold water and squeezed ALMOST dry. A girl who has a very oily skin might prefer to buy a liquid skin cleanser, such as Innoxa Cleansing Milk.

Gay and pretty as the Christmas-tree, Beverly, our model, has achieved the effect that every young girl should aim at; a make-up that is clever enough to enhance her best features and natural enough to be unnoticeable. Right now she knows she is looking her best and the knowledge gives her the confidence to face the party season with happy anticipation. More important still, she knows that her pretty skin will be protected by using the right beauty aids. Beverly wrote to me describing her type of skin; then, taking my advice, she bought small sizes to start with. This saved her from making some expensive mistakes. Even a know-all like me can't always guess colours correctly by post, and experiments may sometimes be needed!

Photographed by BERT HARDY

Christmas Decorations by JILLIAN COWIE LIMITED

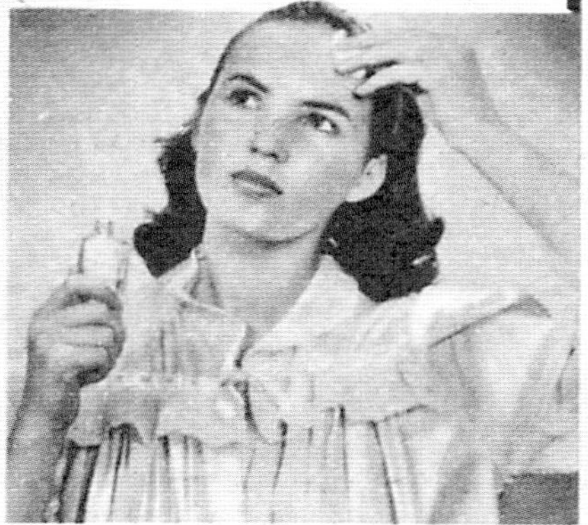

Next comes a toning lotion. here are a number of effec-ive brands – or witch hazel an be obtained from a chem-st. For oily skins or open ores an astringent lotion is dvisable; for normal or deli-ate skins the skin tonics or o-called fresheners are better. everly is paying particular ttention to her hairline, where oap or creams can so easily log the skin and make a way or spots. A dab of ten volume eroxide is all that she uses if the odd spot does appear.

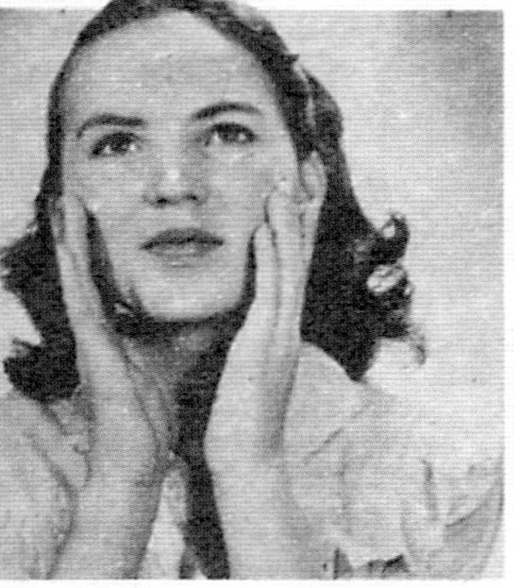

Foundation cream comes next, and Beverly has chosen Max Factor's Invisible foundation. It is an untinted base, excellent for a delicate young skin, and grand for holding powder. She places tiny dabs on nose, forehead, cheeks, chin and neck, then blends them with her fingertips until there is an even covering. She takes great care to use only the smallest quantities, and works upwards and outwards, going VERY GENTLY round her eyes.

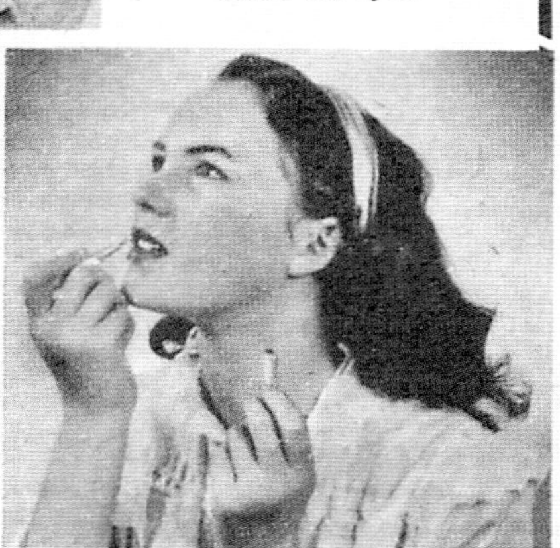

Powder must be fine and linging – I gave Beverly a ist of my favourites and she hose Coty, applying it lavishly vith cotton wool (which can e changed daily) and brushing way the surplus. Her lipstick s Yardley's Pink Magic, as oft and youthful as lip-colour an be, and as you see, she's utlining with a brush before illing in the centre. Two min-ites at least must be allowed or the colour to develop. Then the surplus colour is blotted' on to a face tissue.

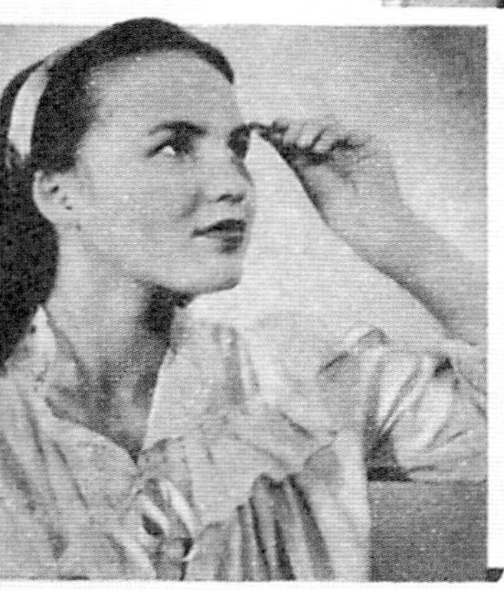

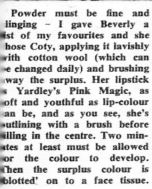

Beverly has eyebrows and lashes several shades darker than her hair, so uses her mascara brush only to dislodge powder particles and give her brows a tidy curve. On party evenings she brushes on a trace of hair-oil. For fair-lashed girls I advise a brown mascara, never a black one. Rimmel sells one for only 1/3. Use almost dry so that it does not clog, and lengthen eyebrows which finish too soon with light, feathery strokes with a brown eyebrow pencil.

The pick of the presents for Christmas

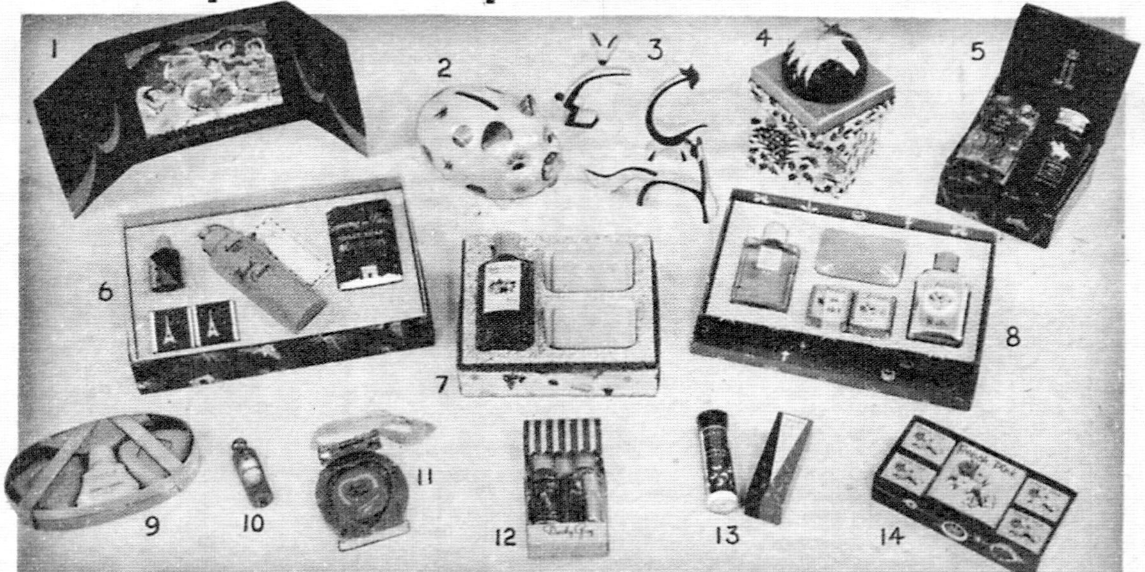

1
2
3
4
5
6
7
8
9
10
11
12
13
14

1. Christmas card of four Gala perfume miniatures, 2s. 6d. 2. A piggy bank from Boots, 5s. 6d. 3. Three unusual ornaments by Boots, one at 4s. 6d., two at 3s. each. 4. Bath soap Christmas pudding, by Bronnley, 7s. 6d. 5. For father: Lentheric's after-shave lotion and talc, 10s. 9d. 6. Bourjois's 'Evening in Paris' coffret, 9s. 7. Morney's bath essence and soap, 8s. 9d. 8. Saville's 'June' coffret, 10s. 3d. 9. Gala's soap and hand lotion at 5s. 3d. 10. Purse Perfume, by Bronnley, 5s. 9d. 11. Outdoor Girl lipstick and Secret Magic, 5s. 9d. 12. Skin perfumes 'Midnight' and 'White Lilac', by Dorothy Gray, 9s. 13. Yardley's crystallized cologne 'Bond Street', 7s. 14. Fields' 'French Pink' soap, bath cubes, 2s. 10d.

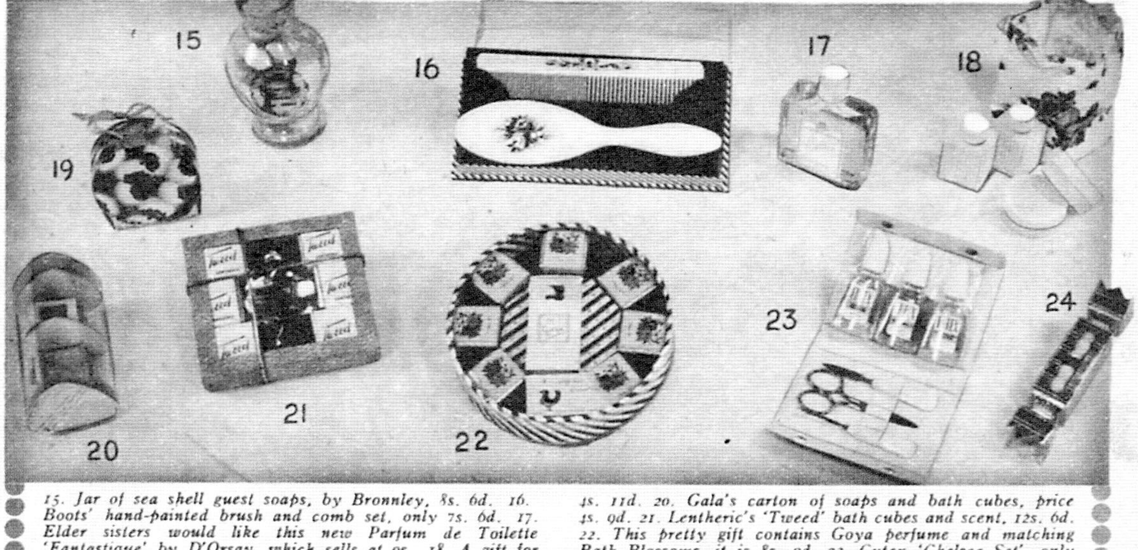

15
16
17
18
19
20
21
22
23
24

15. Jar of sea shell guest soaps, by Bronnley, 8s. 6d. 16. Boots' hand-painted brush and comb set, only 7s. 6d. 17. Elder sisters would like this new Parfum de Toilette 'Fantastique' by D'Orsay, which sells at 9s. 18. A gift for anyone who travels: Boots' plastic kit bag holds five Polythene containers, 5s. 19. 'Airspun' Face Powder by Coty, 4s. 11d. 20. Gala's carton of soaps and bath cubes, price 4s. 9d. 21. Lentheric's 'Tweed' bath cubes and scent, 12s. 6d. 22. This pretty gift contains Goya perfume and matching Bath Blossoms, it is 8s. 9d. 23. Cutex 'Chelsea Set', only 13s. 6d. 24. Goya's Christmas cracker, an ideal gift for a friend, 5s. – in Gardenia, Passport, Black Rose and No. 5.

Registered at the G.P.O. for transmission by Magazine Post to Canada (including Newfoundland). GIRL printed in Great Britain by Eric Bemrose Ltd., Long Lane, Liverpool 9, for the Proprietors

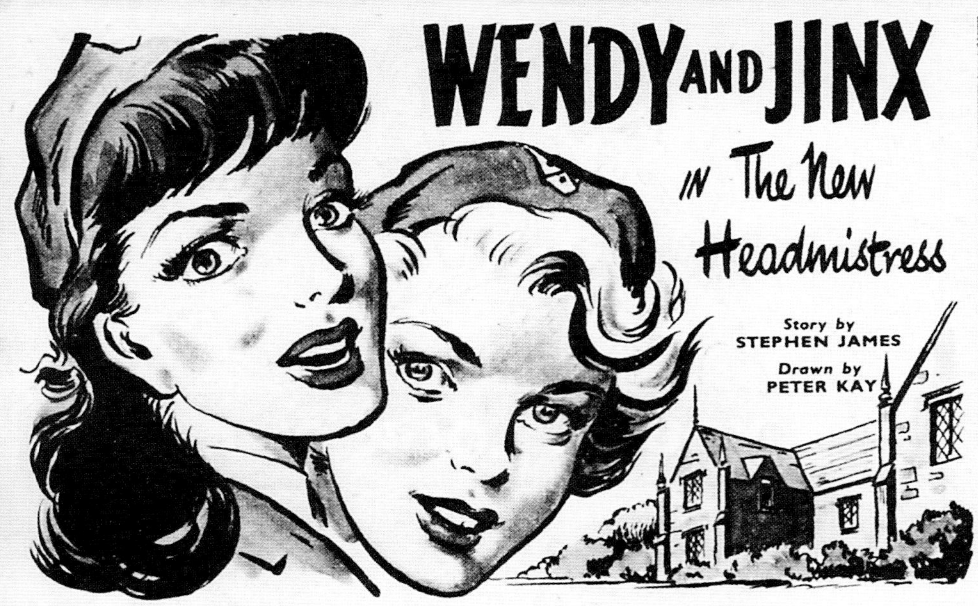
WENDY AND JINX
in The New Headmistress
Story by STEPHEN JAMES
Drawn by PETER KAY

Wendy and Jinx, inseparable friends of Manor School, become estranged when Jinx refuses to join in the activities started by the new headmistress, Miss Kent. This is because Jinx is using all her spare time to earn money in order to help her cousin Peter pay off a huge gambling debt. The whole story finally comes out when Peter falls ill and has to be taken to hospital. Wendy and Jinx, now firmer friends than ever, get together the remainder of the money and pay off Peter's debt, and the good news helps him to get better. Then a measles epidemic breaks out at the school, and Miss Kent is afraid she will have to close it down before the end of term. But Wendy and Jinx have a wonderful idea . . .

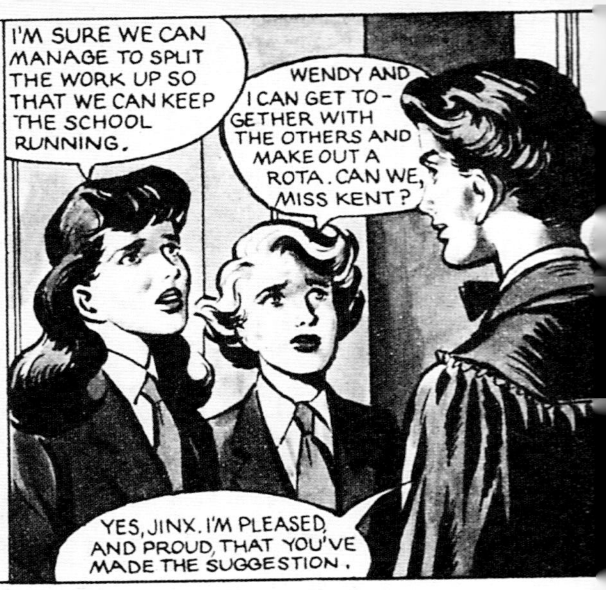
I'M SURE WE CAN MANAGE TO SPLIT THE WORK UP SO THAT WE CAN KEEP THE SCHOOL RUNNING.
WENDY AND I CAN GET TOGETHER WITH THE OTHERS AND MAKE OUT A ROTA. CAN WE, MISS KENT?
YES, JINX. I'M PLEASED, AND PROUD, THAT YOU'VE MADE THE SUGGESTION.

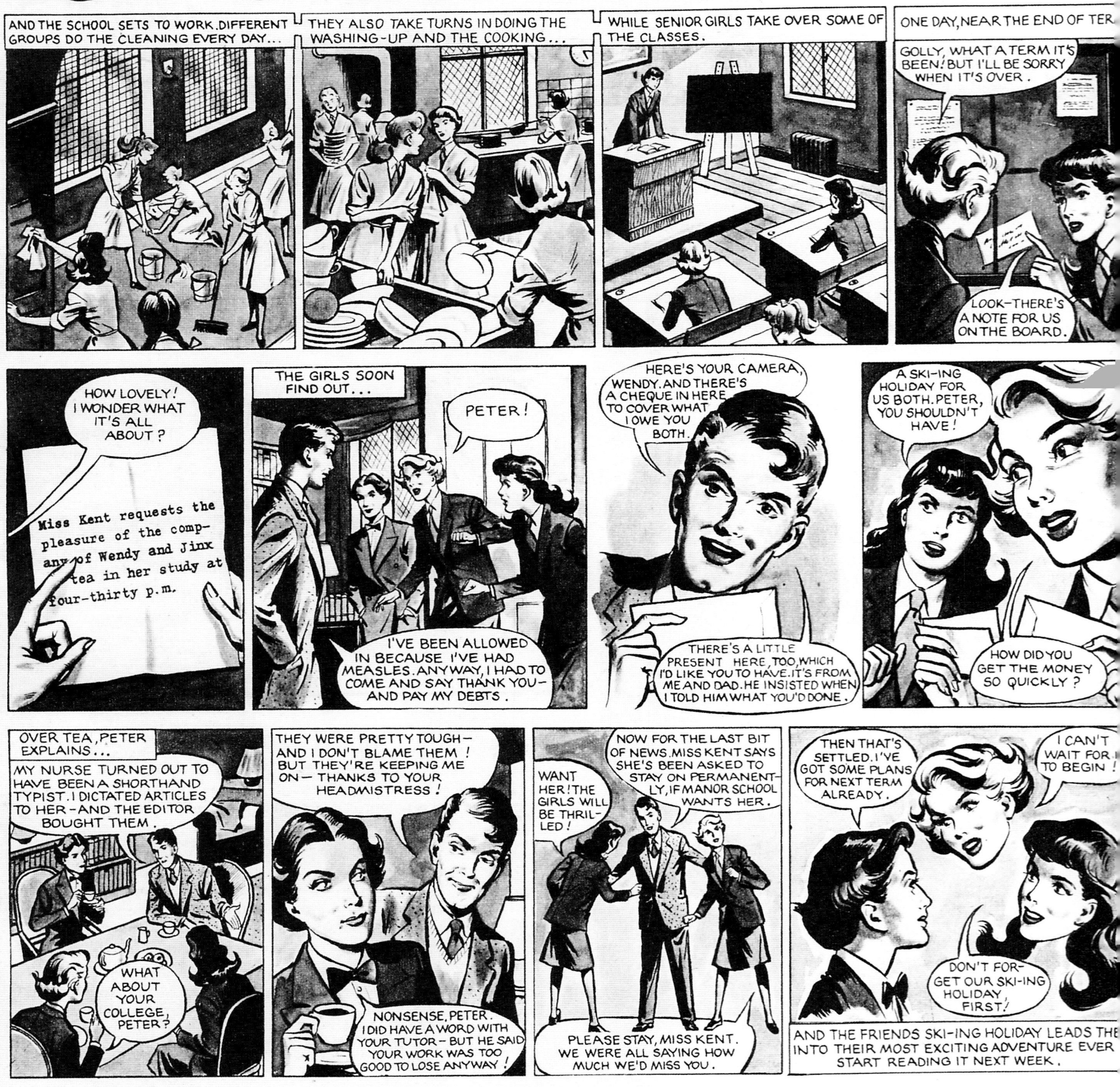
AND THE SCHOOL SETS TO WORK. DIFFERENT GROUPS DO THE CLEANING EVERY DAY...
THEY ALSO TAKE TURNS IN DOING THE WASHING-UP AND THE COOKING...
WHILE SENIOR GIRLS TAKE OVER SOME OF THE CLASSES.
ONE DAY, NEAR THE END OF TER
GOLLY, WHAT A TERM IT'S BEEN! BUT I'LL BE SORRY WHEN IT'S OVER.
LOOK–THERE'S A NOTE FOR US ON THE BOARD.
HOW LOVELY! I WONDER WHAT IT'S ALL ABOUT?
Miss Kent requests the
pleasure of the comp-
any of Wendy and Jinx
tea in her study at
four-thirty p.m.
THE GIRLS SOON FIND OUT...
PETER!
I'VE BEEN ALLOWED IN BECAUSE I'VE HAD MEASLES. ANYWAY, I HAD TO COME AND SAY THANK YOU– AND PAY MY DEBTS.
HERE'S YOUR CAMERA, WENDY. AND THERE'S A CHEQUE IN HERE TO COVER WHAT I OWE YOU BOTH.
THERE'S A LITTLE PRESENT HERE, TOO, WHICH I'D LIKE YOU TO HAVE. IT'S FROM ME AND DAD. HE INSISTED WHEN I TOLD HIM WHAT YOU'D DONE.
A SKI-ING HOLIDAY FOR US BOTH. PETER, YOU SHOULDN'T HAVE!
HOW DID YOU GET THE MONEY SO QUICKLY?
OVER TEA, PETER EXPLAINS...
MY NURSE TURNED OUT TO HAVE BEEN A SHORTHAND TYPIST. I DICTATED ARTICLES TO HER–AND THE EDITOR BOUGHT THEM.
WHAT ABOUT YOUR COLLEGE, PETER?
THEY WERE PRETTY TOUGH– AND I DON'T BLAME THEM! BUT THEY'RE KEEPING ME ON– THANKS TO YOUR HEADMISTRESS!
NONSENSE, PETER. I DID HAVE A WORD WITH YOUR TUTOR–BUT HE SAID YOUR WORK WAS TOO GOOD TO LOSE ANYWAY!
NOW FOR THE LAST BIT OF NEWS. MISS KENT SAYS SHE'S BEEN ASKED TO STAY ON PERMANENTLY, IF MANOR SCHOOL WANTS HER.
WANT HER! THE GIRLS WILL BE THRILLED!
PLEASE STAY, MISS KENT. WE WERE ALL SAYING HOW MUCH WE'D MISS YOU.
THEN THAT'S SETTLED. I'VE GOT SOME PLANS FOR NEXT TERM ALREADY.
I CAN'T WAIT FOR I TO BEGIN!
DON'T FORGET OUR SKI-ING HOLIDAY, FIRST!
AND THE FRIENDS SKI-ING HOLIDAY LEADS THE INTO THEIR MOST EXCITING ADVENTURE EVER START READING IT NEXT WEEK.

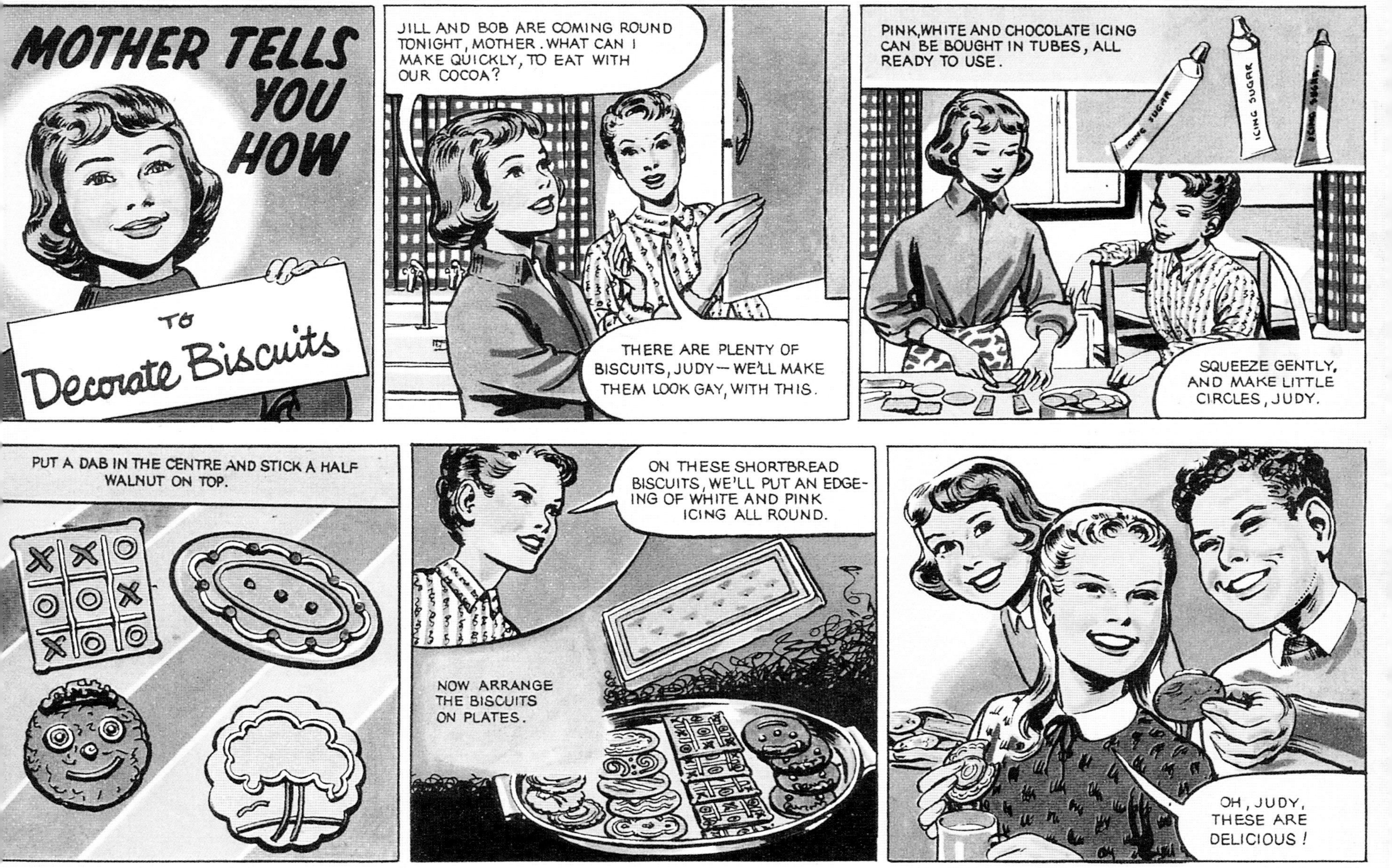
MOTHER TELLS YOU HOW
TO Decorate Biscuits
JILL AND BOB ARE COMING ROUND TONIGHT, MOTHER. WHAT CAN I MAKE QUICKLY, TO EAT WITH OUR COCOA?
THERE ARE PLENTY OF BISCUITS, JUDY — WE'LL MAKE THEM LOOK GAY, WITH THIS.
PINK, WHITE AND CHOCOLATE ICING CAN BE BOUGHT IN TUBES, ALL READY TO USE.
ICING SUGAR
SQUEEZE GENTLY, AND MAKE LITTLE CIRCLES, JUDY.
PUT A DAB IN THE CENTRE AND STICK A HALF WALNUT ON TOP.
ON THESE SHORTBREAD BISCUITS, WE'LL PUT AN EDGE-ING OF WHITE AND PINK ICING ALL ROUND.
NOW ARRANGE THE BISCUITS ON PLATES.
OH, JUDY, THESE ARE DELICIOUS !

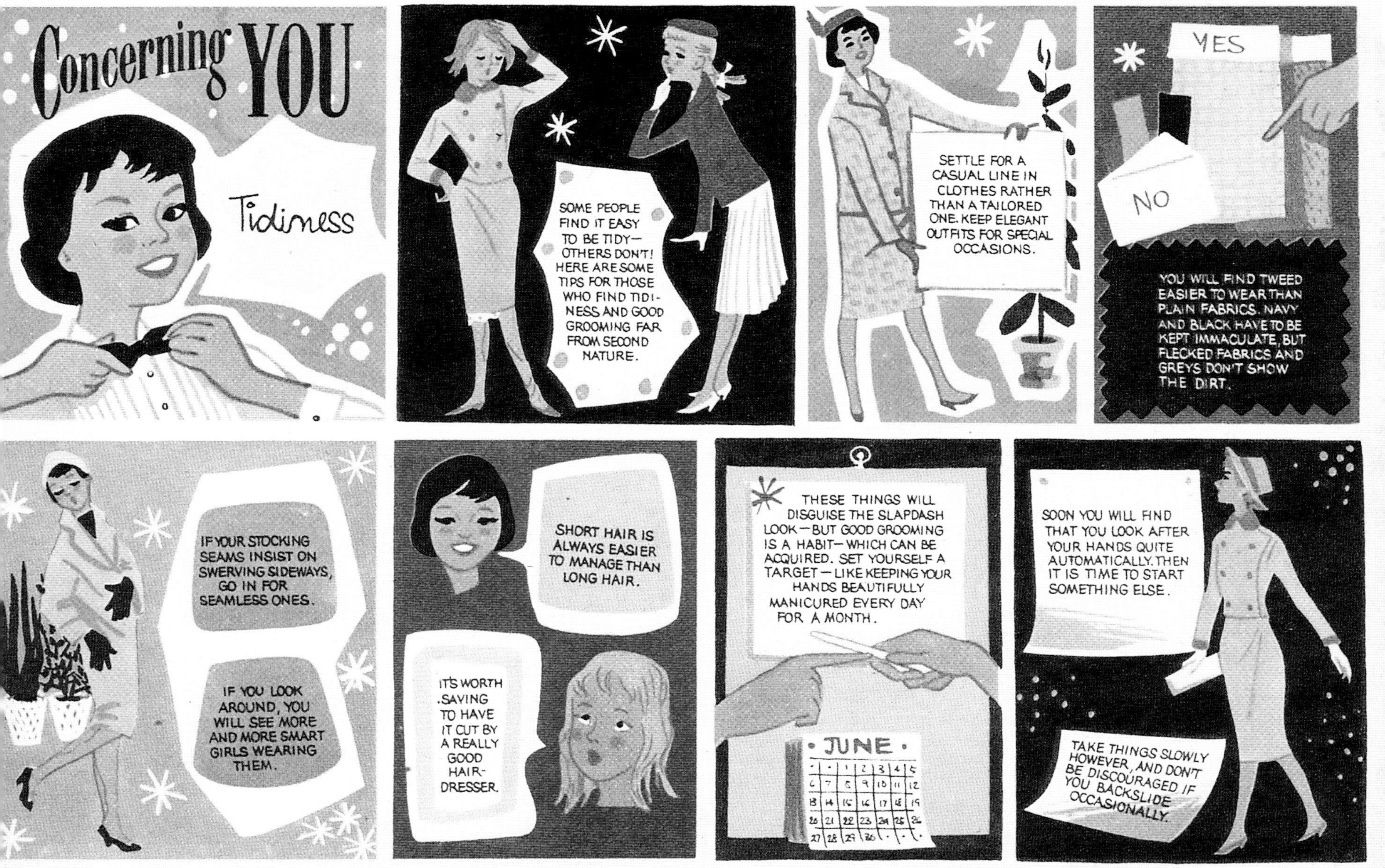
Concerning YOU
Tidiness
SOME PEOPLE FIND IT EASY TO BE TIDY— OTHERS DON'T! HERE ARE SOME TIPS FOR THOSE WHO FIND TIDI-NESS AND GOOD GROOMING FAR FROM SECOND NATURE.
SETTLE FOR A CASUAL LINE IN CLOTHES RATHER THAN A TAILORED ONE. KEEP ELEGANT OUTFITS FOR SPECIAL OCCASIONS.
YES
NO
YOU WILL FIND TWEED EASIER TO WEAR THAN PLAIN FABRICS. NAVY AND BLACK HAVE TO BE KEPT IMMACULATE, BUT FLECKED FABRICS AND GREYS DON'T SHOW THE DIRT.
IF YOUR STOCKING SEAMS INSIST ON SWERVING SIDEWAYS, GO IN FOR SEAMLESS ONES.
IF YOU LOOK AROUND, YOU WILL SEE MORE AND MORE SMART GIRLS WEARING THEM.
SHORT HAIR IS ALWAYS EASIER TO MANAGE THAN LONG HAIR.
IT'S WORTH SAVING TO HAVE IT CUT BY A REALLY GOOD HAIR-DRESSER.
THESE THINGS WILL DISGUISE THE SLAPDASH LOOK — BUT GOOD GROOMING IS A HABIT — WHICH CAN BE ACQUIRED. SET YOURSELF A TARGET — LIKE KEEPING YOUR HANDS BEAUTIFULLY MANICURED EVERY DAY FOR A MONTH.
JUNE
SOON YOU WILL FIND THAT YOU LOOK AFTER YOUR HANDS QUITE AUTOMATICALLY. THEN IT IS TIME TO START SOMETHING ELSE.
TAKE THINGS SLOWLY HOWEVER, AND DON'T BE DISCOURAGED IF YOU BACKSLIDE OCCASIONALLY.

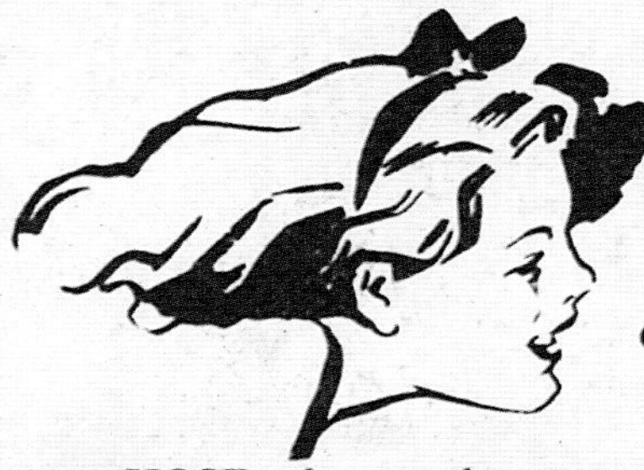

A Letter from the Editor

GIRL OFFICE, 161/166 FLEET STREET, LONDON, E.C.4.

THOSE of you who went to the Boys and Girls Exhibition last month are bound to have paid a visit to the Fashion Theatre. Do you remember the GIRL Sweater which was modelled then? It has been specially designed for GIRL by the Hand Knitting Wool Council and you'll find a picture of it on Page 14 next week – together with full instructions on how to get a free copy of the pattern. Look out for it – it's a very good design and you will all want to knit it for yourselves.

This week, on Page 14, our experts are writing about the question of crushes, which most people have to deal with at one time or another. If you have any problems of this kind – or of any kind, for that matter – our experts will be only too pleased to help if you write to them.

Yours sincerely,

Marcus Morris

READERS' LETTERS

5/- will be paid for every reader's letter printed on this page

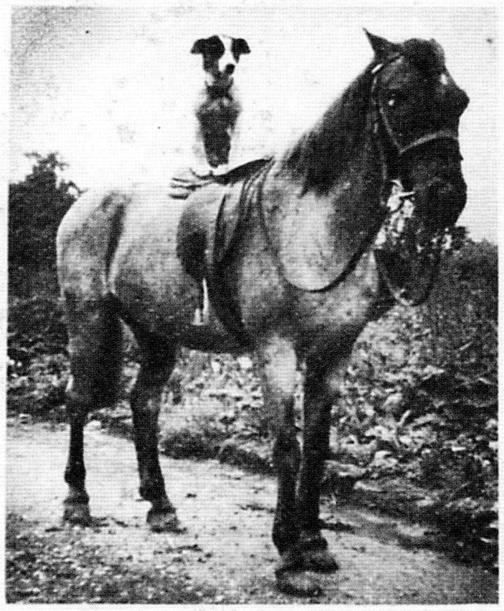

Tosca goes riding

I WAS very interested in a reader's letter in GIRL some time ago, about her dog Kim riding the seventeen-hand practice horses. I have a fox terrier called Tosca, who loves to ride my pony, Lassie, who is 13 hands high.

Tosca jumps on by himself, and he can stay on at a walk, trot or canter. He loves to come with me on foot when I go for rides, and if I do not take him with me he pines for a long time. If he is loose in the garden and I go for a ride, he always follows me. He can ride bare-back or with a saddle. – *Judith Evans, Shrewsbury.*

★ ★ ★ ★ ★ ★ ★ ★

Anne's pets are all called after GIRL characters

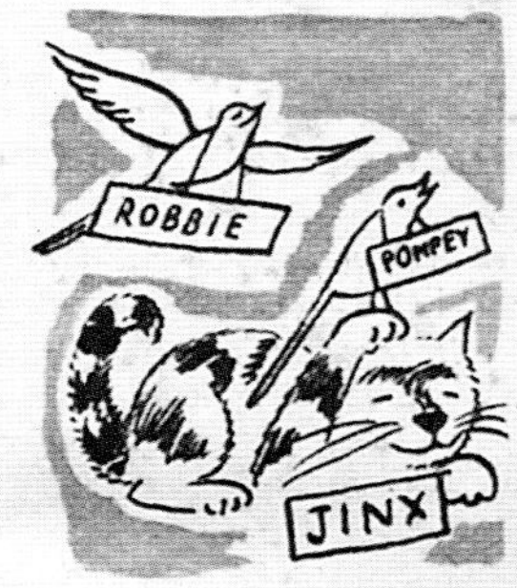
ROBBIE
POMPEY
JINX

I am writing to tell you about my pets. I have two budgies and a kitten. They have all been named after people in our GIRL paper. The budgies are called Robbie and Pompey and our third one, which died a few weeks ago, was called Vicky. The kitten is called Jinx and she is very lively and naughty sometimes. She is a tortoiseshell cat and very pretty. The birds are also very pretty. Robbie is green and yellow and Pompey is turquoise with lovely pale lemon trimmings; he is very unusual.

Vicky was a lovely turquoise blue with a white head. I expect I shall get another bird, and I shall certainly call it after another famous GIRL character. Have any other GIRL readers got pets named like these?

Anne Herdman, Sutton, Surrey.

FILM STAR SPECIAL

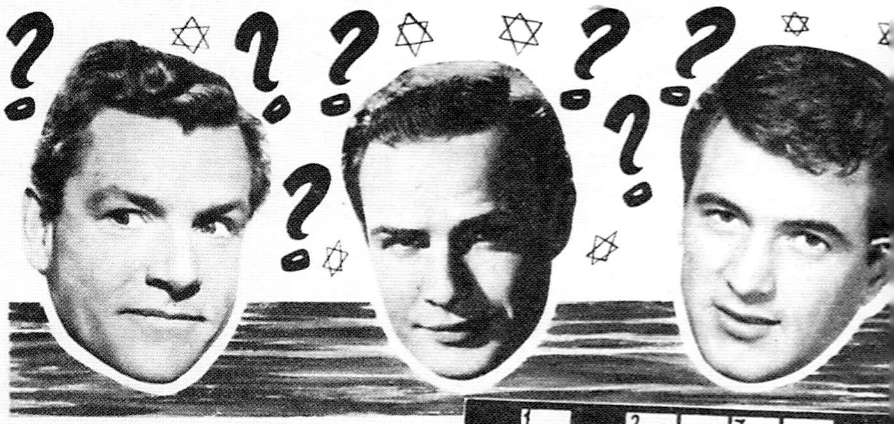

60 DRESSING-TABLE SETS TO BE WON!

Now, you film fans – here's your chance to win one of the 60 lovely Spa dressing-table sets which we are offering as prizes to the winners of this week's competition. Each set consists of a pretty pastel coloured comb, brush and mirror. Not only would they look charming on your dressing-table, but they're a 'must' for good grooming. So set to work now and solve our simple film star crossword.

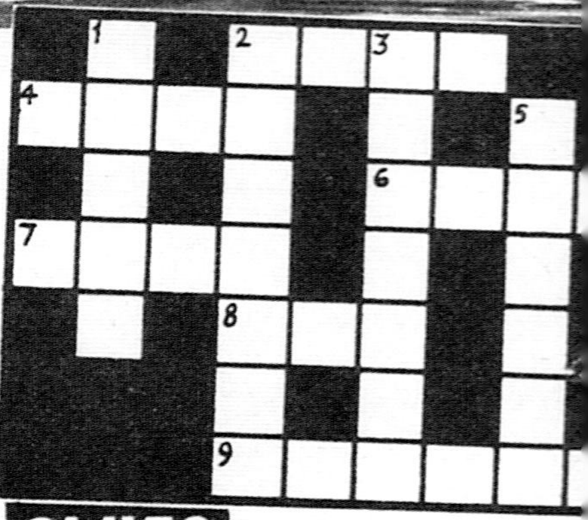

CLUES

ACROSS

2. . . . . Douglas
4. Danny . . . .
6. . . . . Grant
7. . . . . Mills
8. . . . Bartok
9. Rock . . . . . .

DOWN

1. James . . . . .
2. . . . . More
3. . . . . Basehear
5. Marlon . . . .

HERE ARE THE RULES

When you have solved this week's crossword, either copy it or cut it out and paste it on a postcard – remembering to add your name, age and address. Post it to: GIRL Competition No. 39, GIRL Reader Services, Long Lane, Aintree, Liverpool 9, to arrive not later than 6th October. Age and neatness will be taken into consideration in the judging, and all girls under 17 are eligible. The Editor's decision is final. No correspondence will be entered into.

WINNERS

There are many happy hours in store for the fifteen winners of GIRL Competition No. 24, who each won a Slazenger Tennis Racket. They are: Ann Billing of Kent, Christine Challis of Warwickshire, Pamela Grant of London, Carolyn A. Hicks of Essex, Rosemarie A. Hams of Hants., Mair Jenkins of Glamorgan, Evelyn Mitchell of Edinburgh, Kathleen McIntoch of Aberdeen, Lesley Owen of Berks., Pauline O'Dea of Southampton, Christine Russell of Rutland, Margaret A. Shaw of Kent, Jean Vallance of Derbyshire, Susan B. Walters of Devon and Rita Yeates of Southampton.

PEOPLE TO PEOPLE

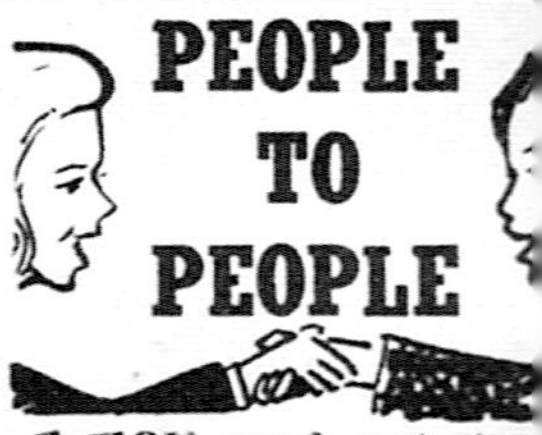

YOU need not tra abroad to meet pe from other countries learn about their way of **A special week of Internati Friendship – called 'Peopl People Week' – is b arranged in Britain from September to 4th October. is your chance to make frie with children from abroad.**

There are probably som your school, so why not your mother if you can h one home to tea? If you wo like help in finding some you can ask a clergyman write to the Internatic Friendship League at Pe Haven, Creswick Road, Ac London, W.3.

By the way, the Internatic Friendship League will be happy to arrange a pen-frie with similar hobbies to y own, in almost any part of world. Just write to th giving all the information ab yourself you can think of, telling them which count interest you particularly.

TEAM PRIZE

I also wish to represent my School/Club in the TEAM Competition.

School or Club . . . .

Address . . . .

INDIVIDUAL ENTRY

Complete this form in ink, using BLOCK LETTERS, and post it to: EAGLE/GIRL Table Tennis Championship, Hulton House, Fleet Street, London, E.C.4, before 13th October, 1958.

Surname . . . .

Christian Names . . . .

Address . . . .

. . . .

Date of Birth: . . . . . . **Day** . . . . . . **Month** . . . . . . **Year**

The event I wish to enter *(strike out event not applicable)*

1. Girls' Singles *(under 15 years on 1st September, 1958)*

2. Girls' Singles *(under 13 years on 1st September, 1958)*

I wish to play my qualifying round at . . . .

(Enter above: LONDON, BIRMINGHAM, MANCHESTER, LIVERPOOL, BRISTOL, CARDIFF or EDINBURGH or, if you are unable to play at any of those main centres, enter instead the name of your nearest large town.)

I ACCEPT THE CONDITIONS OF ENTRY

Signature of Parent, Guardian or Teacher . . . .

Your Signature . . . .

THERE IS STILL TIME!

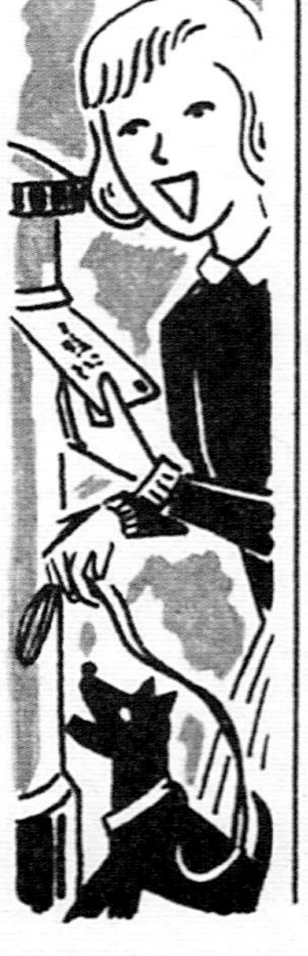

Yes, there is still time to enter our EAGLE/GIRL Table Tennis Championship, if you have not yet had an opportunity to do so. Entry is FREE and open to all readers in Great Britain who are under fifteen years of age on 1st September, 1958.

There are team as well as individual prizes to be won. Fill in the entry form NOW – the team portion, too, if you would like to help your school or club win a super table. However, remember that this form should only be completed if you are not taking part in your own school or club Qualifying Tournament. If you think your school or club would like to organize its own Qualifying Tournament ask your school-teacher or club leader to send a postcard to: Admin. Secretary, EAGLE/GIRL Table Tennis Championship, 161, Fleet Street, London, E.C.4. He will supply full details.

PERSONAL PAGE

This is a problem that many girls worry about

HAVING A 'CRUSH'

At some time during their school reer, most girls get a crush on a acher, or an older girl. What *is* crush? It is an intense feeling of fection and admiration. The girl 10 has a crush finds herself often inking about the person she ces; she is eager to be near her, d very much wants to be liked her. These feelings usually come a surprise, because the girl who s a crush for the first time can- t remember ever before feeling ite so intensely about another rson. And probably she hasn't, cause, during the teens, the notions become more intense. at is what makes a crush a com- etely new kind of experience.

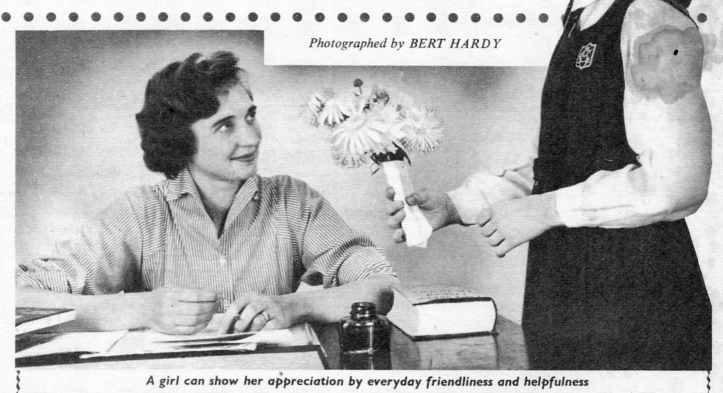

Photographed by BERT HARDY

A girl can show her appreciation by everyday friendliness and helpfulness

CRUSHES are normal and are nothing to feel anxious or ashamed about. But they can lead to difficulties. Just because the experience is new, the girl is likely to have problems about dealing with it. For example, she is tempted to wander around, using every stratagem to be with the person she admires. But, if she yields to that temptation, she may make her feelings so obvious that the object of her admiration may become embarrassed and aloof. Then she will be hurt. A better way is to take what opportunities come naturally of being together.

That leads to another problem – conversation. Some girls long to be with their crush, only to find, when they are with her, that they are tongue-tied. A certain amount of embarrassment is unavoidable, but it can be kept within bounds if the girl does not become too much wrapped up in thinking about her crush. *She should certainly not neglect her other friends and interests.* Then, once the ice is broken, when she meets her crush there will be plenty to talk about.

A full and active life is the best basis for lively conversation. The girls with a crush who find conversation most difficult are the ones who mope around so much that their life is empty except for their crush.

How can a girl tell whether the person she likes likes her? This is a difficult one. What she would like is some special sign from her crush. But a teacher, or senior girl, has to be careful not to seem to have favourites so, whether or not she knows the girl concerned is fond of her, she cannot treat her in a special way. In fact, hard as it will appear to her, the girl with a crush will have to be content to be treated like the others.

Then the question arises of how the girl may show her liking. The answer is – in simple, unobtrusive ways. A teacher will always be glad to receive a card from a pupil who is on holiday, or a greeting at Christmas. In such simple ways, and by everyday friendliness and helpfulness, a girl can show her appreciation without being obtrusive.

How about the teasing of friends? The rule of fair play is 'Do as you would be done by'. No girl likes to have her private feelings made fun of, so it is a little mean to take it out of those who have made it rather plain what their private feelings are. Don't you agree?

What's Your Worry?

A crush on an older girl

Q. My friend and I have a crush on an older girl who is going to live abroad. Do you think we should ask her to go out with us before she leaves and do you think we should write to her?

A. If you know her quite well already, we see no reason why you should not ask her to go out with you. She may not say yes, and you must not be worried if she doesn't. We think she will probably be a little lonely at first when she is away from England and we feel sure she will be glad to have news of her old school. But don't expect her to reply as often as you write. She will be sure to be much occupied adjusting herself to life abroad.

★ ★ ★

Teachers are human beings

Q. Do you think teachers are fair?

A. Mostly they are, but not always. They are human beings too, you know. It is very hard for any of us to be absolutely fair all the time.

FOR GIRL ADVENTURERS

Star Adventurer of the Month

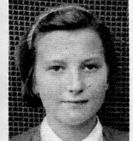

10-year-old Ann Baldwin of Bewdley, Worcestershire, has shown a sense of responsibility of a very high order on two occasions when her mother was in hospital. Her many tasks have included taking care of her baby brother, getting meals for her father and looking after the poultry. Ann has shown exceptional organizing ability by fitting in all the extra jobs as well as carrying on with her school work as usual. Ann has been selected as Star Adventurer of the Month for December.

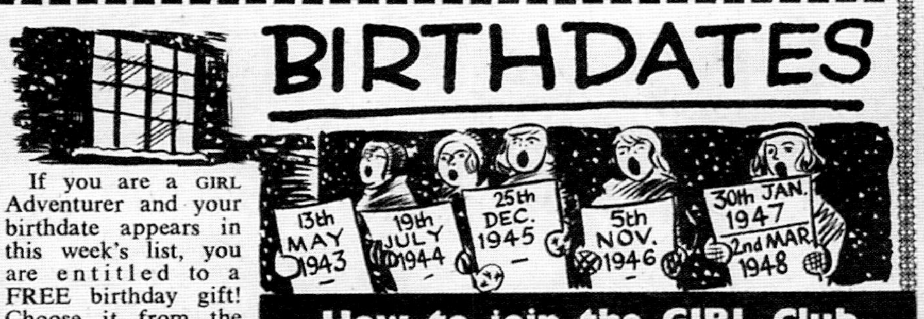

BIRTHDATES
13th MAY 1943
19th JULY 1944
25th DEC. 1945
5th NOV. 1946
30th JAN. 1947
2nd MAR. 1948

If you are a GIRL Adventurer and your birthdate appears in this week's list, you are entitled to a FREE birthday gift! Choose it from the following: **GIRL handbag badge, stamp album, propelling pencil, GIRL autograph book, bicycle bell, ballpoint pen or coloured pencils.** State your choice on a postcard, giving us your name, address, Club number and the date you were born. Send it to: BIRTHDATES (51), GIRL Club, Long Lane, Liverpool 9, to reach us by Tuesday, 23rd December. Overseas members whose birthdates appear here will automatically be sent a present.

How to join the GIRL Club

Fill in this coupon in block capitals, taking great care to put your full address. Then send it, with a postal order for 2/- (made payable to Hulton Press Ltd., crossed '& Co.'), to: GIRL Club, Long Lane, Aintree, Liverpool 9.

NAME ....

ADDRESS ....

DATE OF BIRTH..........**Month**..........**Year**..........

I have placed a regular order for GIRL with:

NEWSAGENT'S NAME ....

ADDRESS ....

Address this label to yourself, using block capitals.

NAME ....

ADDRESS ....

GM

Registered at the G.P.O. for transmission by Magazine Post to Canada (including Newfoundland), GIRL printed in Great Britain by Eric Bemrose Ltd., Long Lane, Liverpool 9, for the Proprietors and Publishers, Hulton Press Ltd., 161/166 Fleet Street, London, E.C.4. Sole agents for Australia and New Zealand, Gordon & Gotch (A/sia) Ltd.; South Africa, Central News Agency Ltd. Subscription Rate: Inland, 12 months 28/2; 6 months 14/1; abroad 12 months 26/-; 6 months 13/-. Postage for single copies: Inland 2d.; Foreign 1½d.; Canada 1d. You can have GIRL sent to any address in this

Concerning YOU
SHOPPING HINTS
NEVER BUY A COAT OR SUIT WITHOUT SITTING DOWN IN IT FIRST. THIS TEST WILL TELL YOU WHETHER A SKIRT HAS EASE OF MOVEMENT AND IF A COAT HAS A LARGE ENOUGH WRAPOVER.
IF ALTERATIONS ARE NECESSARY, MAKE SURE THAT THEY WILL NOT SPOIL THE PROPORTIONS OF THE GARMENT. THINK TWICE ABOUT BUYING A SUIT IF THE JACKET NEEDS EXTENSIVE ALTERATIONS.
WHEN SHOPPING FOR A SWEATER OR A TWINSET, BUY A SIZE LARGER THAN YOUR BUST MEASUREMENT. CLOSE-FITTING KNITWEAR IS NOT SMART, AND IF IT SHOULD SHRINK EVEN SLIGHTLY THE GARMENT BECOMES UNWEARABLE.
MOST SWEATERS HAVE WASHING INSTRUCTIONS ATTACHED TO THEM. IF YOU DO NOT SEE ANY, ASK THE ASSISTANT.
WHEN CHOOSING SHOES, COMFORT COMES FIRST. ALWAYS REJECT SHOES, HOWEVER ATTRACTIVE THEY ARE, IF THEY HURT ANYWHERE. IF YOU ARE BEWILDERED BY A WIDE CHOICE OF STYLES, ALWAYS GO FOR THE PLAINEST.
WHEN BUYING MATERIAL FOR A DRESS, REMEMBER THAT FLUORESCENT LIGHTING ALTERS COLOURS. ALWAYS TEST THEM IN DAYLIGHT BEFORE BUYING THE FABRIC.

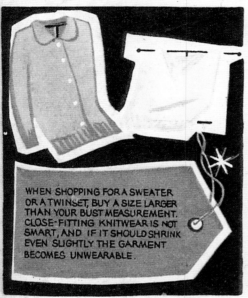

RESULTS

This is the news you have all been waiting for!

GIRL Ballet Scholarship Scheme

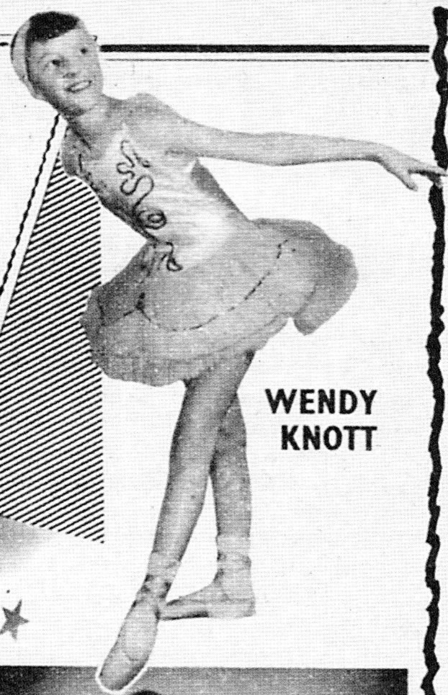

WENDY KNOTT

Every year, in association with the Royal Academy of Dancing, GIRL magazine awards dancing scholarships to the Royal Academy of Dancing. This entitles the holders to two free ballet lessons a week at their nearest R.A.D. Scholarship Centre. Here are the names of this year's Royal Academy of Dancing Scholarship winners: –

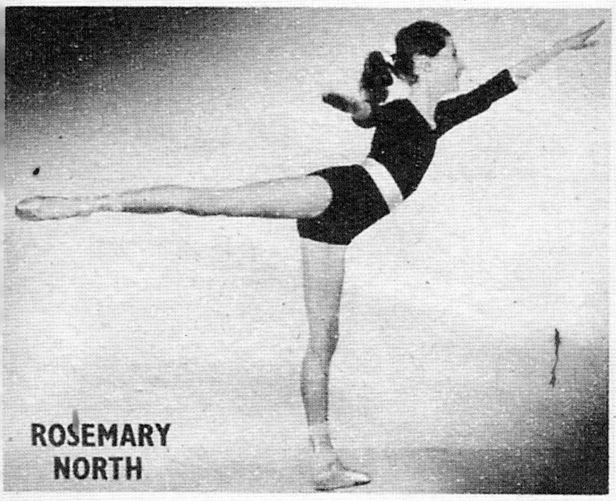

ROSEMARY NORTH

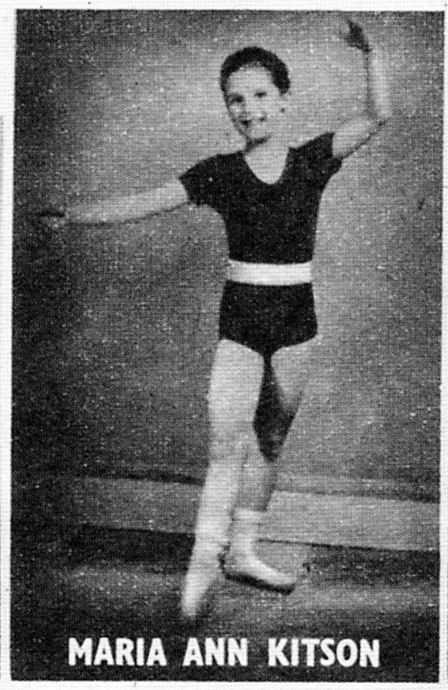

MARIA ANN KITSON

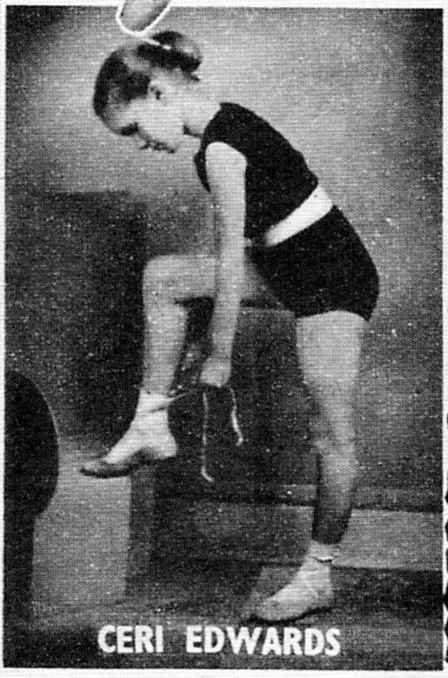

CERI EDWARDS

Yvonne Quin, *Northolt, Middlesex.*
Andrea Rutherford, *St. Mary Cray, Kent.*
Wendy Knott, *Rochester, Kent.*
Angela Savill, *Dagenham, Essex.*
Diane Winnett, *Rayleigh, Essex.*
Elizabeth Hurst, *Ewell, Surrey.*
Beverley Wallis, *Southend-on-Sea, Essex.*
Carol Burke, *Roath, Cardiff.*
Ann Kitson, *Newport, Mon.*
Vivienne Robinson, *Sketty, Swansea, Glam.*
Janet Ladd, *Ely, Cardiff.*
Susan Theodore, *Bridgend, Glam.*
Ceri Edwards, *Penmaen, Blackwood, Mon.*
Gillian Reed, *Sully, nr. Penarth, Glam.*
Diane Tremeer, *West Pontnewydd, Newport.*
Denise Chapple, *Hengrove, Bristol 4.*
Marion Slark, *Clifton, Bristol 8.*
Charlotte Onslow, *Rangeworthy, Glos.*
Judith McDonald, *Horfield, Bristol 7.*
Pia Harper, *Compton Greenfield, nr. Bristol.*
Anne Begley, *Filton, Bristol.*
Gay Phillips, *Filton, Bristol.*
Anne Morgan, *Henbury, Bristol.*
Linda Durrant, *Boscombe, Bournemouth, Hants.*
Marilyn Hewlett, *Weston-super-Mare, Somerset.*
Denise Witcomb, *Sutton Coldfield, Warwick.*
Angela Errington, *Ledbury, Herefordshire.*
Yvonne Pike, *Birmingham 1.*
Anna Smith, *Birmingham 34.*
Diane Cook, *Great Barr, Birmingham 22A.*
Sheryll Stringfellow, *Mansfield, Notts.*
Penelope Perry, *Enderby, Leicester.*
Linda Carpenter, *Old Basford, Nottingham.*
Rosemary North, *Mansfield, Notts.*
Lesley Mason, *Glapwell, Chesterfield, Derbys.*
Ann Du Boisson, *Lincoln.*
Deirdre Lee, *Woodthorpe, Notts.*
Jacqueline Hamer, *Walshaw, nr. Bury, Lancs.*
Jacqueline Kelly, *Woolfold, Bury, Lancs.*
Susan Lamb, *Levenshulme, Manchester 19.*
Gaynor Ward, *Denton, Manchester.*
Susan Chippendale, *Colne, Lancs.*
Barbara Stones, *Farnworth, Lancs.*
Pamela Calf, *Rusholme, Manchester 14.*
Judith Abbott, *Bank Top, Bolton, Lancs.*
Bronwen Cross, *Leeds 16.*
Elizabeth Ridehalgh, *Scarborough, Yorks.*
Ann Curry, *Baildon, Shipley, Yorks.*
Helen Firth, *Leeds 11.*
Valerie Hunt, *Scunthorpe, Lincs.*
Stella Wilson, *Middleton, Pickering, Yorks.*
Anne Parr, *Oakes, Huddersfield, Yorks.*
Sylvia Barker, *Skipton, Yorks.*
Gladys Hand, *West View Estate, Hartlepool.*
Enid Ingram, *West Hartlepool, Co. Durham.*
Pamela Buckley, *Fulwell, Sunderland.*
Heather Forster, *Ashington, Northumberland.*
Gwenda Garvey, *Sunderland, Co. Durham.*
Pixie Routh, *Darlington, Co. Durham.*
Margaret Lindsay, *Edinburgh 9.*
Jean Halliday, *Edinburgh 9.*
Fiona Grant, *Edinburgh 9.*
Jeannette Henderson, *Prestonpans.*
Alice Wilson, *Edinburgh 9*
Iris Scott, *Edinburgh 5.*
Muriel Guthrie, *Edinburgh 9*
June Smith, *Gilmerton, Edinburgh 9.*

ROYAL BALLET SCHOOL SCHOLARSHIP WINNER

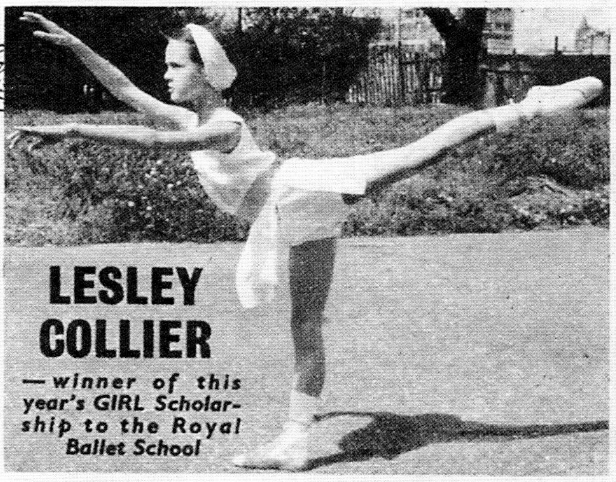

LESLEY COLLIER

— winner of this year's GIRL Scholarship to the Royal Ballet School

The highest award our Scholarship Scheme can offer is a full-time Scholarship to the Royal Ballet School. The candidates are chosen from among the first-year GIRL Scholars of the R.A.D. There is only one Royal Ballet School Scholarship awarded annually, and it is only awarded if the standard is high enough. The candidates for this year's Royal Ballet School Scholarship were: – Sylvia Lock, of Sunderland; Gwyneth Plumb, of Crowborough; Marvyn Parkes, of Ilford; Joan Lewis, of Bridgend; Claire Murthwaite, of Harrow; Pamela Hemstock, of Mansfield; Anne Wheatley, of Nottingham; Elizabeth Field, of London, S.W. 16; Margaret Wilkinson, of Newcastle-upon-Tyne, 7; and Lesley Collier, of Orpington, Kent.

This year the judges were Dame Margot Fonteyn de Arias, D.B.E., Arnold Haskell, C.B.E., Frederick Ashton, Ursula Moreton and Ailne Phillips, and they were all impressed by the high standard shown. However, they unanimously awarded the GIRL Royal Ballet Scholarship to Lesley Collier, of Orpington, whose work they consider shows really great promise. A special GIRL award is also being made to Elizabeth Field, of London, S.W.16. We should like to congratulate all the candidates, both for the Royal Ballet Scholarship and for the Royal Academy of Dancing Scholarships mentioned above, on the very high standard. Good luck to you all!

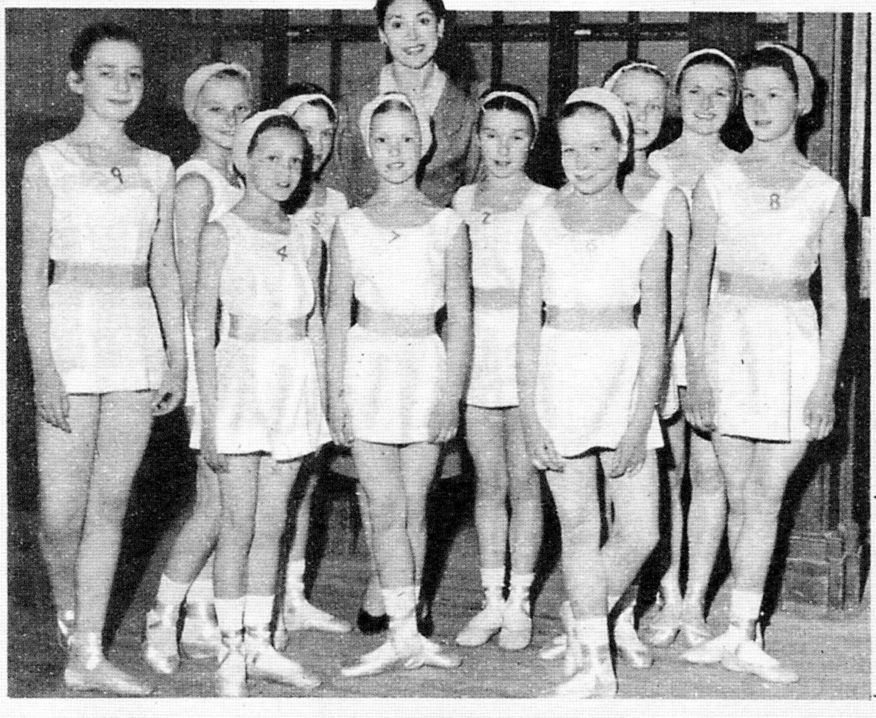

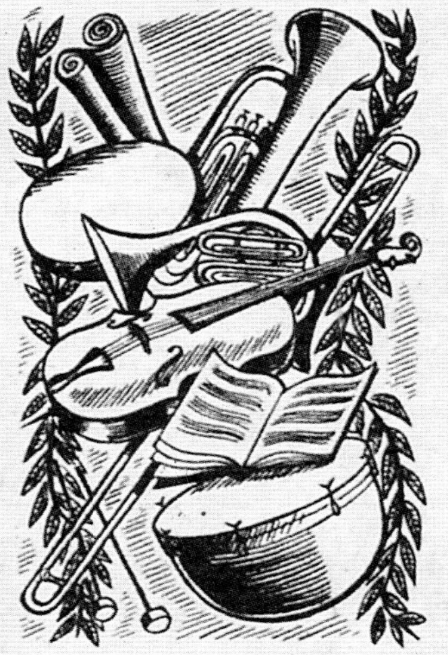

Dame Margot Fonteyn de Arias, D.B.E., President of the Royal Academy of Dancing, and a judge for the Royal Ballet School Audition, is photographed with the candidates.

Registered at the G.P.O. for transmission by Magazine Post to Canada (including Newfoundland). GIRL printed in Great Britain by Eric Bemrose Ltd., Long Lane, Liverpool 9, for the Proprietors

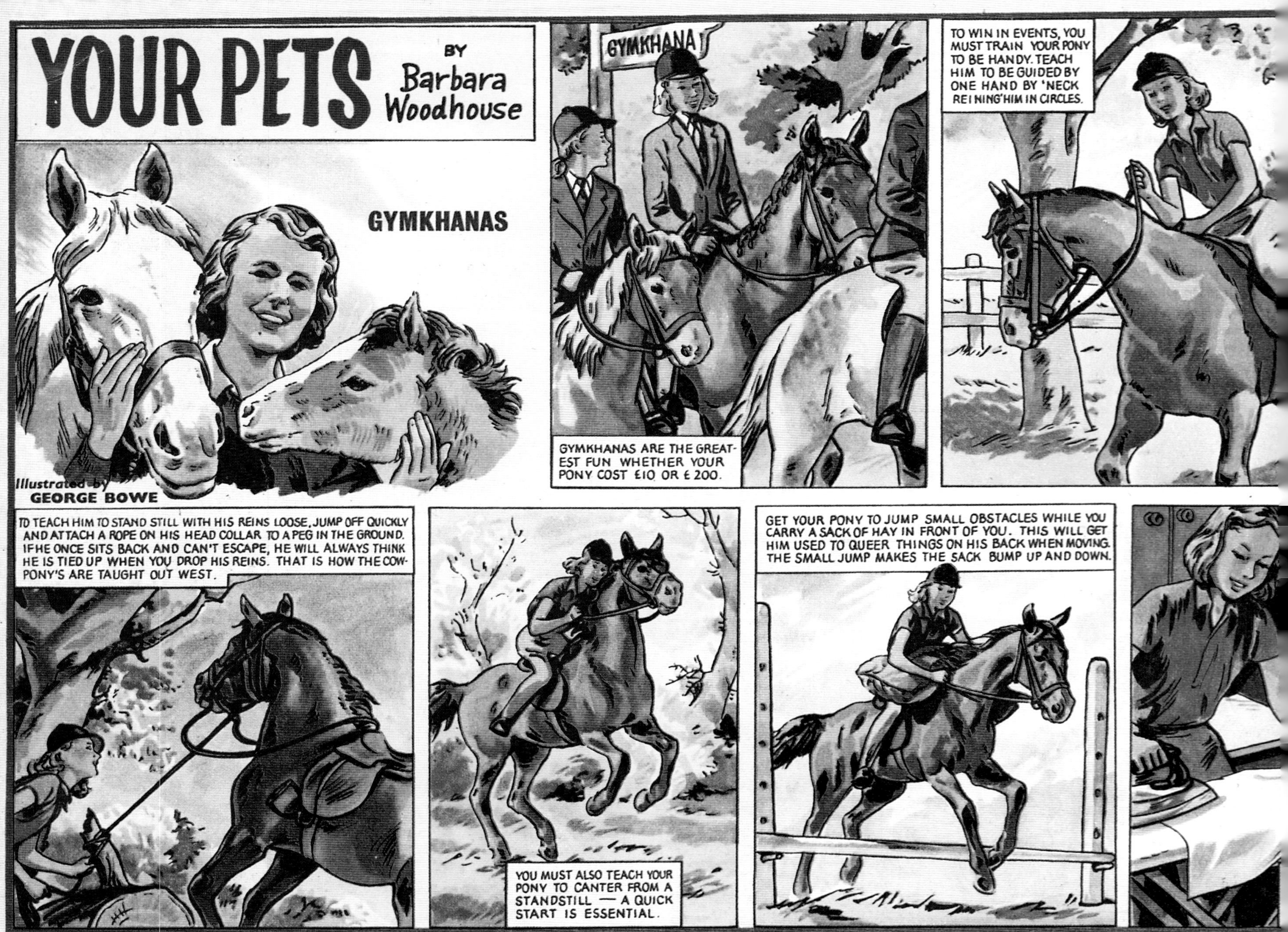
YOUR PETS
BY Barbara Woodhouse
GYMKHANAS
Illustrated by GEORGE BOWE
GYMKHANA
GYMKHANAS ARE THE GREAT-EST FUN WHETHER YOUR PONY COST £10 OR £200.
TO WIN IN EVENTS, YOU MUST TRAIN YOUR PONY TO BE HANDY. TEACH HIM TO BE GUIDED BY ONE HAND BY 'NECK REINING' HIM IN CIRCLES.
TO TEACH HIM TO STAND STILL WITH HIS REINS LOOSE, JUMP OFF QUICKLY AND ATTACH A ROPE ON HIS HEAD COLLAR TO A PEG IN THE GROUND. IF HE ONCE SITS BACK AND CAN'T ESCAPE, HE WILL ALWAYS THINK HE IS TIED UP WHEN YOU DROP HIS REINS. THAT IS HOW THE COW-PONY'S ARE TAUGHT OUT WEST.
YOU MUST ALSO TEACH YOUR PONY TO CANTER FROM A STANDSTILL — A QUICK START IS ESSENTIAL.
GET YOUR PONY TO JUMP SMALL OBSTACLES WHILE YOU CARRY A SACK OF HAY IN FRONT OF YOU. THIS WILL GET HIM USED TO QUEER THINGS ON HIS BACK WHEN MOVING. THE SMALL JUMP MAKES THE SACK BUMP UP AND DOWN.

Look out for CLAU

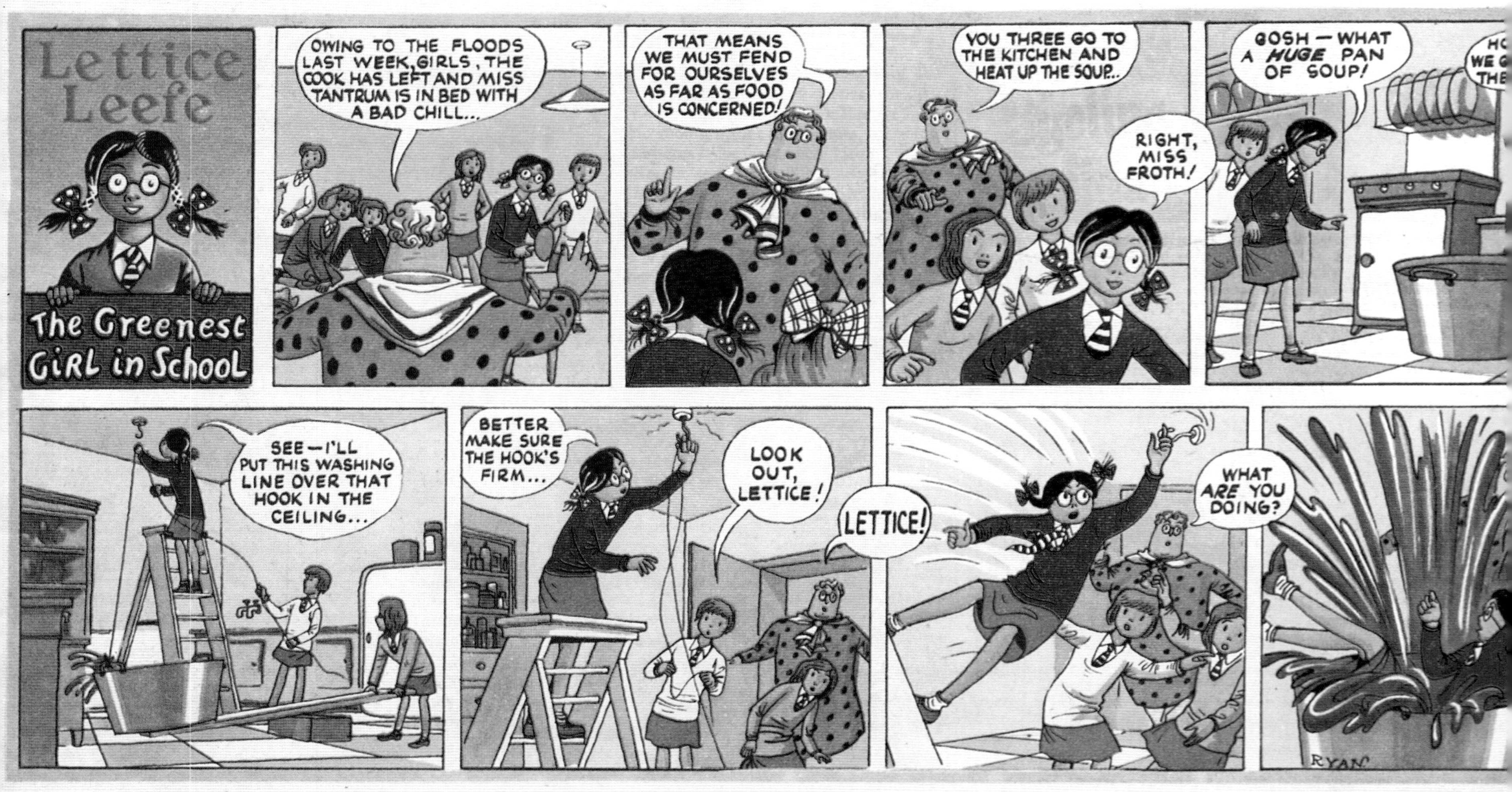
Lettice Leefe
The Greenest GIRL in School
OWING TO THE FLOODS LAST WEEK, GIRLS, THE COOK HAS LEFT AND MISS TANTRUM IS IN BED WITH A BAD CHILL...
THAT MEANS WE MUST FEND FOR OURSELVES AS FAR AS FOOD IS CONCERNED!
YOU THREE GO TO THE KITCHEN AND HEAT UP THE SOUP...
RIGHT, MISS FROTH!
GOSH — WHAT A HUGE PAN OF SOUP!
SEE — I'LL PUT THIS WASHING LINE OVER THAT HOOK IN THE CEILING...
BETTER MAKE SURE THE HOOK'S FIRM...
LOOK OUT, LETTICE!
LETTICE!
WHAT ARE YOU DOING?
RYAN

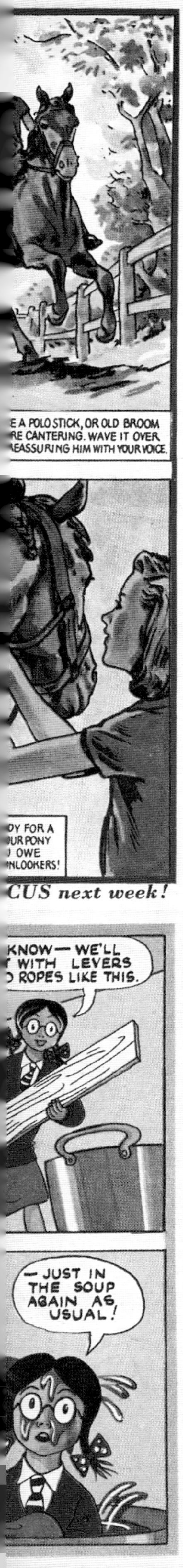
E A POLO STICK, OR OLD BROOM
RE CANTERING. WAVE IT OVER
REASSURING HIM WITH YOUR VOICE.
DY FOR A
UR PONY
U OWE
NLOOKERS!
CUS next week!
KNOW—WE'LL
WITH LEVERS
D ROPES LIKE THIS.
—JUST IN
THE SOUP
AGAIN AS
USUAL!

Girl Picture Gallery

No. 304

Here, in response to your repeated requests for a 'horsey' picture, is a charming study of a mare with her foal.

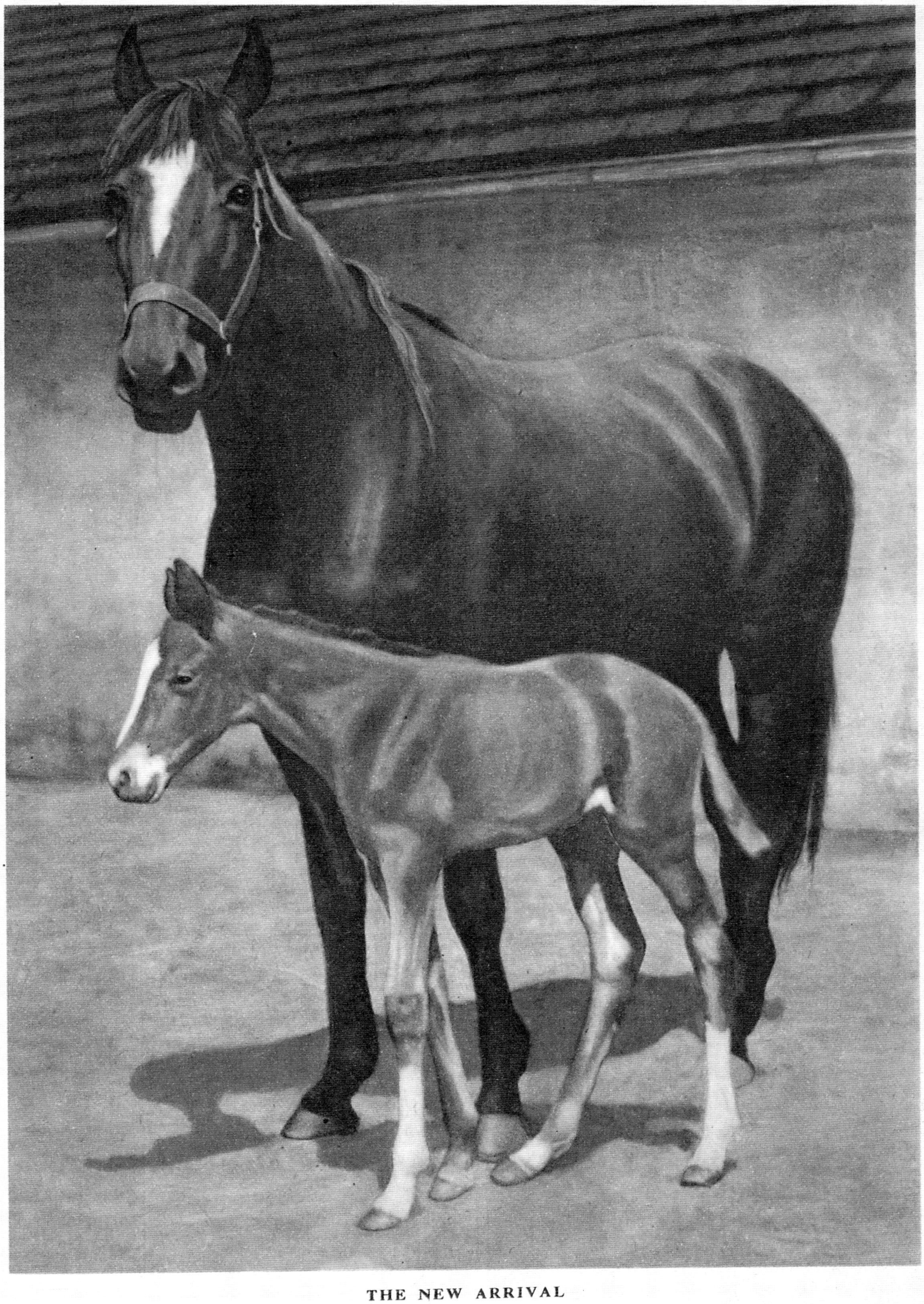

THE NEW ARRIVAL

PERSONAL PAGE

VIRGINIA GRAY tells you how to make it a

BEAUTIFUL CHRISTMAS

CHRISTMAS is here – the season you've looked forward to with such excitement. It's the time for parties, family celebrations – and having fun. Of course, it's a busy time, and you may find yourself the focus of critical observation by relatives you hardly know – which is always a bit of a strain. I can't tell you how to Deal with Relatives, but I can suggest ways of looking your best on this very special day.

If you have neglected your basic beauty chores during the past weeks and have developed spots, now is not the time to fuss about them. Spots are spots and can only be disguised. Don't aggravate the trouble by messing about with them; just dab with an antiseptic lotion and disguise with calomine. If you have no calomine, then beg or borrow some tinted face cream from mother, and apply it as an emergency measure only. Spots thrive on creams, remember, so put calomine lotion on your shopping list.

You are going to have a great deal of rich food during the day, so keep breakfast as simple as possible. Fruit alone should be sufficient to keep all but the most ravenous going, but if you do need something more filling, keep fat to a minimum.

Brush your way to beauty

Give five minutes by the clock to hair-brushing, just as soon as you hop out of bed. The exercise of brushing will zip up your circulation and give a glow to your whole body as well as a beautiful gleam to your hair – and you'll find it's quite wonderful how much more manageable hair can be after brushing.

Mother will need a good deal of help in the kitchen and, indeed, the more you give her the happier will be the celebrations. I suggest that you tie your hair in a chiffon scarf to prevent cooking smells clinging to it, and if you can spray the scarf with toilet cologne, so much the better. (Mother may well take a tip from you on this point.) When you've finished the chores, give the shoes you intend to wear a thorough beauty treatment.

I hope you have a pair of gloves to wear while you are doing the grubby work, but if not, dig your nails into a bar of soap to keep dirt out; then, before you make your preparations for dinner, wash something small – hankies or underclothes – in soap flakes. This is a far gentler way of removing deep-seated grime than scrubbing with a nailbrush – and it's equally effective. Do follow it up with an application of hand-cream. It is advisable to keep a jar of your favourite cream or lotion beside the sink, as well as in the bathroom, so that your hands don't get the opportunity to become chapped. Red hands often need massage, for redness can be caused by bad circulation as well as by exposure and failure to protect them while you help with housework.

As a long-term policy, keep half a lemon handy and use it once or twice a day. It will act as a mild skin bleach and, in addition, give a silky softness to your hands.

Last-minute touches are the same for girls of any age. Straight stocking – or sock – seams, a clean hanky, well-brushed clothes – and a little talcum powder on the palms of your hands to absorb perspiration.

Now you're all set to have a wonderful time.

FOUR STEPS TO BEAUTY

Photographed by BERT HARDY

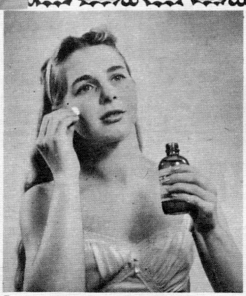

1 Start the day right!

1. Start the day with a long, refreshing drink of fruit juice – hot or cold, whichever you prefer. Fresh fruit is ideal, but the tinned variety is a good substitute. Alternatively, you can try bottled lemon or blackcurrant juice.

2. Cold water is a splendid skin tonic, particularly for the girl with an oily skin. After washing you can either splash with water straight from the tap, or make a little pad of cotton wool, damp it and tap your face and neck with it.

3. To freshen up your hair, push cotton wool soaked in cologne between the bristles of your hairbrush and use it lightly. If mother won't lend you cologne, a spirit setting lotion will do, removing oil and grime, making hair fluffier.

4. For a real before-party treatment, cover your face and neck with cold cream and massage it well into your skin before lathering with soap and water. It makes a soothing emulsion which deep-cleans effectively without over-drying.

2 Dab the odd spot with peroxide (ten volume), to dry it speedily.

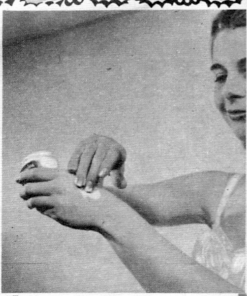

3 Use a medium-soft bristle brush. Harsh treatment never grew long locks.

4 Learn to relax your hands as you use them – it looks feminine and pretty.

Registered at the G.P.O. for transmission by Magazine Post to Canada (including Newfoundland), GIRL printed in Great Britain by Eric Bemrose Ltd., Long Lane, Liverpool 9, for the Proprietors and Publishers, Hulton Press Ltd., 161/166 Fleet Street, London, E.C.4. Sole agents for Australia and New Zealand, Gordon & Gotch (A/sia) Ltd.; South Africa, Central News Agency Ltd. Subscription

ANGELA AIR HOSTESS

the story of a girl who longed for adventure

Written by
BETTY ROLAND
Drawn by
DUDLEY POUT

Air hostess Angela Wells is posted to the Cairo flight with her spoilt cousin, Sandra, and Captain Ian Lewis, on whom the girls are both keen. At Cairo, a wealthy Egyptian, Mr Salem Hassid, asks Angela to take his little son back to London to visit his English cousins. At Athens, Sandra lets Ahmed wander off. Angela sees a strange woman drive off with him and unsuccessfully pursues her. Later, Ahmed is returned, but Angela's 'plane has left. She is sent back aboard another 'plane to London, and learns that Ian's 'plane has crashed. Ian is safe, but Sandra, who rescued injured passengers, is badly burnt. When Angela goes to the hospital to see her . . .

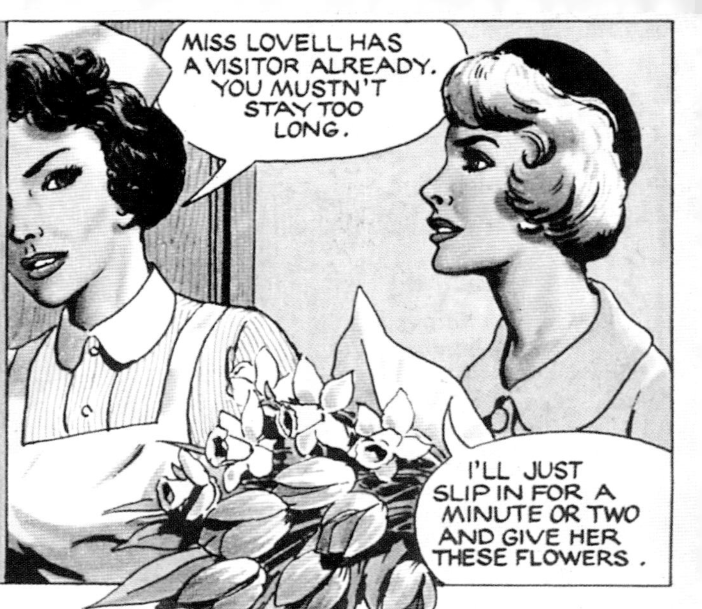
MISS LOVELL HAS A VISITOR ALREADY. YOU MUSTN'T STAY TOO LONG.
I'LL JUST SLIP IN FOR A MINUTE OR TWO AND GIVE HER THESE FLOWERS.

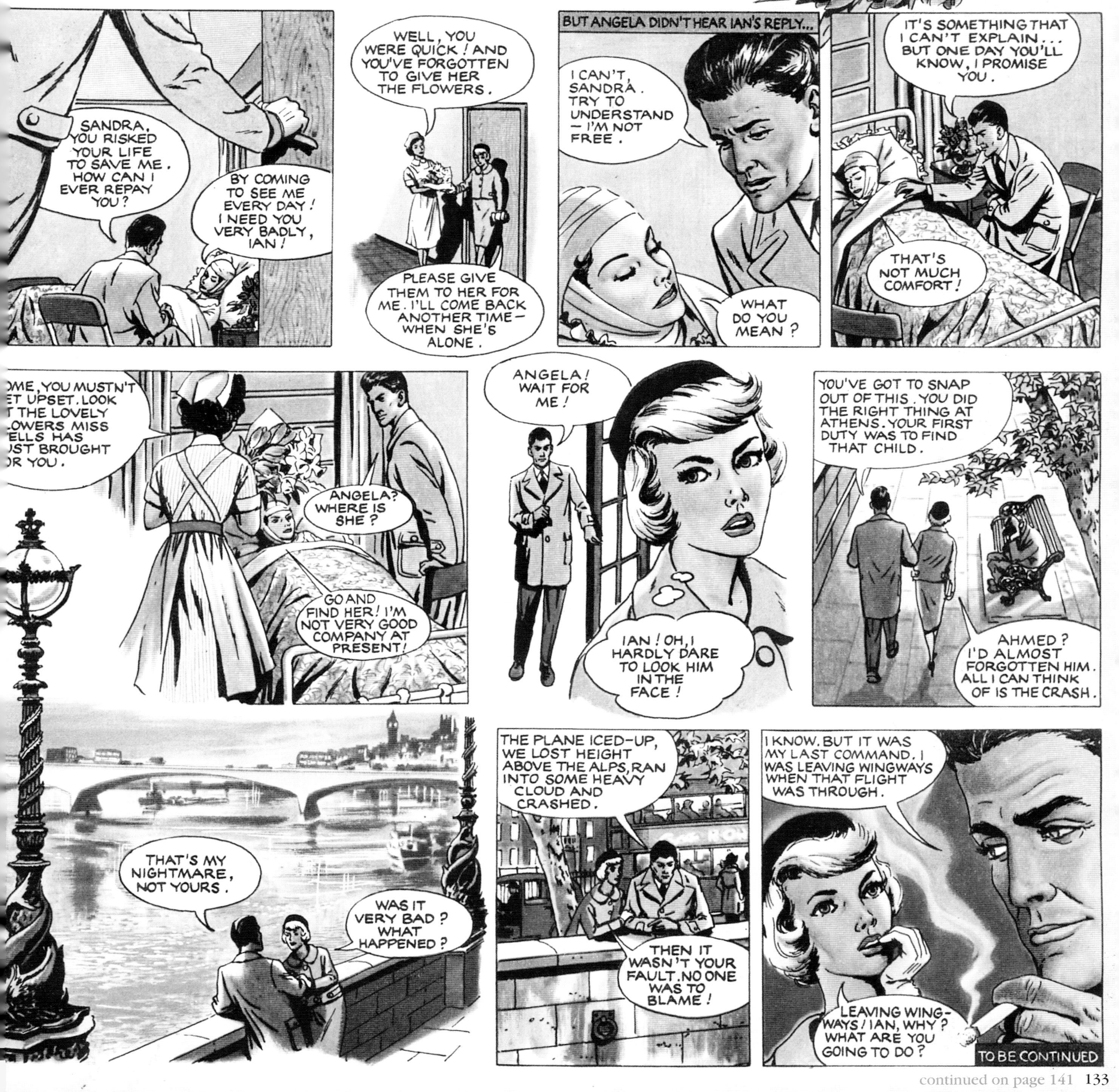
SANDRA, YOU RISKED YOUR LIFE TO SAVE ME. HOW CAN I EVER REPAY YOU?
BY COMING TO SEE ME EVERY DAY! I NEED YOU VERY BADLY, IAN!
WELL, YOU WERE QUICK! AND YOU'VE FORGOTTEN TO GIVE HER THE FLOWERS.
PLEASE GIVE THEM TO HER FOR ME. I'LL COME BACK ANOTHER TIME — WHEN SHE'S ALONE.
BUT ANGELA DIDN'T HEAR IAN'S REPLY...
I CAN'T, SANDRA. TRY TO UNDERSTAND — I'M NOT FREE.
WHAT DO YOU MEAN?
IT'S SOMETHING THAT I CAN'T EXPLAIN... BUT ONE DAY YOU'LL KNOW, I PROMISE YOU.
THAT'S NOT MUCH COMFORT!
OME, YOU MUSTN'T ET UPSET. LOOK T THE LOVELY LOWERS MISS ELLS HAS UST BROUGHT OR YOU.
ANGELA? WHERE IS SHE?
GO AND FIND HER! I'M NOT VERY GOOD COMPANY AT PRESENT!
ANGELA! WAIT FOR ME!
IAN! OH, I HARDLY DARE TO LOOK HIM IN THE FACE!
YOU'VE GOT TO SNAP OUT OF THIS. YOU DID THE RIGHT THING AT ATHENS. YOUR FIRST DUTY WAS TO FIND THAT CHILD.
AHMED? I'D ALMOST FORGOTTEN HIM. ALL I CAN THINK OF IS THE CRASH.
THAT'S MY NIGHTMARE, NOT YOURS.
WAS IT VERY BAD? WHAT HAPPENED?
THE PLANE ICED-UP, WE LOST HEIGHT ABOVE THE ALPS, RAN INTO SOME HEAVY CLOUD AND CRASHED.
THEN IT WASN'T YOUR FAULT. NO ONE WAS TO BLAME!
I KNOW. BUT IT WAS MY LAST COMMAND. I WAS LEAVING WINGWAYS WHEN THAT FLIGHT WAS THROUGH.
LEAVING WING-WAYS! IAN, WHY? WHAT ARE YOU GOING TO DO?
TO BE CONTINUED

continued on page 141

Belle of the Ballet

and her friends in a grand adventure

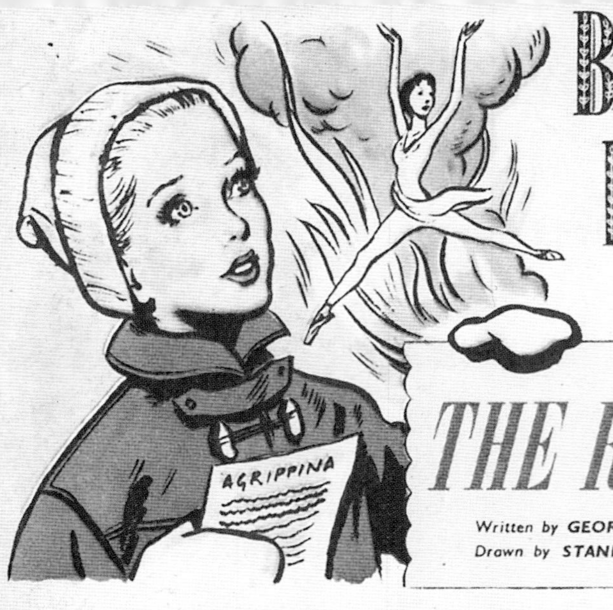
AGRIPPINA

THE REBEL

Written by GEORGE BEARDMORE
Drawn by STANLEY HOUGHTON

Belle Auburn and her friends, pupils of the Arenska Dancing School, take pity on Sylvine, a marvellous dancer whose career is being ruined by her jealous aunt, famous actress Erica Brand. Belle rescues Sylvine from the finishing-school to which Erica sends her, and returns her to her parents. Sylvine then marries Felix, a young musician. After the ceremony they rush to the Throne Theatre, where Sylvine dances, instead of Belle, in the first performance of the new ballet *Agrippina*. She is a great success, and . . .

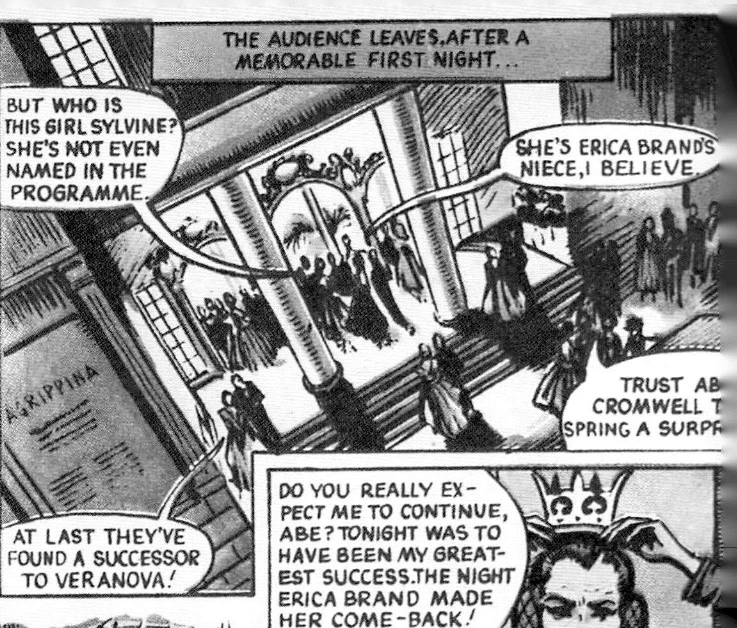
THE AUDIENCE LEAVES, AFTER A MEMORABLE FIRST NIGHT...
BUT WHO IS THIS GIRL SYLVINE? SHE'S NOT EVEN NAMED IN THE PROGRAMME.
SHE'S ERICA BRAND'S NIECE, I BELIEVE.
AGRIPPINA
TRUST AB
CROMWELL T
SPRING A SURPR
AT LAST THEY'VE FOUND A SUCCESSOR TO VERANOVA!

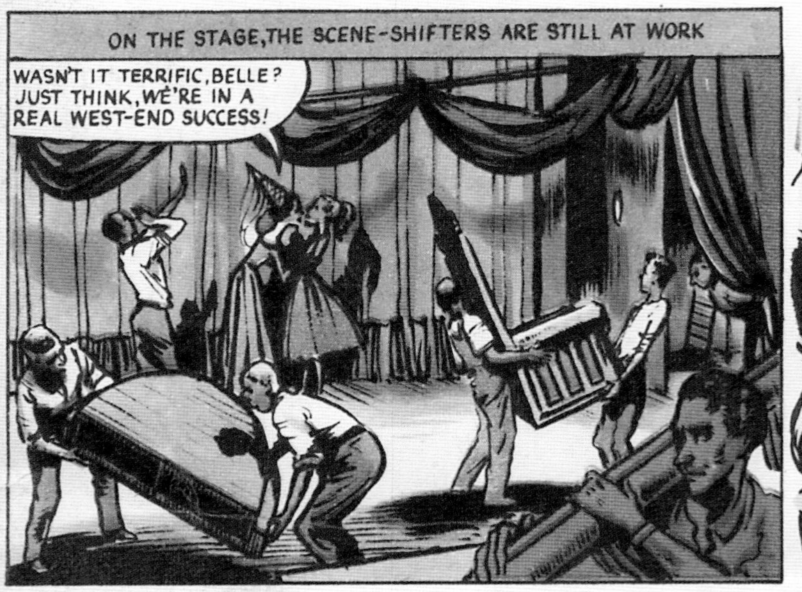
ON THE STAGE, THE SCENE-SHIFTERS ARE STILL AT WORK
WASN'T IT TERRIFIC, BELLE? JUST THINK, WE'RE IN A REAL WEST-END SUCCESS!

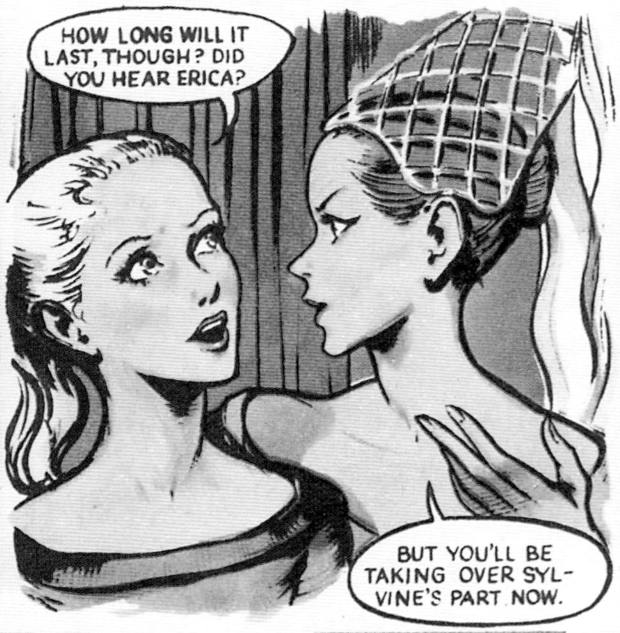
HOW LONG WILL IT LAST, THOUGH? DID YOU HEAR ERICA?
BUT YOU'LL BE TAKING OVER SYLVINE'S PART NOW.

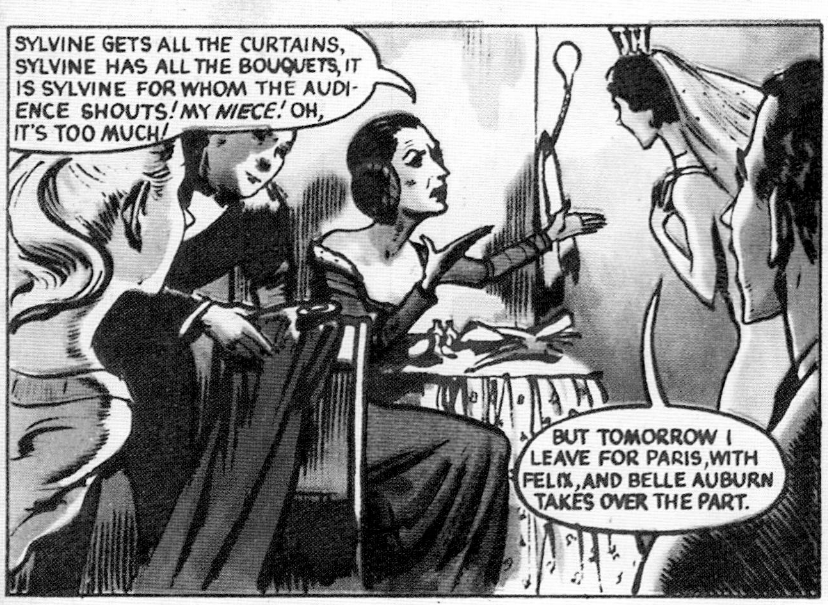
SYLVINE GETS ALL THE CURTAINS, SYLVINE HAS ALL THE BOUQUETS, IT IS SYLVINE FOR WHOM THE AUDIENCE SHOUTS! MY *NIECE!* OH, IT'S TOO MUCH!
BUT TOMORROW I LEAVE FOR PARIS, WITH FELIX, AND BELLE AUBURN TAKES OVER THE PART.

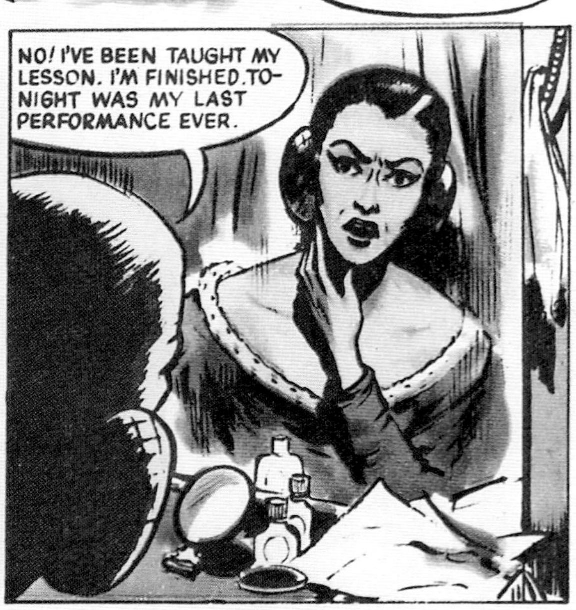
NO! I'VE BEEN TAUGHT MY LESSON. I'M FINISHED. TONIGHT WAS MY LAST PERFORMANCE EVER.

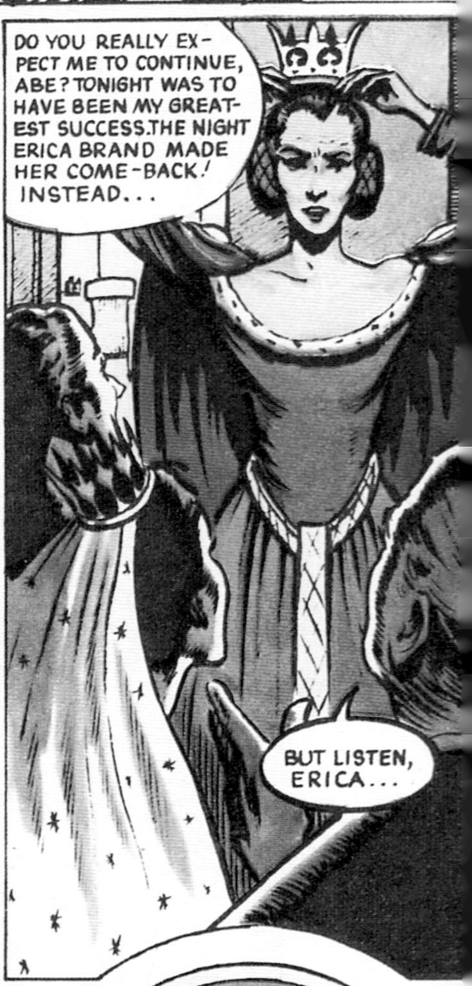
DO YOU REALLY EXPECT ME TO CONTINUE, ABE? TONIGHT WAS TO HAVE BEEN MY GREATEST SUCCESS. THE NIGHT ERICA BRAND MADE HER COME-BACK! INSTEAD...
BUT LISTEN, ERICA...

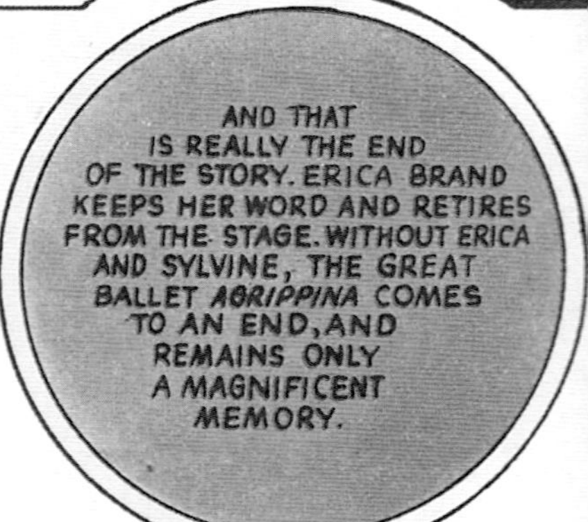
AND THAT IS REALLY THE END OF THE STORY. ERICA BRAND KEEPS HER WORD AND RETIRES FROM THE STAGE. WITHOUT ERICA AND SYLVINE, THE GREAT BALLET *AGRIPPINA* COMES TO AN END, AND REMAINS ONLY A MAGNIFICENT MEMORY.

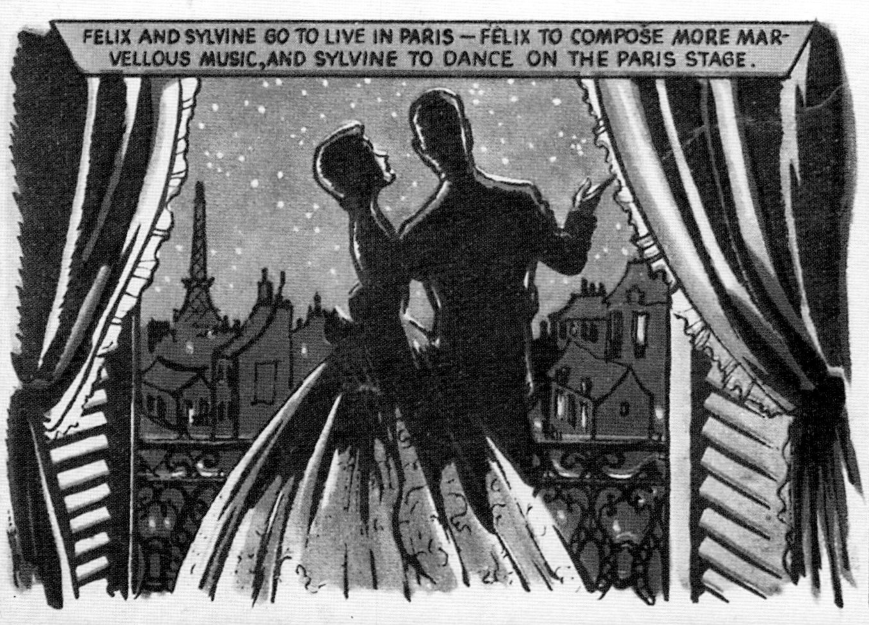
FELIX AND SYLVINE GO TO LIVE IN PARIS — FELIX TO COMPOSE *MORE* MARVELLOUS MUSIC, AND SYLVINE TO DANCE ON THE PARIS STAGE.

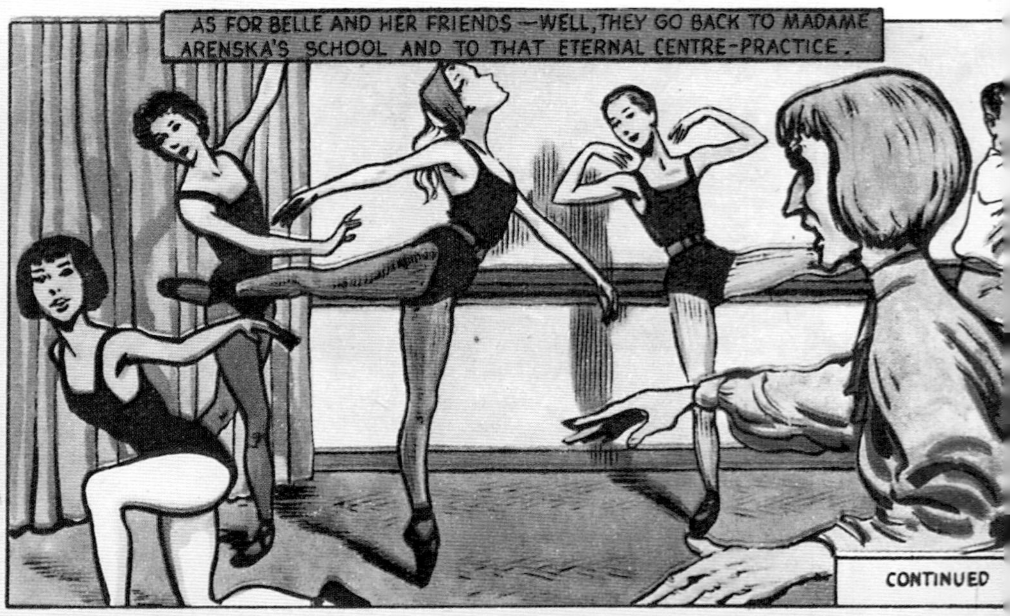
AS FOR BELLE AND HER FRIENDS — WELL, THEY GO BACK TO MADAME ARENSKA'S SCHOOL AND TO THAT ETERNAL CENTRE-PRACTICE.

CONTINUED

ADVENTURE CORNER

If you lead an interesting life write in to 'Adventure Corner' and tell us all about it.

JUNE PALMER

Fifteen-year-old June lives in Bournemouth and spends as much time as she can at the local skating rink. During the holidays she takes part in Exhibitions at the rink and here she is miming "Annie Get Your Gun", during one of the Christmas shows.

June also loves horse riding and she regularly goes to a riding camp at the weekends.

But June's main hobby is skating and she is working hard for her Silver Medal (figures). Here she is practising.

When Poole Park Lake froze June skated there, and showed her skill by jumping over five barrels.

There are school examinations this year as well as skating ones, and we wish June good luck!

What's your Worry?

STARTING SOMETHING NEW

Q. I am going to a different school in order to get ready for my career. You have to pay there, and I am afraid I may let my parents down and waste their money. Can you advise me please?

A. You are making the mistake of expecting yourself to be no good at things before you even start. You feel nervous in case you cannot manage to do as well as will be expected of you. We can assure you that everybody feels like this before starting to learn something new. Go to your new school determined to do your best, but expecting a certain number of ups and downs, and we feel sure you will do well in the end.

★ ★ ★

HOW CAN WE HELP A FRIEND?

Q. How can we help an awkward and spiteful friend who seems to be unhappy at home?

A. Don't fuss over her too much. Show your friendliness, bring her into things with you, and give her an opportunity of being useful and helpful so that she can feel she is being appreciated for the assistance she is giving you.

★ ★ ★

HER BOY FRIEND IS ILL

Q. I am sixteen. I have a boy friend in hospital and he will not be out for a long time. Another boy has been asking me to go for walks with him. I would like to do so. Please, do you think I should?

A. The answer to your question depends on a number of things. Consequently, we are not prepared to give an absolute opinion one way or the other. But, in general, in a case like this, most attention should be given to the person who most needs consideration. This is the boy in hospital.

★ ★ ★

SHOULD SHE SPEAK TO HIM?

Q. I sometimes go out with my parents and some friends, and there is a rather shy boy there. He never speaks to me, and I wonder if I should speak to him. What do you think?

A. Ask this boy some questions about his interests; it will help him to overcome his shyness in company.

★ ★ ★

THEY SEEM TO BE AGAINST HER

Q. All my life I have lived with my grand-parents and my parents. I am 13 now, and I am beginning to find it very hard, because everybody seems to be against me.

A. You have reached an age when you want to feel more independent as a person. This makes you challenge the point of view of older people and probably ends up in your getting criticised by them. Try not to be too challenging. But you are certainly old enough to have a point of view of your own, just as certainly as you are old enough to undertake some of the household chores. Have a talk with your mother and try to work out a give and take plan which will help you all to live more happily together.

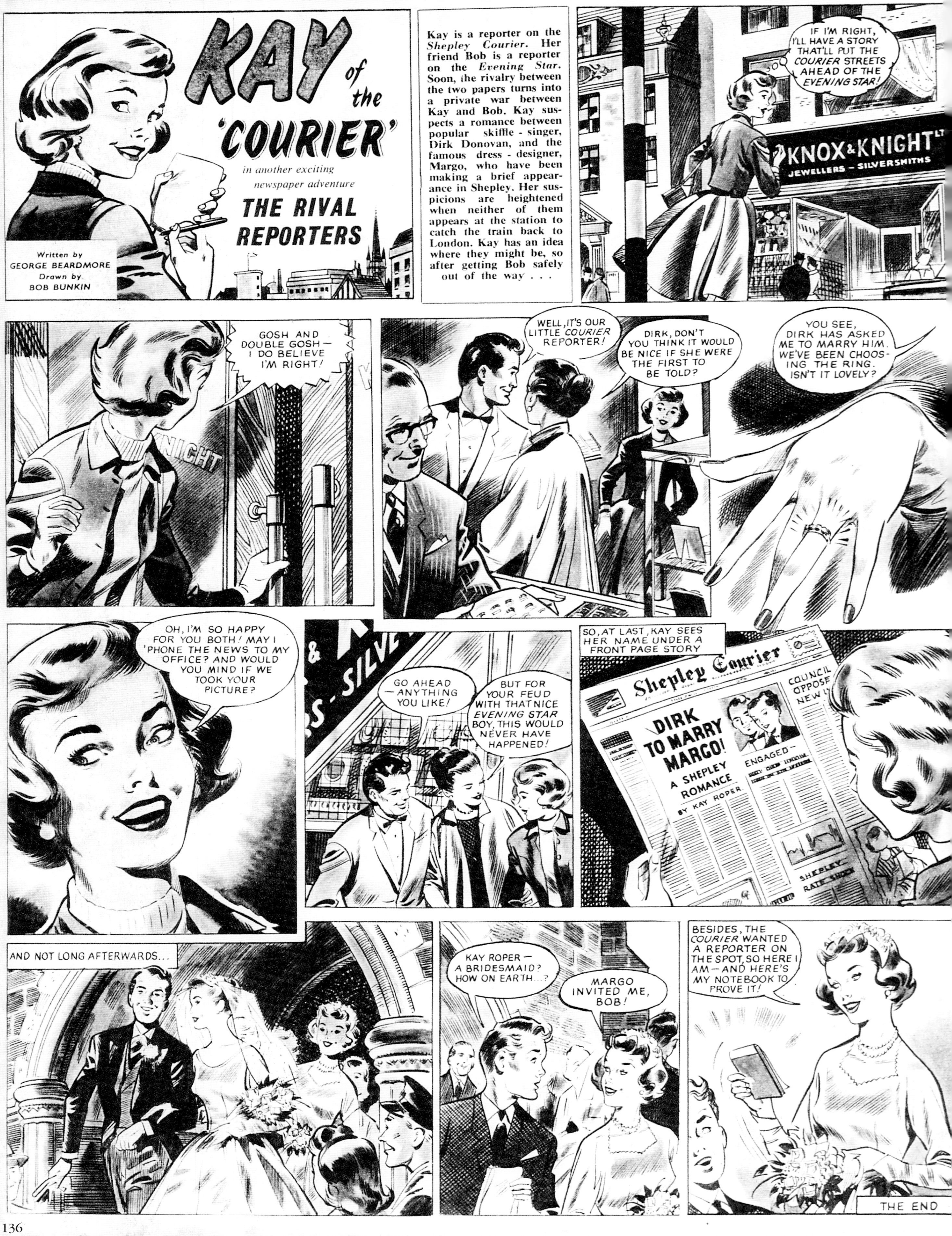
KAY of the 'COURIER'
in another exciting newspaper adventure
THE RIVAL REPORTERS
Written by GEORGE BEARDMORE Drawn by BOB BUNKIN
Kay is a reporter on the *Shepley Courier.* Her friend Bob is a reporter on the *Evening Star*. Soon, the rivalry between the two papers turns into a private war between Kay and Bob. Kay suspects a romance between popular skiffle - singer, Dirk Donovan, and the famous dress - designer, Margo, who have been making a brief appearance in Shepley. Her suspicions are heightened when neither of them appears at the station to catch the train back to London. Kay has an idea where they might be, so after getting Bob safely out of the way . . .
IF I'M RIGHT, I'LL HAVE A STORY THAT'LL PUT THE *COURIER* STREETS AHEAD OF THE *EVENING STAR*!
KNOX & KNIGHT LTD
JEWELLERS – SILVERSMITHS
GOSH AND DOUBLE GOSH — I DO BELIEVE I'M RIGHT!
KNIGHT
WELL, IT'S OUR LITTLE *COURIER* REPORTER!
DIRK, DON'T YOU THINK IT WOULD BE NICE IF SHE WERE THE FIRST TO BE TOLD?
YOU SEE, DIRK HAS ASKED ME TO MARRY HIM. WE'VE BEEN CHOOSING THE RING. ISN'T IT LOVELY?
OH, I'M SO HAPPY FOR YOU BOTH! MAY I 'PHONE THE NEWS TO MY OFFICE? AND WOULD YOU MIND IF WE TOOK YOUR PICTURE?
GO AHEAD — ANYTHING YOU LIKE!
BUT FOR YOUR FEUD WITH THAT NICE *EVENING STAR* BOY, THIS WOULD NEVER HAVE HAPPENED!
SO, AT LAST, KAY SEES HER NAME UNDER A FRONT PAGE STORY
Shepley Courier
DIRK TO MARRY MARGO!
A SHEPLEY ROMANCE
BY KAY ROPER
ENGAGED—
COUNCIL OPPOSE
AND NOT LONG AFTERWARDS . . .
KAY ROPER — A BRIDESMAID? HOW ON EARTH . . . ?
MARGO INVITED ME, BOB!
BESIDES, THE *COURIER* WANTED A REPORTER ON THE SPOT, SO HERE I AM — AND HERE'S MY NOTEBOOK TO PROVE IT!
THE END

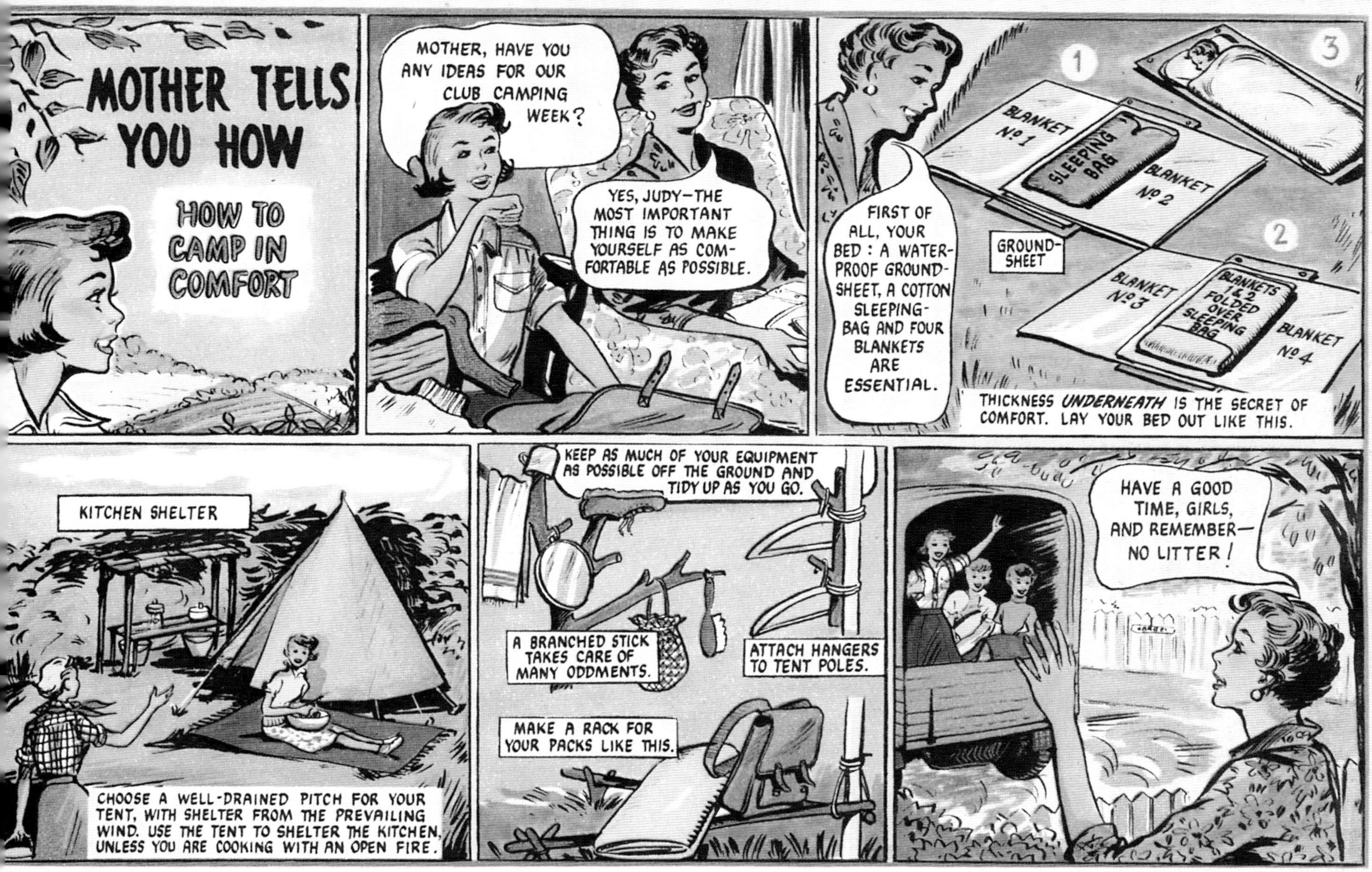
MOTHER TELLS YOU HOW
HOW TO CAMP IN COMFORT
MOTHER, HAVE YOU ANY IDEAS FOR OUR CLUB CAMPING WEEK?
YES, JUDY—THE MOST IMPORTANT THING IS TO MAKE YOURSELF AS COMFORTABLE AS POSSIBLE.
FIRST OF ALL, YOUR BED : A WATER-PROOF GROUND-SHEET, A COTTON SLEEPING-BAG AND FOUR BLANKETS ARE ESSENTIAL.
1
3
2
BLANKET Nº 1
SLEEPING BAG
BLANKET Nº 2
GROUND-SHEET
BLANKET Nº 3
BLANKETS 1 & 2 FOLDED OVER SLEEPING BAG
BLANKET Nº 4
THICKNESS UNDERNEATH IS THE SECRET OF COMFORT. LAY YOUR BED OUT LIKE THIS.
KITCHEN SHELTER
CHOOSE A WELL-DRAINED PITCH FOR YOUR TENT, WITH SHELTER FROM THE PREVAILING WIND. USE THE TENT TO SHELTER THE KITCHEN, UNLESS YOU ARE COOKING WITH AN OPEN FIRE.
KEEP AS MUCH OF YOUR EQUIPMENT AS POSSIBLE OFF THE GROUND AND TIDY UP AS YOU GO.
A BRANCHED STICK TAKES CARE OF MANY ODDMENTS.
ATTACH HANGERS TO TENT POLES.
MAKE A RACK FOR YOUR PACKS LIKE THIS.
HAVE A GOOD TIME, GIRLS, AND REMEMBER—NO LITTER!

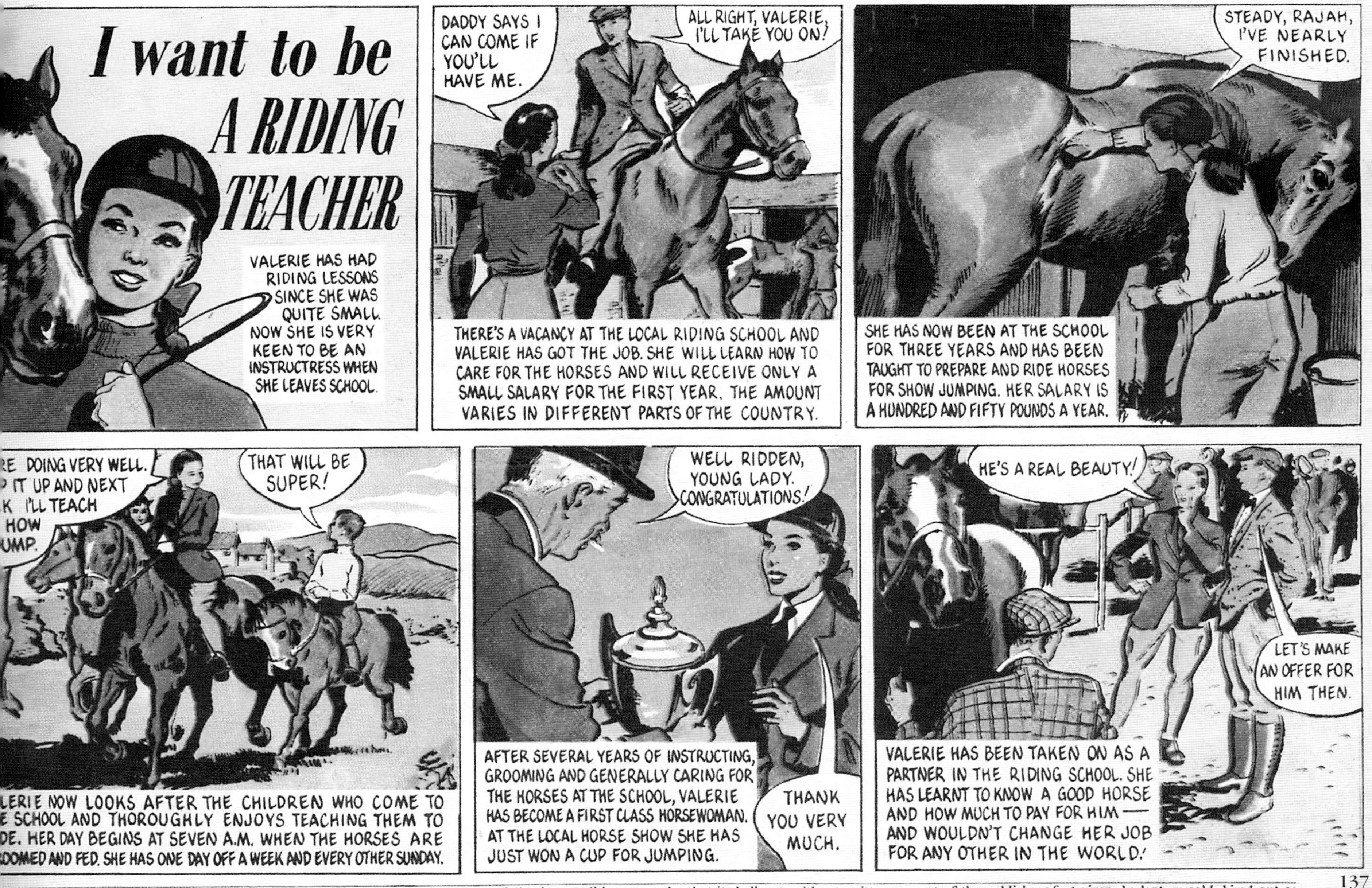
I want to be A RIDING TEACHER
VALERIE HAS HAD RIDING LESSONS SINCE SHE WAS QUITE SMALL. NOW SHE IS VERY KEEN TO BE AN INSTRUCTRESS WHEN SHE LEAVES SCHOOL.
DADDY SAYS I CAN COME IF YOU'LL HAVE ME.
ALL RIGHT, VALERIE, I'LL TAKE YOU ON!
THERE'S A VACANCY AT THE LOCAL RIDING SCHOOL AND VALERIE HAS GOT THE JOB. SHE WILL LEARN HOW TO CARE FOR THE HORSES AND WILL RECEIVE ONLY A SMALL SALARY FOR THE FIRST YEAR. THE AMOUNT VARIES IN DIFFERENT PARTS OF THE COUNTRY.
STEADY, RAJAH, I'VE NEARLY FINISHED.
SHE HAS NOW BEEN AT THE SCHOOL FOR THREE YEARS AND HAS BEEN TAUGHT TO PREPARE AND RIDE HORSES FOR SHOW JUMPING. HER SALARY IS A HUNDRED AND FIFTY POUNDS A YEAR.
RE DOING VERY WELL. P IT UP AND NEXT K I'LL TEACH HOW UMP.
THAT WILL BE SUPER!
LERIE NOW LOOKS AFTER THE CHILDREN WHO COME TO E SCHOOL AND THOROUGHLY ENJOYS TEACHING THEM TO DE. HER DAY BEGINS AT SEVEN A.M. WHEN THE HORSES ARE OOMED AND FED. SHE HAS ONE DAY OFF A WEEK AND EVERY OTHER SUNDAY.
WELL RIDDEN, YOUNG LADY. CONGRATULATIONS!
THANK YOU VERY MUCH.
AFTER SEVERAL YEARS OF INSTRUCTING, GROOMING AND GENERALLY CARING FOR THE HORSES AT THE SCHOOL, VALERIE HAS BECOME A FIRST CLASS HORSEWOMAN. AT THE LOCAL HORSE SHOW SHE HAS JUST WON A CUP FOR JUMPING.
HE'S A REAL BEAUTY!
LET'S MAKE AN OFFER FOR HIM THEN.
VALERIE HAS BEEN TAKEN ON AS A PARTNER IN THE RIDING SCHOOL. SHE HAS LEARNT TO KNOW A GOOD HORSE AND HOW MUCH TO PAY FOR HIM—AND WOULDN'T CHANGE HER JOB FOR ANY OTHER IN THE WORLD!

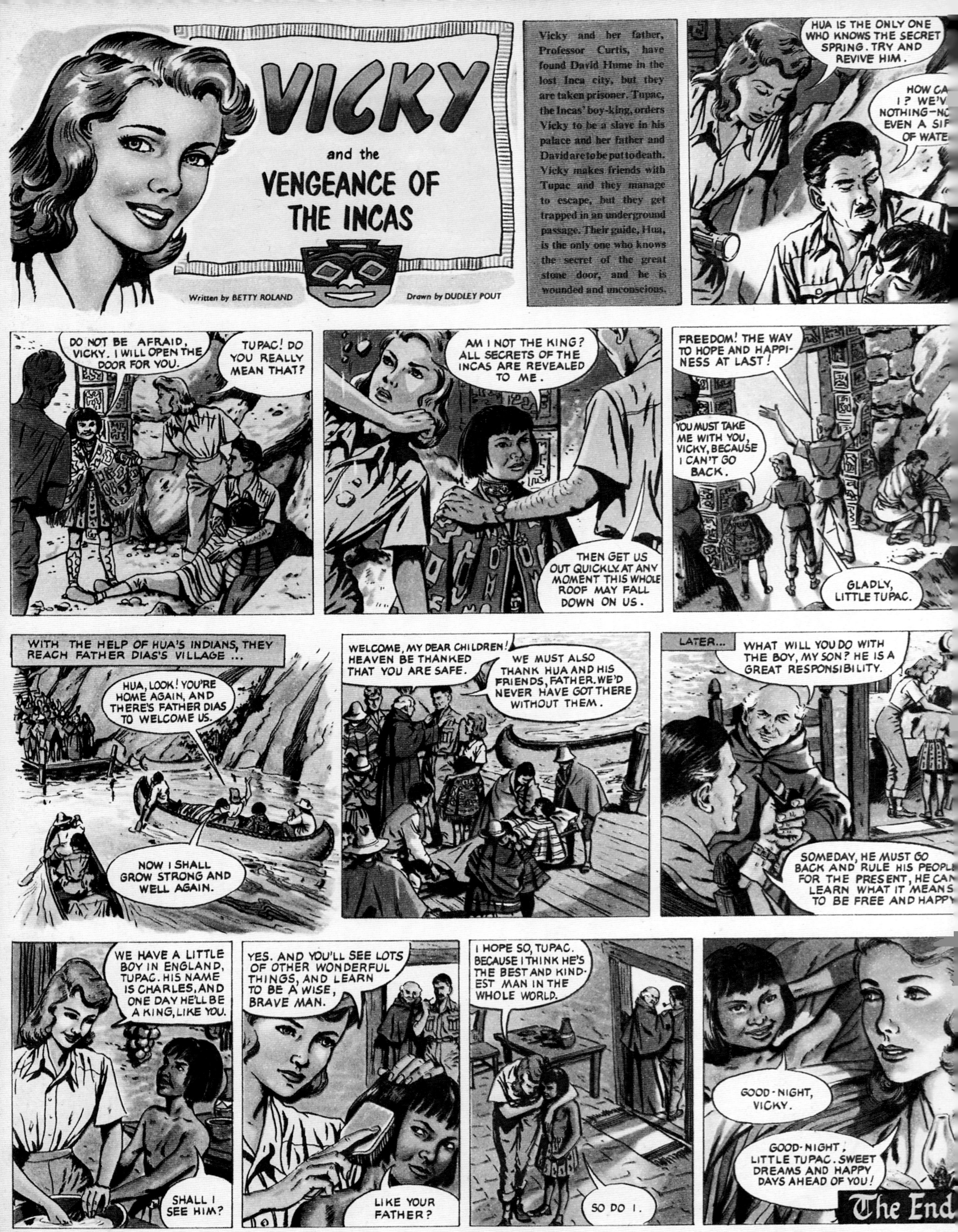
VICKY
and the
VENGEANCE OF THE INCAS
Written by BETTY ROLAND
Drawn by DUDLEY POUT
Vicky and her father, Professor Curtis, have found David Hume in the lost Inca city, but they are taken prisoner. Tupac, the Incas' boy-king, orders Vicky to be a slave in his palace and her father and David are to be put to death. Vicky makes friends with Tupac and they manage to escape, but they get trapped in an underground passage. Their guide, Hua, is the only one who knows the secret of the great stone door, and he is wounded and unconscious.
HUA IS THE ONLY ONE WHO KNOWS THE SECRET SPRING. TRY AND REVIVE HIM.
HOW CA I? WE'V NOTHING—NO EVEN A SIP OF WATE
DO NOT BE AFRAID, VICKY. I WILL OPEN THE DOOR FOR YOU.
TUPAC! DO YOU REALLY MEAN THAT?
AM I NOT THE KING? ALL SECRETS OF THE INCAS ARE REVEALED TO ME.
THEN GET US OUT QUICKLY. AT ANY MOMENT THIS WHOLE ROOF MAY FALL DOWN ON US.
FREEDOM! THE WAY TO HOPE AND HAPPINESS AT LAST!
YOU MUST TAKE ME WITH YOU, VICKY, BECAUSE I CAN'T GO BACK.
GLADLY, LITTLE TUPAC.
WITH THE HELP OF HUA'S INDIANS, THEY REACH FATHER DIAS'S VILLAGE ...
HUA, LOOK! YOU'RE HOME AGAIN, AND THERE'S FATHER DIAS TO WELCOME US.
NOW I SHALL GROW STRONG AND WELL AGAIN.
WELCOME, MY DEAR CHILDREN! HEAVEN BE THANKED THAT YOU ARE SAFE.
WE MUST ALSO THANK HUA AND HIS FRIENDS, FATHER. WE'D NEVER HAVE GOT THERE WITHOUT THEM.
LATER...
WHAT WILL YOU DO WITH THE BOY, MY SON? HE IS A GREAT RESPONSIBILITY.
SOMEDAY, HE MUST GO BACK AND RULE HIS PEOPLE FOR THE PRESENT, HE CAN LEARN WHAT IT MEANS TO BE FREE AND HAPPY
WE HAVE A LITTLE BOY IN ENGLAND, TUPAC. HIS NAME IS CHARLES, AND ONE DAY HE'LL BE A KING, LIKE YOU.
SHALL I SEE HIM?
YES. AND YOU'LL SEE LOTS OF OTHER WONDERFUL THINGS, AND LEARN TO BE A WISE, BRAVE MAN.
LIKE YOUR FATHER?
I HOPE SO, TUPAC. BECAUSE I THINK HE'S THE BEST AND KINDEST MAN IN THE WHOLE WORLD.
SO DO I.
GOOD-NIGHT, VICKY.
GOOD-NIGHT, LITTLE TUPAC. SWEET DREAMS AND HAPPY DAYS AHEAD OF YOU!
The End

Recipe Results

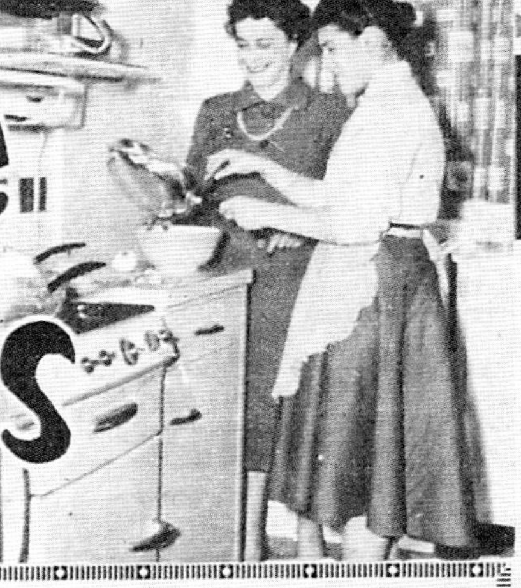

Here are some of the winning recipes, sent in by readers for our recipe competition. The first winner was Ewa Staruszkiewicz, of Kilmaurs, Ayrshire, who gave us this delicious Polish recipe Golabki – which wins her a guinea. The recipes were tested in the Housewife model kitchen by cookery expert Kato Frank and GIRL reader Cathy Sebastien.

GOLABKI

[Stuffed Cabbage Leaves]

You will need:

- ½ lb COOKED RICE
- SLICE OF BACON
- NUT OF BUTTER OR MARGARINE
- 1 EGG
- ½ lb SAUSAGE MEAT
- 1 LARGE CABBAGE
- 1 ONION
- SALT AND PEPPER TO TASTE

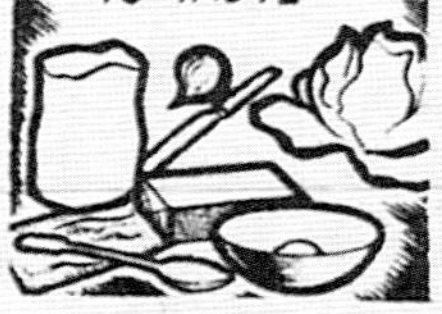

Method: Part boil the whole cabbage to soften the leaves. Fry the finely sliced onion and bacon in the butter or margarine. Add to the cooked rice along with the sausage meat. Add salt and pepper to taste. Bind everything together with the raw egg, and mix well. Divide the cabbage into separate leaves and roll up a tablespoonful of the mixture in each one. Put a few left-over leaves at the bottom of a pot to prevent sticking, and then pack the rolls tightly on top. Add a cupful of stock or water and simmer for one hour.

Serve with either freshly made tomato sauce or breadcrumbs fried in butter. This is enough for six people.

Here are the recipes from the runners-up. They each receive 5/-

French Pancakes

Sent in by Carol Broomer of Cosely, Staffs.

You will need:

- 6 ozs OATMEAL
- 2 ozs BUTTER OR MARGARINE
- 1 EGG
- 2 GILLS OF MILK
- 1 TEASPOONFUL OF RUM
- 1 PINCH OF SALT

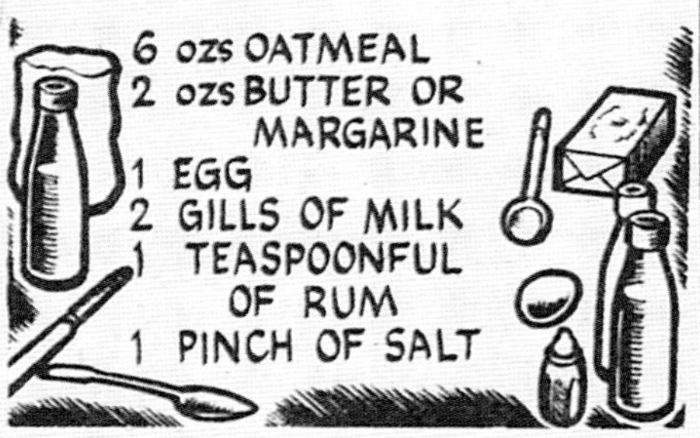

Method: Put the oatmeal into a bowl and make a well in the centre. Then add the egg, which must be whisked first. Mix well. Boil the milk with the butter, pour into the bowl and mix with a wooden spoon. Add the salt and rum and mix again. Melt some fat in a frying-pan and pour half the mixture into it, letting it cover all the surface of the pan. When the pancake rises, loosen the edges with a knife and turn it over to cook the other side. Again loosen the edges, and shake the pan a little. Slide the pancake on to a warm plate. Melt more fat in the frying-pan and cook the remainder of the mixture.

Serve the pancakes hot, with sugar dredged over them. They make a delicious snack for lunch or tea.

Fried Marrow with Poached Eggs

Sent in by Jennifer Shannon of Lincoln

You will need:

- A MARROW
- 5 EGGS
- BREADCRUMBS
- 4 RASHERS OF BACON

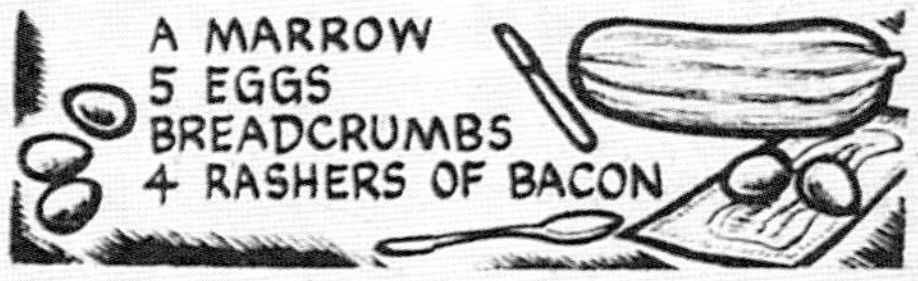

Method: Cut the marrow into slices about ½ inch thick. Pare off the rinds and remove the seeds. Flour each side and brush over lightly with beaten egg. Dip into breadcrumbs and fry in hot fat until a golden brown. Keep hot while the eggs are poached. Serve hot, allowing 3-4 slices to each egg. Alternatively, the marrow may be dipped into batter instead of breadcrumbs, and the dish served with fried bacon rashers.

Dandelion Omelet

Sent in by Elizabeth Field of Bedford

You will need:

- 1 CUP DANDELION HEARTS
- 4 EGGS * BUTTER

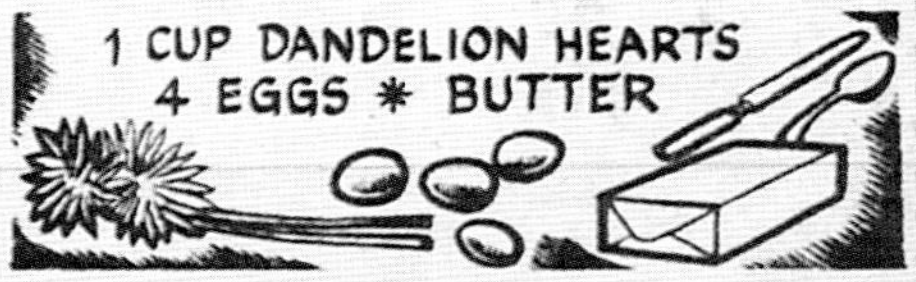

Method: Fry the hearts of very white dandelions in butter, and mix them with well-beaten eggs. Cook like an ordinary omelet. You will find that they taste just like asparagus omelets.

What's Your Worry?

Cruelty to animals

Q. If you see animals being very cruelly treated should you report it to anyone?

A. We think you should first talk to the people concerned about it and then, if they go on in spite of that, you should get in touch with a local branch of the Royal Society for Prevention of Cruelty to Animals.

* * *

Am I too busy?

Q. I have a boy friend whom my parents do not mind, but I am so busy with other things that I only see him once a week. What can I do about it?

A. We think it is a great mistake, when a boy and girl are friendly with each other, to spend too much time together. It is much better to have a varied life. Then you will have lots to talk about when you do meet.

* * *

No longer a child

Q. I am getting on for 14. My father wants to keep me in the same kind of clothes that I wore as a child. How can I persuade him that I am not a child any more?

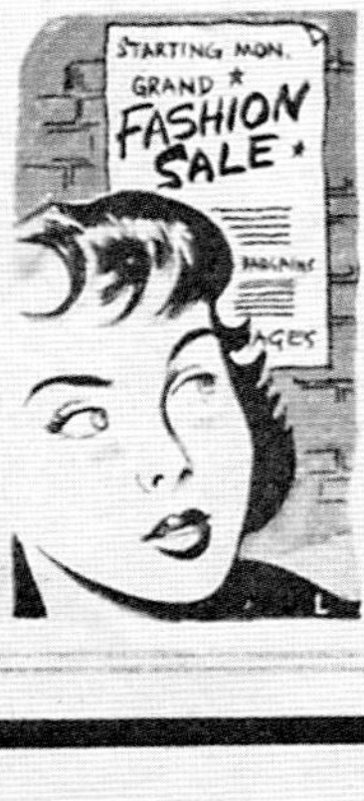
STARTING MON.
GRAND
FASHION SALE

A. Have a talk with your mother and ask if you can have, as an advanced birthday present, an outfit more suitable for your age. When your father sees how nice you look in your new clothes, we think he will accept the fact that you are no longer a child.

* * *

Telling tales

Q. A girl who lives near me keeps on telling the most dreadful tales about me. How can I stop her doing this?

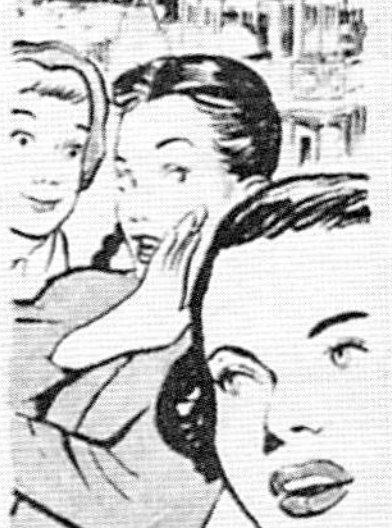

A. For some reason or other she wants to score off you. This may be because she is jealous of you, or because you have offended her in some way. Just be friendly towards her, not critical, and then you may be able to find out what the trouble is.

* * *

If you have a worry with which you feel our experts can help, just write to:– GIRL, 161/166 Fleet Street, London, E.C.4, and mark your letter 'WHAT'S YOUR WORRY?' No names will be printed, but let us have a stamped, self-addressed envelope if you would like a personal reply by letter. A published reply will always involve some delay. It is of help if the age of the reader is included in the letter.

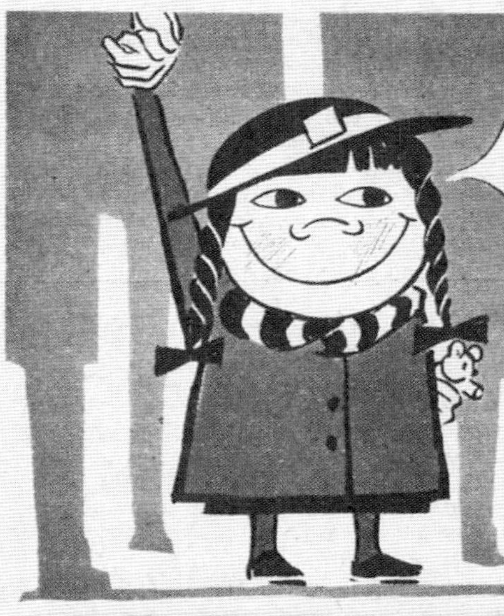

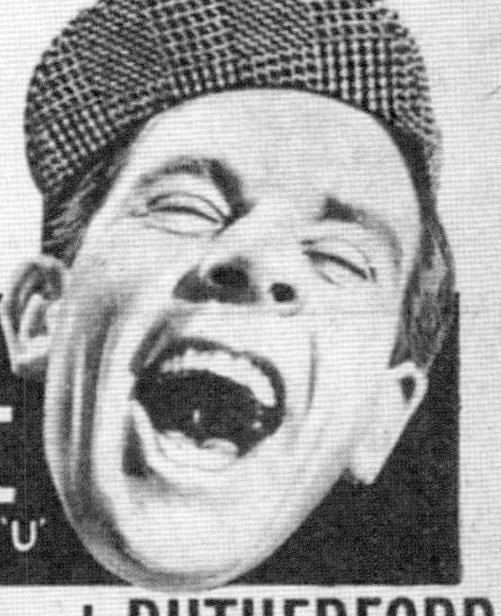

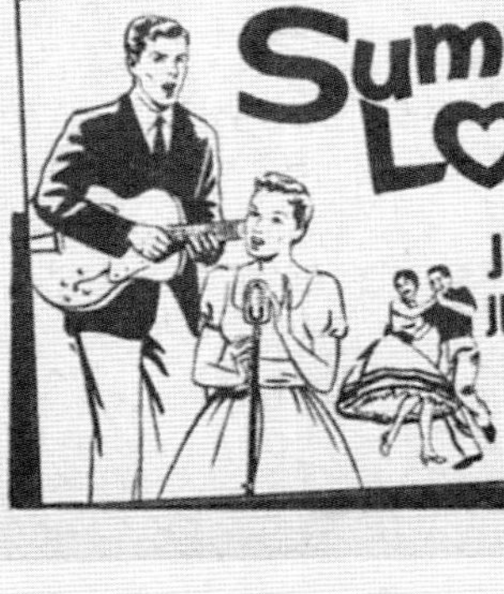

ADVENTURE CORNER

If you lead an interesting life write in to 'Adventure Corner' and tell us all about it.

Peggy Dicker

of Streatham

Fourteen-year-old Peggy's one ambition is to teach dancing – ballet, National dancing, and tap-dancing. She is very rapidly reaching her goal!

She has a large collection of long-playing records, including classics and calypsos.

Peggy has been dancing sinc she was four years old. She now has over seventy certificates

She loves all types of dancing and was the most promising ballroom-dancing pupil in 1956.

STECK

One of her pastimes is playing the family's very old pianola.

After all her dancing classes, she still has time left for her china collection.

Your Easter Books

Picked for you by **Wilfred Ashworth**

THE *White Horse of Hungary* by Margaret Ruthin (Warne, 7/-) is packed brimful with excitement from beginning to end. The background of the Great Plain of Hungary is unusual and enthralling and there is a jewel robbery, stampeding cattle, wild horses, ghost riders, a farm fire and a rescue in the nick of time to sustain the thrilling pitch of interest.

Twins at Highfield by Susan Wilcox (Hutchinson, 6/-) is a school story with an atmosphere of mystery. One of the twins, called Penny, tries to be a detective. Though not anything like so experienced at it as our own Penny Wise, she does help in unravelling the tangle.

A book about ballet

Do you know what ballet is all about, or do you feel lost when your friends talk of it or when you go to a performance? To help you to appreciate ballet and to know something of its history and development James Audsley has written ***The Book of Ballet*** (Warne, 5/-). There are chapters about ballet steps, stories of famous classical and modern ballets and interesting facts about dancers. The photographs and drawings are expressively full of life and movement and make the book a pleasure to read and own.

For nature-lovers

Wherever there is water in our countryside, Nature is in her most varied mood. There are animals and plants, birds and insects which flourish in, or keep close to, rivers and streams and provide plenty for nature-lovers to study. ***By River and Stream*** by Cecily M. Rutley (Warne, 6/-) describes what you should look for and enjoy in these places.

Teenagers forward!

Growing up is a tremendously exciting, yet sometimes complicated, process! To help teenage girls gain the most pleasure from this time in their lives Constance Holt has edited a book which is as up-to-date as its name – ***Modern Miss.*** This review will, I hope, stimulate your interest; if you write your *own* review you may win a handsome prize. Details of the competition are in the book, which is published by the Naldrett Press at 10/6.

(All of these books can be obtained from your local bookshop.)

Your Easter Films

Reviewed for you by

Lia Low

COMING to the screen at Easter, together with her friend Peter, Grandfather and – of course – the goats, is **HEIDI.** In case you haven't read the famous book by Johanna Spyri, she is a small Swiss girl who has to leave her beloved Alps for a starchy town household. And there's no film trickery about those Alps: they are the exact mountains mentioned in the book.

Elspeth Sigmund, who plays the title role of **Heidi**, *is 10 years old – and a Swiss girl in real life as well as in this new picture.*

From the Swiss Alps to Scotland, and a host of Scottish characters. First, there's **THE MAGGIE.** She is an old and sooty puffer boat, the pride of Skipper MacTaggart and his crew. This includes the Wee Boy, ship's cook and poacher, who is as wily as any of them in proving the 'Maggie's' worth to the unfortunate American who hires her. Sandy Mackendrick, the director of the film, says that young people are wonderful to work with. Needless to say, he comes from Scotland himself.

Sandy Mackendrick shows Lia Low a model of the boat after which **The Maggie** *film is named.*

Then there are **THE KIDNAPPERS** – Harry (8) and Davy (5) to be exact. Their parents are dead and they come to live with their grandfather in a grim little settlement in Scotchtown, Nova Scotia. His farm is poor and there's not even a dog to play with. Then, in the wood, they find a baby and decide to keep it. Two days later a sheriff's posse comes riding in search of the kidnapped child – but all ends happily.

In **The Kidnappers** *Vincent Winter plays the part of Davy, who longs for a dog of his own.*

ANGELA

AIR HOSTESS

the story of a girl who longed for adventure

Written by
BETTY ROLAND
Drawn by
DUDLEY POUT

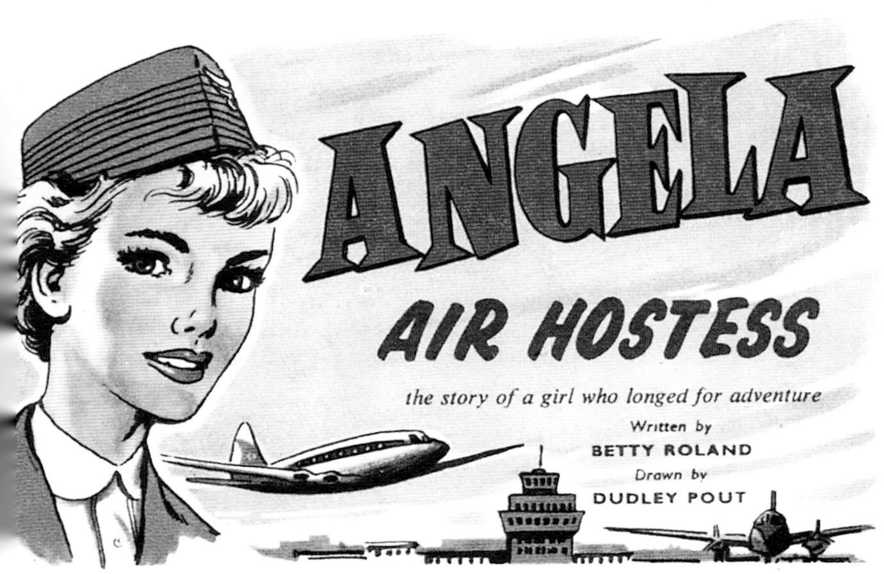

Air hostess Angela Wells grows very fond of Ian Lewis, Wingways' Chief Pilot. Ian leaves Wingways in order to do experimental work on a rocket ship, but before he leaves for the Rocket Range in Australia, he asks Angela to look after Mandy, his dog, and promises to return when his work is done. While Angela is at a ball with her brother's friend, Ron, Ian telephones from Sydney, and, when he hears where Angela is, he ruefully tears up the letter he has written her. Mrs Wells, who thinks Ian is too old for Angela, does not tell her about the call. Next day, Angela sets off on a special charter-flight to Grodnik, a trouble spot . . .

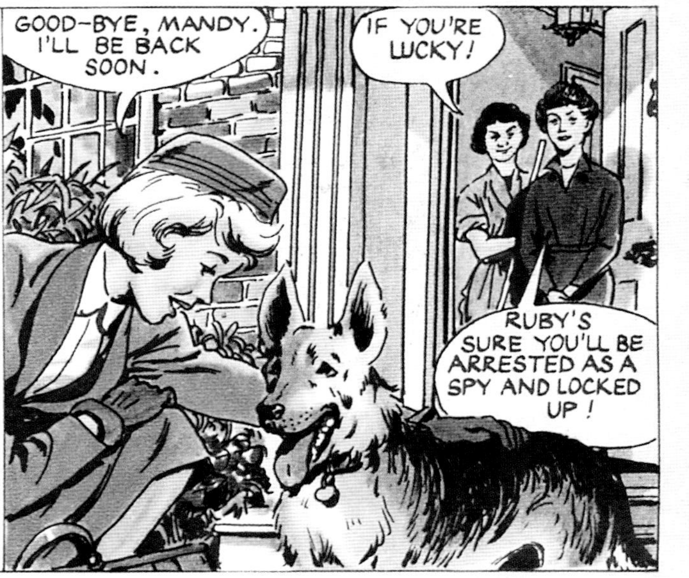
GOOD-BYE, MANDY. I'LL BE BACK SOON.
IF YOU'RE LUCKY!
RUBY'S SURE YOU'LL BE ARRESTED AS A SPY AND LOCKED UP!

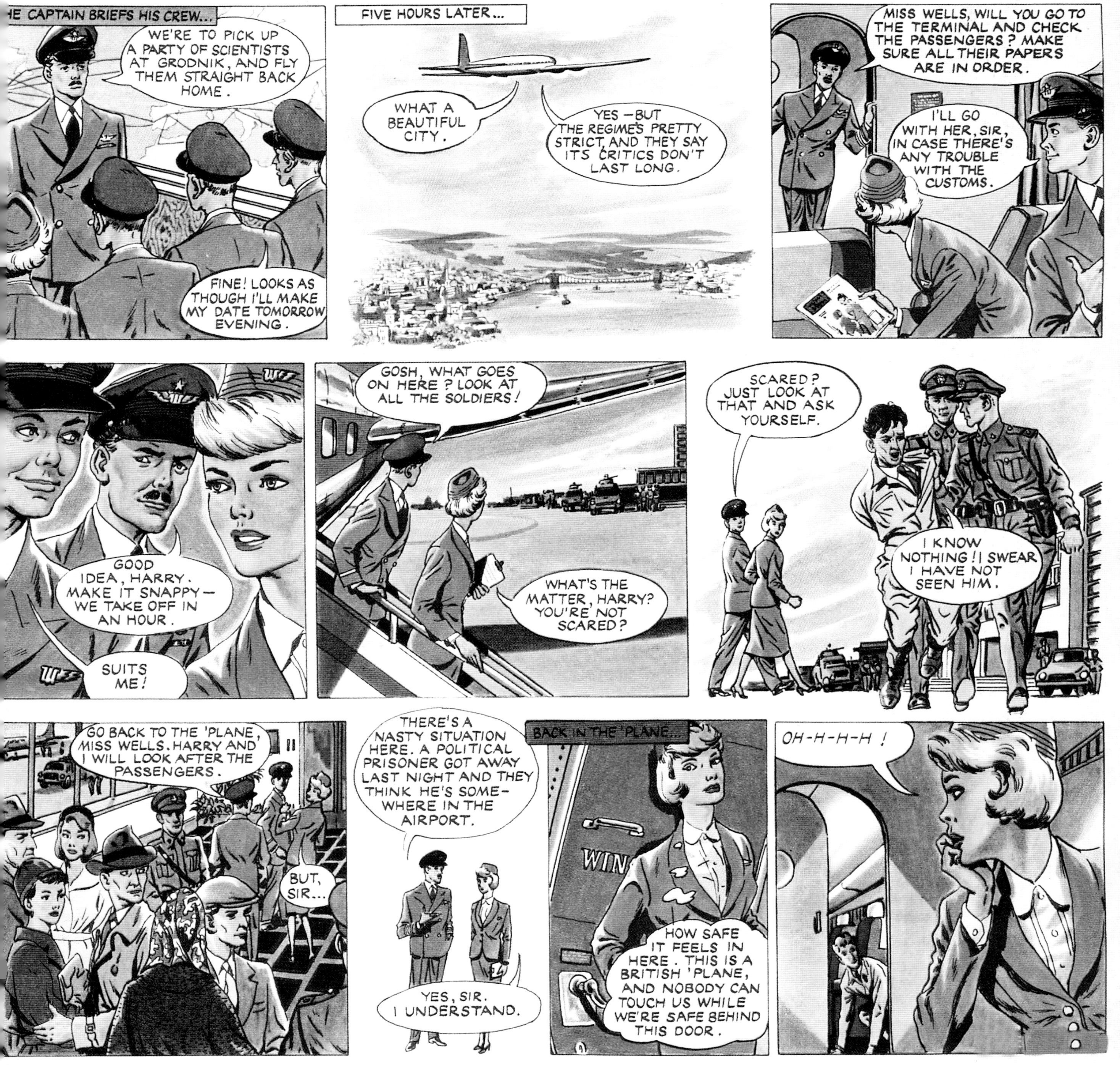
THE CAPTAIN BRIEFS HIS CREW...
WE'RE TO PICK UP A PARTY OF SCIENTISTS AT GRODNIK, AND FLY THEM STRAIGHT BACK HOME.
FINE! LOOKS AS THOUGH I'LL MAKE MY DATE TOMORROW EVENING.
FIVE HOURS LATER...
WHAT A BEAUTIFUL CITY.
YES — BUT THE REGIME'S PRETTY STRICT, AND THEY SAY ITS CRITICS DON'T LAST LONG.
MISS WELLS, WILL YOU GO TO THE TERMINAL AND CHECK THE PASSENGERS? MAKE SURE ALL THEIR PAPERS ARE IN ORDER.
I'LL GO WITH HER, SIR, IN CASE THERE'S ANY TROUBLE WITH THE CUSTOMS.
GOOD IDEA, HARRY. MAKE IT SNAPPY — WE TAKE OFF IN AN HOUR.
SUITS ME!
GOSH, WHAT GOES ON HERE? LOOK AT ALL THE SOLDIERS!
WHAT'S THE MATTER, HARRY? YOU'RE NOT SCARED?
SCARED? JUST LOOK AT THAT AND ASK YOURSELF.
I KNOW NOTHING! I SWEAR I HAVE NOT SEEN HIM.
GO BACK TO THE 'PLANE, MISS WELLS. HARRY AND I WILL LOOK AFTER THE PASSENGERS.
BUT, SIR...
THERE'S A NASTY SITUATION HERE. A POLITICAL PRISONER GOT AWAY LAST NIGHT AND THEY THINK HE'S SOME-WHERE IN THE AIRPORT.
YES, SIR. I UNDERSTAND.
BACK IN THE 'PLANE...
WIN
HOW SAFE IT FEELS IN HERE. THIS IS A BRITISH 'PLANE, AND NOBODY CAN TOUCH US WHILE WE'RE SAFE BEHIND THIS DOOR.
OH-H-H-H!

A Letter from the Editor

GIRL OFFICE, 161/166 FLEET STREET, LONDON, E.C.4.

30th April, 1958

IN the 'Mystery of the Magpies' today, you'll see a reference to a whistled language, the Silbo. I was rather intrigued by this so I asked the author, Stephen James, to tell me more about it. He says that it really exists and is used in the Canary Islands, where Spanish is the language used. There is no telegraph but, by means of this shrill whistle, people can talk to one another over distances of nearly four miles! It is not a code, but Spanish 'spoken' in a particular kind of way. Just as good as a telephone, in fact, and all you need are strong teeth and even stronger lungs!

Yours sincerely,

Marcus Morris

COME TO OLYMPIA — *by Coach!*

LONDON

Soon it will be time for the 1958 Hulton's Boys and Girls Exhibition. This year we would like a great many more of you to have the opportunity of coming to London to visit OLYMPIA. So here's our suggestion. Get together with your parents, schoolteachers, youth leaders or club secretaries and form a party! Explain to your leaders that, this year, your local coach operator will be pleased to organize party bookings for you. Ask them to go along and see him, and he will tell them all about it. Don't forget the date — 12th to 23rd August.

HULTON'S BOYS AND GIRLS EXHIBITION

WIN THREE DRESSES!

Styled by Sally Pigtails

There are 150 autograph books for the runners-up!

THIS week we are again offering three dresses from the Sally Pigtails range to the winner of this week's simple competition. All you have to do is find the odd man out. In each set of objects there is one which shouldn't be there. Can you discover which one it is? Set to work now and perhaps you will be lucky enough to win three super dresses to wear on your summer holiday.

HERE ARE THE RULES:

Write your answers on a postcard, remembering to add your name, age and address, and post to: – GIRL Competition No. 18, GIRL Reader Services, Long Lane, Liverpool 9, to arrive there not later than 12th May, 1958. All girls under 17 are eligible, and age and neatness will be taken into consideration in the judging. The Editor's decision is final and no correspondence can be entered into.

A
B
C
D
E
F
CREAM
BUTTER

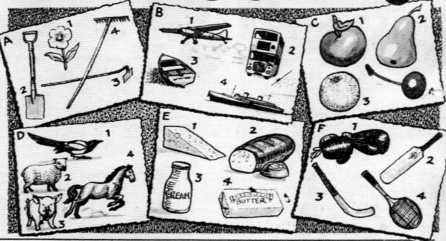

READERS' LETTERS

5/- will be paid for every reader's letter printed on this page.

One ear each!

WHEN MUMMY and I spent a holiday at my grandmother's, she took us to the park to see the animals. Mummy took some photographs, and how we laughed to see the one of the donkeys, for they look as if they have only got one ear each. I thought you might like to see them.

Susan Parchment, Hailsham, Sussex.

A relaxing position

I WAS very surprised at June Paul ('Try Anything Once', GIRL 19th February, 1958) saying that it was terrible hanging from a trapeze.

I have a fairly low trapeze in my garden and I find that hanging from it is the most relaxing position possible. As for getting up again – that's easy after a little practice. My brother, sister and I can do all sorts of acrobatics on our trapeze – but, of course, we are very far from being trapeze artistes.

Hanging by your knees is very easy once you have dared let go with your hands. When you are upside down you just let yourself go limp and swing a bit – it's lovely. *Genevieve Hawkins, Louveciennes, France.*

Vicky and Geography

YOU MIGHT like to know that the Vicky stories in GIRL have been a great help in my Geography lessons.

Quite a long time ago one of our stories was about the Incas. At that time we were learning about the Incas in our Geography lessons at school. I cut out the pictures and stuck them in my Geography best book. The mistress gave me a very high mark for the work.

I would like to thank you for putting such an interesting series in the magazine. I think it is well worth 4½d. *Judith Spencer, Droitwich.*

COLUMBIA
BRAZIL
CHILE
MAP OF PERU

WINNERS

Congratulations to the winners of the fifty sling bags offered as prizes for GIRL Competition No. 5. I am afraid we have no room to print their names, but a full list may be obtained from: – GIRL Reader Services, Long Lane, Aintree, Liverpool 9. Please remember to enclose a self-addressed, stamped envelope.

FOR GIRL ADVENTURERS

Walking AND Cycling Holidays!
EAGLE-GIRL HOLIDAYS 1958

What could be more exciting than a holiday in the open air, exploring the beautiful countryside of the British Isles, in the company of fellow GIRL Adventurers. You can be sure of a wonderful time if you choose to go on a GIRL/Y.H.A. walking or cycling tour. Write for a copy of our brochure, which includes a very wide range of super holiday tours. Address your letter to: GIRL Summer Holidays, Long Lane, Aintree, Liverpool 9. Please tell us your Club number, and enclose a self-addressed, gummed label, bearing a 2d. stamp. These holidays are for members aged 12-16.

BIRTHDATES

26th FEB. 1943
1st NOV. 1944
13th JULY 1945
20th JAN. 1946
21st SEPT. 1947
8th MARCH 1948

If you are a GIRL Adventurer and your birthdate appears in this week's list, you are entitled to a **FREE** birthday gift! Choose it from the following: **GIRL handbag badge, stamp album, propelling pencil, GIRL autograph book, bicycle bell, ballpoint pen** or **coloured pencils.** State your choice on a postcard, giving us your name, address, Club number and the date you were born. Send it to: BIRTHDATES (18), GIRL Club, Long Lane, Aintree, Liverpool 9, to reach us by Thursday, 8th May. Overseas members whose birthdates appear here will automatically be sent their presents.

WHAT'S COOKING? with *Carol and Chris*

CAROL, LOOK WHAT I GOT FROM AN AUSTRIAN GIRL IN THE STUDIO. A LOVELY NEW RECIPE!

VIENNESE HAZELNUT KISSES. GOOD! LET'S MAKE THEM RIGHT AWAY.

INGREDIENTS
4 ozs. ground hazelnuts
4 ozs. caster sugar
1 egg
1 tablespoon flour
1 tablespoon cocoa
A little red jam

WE HAVEN'T GOT A NUT GRATER, BUT MINCING NUTS SEEMS TO BE QUITE EASY.

THESE 'KISSES' NEED A MODERATE OVEN. I'LL SET IT AT MARK FOUR.

Mix all the ingredients together in a basin.

© Gas Council

Moisten your hands and roll small portions of the mixture into balls. Place them in a greased baking-tin.

Press your forefinger lightly in the centre of each portion, to make a small well. Drop a blob of jam into each well. Bake the 'Kisses' for 30 minutes. Let them cool before taking them out of the baking-tin.

A KISS FOR A KISS, MR THERM!

Hazelnut kisses can be prepared a few days before you need them and kept in an airtight tin.

Girl Picture Gallery

No. 332

This delightful little creature is our native squirrel. It is smaller and lighter in build than the imported American grey squirrel.

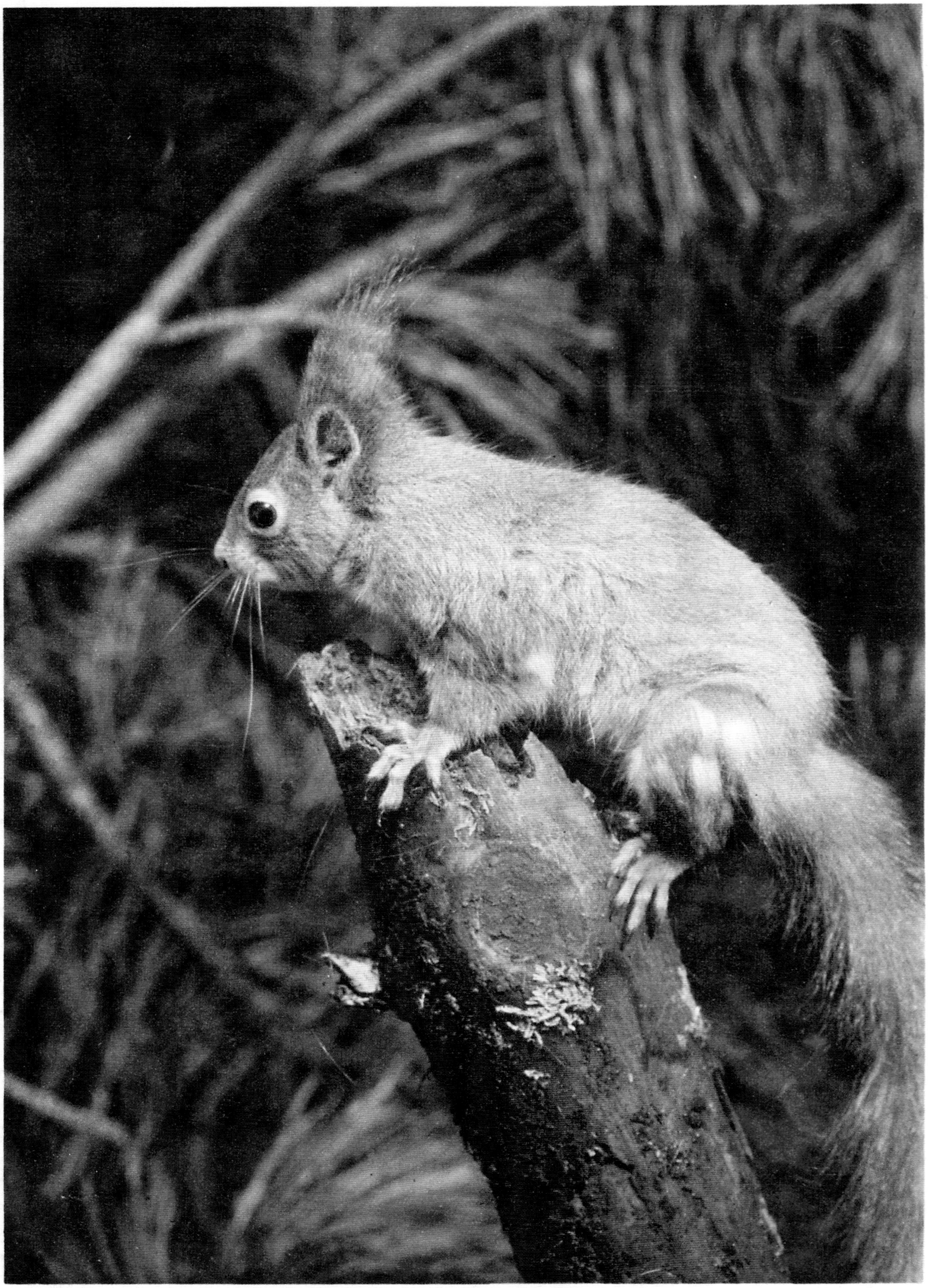

by John Markham, F.R.P.S.

RED SQUIRREL